D1882596

THE EDUCATIONAL SYSTEM

OF

THE ANCIENT HINDUS

THE EDUCATIONAL SYSTEM
OF
THE ANCIENT HINDUS

BY

SANTOSH KUMAR DAS

GYAN

GYAN PUBLISHING HOUSE

New Delhi - 110002

THE EDUCATIONAL SYSTEM OF THE ANCIENT HINDUS

ISBN :9788121202084

SANTOSH KUMAR DAS

All rights reserved. No part of this book may be reproduced in any manner without written permission.

Published in 2025 in India by
Gyan Publishing House
5, Ansari Road, Daryaganj,
New Delhi - 110002
Phones : 011-47034999, 9811692060
e-mail : books@gyanbooks.com
website : gyanbooks.com

Printed at: G. Print Process, Delhi.

"प्रथम प्रभात उदय तव गगने,
प्रथम सामरव तव तपोवने,
प्रथम प्रचारित तव वन भवने,
ज्ञान धर्म्म कत काव्य काहिनी ।"

—रवीन्द्र नाथ ।

Thine the skies where dawned the first bright morn,
The hermitage thine where the earliest *Samans* were sung,
Thine, too, the forests where first went forth sublime,
Knowledge, Religion—Store of Lore Divine!

—*Rabindranath.*

Dedicated

by kind permission

to

His Highness the Maharaja
Projjvala Nepal-taradhisha Sir Bhim
Shum Shere Jung Bahadur Rana
K.C.S.I., K.C.V.O., Honorary G.C.S.I.,
Honorary Major-General : British Army,
Honorary Colonel :
Fourth Gurkhas,
Prime Minister and Supreme Commander-in-chief,
Nepal.

PREFACE.

In this work an attempt has been made to furnish a comprehensive account of the Educational System of the Ancient Hindus. The difficulties of a work of this kind are considerable in India, specially in Nepal, where up to date libraries are few and far between and the verification of the references proportionately laborious and difficult. Moreover, in a secluded country like Nepal it is difficult to obtain co-operation and guidance in research from others and so the present work was conducted independently by the author from start to finish. Nevertheless, the author begs to acknowledge the invaluable help and guidance he has received from the researches of many savants, specially from those of Rev. F. E. Keay and Professors S. V. Venkateswara, Radhakumud Mukerji and Nagendra Nath Mazumdar who are the pioneers in this particular branch of Indology.

Ever since the author began this work he as a Hindu servant in the Education Department of a Hindu state like Nepal, cherished the desire that his work on the Educational System of the Ancient Hindus should, in the fitness of things, be dedicated to its Hindu ruler. The author, therefore, begs to acknowledge his heart-felt gratitude to His Highness the Maharaja Projjvala Nepal-taradhisha Sir Bhim Shum Shere Jung Bahadur Rana K. C. S. I., K. C. V. O., Honorary G. C. S. I., Honorary Major-General, British Army, Honorary Colonel, Fourth Gurkhas, Prime Minister and Supreme Commander-in-chief, Nepal, for kind permission to dedicate the work to His Highness. The author is no less indebted to His Excellency Supradipta Manyabara Sir Kaiser Shum Shere Jung Bahadur Rana K. B. E., General, Nepal Army, without whose princely help in the shape of books it would have been well nigh impossible for him to complete the present work. The author also takes this opportunity of expressing his heart-felt gratitude to His Excellency General Hiranya Shum Shere Jung Bahadur Rana for kind encouragement and sympathy which it is alike his pleasure and duty to gratefully acknowledge.

Tri-Chandra College
Nepal
The 5th August, 1930.

Santosh Kumar Das.

Contents.

CHAPTER I.

THE FACTORS IN ANCIENT INDIAN EDUCATION.

CHAPTER II.

ANCIENT HINDU EDUCATION: ITS AIMS AND OBJECTS.

CHAPTER III.

HOME EDUCATION OF THE CHILD IN ANCIENT INDIA.

CHAPTER IV.

ELEMENTARY EDUCATION IN ANCIENT INDIA.

CHAPTER V.

SECONDARY AND HIGHER EDUCATION IN THE BRAHMINIC SEATS OF LEARNING.

CHAPTER VI.

THE ORGANISATION OF SECONDARY AND HIGHER EDUCATION IN THE BRAHMINIC SEATS OF LEARNING.

CHAPTER VII.

SECONDARY AND HIGHER EDUCATION IN THE BUDDHIST SEATS OF LEARNING.

CHAPTER VIII.

VOCATIONAL EDUCATION IN ANCIENT INDIA.

CHAPTER IX.

FEMALE EDUCATION IN ANCIENT INDIA.

CHAPTER X.

THE EDUCATION OF THE PRINCE IN ANCIENT INDIA.

CHAPTER XI.

THE EDUCATIONAL INSTITUTIONS IN ANCIENT INDIA.

CHAPTER XII.

AGENCIES OF EDUCATION IN ANCIENT INDIA.

CHAPTER XIII.

EDUCATION AND THE STATE IN ANCIENT INDIA.

CHAPTER XIV.

EDUCATION AND THE SOCIETY IN ANCIENT INDIA.

one, 461—hence the emphasis on the acquisition of all knowledge, 432 specially Vedic learning, 433—hence the gift of learning is the best gift, 434—hence even house-holders 434 and Vānaprasthins 435 are asked to study the Vedas—hence the acquisition of Vedic learning is the compulsory duty of all Brahmins, 436—hence unlearned Brahmins are looked down by society, 436—hence gifts should *not* be made to unlearned Brahmins, 437—learning could be acquired even from *learned non-Brahmins*—hence people are asked to show *greater* respect to the learned than to the king, 439—*special privileges* granted to the learned, 441—*special privileges* granted to the students, 442—education was a consideration as regards the selection of bridegrooms, 443 and government servants, 443 and membership of the village assembly, 445.

CHAPTER XV.

Conclusion: effects of the educational system.

Age-long continuity shows the vitality of the educational system, 447—but as the ideals of the past guided its growth, education and educational methods became stereotyped, 447—the individual was educated not so much for his own sake as for the sake of society and individualism came to have very little scope for development, 448—nevertheless, it produced the most comprehensive literature and the *best type of men*, 448—it was also responsible for the *high level of average men* in Ancient India, 448—*internally* it made India fit for a free and full self-expression 209*f* and *externally* it enabled her to build up a Greater India beyond her northern mountains and southern seas, 451.

THE EDUCATIONAL SYSTEM OF THE ANCIENT HINDUS.

CHAPTER I.

THE FACTORS IN ANCIENT INDIAN EDUCATION.

In the infancy of humanity education was quite unconscious. In trying to get food, shelter and safety man originally learnt to observe Nature, to use it to his ends and to save himself from its destructive forces. Thus in addition to the inborn instincts, which he had in common with other animals, he brought into play his own special powers physical and mental. Experience was the next means of training. The younger generation learnt from the elders what was wholesome and what was harmful, how to enjoy pleasures and to keep away from pain. The arts of cutting, hunting, building and defending contributed to the development of human intellect, the observation of the striking phenomena in Nature laid the foundation of man's ideas of worship and religion and both increased his knowledge of the physical world. The inventions of fire and language were also great steps in the advancement of his worldly welfare, of a settled life and of his idea of social relations. Man learnt to rise above his brutal instincts first in the family under the power of the patriarch, later in the village under the rule of the headman and again in the society under the bonds of customs and laws. This was the beginning of conscious education.

§ 1—THE ETHNIC FACTOR.

But this conscious education is not a physical science. Its aim and organisation have always been determined by man according to his ideals and convenience. Hence in order to understand properly the nature of Education in Ancient India *we shall have to consider on the one hand the original nature of the people who lived there and on the other, the character of the environment in which their inherited capacities were called into active development.* But the people who lived in Ancient

India did not belong to one race but to many. At different times, waves of different people reached India and left their mark on society to a more or less lasting degree. Anthropological enquiries have revealed that four main types of races had come and lived in Ancient India, viz., Dravidian, Aryan, Scythian and Mongolian. The four main types are not to be traced as distinct from one another but there has been a fusion of them all on a large scale. But it is the Aryans who have carried the lion's share in controlling the destiny of the country.

Anthropologists scarcely need be reminded that humanity is not a democracy but a hierarchy, ascending in successive gradation from the lowest Negroid to the highest Caucasian type, from the man of muscle to the man of mind, from the creature of appetite to the being of thought; and the grandest problem yet awaiting solution is the due relegation of each great family to its proper place in the ethnic scale. Of the relative place of the Negro, the Turanian and the Caucasian, there can be no doubt; the order of these primary divisions may be regarded as settled. But when we come to their minute sub-divisions, specially those of the last, opinions differ, a satisfactory indication that our data are insufficient or that our principles are unsettled. We all admit that the Foulah and the Kaffir are superior to the Negro of the coast of Guinea; nor do we deny that the Turcoman and the Finn stand higher in the ethnic scale than the Samoyede and the Lapp. And perhaps, one reason why we see all this so clearly is, that we are outside these races, so that we have no feelings of jealousy to disturb our perception and warp our judgment. But it is otherwise with our own more exalted type. Here the rival claims of Semite and Aryan, of Greek, Roman, Teuton and Celt afford a never-ending subject of controversy in which it is to be feared passion and prejudice have but too often supplied the place of fact and argument.

The speculation, however, which regards humanity as the collective or grand man is not, perhaps, altogether fanciful or ungrounded. It, at all events, has the recommendation of comprehensiveness and enables us the more readily to arrange subordinate topics as parts of a large whole. Thus contemplated, then, we may say that the Negroid races represent the vascular, the Turanian the muscular, the Caucasian the nervous portion of the mundane structure. Were we inclined to enlarge our comparison by taking in a wider and, therefore, more diversified range of vitality, we would say that the Negro represents the vegetative, the Turanian the animal and the Caucasian the more purely human attributes of this collective organism. We shall not, perhaps, greatly err, if we speak of these great types as successive stages of advancement from alimentation and reproduction to respiration and cerebration.

The Indo-Aryans, therefore, who belonged to this Caucasian type were remarkable for their manly virtues and strength of intellect. Hence it is no wonder that "whatever sphere of the human mind you may select for your special study, whether it be language, or religion, or mythology, or philosophy, whether it be laws or customs, primitive art or primitive science, everywhere you have to go to India, whether you like it or not, because some of the most valuable and instructive materials in the history of man are treasured up in India and in India only".[1]

Let none however imagine that the non-Aryans have contributed nothing of value to Indian life. Contact with them made Hindu civilisation varied in aspect and deeper in spirit. The Dravidian was no theologian but expert in imagination, music and construction. He excelled in the fine arts. The pure spiritual knowledge of the Aryans mingling with the Dravidian's emotional nature and power of æsthetic creation formed a marvellous compound which was neither Aryan nor non-Aryan but Hindu. Thus the spiritual and moral ideals of Ancient Indian Education were essentially the product of the Aryan mind, while its vocational and æsthetic aspects were mainly inspired by the material and emotional nature of the Dravidians.

§ 2. THE GEOGRAPHICAL FACTOR.

After the Indo-Aryans had entered India their martial spirit was for a long time kept alive by the necessity of holding their own against the enemy. When this had been effected and the resistance of the non-Aryans was broken, there was left very little scope for the

---

[1] India: What can it teach us ?—Max Muller, p. 15.

development of the manly virtues. Henceforward they began to develop in their character a deep delight in the contemplation of the secrets of Nature and an enthusiastic devotion for subtle speculation. For, no country in the world displays such luxuriant productiveness, combining in the north, the natural phenomena of all the Zones from the eternal ice and scanty vegetation of the glacier world to the exhuberant undergrowth and majestic palms of the tropics. Under the glaring tropical Sun, the moist soil becomes fertile beyond imagination, producing for man, in lavish abundance, all that he needs for life. But it also subdues the mind with the overwhelming force of its fecundity. It could not have been otherwise than that the exhuberance of tropical Nature should have captivated the mind of man, stirring up his imagination, filling it with brilliant pictures and fostering in him a love of contemplation and luxurious ease. Indeed, the rich soil and the genial climate bringing the means of subsistence within easy reach made the struggle for existence an easy one and left men sufficiently at leisure to develop the various arts of civilisation. Thus while in Europe long cold winter, barren soil and conflict of interests between small countries have developed in the Aryans there '*the instinct of self-preservation*' to the highest pitch and have made them comparatively more '*active*', '*combative*' and '*enterprising*', the peculiar geographical conditions of India have tended to make her people more '*passive*', '*meditative*' and '*philosophical*'. The absence of any keen struggle for existence has enabled the people to maintain at the head of their society a thinking class that made light of worldly concerns and devoted themselves almost wholly to philosophical contemplation. Hence owing to differences in the geographical conditions of the two countries the people in them though they originally belonged to the same stock and possessed similar virtues, now present such marked distinctions in the development of their character. The different geographical conditions of the two countries have not only affected their nature but have also influenced their institutions, their sciences, arts and literature. Thus while in Europe the various institutions, arts and sciences have been developed more or less to meet the material needs of the people and to enable them to hold their own in their political and economic relations, in India they had had their origin in the '*exigencies of religion*'. Moreover, the lofty mountains and seas that shut the country off from the world outside not only rendered the Indian civilisation at once original and unique in character but also allowed time to the Hindu institutions, educational or otherwise, to become deep-rooted and in a great measure able to withstand the modifying influence of later invaders.

§ 3. THE SOCIAL FACTOR.

Coming to the social environment we find that the most characteristic feature of the Hindu society is its caste system. It is a matter of common knowledge that in the Rigvedic age the caste system was not well developed, if indeed, it existed at all. Each man was a priest, a warrior and a husbandman. But even then some families obtained pre-eminence by their special knowlegde of the ways of performing religious sacrifices and their gift of composing hymns ; others again excelled in military prowess. In course of time to keep pace with the growing needs and complexity of society differentiation became a necessity. Hence the Indo-Aryans like Plato, made an intelligent application of the principle of division of labour and became gradually divided into four castes according to their occupation and innate qualities. The ancient Hindus looked upon society as an organic whole and each member in the beginning picked up that branch of human activity which was suited to his innate qualities ; and afterwards his descendants followed the same, because on the strength of heredity they were best fitted for it. Experimental Psychology tells us that a long and continuous line of impressions goes to produce a high degree of efficiency in any branch of science or in any field of industry. Hence though the study of the Vedas was enjoined on all Aryans, yet as appears from the following śloka the respective occupation of each and the corresponding training were held to have been far more important :—

> " Śreyān swadharmo biguṇaḥ paradharmāt swanuṣṭitāt
> Swabhābaniyataṃ karma kurban nāpnoti kilbiṣam."

"One's own duty though defective, is better than another's duty well performed. Performing the duty *prescribed by nature* one does not incur sin." (Gītā, XVIII. 47) Herbert Spencer speaks in the same strain. "It is" says he, "a trite remark that, having the choicest tools, an unskilled artisan will botch his work ; and bad teachers will fail even with the best methods. Indeed, the goodness of the method becomes in such a case a cause of failure ; as, to continue the simile, the perfection of the tool becomes in undisciplined hands a source of imperfection in results."[2] Hence we have in the Gītā[3] the warning :

"Śreyān swadharmo biguṇaḥ paradharmāt swanuṣtitāt
Swadharme nidhanaṃ śreyaḥ paradharmo bhayābahaḥ."

"One's own duty, though defective, is better than another's duty well performed. Death in (performing) one's own duty is preferable ; the (performing of the) duty of others is dangerous.".

Again, though our philosophers warned us against changing our duties for those of a better class, yet the Platonic ideal did not remain unrealised and no inseparable barrier was set up between the orders. "If one brahmin by birth behaves like a śūdra, he can be desinated as a śūdra and if one, śūdra by birth, lives the regulated life of a brahmin, he can be designated as a brahmin."[4] Indeed, as the following ślokas will show, if a child of the inferior class possessed qualities characteristic of a superior class, he was admitted to that class :—

"Śriṇu yakṣha kulaṃ tāta na swādhyāyo na cha śrutam
Kāraṇaṃ hi dwijatwe cha brittameba na saṃśayaḥ".

"O honoured Yakṣha, hear (me), doubtless the actions alone and not lineage, perusal of sacred books and Vedic learning are the determinants of brahminhood."[5]

"Śūdre cha yadbhabellakṣhma dwije taccha na bidyate
Na bai śūdro bhabechchhūdro brāhmaṇo na cha brāhmaṇaḥ
Yattṛaitallakśhte Sarpa bṛittyaṃ sa brāhmaṇah smṛitaḥ.
Yattṛai tanna bhabet Sarpa taṃ śūdramiti nirdiśhet."

"What is noticed in a śūdra does not exist in a brahmin. A śūdra is not necessarily a śūdra nor a brahmin, a brahmin. Sharpa, only he is

---

[2] Education—Spencer, p. 83.
[3] III. 35.
[4] Mahābhārata, Banaparba, 189th Adhyāya.
[5] Mahābhārata, Banaparba, 311th Adhyāya.

called a brahmin, in whom such (characteristics of a brahmin) actions are found and O Sharpa, where these are lacking one should designate him a śūdra."[6]

"Yasya yallikhitaṃ proktaṃ puṃso varṇābhibyāñjakam
Yadanyatrāpi dṛishyet tat tenaiba binirddishet."

"If in an individual there appears worth other than that characteristic of his class he should be designated accordingly."[7]

Thus in agreement with the tendency of the modern world, there was in ancient India sufficient scope for the development of one's own individuality. In fact, *by the system of caste alone was self-realisation made compatible with social service.* Thus, it may well be said that even in those early times the Indo-Aryans saw that, for social efficiency, the individual should be allowed to develop along the lines of his greatest power. From this there follows the pedagogical principle that it is the function of education to determine the line of the greatest power of each individual and then to prepare him for service in that direction. This is the formulation of the ancient Indian ideal of a liberal education.

In fact, in ancient times the greatest care was taken to discover the aptitute and fitness (adhikāra) of an individual to receive any particular kind of education. The śūdras were, in general, denied the study of the Vedas only because they had neither the tradition nor the aptitude for acquiring the language and spirit of the Vedic literature. Indeed it is bad policy to spend time and energy in making an 'indifferent' priest out of a citizen who could have become an 'excellent' soldier or an 'expert' craftsman. The teachers then thoroughly realised that disastrous results were sure to ensue if knowledge were to be imparted without any consideration of what suited one's tastes and ways of doing things. Thus we have—

"Vidyayā sārdhaṃ mṛiyeta na vidyā muṣare bapet."

"Better die with learning rather than plant it in a barren soil."[8]

---

[6] Mahābhārata, Banaparba, 179th Adhyāya.

[7] Śrīmadbhāgavat, Canto VII. Ch. XI.

[8] Chāndogya Brāhmaṇa.

"Vedante paramaṃ gujhyaṃ purākalpe prachoditam
Nāpraśāntāya dātabyaṃ nāputrāyāśiṣyāya bā punaḥ."

"The highest mystery in the Vedānta, delivered in a former age, should not be given to one whose passions have not been subdued, not even to the son or disciple, if he is unworthy."[9]

Also—

"Let no man preach this most secret doctrine to any one who is not his son or his pupil or who is not of a serene mind. To him alone who is devoted to his teacher and endowed with all necessary qualities, may he communicate it."[10]

"Vidyā brāhmaṇametyāha śebadhistesmi rakṣha mām
Asuyakāya māṃ mādāstathā syāṃ bīryabartamā."

"(The Goddess of) learning came to a brahmin and said: "Preserve me, I am thy highest treasure. Do not impart me to a malicious person, thereby my potency will be kept unimpugned."[11]

"Yameba tu śuchiṃ vidyā niyataṃ brahmachāriṇam
Tasmai māṃ bruhi biprāya nidhipāyāpramādine."

"To him whom thou shalt know to be pure, perfectly continent and free from the follies of the world, to that brahmin shalt thou impart me."[12]

"Vidyayaiba samaṃ kāmaṃ martabyaṃ brahmabādinā
Āpadyāpi hi ghorāyāṃ natwenāmiriṇe bapet."

"Even in the absence of a means of livelihood, rather let a Vedic preceptor die with his knowledge than impart it to an unworthy recipient"[13]

We similarly find the striking feature constantly recurring in the Upaniṣhads that a teacher refuses to impart any instruction to a pupil until he proves to his satisfaction his competence, mental and moral, to receive the instruction, especially when that instruction is connected

---

[9] Śvetāśvatara Upaniṣhad, VI. 22.

[10] Maitrāyaṇīya Brāhmaṇa Upaniṣhad, VI. 29.

[11] Manu II. 114.

[12] Manu II. 115.

[13] Manu II. 113.

with the highest truths of life. The typical instance of this kind of pupil is Nachiketas in the Kaṭhopanishad approaching Yama for instruction on the nature of the soul and its destiny when Yama first satisfies himself as to his sincerity and zeal in the pursuit of truth by offering him the strongest temptation that might divert him from his end,—"sons and grandsons who shall live a hundred years, herds of cattle, elephants, gold and horses, sovereignity of the wide abode of the earth, fair maidens with their chariots and musical instruments and control over death." Nachiketas answers like a true sannyāsin "Keep thou thy horses, keep dance and song for thyself. No man can be made happy by wealth." Then Yama ultimately is compelled to admit: "I believe Nachiketas to be one who desires knowledge, for even many pleasures did not tear him away." Indra deals similarly with Pratardana by asking him to choose a boon but Pratardana is wise enough to leave the choice to Indra.[14] King Janaśruti Pautrāyaṇa similarly approaches Raikva for instruction with 600 cows, a necklace and a carriage with mules, whereupon Raikva answers: "Fie, necklace and carriage be thine, O Śūdra, together with the cows."[15] Satyakāma Jābāla did not impart instruction to Upakośala Kāmalayana even after his tending his fires for twelve years.[16] Pravāhaṇa approached by Āruṇi for instruction, says to him: "Stay with me for some."[17] Similar is the treatment meted out by Prajāpati to Indra and Vairocana [18] and by Yājñabālkya to Janaka[19] and by Śākāyanya to king Bṛhadratha.[20] All these cases but emphasise the pupil's own efforts along with those of his teacher as factors in education. The Upanishads[21] require that the pupil before he is taught the highest knowledge should show that he is calm and unperturbed in

---

[14] Kauś. III. 1.

[15] Chāndogya IV. 2.

[16] Chāndogya IV. 10. 2.

[17] Chāndogya V. 3. 7; Bṛhad. VI. 2. 6.

[18] Chāndogya VIII. 8. 4.

[19] Bṛhad. IV. 3. 1.

[20] Maitryā. I. 2.

[21] Bṛhad. IV. 4. 23 enumerates all the five attributes.

mind (śānta)[22] self-restrained (dānta), self-denying (uparata),[23] patient (titikṣhu) and collected (samādita).[24] To these are sometimes added purity of food and as a consequence purity of nature (sattva-śuddhi);[25] the fulfilment of the vow of the head (śirobratam)[26] which indicates either the rite of carrying fire on the head or as Deussen suggests[27] the shaving of the head bare (as implied by the term muṇḍaka).[28]

§ 4. THE RELIGIOUS FACTOR.

But the most potent influence on Ancient Indian Education was that of the religious environment. The Indo-Aryans when they first settled in the Indus valley were deeply impressed with the most imposing manifestations of Nature. They picked up what was beautiful and striking in Nature. looked upon that as the governing force in their regions and tried to propitiate it by prayers for their own welfare. The sky, the atmosphere and the earth exhibited such attractive phenomena at different times that they sang out praises to them: from the first, the Sun received the greatest attention followed by the Dawn;[29] from the second, Indra, Parjanya, Vāyu and Rudra were offered frequent worship;[30] and from the third, Agni, Soma, Varuṇa and Puṣhan carried the highest respect.[31] They sometimes rose above this Nature-worship, caught a glimpse of the Head of all these deities and praised Him in stirring and sublime verses.[32] Agni

---

[22] Kaṭha. II. 24; Muṇḍaka. I. 2. 13; Śvet. VI. 22; Maitrā. VI. 29 and X. 22; Kaivalya. III. 4.

[23] Kaṭha. II. 24.

[24] Kaṭha. II. 24.

[25] Chāndogya. VII. 26. 2; Muṇḍaka. III. 2. 6; c. f. also Mahānārāyaṇa.

[26] Muṇḍaka. III. 2. 10—11.

[27] Philosophy of the Upaniṣhads, p. 73.

[28] For other passages proving the doctrine of Adhikārabād see Aitareya Āraṇyaka III. 2. 6. 9 and V. 3. 3. 4; Chāndogya. III. 2. 5; Bṛhad. VI. 3. 12; Mahābhārata, Śāntiparba, 309th Adhyāya; Vaśiṣṭha Chs. II and XIII; Viṣhṇu XXIX. 7 and XXIX. 9 and XXIX. 10; Yājnabālkya I. 28; Hārīt I. 20; I. 21; Uśanā III. 35-37; Atṛī I. 8; Gautama XII; Manu II. 16; II. 109; XI. 181; Vātsyāyana's Kāmasūtra Bk. VII. Ch. II. śl. 55.

[29] Ṛgveda I. 115; III. 61; VII. 75.

[30] Ṛgveda II. 12; IV. 46; V. 83. etc.

[31] Ṛgveda I. 1; V. 26; VI. 53; VII. 86 etc.

[32] Ṛgveda X. 90, 121 etc.

making his appearance in the form of the Sun in the heavens, of the lightning in the atmosphere and of fire on the earth was soon considered to be the mouth or representative of all the gods. While sharpening a stone into some weapon men originally saw sparks and then found out how to produce fire, or a conflagration due to friction (caused by roaring winds) of branches of Aruṇi was observed clearing forests, burning down various animals, melting ores, and he got the idea of keeping fire, of using it for cooking and of offering oblations to it. In this way probably they marked the usefulness of the various phenomena in Nature and out of cheerful simplicity made them objects of their worship. Fire was to be kept up by every householder, oblations offered to it and hymns sung in its praise. In the morning and evening, prayers were also said by the river-side to the Sun as it rose and set. Thus even in the Ṛgveda sacrifice appears to be the centre of all religious activities, though its elaborate development and varied classification was the work of the second stage of the development of Indo-Aryan religion. There are hundreds of allusions to the materials and performances of sacrifices and the designations of priests at them in all the maṇḍalas of the Ṛgveda, which it is not necessary here to quote.[33]

Each of the Vedic poets was probably the family priest at the court of some chieftain or nobleman who wanted to propitiate the gods for prosperity and success by sacrifice with his help. Each poet handed down his own hymns to his descendants some of whom probably made additions to the original composition. Each maṇḍala of the Ṛgveda was thus a family collection, handed down from generation to generation and no doubt guarded jealously as a family inheritance. Later on, a sort of competition probably arose among such priestly families to possess the best hymns and led to the formation of a dignified and expressive literary dialect.

As the influence of the priests increased the ritual of the sacrifice became more complex. The technical lore of language and of hymns was taught by the poet-priest to his sons or nephews and this was no doubt the beginning of Ancient Hindu Education. In course of time probably due to

[33] Mahārāṣṭrīya Dnyānakoṣa, Part II. pp. 359-371.

the action of some powerful chieftain who wished to gather for his own benefit all the sacrificial literature, these family collections of hymns came to be amalgamated and taught together.

There were three functions which the priest might perform in the ritual and to those who performed them different names were given. The 'hotṛi' was the leading priest who while the sacrifice was being made recited hymns of praise in honour of the particular god he was worshipping (Indra, Agni, etc). And then part of the ritual was done by 'udgātṛi' whose duty was to sing the sāmans or hymns in praise of the Soma plant hypostatised and regarded as a god. Another priest was concerned with the manual acts of sacrificing and he was called an 'adhvaryu'. There was, at first, however, no distinct order and each priest might perform any of these functions. There was but one education for all, and each priestly student received a triple training so that he might perform any one of these three duties. Gradually, however, the ritual of the sacrifices became elaborated, and with its growing complexity some division of priestly labour became unavoidable. No one priest could become an expert in the three branches of the ritual and specialist training became necessary. Probably at first it consisted in a priestly student first learning the ritual of all the three branches and then specialising in one of them. The collection of Soma hymns into the nineth book of the Ṛgveda seems to show traces of this. But eventually something more than this was needed and there came to be three orders of priests, each possessing its own particular Veda and having its own training schools.

All the hymns to be chanted at the Soma sacrifice were gathered into a separate collection called the Sāmaveda. All its verses except seventy-five were taken from the Ṛgveda and formed a special musical collection for the Soma ritual. It consists of two parts called ārchikas. The first ārchika consists of stanzas, each of which was associated with a separate tune, of which there were no less than 585. The second part, or uttarārchika, contains the strophes which were required for use in the ritual. The udgātṛi had to learn to sing all the tunes required for the Soma ritual and to know which particular strophe was required for each sacrifice. The complicated work of the udgātṛi priest thus led to the creation of a special school for those who wanted to specialise in this branch of study. At a later date tune books called gānas were prepared.

Although the recitation of the appropriate hymns of praise at the ordinary sacrifices was the special duty of the 'hotṛi' priest, the 'adhvaryu' who performed the manual acts of the sacrifice, was required to utter certain ritual formulas (yajūṃshi), and at different points of the ritual had also to utter certain prayers and praises. For the training of the 'adhvaryu' priests also, special schools arose, and their particular Veda was the Yajurveda.[35] This collection consists of prose formulas or mantras, among which many verses, mostly taken from the Ṛgveda, are also interpolated. When these special schools were formed for the udgātṛi and adhvaryu priests, the older schools connected with the Ṛgveda came to be regarded as special schools for the hotṛi priests.

By the time these various types of priestly schools had been formed, the centre of the Aryan civilisation had shifted eastwards and lay somewhere between the Sutlez and the Jumna rivers. There came to be slight differences in the Vedic texts and each recension was called a śākhā. Those who followed a particular śākhā of a Veda were said to form a charaṇa or school of that Veda. At sometime, however, precautions were taken for the preservation of the sacred text, and this led to the constitution of the padapāṭha[36] and other forms of the sacred texts.

The different kinds of priestly schools had now become well developed, and were learned associations with a growing reputation and a priest was proud of the school in which he had received his training and he could not perform his duties as a priest without having passed through one of these schools. The first duty of the student was to learn by heart the particular Veda of his school. This he did by repeating after his teacher till perfect accuracy was obtained. He would also receive a great deal of instruction on his duties as a priest and also explanations of the hymns and ritual acts. The instruction was called 'viddhi' and the

---

[34] Macdonell's History of Ancient Sanskrit Literature, p. 171 ff.

[35] Ibid. pp. 174 ff.

[36] Ibid. p. 51.

explanation 'arthavāda.' For a long time these discourses were given orally by the teacher in his own language but in course of time in each school the didactic material contained in the text tended to follow precedent more and more and finally became stereotyped in the Brāhmaṇas.[37] These treatises written in prose were supposed to elucidate the texts and contained the speculation of generations of priests. A single discourse of this kind was called a Brāhmaṇa and later on all collections or digests of such discourses were called by the same name. Besides instruction and explanation relating to the sacrificial ritual, they contain mythological stories and legends, speculation and argument and we can find in them the first beginnings of grammar, astronomy, etymology, philosophy and law. Their intellectual activity was centred, however, on the sacrifice.

But though the Hindu education started out with the idea of the teacher passing on to the pupil the traditions he had himself received, yet even from the earliest times, the contents of the education must have begun to widen out. The sacrificial ritual itself gave birth to some of the sciences. The elaborate rules for the construction of altars led to the sciences of geometry and algebra being developed, and as it was sometimes desired to erect a round altar covering the same area as a square one, problems like squaring the circle had to be faced.[38] The desire to find out propitious times and seasons for sacrifices and other purposes gave rise to astrology, from which astronomy doveloped. The dissection of sacrificial victims was the beginning of anatomy. The care taken to preserve the sacred text from corruption led to the development of grammar and philology, while the deep questions with regard to the universe and man's place in it, which were already being referred to in the saṃhitās of the Vedas and discussed more fully in the Āraṇyakas and Upanishads led to the formation of elaborate philosophical systems and the study of logic.

According to tradition,[39] there are six subjects "the study of which was necessary either for the reading, the understanding or the proper

[37] Macdonell's History of Ancient Sanskrit Literature, p. 202.

[38] R. C. Dutt's Civilisation in Ancient India, pp. 93 ff.

[39] Kautilya in his Arthaśāstra confirms this tradition, (R. Shāmśāstrī's Eng. Trans., p. 7.)

sacrificial employment of the Veda." These are called the Vedāngas and comprise the following subjects :—Śikshā (or phonetics), Chhandas (or metre), Vyākaraṇa (or grammar), Nirukta (etymology or explanation of words), Jyotiṣha (or astronomy) and Kalpa (or ceremonial or religious practice). "The first two are considered necessary for reading the Veda, the two next for understanding it, and the last two for employing it at sacrifices."[40] From these, however, other subjects developed, as for example, the study of law from Kalpa. Thus the education of the ancient Hindus had its origin and development in sacrifice which occupied so prominent a place in the first and more specially in the second stage of the evolution of Vedic religion.

But in the next stage some impatience appears to have been felt with the elaborate rites and sacrifices which the thinking section of the people regarded as useless. Hence the mind of the great ṛṣis passed beyond the natural phenomena to the consideration of their cause and purpose :

"Kiṃ kāraṇaṃ brahma kutaḥ sma jātā jībāma kena kwa cha
sampratiṣṭhāḥ
Adhiṣṭhitāḥ kena sukhetareṣu bartāmahe brahmabido byābasthām".

"Is Brahman the cause ? Whence are we born ? Whereby do we live and whither do we go ? O, ye who know Brahman, (tell us) at whose command we abide, whether in pain or in pleasure."[41]

The thought that was thus set up culminated in the doctrine :

"Sarbaṃ khalbidaṃ brahma tajjalāniti śānta upasita."

"All the universe indeed is Brahma ; from Him does it proceed ; into Him is it dissolved ; in Him it breathes. So let every one adore Him calmly".[42]

Hence like the modern educators the ancient Hindus saw that complete self-realisation was possible only through finding one's own relations to the world around one and thus realising that all things have their beginning,

---

[40] Quoted in R. C. Mazumdar's Outline of Ancient Indian History and Civilisation, pp. 30-31..

[41] Śvetasvatara Upaniṣhad I. 1.

[42] Chāndogya Upaniṣhad.

life and end in God.[43] So according to them the final emancipation was possible only through "communion with one's fellowmen and with the beauty and truth of the universe." In fact, the ideal of the Hindu educational theorist was to know oneself in relation to society and the universe and to find out the identity between the individual and the eternal self, for, this is "the only way in which we can conceive the satisfaction of human aspirations, the completion of human knowledge and the sanctification of human life."

The Hindus from a very early time have held that each man is born a debtor, that he has obligations first to the sages who were the founders of his religion and culture; secondly to the gods; thirdly to his parents.[44] The first debt he repays as a student by the careful study of the Vedas; the second he repays as a householder by the performance of a number of sacrifices; the third debt he repays by offerings to the manes and by becoming himself the father of children.[45] When a man has thus paid all the three debts he is considered free and becomes fit for applying himself to the attainment of final liberation. The early Hindus, therefore, considered education as a life-process and divided the life of an individual into four stages to each of which different duties were assigned[46] in such a way that their due performance in any stage might prepare the individual for the next higher stage. In the first stage, the mind was opened and disciplined and the body made fit to carry out the orders of the mind. In the second, the individual put the principles he had learnt into practice and realised their true nature and that of the things of the world and its round of duties; and thus becoming pure in mind and body, in the third, he turned his attention inward to recognise the true and intimate relation between the individual and the eternal self in which

---

[43] Compare—"Nityonityānāṃ chetanaschetanāmeko bahunāṃ yo bidadhāti kāmān Tamātmaṣthaṃ yenupaśyanti dhīrāsteṣām śāntiḥ śaśtwatī:netāreṣam". "Who is eternal in the non-eternal, who is life of the living, who though One, fulfills the desires of Many. The wise who perceive Him within their self, to them belongs eternal peace, to none else."—Kaṭhopaniṣhad V. 13.

[44] Mahābhārata, Ādiparba, 229th Adhyāya.

[45] Mahābhārata, Anuśāsanaparba, 37th Adhyāya.

[46] Jābāla Upaniṣhad, 4. says "Brahmachārī bhūtwā gṛhī bhabet, gṛhī bhutwā banī bhabet, banī bhutwā prabrajet." *See* also Manu VI. 34-35.

was found the explanation of the origin and the meaning of existence. Hence with the ancient Hindus as with Frœbel " the purpose of education was to expand the life of the individual until it should comprehend this existence through participation in the all-pervading spiritual activity."

Hence we have in the Gītā[47] : "Let no wise man unsettle the mind of ignorant people attached to action." Thus the Gītā forbids the wise to thrust on the individual the divine wisdom before he becomes fit for receiving it. It urges that the individual should perform action so that he may learn by *doing*, the true nature of his own self. This goes to show that the Hindu system was not in favour of dogmatic instruction and aimed at the development of the personality of the individual.[48] " Indeed in the last stage of his life the individual becomes free from all fetters of law, of custom and of tradition and enjoys a life of perfect spiritual freedom and eternal bliss."[49] It is thus clear that the Hindu philosophers instead of giving an 'expression to the hostility to individuality' as has been suggested by some writers[50] aim at the greater development of individuality. In fact, instead of suppressing their individuality, " they attain their real individuality, infinitely beyond these little selves which we now think of so much importance. No individuality will be lost; an infinite and eternal individuality will be realised. Pleasure in little things will cease. We are finding pleasure in this little body, in this little individuality, but how much greater the pleasure will be when the whole universe appears as our own body? If there be pleasure in these separate bodies how much more pleasure when all bodies are one? The man who has realised this, has attained to freedom, has gone beyond the dream and known himself in his real nature."[51] So not only does the identification of the individual self with the eternal self 'not imply the loss of individuality but it is the only means by which individuality can be conserved and developed.'

[47] III. 26.

[48] Also *compare* Gītā III. 29; Praśna Upaniṣad, 1st Praśna, 2; Taittirīya Upaniṣad—Vṛgu Vallī; Chāndogya Upaniṣad—Satyakāma Jābāla.

[49] Lectures on the Origin of Religion—Max Muller, p. 365.

[50] A Brief Course in the History of Education—Monroe, p. 21.

[51] The Science and Philosophy of Religion—Swāmī Vivekānanda, pp. 188-89.

CHAPTER II.

ANCIENT HINDU EDUCATION: ITS AIMS AND OBJECTS.

Three or four words are to be met with in Ancient Indo-Aryan literature which roughly correspond to the modern word "education." Firstly the word "śikṣh" is to be found in the Vedic hymns which means "to learn to recite." In the Brāhmaṇic, Upaniṣadic and Sūtra literature the word "adhyayana" is to be met with which literally means "to go near" and expresses the idea of pupils going to some teacher for education. Thus the initiation ceremony "upanayana" was instituted which literally means "taking near." Young children were taken near a teacher for their education. In early Vedic times instruction was confined to particular families where the father generally taught his sons and there was no such initiation ceremony; but later on it came to be regarded as the preliminary to school-life. Thirdly, the word "vinaya" is to be met with in classical literature which comes from a root meaning "to lead out in a particular way." Thus it literally means "an action in which (inborn faculties) are led out (*i. e.*, trained) in a particular way" or "an action in which (one) leads (oneself) in a particular manner." The first meaning is identical with that of "education" and the second expresses the idea of the formation of character. Kālidāsa carries the credit of having used it very often in that sense. Here is a reference to the 'development theory' of education: the inborn powers of man are to be drawn out and developed. "Probodha" is used by the same poet to express the results of education. It means "awakening" or "enlightenment." Indeed an idea of the all-sided development of man was conceived by the Indo-Aryans and this will be further evident from the following passages:—

> "Learning brings on Vinaya (development of inborn power or modesty) which it its turn enhances the worth of man."[52]

---

[52] Hitopadeśa.

"Whoever learns by heart, writes, observes, asks questions (to get difficulties solved) and waits upon the learned, has his intellect developed like a lotus by the Sun's rays."[53]

"Just as well-secured learning brings on enlightenment and leads to the formation of character."[54]

But an all-sided development of man cannot be complete unless he is prepared by the education he receives, not only for this life but also for a future existence. The harmonising of these two purposes in due proportion has always been a difficult task for educators. Thus in the Middle Ages in Europe stress was laid upon preparation for the world to come, while modern European systems often tend unduly to ignore this side of education. But the ancient Hindus attempted a happy synthesis of both these purposes. Thus a young Brahmin was prepared by the education he received for his practical duties in life as a priest and teacher but the need of preparing him for the life after death was also included in the education he received. The same may be said of the young Kṣhatriyas and Vaiśyas who were required not only to fit themselves for their respective vocation in life but also to study the Vedas and give heed to the teachings of religion.

Hence the object of Ancient Hindu education was made three-fold: the acquisition of knowledge, the inculcation of social duties and religious rites and above all the formation of character.

The technical name for study proper i. e., Vedic study is "swādhyāya." The object in view was the three-fold knowledge (trayī), that of Ṛk, Yajus and Sāman.[55] Besides the three Vedas the branches of knowledge cultivated by the Hindus included not only literature, both sacred and secular with its accessories, Grammar, Phonetics, Exegetics and Metrics but also Logic, Philosophy. Itihāsa, Vārtta (Economics), Daṇḍanīti (science of government), Dhanurveda (science of war), Astronomy, Law, Medicine and Mechanical and Fine Arts of all descriptions.

---

[53] Subhāṣita.

[54] Raghuvaṃśam.

[55] Śatapatha Brāhmaṇa I. 1. 4. 2. 3; II. 6. 4. 2-7; IV. 6. 7. 1. 2.; V. 5. 5. 9; VI. 3. 1. 10. 11. 12; X. 5. 2. 1. 2.; XI. 5. 4. 18; XII. 3. 3. 2; etc., etc.

Besides these we find innumerable references to the supreme or highest knowledge, technically called parā-vidyā, as distinguished from all other knowledge termed aparā, as is done in the Muṇḍakopaniṣad.[56] The Muṇḍaka[57] defines aparāvidyā as comprising the four Vedas and the six Vedāngas. By the parā-vidyā, the Muṇḍaka understands that knowledge through which the ultimate Reality is known. All knowledge, parā or aparā, is opposed to ignorance, avidyā. Parā-vidyā, however, is extolled as sarva-vidyā-pratiṣṭhā, the foundation of all arts and sciences,[58] as vedānta, the final and highest stage of Vedic wisdom[59] and as verily the science of sciences wherein lies implicit the knowledge of everything.[60] A few citations would show clearly how the insufficiency of even the knowledge of the Vedes and indeed of all existing knowledge is recognised in the Upaniṣads.

In the Chāndogya Upaniṣad[61] Nārada acknowledges to Sanatkumāra:

"I have studied, most revered Sir, the Ṛgveda, the Yajurveda, the Sāmaveda, the Atharvaveda as fourth, the epic and mythological poems as fifth Veda, grammar, necrology, arithmetic, divination, chronology, dialectics, politics, theology, the doctrine of prayer, necromacy, the art of war, astronomy, snake-charming and the fine arts—these things most revered Sir, have I studied: therefore am I, most revered Sir, learned indeed in the scripture (mantrabit), but not learned in the Ātman (ātmabit). Yet have I heard from such as are like you that he who knows the Ātman vanquishes sorrow. I am in sorrow. Lead me then over, I pray, to the farther shore that lies beyond sorrow."

Sanatkumāra said to him: "Whatever you have studied is but words."

Similarly in the Chāndogya,[62] Bṛhadāraṇyaka[63] and Kauśitakī[64] treating of the same topic, Śvetaketu professes to have been taught by his father Āruṇi, but fails to answer the eschatological questions propounded by King Pravāhaṇa (in the Kauśitakī Citra Gāṅgyāyani) and returning in anger to his father reproaches him: "So then, without having really

---

[56] I. 1. 4.
[57] I. 1. 5.
[58] Muṇḍakopaniṣad, I. 1. 2.
[59] Ibid., III. 2. 6.
[60] Ibid., I. 1. 3.
[61] VII. 1.
[62] V. 3. 10.
[63] VI. 2.
[64] I.

done so, you have claimed to have instructed me";[65] "it was imagination then when you previously declared that my instruction was complete."[66]

Again in the Chāndogya[67] it was shown that Śvetaketu's "thorough" study of "all the Vedas" for full twelve years leaves him only full of conceit and confidence in his study and wisdom but ignorant of the questions put to him by his father regarding the One and Self-existent, through knowing whom every thing is known.

Accordingly we find several emphatic declarations of the principle as pointed out by these examples. "Therefore let a brāhmaṇa, after he has done with learning wish to stand by real strength (knowledge of the Self which enables us to dispense with all other knowledge)" says the Bṛhadāraṇyaka Upaniṣad.[68] "He should not seek after the knowledge of the books, for that is mere weariness of the tongue" says the same Upaniṣad elsewhere.[69] The Taittirīya Upaniṣad[70] says "Before whom words and thoughts recoil, not finding him" while the Kaṭha Upaniṣad[71] emphatically states that "Not by the Veda is the Ātman attained, nor by intellect, nor by much knowledge of books."

In this view the Kaṭha Upaniṣad[72] even regards aparā-vidyā as avidyā and emphasises its essential inferiority and worthlessness, although the aparā-vidyā includes, according to the Muṇḍaka[73] the four Vedas together with the six Vedāngas.

From the same ideal standpoint and standard of knowledge Kalpa or ritualism comes in for its special share of condemnation.[74] The Muṇḍaka[75] openly brands as fools those that seek to perform mere rites and ceremonies. The Bṛhadāraṇyaka[76] in a spirit of depreciation thinks

---

[65] Chāndogya Upaniṣad, V. 3. 4.

[66] Bṛhadāraṇyakopaniṣad, VI. 2. 3.

[67] VI. 1.

[68] III. 5. 1.

[69] IV. 4. 21.

[70] II. 4.

[71] I. 2. 23.

[72] I. 2. 4-5.

[73] I. 1. 5.

[74] For the entire evidence see Dr. R. K. Mookerji's article in Sir Āśutoṣa Mukerji Silver Jubilee volumes, Vol. III. Part I. Orientalia, pp. 220f., upon which I have freely drawn.

[75] I. 2. 7.

[76] I. 4. 10.

it fit to compare those who instead of knowing and recognising the Ātman as the only Reality, merely offer sacrifices to the gods, to domestic animals, ministering to the comforts of their owners. We read there:[77] "By sacrifice the world of the fathers, by knowledge the world of the gods is gained". In the Aitareya Āraṇyaka[78] we find the following: "To what end, shall we repeat the Veda, to what end shall we sacrifice? For, we sacrifice breath in speech or in breath speech."

In the later Upaniṣads, however, we find a more friendly attitude towards the sacrificial cult. In Kaṭha[79] the performance of certain ceremonies and works leads to the "overstepping of birth and death" and to "everlasting rest." This tendency towards reconciliation and synthesis attains its climax in the Maitrāyaṇa Upaniṣad, of which the very first passage affirms that the laying of the sacrificial fires leads to a knowledge of Brahman, while in IV. 3, it is expressly laid down that a knowledge of the Veda, observance of caste-duties and āśrama-duties are all essential to the emancipation of the natural ātman and its re-union with the Supreme Ātman. In Yājñabālkya Saṃhitā[80] we read: "brāhmaṇas endowed with Vedic studies are superior to all (the other castes); of them those given to the performance of religious acts, are superior; of them those gifted with the knowledge of the Self (are superior). The worthiness of a person is not determined by mere learning or asceticism; but he is known as a worthy person in whom both these exist." Again[81]: "The study of the Vedas, sacrifice, celibacy, penance, self-control, faith, fasting and control over the senses are the instruments of the knowledge of the Self." Hārit Saṃhitā[82] speaks in the same strain: "So long one enjoys the pleasure of seeing the Ātman he should not act against the religious practices mentioned in the śruti and the śmṛiti (such as penances, meditation, etc.). It should be noted, however, that orthodox and traditional Brahminical opinion does not find any real antagonism between the sacrificial cult, the scheme of practical life under the orders of caste and āśrama on the one hand and the Upaniṣadic spirit of the quest of

[77] I. 5. 16.
[78] III. 2. 6.
[79] I. 17.
[80] I. 199-200.
[81] III 190; *compare* III. 191.
[82] VII. 8.

the Brahman on the other. The importance of the passages expressing such attitude is only to emphasise the supreme importance and worth of parāvidyā.

It is obvious, however, that all men are not physically and mentally fit for the acquisition of parāvidyā, nor can they be fit for it, all at once. It was to meet this difficulty, that the ancient Hindus considered education as a life-process and divided the life of an individual into four stages to each of which different duties were assigned in such a way that their due performance in any stage might prepare the individual for the next higher stage. Thus the ancient Hindus did not ignore this mundane existence but on the other hand prepared the people for it by providing for education on a caste basis; so that on the completion of their education they found no difficulty in obtaining a means of livelihood.

Indeed social efficiency was one of the aims of Ancient Hindu Education. From the modern point of view a socially efficient man is he who is not a drag on his society and who far from interfering with the efforts of others, contributes to the progress and development of the society from which he has freely received nourishment for his body and soul. Hence every student was taught the rights and duties holding all together (Dharma), and even an advanced soul had no right to give up the duties pertaining to its position until it had shuffled off the mortal coil. We have the explicit mention of the value of philosophy as sustaining man n unremitting social service. 'Infinity is bliss, and only one who obtains bliss performs social duties.' [Ch. Up., VII. 22. *Compare* "Ātmā iva Sevaḥ" (Ṛgveda 1. 73. 2) and "Eṣa hyevānandayti" (Taitt. Up.).] 'None would strive to work or even to live, if only this bliss in the human heart (ānanda) ever ceased to be. Then joy would cease, and the thought of its ceasing smites humanity with horror.'[83] Thus the vedic ideal was the harmony of work and worship attained through perfect obedience to the divine will. Education aimed at developing the power

[83] Yadā hyevaiṣa etasmin udaramantaram kurute atha tasya bhayam bhabati (Taitt. Up.).

Upastaraṇamaham prajāyai paśūnām bhūyāsam

Vācham............śuśrūṣeṇyām manuṣyebhyaḥ

(T. A., IV. 1.),

and gifts of the people along these lines. It took advantage of the natural reactions of the child, and developed his individuality, only to lose it finally in the larger life of the universe.

Again, as the development of the spiritual side concerned the Hindus more than anything else, the moral purpose completely dominated the school-life of the Hindu student. He had to go through a course of discipline which helped to form his mind and to make his body fit to carry out its orders. Frœbel rightly observes: "To give firmness to the will, to quicken it and to make it pure and strong and enduring is the chief concern in education." The German educator Herbert was also a staunch supporter of the formation of character as the aim of education. That the ancient Hindu educators also laid the greatest emphasis on the formation of character will be evident from the following:—

"The result of education is good character and good behaviour."[84]

"The result of studies is good character and good conduct."[85]

"O Yakṣa, listen, high moral character is undoubtedly the only valuable qualification for being a brāhmaṇa, not so much race nor learning. Character should be scrupulously cultivated by all and in particular by the brāhmaṇa..................a brāhmaṇa without good character is less than a śūdra.[86]

"A conquest does not make a hero, nor studies a wise man. He who has conquered his senses is the real hero. He who practises virtues is really wise."[87]

"Neither austerities nor the Veda nor the Agnihotra nor gift of sacrifical presents can save one who has resorted to low conduct and deviated (from the path of duty)."[88] "The Vedas do not purify him who is void of good conduct, though he may have studied them together with the six Angas; the metres leave this man at death as full-fledged birds leave their nest."[89] "Like unto doors (unable to please) a blind

[84] Mahābhārata, Savāparba, 5th adhyāya.

[85] Mahābhārata, Udyogaparba, 38th adhyāya.

[86] Mahābhārata, Banaparba, 312th adhyāya.

[87] Vyāsa Saṃhitā, IV. 59-60.

[88] Vaśiṣṭha Saṃhitā, Ch. VI.

[89] Vaśiṣṭha Saṃhitā, Ch. VI.

man how can all the Vedas with the six Angas and esoteric sciences please a brāhmaṇa who is devoid of good conduct."[90]

"Conduct is the highest virtue as inculcated by the śmṛti and the sruti."[91] "Devoid of conduct, a brāhmaṇa does not obtain the merit of reading the Vedas. Possessed of good conduct he reaps the entire fruit (of such study)."[92] "Having thus observed the origin of virtue from (good) conduct, the sages accepted conduct as the basis of all austerities."[93]

Kautilya speaks in the same strain: "Restraint of the organs of the sense on which success in study and discipline depends can be enforced by abandoning lust, anger, greed, vanity (māna), haughtiness (mada) and overjoy (harṣa). Absence of discrepancy (avipratipatti) in the perception of sound, touch, colour, flavour and scent by means of the ear, the eyes, the tongue and the nose is what is meant by the restraint of the organs of the sense. Strict observance of the precepts of sciences also means the same; for *the sole aim of all the sciences is nothing but restraint of the organs of sense.* Whosoever is of reverse character, whoever has not his organs of sense under his control, will soon perish, though possessed of the whole earth, bound with the four quarters."[94]

Atri[95] says: "The panegyrists, the flatterers, cheats, those who act harshly and those who are avaricious—these five brāhmaṇas should never be adored, even if they are equal to Bṛhaṣpati in learning." A brāhmaṇa who knows only Gāyatrī but who is thoroughly self-restrained is better than he who knows the three Vedas (but) who is not self-restrained, who eats all (sorts of) food and sells everything (*i.e.*, prohibited things)."[96] "Neither the study of the Vedas nor liberality nor sacrifices nor any self-imposed restraint, nor austerities ever procure the attainment of rewards to a man whose heart is contaminated by sensuality". For, "when one among

---

[90] Vaśiṣṭha Saṃhitā Ch. VI; c. f. the four ślokas in this chapter which immediately follow those quoted above.

[91] Manu I. 108.

[92] Manu I. 109.

[93] Manu I. 110; c. f. Manu II. 118.

[94] Arthaśāstra, R. Śyāmaśāstrī's Eng. Trans., p. 12; c. f. Kāmandakīya Nītisāra, 1st Sarga, śloka 20.

[95] I. 379.

[96] Manu II. 118.

all the organs steps away from him, even as the water (flows) through the one (open) foot of a (water-carrier's) skin." Śukrāchārya says: "One should bring to bay or discipline by the hook of knowledge, the elephant of the senses which is running to and fro in a destructive manner in the vast forest of joyable things."[97] "Discipline is the chief thing to the guide or King. This comes through the dictates or precepts of the śāstras. This gives mastery over the senses and one who has mastered the senses, acquires the śāstras."[98] In Kādambarī we find a young ascetic admonishing Puṇḍarika for losing his self-control, thus: "Verily all knowledge is fruitless, study of holy books is useless, initiation has lost its meaning, pondering the teaching of gurus avails not, proficiency is worthless, learning leads to naught, since even men like thee are stained by the touch of passion and overcome by folly."[99]

In order to achieve this high ideal of perfect mastery over the senses, a life of strict discipline was prescribed for the student. He had to shun sensual pleasures of all kinds and lead a simple austere life. He was inspired by the high ideals of the teacher with whom he lived in close and intimate contact and imbibed social and moral virtues by his precept and example. At the same time the tender side of his nature was nourished and domestic virtues developed by the sweet and affectionate relationship with the wife and children of the teacher.

---

[97] Ch. I. lines 193-94.

[98] Śukranītisāra, Ch. I. lines 181-82; c. f. Ch. I. lines 183-85; 191-92.

[99] Kādambarī, C. M. Ridding's Eng. Trans., pp. 110-111.

CHAPTER III.

HOME EDUCATION OF THE CHILD IN ANCIENT INDIA.

We have already referred to the acquisition of knowledge as one of the aims of Ancient Indian Education ; but it was the acquisition of such knowledge as would enable a man to attain a right attitude in life. In one of the Upanishads we are told that the Right and the Real are concealed under the glamour and glitter of knowledge, as the real form of the Sun is obscured from our view by the halo of light surrounding that luminary.[100] We are told also that the knowledge of the self, of eternal life, is not obtained by learning, by the recitation of texts or even by listening to the experiences of others, but is entirely a matter of the individual's interiorisation[101] which finds all things in the universe in their proper place and proportion and fills the earnest seeker with sweetness and light, born of love for all and renunciation of the self. Indeed, Education in Ancient India was not merely concerned with the instruction of the young ; nor even with the formation of habit and the development of will-power. It sought to build up the whole being of the individual and to enable him to lead the best and the highest kind of life possible for him in the circumstances in which he was placed. Educative influences were so planned as to mould his life from the moment he was conceived to the moment of his death. The system included the anxious care-taking of the babe, the efficient breeding of the child, the delicate training of adolescence and the gradual developing of the sense of values in the little thought of acts of daily life. His domestic and social duties were so arranged as to develop a life of constant social service and spiritual drill, to lead finally to a surrender of the realised self in communion with the Divine. If education was conterminous, it was also co-extensive with life.

---

100 Satyasyāpihitam mukham.........apāvṛṇu satyadharmāya drishtaye—Iśa Up.

101 Nāyamātmā prabachanena labhyo na medhayā na bahunā śrutena—Kaṭha Up.

The embryo was treated through the expectant mother and a ceremonial or a festivity ensured emphatic attention at every stage to matters of embryonic and babe welfare. Numerous Vedic hymns which are outside the regular collection impress on the parents the need for complete concord and agreement and for harmony with the laws of Nature, to ensure the real happiness of the babe to be born. It is clearly recognised that the mother, as she is the first, is also the most powerful of educators whose influence just before and during pregnancy would make or mar the child's welfare in after life. If she thinks of things holy and serene, enjoys peace and happiness and finds her atmosphere congenial, she can stimulate the child's mental faculties, induce patriotic and other virtues and instill spiritual force into its mind. When she is *enceinte* the prayer is to secure her health and that of the fœtus, so that both might be alive after the parturition. The expectant mother has her surroundings solemn and silent, which lay the foundations of the spiritual training of the future child.[102]

After confinement the mother is placed under pollution for a month and a half, to ensure the concentration of her attention on the infant. The hymns used at the jātakarma draw attention to the need for the service of humanity with an abiding faith in the Omnipotent, for building the babe's physique by attention to the breast-milk of the mother. On this latter circumstance depended not only the life of the tender one, but its natural endowment of strength and its mental and moral qualities

---

[102] Pregnant women must not bathe in bathing places, allow hair to be loose or lie with head high or low and must not walk in the open air. They must avoid the cemetery, burial ground, large trees, etc. (Suśruta, III, 10). c. f. Petavattu I. 5; Dīvyābadāna, pp. 2, 79, 167, 441 and 523.

c. f. Megasthenas: 'The Brachmanes are the best esteemed, for they are more consistent in their opinions. From the time of their conception in the womb they are under the guardian care of learned men who go to the mother and under the pretence of using some incantations for the welfare of herself and her unborn babe, in reality give her prudent hints and counsels. The women who listen most willingly are thought to be most fortunate in their children. After the birth, the children are under the care of one person after another, and as they advance in age, each succeeding master is more accomplished than his predecessor.'—Fragment 41.

(āyur varcho yaśo balam). At the niṣkramaṇa the child was taken into the open, to admire the gay flowers and the green leaves on the background of the Sun-lit sky. It breathed the pollen driven by the wanton wind, witnessed the bright plumage of the dancing peacock and was treated to the music of the gurgling brook and the sweet song of the birds. A spirit of cheery optimism and a sense of the joyousness of life are sought to be instilled into the child almost from birth as at the name-giving ceremony (nāma-karaṇa)—which was certainly in vogue at least as early as the Yajurveda—by the friends and relatives assembled for the purpose. After the celebration of the first birthday it was given its food in the placid moon-light and taught to trace the course of the Moon and the stars as they appear on the heavens unwearied night after night. In fact, its individuality was respected and emotions aroused at every ceremonial.

'The parents of little Goyama performed in due order the rites of the birthday, the sight of the Sun and the Moon, the vigil, the name-giving, the walking and moving of legs, the feasting, the increase of food, the teaching to speak, the boring of ears, the cleansing of the ear, the dressing of the hair, the taking to school etc.,[103] This attention to the child in the first four or five years must be of high educative value. Jung and Freud have proved by psycho-analysis that the habits formed in these years have great influence in determining not only the physical status of the child but the future emotional and volitional life of the adult.

The ceremony of tonsure (chaula) is at the age of three or five, when the consciousness of self appears and asserts itself. Advantage is now taken of his growing egoism for establishing regularity in daily life. He is to rise early, and wash specially his teeth and eyes, to have regular meal times and retire to bed an hour or two after sun-set. His home-education would begin from now. Comenius calls the first years the mother's school and finds here the rudiments of all later education. And this was true of the Indian mother whose share in education is well brought out by the epithet Vīrasū—'The mother of heroes'—of a Kshatriya lady and by invoking the name of the mother when trying to

[103] Antagado Dasao, Barnett's Trans., p. 29 Mantra Pāṭha of the Āpastambins, 13, 2; Aśoka's Rock Edict, IX.

appeal to a sense of heroism. We have good examples in the epithets Āñjaneya for Hanumāna ; Kuntīmāta applied to Bhīma and Kaunteya to Arjuna. The child was taught that he was a brother to the Nature's dumb creation, to the guileless calf of the milchcow and even to the noisy Indian crow. The high rocks and giant trees were to him embodiments of a mysterious power which he was taught to reverence. Nature's phenomena like thunder and lightning were explained as the results of the working of this Unseen Being, as much as the soft stillness of the night and the motions of the spheres. He was led from Nature to Nature's God. This was the foundation of his spiritual training.

The family under the guidance of the father was the next factor in the child's education. Kālidās calls a child 'well-trained at home' as 'having a real father' and exhorts each and every father to bring up his children according to the religious instructions by example as well as by precept. Pestalozzi says that life educates more than the school and that the centre of elementary education is the sympathy of ideas, the speech and the intelligent activities of a well-organised family-life. The Hindu joint family furnished the child with his first lessons in the art of co-operation. It is the schooling ground of the social virtues—of sympathy with distress, of unselfish affection, of gratitude for service, of regard for elders, of social service without a sense of patronage and of self-sacrifice in the interest of the other members of the community. In family life alone, in other words, is there complete provision for what Froebel [104] calls 'the fundamental need of childhood'—self-expression.

The Indian home was not so much a preparation for the school as a supplement to it. The father, sitting under the bounteous mango or the shady banyan and the grand-mother at her leisure, kindled not only the child's love of Nature but his interest in literature, by telling him stories and reading aloud to him extracts from the golden deeds of the epic heroes and heroines. The child's personality was worked and developed and his work assessed and appreciated in his treatment of nursery rhymes as well as in the reproduction of these stories. In a joint family, trained to share

---

[104] The Education of Man., p. 102.

what he had with others one could expect the idea of giving foremost in the mind of every juvenile Nachiketas and the incipient spirit of commercialism clean wiped out of his mind. Thus the Indian family training did not aim at enabling the child to be useful to the family at the earliest possible moment by training him in some practical art but aimed at the harmonious development of his powers.

CHAPTER IV.

ELEMENTARY EDUCATION IN ANCIENT INDIA.

The weaning of the child from the sweet and softening influences of family life was signalised by a great ceremony which took place probably at the age of five. Sometime later, at the age of seven or eight, was initiation into sacred lore at the hands of a spiritual teacher. But in a system where the boy generally followed the occupation of his father, it is probable that he was trained by actual participation in those activities that were required of him in adult life. So primary schools in the modern sense probably did not exist in the earliest times. Even in the Sūtras there is no mention of different curricula for the different stages of education. Indirectly we can gather some information about them from the references in almost all the works of the later systems of philosophy as to the competency of the student to enter upon the study. For instance, the study of Nyāya and Tarka required a student to have gone through the course of grammar, literature and lexicon.[105] For Vedānta, a previous knowledge of Vedic hymns, of Vedāngas and a course of regular religious instruction and a pure righteous mind were necessary.[106] Whoever was authorised to enjoy the fruit of the religions rites could study Mimānsā.[107] Thus the different sciences laid down different standards of previous preparation, the highest of them being that of the Vedānta. The Sāṇkhya, Nyāya and Vaiśheśikā systems were a sort of realism and a student who understood written Sanskrit could commence their study, which made him observe and think of the matter and of its properties. No hard and fast rules were laid down anywhere as regards the primary or higher course. That was all left to the discretion of the teacher who marked the capacity of the pupil and led him on step by step from one book to another.

---

105 Adhītavyākaraṇakābyakoṣonadhītanyāyo bālaḥ.

106 Adhikārī tubidhibadaditavedavedāngatwenāpātato nitāntanirmalaśwāntaḥ.

107 Falaswāmyamadhikāraḥ.

In a book on astrology,[108] however, auspicious days and hours are mentioned for the commencement of the teaching of the alphabet to small children. But our authorities differ as to the earliest age for the commencement of such studies. Works on astrology permit education to begin as early as the third year but this was considered too early by writers on medicine. Charaka, for instance, insists on the postponement of the school-going age to the fifth year. According to Viṣṇu Purāṇa the period from birth to the fifth year of the child was regarded as the time for play,[109] after which[110] the time for study commenced. Nevertheless, in the case of precocious children, there was introduction to letters at the age of three and initiation to Vedic studies a few years later. According to Kautilya[111] "having undergone the ceremony of tonsure the student shall learn the alphabet (lipi) and arithmetic. After investiture with the sacred thread he shall study the triple Vedas etc." From the Raghuvaṃśa[112] of Kālidāsa we learn that when the tonsure ceremony was over, Prince Raghu learnt the proper grasping of the alphabets along with the ministers' sons of equal age and then entered the extensive field of learning like one entering the vast expanse of the sea through the mouths of a river. Kālidāsa would not have mentioned the fact of ministers' sons being likewise fit for school, if the prevailing sentiment of the time had looked at such juvenile training as incredible or impossible. According to I-Tsing[113] the children learn the letters of the alphabet etc., when they are six years old. Yuan Chwang informs us that boys passed on to the study of arts and sciences at seven years of age, so that elementary education must have begun earlier.

---

108 Mūhurta Mārtaṇḍa.

109 Kālāḥ krīḍanakam te tadante adhyayanasya cha
Tataḥ samastabhogānāṃ teṣyānte tapaḥ
—Viṣṇu Purāṇa. Part I, XII. 18.

110 Manu II. 37.

111 Arthaśāstra, R. Śyāma Śāstri's Eng. Trans., pp. 10-11.

112 Canto III. śloka 28.

113 Takakusu's Eng. Trans., pp. 171-72.

Kalhaṇa's Rājataraṅgiṇī also refers to elementary education in the following passages :—

> "Taking the name of Suyya, he grew into an intelligent (youth) and having learnt his letters, became a teacher of small boys in the house of some householder."[114]

> "Kāmadeva..........having acquired a knowledge of the akṣaras became a boy's teacher in the house of Merubardhana (a minister)."[115]

But the Hindu Dharmasūtras and Gṛhyasūtras have no reference to any form of literary education outside the Brahminic schools. But silence in works of this kind is not certain evidence that facilities for primary education did not exist and the Brahmins may have had reasons for wishing to ignore any form of education which was not in their hands. We have numerous references to the various and wide-spread uses of writing in the Jātakas; to the writing of epistles, sealing a letter, the forging of letters, inscriptions on a gold plate, inscription over hermitage, letters of the alphabet engraved on gold necklets, inscriptions upon garments and accoutrements, the scratching of a message on an arrow, writing on a leaf etc.[116]

A Buddhist tract called the Silās which dates from about 450 B. C.[117] gives a list of children's games. One of them is Akkharikā (Lettering) which is explained as "guessing at letters traced in the air or on a play-fellow's back." Such a game amongst children seems to show that the knowledge of the alphabet was prevalent at least among a certain section of the community. The Greek writers Nearchos and Curtius,

---

114 Stein's Rājataraṅgiṇī, Vol. I. p. 196.

115 Stein's Rājataraṅgiṇī, Vol. I. p. 134.

116 Jātaka II. 95 ; 174 ; VI. 370, 385, 403 ; I. 451, IV. 124 ; II. 36, 372, 376 ; IV. 7, 257, 355, 488 ; V. 59, 67, 125 ; VI. 29 ; VI. 520 ; IV. 489 ; VI. 390 ; VI. 408 ; II. 90 ; II. 174 : IV. 55 ; VI. 369, 400.

117 Rhys Davids—Buddhist India, p. 108.

in the last quarter of the fourth century B. C., refer to the custom of the Indians of writing letters on cloth and bark. No doubt, Megasthenes, at a slightly later date, relates that judicial cases in India were decided according to unwritten laws and that the Indians knew no letters but in another passage, he speaks of the use of mile-stones to indicate distances and halting places on the high roads.[118] Taking these passages together it seems that at that time, writing was used for public and private notifications, though this does not necessarily imply the existence of schools for teaching these arts.

But there is a passage in Jataka I. 451 which indicates that there were elementary schools where the art of writing was regularly taught. It tells us how when a rich man's son "was being taught to write" his "young slave used to go with his young master's tablets and so learnt at the same time to write himself." There is a passage also in Lalitavistāra "[119] which shows that at the time when it was composed it was not uncommon for some boys at least to learn writing and arithmetic and there were some facilities for this in the shape of elementary schools of some sort and that these were outside the monasteries. Here we are told that following the usual custom of the world Gautama Buddha went to the 'writing' school to practice well all figures, letters, calculation and reading and writing and moral precepts. It is interesting to note here that a modern system of teaching the letters of the alphabet was also then known as the teacher then taught each of them in association with a sentence beginning with the letter.[120] The first lesson in writing delineated in sculpture is at Peshwar. The writing board shows a few kharoshti characters, which the infant Buddha is supposed to have written.[121] According to the Elephant Cave Inscription of the year 165 of Mauryan era (157 or 148 B. C.) King Khāravela of Kalinga leart reading, writing and arithmetic in

---

118 Indian Palæography, J. G. Buhler, p. 6.

119 Ch. X.

120 Lalitavistāra—R. L. Mitra, p. 184.

121 Sculpture No. 347. (Spooner's Hand book, p. 54).

his childhood.[122] The Śikṣā enumerates the course of elementary study as comprising the art of writing (lipi), prayers and psalms (stuti), meanings of words and their mutual relationships (nighaṇṭu) and elementary grammar including terminations and tenses, declensions and inflections (śabha). The Divyābadāna[123] has reference to school-room (lekha-śāla), to sciences taught (ketubham), to stories which delight the young learners (parikathā), to pencils used in writing (tulā) and the abacus (janitra) used in teaching arithmetic. The Lalitavistāra[124] refers also to the wooden writing-board (phalākā). Jātaka No. 125[125] refers not only to the wooden writing board (phalākā) but also to the wooden pen (barṇaka). And it is interesting to note that both of these are still used in Indian elementary schools.

It is well known that Aśoka issued his Inscriptions with a view to promote amongst his people Dharma or the Law of Piety. These inscriptions were composed in vernacular dialects and inscribed in two different scripts. This shows that they were meant to suit the people of the different provinces and implies a certain percentage of literacy among the people. In the words of Mr. V. A. Smith[126] "the care taken to publish the imperial edicts and commemorative records by incising them in imperishable characters, most skilfully executed, on rocks and pillars in great cities, on main lines of communication or at sacred spots frequented by pilgrims, implies that a knowledge of reading and writing was widely diffused, and that many people must have been able to read the documents. The same inference may be drawn from the fact that the inscriptions are composed, not in any learned scholastic tongue, but in vernacular dialects intelligible to the common people and modified when necessary to suit local needs."

---

[122] J. G. Buhler, Indian Palæography, p. 5.

[123] Cowell and Neill's edition, p. 532.

[124] Chapter X.

[125] J. G. Bühler, Indian Palæography, p. 5.

[126] Aśoka, third edition, pp. 138-39.

The next question which awaits solution is how far during all the centuries that Buddhism existed in India, Buddhist monasteries influenced the general mass of the people, at least those who adhered to Buddhism and provided opportunities of elementary instruction. Before we can give our verdict we shall do well if we bear in mind that in breaking down the monopoly of higher learning which has been in the hands of Brahmin teachers and in offering the possibilities of education to men of all castes, Buddhism may have done something to extend amongst the people of India the desire for some elementary education. It is also quite certain that Buddhist educational ideals and practices were mostly derived from or closely connected with, those of Brahminism. No doubt the persuit of secular knowledge would almost seem, from one point of view, to be contrary to the spirit and purpose of Buddhism and yet the monasteries had to make provision for some sort of general and secular education when they found that their rivals—the Brahminical schools—were open not only to young brāhmaṇas who were destined for the priestly office, but to others of the twice-born castes as well. Moreover, elementary instruction was also imparted by the Buddhist monasteries of Burma,[127] Ceylon,[128] Tibet[129] and China.[130] All these considerations may lead one to the not improbable conclusion that Buddhist monasteries in India also began to impart elementary education of a secular kind, at sometime or other. Mr. V. A. Smith remarks :[131] " It is probable learning was fostered by the numerous monasteries and that the boys and girls in hundreds of villages learned their lessons from the monks and nuns as they do now in Burma from the monks. Aśoka it should be noted, encouraged nunneries, makes particular reference more than once to female lay disciples as well as to nuns. I think it likely that the percentage of literacy among the Buddhist population in Aśoka's time was higher than it is now in many provinces of British Iudia. The returns of 1901 show[132] that in the

---

[127] Shway Yeo, Ch. II.; Burma Past and Present—Albert Fytche, pp. 190-92.

[128] R. S. Hardy, Eastern Monachism, pp. 18 and 313ff.

[129] S. C. Das, Indian Pundits in the Land of Snow, pp. 3-11.

[130] Fa-Hien, Legge's Eng. Trans., p. 78.

[131] Aśoka, third edition, p. 139.

[132] The Indian Empire, Imperial Gazeteer, Vol. IV. (1907), p. 416.

United Provinces of Agra and Oudh which include many great cities and ancient capitals, the number of persons per 1000 able to read and write amounts to only 57 males and 2 females. In Burma where Buddhist monasteries flourish, the corresponding figures are 378 and 45." There is not, however, any very clear evidence of the fact that Buddhist monasteries began to impart popular secular education as early as the days of Aśoka; but we should bear in mind that the rise of Buddhism is synchroneous with the rise of mighty Indian Empires and the welding together of a large part of India into one Empire, under the strong rule of Mauryan sovereigns, must have given increased opportunities for trade and commerce and this may have also led to an increased demand for popular schools where the three R's could be learnt. Moreover, the prevalence of the Vaiṣṇava cult, centuries before the Christian era, which held out the possibility of the attainment of salvation by an earnest layman who does his duty as expounded in the Bhāgabad Gītā is the evidence of a widespread movement amongst laymen in India and it would be not unlikely that it would be also characterised by a growing desire for education. And the growth of the popular form of Buddhism of the Mahāyāna school which similarly held out hopes of spiritual progress to those who are not able to forsake the world and become monks must have given a keener edge to this hankering for secular education.

As a matter of fact we find that at the time of the visit of Fa-Hien (399-414 A. D) the monasteries seem to have begun to undertake instruction of a more general kind than merely instructing those who joined the saṃgha in the precepts of Buddhism. In speaking of the monastery at Pātaliputra or Patna, he says[133]: "By the side of the Tope of Aśoka there has been made a Mahāyāna monastery, very grand and beautiful; there is also a Hīnayāna one; the two together containing six or seven hundred monks. The rules of demeanour and the scholastic arrangements in them are worthy of observation. Śāmans (monks) of the highest virtue from all quarters and students, inquirers wishing to find out truth and the grounds of it all resort to these monasteries." In a note on Fa-Hien's

[133] Fa-Hien—Legge's Eng. Trans., p. 78.

reference to the "scholastic arrangements" at Patna Prof. Legge says: "Why should there not have been schools in those monasteries in India as there were in China? Fa-Hien himself grew up with other boys in a monastery and no doubt had to go to school. And the next sentence shows us that there might be schools for more advanced students as well as for the śramaners." Thus there seems no reason to doubt that by the time of Fa-Hien the monasteries may have given some general instruction not only to young novices but even to pupils who had no intention of joining the saṃgha. At all events the system was in full swing at the time of I-Tsing's visit. He says[134]: "To try the sharpness of their wit they proceed to the King's court to lay down before it the sharp weapon of their abilities; there they present their schemes and show their (political) talents *seeking to be appointed in the practical government*...........They receive grants of land and are advanced to a high rank; their famous names are, as a reward, written in white on their lofty gates. After this they can *follow whatever occupation they like.*" But there is a passage[135] which puts the matter still more clearly and leaves no doubt upon the question: "Those white-robed (laymen) who come to the residence of a priest and read chiefly Buddhist scriptures with the intention that they may one day become tonsured and black-robed are called "Children" (mānava). Those who (coming to a priest) want to learn secular literature only, without having any intention of quitting the world, are called "students" (brahmachāri). These two groups of persons residing in a monastery, have to subsist at their own expense. In the monasteries in India there are many "students" who are entrusted to the bhikṣus and instructed by them in secular literature. On the one hand the "students" serve under priests as pages, on the other the instruction will lead to pious aspirations. It is, therefore, very good to keep them in as much as both sides are benefitted in this way."

These passages make it quite clear that arising out of the duty of the bhikṣus to teach and spread their doctrines and of the relation of the teacher and pupil which the discipline of the order required, the Buddhist monastery had become a place where lived not only those who were studying

---

[134] I-Tsing, pp. 177-78.

[135] I-Tsing, pp. 105-106.

the Buddhist doctrines with a view to joining the order but also those who had no intention of doing so but were residing only for the sake of secular knowledge and education. This practice may have been inflenced by tne Brahminical schools which were open not only to young brāhmaṇas but to others of the twice-born castes as well.

The Chinese travellers furnish us with some idea of the curricula of studies carried on in these monastic schools. Yuan Chwang says that children began by learning the alphabet and the siddhir-astu, a primer of twelve chapters. Then began the study of the five Vidyās—śabda-vidyā (grammar), Śilpasthāna-vidyā (arts and crafts), Chikitsā-vidyā (medicine), Hetuvidyā (logic), and Adhyātma-vidyā (philosophy). I-Tsing gives more details; says he:[136] "The name for the general secular literature in India is Vyākaraṇa, of which there are about five works, similar to the Five Classics of the Divine Land (China).

I. The Si-t'an Chwang (Siddha-composition) for beginners—This is also called Siddhirastu, signifying 'Be there success' (Ch. lit. 'complete be good luck!') for, so named is the first section of this small (book) of learning.

There are forty-nine letters (of the alphabet) which are combined with one another and arranged in eighteen sections; the total number of syllables is more than 10,000 or more than 300 ślokas..............children learn this book when they are six years old and finish it in six months. This is said to have been originally taught by Maheśwara-deva.

II. The Sūtra—The sūtra is the foundation of all grammatical science. This name can be translated by 'short aphorism' and signifies that important principles are expounded in an abridged form. It contains 1000 ślokas and is the work of Pāṇinī......................Children begin to learn the Sūtra when they are eight years old and can repeat it in eight months' time.

III.—The Book on Dhātu—This consists of 1000 ślokas and treats particularly of grammatical rules. It is as useful as the above Sūtra.

---

[136] I-Tsing, pp. 175-179.

IV. The Book on the Three Khilas—Khila means 'wasteland', so called because this (part of grammar) may be likened to the way in which a farmer prepares his field for corn. It may be called a book on the three pieces of waste land; (1) Aṣtadhātu consists of 1000 ślokas (2) Wench'a (Manda of Munda) and consists of 1000 ślokas; (3) Unādi too consists of 1000 ślokes. (The first deals with cases and conjugations and the two others with the formation of words from root and suffix or suffixes).

V. Vritti-sūtra (Kāsikāvritti)—This is a commentary on the foregoing Sūtra (i. e., Pāniṇī's Sūtra)................It cites the text of of the Sūtra and explains minutely its manifold meaning, consisting altogether of 18,000 ślokas..............Boys of fifteen begin to study this commentary and understand it after five years.

There thus seems to have been a long course of grammatical study of Sanskrit language, beginning when a boy was six years of age and lasting till he was twenty, which was a preliminary to the study of higher subjects in the secondary stage of education. But this profound study of Sanskrit grammar was of a higher rather than of an elementary type and it is curious that I-Tsing makes no mention of any arrangement for the teaching of reading and writing to the lads who were taking up this course nor of the teaching of arithmetic. It would seem, however, not unlikely that when once the monasteries had begun to receive pupils who were not intending to join the community, the system might have been generally extended and to have catered even for children who only came to learn the three R's and receive some simple religious instruction, and the analogy of Buddhist schools as they exist in Burma and Ceylon even down to the present day would seem to confirm this.

A description of the elementary education carried on in Burma in Buddhist monasteries as given by Lieutenant-General Albert Fytche may help us to form some picture of what the Buddhist elementary schools in India were probably like, though difference of country and lapse of time may have brought about many changes. "It is almost the universal custom for Burmese parents in every class of life, to cause their sons to enter the monasteries as novices, for the purpose of learning to read and write. As soon as the boys are able to read and write, religious books are put into their hands, from which they imbibe religious notions and become acquainted with at least some portions of their creed... ....Before a lad can obtain the novitiate he must be at least eight years of age, and his entrance into a monastery is a marked event in his life. He proceeds through the streets to the monastery, dressed in the richest apparel his parents can afford, riding on a horse gaily caprisoned, or sitting in a handsome litter borne on the shoulders of four or more men, with gold umbrellas held over their head, and accompanied by music and a large procession of kinsfolk and acquaintances. On reaching the threshhold of the monastery, the postulant is delivered by his parents over to the Superior or Tsaya-dau, after whom he repeats the two Buddhist formularies of the "Three Refuges" (tun-surana) and the ten obligations (das-sil). His head is then shaved and his fine secular dress is changed for the yellow-robe. From that time his identity is lost, he is subjected to monastic discipline, the monastery becomes his home and he must go round every morning with his alms-bowl and subsist on the daily food that is given him.....................The novices do not generally remain in the monasteries beyond a few years and then they return to secular life; but in the event of their remaining until they are twenty years of age, they can then, if they wish it, receive full ordination, and become patsengs or professed members of the order."[137]

"Some boys are boarders, others attend the monastery every day. The instruction begins by teaching a boy the letters of the alphabet written on a rough wooden slate. These he learns by shouting them out at the top of his voice. All the books which are learnt are religious ones, and the curriculum includes the learning of Pali formulæ and prayers necessary for religious worship. The life and sayings of Buddha and the Jātakas are the chief elements of instruction. The pupils repeat their lessons word for word after their teacher, as they sit in rows before him and chant after him all in the same way."[138]

---

[137] Burma Past and Present, Lieut-General Albert Fytche, pp. 190-92.
[138] Shway Yeo, Ch. II.

"The monastic system in Burma has a practical interest from its being connected with national education. Every monastery has its school, where in harmony with the national religion are learnt the same lessons which have been taught from generation to generation for a couple of thousand years. On arriving at some obscure spot in the interior of the country, the first sign of life that often strikes the ear, is the murmuring sound proceeding from the monastery school; and there is not a town or village, scarcely even a hamlet, I think, that has not at least one of such schools."[139]

In schools in Buddhist monasteries in Ceylon the condition of affairs was very similar.[140] There was generally a school attached to the pansal or residence of a Buddhist priest. The children did not all attend at the same period of day but as they had leisure went to the pansal to repeat their lessons and then returned home or went to their employment in some other place. The school was a mere shed open at the sides, with a raised platform in one corner covered with sand on which letters were traced by the finger of the child learning to write. Lessons were usually repeated aloud and were recited in a singing tone, several boys frequently joining in chorus. The alphabet was first learnt and was usually copied on tāl leaves; after that the union of vowels and consonants. Then the pupil began to write the letters upon sand, holding in the left hand a piece of wood to erase what had been written. The course of reading included about fourteen books. (1) A name book which was a collection of names of villages, countries, temples, caves, etc.; (2) an enumeration of the various signs and beauties upon the person of Buddha; (3) stanzas in honour of Buddha, Truth etc., with some grammatical rules also; (4) an account of the birth of Gaṇeśa, etc.,; (5) stanzas in praise of Buddha in Elu, Pali and Sanskrit; (6) Navaratna ("The nine Jewels")—a description and eulogy of nine most precious things in the world, the principal of which is Buddha; (7) Sanskrit proverbs with explanations; (8) Sanskrit stanzas in honour of Buddha with explanation; (9) Sanskrit stanzas containing the names of the last twenty-four Buddhas, etc.; (10) Pali

---

139 Burma Past and Present, Albert Fytche, p. 205.

140 R. S. Hardy, Eastern Monachism, pp. 18 and 313 ff.

stanzas in nonour of Buddha ; (11) Sanskrit stanzas in honour of the Sun ; (12) Sanskrit stanzas on the management of the voice in recitation; (13) Pali stanzas in honour of Buddha ; (14) the Amarakoṣa or Sanskrit lexicon, with a Singhalese commentary. There was a course of further studies for those Singhalese students who wanted to prepare themselves for the priesthood or for the medical profession.

In the primary schools attached to Buddhist monasteries education was imparted through the medium of Pali which was the language of the masses and not through Sanskrit as was the case in Brāhmaṇic schools. Once two bhikkhus named Yamelu and Tekula, brahmins by birth but converted to Buddhism, complained to their Lord that the priests 'differing in lineage, in birth, in family' corrupted the language by their own dialect and offered that they would put down his teachings into Sanskrit verse. Gautama said to them "You are not, O bhikkhus, to put the word of the Buddha into Sanskrit verse.........I order you O bhikkhus, to learn the word of the Buddha each in his own dialect."[141]

In Southern India the Jaina ascetics who established the Digambara sect of Jainism in Tamil land, in Andhra and in Karṇātaka from the early centuries of the Christian era enriched the three vernacular languages of these three countries. They did not use the modulated Prākṛt forms like the Buddhists but used Sanskrit words in their unchanged or tatsama forms in vernacular writing and thus embellished Telegu, Tamil and Kanarese literatures. They also wrote the grammars of these local vernaculars in Sanskrit. They again appear to have started elementary schools for children, as strangely enough we find in Andhra, Tamil and Karṇātaka and even in Mahārāṣṭra that the first sentence taught to children in writing varṇamālā is still the Jaina salutation "Om namaḥ Siddham". The Telegu people use the formula "Om namaḥ Śivāya, Siddham namaḥ".[142] "The first part has been added subsequently by the Śaivas in the South to obliterate the influence of the Jainas when they

---

[141] Chullavagga V. 33. 1.

[142] Rāmaswāmī Ayyanger, Andhra-Karṇātaka Jainism. p. 64 ; also Studies in South Indian Jainism. The latter portion is said to be Buddhist by Mr. Ayyanger but it seems to be Jain.

themselves started Matams and Pāṭhśālās or primary schools in villages and towns." "In Kalinga or Ooriya the formula is "Sidhirastu" which is clearly Jain.[143] In Mahārāṣṭra " Śrī Gaṇeśāya namaḥ " is added to "Om namaḥ Siddham." These relics show that formerly the Jain ascetics took a great share in teaching children in the southern countries.

The effect of Muhammadan domination upon these primary schools must have been very considerable. Muhammadanism, at any rate, helped the development of Indian vernaculars and might have given a great impetus not only to the teaching of vernaculars but also to instruction through them. But the growth of a large Muhammadan population might have lessened the number of such Hindu elementary schools and the use of Persian as the official language by the Muhammadan rulers made even Hindus resort to Muhammadan teachers in order to obtain a knowledge of this language and with it the possibility of obtaining Government employment. These Persian elementary schools must then have become numerous in the Muhammadan period. As Abul Fazl, Akbar's personal friend and minister says[144] : " In every country, but specially in Hindusthan, boys are kept for years at schools, where they learn the consonants and vowels. A great portion of the life of the student is wasted by making them read many books. His Majesty orders that every school-boy should first learn to write the letters of the alphabet and also learn to trace their various forms. He ought to learn the shape and name of each letter, which may be done in two days, when the boy should proceed to write the joined letters. They may be practised for a week, after which the boy should learn some prose and poetry by heart and then commit to memory some verses to the praise of God or moral sentences, each written separately. Care is to be taken that he learns to understand everything himself but the teacher may assist him a little. He then ought for some time to be daily practised in writing a hemistich or a verse and will soon acquire a current hand. The teacher ought specially to look after five things, knowledge of the letters ; meanings of words ; the hemistich ; the verse ; the former lesson. If

---

143 Ibid.

144 Āin-Ākbarī (Blochmann and Jarret's edition) p. 278 ; Gladwin's edition I. 223.

this method of teaching be adopted, a boy will learn in a month or even in a day, what it took others years to understand, so much so that people will get astonished. Every boy ought to read books on morals, arithmetic, the notation peculiar to arithmetic, agriculture, mensuration, geometry, astronomy, physiognomy, household matters, the rules of Government, medicine, logic, the tabī'ī, riyāzī and ilāhī sciences and history; all of which may be gradually acquired. In studying Sanskrit students ought to learn the Vyakarana, Niyaī, Vedānta and Patanjal. No one should be allowed to neglect those things which the present time requires." This passage, however, does not refer to Hindu primary schools although it mentions Hindu Sanskrit education. But such schools no doubt continued to exist and would be used by the Hindu trading and agricultural classes.

Pietra della valle[145] who visited India in 1623 thus describes a Hindu primary school in South India :—"In the meantime, while the burthens were getting in order, I entertained myself in the porch of the temple, beholding little boys learning arithmetic, after a strange manner, which I will here relate. They were four and having all taken the same lesson from the master, in order to get that same by heart and repeat likewise their former lessons and not forget them, one of them singing musically with a certain continu'd tone (which hath the force of making a deep impression upon the memory) recited part of the lesson; as for example, "one by itself makes one"; and while he was thus speaking, he writ down the same number, not with any kind of pen, nor on paper but (not to spend paper in vain) with his finger on the ground, the pavement being for that purpose strew'd all over with very fine sand; after the first had writ what he sung, all the rest sung and writ down the same thing together. Then the first boy sung and writ down another part of the lesson; as for example, "two by itself makes two", which all the rest repeated in the same manner and so forward in order. When the pavement was full of figures they put them out with the hand and if need were, strew'd it with new sand from a little heap which they had before them wherewith to write further. And thus they did as long as the exercise

[145] Travels of Pietra delle valle (Hakluyt Society's Publication) II. 227.

continu'd, in which manner likewise, they told me, they learnt to read and write without spoiling paper, pens or ink, which certainly is a pretty way." Mr. William Adam in his Reports on Vernacular Education in Bengal (1835-38)[146] mentions that one of the text-books used in the Hindu vernacular schools was Subhankar's rhyming arithmetic rules which he says were evidently composed during the existence of Muhammadan power, as it was full of Persian terms and reference to Muhammadan usages. This shows how even the Hindu elementary schools had to accommodate themselves to some extent to the altered circumstances which were brought about by Moslem rule.

---

[146] Edited by Rev. J. Long, p. 97.

CHAPTER V.

SECONDARY AND HIGHER EDUCATION IN THE BRAHMANIC SEATS OF LEARNING.

We have already seen that before the upanayana and the commencement of Vedic study the Hindu child did not pass his days idly but received an elementary training in the writing schools in one of which Gautama Buddha received his primary education. But in earlier times the education of the child up to the age of seven seems to have been more in the home than in these schools. But later on when the religious ceremonials were beginning to increase in complexity and the literal sense of the hymns was becoming foreign to the people in general, it became necesary to take precautions for securing and establishing their sense. "To attain these objects" says Weber "those most conversant with the subject were obliged to give instruction to the ignorant and circles were formed around them of travelling scholars who made pilgrimages from one teacher to another according as they were attracted by the fame of special learning". [147]

Thus there gradually came into existence a large mass of literature composed by eminent teachers, containing explanations and discussions of various texts and allusions and references to their application to rituals. The Yajurveda and the Brāhmaṇas teem with discussions of the meaning, significance and application to several Vedic passages.[148] These discussions and dissertations were later classified and arranged under different heads. The Śatapatha Brāhmaṇa mentions the Anuśāsanas [149] which are commandments issued to the learners of the Veda in conformity with the spirit of these texts ; the Vidyās or mystic and sacred lore ; Vākovākya or logic ; Itihāsa or legendary history ; Purāṇa or legendary lore ; Nārāśṃsis or verses in commemoration of patrons and heroes ; Gāthās or sententious

---

[147] History of Indian Literature—Weber, p. 21.

[148] Ṛgveda X. 85, 6.

[149] Śāsana means instruction. C. f. Śāstā (teacher), Śāstrā (treatise), Śādhi (teacher), Anuśāstṛ (teacher).

sentences. The Taittirīya Āraṇyaka has practically the same list but puts the two last together. [150]

It is as a result of this process and further specialisation of the various branches of learning that we have the systematisation of the Vedāngas. The first reference to the Vedāngas is to be found, I believe, in the term Anuśāsana, which occurs in the Śatapatha Brāhmaṇa. Sāyaṇa explains the term as meaning the vedāngas and his explanation is not inherently impossible, as the Vedāngas were then already in the embryo, and it might be included under the general term anuśāsana, which literally means only studies and directions auxiliary to the study of the Vedic texts.[151]

The earliest of the Vedāngas appears to have been Kalpa, which contains not only directions for sacrifices, as is usually believed, but also general rules of conduct and regulations in regard to study and teaching. It is mentioned in the Śvetāśvatara Upanishad, [152] for instance, that it was laid down in the early Kalpas that knowledge of the highest kind should not be imparted to one who was not calm and tranquil in spirit and who was not a son or resident disciple. The Nirukta was the crystallisation of the discussions stimulated by the spirit of enquiry prevalent in the age of ritualism The riddle verses of the Atharvaveda represent probably the earliest step in this direction. The Yajurveda has the expression "praśnam etc." and the Brāhmaṇa has praśnin, abhiprasnin and praśnavivāka—questioner, cross-questioner and answerer. There can hardly be any reference here to 'parties in law-suit' which is a gratuitous assumption. The significance is educational rather than legal. Praśna in course of time, came to denote a section or division of a thesis. Along with the praśnin of the Yajurveda and the Provāchika of the Atharvan, we may take the Nirvachana of the Brāhmaṇa literature, which is certainly connected etymologically with Nirukta, [153] the science of etymology. The best known work under this head is that of Yāska, who mentions no

150 Śatapatha Brāhmaṇa X. 1 ; Taitt. Āraṇyaka II. 9 ; Atharvaveda XV. 6. The meanings of these terms are clear from Taitt. Āraṇyaka I, 1, 1, 6 etc.

151 As in Taitt. Up. 1, 1, 13.

152 Svet. Up. VI. 22 ; c. f. Maitrā. Br. Up. VI. 29.

153 Nirukta is derived from nirvach to explain.

fewer than a dozen predecessors of whom Aupamanyava, Aruṇavābha, Śākapuṇi and Sthaulashṭhīvi are otherwise known. [154]

Of the other Vedangas Śikṣhā and Chhandas are already in evidence through the evolution of Vedic phonology and early works on Chhandas are known to have existed, bearing the names of Yāska and Saitava and on Śikṣhā as preserved in the Māṇḍukī school. The earliest of the existing works is that of Piṅgala Nāga on Metrics and of Vyāsa on Phonetics. Vyākaraṇa had a long history and development before the days of Pāṇinī who mentions at least sixty-four distinguished predecessors. In Yāska's day the Vyākaraṇa school of Gārgya stood in opposition to the Nairuktaka school founded by Śākaṭāyana. Stages in the evolution of stellar astronomy are marked by the mention of lunar asterisms and years in the hymns ; the solar year, intercalation and cyclic years in the Brāhmaṇas ; and the references to planets, vague in the Brāhmaṇas but clear in the Upaniṣhads. All this formed the subject-matter of Vedānga-Jyotiṣa.

As long as the six Vedāngas consisted of short simple treatises there existed only Vedic schools. But as the materials for the study of the subjects included in the six Angas accumulated, such an enormous amount of matter would have to be worked through by the intending students that it evidently became impossible for one student to acquire a mastery of all the subjects and so special schools arose for the study of special subjects. The members of the former devoted their energy to get full and accurate knowledge of the sacred texts together with the accompanying Angas but took very little care to understand the subject matter, so that they became "living libraries" ; while the special schools taught their special subjects thoroughly and intelligently. This is made clear by the state of Hindu learning in modern times. It is said that there are men called Vaidics who can recite whole volumes of the Vedic texts. But besides this there are specialists who have an expert knowledge of some part of ancient learning such as the performance of sacrifices, grammar, law or astronomy. This specialisation must have begun in very early times, as the work of grammarians like Pāṇinī shows. Thus were formed special schools of grammar, law and astronomy.

---

[154] Taitt. Br. III. 4.

These special schools helped in the growth of a vast body of literature bearing on the Vedic texts which were further developed in the various schools of study and interpretation :—Śākhās, Vyūhas and Charaṇas. There were at least four different schools of Vedic interpretation, known to Yāska :—aitihāsika, ādhyātmika, ādhiyajñika and svābhāvika. The traditional learning was preserved and propagated by various families in different parts of the country. The patriarchal Gotras of the Āryas and the Kulas of spiritual teachers became special guardians of the composition of these schools and of the improvements effected by them in the arrangement and order of studies. In course of time, these gave place to new integrations of scholars—teachers and students—in the Charaṇas. Each Charaṇa or school of Vedic study had its own arrangement of texts, its own manner of application of texts to rituals and its own rules for the conduct and discipline of its members. The relationship by blood characteristic of the Gotra was now replaced by one of cultural relationship and socio-religious observances. In a work named Charaṇayavyuha (a catalogue of all schools or charaṇas) there are mentioned five charaṇas of the Ṛgveda, twenty-seven of the Black Yajurveda, fifteen of the White Yajurveda, twelve of the Sāmaveda and nine of the Atharvaveda.

In course of time the sacred books which had to be mastered by the student had increased to a huge bulk and it became necessary to condense their teaching into some convenient form. This literature is known as the Sūtras. These Sūtra schools multiplied rapidly and came to fall into three classes according to their subject of teaching. The Śrauta Sūtra schools taught the details of ceremonials relating to Vedic sacrifices. Each Veda had its own Śrauta Sūtras and the noteworthy teacher of them are Aśvālāyana and Sānkhālāyana belonging to the Ṛgveda, Lātyāyana and Drāhyāyana to the Sāmaveda, Baudhāyana, Āpasthamba and Hiraṇyakeśhin to the Black Yajurveda and Kātyāyana to the White Yajurveda. Next come the Dharma Sūtra schools which taught the students the customs, manners and laws of the society. Then come the Gṛhya Sūtra schools which taught the rights and obligations of the son, husband, the wife, the father etc., towards one another and set forth distinct rules for the conduct of each one. The present codes of Manu and Yājñabālkya grew up in one of these Dharma

Sūtra schools. The Shulba Sūtra schools taught geometry, purely as was required for the preparation of sacrificial altars. All these classes of Sūtra school branched off from the school of Kalpa.

In course of time there grew up the different schools of Hindu Law. The notion that Hindu religion is exclusively the source of Hindu law is mainly responsible for the idea too often entertained that Hindu law is incapable of growth but the most superficial student of Hindu law will not fail to observe that in reality its history has been otherwise. Indeed the chief agencies of this development have been custom and the commentaries. These commentaries written either by kings like Aparaka of Konkan or by learned Brahmins have twisted and tortured a text of the Smṛti according to the views of justice and practical utility entertained by their authors and according as these views have been accepted in one place and rejected in another, have grown up the different schools of Hindu law. Thus Vijñāneśwara, the author of the Mitākṣarā, when discussing the text prescribing unequal shares for sons according to priority of birth, lays down the general principle that practices expressly inculcated by the sacred law-codes may become obsolete and should be abandoned if opposed to public opinion. So also Nilkaṇṭha, the author of Mayukha in discussing the right of a Śūdra to adopt expressly refers on the authority of his own father, to custom as justifying him in the particular interpretation put by him on the following text of Saunaka :—"But a daughter's son and a sister's son are affiliated even by Śūdras". Again relying on custom he comes to the conclusion that a boy can be adopted even after marriage.

Professor Winternitz[155] has profounded the theory that the Arthaśāstra was originally taught in the schools of Dharmaśāstra among the "duties of the king" but at the same time it branched off from the Dharmaśāstra and was taught in separate schools of Arthaśāstra, the reason being that the same teachers appear in the Mahābhārta and elsewhere as authors of both Dharmaśāstras and Arthaśāstras. But Prof. Winternitz ignores the fact that Kautilya's Arthaśāstra itself refers to the existence of Vārta (Economics) and Daṇḍa-nīti (Polity) as separate branches of learning which developed very early in separate

[155] Calcutta Review, April, 1924.

schools and the Arthaśāstra and the Dharmaśāstra utilised the results of the study of these two branches of learning in those schools. There are evidences in Kautilya's Arthaśāstra showing that treatises on Polity made use of sūtra style. This together with the existence of separate works on Polity, *e. g.*, the Chāṇakyasūtra and Bṛhaṣpatisūtra make it very probable that there was a sūtra period in the development of treatises on Polity just as these was a sūtra period in the development of the law-codes like that of Manu. It is not, therefore, likely at all that Arthaśāstras should branch off from the Dharmaśāstras. It was in the treatises on Daṇḍanīti and Vārta that full treatment can be made of the subjects of Polity and Economics. The Dharmśāstras made only a very meagre treatment of those subjects because their full treatment was not the province of a code of law. It would, therefore, be proper to hold the view that the Arthaśāstras and the Dharmaśāstras developed on parallel lines and just as the Dharmaśāstras had a sūtra period, so also the branches of learning—Vārta and Daṇḍanīti—utilised by the Arthaśāstras passed through a similar sūtra period and could well have been contemporaneous with the works of the corresponding stages of development of the Dharmaśāstras.

The growth of these special schools began not later than the 5th century B. C.[156] It is thought that Law became a special subject of study at a somewhat later date than Grammar or Astronomy. But even in the Rāmāyaṇa and in some of Dharmasūtras there are traces that the specialisation had already begun. Thus in the Rāmāyaṇa[157] we find a reference to professors of the Tattirīya branch and to students who are specialising in the Kaṭha branch of Vedic studies. On the eve of his journey to Daṇḍakāraṇya Rāma ordered Lakṣhmaṇa to make various gifts to such men living under his protection.[158] Reference to paṇḍits who have specialised in Vedic learning, in the Purāṇas, Swara-lakṣhmaṇa, in the science of music, in Chhanda-lakṣhmaṇa,

---

[156] For the beginnings of specialisation, see Buhler, Sacred Books of the East, Vol. XXV. (The Law code of Manu), p. XLVI ff.

[157] Ayodhyākāṇḍa, 32nd Sarga.

[158] Ibid.

in Sāmudṛk lakṣmaṇa, in Tāla, in Astrology, in Kalpasūtra, in sacrificial ceremonies, in Logic, in Grammar, etc, authors of books on a painting (Chitra-Kābya-praṇetā) is also to be found.[159] Rāma brought all of them in connection with his sacrifice and then summoned Kuśa and Laba to sing Rāmāyaṇa in their presence.[160] Again in Gautama[161] regarding the composition of the Pariṣad we find that besides the men who have completely studied the Veda, there are those who know the different Dharmasūtras, besides the three representatives of the first three āśramas. In Vaśiṣtha[162] and Baudhāyana,[163] the three specialists are student of the Mīmānsā, that is, one who knows the sacrificial rules, one who knows the Angas and one who recites the works on the sacred law. In Manu[164] those who know the Vedas are reduced to three and the specialists are a Logician, a Mīmānsaka, one who knows the Nirukta and one who recites the Institutes of the sacred law. Similarly we find in Vaśiṣtha Saṃhitā[165] the following specialists who along with others are called the sanctifiers of the rows of learned Brahmins :—one who knows the text of the four sacrifices (Aśvamedha, Purushamedha, Sarvameda and Pitṛmedha), one who knows Vājasena (branch of the White Yajurveda), one who knows the six Angas, one who knows Chhandas (Vedic metre) and the brāhmaṇa who studies the sacred law treatises.

These Vedic schools and Special schools were run by a teacher who admitted to his family as many pupils as he could manage. Such teachers were householders. To them students came from all sides "as water runs downwards, as months go to the year". [166] In a hymn of the Ṛgveda[167] there is a reference to such a school which compares the meeting together of the teacher and the taught with the gathering of the frogs in the rainy season :

---

[159] Rāmāyaṇa, Uttarakāṇḍa, 94th Sarga.

[160] Ibid.

[161] Chapter XXIX.

[162] III. 20.

[163] i, 1, 5-13.

[164] XII. 110-112.

[165] III. 19.

[166] Taittirīya Upaniṣhad I. 4. 3.

[167] Ṛgveda VII. 103. Griffith's translation.

"Each of these twain receives the other kindly,
while they are revelling in the flow of waters.
When the frog moistened by the rain springs forward
and Green and Spotty both combine their voices.
When one of these repeats the other's language, as he who
learns the lesson of the teacher,
Your every limb seems to be growing larger, as ye
converse with eloquence on the waters."

That such seats of learning continued to be popular down to the time of Harṣa Śilāditya will be evident from Bāṇa's Harṣacharita where a province is described as being resorted to quite joyfully by multitudes of people "like a school by pupils". Bāṇa, [168] greeted by his numerous relatives, on his return from Harṣa's court made among others the following enquiries : "Do the boys pursue their studies at the proper time ? Is there the same unbroken daily application to the Veda ? The old earnestness in the practice of the art of sacrifice ? Are there the same classes in grammar exposition, showing respect by days not idly spent in series of emulous disscussions ? Is there the old logic society, regardless of all other occupation ? The same excessive delight in the Mīmānsā, dulling all pleasure in other authoritative books ?"

But the most important seats of learning were the Brāhmaṇic settlements and in connection with them Pariṣads or assemblies of learned brahmins who gave decisions on all points connected with the Brāhmaṇic religion and learning.[169] These were in some respects like judicial assemblies[170] and in others like ecclesiastical synods[171] but as those who composed them were most of them also teachers, they corresponded to a certain extent to the associations of teachers in the Middle Ages of Europe which developed into Universities. The settlement of brahmins proficient in different branches of the ancient learning in various centres must have meant the gathering together

---

168 Harṣacharit—Cowell and Thomas, p. 71.

169 Civilisation in Ancient India—R. C. Dutt, Vol. I. p. 163.

170 Manu XII. 110 ; Vaśiṣṭha III ; Gautama XXIX ; Parāśara VIII. 6-7.

171 Yājñbālkya I. 9.

also of a number of students who were receiving instruction from them, and thus these Parişads would form the nucleus of something corresponding to a University. In the Bṛhadāraṇyaka Upanişhad[172] we read that Śvetaketu went to the Parişad of the Pāñchālas. King Pravahana Jaibali was the member of Pāñchāla Parişhad of scholars which he attended every day.

Max Muller says[173] that according to modern writers a Parişad ought to consist of twenty-one brahmins, well versed in philosophy, theology and law. But in early times it seems that a smaller number would have been sufficient. According to Manu[174] "Whatever an assembly of ten or three qualified brahmins, faithful to their duties, shall lay down as the law, must be accepted as such. Such an assembly shall consist of at least ten brāhmaṇas consisting of three persons who each know one of the three principal Vedas, a Logician, a Mīmāṃsaka, one who knows the Nirukta, one who recites the institutes of the sacred law and three men belonging to the first three āśramas. One who knows the Yajurveda, one who knows the Sāmaveda shall be known to form an assembly consisting of at least three members and competent to decide doubtful points of law." According to Gautama[175] "All matters of doubt should be submittod to the deliberations of at least ten honest, greedless, impartial men of wisdom of the following type for settlement: Four of them must be brahmins well-versed in the Vedas; one member of good conduct from each of the following orders, *viz.*, brahmachārins, householders and vānaprasthas and three men who know the different institutes of law. A council consisting of the aforesaid type is called a Parişad." According to Vaśiṣṭha.[176] "Four men who each know one of the four Vedas, one who knows Mīmānsā, one who knows the Angas, a preceptor of the sacred law and three leading men of the first three āśramas constitute a Parişad consisting of at least ten (members)." According to Baudhāyana[177] "it shall consist ten members consisting of four men

---

172 VI. 2.

173 History of Sanskrit Literature—Max Muller, pp. 128-132.

174 Manu XII. 110-112.

175 Chapter XXIX.

176 III. 20.

177 i, 1, 5-13.

who each know one of the four Vedas, one well-versed in Mīmānsā, one who knows the Angas and three brahmins belonging to the first three āśramas." According to Yājñabālkya[178] "Four persons well-read in the Vedas and religious codes or a number of brahmins versed in the three Vedas, form a synod. Whatever this synod or a person foremost among those well-versed in spiritual science declares is religion." According to Parāśara[179] "An assembly consisting of three or five brahmins who are well-versed in the Vedas and Vedāngas even without consecrating the sacred fire is called a Pariṣad. Even a single brahmin who is a muni with a knowledge of his self and devoted to prayers, performances of Vedic sacrifices and ceremonial oblations, may constitute a Pariṣad in his individual capacity. In the absence of five brahmins of the aforesaid type, an assembly consisting of brahmins who are content with their own profession should be regarded as a Pariṣad." Further we are told "He who is well-versed in the four Vedas and Vedāngas, who studies the scriptures and has got a mind free from all hesitations or waverings should be regarded as constituting the best Pariṣad in his individual self. In the absence of such a man, a council consisting of ten brāhmaṇa householders should be reckoned as a Pariṣad of the middling class."[180] These details about the composition of the assembly are interesting as showing how specialisation in Vedic study had begun in very early times. It is equally interesting to find that not only were the different faculties represented in this nucleus of a University but even a student (brahmachārin) was a member of the Pariṣad.

Some of the centres of learning were the hermitages of ṛṣis or other learned men who retired to the forests in their old age. We learn from Buddhist literature that the Buddha after stealing away from his father's palace went to the hermitage of one of the ascetics living in the forest near the Rājagṛha hills, Ālāra Kālāma by name. He taught Gautama the doctrine of nothingness. Gautama describes his progress thus: "Very speedily I learned the doctrine and so far as concerns uttering with mouths

---

[178] I. 9.

[179] VIII. 19-21.

[180] Parāśara VIII. 34.

and lips the words, "I know, I understand", I and others with me knew the word of wisdom and ancient lore. Then the thought occurred to me "When Ālāra Kālāma declares : "Having myself realised and known this doctrine, I abide in the attainment thereof", it cannot all be a mere profession of faith ; surely Ālāra Kālāma sees and knows this doctrine."

Knowledge in ancient India was not a mere matter for memory, study or intellectual apprehension, it was something to be realised and lived. Thus the Buddha strove hard to reach as far as his teacher in that doctrine so as ultimately "to dwell in the attainment of a knowledge and realisation thereof". He achieved success in his efforts in no long time, whereupon his teacher unable to contain himself, burst out as follows : "Happy friend, are we ; yea, doubly happy, in that we look upon such a venerable one, such a fellow-ascetic as thee ! The doctrine which I know, that thou knowest ; and the doctrine which thou knowest, that I know. As I am, so art thou ; as thou art, so am I. Come friend, you and I together lead this company of ascetics" Thus did the teacher put his pupil "on a perfect level with himself, so honouring him with exceeding great honour". But Gautama could not remain satisfied with that doctrine and seeking the highest good, the incomparable path to Peace Supreme, he sought another teacher and went where dwelt Uddaka, the disciple of Rāma and thus addressed him : "I wish, friend, to lead the ascetic life under this discipline and doctrine". As before he "speedily acquired this doctrine so far as concerns lip-profession" and later on achieved sufficient mastery to be able "to abide in a realisation and knowledge of the doctrine" and was treated by his teacher as fully his equal. With the knowlege and training in Yoga received from his brāhmaṇa teachers, the Buddha then resolved to depend upon himself for his further progress and retired to the jungles of Uruvelā near the present temple of Bodh Gayā. There he "spied a beautiful secluded spot among the trees, with a pleasant, shallow clear-flowing river close by, easily accessible, with field and pastures all around" and immediately settled down, saying "this suits well for effort". Early Buddhism with its scheme for self-suppression was not dead to the objective beauty of Nature as an aid to the inner spiritual life.

An idea of the free academic life and the variety and catholicity of studies in these hermitages will be evident from the description given in the Mahābhārata [181] of the hermitage of Kaṇva. It was situated on the bank of the Mālini river and there many ṛṣis were reciting the hymns of the Ṛgveda and many others were singing passages from the Sāmaveda and the Atharvaveda. In another part of the hermitage ṛṣis who had seen the end of various śāstras like the Purāṇas, Nyāya, Tatva, Ātmaviveka, Śabdaśāstra, the Vedas with their Vedāngas and who were well-versed in the science of matter with its actions and qualities, in the speech of birds and lower animals were discussing with one other the subtle points of their respective branches of study. Followers of Buddhism also were studying their own sacred texts.

The ṛṣis who lived in these hermitages were not all lonely recluses or celibate anchorites cut off from the soceity of women and the family. Some of them formed family groups, living with their wives and children, but not pursuing wealth or fame or material advancement like ordinary householders. Thus they lived in the world but were not of it. They had frequent touch with the cities and the royal court by means of respectful invitations to the domestic ceremonies of the kings and rich men and the visits made by the latter to their hermitages in a spirit of pilgrimage. Their pupils included their own children and also boys from the busy world, who lived with the hermits, shared their toils, studied under them and served them like their own sons. Then after finishing their education they would bow down to the guru, pay their dakṣhiṇā and come to the busy world to take places among the men of action. In the calm of these sylvan retreats learning was thus fostered by the ṛṣis who were maintained in learned leisure partly by their pupils' foraging in the woods and fields and partly by the gifts of kings and rich householders.

These hermitages were, indeed, as effectual for the promotion of knowledge as the cathedrals of Mediæval Europe, but without the unnatural monachism of the latter. Lecky[182] thus remarks about

---

[181] Ādi Parva, 70th Adhyāya.

[182] History of European Morals, cabinet edition, II. 137, 334-35.

the celibate clergy of the Catholic world: "The effect of the mortification of the domestic affections upon the general character was probably very pernicious. In Protestant countries, where the marriage of the clergy is fully recognised, it has, indeed, been productive of the greatest and most unequivocal benefits. Nowhere does Christianity assume a more beneficial or a more winning form than in those gentle clerical households which stud our land, constituting as Coleridge said, 'the one idyl of modern life' the most perfect type of domestic peace, the centre of civilisation in the remotest village..................... Among the Catholic priesthood, on the other hand, where the vow of celibacy is faithfully observed, a character of a different type is formed, which with very grave and deadly faults, combines some of the noblest excellences to which humanity can attain." This evil was avoided in Ancient India.

The sanskrit poets like Kālidās, Bhababhūti and others love to depict the beautiful surroundings of these hermitages and the simple life of their inhabitants in contact with both animate and inanimate Nature. The Parāśara Saṃhitā [183] describes the Badarikāśrama of Parāśara, son of Śakri, father of the holy Vyāsa, thus: "Trees of wonderful fruit and foliage enhanced the beauty of that holy forest where fountains and rivulets of crystal flow ran babbling into sacred pools. Herds of deer were found to roam about and birds of beautiful plumage were heard to join their melodious notes in a chorus of harmony". It is also a noteworthy fact that in each of the places of preaching and places of his retreat the Buddha preferred the forest near by to the city itself. Thus at Rājagṛha he would reside in the Veluvana or Yaṣṭivasa or the Uruvelā village; at Śrāvastī there were the famous Jetavana and its elaborately constructed vihāra, as well as the Pubhārāma; at Kauśāmbi, he had the Ghoṣitārāma at his disposal; at Vaiśali he had the Mahāvana with its Kutāgāra hall and for his second residence the mango-grove or Āmrapālī; at Pāva he would stay in Chunda's mango-grove; Kapilāvastu has its Nyagrodha grove, and Benares had its deer-park at Isipatana. Hence the remark of Dr. Rabindranāth [184] "A most wonderful thing

[183] I. 6-7.

[184] Biśwa-bhāratī Quarterly, April, 1924, p. 64.

that we notice in India is that there the forest, not the town, is the fountain-head of civilisation. Wherever in India its earliest and most wonderful manifestations are noticed, we find that there men have not come into so close a contact as to be rolled or pushed into a compact body or mass or whole. There, trees and plants, rivers and lakes, had an ample opportunity to live in close relationship with men. In these forests, though there was human society, there was enough of open space or aloofness; there was no jostling. Still this aloofness did not produce an inertness in the Indian mind; on the other hand it rendered it all the brighter. It is the forest that has nurtured the great ancient sages of India, the Vedic and the Buddhistic. Not only the Vedic ṛṣis but Lord Buddha also preached in many woods of India. The royal palace had no room for him, it was the forest that took him into its lap. The current of civilisation that flowed from the forest inundated the whole of India".

"Here is an Indian ideal that it would be well to revive, for this planting of universities in the midst of great cities is European and not Indian. Oxford and Cambridge alone in England have kept up the tradition of their Aryan forefathers. The modern "Civic Universities" as they are called, are planted in the midst of the most tumultuous, hurrying noisy cities in England. Not from them will come sublime philosophies or artistic master-pieces, but they will doubtless produce men of inventive genius, miracles of machinery, new ways of annihilating space. But in a country in which a man is valued for what he is, not for what he has, in which a man's life consisteth not in the abundance of the things which he possesseth, the Indian ideal is the most suitable. The essence of that Ideal is not the forest as such but the being in close touch with Nature; to let her harmonies permeate the consciousness and her calm soothe the restlessness of the mind. Hence it was the forest, which best suited the type and the object of the instruction in the days which evolved ṛṣis; instruction which aimed at profound rather than at swift and alert thought; which cared not for lucid exposition by the teacher, but presented to the pupil, a kernel of truth in a hard shell, which he must crack unassisted with his own strong teeth if he would enjoy the kernel; if he could not break the shell, he could go without the fruit; instruction which thought less of an accumulation of facts poured out into the pupil's memory than of the drawing out in him the faculty which could discover the truth, hidden beneath a mass of irrelevancies; of such fruitful study the Hindu Āśrama in the forest is the symbol".[185]

---

[185] Kamalā Lectures, 1925—Annie Beasant, pp. 26-27.

CHAPTER VI.

THE ORGANISATION OF SECONDARY AND HIGHER EDUCATION IN THE BRAHMANIC SEATS OF LEARNING.

An idea of the educational organisation of the Brāhmaṇic seats of learning can be formed from an intelligent study of the Brāhmaṇas and the Upanishads but more fully from that of the Śrautasūtras, the Gṛhyasūtras, the Dharmasūtras and the Dharmaśāstras.

§ 1.—THE IMPORTANCE OF A TEACHER IN EDUCATION.

The Upanishads fully recognise the futility of mere self-study. In the Kaṭha Upanishad [186] the teacher is represented as indispensible to knowledge: "Apart from the teacher there is no access here". The Muṇḍaka Upanishad [187] says "Let him in order to understand this, take fuel in his hand and approach a Guru who is learned and dwells entirely in Brahman". Again, "Not by self-study is the ātman realised, not by mental power, nor by amassing much information".[188] That a teacher is necessary to disperse the mist of empirically acquired knowledge from our eyes is explained beautifully in the following passage from the Chāndogya Upanishad: [189] "Precisely, my dear Sir, as a man who has been brought blind-fold from the country of Gāndhāra and then set at liberty in the desert, goes astray to the east, north or south, because he has been brought thither blind-fold and blind-fold set at liberty; but after that some one has taken off the bondage and has told him "In this direction Gāndhāra lies, go in this direction", instructed and prudent, asking the road from village to village, he find his way home to Gāndhāra; even so the man, who in this world has met with a teacher becomes conscious, 'To this (transitory world) shall I belong only until the time of my release, thereafter shall I go home,". In the Śatapatha Saṃhitā [190] we are told that "the pilferer of learning and books is born dumb". In the Mahābhārata [191] there is a story of Yavakṛta who studied the

---

186 II. 8. 187 I. 2. 12. 188 III. 2. 3.

189 VI. 14. 1-2.

190 IV. 22. 191 Banaparva 134th and 137th Adhyāyas.

Vedas without a Guru and then had to suffer a lot of misery for that. Indeed the Vedas cannot be wellread even from mere books (because of the accents), much less learnt. From a teacher alone one can learn the proper pronunciation. Hence it became the custom that only from a teacher one should learn and the people believed that the lore learned from a teacher could alone be successful and beneficial.

§ 2.—THE SELECTION AND ADMISSION OF STUDENTS.

There was the custom of selecting students for admission into the school. According to Manu [192] the teacher should select only ten classes of pupils for instruction—the son of one's teacher, one who did personal service, one who taught some other subject, a good man, a man pure in mind and heart, a reliable friend, one capable of comprehending and applying the knowledge acquired, a patron and a recluse. Uśanā Saṃhitā [193] says: "An Āchārya's son, one who wishes to hear attentively, one who has given knowledge (in any other subject), a virtuous person, a person pure in body and mind, a relative, one who is capable of understanding the scriptures, one who is liberal in giving away money, a good man and a kinsman—these ten should be taught according to the rules of religious teaching. A Kṣhatriya who is grateful, shorn of malice, intelligent and always doing good; a Vaiśya, endowed with similar qualifications, a grateful Brāhmaṇa, a non-injuring Brāhmaṇa, an intelligent Brāhmaṇa and a Brāhmaṇa doing good unto all—these six should also be taught by the leading twice-born ones. Even though it be quite contrary to the established rules of religious instruction, when a Bipra, invested with the sacred thread by another, comes he should be taught. Instruction in the Vedas should be given to those only and not to any one else; so it is said." According to Yājñabālkya Saṃhitā [194] "The grateful, the submissive, the intelligent, the pure, those who do not suffer from mental and physical ailments, those who are shorn of jealousy, the good-natured, those who are clever in serving friends, those who distribute learning and riches, are worthy of receiving religious instructions". According to Śukrāchārya[195]

---

[192] II. 138, 240, 241.

[193] III. 35-37.

[194] I. 28

[195] Śukranītisāra, Ch. III. line 637.

"one should, educate his own child as well as other's children but not the offenders". From Uśanā Saṃhitā [196] we learn that the student used to live in the house of his teacher without being taught for some time. During this period the teacher had enough opportunity to test or examine his pupil. He would give him instructions in Vedic study only when he thought the pupil fit for it. If the pupil had anything wrong in his conduct the teacher during this one year would correct him his faults and then teach him. The Indian teacher was thus not a believer in making higher education open to all; he imparted instruction to a student only when he was duly qualified for it by his character and capacity, by his heredity and environment. To those times may be applied the observations made recently by Lord Hugh Cecil: "Uniformity is the essence of any and every system, whereas infinite variety and infinite irregularities are the characteristics of people. The only education, therefore, that deserves the name or is really beneficial, is that which ministers to individual capacity and personality. When that connection and response are lacking, teaching and being taught are a funeral waste of time."[197]

§ 3.—THE INITIATION CEREMONY: THE SYMBOL OF ADMISSION AS A STUDENT.

In the Atharvaveda [198] there is a mystic hymn which describes the Sun or the primeval principle, under the figure of a Brāhmaṇa student who brings firewood (samidh) and alms for his teacher. This offering of sacrificial fire to a teacher became the regular way by which a youth sought to be recognised as his pupil and implied a desire to partake in his domestic sacrifice and to accept the duty of helping to maintain it.[199] This is the earliest reference to Upanayanam. In the Śatapatha Brāhmaṇa we are given a line of teachers who have transmitted the sacrificial science to that time.[200] This line is traced back to

196 III. 33-34.

197 Sunday Times, London, August 7, 1925.

198 XI. 5.

199 Kauś. Up. IV. 19; Chāndogya Up. IV. 5; V. 13, 17; VIII. 7. 2; X. 3; XI. 2; Muṇḍaka Up. I. 2. 12; Praśna Up. I. 1.

200 Śatapatha Brāhmaṇa X. 6, 5, 9.

Prajāpati (the creator) and Brāhmaṇa students are spoken of as guarding their teacher, his house and cattle, lest he should be taken away from them.[201] There are references also to a lad going to a teacher with firewood in his hand and asking to become his pupil[202]. This book contains an account of the Upanayana (initiation) ceremony of a Brāhmaṇa student.[203] He is made to say to the preceptor "I have come for brahmacharya (studentship); let me be a brahmachārī (student)". The request to be received by the preceptor was to be duly made *i. e.*, according to the Bṛhadāraṇyaka Upaniṣhad[204] with the words "Upaimyaham vabantam".[205] Before receiving him, the teacher makes enquiry into his name, his birth and family. Satyakāma Jābāla going to Gautama Hāridrumata said to him: "I wish to become a brahmachārin with you, Sir. May I come to you, Sir?" He said to him: "of what family are you, my friend?"[206] The manner of enquiry shows that it was made in a very indulgent fashion and the uncertainty regarding his parentage was not in actual practice admitted as a bar to the teacher's acceptance of the pupil.

The duties pertaining to his new life are now impressed upon the student: "Put fuel into fire. Cleanse internally with water. Do service. Do not sleep in day-time."[207] He was enjoined to move along the Sun's course after Him, symbolising the teaching to follow Nature and her forces as far as possible. He was made to tread on a stone; he was to be 'firm like a stone' and overcome his foes—the temptations within and the slanderers without. The food taken by him was to make him 'strong, long-lived and covered with splendour'. The teacher then touches the chest of the boy with his fingers upwards and repeats the words[208]: "Thy heart shall dwell in my heart; my mind thou shalt follow with all thy heart; may Bṛhaspati join thee to me." "To me alone thou shalt adhere. In me thy thoughts shall dwell. Upon me thy veneration shall be bent. When I speak thou shalt be silent." "May I be dear to thee; let us

---

201 Ibid., III. 2, 6, 15.
202 Ibid., XI. 4, 1, 9.
203 Ibid., XI. 5, 4.
204 VI. 2, 7.
205 c. f. vidhivat in Muṇḍaka Up. I 1, 3.
206 Chāndogya Up. IV. 4, 4.
207 Divā mā Susupthāh (Mantrapāṭha, II, 6, 14).
208 This hypnotism induced into the boy stronger personality.

dwell here in breath and life." After these prayers for concord the teacher bestows on him the blessing. "The bliss in which the Fire, the Sun, the Moon and the Waters go their way, even in that bliss go thou that way. Thou hast become the pupil of Breath. May Indra, Saraswatī and the Aświns bestow intelligence on thee." For himself, the teacher prays that he may through his pupil, "become rich in holy lustre." The ceremonial is equally impressive in all the texts; the only point of difference is that instead of styling him "the pupil of life" one text has the reading "the pupil of Kāma." [209]

In course of time the sacred thread came to be used for the performance of sacrifice.[210] In the Śatapatha Brāhmaṇa[211] it is told that the god and the father went to Prājāpati, wearing the 'sacrificial cord': and also in the Kaushitaki Upanishad [212] the all-conquered Kaushitaki adores the Sun at its rise having put on the 'sacrificial cord'. The spiritual significance of the details of the Upanayana ceremony is thus indicated in the Śatapatha Brāhmaṇa:[213] "The teacher lays his right hand on the head of the pupil whereby he becomes pregnant with him [214] and then in the third night the embryo issues out of the teacher and being taught the Sāvitrī obtains true Brāhmanhood".[215] "He is like a divine creature born from his teacher's mouth".[216] Sāṃkha Saṃhitā [217] says "Brāhmaṇas, Kshatriyas and Vaiśyas are the three twice-born castes: their second birth takes place on the occasion of putting on the girdle of sacred rush. On his second birth symbolised by the wearing of the sacred girdle, the preceptor of a Brāhmaṇa, Kshatriya or Vaiśya who imparts the Gāyatrī Mantra, should be regarded as his father, while the Mantra itself should be looked upon as fulfilling the office of his mother. Until the commencement of his study of the Vedas, a Brāhmaṇa continues in the status of a Śūdra; he becomes a

---

209 Śāṃkhyāyana, IV, 4, 2.

210 It was called the 'Yajñopabīta' i. e., the sacrificial cord. The followers of Āvesta also uses such a cord at the worship of Fire.

211 II. 4. 2.

212 II. 7.

213 XI. 5. 4.

214 Tena garvī bhabati.

215 For fuller explanations see Sāyaṇa's commentary.

216 Śatapatha Brāhmaṇa XI. 5. 4. 17.

217 I. 6-8; c. f. Vishṇu Saṃhitā XXVIII. 37-40.

twice-born after that". Vyāsa Saṃhitā [218] says "Brāhmaṇas, Kshatriyas and Vaiśyas are called the twice-born. Their first birth takes place when they are delivered of their mother's womb; their second, when they duly accept Gāyatrī Mantra from their preceptors". Vaśiṣṭha Saṃhitā [219] says "Their first birth is from their mother and the second from the investiture of the sacred girdle. There (*i. e.* in the second birth) Sāvitrī is the mother and the preceptor is said to be the father. They call the preceptor the father because he gives instructions in the Veda. They quote the following example:—Indeed the virile energy of a man learned in spiritual science, is of two sorts, that which is above the navel and the other such is situated below; through that which is above the navel his offspring is produced when he invests one with the sacred thread and makes him holy. By that which resides below his navel, the children of his body are produced on their mother. Therefore they should never say to a Śrotrīya who teaches the Veda 'Thou art destitute of a son'. Hārīt quotes the following verse:—"There is no religious rite for a child of the twice-born before he has been invested with the sacred girdle. His conduct shall be known as equal to that of a Śūdra before his new birth from the Veda. (The above prohibition relates to all rites except those connected with libations of water, the exclamation Swāhā and the rites to departed names)" Vishṇu Saṃhitā [220] says "The birth of a child in its mother's womb through the union of its parents, out of carnal desire, is a mere organic existence, which he has in common with the beasts. The birth which his teacher, conversant with the Vedas, effects for him, by uttering the Sāvitrī Mantra is the only true, deathless, decayless existence".

In the older Upanishads we come across the prohibition to communicate a doctrine or ceremony to any one except a son or a pupil adopted by the rite of Upanayanam. According to the Aitareya Āraṇyaka [221] the mystical meaning of the combinations of letters must be "communicated to no one who is not a pupil, who has not been a pupil for a whole year, who does not propose himself to be a teacher". Again the Chāndogya Upanishad [222] states: "A father may, therefore, tell that doctrine (*i. e.*,

---

[218] I. 20-21. [219] Ch. II. [220] XXX. 45-46.

[221] III. 2. 6. 9. [222] III. 2. 5.

the doctrine of Brahman as the sun of the universe) to his eldest son or to a worthy pupil. But no one should tell it to any body else, even if he gave him the whole sea-girt earth, full of treasure". In the Bṛhadāraṇyaka Upaniṣhad [223] we are told that the ceremony of the mixed drink, must be communicated to none but a son or a pupil. Similarly the Śvetāsvatara Upaniṣhad [224] says: "This highest mystery in the Vedānta delivered in a former age should not be given to one whose passions have not been subdued nor to one who is not a son or who is not a pupil". And the Maitrāyaniya Upaniṣhad: [225] "Let no man preach this most secret doctrine to any one who is not his son or his pupil". So great was the importance put on this Upanayanam that according to Viṣhṇu Saṃhitā [226] "to suffer one's self to remain uninitiated beyond the proper age-limit (vrātyatā) is one of the Upapātakas", and "such a Vrātya is to be avoided". [227] Manu [228] speaks in the same strain: "A Brāhmaṇa even in time of distress, must not hold any connection with these Vrātyas, not duly expiated according to regulation, either by marriage or by Vedic study".

We accordingly find men and gods taking fuel in their hands and submitting to the conditions of pupilage. The Chāndogya Upaniṣhad [229] relates how Indra himself was obliged to live with Prajāpati as a pupil for 101 years in order to obtain the perfect instruction. In the Kauṣitaki Upaniṣhad [230] Āruṇi takes fuel in his hand and becomes a pupil of Citra Gāṅgyāyani. In the Bṛhadāraṇyaka [231] Gārga says to Ajātaśatru: "Then let me come to you as a pupil". In the Praśna Upaniṣhad [232] Sukeśas, Satyakāma, Sauryāyaṇin, Kauśalya, Vaidarbhi and Kabandhiṇ take fuel in their hands to become pupils of Pippalāda.

At the same time the evidence seems to indicate that a formal pupilage was not absolutely binding in the earlier period. Thus in the Chāndogya [233] it is merely said that "the knowledge which is gained

---

[223] VI. 3. 12.
[224] VI. 22.
[225] VI. 29.
[226] XXXVII. 19.
[227] Viṣhṇu Saṃhitā LVII. 1-2.
[228] II. 40.
[229] V. 3.
[230] I. 1.
[231] II. 1-14.
[232] I. 1.
[233] IV. 9. 3.

from a teacher (as opposed to supernatural instruction by beasts, fire, geese or ducks) leads most certainly to the goal". In another passage [234] the King Aśvapati, instructs the six brāhmaṇas who approach him with fuel in their hands anupanīya *i. e.*, "without first admitting them as his pupil or demanding any preparatory rites". In still another passage [235] we read: "There lived once Śvetaketu Āruṇeya. To him his father (Uddālaka, the son of Aruṇa) said "Śvetaketu, go to school; for there is none belonging to our race, darling, who not having studied the Veda is, as it were, a brāhmaṇa by birth only". From this remark it may reasonably be inferred that at that time entrance upon the life of a brāhmaṇa-student while it was a commendable custom, was not yet universally enjoined upon brāhmaṇas. Again in the Bṛhadāraṇyaka [236] Yājñabālkya instructs his wife Maitreyī when she was not strictly his pupil; he also teaches King Janaka [237] when he was not strictly his pupil; he also imparts knowledge on the deepest problems (*e. g.*, in the conversation with Gārgī) [238] in the presence of a numerous circle of hearers; and only exceptionally, when he desires to explain to Ārtabhāga [239] the mystery of the soul's transmigration, does he retire with him into privacy.

It is also evident from the passages just cited that it was possible in those days for a man to receive instruction from his father or from other teachers. Śvetaketu did both.[240] The Śatapatha Brāhmaṇa [241] shows that the Brāhmaṇa was expected to instruct his own son in both study and spiritual ritual and furnishes an illustration of this in Varuṇa, the teacher of his son Bhṛgu. This fact is also borne out by the evidence of some of the names in the Vaṃśa Brāhmaṇa of the Sāma Veda and the Vaṃśa or list of teachers of the Śāṃkhyāyana Āraṇyoka.[242] It should, however, be noted that these Vaṃśas and those of the Śatapatha Brāhmaṇa also show that a father often preferred that his son should have a famous teacher.

---

[234] Chāndogya Upaniṣhad V. 11. 7.

[235] Chāndogya Upaniṣhad VI. 1. 1.

[236] II. 4.

[237] Bṛhad. Up. IV. 1-2, 3-4.

[238] Bṛhad. Up. III. 8.

[239] Bṛhad. Up. III. 2. 13.

[240] Chāndogya Up. V. 3. 1; Bṛhad. Up. VI. 2. 1; Kauś. Up. I. 1; and Chāndogya Up. VI. 1. 1.

[241] I. 6. 2. 4.

[242] XV. 1.

§ 4.—THE AGE TO COMMENCE VEDIC STUDIES.

The age at which such studentship commenced probably varied from time to time. Thus Śvetaketu "began his apprenticeship with a teacher when he was twelve years of age".[243] According to Vishṇu Purāṇa [244] "the period from birth to the fifth year was regarded as the time for play. After which the time for study commenced". The initiation ceremony which marked the beginning of a boy's student-life was fixed by Manu [245] at the 8th, the 11th and the 12th year in the case of a Brāhmaṇa,, Kshatriya or a Vaiśya boy respectively. But it might take place between 8 and 16 in the case of a Brāhmaṇa, between 11 and 22 in the case of Kṣhatriya and between 12 and 24 in the case of Vaiśya.[246] Gautama [247] says "The initiation of a Brāhmaṇa boy shall ordinarily take place in his 8th year. It may also be performed in the ninth or fifth year for the fulfilment of some particular wish. The number of years is to be calculated from conception. That initiation is the second birth.................The initiation of a Kṣhatriya shall ordinarily take place in the eleventh year after conception, and that of a Vaiśya in the twelvth. Up to the 16th year the time for the Sāvitrī (initiation) of a Brāhmaṇa boy has not passed. Nor (for the initiation) of a Kṣhatriya up to the 20th year. And the limit for that of a Vaiśya extends two years beyond the latter term". According to Yājñabālkya[248] "the Upanayana of a Brāhmaṇa is performed in the eight year (continuing from the time) of conception, that of a Kṣhatriya, in the eleventh or according to the practices of the family". "The period up to the sixteenth, twenty-second and the twenty-fourth is laid down as the time for Upanayanam respectively for the Brahmaṇa, Kṣhatriya and the Vaiśya".[249] According to Uśanā Saṃhitā [250] the investiture of the foremost of the twice-born should take place in the eighth year, either counting from the period of conception or from the date of birth, according to the regulation laid down in one's own family

---

[243] Chāndogya Up. VI. 1. 2.

[244] Part I. XII. 18.

[245] II. 36.

[246] Manu II. 38.

[247] I. 5-14.

[248] I. 14.

[249] Yājñabālkyā Saṃhitā I. 37.

[250] I. 4.

code of rites. According to Vyāsa,[251] Sāṃkhya,[252] Vaśiṣtha[253] and Vishṇu[254] Saṃhitās "the son of a Brāhmaṇa should be invested with the holy thread at the eighth year of his age reckoned from the period of his inter-uterine life. Similarly, the investiture with the holy thread in the case of a Kṣhatriya or Vaiśya child should be made at the eleventh and twelvth year respectively".

The age fixed was no doubt regarded as the ideal to be aimed at, though we see that considerable latitude was provided for. A young Brāhmaṇā was thus about seven years of age (according to our reckoning) when he entered upon the obligations of studentship and this age is that which has been considered a suitable one by many educationists as then the brain has its physical form fully developed. It was expressly provided in a later verse that a child should not be made to recite Vedic verse before initiation. Why a later age was provided for Kṣhatriyas and Vaiyas śis not quite clear. They were of course, not expected to attain to the same proficiency in the Vedic lore as the young Brāhmaṇa, as he alone could perform the sacrifical ritual, and certain portions of the sacred knowledge were reserved for him and their course was, therefore, it may be supposed, not expected to last as long as his. But in this case we should have expected them to have started at the same time and to have left their studentship at an earlier age, especially as they had also to learn their own particular crafts. It seems probable, however, that the difference in age was to emphasise the supposed intellectual superiority of the Brāhmaṇa who was thus ready to begin the study at a younger age than his non Brāhmaṇa fellows ; or the difference was deemed necessary as the young Brāhmaṇa in nine cases out of ten commenced his study at home with his father while his non-Brāhmaṇa fellows were to leave their home and to live with their teacher away from their parents or guardians, for which an older age was quite suitable.

The Upanayana ceremony of a Brāhmaṇa takes place in spring, that of a Kṣhatriya in summer and that of a Vaiśya in autumn.[255]

---

[251] I. 19.
[252] II. 6.
[253] Ch. X.
[254] XXVII. 15-17.
[255] Indische Studien—Weber, Vol. X. p. 22.

It may be noted in this connection that a mystic significance was attached not only to the number of years but also to the particular seasons in which Vedic initiation should take place. Thus according to Āpastamba a boy initiated in the seventh year shows progress in learning, while one who begins in the eighth year lives long, in the nineth gets vigour, in the eleventh strength ; and the tenth and the twelfth make for prosperity. Similarly spring in India is the season of peace and plenty, summer is the time when the tropical sun is at the height of its power and glory, and autumn is the season for harvest.

§ 5.—THE PERIOD OF STUDENTSHIP.

The period of studentship varied according to the aptitude of the pupil to learn and to the vow to learn one or more Vedas. Manu [256] says : "In his preceptor's house, a brahmachārin having practised the vow of studying the three Vedas (Atharva being included within the Ṛgveda) for thirty-six years or for a half or for a quarter of that period necessary to fully comprehend them ; or having studied (all the Vedas or two Vedas or a single Veda, in the proper order of Mantra, Brāhmana etc., without the least deviation from his vow shall enter the order of the householder". According to Yājñabālkya Saṃhitā [257] "In studying each Veda one should lead the life of a religious student for twelve years or five years (at the lowest)". According to Gautama Saṃhitā [258] "Each Veda should be studied for 12 years ; or until it is thoroughly mastered and understood." According to Baudhāyana[259] the total duration of studentship was twelve years for each Veda, at least one year for each division thereof and twenty-four, thirty-six or forty-eight years in all. Manu [260] says elsewhere : "A twice-born one shall reside for the first quarter of his life in the residence of his preceptor" (*i. e.*, for 25 years, since according to smṛti, a hundred years is the ordained space of human existence).[261] In the Mahābhārata [262] we are told : "One should lead a fourth of one's life

---

[256] III. 1-2. [257] I. 36. [258] Ch. II.

[259] I. 2. 3. [260] IV. 1. [261] Śatāyurvai puruṣaḥ.

[262] Śāntiparva, 243rd Adhyāya.

as a brahmachārī". Even after the regular term was over there was no reluctance to continue the study under the teacher. Śvetaketu declares that a further residence of two months every year was advisable, for, by this means he had learnt more than during the period of his formal studentship.[263] Śukrāchārya[264] says: "'I shall live for one hundred years and enjoy life with wealth'—one should ever earn learning and wealth in this hope for twenty-five years or half or quarter of that period." We need not be surprised at the long period of twelve years which was considered necessary to become acquainted even with one Veda. Max Muller[265] quotes from a letter which he received in 1878 from an Indian gentleman giving an account of the system as it was then: "A student of Ṛgveda śākhā, if sharp and assiduous, takes about eight years to learn the Daśagranthas, the ten books which consist of (1) the Saṃhitās or the hymns; (2) the Brāhmaṇas, the prose treatises on sacrifices etc.; (3) the Āraṇyakas; (4) the Gṛhyasūtras, the rules on domestic ceremonies; (5)—(10) the six Angas, treatises on pronunciation, astronomy, ceremonial, grammar, etymology and metre. A pupil studies every day during the eight years, except on the holidays, the so-called anadhyāya *i. e.*, non-reading days. There being 360 days in a lunar year, the eight years would give him 2880 days. From these, 384 holidays have to be deducted, leaving him 2496 work-days during the eight years. Now the ten books consist, on a rough calculation, of 29, 500 ślokas, so that a student of the Ṛgveda has to learn about 12 ślokas a day, a śloka consisting of 32 syllables"

But Śvetaketu[266] returned home after studying all the Vedas foı 12 years with his preceptor. Upakośala Kāmalāyana[267] dwelt as a brahmachārin in the house of Satyakāma Jābāla and "tended his fires for twelve years". There also seems to have been longer terms than that of 12 years. Satyakāma Jābāla[268] spent a series of years with his preceptor

---

[263] Āpastamba, I. 4, 13, 19.

[264] Śukranītisāra, Ch. III., lines 357-59.

[265] Lectures on the Origin and Growth of Religion—Max Muller, Lec. III., pp. 165-66.

[266] Chāndogya Up., VI. 1. 2.

[267] Ibid., V. 10. 1.

[268] Ibid., IV. 4. 5.

during which "four hundred cows had become a thousand". Studentship for thirty-two years is also mentioned [269] and also for 101 years.[270] Megasthenes who came to India in the fourth century B. C. refers to Indian pupils spending thirty-seven years in study. Indeed it was already being recognised that for the cultivation of Vedic studies a long period of studentship was necessary. In the Taittirīya Brāhmaṇa[271] we read: "Bharadvāja lived through three lives in the state of a religious student. Indra approached him when he was lying old and decrepit and said to him, 'Bharadvāja, if I give thee a fourth life, how wilt thou employ it?' 'I will lead the life of a religious student', he replied. He (Indra) showed him three mountain-like objects, as it were unknown. From each of them he took a handful and calling to him, 'Bharadvāja' said: 'These are the three Vedas, The Vedas are infinite. This is what thou hast studied during these three lives. Now there is another thing which thou hast not studied. Come and learn it. This is the universal science.........He who knows this (ya evam Veda) conquers a world as great as he would gain by the triple Vedic science". Indra [272] is said to have lived with Prajāpati as a pupil for no less than 105 years. More often, as might naturally be expected, the realisation of the knowledge of Brahman, with its hard conditions and pre-requisites, required the dedication of a whole life and not merely a part of it. Śvetaketu [273] coming home after twelve years of studentship "conceited, considering himself well-read and stern" and ignorant of the knowledge of Brahman was probably typical of such students as failed to attain the highest knowledge during the comparatively brief period of their pupilage and were deemed unworthy of that instruction. Upakośala Kāmālāyana [274] was probably another such student who inspite of his twelve years of austere studentship was not deemed worthy of that instruction by his teacher. Hence in some cases students chose to become life-long pupils of their teacher.[275] Dakṣa Saṃhitā[276] says: "Two classes of brahmachārin have

---

[269] Ibid., VIII. 7. 3.

[270] Ibid., 11. 3.

[271] III. 10. 11. 3.

[272] Chāndogya Up., VIII. 2. 3.

[273] Ibid., V. 1.

[274] Ibid., IV. 10.

[275] Bṛhad. Up., II. 23, 2.

[276] I. 8-9.

been mentioned by the wise in smṛiti. The first is Upakurvaṇaka (a pupil who wishes to pass on to the state of a householder); the second is Naiṣṭhika (one who lives a life of perpetual celibacy and studentship). He who after having adopted the life of a householder, becomes a religious student again,—is neither a Yatin nor a Vānaprasthin,; he is divorced from all the āśramas". According to the Rāmāyaṇa [277] the former is a Gauṇa brahmachārin, while the latter is a Mukhya brahmachārin. According to Vyāsa Saṃhitā [278] "The twice-born one who practises the vow of Vedic study for 36 years is an Upakuvaṇaka". Life-long or perpetual students are also mentioned in Yājñabālkya, [279] Uśanā, [280] Vyāsa, [281] Manu, [282] Vaśiṣṭha [283] and Viṣṇu [284] Saṃhitās. Indeed it is reasonable to assume that some of the moral attributes insisted upon as essential pre-requisites of instruction, being as they are, but the preparatory means to the highest end of human life—the attainment of the knowledge of Brahman—belong to the last stages of a disciplined life, as the fruits of a long struggle, rather than to its first stage. They cannot be regarded as the normal initial endowments with which a youthful student starts in his career. The epithets śānta, dānta, uparata and the like are hardly applicable, for instance, to an immature stripling who has had no experience of the struggles and temptations of life and of "the ills that flesh is heir to".

This view is supported by several passages in the Upaniṣads in which the conception and scope of brahmacharya is widened so as to embrace, not merely the student-period proper, but the entire course of life, regulated by the disciplines of the four successive stages or āśramas as the way that leads to the Ātman so that the whole of life was looked upon as an education for the life beyond. But many scholars like Deussen, [285] Rhys Davids [286] and Rev. F. E. Keays [287] deny the existence of the

---

277 Bālakāṇḍa 9th Sarga.

278 I. 41.

279 I. 49.

280 III. 83.

281 I. 40.

282 II. 243, 249.

283 Ch. VII.

284 XXVIII. 43.

285 The Philosophy of the Upaniṣads—Deussen, pp. 367, 368.

286 The Dialogues of the Buddha—Rhys Davids, Vol I. pp. 212, 213.

287 Ancient Indian Education—Keays, p. 28; c. f. p. 25.

successive four āśramas or stages in the age of the Upaniṣads. But Dr. N. N. Law [288] has adduced evidences which go to prove that the four āśramas existed as a firmly established institution as early as the time of the two oldest Upaniṣads—the Chāndogya and the Bṛhadāraṇyaka. Further evidences are available which go to show that the knowledge aimed at in the Upaniṣads implies the application of the whole life, through all its stages. Thus in the Chāndogya Upaniṣad [289] the brahmachārin is exhorted after completing his studentship, to become a householder (kutumbe sthitwā) and attain fruition in a life of self-study and self-discipline. In another passage [290] the observances of the last three āśramas such as sacrifices, vow of silence, fasting and living an anchorite's life in the forest are recognised as being ultimately but forms of brahmacharya as the underlying principle of life. In the Kena Upaniṣad [291] asceticism, self-restraint, and sacrifice (tapas, dāma and karman) are specified as the preliminary conditions (pratiṣṭhaḥ) of the Brāhmi Upaniṣad *i.e.*, of the real mystical doctrine which reveals Brahman. In the Kaṭhopaniṣad [292] all the Vedas, all the practices of tapas and brahmacharya are described as means by which the One (Brahman) is to be sought as the final aim.

That the acquisition of knowledge was not always confined to the first period of life is also evident from a few concrete examples. Śvetaketu Āruṇeya, [293] on reporting to his father Gautama, the imperfect character of the instruction he received from him as proved by his inability to answer some questions put to him by the king (rājanya) Pravahana Jaivāli was thus told by his father : "You know me, child, that whatever I know, I told you. But come, we shall go thither and dwell there as students". Gautama then goes to the king who asks him "Gautama, do you wish (for instruction from me) in the proper way ?" Gautama replied : "I come to you as a pupil". There are other examples which point to temporary connections between teachers and elderly pupils or

[288] Studies in Indian History and Culture—N. N. Law, pp. 1-20.

[289] VIII. 15.

[290] Chāndogya Up., VIII. 5.

[291] IV. 8.

[292] II. 15.

[293] Bṛhad. Up., VI. 2. 1-7 ; also Chāndogya Up., V. 3.

householders, for the imparting of the knowledge of some special doctrines and truths. In the Bṛhadāraṇyaka Upaniṣad[294] Yājñabālkya instructs Maitreyī, Janaka, Gārgī and Ārtabhāga. In the Chāndogya Upaniṣad [295] "five great householders and five great theologians"—Prāchinaśala Aupamanyava, Satyayajña Paulusī Indradyumna Bhāllaveya, Jana Śārkarākṣya and Buḍila Āsvatarasvi—first go for some special instruction to Uddālaka Āruṇi. The latter diffident as to the fullness of his knowledge of the subject went with them to Aśwapati Kaikeya as the best teacher for the purpose. In the Muṇḍaka [296] Upaniṣad Saunaka who is described as great householder (Mahāśālaḥ) approaches Angiras for instruction. In the Chāndogya Upaniṣad [297] Nārada approaches Sanatkumāra after completing the period of ordinary studentship during which he has studied a variety of subjects, and says: "I, sir, have learnt all the mantras, but do not yet know what ātman is". In another passage [298] Indra grows old in learning at the house of his preceptor. In the Mahābhārata[299] we are told of Kacha, son of Bṛhaspati, who approached Śukra and agreed to remain with him as a student for 1,000 years.

§ 6. CONDITIONS AND DUTIES OF STUDENTSHIP.

We shall now consider the conditions and duties of studentship.

(a) *Residence in the teacher's house*—The first condition was that the student should live in the house of his teacher. Even the Atharvaveda [300] refers to this condition in the phrase "if we have dwelt in studentship". It is also referred to in the Śatapatha Brāhmaṇa [301] as also in the Aitareya [302] and Tattirīya [303] Brāhmaṇas. The Chāndogya

[294] Bṛhad. Up., II. 4; IV. 1-2, 3-4; III 2, 13.

[295] V. II.

[296] I. 1. 3.

[297] VII. 1.

[298] Chāndogya Up., VIII. 7-11.

[299] Ādiparva, 76th Adhyāya.

[300] Brahmacharya yaduṣima, VII. 109. 7.

[301] XI. 3. 3. 2.

[302] In the story of a boy whose brothers divided the paternal property among themselves, while he lived with his teacher studying the Vedas, brahmacharyaṃ basaṃtaṃ, Ait. Br., V. 14.

[303] Yo bo devāścharati brahmacharyam, Taitt. Br., III. 7. 63.

Upaniṣad applies to the student the epithets "achārya-kula-vāsin"[304] and "ante-vāsin".[305] The latter epithet is also used in the Bṛhadāranyaka[306] and Taittirīya[307] Upaniṣads. Residence in the house of the preceptor is referred to also in Manu,[308] Hārīt,[309] Vyāsa,[310] Viṣṇu[311] and Vaśiṣṭha[312] Saṃhitās. Manu[313] says: "Let not the rising or setting sun find the brahmachārin within the precincts of a village". Thus the student must be in his preceptor's house before the sun sets and should not quit it for a village before the sun rises in the morning. While on duty in his preceptor's house the brahmachārin was free from all fear of injury or death. "The Brahmā delivered the creatures over to Death, the brahmachārin alone He did not deliver over to him".[314]

In this connection we shall do well to bear in mind that the modern educators recognise two factors in education: (1) the internal and (2) the external. The first includes all the congenital tendencies and innate capacities of the child. The second is the child's environment. We have seen that early Hindu teachers by developing the doctrine of Adhikāra took into consideration the tastes and innate capacities or potentialities of the child. They also clearly saw the far-reaching effect of the child's environment on his education. Hence as soon as the mind began to develop the child was translated from his home to an atmosphere where he could breathe freely moral health and strength and which was, therefore, most favourable to the development of a spiritual life which concerned the Hindus more than anything else. Indeed the cheerfulness and calmness of the school environment, the peace that reigned there and the orderly and pure life lived by every one there, were stimulating to a healthy and pure life in the student. In fact, the principle underlying the ancient Brāhmaṇic educational system is the same that urges the modern educators to advocate the system of Residential Universities. But as the student lived in the house of his preceptor as one of his family and breathed there the atmosphere of his own home, the ancient Hindu

---

[304] II. 23. 2. [305] III. 11. 5; IV. 10. 1. [306] VI. 3. 7.
[307] I. 3. 3; II. 1 [308] II. 175. [309] III. 1.
[310] I. 23. [311] XXVIII. 1. [312] Ch. VII.
[313] II. 219. [314] Śatapatha Brāhmaṇa, XI. 3. 3.

residential system was free from most of the defects and artificialities which take from the value of the modern Boarding Schools a: d Residential Universities. In this respect the Hindu residential system was also superior to the Buddhist residential system in the monasteries. This ancient Hindu system still survives in our tols.

But residence with the teacher was not a compulsory condition of studentship in all educational institutions. Day-scholars were also admitted to instruction. We read of Prince Junha of Benares setting up independent house for nimself from which he attended the College at Taxila (Jāt. IV. 96). We read of 'a country Brahmin' who finishing his studies in the three Vedas and the eighteen sciences under a famous teacher in Benares, stopped on there to look after his estate, married and become a regular house-holder. And yet he was allowed to continue his studies as an external student. He could however come but "two or three times every day to listen to his master's teaahings" owing to the obstructions of his mischievous wife who always feigned sickness whenever he wanted to get away to the school. A similer case is that of 'a young Brahmin from a foreign land' who while studying as one of the 5,0 pupils of a famous teacher in Benares, "fell in love with a woman and made her his wife. Though he continued to live on in Benares he failed two or three times in his attendance on the master". Sometimes he was so worried and harassed by his unmanageable wife that he absented himself altogether from waiting on the master. "Some seven or eight days later he renewed his attendances" when his master gave him necessary instruction after which he "paid no heed to his wife's caprices", while his wife also "ceased from that time forward from her naughtiness. There is another instance of a student being handicapped in his studies by the wicked ways of his wife. (Jāt. I. 463 ; I. 300 ; Ibid., 301-302).

(b) *Begging alms.*—It was the usual rule for the brahmachārin to go about *begging for his teacher*. In the Chāndogya Upaniṣad[315] while the householders Saunaka Kāpeya and Abhipratarin Kākṣaseni were being waited on at their meal a religious student begged of them.

[315] IV. 3. 5.

The Śatapatha Brāhmaṇa[316] also refers to the brahmachārin begging tor alms as well as the Atharvaveda.[317] It is also clear from the Śatapatha Brāhmaṇa [318] that begging was prescribed for the student to produce in him a proper spirit of humility: "Having made himself poor, as it were, and become devoid of shame he begs alms". Āpastamba, [319] Manu, [320] Uśanā, [321] Sambarta, [322] Vyāsa, [323] Sāṃkhya, [324] Vaśiṣṭha [325] Viṣṇu [326] Hārit [327] and Yājñabālkya [328] Saṃhitās also refer to begging alms as the duty of the student. "If in health, a brahmachārin fails to beg alms for seven days in succession, he must do the penanace of an Avakirni (of broken vow)".[329] In the Middle Ages in Europe we read of some students in the Universities subsisting by means of begging; but India far surpassed that by making it a rule for all students. A brāhmaṇa student shall beg alms, pronouncing the term 'bhabat' in the first part, a kṣhatriya (should use the term 'bhabat') in the middle and a vaiśya (should use the term 'bhabat') in the end (of his begging formulæ).[330]

He shall beg alms first of his own mother or sister or mother's sister or of any other woman who might not insult him with a refusal. [331] He should beg alms from those who are given to Vedic study, the celebration of sacrifices and are intent on the performance of the duties of their respective castes and orders. [332] He shall not beg alms of his preceptor's family nor of his cognates and relations. [333] In the absence of any other householder, he shall beg alms, leaving each preceeding one of these persons. [334] In the absence of (fit persons of whom the Vedas give the brahmachārin the sanction to beg alms) let him, silent and self-controlled,

[316] XI. 3. 3. 5; X. 6. 5. 9.
[317] VI. 133. 3.
[318] XI. 3. 3. 5.
[319] I. 1.
[320] II. 41; II. 108; II. 182; II. 190.
[321] I. 5.
[322] I. 11.
[323] I. 30.
[324] III. 8.
[325] Ch. VII.
[326] XXVIII. 10.
[327] III. 7.
[328] I. 29.
[329] Manu II. 187.
[330] Manu, II. 49; Yājñabālkya, I. 30; Sāṃkhya, II. 12; Vaśiṣṭha, Ch. X; Uśanā I. 52 Gautama Ch. II.
[331] Manu II. 50; Uśanā I. 53.
[332] Manu, II. 183; Uśanā, I. 55.
[333] Manu, II. 184; Gautama, Ch. II; Viṣṇu. XXVIII. 9.
[334] Manu, II. 184; Uśanā, I. 56; Gautama, Ch. II.

beg alms of the whole village (*i. e.*, of all the four castes) without repeating the proper formulæ of begging.[335] Uśanā Saṃhita[336] says: "It is said that one may receive alms from all of his caste or from all castes but he should shun the outcastes". Sāṃkha[337] and Yājñabālkya[338] Saṃhitās, however, lay down that "a brahmachārin should beg alms of brāhmanas alone".

He should collect daily food (which a brahmachārin may take) except salt and what is stale.[339] "Even while in distress, the acceptance of any wealth except the alms is prohibited."[340]

All articles obtained by begging should be undeceitfully made over to the preceptor.[341] In the event of the preceptor being absent from his house, articles of fare obtained by begging, should be made over to his wife or son or to a senior fellow-student.[342]

(*c*) *Tending the sacred fires.*—Another of his duties was to tend the sacred fires. Upakośala tended the sacred fires for twelve years and yet his teacher does not allow him to return home, but goes away on a journey without having taught him.[343] Looking after the sacrificial fires is also mentioned in the Śatapatha Brāhmaṇa.[344] Elsewhere in the same work[345] the duty of the brahmachārin is stated to be to "put on fuel," the spiritual significance of which is also explained, *viz.*, "to enkindle the mind with fire, with holy lustre." Manu,[346] Yājnabālkya,[347] Hārīt,[348] Gautama,[349] Vyāsa[350] and Sāṃkhya[351] Saṃhitās also enjoin the student to tend the sacred fire. The Mahābhārata[352] also enjoins the student to tend the sacred fire. Manu[353] says, "In health, if a brahmachārin fails to kindle the sacrificial fire with the fuel of samidh twigs for seven days in succession he must do the penance of an Avakirni (of broken vow)."

---

335 Manu, II. 184; Uśana, I. 57.
336 I. 54.
337 III. 8.
338 I. 29.
339 Uśanā, III. 19.
340 Vyāsa Saṃhitā, I. 32.
341 Manu, II. 51; Gautama, Ch. II.; Uśanā, I. 51; Vaśiṣṭha, Ch. VII.
342 Gautama, Ch. II.
343 Chāndogya Up., IV. 10. 1-2.
344 XI. 3. 3. 4.
345 XI. 5. 4. 5.
346 II. 108; II. 176; II. 186.
347 I. 31.
348 III. 2.
349 Ch. II.
350 I. 34.
351 III. 10.
352 Śāntiparva, 191st Adhyāya.
353 II. 187.

(*d*) *Tending the Teachers' House.*—Tending the house of the teacher was also one of the duties. In the Śatapatha Brāhmaṇa[354] we read "wherefore the students guard their teacher, his house and the cattle." In the Chāndogya Upaniṣad[355] Satyakāma is sent away with the teacher's cattle into a distant country where he remains for a series of years during which four hundred cows had become a thousand. The duty of guarding the teacher's cattle and grazing them in the pastures is also referred to in the Sāṃkhāyana Āraṇyaka.[356] In the Aitareya Āraṇyaka[357] Tārukṣya guards his teacher's cows for a whole year. The Hārit Saṃhitā[358] also asks the student to offer unto his preceptor pitcherfuls of water and morsels of grass for his cow. According to Uśanā Saṃhitā[359] "he should daily bring pitcherfuls of water, kuśagrass, flowers and sacrificial fuels." According to Manu[360] "the brahmachārin shall fetch pitcherfuls of water, flowers, cow-dung, clay and kuśa grass as much as his preceptor might require every day." In the Mahābhārata[361] we find that Āruṇi is working on the field of his teacher and Upamanyu is grazing the cattle of his teacher. In the same work[362] we find that Kacha is grazing the cattle of his teacher Śukra and bringing flowers for his teacher's daughter Devayoni.

(*e*) *Serving the teacher by word, mind and deed.*—According to Manu[363] the brahmachārin should "do what is conducive to the good of his preceptor each day." As by digging (the earth) with a digging instrument one gets water, so by faithfully serving him, a pupil acquires (all) the knowledge which is contained in the guru.[364] According to Yājñabālkya Saṃhitā[365] "the service of the preceptor leads one to immortality." "He should secure the preceptor's well-being by his body and mind, words and deeds."[366]

---

354 III. 6. 2. 15. 355 IV. 4. 5.
356 VII. 19. 357 III. 1. 6. 3-4. 358 III. 2.
359 III. 8; c. f. III. 19. 360 II. 182. 361 Ādiparba, 3rd Adhyāya.
362 Ādiparba, 76th Adhyāya.
363 II. 108. 364 Manu II. 218.
365 III. 156; c. f. Kāmandakīya Nītisāra, 1st sarga sls. 66-67.
366 Yajṇabālkya Saṃhitā, I. 27; Mahābhārata, Udyogaparba, 43rd Adhyāya.

Hārit[367] also asks the student to do good unto his preceptor's family by thought, word and deed. According to Samvarta Saṃhitā[368] "Being invested with the sacred thread, a vipra should always do good unto his preceptor." According to Vyāsa Sambitā[369] "He should devote himself to the good of his teacher." According to Sāṃkha Saṃhitā[370] "Humble in spirit and without arrogance, he should do only what is good and beneficial to his preceptor..................and carry out his behests." According to Viṣṇu Saṃhitā[371] he shall do what is pleasant and beneficial to his preceptor. According to the Jaina sacred texts[372] the pupil should avoid doing acts unpleasant and disrespectful to his teacher. According to Gautama Saṃhitā[373] "of all the stages of life that of the brahmachārin entails the perpetual service of one's preceptor." Together with and after these acts of service, "in the time remaining over from work for the teacher" (Guroḥ karmātiśeṣe bā) the pupil should prosecute his studies.[374]

§ 7. Regulations governing student-liee.

Let us now consider the various regulations governing the life of the student in the teacher's house.

(a) *Early rising.*—Discipline was held of much greater value than instruction and the most important work of the educator was to help the student to get into an orderly routine of life. One such discipline consisted in early rising. Thus we are told "he should duly perform the Sandhyā adoration in the morning when the stars are still visible."[375] "A brahmachārin having quitted his bed early in the morning and having bathed and performed the Homa should accost self-controlled his preceptor."[376] "If the sun rises, seeing him asleep, out of wilful laziness let him mutter the Gāyatrī mantra and fast for a whole day."[377] "Indeed a sleeping brahmachārin roused from his sleep by the sun, if he fails to

---

367 III. 1. 368 I. 5. 369 I. 36.
370 III. 9-10. 371 XXVIII. 7.
372 Pṛthibīr Ithihāsa, Part VI., p. 153; c. f. Ibid., p. 81. 373 Ch. III.
374 Chāndogya Up., VII. 15.
375 Sambarta Saṃhitā, I. 6. 376 Sāṃkhya Saṃhitā, III. 2.
377 Manu II. 220; Viṣṇu XXVIII. 53.

do this penance is associated with a great sin."[378] Kālidās also emphasises the habit of the student in getting up in the small hours of the morning. Dilīpa was awakened in the morning by the Vedic chant of the young students in the hermitage. Kumudbatī the Nāga princess got from Kākutsa (*i. e.*, Kuśa) a son named Atithi just as the intellect acquires clearness form the last quarter of the night.[379]

In Jātaka (I. 436) we read of a school of for brāhmaṇa students in Benares who "had a cock that crowed betimes and roused them to their studies." When, the trained cock died, a second cock was obtained which "had been bred in a cemetary and had thus no knowledge of times and seasons and used to crow casually, at midnight, the young brāhmaṇs fell to their studies, so that by dawn they were tired out and could not for sleepiness keep their attention on the subject already learnt (gahit atthanampi) ; and when he fell a-crowing in broad day they did not get a chance of quiet for repeating their lessions. And as it was the cock's crowing at midnight and by day which had brought their studies to a standstill, they took the bird and wrung its neck". We may note in passing that this passage also proves that there was time for the private study of the students which they spent on repeating new lessons and revising old ones.

(b) *Prayer.*—Another discipline consisted in the worship of the Sun as the universal spirit. We have numerous references in the Vedas[380] to the three worships in the day—morning, midday and evening—in the Saṃhitā as well as in the Brāhmaṇa portion. In the Āraṇyaka[381] we have not merely the worship of the Savitr, but clear reference to twilight worship (sandhyā). Manu says " Both in the morning and in the evening, let the student pure and self-controlled, mutter the Gāyatrī and pray, sitting in a holy place."[382] The Mahābhārata[383] also enjoins the student to pray to the Sun in the morning and to Agni in the evening. The Viṣṇu,[384] Sambarta[385] and Uśanā[386] saṃhitās also enjoin the

---

378 Manu II. 221.

379 Raghuvaṃsam, Canto XVII. 1.

380 Ṛgveda, III. 56, 6.

381 Tait. Āraṇ., II. 1.

382 Manu II. 222.

383 Śāntiparva, 191st Adhyāya.

384 XXVIII. 2.

385 I. 6.

386 I. 15.

student to perform the two rites of sandhyā every day. "Standing he shall perform the morning sandhyā and the evening sandhyā seated."[387] According to Gautama Saṃhitā[388] "one should perform the daily sandhyās outside one's room. The rite of morning sandhyā should be performed standing; while that of the evening sandhyā should be performed in perfect silence, till the appearance of the stars and planets in the heavens."

Prof. James in his "Talks to Teacher on Psychology" speaks very highly of the practice of *morning and evening prayers* among the Hindu students. Not only does it help to train up the boy in right moral conduct but also to stimulate his preconscious thought. A modern writer[389] has said that as the child is incapable of forming abstract religious conceptions, the training during this period "should be of the heart rather than of the head and perhaps even more of the hand, *i.e.*, a training in doing, or in other words, taking part in religious forms." So in initiating the child early to religious forms and practices the Hindu system met the demands of the nature of the child most effectively. Indeed the main purpose of these worships and the prayers used in them was to remind the individual that his success in life and spiritual welfare depended on his energies running into line with the principles of the life universal. This is illustrated by the Gāyatri hymn with which handfuls of water are to be offered to the Sun.[390] 'We meditate on that adorable effulgence of the lord Savitr from whom we derive the stimulus for our mental strivings and our activities.' The hymn is so worded that it could be applied as motive power to the student of whatever grade, whether he worships a personal god or the universal spirit. The object of these hymns was to establish a habit of righteousness, apart from intellectual conviction, by working on the sub-conscious region of the mind.

(c) *Bath.*—To relieve nervous tension in a tropical country like India and to obtain physical purity which was intimately connected

---

[387] Viṣṇu Saṃhitā, XXVIII. 3.

[388] Ch. II.

[389] Fundamentals of Child Study—Kirpatrick.

[390] Tait. Āraṇ., II. 1.

with mental purity the student was enjoined to take regular baths every day. According to Manu[391] the (religious) student should take his bath every day; according to Viṣṇu Saṃhitā[392] twice a day, while according to Vaśiṣṭha Saṃhitā[393] and Kāmandakiya Nītisāra[394] thrice a day. "He who takes his food without taking his bath, should recite the Gāyatrī one hundred and eight times.[395] "He should never take such a bath as would remove the filth of his body."[396] "He must not remove the dirt in his body except in a calamity and must not sport in water."[397] The idea was that the student should not be over-zealous in bathing so as to beautify his person. Hence Uśanā Saṃhitā[398] lays down that "he should daily wash his limbs and paste them with earth."

The hymns to the waters repeated by him at his bath not only remind him of the universal water which flow in all the streams from the Ganges onwards, but also of his sins and transgressions, committed in eating forbidden food (fed by the waters) which might excite wrong passions, in drinking or in accepting things from greed. He might bathe in a mountain ravine, but he saw in it the mighty Ganges or the winding Jamunā, or even the confluence of the seven streams familiar to him from the Vedic age onwards.[399] The waters that washed him reminded him of the vast ocean and of the herbs which grew near the milky brine when the Moon shed her silver radiance on it and cured many a benumbed limb and aching heart. Everywhere he learnt to identify his interests with those of Nature's eternal forces.

(d) *Dress.*—Then come the regulations about the dress of the student. "The brahmachārins (of the three social orders) shall respectively wear hempen, silken and woolen cloths."[400] "A twice-born one should put on an excellent white piece of cotton or silk cloth without hole but quite different from the one used before."[401]

---

391 II. 176.
392 XXXVIII. 9.
393 Ch. VII.
394 2nd Sarga, sl. 22.
395 Sambarta Saṃhitā, I. 29.
396 Uśanā Saṃhitā, III. 22.
397 Kātyāyana Saṃhitā, XXV. 15.
398 III. 8.
399 Imam me Gange Jamune, etc.
400 Manu, II. 41.
401 Uśanā, I. 7.

According to Vaśiṣṭha[402] "the wearing cloth of a brāhmaṇa shall be white (and) spotless; that of a kṣhatriya dyed with madder; that of a vaiśya dyed with turmeric or made of raw silk. The undyed cotton cloth (is) for all (religious students)"

"They shall respectively put on upper sheets (uttarīya) respectively made of the skins of the antelope, ruru (a species of deer) and goat."[403] "For the twice-born one, the sacred skin of a black antelope has been described as the cloth for covering the upper part of the body. In its absence, the skin of a ruru deer is allowed to be used."[404] Sāṃkhya[405] and Viṣṇu[406] Saṃhitās prescribe a deer-skin, a tiger-skin and a goat's skin for the first three orders respectively. Vaśiṣṭha[407] prescribes the skin of a black antelope, the skin of a spotted deer, cow-skin or he-goat's skin respectively. From the hymns used at the initiation ceremony we learn that the antelope skin kept him from forgetting what he had learnt—apparently a reference to its power of retaining the human force which we now call electricity.

"The girdle of a brāhmaṇa (student) shall be made of three strings of Munjā grass[408] evenly and smoothly tied, that of a kṣhatriya shall be made of murbā fibre[409] tied in the shape of a bow-string and that of a vaiśya shall be made of hemp[410] twists[411]—symbolical of the professions to be followed in each case in the next stage of life. "In the absence of munjā grass, etc., the girdles (of brāhmaṇas, kṣhatriyas and vaiśyas) shall be made respectively of the fibres of kuśa,[412] ashwantaka and valvaja, consisting of one, three or five ties (according to the family custom), each tie being tied with three strings of such fibre-thread."[413]

"One should always wear the sacred thread."[414] "The holy thread of a brāhmaṇa shall be made of three strings of cotton thread,

---

402 Ch. X. 403 Manu, II. 41. 404 Uśanā, I. 8.
405 II. 9. 406 XXVII. 20. 407 Ch. X.
408 Uśanā, I. 13; Viṣṇu, XXVII. 18. 409 Viṣṇu, XXVII. 18.
410 Viṣṇu, XXVII. 18 prescribes Valvaja. 411 Manu, II. 42.
412 Uśanā, I. 13. 413 Manu, II. 43. 414 Uśanā, I. 9.

that of a kṣhatriya with three strings of hempen thread and that of a vaiśya with three strings of woolen thread, suspended from the upper part of the body."[415] The sacred thread should extend from the left shoulder to the bottom of the right arm.[416]

The student was invested with a staff 'for the sake of a long life of holiness, and of holy lustre'. It symbolised his entering a long sacrificial period. "The staff was to be made of vilva or palāśa wood[417] for a brāhmaṇa student, symbolical of sacredness and purity; of vata or the catechu wood[418] for the kṣhatriya, whose widespreading arms giving shade and shelter represented his functions; and in the case of the vaiśya of the udumvara,[419] reminding one of strength and increase".[420] According to Sāṃkhya Saṃhitā[421] the sacred rods of these three orders should be respectively made of parṇa, pippala and vilva wood. Viṣṇu[422] however allows all the twice-born to use a staff made of palāśa, khadir and udumvara if they like. The staff of a brāhmaṇa shall be made of a height so as to reach to the hair of his head, that of a kṣhatriya shall be of a height so as to reach his forehead, while that of a vaiśya shall be of a height so as to reach the tip of his nose.[423] According to Sāṃkhya Saṃhitā[424] the staff should reach respectively their hair, ears and forehead in height. According the Sāṃkhya Saṃhitā[425] the staff should be whole-skinned,[426] unbent[427] and unburnt. According to Manu[428] besides this, it should be beautiful to look at, not eaten into by worms and uncreative of terror to any person.

The shaving of the head, except the tuft of hair on the crown, should be done by a brahmachārin.[429] According to Viṣṇu[430] and Vaśiṣtha Saṃhitās[431] a religious student shall wear either matted locks or a tuft of hair on the crown of his head. "A twice-born one should always tie up the tuft of hair on his crown."[432]

---

[415] Manu II. 44; Viṣṇu XXVII. 19; Uśanā I. 6.
[416] Uśanā I. 9.
[417] Vaśiṣṭha X; Viṣṇu XXVII. 21.
[418] Viṣṇu XXVII. 21 prescribes khadir wood, while Vaśiṣṭha X. prescribes nyagrodha wood.
[419] Vaśiṣṭha X; Viṣṇu XXVII. 21.
[420] Manu II. 45; Uśanā I. 14.
[421] II. 10.
[422] XXVII. 23.
[423] Manu II. 46; Viṣṇu XXVII. 22.
[424] II. 10.
[425] II. 11.
[426] Vishṇu XXVII. 24.
[427] Ibid.
[428] II. 47.
[429] Kātyāyana Saṃhitā XXV. 15.
[430] XXVIII. 41.
[431] Ch. VII.
[432] Uśanā I. 7.

According to Manu[433] and Viṣṇu[434] Saṃhitās a girdle, a staff, a holy thread or a kamaṇḍalu (ewer) broken or spoiled by use, should be thrown into water, and one should take a new one, consecrated with the mantra.

He should not be covered with too much clothing;[435] he snould renounce personal decorations.[436] He should not put on colour;[437] he should not anoint his eyes;[438] he should not oil his body;[439] he should not rub his body;[440] he should not shave;[441] he should not see his face in a mirror;[442] he should not use garlands of flowers.[443] He should forswear the use of scents;[444] he should not use sandal paste;[445] he should not wear shoes;[446] He should not use umbrellas;[447] he should not rub his teeth;[448] he should not have clean finger, nails and teeth.[450] He should avoid clean teeth;[450] but this does not prove that the student had dirty teeth—only personal beauty is to be avoided, for, we are told[451] that he should use a piece of wood for cleansing the teeth. But according to Hārīt[452] the student should not rub his teeth with wood after having rinsed his mouth at the time of bathing. The prohibition in Gautama[453] of not cleansing the teeth in the presence of the preceptor also shows that the students did not possess dirty teeth.

(e) *Food.*—Then come the regulations about the food of the student. The student should daily support himself with a portion of the food acquired by begging.[454] He should, however, take his food

---

433 II. 61. 434 XXVII. 29. 435 Aitareya Āraṇyaka V.

436 Vyāsa Saṃhitā I. 28. 437 Aitareya Āraṇyaka V. Manu II. 178.

438 Aitareya Āraṇyaka V; Manu II. 178; Yājñbālkya I. 33; Uśanā III. 16; Vyāsa I. 28; Sāṃkhya III. 12; Vaśiṣṭha VII; Viṣṇu XXVIII. 11.

439 Aitareya Āraṇyaka V; Uśanā III. 16; Vaśiṣṭha VII.

440 Aitareya Āraṇyaka V. 441 Aitareya Āraṇyaka V.

442 Uśanā III. 20; Vyāsa I. 28.

443 Aitareya Āraṇyaka V; Manu II. 177; Hārīt III. 8; Uśanā III. 16; Vyāsa I. 29. Sambarta I. 5; Gautama II.

444 Manu II. 177; Hārit III. 8; Vyāsa I. 29; Sambarta I. 5; Gautama II.

445 Vyāsa I. 29. 446 Manu II. 178; Hārīt III. 8; Uśanā III. 16; Gautama II.

447 Manu II. 178; Hārīt III. 8; Uśanā III. 17; Gautama II. 448 Uśanā III. 20.

449 Taitt. Brāh. III. 450 Vaśiṣṭha VII. 451 Hārīt III. 6.

452 III. 7. 453 Ch. II. 454 Hārīt I. 59.

with the previous permission of his preceptor.[455] "He should daily adore his food and take it without speaking ill of it; on seeing it he should be delighted and happy and should welcome it with laudation.[456] For says Manu [457] "Food daily worshipped, gives strength and vitality. Unworshipped food destroys both the worlds of the partaker."

The prayer at his meal is as follows: 'Oh Savita, lord and first cause of production, I see before me the visible effects of thy work (satyam) amidst the mystery of the things unseen (ṛtyam). Oh water, thou art the symbol of the mystery of eternity, being at the bottom of all creation and the cover of all, encompassing all in thy infinite expanse. I take this food for the upkeep of the vital airs in the body, with a drop of moistening water to prepare the alimentary system for its work. May the food I take be an offering to universal Brahman so that I may be fed with the waters of everlasting life'. The food, says another hymn, is of good. In the highest sense of the word, everything in this world is either food or the feeder. Water is the food. Fire the feeder; life's duration is the food for the feeder, this body. Earth is the food for the feeder, space (ākāśa).[458] The food and the feeder depend on each other. He who realises this becomes one with food as well as with the feeder; he feeds on all things that are and is free. [459]

Having drawn a circular figure first, he should place the vessel on it and eat till the recitation of the formulæ amṛtopidhan, etc., at the end of his meal.[460]

He should eat his meal sitting with his face towards the east.[461] He who eats his meal with his face towards the east acquires longevity; by taking his meal with his face towards the south a person acquires fame. He who takes his meal with his face turned towards the west acquires opulence; by eating with his face turned

---

[455] Hārīt I. 58; Yājñabālkya I. 31; Vyāsa I. 31; Viṣṇu XXVIII. 10; Sāṃkhya III. 8; Gautama II; Vaśiṣṭha VII.

[456] Hārīt I. 60; Manu II. 54; Yājñabālkya I. 31.

[457] II. 55.

[458] Taitt. Up., III. 7-9.

[459] Taitt. Up.,—Ahamannam ahamannādah... ..kāmānnī kāmarūpyanusancharan......ahaṃ viśvam bhuvanamabhyabhavām.

[460] Hārīt I. 64.

[461] Manu II. 51; Sāṃkhya III. 8; Sambarta I. 11.

towards the south, he acquires truthfulness." [462] Hārit Saṃhitā [463] lays down that "he should daily take his meal with his face directed towards the east or the south. But he should never eat facing the north."

He should take his meals abstaining from speech. [464]

Vaśiṣṭha Saṃhitā [465] says: "Eight mouthfuls form the meal of an ascetic, sixteen that of a hermit, thirty-two that of a householder and an unlimited quantity that of a religious student." "An ox, a student and a brāhmaṇa who has kindled the sacred fire, can do their work if they eat; without eating (much), they cannot do it." [466] Vyāsā Saṃhitā [467] lays down: "A single meal, which is not incompatible with the spirit of brahmacharya is what is enjoined to be taken by the student, every day". Manu [468] prescribes two meals; but says he "Let him not take a third meal during the interval of his morning and evening ones." Manu [469] says "Let him avoid over-eating". For says he: [470] "Over-eating brings on ill health, shortens the duration of life, proves hostile to acts (sacrifices) which lead to heaven, is sinful and condemned by men. Hence let him avoid over-eating." Hārit [471] speaks in the same strain: "Taking too much or bad food is destructive of health, longevity, attainment of the celestial region and virtue and is condemned by the community. Therefore it should be avoided". According to Gautama Saṃhitā [472] "He shall eat his meal till the appetite is fully satisfied. He shall rise up from his dinner just as he has taken his fill, without casting any greedy look on the food left unconsumed". Indeed true discipline consists in withdrawing the mind from sense-objects, instead of merely checking the senses. The Bhāgabat Gītā forbids gluttony because over-eating stands in the way of success in the practices of Yoga [473] *i. e.*, control of the mind.

---

[462] Manu II. 52. [463] I. 62.
[464] Hārīt I. 58; I. 64; Sambarta I. 11; Yājñabālkya I. 31; Gautama II.
[465] Ch. VI. [466] Vaśiṣṭha VI. [467] I. 33.
[468] II. 56. [469] II. 56. [470] II. 57. [471] I. 61.
[472] Ch. II.
[473] Nātyaśnatastu Yogosti in Bhāg. Gītā. Atomanah chanchalatvam yayau āhārasovayā in śukasaptati, I. 56. (See Z. D. M. G., for 1900., p. 643).

He should not take only cooked rice [474] nor that which is the residue of another's meal. [475] According to Yājñabālkya [476] and Viṣṇu [477] he can take the residue of the food of his preceptor only. He should not, however, take the residue of his preceptor's food willingly for medicinal purposes. [478] "Nor should he take the residue of the food eaten by his guru's son[479] or wife".[480] Yājñabālkya[481] says "while a brahmachārin, one should not partake of boiled rice brought from elsewhere unless he suffers from any disease. And a brāhamaṇa only is allowed to take food as he likes when invited on the occasion of a śrāddha, provided he does not break his vow". Manu [482] says "A brahmachārin having been invited to a repast given in connection with a śrāddha offered to the deities may take to his satisfaction (articles of food which do not soil the vow of a vowist); invited to a repast in connection with a śrāddha offered to the manes, he may take to his satisfaction such food, which a ṛṣi may eat (nirvāra grains and such like food-stuff which a holy sage usually takes in his hermitage) without incurring the sin of eating the food given by one and the same person; thereby his vow is not nullified". According to Vyāsa Saṃhitā [483] "he may dine in connection with a pitṛ śrāddha if thereto invited by a person without any disqualification and if his preceptor approves of it. But a kṣhatriya or a vaiśya brahmachārin is not authorised to partake of a śrāddha repast given by a single person". Sambarta Saṃhitā,[484] however, lays down that "a brahmachārin, who eats boiled rice of a person suffering from the impurity of birth or that at the first śrāddha or that at the monthly (śrāddha) should get himself purified (by fasting) for three nights". According to Viṣṇu [485] and Sāṃkhya [486] Saṃhitās he should avoid meals on the occasion of a śraddha ceremony.

He should avoid flesh;[487] specially of aquatic creatures; [488] he should

---

474 Vyāsa I. 31. 475 Vyāsa I. 31; Manu II. 56; Yājñabālkya I. 33. 476 I. 33.
477 XXXIII. 11. 478 Uśanā III. 21. 479 Viṣṇu XXVIII. 33.; Gautama II.
480 Gautama II. 481 I. 32. 482 II. 188-89. 483 I. 32.
484 I. 24. 485 XXVIII. 11. 486 III. 12.
487 Aitareya Āraṇyaka V; Manu II. 177; Yajñabālkya I. 33; Sambarta I. 5; Viṣṇu XXVIII. 11.
488 Taitt. Brāhmaṇa II. 8, 7.

avoid meat-diet;[489] he should not take honey [490] If however a student happens to take somehow meat or honey he should after performing Prājāpatya, be purified by a mouñji-homa.[491] He should not take articles of sweet taste which acquire an acid flavour when stale.[492] He should avoid prepared betel-leaf.[493] He should not take artificial salt[494] and sweet juice.[495] He should refrain from taking all kinds of stale food.[496]

(f) *Sleep.*—According to Manu,[497] Hārit[498] and Sāṃkhya[499] Saṃhitās the student should lie on the bare ground. According to Vaśisṭha Saṃhitā[500] he should avoid sleep on a cot.[501] According to Gautama[502] and Viṣṇu[503] he should sleep on a lower bed than that of his preceptor and should rise before and sleep after his preceptor.[504]

According Śatapatha Brāhmaṇa[505] he should not sleep in day time.[506] Manu[507] and Viṣṇu[508] Saṃhitās say—" If the sun goes down without the knowledge of the brahmachārin finding him resting in bed out of laziness, let him mutter the Gāyatrī mantra and fast for a whole day." Indeed according to the Mahābhārata sleeping at sandhyā shortens life.[509] Sambarta Saṃhitā[510] lays down that if a brahmachārin, on any occasion, sleeps during the day, in a healthy state, he should after bathing and adoring the sun, recite the Gāyatrī one hundred and eight times.

(g) *Celibacy.* The greatest restraint was as regards the sexual impulses. Herein the Aryans were strong as compared with their enemies the Dasyus who are laughed at as śiśnadevāh',[511] a term which Yāska interprets

---

489 Sāṃkhya III. 12 ; Gautama II.

490 Manu II. 177 ; Yājñbālkya I. 33 ; Sambarta I. 5 ; Sāṃkhya III. 12 ; Viṣṇu XXVIII. 11 ; Gautama II.

491 Sambarta I. 26.

492 Manu II. 177.

493 Parāśara Saṃhitā I. 50.

494 Viṣṇu XXVIII. 11.

495 Uśanā III. 16.

496 Viṣṇu XXVIII. 11.

497 II. 108.

498 III. 2.

499 III. 13.

500 Ch. VII.

501 Compare Taitt. Brāh.,—He should avoid high seats.

502 Ch. II.

503 XXVIII. 12-13.

504 Compare Vyāsa I. 35.

505 XI. 5. 4. 5.

506 Mantrapāṭha II. 6, 14.,—Divā mā susupthāh.

507 II. 220.

508 XXVIII. 53.

509 Anuśāsanaparva, 104, 27 ; 120, 87 ; 100, 5? ; 120, 29.

510 I. 33.

511 Ṛgveda VIII. 2. 1. 5 ; X. 99. 3.

as 'men of loose sexual habits'. Elsewhere we are told that the Aryans were able to vanquish the united army of the Asuras entirely by their brahmacharya tapas, *i. e.*, the stability of character arising from the curbing of the sexual impulses.[512] The Taittirīya Brāhmaṇa,[513] therefore, enjoins the student to observe the vow of continence. According to Hārīt[514] and Vyāsa[515] Saṃhitās the student should lead a celibate life. "He should refrain from sexual intercourse.[516] According to Yājñabālkya[517] he should always avoid women. Uśanā Saṃhitā[518] lays down that he should studiously avoid maidens. Manu[519] says—" Let the student refrain from visiting women." " Let him renounce embracing and casting lustful eyes on females."[520] Vātsyāyana[521] says—" In his boyhood, one should devote himself to education and other equipments as the means of securing worldly objects in after life. He should observe absolute celibacy till he completes his education." Sambarta Saṃhitā[522] says " A student who being stricken with lust knows a woman should, being observant of regulations, perform the distressing penance of Prājāpatya."

Married students were, however, not unknown. Kautilya in his Arthaśāstra[523] refers to "married students studying abroad" The Jātakas also refer to married students who continued their studies at Benares as external students (Jātaka I. 463; I. 300; Ibid., 301-02). Lastly, we may refer to the instance of a teacher of 500 students at Benares who selects by a special test one of them for the hand of his grown-up daughter. With some teachers " there was a custom that if there should be a daughter ripe for marriage she should be given to the eldest pupil" (Jātaka III. 18; VI. 347).

" Let him sleep always alone, and let him not cast his seed (by any unnatural means). A lustful casting of one's seed kills one's vow. "[524] Indeed deliberate acts resulting in loss of seed were regarded as acts of theft and of murder of embryo.[525] And the killing of human

---

512 Tait. Āraṇyaka II. 1. 513 II. 8. 7.
514 III. 1. 515 I. 23; I. 28.
516 Hārīt III. 8; Gautama II; Viṣṇu XXVIII. 11. 517 I. 33.
518 III. 16. 519 II. 177. 520 Manu II. 179.
521 Kāmasūtra Bk. I. Ch. II. sls. 2-3. 522 I. 25.
523 R. Śyāmaśāstrī's Eng. Trans., p. 201. 524 Manu II. 180. 525 Taitt. Brāh. II. 8. 2.

seed (vīryahatyā) was as heinous a sin as the slaughter of a brāhmaṇa or the murder of a fœtus.[526] Even unconscious emission of the vital fluid has its expiatory rites; for it implied not only loss of health and strength, and shortening of life, but also loss of intellectual and spiritual power. It was thus a sin against Indra, Agni and Bṛhaṣpati.[527] A brāhmaṇa student who has unintentionally spent himself in sleep, shall bathe and worship the sun and thrice mutter the Rik running as Punarmām, etc.[528] According to Samvarta Saṃhitā[529] "a brahmachārin who knowingly discharges his seminal fluid, should perform the expiation consequent on the breach of the vow; and if unknowingly, he should be purified by bathing." According to Viṣṇu Saṃhitā[530] "a wilful evacuation of semen by a brahmachārin is pronounced as the breach of the vow by pious Brahmavādins. Having committed this sin he shall put on the skin of an ass and beg at seven houses, confessing his guilt. For a year he shall live on what he shall obtain by thus begging every day and bathe three times a day whereby he shall regain his purity." "Having unconsciously spent his seed in a dream, a brahmachārin shall bathe, and worship the sun and three times recite the Punarmām etc., verse whereby he shall regain his purity."[531]

"So essential was the virtue of continence" remarks Professor Venkateśwara[532] "that brahmacharya came to denote both continence and studentship. All our texts agree that discipline is more important than study. Agni granted Gaya the power to know the Vedas without study, simply as the result of his austerity, chastity, observances, vows and the grace of the gurus.[533] How to make sure of brahmacharya and to steer

[526] Compare the list of offences in the Tṛsuparṇa. The degrees are Brahmahatyā, Vṛūṇahatyā and Vīryahatyā. Yathā Vṛūṇahatyā evam eṣa bhabati yah ayonau retah siñchati (T. A. II. 8. 2). Ā no vīro jāyatām in Taitt. Saṃ., II. 1. Kuṣmāṇḍairjuhuyāt yo āpūtā iva manyate, and yad arvāchino Vṛūṇahatyāyāh tasmāt muchyate (T. A. II. 8. 3).

[527] Tait. Āraṇyaka II. 8.

[528] Manu II. 181.

[529] I. 28.

[530] XXVIII. 48-50.

[531] Vishṇu XXVIII. 51.

[532] Indian Culture Through the Ages, Vol. I. pp. 138-40.

[533] Mahābhārata, Ādiparva, 66, 2f.

clear of passions and temptatious when youth passed into adolescence. This subject was one of anxious care among the ancients. Manu has a simple recipe for counteracting sexual inclinations and the premature awakening of the sexual impulse. 'Give the mind absorbing work and the body plentiful exercise in the open air'. Sexual ideas breed in the darkness of the closed room and in the luxury of comfortable beds and belongings. Hence the unanimous condemnation in all the scriptures Hindu, Buddhist and Jaina, of unguents and perfumes, flowers and high seats, beds, sandal, music etc., which capture the mind through the gateways of the senses. Some of the texts like the Anugītā,[534] forbid secular music even to the family man, on the ground that it would stimulate the senses to an undue extent. Further, the young men were to go out for alms and do other work of a strenuous and tiring nature A story in the Pauṣya-parba of the Mahābhārata illustrates this somewhat Spartan rigour and the privations to which students were inured. Lastly, they were trained up to regard with a brotherly eye all the tender-eyed maidens of the neighbourhood who bestowed alms, and the guru's wife and other members of his household, with whom they were on familiar terms. The Hindu system was thus a contrast to the Egyptian. In the latter, the sight of strange girls was to be avoided; in the former ladies were looked on as mothers and sisters, so that the carnal idea was put out of place inspite of social freedom. The only exception was in the Buddhist and Jaina monasteries, where young men lived in bands and the vice of homosexuality appears to have prevailed, as in modern times in hostels and boarding houses, as described by Havelock Ellis."[535]

(h) *Mental and moral discipline.*—The Gopatha Brāhmaṇa[536] requires the brahmachārin to overcome the same passions, *viz.*, caste-pride (brahma-varchasam), fame, sleep, anger, bragging, personal beauty and fragrance which are correlated respectively with the antelope, the teacher, the python, the boar, the water, maidens, trees and plants. If he clothes himself in the skin of the antelope, he obtains

---

[534] S. B. E. Vol. VIII. p. 208. Compare Gautama II. 13 and Manu II. 178.

[535] Studies in the Psychology of Sex, Vol p. 97.

[536] II. 1. 2. 1-9.

brahmavarchasam; if he works for his teacher, he obtains fame for the latter; if though sleepy, he abstains from sleep, he obtains the sleep that is in the python; if humble in spirit, he does not injure any one in anger, he obtains the anger that is in the boar; if he does not perform braggart tricks in the water, he obtains the braggadocio that is in the water; if he does not look at a naked maiden, he obtains the beauty that is in the maiden; if he does not smell plants and trees, after having cut them, he becomes himself fragrant.[537]

He should have control over his senses.[538] "He should curb his tongue,[539] appetite and arms".[540] He should renounce lust,[541] anger,[542] discontent,[543] greed,[544] fear,[545] hatred,[546] falsehood,[547] pride (māna),[548] idleness,[549] mada,[550] moha,[551] chapalatā,[552] wickncdness,[553] envy,[554] malice,[555] useless conversation,[556] idle gossips[557] lewd talk,[558] obscene words,[559] sleep[560] (too much sleeping), idle glances at the sun,[561] idle strolls,[562] ignorance,[563] abusive language,[564] harsh words,[565] detracting other people,[566] calumny,[567] scandal,[568] intoxication,[569] looking at women,[570] conversing with women,[571] with śūdras[572] and with notorious impure persons,[573]

---

537 Atharvaveda—Bloomfield, p. 111.

538 Manu II. 178; Uśanā III 15.

539 Vaśiṣṭha VII.

540 Gautama II.

541 Manu II. 178; Uśanā III. 17; Gautama II.

542 Manu II. 178; Uśanā III. 15; Uśanā III. 17; Gautama II; Mahābhārata, Udyogaparba, 43rd adhyāya.

543 Vyāsa 1. 29; Mahābhārata, Ādiparba, 91st adhyāya

544 Manu II. 178; Gautama II; Mahābhārata, Udyogaparba, 39th adhyāya.

545 Uśanā III. 17; Gautama II.

546 Vyāsa I. 28.

547 Manu II. 179; Taitt. Brāh. II. 8. 7.

548 Mahābhārata, Udyogaparba, 43rd adhyāya.

549 Mahābhārata, Udyogaparba, 39th adhyāya.

550 Ibid.

551 Ibid.

552 Ibid.

553 Uśana III. 8.

554 Vyāsa I. 28; Sāṃkhya III. 12.

555 Vyāsa I. 28.

556 Hārīt III. 8.

557 Manu II. 179.

558 Viṣṇu XXVIII. 11.

559 Yājñabālkya I. 33.

560 Uśanā III. 17.

561 Vyāsa I. 28; Yājnabālkya I. 33.

562 Vyāsa I. 29.

563 Gautama II.

564 Viṣṇu XXVIII. 11.

565 Yājñabālkya I. 33.

566 Uśana III. 18.

567 Vyāsa I. 28; Sāṃkhya III. 12; Yājñabālkya I. 33; Gautama II.

568 Manu II. 129.

569 Vyāsa I. 28.

570 Uśanā III. 18; Mahābhārata, Śāntiparba, 213th adhyāya.

571 Uśanā III. 18; Uśanā III. 21; Mahābharāta, Śāntiparba, 213th adhyāya.

572 Uśanā III. 21.

573 Uśanā III. 21.

injuring other people,[574] hurtful feelings,[575] female company,[576] thievish propensities and service of the mean.[577] He should be impartial,[578] of sweet speech[579] and devout in spirit.[580] He should abstain from riding on horses and elephants.[581] He should forego the use of vehicles of all kinds.[582] "He was not to run when it rained or to tread on gold or on the lotus flower; he was to refrain from voiding rheum or committing nuissance in the mass of waters intended for bathing in."[583] He must avoid dancing[584] and singing.[585] He should abstain from playing on musical instruments.[586] He should refrain from all music.[587] He should avoid gambling.[588] He should renounce gambling with dice.[589] Manu[590] says:—"Let him (the brahmachārin) refrain from killing animals and doing injury to them."[591] According to Uśanā[592] he should studiously avoid the destruction of small animals. According to Gautama[593] he should renounce all killing propensities.

That some of these rules were actually enforced is evident from the case of Prince Āyu who was expelled from the school by Chyavan for having killed a bird with an arrow near by. Even the royal visitors had to observe the rules of discipline while in the school compound. King Duṣmanta had to withdraw his arrow aimed at a deer at the request of the hermit teacher. When in quest of Rāma Bharata started for Chitrakūta hill he did not dare to enter the hermitage of Varadwāja with his troops but asked them to stay at a respectful distance of two miles lest they caused disturbance (āśramapīḍā) there.[594]

---

574 Uśanā III. 18. 575 Viṣṇu XXVIII. 11.
576 Sāṃkhya III. 12. 577 Gautama II. 578 Uśanā III. 20.
579 Uśanā III. 15; Vyāsa I. 36. 580 Vyāsa I. 36.
581 Hārīt III. 9. 582 Gautama II.
583 Taitt. Āraṇyaka I. 26; II. 8, 7; Taitt. Saṃ., II. 1.
584 Hārīt III. 8; Uśanā III. 17; Vyāsa I. 28; Sāṃkhya III. 12; Viṣṇu XXVIII. 11; Manu II. 178.
585 Hārīt III. 8; Uśanā III. 17; Uśanā III. 20; Vyāsa I. 28; Sāṃkhya III. 12; Viṣṇu XXVIII 11; Manu II. 178. 586 Uśanā III. 17.
587 Sāṃkhya III. 12; Manu II. 178; Gautama II. 588 Uśanā III. 17; Gautama II.
589 Manu II. 179. 590 II. 177.
591 Yājñabālkya I 33. 592 III. 16. 593 Ch. II.
594 Rāmāyaṇa, Ayodhyākāṇḍa, 89th and 91st sargas.

All these conditions of studentship and rules governing Vedic studies seem to be very severe to us now; they seem to have made the life of the student miserable, as he was denied all worldly pleasures and had to live a beggar's or a menial's life in the house of a stranger. Indeed, such restrictions might kill cheerfulness but they materially helped in the attainment of the spiritual ideal of the then education. They made students highly moral in conduct and respectful in behaviour. In doing physical labour at the teacher's house, on his field and pasture, the students developed their limbs and muscles in the fresh air and sunlight. The moral side received direct training in the morning and evening prayers, in the study of the religious texts and in the performance of the sacrificial ritual. The intellectual side was touched in hearing explanations of mantras and hymns, in the observation of Nature and the preparation of the material at the sacrifice, domestic or public. Memory and imagination received the greatest attention, as from start to finish, lessons were learnt by heart and as various mystical ideas about deities and gods were heard from the teachers. In fact the marvellous and elaborate system of sacrifices were the product of the incomparable flights of the imagination of the priesthood. We may laugh at the old brahmachārī not taking sweets, living in a lonely place, having light meals, turning away his ears from music, etc.; but unless the bodily senses are trained up and controlled in some such way, it is impossible for a human being to check his actions and desires. Indeed by means of these external practices and regulations, it was sought to develop in the young pupils those internal conditions (pratyāsanna or direct as opposed to bāhya) or mental and moral attributes which would afterwards fit them for being taught the highest knowlege. Such a regulated life results in "inner freedom" which cannot come off by itself or at will. Philosophers have proved that the unit of change is both physical and spiritual and that the one precedes the other. You cannot begin at the top. The bodily unit is the place where you can commence a change and make a slow but sure progress till in course of time you find your mind as well as your body completely transformed. Hence the ancient Hindus created such an atmosphere as kept the aim of his stay in the teacher's house brightly before the pupil's eye and as such created a necessity for him to put forth great voluntary effort to accomplish it. Educationists tell us that to stimulate the effort on the part of the pupil and to enlist it in line with our aim are the chief purposes of teaching. Pestalozzi did not give so much importance to "interest" in education as to "self-effort" on the part of the student. The Hindus then were so far successful in their attempts though the effort of the student was accompanied with something like ascetic gloom.

§ 8. RESPECT TO TEACHER.

There were rules also for the respect due from pupil to teacher. Respect to teacher was also a part of Aśoka's Law of Piety.[595] Strict obedience was enjoined unless the teacher ordered the pupil to commit crimes which involved loss of caste.[596] Even having been reprimanded by his preceptor, he should not make any reply in retort, nor go away even when driven away by the former. (Vyāsa I. 27). "An infringement of the preceptor's order makes all studies of the Vedas abortive. Hence one should study them in a submissive spirit."[597]

He should not cleanse his teeth or prick his ear-holes or stretch or screw up his legs or sit with his chin supporting on his hand or laugh or yawn or contort his limbs or twist his body, in the presence of his preceptor (Gautama II). By the side of his preceptor he shall eat food and wear garments inferior to those of his preceptor.[598] By the side of his preceptor he shall always occupy a lower bed or seat.[599] He shall lie down in a lower bed than that of his preceptor and sleep after he has slept, leaving his bed before he rises.[600] He should avoid sitting on the same bed or seat with his preceptor or at a place where his preceptor sits;[601] "except in a boat,[602] or in a carriage[603] or on a stone slab"[604] or in a bullock cart, "in a court-yard or in the terrace of a building or a large mattress of reeds."[605] "He must not sit with his guru when

595 Rock Edict IX; Minor Rock Edict II.

596 Āpastamba I. 1.

597 Vyāsa I. 39.

598 Manu II. 174.

599 Manu II. 198.

600 Manu II. 194; Mahābhārata, Ādiparba, 91st adhyāya; Viṣṇu XXVIII. 12-13; Gautama II.

601 Manu II. 119; Viṣṇu XXVIII. 27; Gautama II.

602 Viṣṇu XXVIII. 28.

603 Ibid.

604 Ibid.

605 Manu II. 204.

the wind will be blowing from his direction to that of his guru or the contrary; while in his company he must not say anything which is inaudible to his guru."[606]

Serving a preceptor consists in hearing his behests from a lower seat and in meekly and faithfully carrying them out.[607] "He should not serve the preceptor (by the intervention of another) while he stands aloof nor when he (himself) is angry, nor when a woman is near; if he is seated in a carriage or on a (raised) seat he should get down and salute his preceptor."[608] A disciple should stand up at the sight of his preceptor[609] and follow him whenever he goes out.[610] "Interrogated by his preceptor, he should give true and correct answer to his queries, sit down to study whenever he may be pleased to direct him in that behalf[611] and do nothing but what is pleasant and beneficial to him."[612] Likewise he should behave towards his preceptor's wife,[613] sons,[614] friends[615] and relations.[616] "After performing his sandhyā he shall salute his preceptor. He shall simultaneously catch hold of the two feet of his preceptor with his two hands, the right foot with the right hand and the left foot with the left hand. After salutation he shall mention his own name (as I am such and such) and add the word 'Bhos' at the end of his address."[617] One should catch hold of one's preceptor's feet every day when first meeting him.[618] He must not speak to his preceptor when he is himself sitting, standing, lying down, eating or averting his face.[619] If his preceptor sits, let him speak to him, standing up; if he walks, advancing towards him; if he comes towards him, meeting him; if he runs, running after him;[620] turning round so as to meet him, if his face is averted (Viṣṇu 20; Manu II. 197). Approaching him, if he is at a distance;[621] leaning to him, if he be in a reclining posture.[622] Before his eyes, let

[606] Manu II. 203.
[607] Gautama II.
[608] Manu II. 202.
[609] Manu II. 130; Manu II. 119; Gautama II.
[610] Gautama II.
[611] Mahābhārata, Ādiparba, 91st adhyāya.
[612] Gautama II.
[613] Manu II. 210; Gautama II.
[614] Gautama II; Manu II. 207
[615] Manu II. 207.
[616] Ibid.
[617] Viṣṇu XXVIII. 14-17.
[618] Vaśiṣṭha XI; Gautama VI.
[619] Manu II. 195; Viṣṇu XXVIII. 18.
[620] Manu II. 196; Viṣṇu XXVIII. 19.
[621] Viṣṇu XXVIII. 20; Manu II. 197.
[622] Viṣṇu XXVIII. 22; Manu II. 197.

him not sit in a careless manner. [623] He shall not utter his preceptor's name even at his back. [624] Let him not pronounce his name without due respect. [625] Let him not imitate his speech, gait and manner. [626] Let him not wilfully leap over the shadow of his preceptor. [627] Let him not in any way hurt or injure an ācharya (and an expounder of the Vedas). [628] Let him leave the place where his guru is calumnised or lightly spoken ot. [629] "A calumniator of his own guru shall be born as an ass; and a vilifier of his own guru shall be a dog in his next birth; for having wrongfully enjoyed the property of his own guru, he shall be born as a worm; one who is envious of his guru's excellence shall take his birth as an insect in his next incarnation". [630] "Having used angry words to his preceptor one should bathe at morning, noon and evening each day, live in a thatched cottage of dry leaves and on roots and bulbs of the forest, wearing large clotted hairs, lie down on bare ground in the night, enter a village for alms, proclaiming his guilt to all and sundry. For twelve years he should live the life of penance." [631] For having angrily roared unto a preceptor he should practise the above-mentioned penance. [632] Without the permission of his preceptor, let him not speak to his relatives, parents etc. [633] Even if a preceptor communicates only one letter to a disciple, there is no article on earth, by presenting which he may be free from his debt. [634] He who does not regard a preceptor, the giver of even one letter, is born among the chaṇḍālas, after having gone through a hundred births in the canine species. [635] According to Kautilya's Arthaśāstra the student should be devoted to his teacher even at the cost of his own life or in the absence of his teacher, to the teacher's son or to an elder class-mate. [636] Again "the teacher shall invariably be respected."[637] "As a student his teacher, a son his father and a servant his master, the king shall follow (the high-priest). [638] "One should not sit on

---

623 Viṣṇu XXVIII. 23; Manu II. 198.
624 Manu II. 199.
625 Viṣṇu XXVIII. 24; Gautama II.
626 Viṣṇu XXVIII.25; Manu II. 199.
627 Manu IV. 130.
628 Manu IV. 162.
629 Viṣṇu XXVIII. 26; Manu II. 200.
630 Manu II. 201.
631 Sāṃkhya XVII. 1-2 and 51.
632 Sāṃkhya XVII. 56.
633 Viṣṇu XXVIII. 30; Manu II. 205.
634 Atri Saṃhitā I. 9.
635 Atri I. 10.
636 R. Śyāmaśāstrī's Eng. Trans., p. 8.
637 Ibid., p. 14.
638 Ibid., p. 17.

important seats before the preceptor nor being arrogant, distort his sayings through (false) reasoning." [639] According to Śukrāchārya [640] "the ācharya or preceptor (of the king) like the father (of the king) is to sit on the same kind of good seats." We get a bright example of devotion and obedience to the teacher in the characters of Āruṇi, Upamanyu and Ekalabya. [641]

Show him the respect of a guru, if a preceptor's preceptor is arrived. [642] On a preceptor's son, junior or equal to him in years, happening to be his tutor, he shall pay the same respect to him as to his own preceptor. [643] "The śruti says that one must treat a teacher's son just as the teacher himself." [644] A preceptor's wife happening to be young, a disciple should not touch her feet during an act of obeisance; [645] but returning from a sojourn in a distant country, he may be allowed to catch hold of her feet [646] on the first day; on all subsequent days, he shall simply accost her without clasping her feet. [647] He should not address the sons or wife of his preceptor by their names and avoid using any harsh language. [648]

If a teacher dies, one should not read the Vedas for three nights. [649] A man remains unclean for three days on the death of a spiritual preceptor or of a wife or son of his spiritual preceptor. [650] One becomes purified in one night, if the wife or son of his teacher or his upādhyāya or a fellow-student or a pupil is dead. [651] On the death of his preceptor, unto a qualified son of his or unto his widow or unto a cognate of his, he shall behave as his preceptor. [652] The property of bachelors learning the Vedas shall on their death be taken by their preceptors. [653]

A development of the rules regulating the conduct of the pupil to his preceptor was the exhaltation of the teacher to such a position of

---

639 Śukranītisāra, Ch. III. lines 326-27.

640 Ibid., Ch. I. line 720.

641 Mahābhārata, Ādiparba, 132nd adhyāya.

642 Viṣṇu XXVIII. 29; Manu II. 205; Vaśiṣṭha XI.

643 Manu II. 208; Viṣṇu XXVIII. 31.

644 Vaśiṣṭha XI; Gautama II.

645 Manu II. 212; Gautama II.

646 Manu II. 217; Gautama II.

647 Manu II. 217.

648 Gautama II.

649 Vaśiṣṭha XI.

650 Gautama XIV.

651 Viṣṇu XXII. 43.

652 Manu II. 247.

653 R. Śyāmaśāstrī's Eng. Trans., p. 242.

reverence that he was worshipped by his pupil.[654] In the schools of early Vedānta, the teacher or guru was always one who was himself supposed to have reached emancipation and thus to have come to the realisation that he is Brahman. In his devotion or bhakti for Brahman, it was but a short step for the pupil to feel bhakti also for the guru who was thus identified with Brahman. This is referred to as early as the Śvetāśvatara Upaniṣad[655] but it received a great emphasis in all the chief Bhakti sects. A spiritual guide and a teacher are to be particularly adored.[656] A teacher is the foremost of all superiors.[657] Of one's two fathers, the progenitor and the teacher of the Vedas, more honoured is the teacher of the Vedas in as much as the birth of a twice-born one in the knowledge of Brahman is the only abiding existence both in this world and the next.[658] The pupil should consider his preceptor as his father and mother; he must not grieve them by saying 'I am indebted to none'.[659] One's mother, father and preceptor are called one's great gurus.[660] One must perpetually serve them.[661] Let him obey their commands.[662] Let him do what is pleasant and beneficial to them.[663] Without their leave he should not do anything.[664] "Let him constantly do what is good to his parents and specially what conduces to the comfort of his preceptor. The satisfaction of these three is the consummation of all tapas (penitential austerities)."[665] Serving these constitutes the highest tapas; without their permission let him not practise any other piety.[666] "These three represent the three regions, the three orders of society. They are the three Vedas, they are the three fires. The father is the household fire, the mother is the ceremonial fire, the preceptor

---

654 Furquhar, Crown of Hinduism, p. 402.

655 VI. 23.

656 Uśanā I. 30.

657 Gautama II.

658 Manu II. 146; Viṣṇu XXX. 44; Mahābhārata, Śāntiparba, 108th adhyāya; compare Mahābhārata, Śāntiparba, 243rd adhyāya.

659 Vaśiṣṭha II.

660 Viṣṇu XXXI. 1-2. In the Rāmāyaṇa, (Kiṣkindhyakāṇḍa, 18th sarga we are told that the eldest brother, the progenitor and the teacher are all fathers.

661 Viṣṇu XXXI. 3.

662 Viṣṇu XXXI. 4.

663 Viṣṇu XXXI. 5; Manu II. 235.

664 Viṣṇu XXXI. 6; Manu II. 236.

665 Manu II. 228.

666 Manu II. 229: Manu II. 235, 237.

is the spiritual fire. These three fires are the most glorious in the world." [667] "A householder who does not commit any folly in respect of these conquers the three regions ; effulgent as a god, he even in his mortal frame, is enabled to enjoy the felicity of heaven." [668] By means of devotion to his father he conquers the middle world (firmament) and by devotion to his preceptor he attains to the region of Brahmā. [669] Commendable are all the acts of him by whom these three are respected. Futile are the acts of him by whom these three are dishonoured. [670] By worshipping his preceptor alone and not so much through the merit of oblations, homa or fireworship, that a brahmachārin can attain to heaven. [671] This was, of course, an honour paid to a religious teacher but it had an effect upon the relation of all pupils and teachers and helps to explain the high respect which Indian students of today have even for a teacher of secular subjects.

§ 9. THE ANNUAL TERM.

The session (or annual term) began in the rainy or cold season when the heat was less intense. The commencement (of Vedic study) must take place on the full moon day either of the months of Āṣārḍha, Śrāvaṇa or Bhādra." [672] In the Rāmāyaṇa[673] we are told that "brāhmaṇas of the Sāma school are waiting for the month of Bhādra which is the time for beginning their Vedic studies". According to Gautama Saṃhitā [674] one should read the Vedas in the months of Śrāvaṇa and Bhādra or during the five months the sun follows the southern course. Vaśiṣṭha Saṃhitā[675] says : "The Upakarman (the rite preparatory to Vedic study) shall be done on the full moon day of the month of Śrāvaṇa or Praustha-pada". According to Viṣṇu Saṃhitā [676] the rite of Upakarman is to be performed on the full moon day of the month of Śrāvaṇa and Bhādra. For we are told[677] that it was then that the herbs appeared amid the glad

---

[667] Manu II. 230-31 ; Viṣṇu XXXI. 7-8.

[668] Manu II. 232.

[669] Manu II. 233 ; Viṣṇu XXXI. 10.

[670] Viṣṇu XXXI. 9 ; Mahābhārata, Śāntiparba, 108th adhyāya.

[671] Sāṃkhya V. 9.

[672] Uśanā Saṃhitā III. 55.

[673] Kiṣkindhyākāṇḍa, 28th sarga.

[674] Ch. XVI.

[675] Ch. XI.

[676] Ch. XXX.

[677] Śānkhyāyana, IV, 5, 2.

grass and all Nature smiled with the pulsation of a fresh life. This was also the commencement of the Vedic year, when the frogs broke into a croaking harmony and when the Vedic students returned to their chant. According to Yājñabālkya [678] "when medicinal herbs grow on the full moon day of Śrāvaṇa or on a day under the Śrāvaṇa asterism or on the fifth day of Hasta asterism (name of the 13th lunar mansion consisting of five stars) one should begin the study of the Vedas". The Upakarman rite was performed annually before the commencement of the study of the Veda. [679] "Having kindled the sacred fire he (the student) shall offer oblations to the deities and the sacred metres. Having made oblations to the sacred metres, having made the brāhmaṇas utter words of well-being and after having fed them with curd he shall continue the Vedic study for four months and a half and then perform the Utsarga (a dedicatory rite performed annually after the completion of the Veda)." [680] "After a study of four months and a half" says the Viṣṇu Saṃhitā [681] "the rite of Utsarga shall be done, outside the town, in respect of the Vedas which have been completely studied and not in respect of those whose studies have not then been completed". According to Uśanā Saṃhitā [682] "after a study of four months and a half in a holy place, one should perform the dedicatory rite of the Vedas under the constellation of Puṣyā. Or he should do it in the first part of the first day of the month of Māgha". According to Yājñabālkya Saṃhitā [683] "On a day under the Rohinī asterism in the month of Pouṣ or on an Aṣṭaka tithi, one should, near water, at the outskirt of a village, duly consecrate one's Vedic studies".

After the Utsarga rite the twice-born ones should study the Vedas in the light fortnight.[684] In the dark fortnight a person should study the Vedāngas and the Purāṇas.[685] According to Vaśiṣṭha Saṃhitā (Ch. XI.) after the Utsarga rite he shall study the Vedas during the light fortnight and the Vedāngas at pleasure. According to Viṣṇu Saṃhitā,[686] however,

---

678 I. 142.

679 Kātyāyana Saṃhitā XXVII. 17.

680 Vaśiṣṭha XI ; Kātyāyana XXVII. 17.

681 XXX. 1-2.

682 III. 55-57.

683 I. 143.

684 Uśanā III. 57.

685 Uśanā III. 58.

686 XXX. 3.

the Vedāngas should not be studied between the rites of Utsarga and Upakarman."

The length of the annual term to be spent in Vedic study was thus usually four months and a half,[687] though the term may be two months,[688] five months,[689] five months and a half or six months and a half[690] and six months[691] in duration.

§ 10. DAYS OF NON-STUDY.

During the academic year there were numerous holidays and interruptions of study. Thus at Upakarman and at Utsarga the Vedas should not be studied for three days.[692] The study should be stopped for one whole day or night on Amābasyā.[693] The Vedas should not be studied on the new moon day;[694] according to Gautama (Ch. XVI.) for two days from the day of the new moon; on the full moon day;[695] on the fourteenth day of the two fortnights;[696] on the eighth day of the two fortnights;[697] on the twelfth day of the fortnight;[698] on the day of solar eclipse;[699] or for three days on the solar eclipse (for brāhmaṇa students);[700] when the sun is observed to be surrounded by a ring of haloe;[701] on the day of lunar eclipse;[702] or for three days on the lunar eclipse (for brāhmaṇa students);[703] when the moon is observed to be surrounded

687 Uśanā III. 56; Viṣṇu XXX. 1; Vaśiṣṭha XI.

688 Gautama XVI.

689 Gautama XVI.

690 Śānkhyāyana IV, 6, 7; Vaśiṣṭha XI.

691 Āśwalāyana, III, 5, 14.

692 Yājñabālkya I. 142; Uśanā III. 71; Vaśiṣṭha XXX. 24-25; Manu IV. 119.

693 Yājñabālkya I. 146; Hārīt IV. 71; Uśanā III. 70.

694 Vaśiṣṭha XI; Manu IV. 113; Sāṃkhya III. 15; compare Manu IV. 114.

695 Yājñabālkya I. 146; Hārīt IV. 71; Uśanā III. 70; Sāṃkhya III. 5; Manu IV. 113; Gautama XVI; compare Manu IV. 114.

696 Yājñabālkya I. 146; Uśanā III. 70; Sāṃkhya III. 5; Vaśiṣṭha XI; Manu IV. 113; compare Manu IV. 114.

697 Yājñabālkya I. 146; Uśanā III 70; Sāṃkhya III. 5; Viṣṇu XXX. 4; Vaśiṣṭha XI; Manu IV. 113.

698 Hārīt IV. 71; Manu IV. 105; Viṣṇu XXX. 5; Sāṃkhya III. 5; Vaśiṣṭha XI; compare Manu IV. 110.

699 Yājñabālkya I. 146.

700 Uśanā III. 67.

701 Gautama XVI; Manu IV. 105; Viṣṇu XXX. 5; Sāṃkhya III. 5; Vaśiṣṭha XI; compare Manu IV. 1.0.

702 Yājñabālkya I. 146.

703 Uśanā III. 67.

by a ring of haloe;[704] on the junction of the seasons (i. e., on the Pratipada day of Chaitra, Srāvaṇa and Agrahāyaṇa);[705] at the termination of the seasons;[706] in the unnatural season of the year;[707] on the Mahānavamī day;[708] on the third day of the bright half of Vaiśākha;[709] on the seventh day of the fortnight in the month of Māgha; [710] on the Rathya Saptamī;[711] on the Bharaṇī;[712] on the Aṣṭakas;[713] on the birth of the king's son for three days (for brāhmaṇa students only);[714] on the death of the king of one's country;[715] on the day of the hoisting or throwing down of the enemy's standard.[716] It is interesting to follow the reasons assigned for these breaks. Manu says that study in the prohibited lunar days was detrimental to the health of the teacher or of the student and did not conduce to the growth of learning. The first day of the fortnight was considered the most objectionable and we have reference to this in the Rāmāyaṇa[717] where Sītā is described as emaciated 'even as the learning of one who habitually studies on the first day of the fortnight'. Aśoka in his Pillar Inscription V, attaches special importance to these days, on which he forbids the castration of bulls and the killing of fish and

---

704 Gautama XVI.

705 Yājñabālkya I. 146.

706 Uśanā III. 71 ; Viṣṇu XXX. 5.

707 Gautama XVI.

708 Hārīt IV. 71.

709 Hārīt IV. 71.

710 Hārīt IV. 72.

711 Hārīt IV. 72.

712 Hārīt IV. 71.

713 Uśanā III. 71 ; Vaśiṣṭha XI ; Manu IV. 113 ; Compare Manu IV. 114 and IV. 119. According to Gautama (Ch. XVI.) one should refrain from studying the Vedas for three nights on the advent of the Aṣṭakas. "According to other authorities" says he (Ch. XVI.) "such prohibition exists only in respect of the last Aṣṭaka".

714 Uśanā III. 67 ; Manu IV. 110. In Bhababhūti's Uttara-Rama-Charita Act. IV. (Belvarkar's Eng. Trans., p. 60) we find the pupils of Vālmīkī's hermitage delighted at the thought that the royal guests would bring with them a holiday for the school.

715 Gautama XVI. In the Rāmāyaṇa, (Ayodhyākāṇḍa, 48th sarga) we find that all study and śāstric discussions were stopped when Rāma left Ayodhyā for Daṇḍakāraṇya forest where he was banished.

716 Yājñabālkya I. 147.

717 Sundarakāṇḍa, LIX. 34 : Pratipatpāṭhaśīlasya vidyeva tanutām gīta.

other creatures. We are to seek for an explanation probably in the ritualistic importance of these days, and it was based on the phases of the Moon, as was natural among a people following a luni-solar calendar.

The Vedas should not be studied on the following occasions :—For three days on the death of either a disciple,[718] or a ritwik,[719] or a priest,[720] or a preceptor,[721] or a friend,[722] or a śrotrīya studying the same branch of the Veda,[723] or a fellow-religious student (Uśanā III. 74; Vaśiṣṭha XI). The Vedas should not be studied on the death of a teacher's son or wife for one day.[724] The Vedas should not be studied for one whole day and night when one partakes of food and accepts presents on the occasion of a śrāddha ; [725] or when he had touched the leavings of food offered at a śrāddha ; [726] and for three days on a brāhmaṇa's accepting invitation for the Ekoddhiṣta śrāddha. [727] The study should also be stoppoed during the period of uncleanness incidental to the death of a sapiṇḍa or cognate relation ; [728] during a period of uncleanness ; [729] during birth-uncleanness ; [730] during death-uncleanness ; [731] on the occasion of a śrāddha ceremony (Gautama XVI.) ; after offering food at a śrāddha ; [732] and on the occasion of a friendly feast.[733]

The fundamental condition of inspiring thought is peace within oneself and harmony with Nature's forces. Hence when one shall see thunder, lightning, etc., rise in the morning and evening when the sacred fire is lit up, he should not study the Vedas ; in any other seasons except the rainy, on seeing a cloud.[734] According to Manu,[735] however, if these phenomena

---

718 Yājñabālkya I. 144. 719 Yājñabālkya I. 144. 720 Vaśiṣṭha XI.

721 Yājñabālkya I. 144 ; Uśanā III. 74 ; Vaśiṣṭha XI.

722 Yājñabālkya I. 144. 723 Uśanā III. 74 ; Yājñabālkya I. 144.

724 Vaśiṣṭha XI.

725 Yājñabālkya I. 146 ; Uśanā III. 66 ; Vaśiṣṭha X ; Vaśiṣṭha XI ; Manu IV. 109 ; compare Manu. IV. 116 and IV. 117.

726 Uśanā III. 66. 727 Uśanā III. 67 ; Manu IV. 110.

728 Sāṃkhya III. 6. 729 Sāṃkhya XV. 24.

730 Manu IV. 112 ; Gautama XVI. 731 Manu IV. 112 ; Gautama XVI.

732 Vaśiṣṭha X. 733 Gautama XVI.

734 Uśanā III. 61 ; Manu IV. 104 ; compare Uśanā III. 63. 735 IV. 104.

occur at the time of kindling the homa fire in the evening during the rainy season they should not be regarded as occasions of non-study. The finishing of the Veda and the study of the Āraṇyakas should be stopped for one day and night when there is roaring of clouds in the morning and evening.[736] When there is an ominous sound in the sky,[737] when a downpour of rain takes place accompanied by the flashing of lightning and the roaring of clouds[738] the Vedas should not be studied. From the time of rain with thunder and lightning to the next day the Vedas should not be studied.[739] When there is an ominous sound in the mountains[740] or an earthquake[741] or showering of sand[742] or showering of stones[743] or showering of blood[744] or dropping of fire-brands,[745] the Vedas should not be studied; nor when luminous bodies fall[746] nor during the appearance of the magnetic light in the western sky[747] nor when the muttering of thunder is heard[748] nor on the descent of thunder-bolts in unnatural seasons of the year[749] nor on a day covered with mist[750] nor when purple rainbows are observed to separate the firmament[751] nor when the Sāmans are sung[752] nor at the two sandhyās[753] nor when there is any sound of arrow,[754] any sound of trumpet,[755] any sound of drum[756] nor where the crying

736 Yājñabālkya I. 145; Yājñabālkya I. 149; Sāṃkhya III. 6; Gautama XVI; Vaśiṣṭha XI.

737 Yājñabālkya I. 145; Uśanā III. 62; Vaśiṣṭha XI.

738 Uśanā III. 49; Viṣṇu XXX. 8; Gautama XVI.

739 Manu IV. 103.

740 Vaśiṣṭha XI.

741 Yājñabālkya I. 145; Uśanā III. 62; Sāṃkhya III. 5; Viṣṇu XXX. 9; Manu IV. 105; Gautama XVI; Vaśiṣṭha XI.

742 Vaśiṣṭha XI.

743 Vaśiṣṭha XI.

744 Vaśiṣṭha XI.

745 Yājñabālkya I. 145; Uśanā II2. 49.

746 Uśanā III. 62; Sāṃkhya III. 5; Gautama XVI; Vaśiṣṭha XI, Viṣṇu XXX. 9; Manu IV. 103; compare Manu IV. 115.

747 Viṣṇu XXX. 9.

748 Yājñabālkya I. 199; Vaśiṣṭha XI; Viṣṇu XXX. 8; Uśanā III. 61; Sāṃkhya III. 6; Gautama XVI.

749 Gautama XVI.; Vaśiṣṭha XI.

750 Uśanā III. 70; Gautama XVI.

751 Gautama XVI.

752 Yājñabālkya I. 148; Gautama XVI; Vaśiṣṭha XI; Viṣṇu XXX. 26; Manu IV. 123.

753 Uśanā III. 70.

754 Yājñabālkya I. 148; Uśanā III. 70; Vaśiṣṭha XI; Manu IV. 113.

755 Gautama XVI.

756 Gautama XVI.

sound is heard (Uśanā III. 65 ; Manu IV. 108) nor when the cry of a person in danger is heard [757] nor when a king, a śrotrīya or a brāhmaṇa has met with an accident [758] nor on hearing the sound of weeping in the evening [759] nor when hearing the sound of music [760] nor when high winds blow [761] nor on the night when a roaring wind blows [762] nor when ominous dust is showered [763] nor on the day when a dusty wind blows (Uśanā III. 59) nor when the quarters are ablaze [764] nor at the periods of conjunction[765] nor in the evening [766] nor in the middle of the night [767] nor in the nights (Uśanā III. 71). "Several authorities aver that the study of the Vedas is prohibited during the first three hours and a half of each night". [768]

The Vedas should not be studied for one whole day and night on a paśu (animals which are 14 in number, viz., cow, sheep, goat, horse, mule, ass and man—these domestic and buffalo, monkey, bear, reptile, ruru-deer, spotted antelope and deer—these wild ones) happening to pass between a student and his preceptor ; [769] on the passing of a five-toed animal between the pupil and his preceptor ;[770] on the passing of a toad, a cat, a dog, a snake, mungoose or a mouse between the pupil and his preceptor.[771] The Vedas should not be studied for one whole day and night when a dog ;[772] a jackal [773] an ass[774] or an owl (Yājñabālkya I. 148) emits a noise and when camels scream.[775]

---

757 Yājñabālkya I. 148. 758 Viṣṇu XXX. 23. 759 Hārīt IV. 73.
760 Sāṃkhya III. 6 ; Viṣṇu XXX. 13.
761 Yājñabālkya I. 149 ; Manu IV. 122 ; Viṣṇu XXX. 7.
762 Uśanā III. 59. Manu IV. 102.
763 Yājñabālkya I. 149 ; Gautama II. ; Manu IV. 102 ; Manu IV. 115.
764 Yājñabālkya I. 149 ; Sāṃkhya III. 6 ; Gautama XVI ; Manu IV. 118.
765 Yājñabālkya I. 150 ; Vaśiṣṭha XI. ; Manu IV. 113.
766 Yama Saṃhitā I. 76 ; compare Ibid., 77.
767 Yājñabālkya I. 150 ; Uśanā III. 66 ; Manu IV. 109. 768 Gautama XVI.
769 Yājñabālkya I. 147 ; Manu IV. 126. 770 Viṣṇu XXX. 22.
771 Manu IV. 126 ; compare Gautama I.
772 Yājñabālkya I. 148 ; Gautama XVI ; Viṣṇu XXX. 12 ; Manu IV. 115.
773 Yājñabālkya I. 148 ; Gautama XVI ; Viṣṇu XXX. 12 ; Manu IV. 115.
774 Yājñabālkya I. 148 ; Gautama XVI ; Viṣṇu XXX. 12 ; Manu IV. 115.
775 Manu IV. 115.

The Vedas should not be studied in a very loud voice,[776] in an impure state,[777] when feeling amative propensities (Sāṃkhya III. 6), when within water,[778] in a town,[779] in a forest,[780] in unwashed mouth after eating,[781] when the hand is yet wet after eating,[782] after meals,[783] where the four roads meet,[784] by the side of a high road,[785] near an unholy place,[786] in a pasture ground,[787] near a cremation ground,[788] near a divine temple,[789] near an unholy object,[790] seated on an ant-hill,[791] near the side of an ant-hill,[792] near a Phallic emblem,[793] near a dead body,[794] at places containing carcasses,[795] at the outskirt of a village (Manu IV. 116), near a śūdra,[796] near a chaṇḍāla (divakirti),[797] near a man of degraded caste,[798] near an impious man,[799] near a fallen person,[800] near the performer of a śrāddha ceremony who has not fed the brāhmaṇas with boiled rice,[801] near an irreligious person;[802] in a village inhabited by low caste people,[803] near a troop of soldiers,[804] and where there is a multitude of men.[805] The brāhmaṇas should not read the Vedas in a company.[806] The Vedas should not be studied while fighting or

---

776 Sāṃkhya III. 7. 777 Yājñabālkya I. 149.

778 Yājñabālkya I. 150; Uśanā III. 66; Viṣṇu III. 16; Manu IV. 109.

779 Gautama XVI. 780 Manu IV. 113.

781 Manu IV. 109. 782 Yājñabālkya I. 149; Vaśiṣṭha XI.

783 Manu IV. 121; Vaśiṣṭha XI. 784 Viṣṇu XXX. 15.

785 Viṣṇu XXX. 15; Gautama XVI. 786 Yājñabālkya I. 148.

787 Manu IV. 116.

788 Sāṃkhya III. 7; Gautama XVI; Viṣṇu XXX. 15; Manu IV. 116.

789 Sāṃkhya III. 7; Viṣṇu III. 15. 790 Yājñabālkya I. 148.

791 Gautama XVI. 792 Sāṃkhya III. 7. 793 Sāṃkhya III. 7.

794 Yājñabālkya I. 149. 795 Gautama XVI.

796 Yājñabālkya I. 199; Gautama XVI; Viśṇu XXX. 14.

797 Gautama XVI. 798 Yājñabālkya I. 148; Viṣṇu XXX. 14.

799 Manu IV. 108. 800 Yājñabālkya I. 149.

801 Gautama XVI. 802 Uśanā III. 65. 803 Uśanā III. 65.

804 Manu IV. 121. 805 Uśanā III. 65; Manu IV. 107, 108.

806 Manu IV. 15. Compare:

"Uneven grounds, unsafe and windy spots,
And hiding places and god-haunted shires,
High roads and bridges and all bathing ghats,
These eight avoid when talking of high things."
—Milindā-Pañha, IV. 1. 8.

wrangling, [807] while running,[808] while in a state of fright, [809] when any fear proceeds either from a king[810] or a robber or a thief, [811] when there are village disturbances; [812] in a battle, [813] in a camp,[814] when a bad smell comes; [815] when a good person arrives at the house,[816] on the return of a friend from a foreign country,[817] without taking the permission of the guest in the house;[818] while going on an ass, [819] or on a camel, [820] or on a chariot, [821] or on an elephant,[822] or on a horse, [823] or in a boat,[824] or in a carriage; [825] while on a tree, [826] or under the shade of śleśmataka, śālmalī, madhuka, kovidara and kapithwa trees; [827] in a desert; [828] during an indigestion, [829] after a sour rising, [830] while passing excreta, [831] after having purged, [832] while rubbing oil, [833] while passing urine, [834] on the day he has vomited, [835] while bathing, [836] while he leaps, [837] while leaning against something; [838] on seeing a dead body carried, [839] in a town where a corpse lies, [840] in a town where chaṇḍālas live (Vaśiṣṭha XI), on seeing a dead body placed on earth; [841] while lying down, [842] while seated with a leg cocked

---

[807] Manu IV. 121. [808] Yājñabālkya I. 150; Vaśiṣṭha XI.
[809] Gautama XVI. [810] Manu IV. 118.
[811] Yājñabālkya I. 150; Manu IV. 118.
[812] Sāṃkhya III. 6. [813] Manu IV. 121; Viṣṇu XXX. 11.
[814] Vaśiṣṭha XI.
[815] Yājñabālkya I. 150; Uśanā III. 64; Gautama XVI; Vaśiṣṭha XI; Manu IV. 107.
[816] Yājñabālkya I 150. [817] Gautama XVI. [818] Manu IV. 122.
[819] Yājñabālkya I. 151; Manu IV. 120.
[820] Yājñabālkya I. 151; Manu IV. 120; Viṣṇu XXX. 17.
[821] Yājñabālkya I. 151. [822] Viśṇu XXX. 17; Manu IV. 120.
[823] Yājñabālkya I. 151; Viṣṇu XXX. 17; Manu IV. 120.
[824] Yājñabālkya I. 151; Vaśiṣṭha XI; Viṣṇu XXX. 17; Manu IV. 120.
[825] Gautama XVI; Viṣṇu XXX. 17; Manu IV. 120.
[826] Yājñabālkya I. 151; Vaśiśṭha XI; Manu IV. 120. [827] Uśanā III. 73.
[828] Yājñabālkya I. 151. [829] Viṣṇu XXX. 21; Manu IV. 121.
[830] Manu IV. 121. [831] Uśanā III. 62; Gautama XVI; Vaśiṣṭha XI; Manu IV. 109.
[832] Viṣṇu XXX. 20. [833] Hārīt IV. 72
[834] Manu IV. 109; Uśanā III. 66; Gautama XVI; Vaśiṣṭha XI.
[835] Viṣṇu XXX. 19; Manu IV. 121; Gautama XVI; Vaśiṣṭha XI.
[836] Hārīt IV. 72. [837] Vaśiṣṭha XI. [838] Vaśiṣṭha XI.
[839] Hārīt IV. 73. [840] Vaśiṣṭha XI; Viṣṇu XXX, 10; Manu IV. 108.
[841] Hārīt IV. 73. [842] Uśanā III. 79; Manu IV. 112.

up, [843] while seated by placing the soles of the feet on the seat, [844] while stretching his feet out, [845] while sitting on his haunches, [846] while sitting with a cloth girt round the legs and knees, [847] and while taking food rendered impure by birth or death. [848] As long as the scent and paste dedicated at the Ekoddhiṣta śrāddha exist on the person of a learned brāhmaṇa, he should not study the Vedas.[849] The Vedas should not be studied after bleeding from any part of the body [850] and after a cut from a weapon. Thus we see that "the impurity of the place of Vedic study and personal uncleanness of the reader—these two are the permanent causes of non-study." [851]

On the Aṣtaka day, when a high wind blows or in any other calamity, a twice-born one should study one Ṛk or one Yajus or one Sāma mantram.[852] "There is no prohibition in respect of reading the allied branches of Vedic study such as Prosody, Grammar, etc., or in respect of the homa mantras or in respect of that portion of the Veda which should be read each day (i. e., the sandhyā mantras) during the period in which the study of the Vedas is ordinarily prohibited.[853] "There is no prohibition as regards the study of the Vedāngas, of the Itihāses and the Purāṇas, or of the Dharmaśāstras and other works ; but a twice-born one should abstain from studying all these on the Parba days (*i.e.*, on the full moon, the last day of the dark night, and the third day of the bright half of Vaiśākha)".[854] According to Vyāsa Saṃhitā [855] on the interdicted days subjects collateral to the Vedas should be studied with the preceptor's permission. "For the six months when the sun is in the southern solstice, a wise man should not study the subsequent mysterious subjects and the Upaniṣads."[856]

§ 11. CLASSES OF TEACHERS.

There were three classes of teachers—the guru, the āchārya and the upādhyāya. He is called guru who, having performed all the rites

[843] Gautama XVI. [844] Uśanā III. 69 ; Viṣṇu XXX. 18.
[845] Vaśiṣṭha XI. [846] Manu IV. 112. [847] Uśanā III. 69.
[848] Uśanā III. 69. [849] Uśanā III. 68 ; Manu IV. 111.
[850] Manu IV. 122. [851] Manu IV. 127. [852] Uśanā III. 77.
[853] Manu II. 105. [854] Uśanā III. 98. [855] I. 38.
[856] Kātyāyana Saṃhitā XXXVIII. 2.

(beginning with garvadhānam) delivers instructions in the Vedas.[857] He is called āchārya who teaches the Vedas after having performed only the ceremony of upanayanam.[858] According to Manu[859] and Vyāsa[860] Saṃhitās "a brāhmaṇa who practises penitential austerities and performs the rite of homa every day and teaches the Vedas with their Kalpas (the branch of Vedic literature which deals with ceremonials and the celebration of religious sacrifices) and Rahasyas (the transcendental truths inculcated in the Upaniṣads) is called an āchārya." "He is called upādhyāya who teaches only a portion of the Vedas;"[861] "one who teaches the Angas of the Vedas is also an upādhyāya."[862] According to Viṣṇu Saṃhitā[863] "he who teaches an entire Veda in consideration of fees or a portion of the Veda without fees is called an upādhyāya." According to Sāṃkhya Saṃhitā[864] "one who gives lessons in the Vedas for money is an upādhyāya." Manu[865] says: "He who in consideration of fees, teaches a portion of the Veda and any of the Vedāngas is said to be an upādhyāya."

§12. Teaching—the Monopoly of the Brahmin?

In course of time teaching the Vedas came to be the exclusive duty of the brāhmaṇa. In the Hārit,[866] Atri[867] and Manu Saṃhitās[868] where the duties of the four castes are enumerated we find that the brāhmaṇas alone are entitled to give instructions in the Vedas. Manu[869] explicitly says: "The brāhmaṇas alone shall teach the Vedas and none else, this is the conclusion." In another place he says: "Teaching the Vedas, etc., shall never revert to the kṣhatriya as against the brāhmaṇa;"[870] "nor to the vaiśya as against the brāhmaṇa."[871] "Rather should the kṣhatriya in distress live by following the low trades, but under no circumstances should he embrace the vocation of a brāhmaṇa.'[872] According to Manu[873] his law-code should be taught in its entirety

---

[857] Yājñabālkya I. 34. [858] Yājñabālkya I. 34; Vaśiṣṭha III; Viṣṇu XXIX. 1.
[859] II. 140. [860] IV. 43. [861] Yājñabālkya I. 35; Vaśiṣṭha III.
[862] Vaśiṣṭha III. [863] XXIX. 2. [864] III. 1.
[865] II. 141. [866] I. 18. [867] I. 13-15.
[868] I. 88-91. [869] X. 1.
[870] Manu X. 77. [871] Manu X. 78.
[872] Manu X. 95. Compare Manu X. 96-97. [873] I. 103.

by an erudite brāhmaṇa and not by a member of any other caste. In the Mahābhārata[874] Viṣṇu says to Yudhiṣṭhir "Begging, officiating as a priest and teaching are strictly forbidden in the case of a kṣhatriya." Alberuni[875] says: "The brāhmaṇas teach the Vedas to the kṣhatriyas. The latter learn it, but are not allowed to teach it, not even to a brāhmaṇa. The vaiśya and the śūdra are not allowed to hear it, much less to pronounce and recite it." According to Atri Saṃhitā[876] giving instructions in the Vedas would outcaste the kṣhatriya and the vaiśya.

But these rules forbidding non-brāhmaṇas to teach and the injunction of Angīras Saṃhitā[877] that acquiring knowledge from a śūdra would degrade even one burning with Brahma energy indirectly prove that non-brāhmaṇa teachers were not altogether rare. This is corroborated by other evidences from Gautama and Manu Saṃhitās. "In times of distress a brāhmaṇa student may take lessons from a non-brāhmaṇa teacher and he shall serve his guru only so long as he shall actually study."[878] "Wishing the most exalted existence (*i. e.*, liberation of the self) after death, let not a brāhmaṇa student live for good in the house of his non-brāhmaṇa preceptor".[879] "Women (wives), gems, *knowledge*, virtue, purity, good words (counsels) and *the various kinds of arts* may be acquired from anywhere."[880] Again, teaching sciences other than the Vedas is mentioned by Manu as one of the ten means of livelihood in times of distress for men of all castes.[881] Gautama Saṃhitā[882] says: "In times of distress a brāhmaṇa may learn an art and a science from a non-brāhmaṇa teacher and he should serve and follow the preceptor until the close of his study." Again, the injunction of Manu that "the king shall learn from the people the theory of the various trades and professions" seems to imply that in secular subjects like Vārttā, others besides brāhmaṇas may be called in to give instruction to the young princes and this seems probable also in the matter of military skill. Viśwāmitra

---

874 Śāntiparva, 60th adhyāya.

875 Sachau's Eng. Trans., Vol. I., p. 125.

876 II. 20.

877 Śloka 49.

878 Manu II. 241.

879 Manu II. 242.

880 Manu II. 240

881 Manu X. 116.

882 VII.

thus gave to Rāma a training in the use of missils and weapons.[883] It is needless to point out that technical education was mostly imparted by non-brāhmaṇas, so that the prohibition of teaching by non-brāhmaṇas seems to be confined only to sacredotal knowledge.

§ 13. TUITION FEE.

All the time the pupil was under instruction the teacher was not to receive any fee. The Mahābhārata[884] condemns teaching for pay and even goes so far as to hold that "those who accept remuneration for teaching are designated as equal to a śūdra."[885] Manu[886] says: "Let not a virtuous Vedic student pay any (money) to his preceptor ere he returns from his house after finishing his career." Viṣṇu[887] says: "He who having acquired knowledge sells it for a living in this world, shall derive no benefit from it in the next." Indeed to teach in consideration of fees was looked upon as an upapātaka (minor sin).[888] Receiving lessons on payment of a fee was similarly looked upon as an upapātaka.[889] According to Vyāsa Saṃhitā[890] mercenary teaching of the Vedas rank equally with an act of brahminicide in respect of sin. According to Manu[891] and Uśanā[892] Saṃhitās both he who studies the Vedas by paying fees and he who gives instructions on receiving fees should be studiously avoided on the occasion of a śrāddha ceremony. Uśanā[893] calls them as vṛttakas while Manu[894] asks all good and erudite brāhmaṇas to avoid these vile and condemnable persons. In Mālavikāgñimitra[895] we are told: "He whose learning is merely for a livelihood, is called a trader that traffics in knowledge." Indeed teaching for money was allowed as a means of livelihood only in times of extreme distress.[896] King Amar Śakti wanted to pay Viṣṇuśarmā

[883] Rāmāyaṇa, Bālakāṇḍa, 27th and 28th sargas.

[884] Śāntiparva, 260th adhyāya.

[885] Anuśāsanaparva, 135th adhyāya.

[886] II. 245.

[887] XXX. 39.

[888] Viṣṇu XXXVII. 20 and 34; Yājñabālkya III. 236, 242.

[889] Viṣṇu XXXVII. 21, 34; Yājñabālkya III. 236, 242.

[890] IV. 70.

[891] III. 156.

[892] IV. 24.

[893] IV. 24.

[894] III. 167.

[895] M. R. Kale's Eng. Trans., p. 12.

[896] Yājñabālkya III. 42.

"śata-śāsana" for teaching his ill-behaved sons, whereupon the spirited brāhmaṇa replied : "Nāhaṃ śāsana śatenāpi vidyā-vikrayaṃ kariṣyāmi".

When, however, the course was completed the pupil performed certain bathing ceremonies and "after having bathed with the permission of his guru he was to pay him an honorarium according to his pecuniary circumstances."[897] This honorarium was a mere symbol of the respect on the part of the pupil to his teacher. Vājaseniya Saṃhitā[898] says : "Dakṣhiṇā śraddhāṃ dadāti, śraddhayā āpyati jñānam." "A plot of land, gold, a cow, a horse, an umbrella, a pair of shoes, paddy, vegetables, clothes or whatever he is capable of giving him, with that he shall evoke the pleasure of his preceptor."[899] Thus we see that in return for the knowledge acquired from him, the student can give to his preceptor a few vegetables if his worldly circumstances do not admit of giving any other (more costly) thing. At the same time a gift, however precious or costly, was considered no adequate return for the benefit which a preceptor accords to his pupil. Laghu Hārita says : "There is no such thing in this world, by giving which a pupil can discharge his debt to a teacher, who has taught him no more than a single letter of the alphabet." In the case of technical education, however, we have instances of fees being paid by the apprentices to teachers. Thus in the Jātakas[900] we find that two merchant-sons paid 2000 pieces each.

At Taxila, the students were usually admitted on payment in advance of the entire tuition fees. A fixed sum seems to have been specified for the purpose amounting to 1,000 pieces of money.[901] In lieu of paying the fees in cash, a student was allowed to pay them in the shape of services to his teacher.[902] To this class apparently belonged the majority of the students who attended on their teacher by day, and received instruction at night. We read of a school of five hundred brāhmaṇa pupils whose duties were among others, to gather fire-wood from the forests for their teacher.[903]

---

[897] Manu II. 245.

[898] 19, 30.

[899] Manu II. 246.

[900] IV. 224, 225, 38, 39.

[901] Jātaka I. 272, 285 ; IV. 50, 224 etc.

[902] Compare-Milindā Pañha VI. 71.

[903] Jātaka I. 317-318.

Sometimes a student would prefer to devote his whole time to studies without sparing any time for such services or menial work, while at the same time he was too poor to be able to pay the teacher's fees in cash in advance. In such a case the student was trusted to pay the fees after the completion of his studies. We read of one such student, a brāhmaṇa boy of Benares, who, after completing his education at Taxila, paid his teacher's fees by begging for them in distant countries beyond the Ganges.

Where students were unable to pay the teacher's fee in any of the several ways aforesaid, a charitable community often came forward to provide for them a free education. We read of 'a teacher of world-wide fame at Benares' who had in his school five hundred young brāhmaṇa pupils. The difficulty of maintaining such a school was removed by the generosity of the Benares folk who used "to give day by day commons of food to the poor lads and had them taught free". The cost of education was also to some extent taken over from the teachers and the taught by the occasional invitations to dinner extended to them by philanthropic householders. We read of a school of five hundred students being invited to take meals by a country-family at at Taxila and of a similar entertainment given by an entire village.[904]

There was again another class of students who paid the teacher's fees from the scholarships awarded to them by the states to which they belonged. Generally such students would be sent as companions of the princes of their respective countries who were deputed to Taxila for education. We read of the sons of the royal chaplains of the courts of Benares and Rājagaha accompanying their respective princes to Taxila. Cases, however, are not wanting of students being sent on their own account for higher studies to Taxila at the expense of the State. Thus we read of a Brahmin boy of Benares, being sent by the King at his expense to Taxila for the purpose of specialising in the science of archery.[905]

---

[904] Jātaka I. 239; I. 317; III. 171.

[905] Jātaka V. 263; III. 238 and V. 247; V. 127.

§ 14. QUALIFICATIONS REQUIRED OF THE TEACHER.

The teacher was generally called "guru" which means 'heavy' or 'great' and he was to be really great in learning and moral conduct. He was also called "āchārya" which comes from the word "char" to behave and means 'one who trains up others in good behaviour' (āchāraṃ grāhayati iti āchāryaḥ); it is also taken by some to mean the source of all religion (dharmaṃ āchinoti iti āchāryaḥ). In either sense the teacher was expected to train up the pupils in good behaviour, the essence of religion, and naturally to possess those qualities himself. "This truth is not grasped when taught by an inferior man" says the Kaṭhopaniṣad.[906] The Muṇḍakopaniṣad[907] asks the teacher to be a śrotriya (*i. e.*, one whose ancestors had been Vedic scholars for at last three generations) and brahmaniṣṭha (dwelling entirely in the Brahman). Various descriptions are met with in the Rāmāyaṇa and the Mahābhārata of celebrated gurus like Vaśiṣṭha, Viśwāmitra, Sandipani, Droṇa, Paraśurāma and Kaṇva and they are said to be vastly learned men of ideal character, quite contented with their lot, free from all worldly hankerings and respected even by kings who put their sons under them for instruction. Of course every teacher could not be like them but he was expected to possess these qualities.

The Prātiśākhya[908] of the Ṛgveda gives us some idea of the intellectual qualifications of a teacher: 'he must himself have passed through the recognised curriculum and have fulfilled all the duties of the brahmachārin, before he is allowed to become a teacher'. Moreover, the success in debate[909] was also necessary to make one's name known to the public as being well-versed in learning. In the Upaniṣads we have a further list of the qualifications expected of a teacher. He was to come of a family of Vedic teachers and be intent on the acquisition of the highest experience. He must work heart and soul and be like a parent unto his disciples. He must add the force of his example to the influence of precept. "As one acts, he becomes, good by good deeds, bad by evil; what action he performs, into that

[906] I. 2, 8. [907] I. 2, 12. [908] Ch. XV.
[909] Compare Ṛgveda X. 71.

does he become changed".[910] He should conceal nothing from his pupil if he had stayed with him for a year. He should impress the essential points and impart true knowledge after making sure of the earnestness and the level of intelligence of the pupil, and satisfying himself as to his character. In one of the Upaniṣads we are introduced to the sage Pippalāda who asks his questioners to spend a year with him in austerity, purity and single-minded devotion to knowledge. The teacher was to be remarkable for his humility. He should answer the questions put 'if he had the knowledge needed.' When five brāhmaṇas came to Uddālaka Āruṇi to learn Vaiśwānara-vidyā Āruṇi, diffident as to the fullness of his knowledge of the subject asked them to go to King Aśwapati Kaikeya. Thus there was no idea of palming off false knowledge as true, or posing as an authority on matters outside the direct range of one's own study and experience. It is a part of the valedictory address of the teacher to his disciple, that the latter should listen with respect and veneration to those who were greater than the former and that the teacher's example might be followed only in so far as his conduct was above reproach.[911]

The individual skill in communicating one's knowledge to others was recognised to distinguish between teachers and teachers. In the Sabhāparba[912] of the Mahābhārata we are told that Devarṣi Nārada alone really knew the method of imparting instruction to pupils. In Kālidāsa's Mālavikāgñimitra we find that when a dispute arose about the superiority in knowledge between two teachers of the dramatic art, Gaṇadāsa and Haradatta, Paribrājikā suggested that the decision be arrived at by practical display of teaching. In this connection we find the following observations :—

"The acceptance of an unpromising pupil shows a want of *discernment* on the part of the teacher."[913]

"The *skill* of a teacher when imparted to a worthy object attains greater excellence, as the water of a cloud when dropping into a sea-shell, acquires the state of (is converted into) a pearl."[914]

---

[910] Bṛhad. Up., III. 88; IV. 1; VI. 3. 12; Chāndogya Up., III. 1, 5; Śvet. Up., VI. 22.

[911] Praśna Up., I. 1.; Taitt. Up., I. 11.

[912] 5th adhyāya.

[913] Mālavikāgñimitra, M. R. Kale's Eng. Trans., p. 11.

[914] Ibid., p. 5.

"If you do not permit me who am now desirous of showing in the present contest, my *power of imparting instruction*, then (I must say) I am given up by you."[915]

"Then exhibit, both of you, your *skill* in instruction."[916]

"Your Majesty will, therefore, kindly tell me in what subject-matter of dramatic representation I shall show my *ability* to impart instruction."[917]

"Every person, though well-educated, has not the *skill* to impart instruction to others."[918]

"One man is at his best when exhibiting his art in person; another has as his special qualification the power of *communicating his skill*; he who possesses both (these excellences) should be placed at the head of teachers."[919]

Here we clearly see the recognition of the teacher's skill as an independent art.

That some of these equipments were thought necessary for a teacher would be evident from the fact that students after finishing their education in the house of the preceptor were under an obligation to teach and thus transmit learning from age to age. The Aitareya Āraṇyaka[920] says: "Naprabaktre," "Do not teach one who will not himself teach". In the Bower manuscript which is really a collection of two manuscripts we have a portion called Nābanītaka in which the instructions at the beginning say that 'it should not be taught to anyone who has no disciple.'[921] In the Taittirīya Upaniṣad[922] learning and teaching the Vedas are both enjoined on the pupil. In another passage of the same Upaniṣad[923] the student is asked, after finishing his education in his preceptor's house not to neglect the learning and the 'teaching' of the Veda.

---

[915] Ibid., p. 13. [916] Ibid., p. 12.
[917] Ibid., p. 13. [918] Ibid. [919] Ibid., p. 11.
[920] III. 2. 6.
[921] India and Centra Asia—Dr. Nirañjana Prosāda Chakravartī, pp. 41-42.
[922] I. 9. [923] 1. 11.

Many European Indologists have spoken of the fine genius of the ancient Indian teacher; of them Mr. F. W. Thomas says: "What was taught was well taught and the attainments of the Hindus were not inferior to those of any ancient nation, or to those of European scholars prior to the Renaissance". Moreover, it was in moral and religious qualifications that the Hindu teacher stood worthy of the name. His plain-living, high-thinking, disciplined routine, abstinence from pleasures, mental control and above all, his sincerity of purpose were the principal factors in the success of his work. Such qualities could never fail to command respect from any body; they were a living model for the pupils to follow and carried the lion's share in the creditable educational results when there was no state-organisation for education. The Jesuits offer a fine comparison. Both were devoted, religious, learned and disciplined body of men. Both produced good results in their own spheres. Both imparted religious and secular knowledge and were respected wherever they went. The latter however kept no household and lived celibate lives, in which respects the Buddhist monk had much in common with them. These very conditions of life were the cause of those defects and artificialities which ultimately led to the decline of both the Jesuits and the Buddhist monks, when the individual fervour, sincerity and virtue were on the wane. On the other hand, the Hindu teacher kept his household, enjoyed his simple family-life and at the same time abstained from throwing himself headlong into intemperate worldly pleasures. He managed his own school except in the case of a large institution where many like him worked under a kulapati. Of the three the ancient Hindu institution appears to be the most natural and lasting, though the least dazzling.

§ 15. METHOD OF TEACHING.

The actual teaching was to proceed in the following manner. "A brahmachārin, having quitted his bed early in the morning and having bathed and performed the homa should accost self-controlled, his preceptor. Then having been commanded by his preceptor and having cast a look at his face, he should commence the study of the Vedas".[924] Before reading the Vedas he must put off his shoes.[925]

[924] Sāṃkhya Saṃhitā III. 2-3.

[925] Āpastamva Saṃhitā IX. 20.

The study commenced in the last watch of the night[926] after which the student was not to sleep again.[927] For the purpose of studying the Vedas, the student self-controlled, clad in a light garment, looking towards the north shall do the āchamanam, and unite his palms in the manner of brahmāñjali, after which lessons should be given to him.[928] At the commencement and at the close of his Vedic study, a student shall catch hold of the feet of his preceptor.[929] With his arms parallelly outstretched, he shall make obeisance unto his preceptor, by touching his (preceptor's) right foot with the right and his left foot with the left hand of his own.[930] The preceptor then free from idleness, shall take hold of the small finger of the pupil's left hand and shall address him as "O you read now".[931] Then the pupil should touch his eyes, ears and the regions of his life and intellect with a blade of kuśa grass and shall purify his body by three prāṇāyāmas consisting of fifteen mātrās (*i. e.*, lasting for a time necessary to utter fifteen short vowels).[932] "After this he shall utter the Praṇava,"[933] for, "Praṇava (*i. e.*, Om or Omkāra) not uttered at the commencement leads to the destruction of the reading".[934] "Sitting on a cushion previously spread out, he should recite five or seven vyāpritis preceded by the Praṇava, each morning at the commencement of Vedic study.[935] He should make formally obeisance to his preceptor; and seated on his right, with his face turned towards the north or to the east, he should recite the Gāyatri,[936] and the Praṇava mantra (Om) after the recitation of the Gāyatrī.[937] Placing the two hands firmly on the two thighs, with the permission of the preceptor he should begin his course. He should not have his mind strayed away (to any other subject).[938]

---

926 Manu IV. 99; Viṣṇu XXX. 27.
927 Manu IV. 99; Viṣṇu XXX. 27.
928 Manu II. 70.
929 Manu II. 71; Viṣṇu XXX. 32.
930 Manu II. 72.
931 Manu II. 73; Gautama, Ch. I.
932 Manu II. 75; Gautama, Ch. I.
933 Manu II. 75.
934 Manu II. 74.
935 Gautama, Ch. I.
936 Gautama, Ch. I; Sambarta Saṃhitā, śl. 9.
937 Gautama, Ch. I.
938 Sambarta Saṃhitā, śl. 10.

The fifteenth chapter of the Prātiśākhya of the Ṛgveda gives in brief the method of teaching that was in vogue in those early times. 'At the beginning of each lecture the pupils embrace[939] the feet of their teacher and say "Read sir." The teacher says "Om" and then pronounces two words or if it is a compound, one. When the teacher has pronounced one word or two, the first pupil repeats the first word; but if there is anything that requires explanation, the pupil says "Sir;" and after it has been explained to him, the teacher says "Om." In this manner they go on till they have finished a praśna (question) which consists of three verses, or if they are verses of more than 40 to 42 syllables, of two verses. If they are paṃkti verses of 40 to 42 syllables each, a praśna may comprise either two or three; and if a hymn consists of one verse only, that is supposed to form a praśna. After the praśna is finished, they have all to repeat it once more, and then to go on learning it by heart, pronouncing every syllable with high accent. After the teacher has first told a praśna to his pupil on the right, the others go round him to the right and this goes on till the whole adhyāya or lecture is finished, a lecture generally consisting of 60 praśnas. At the end of the last half-verse, the teacher says "Om," and the pupil replies "Om," repeating also the verses required at the end of a lecture.' "The pupils then embrace the feet of their teacher."[940]

The teacher probably used to give a general idea of the subject to the pupils either at the commencement or at the end of its study. This is illustrated by a well-known story about Vyāsa. He had four disciples—Vaiśāmpāyana, Sumantu, Paila and Jaimini. To each of them, he explained the comprehensive view of each of the Vedas.

The reading lesson was followed by instruction (viddhi) and explanation (arthavāda). In 'viddhi' the teacher showed the pupils the acts and actions to be actually performed during the ritual ceremony described in the text; and in 'arthavāda' the meaning of the sentences was made clear. We cannot say what this explanation amounted to in the earliest times but when other subjects and sciences arose,

---

[939] Sambarta Saṃhitā, śl. 10; Manu II. 71; Viṣṇu XXX. 32.

[940] Manu II. 71; Viṣṇu XXX. 32.

explanation must have been given a very large place. We are told in the Uśanā Saṃhitā[941]: "This foremost of the twice-born one should not be satisfied with merely reading the Vedas. The mere recitation of the Vedas becomes useless like a cow in mire. He who studying duly the Veda, does not *discuss* (*i. e.*, masters) the Vedānta, becomes like a śūdra with his entire family. And he is not entitled to have water for washing his feet." Dakṣa Saṃhitā[942] says: "The first is the admission (of the superiority) of the Vedas; then *discussion* (on the Vedas); then the study; then the recitation (of the Vedas); and then the deliverance of instructions unto disciples. This is the five-fold practice of the Vedas." As a matter of fact we find that as the systems of philosophy arose, for the full understanding of the text, a three-fold explanation was given: (1) Pada or word, (2) Vākya or sentence, (3) Pramāṇa or argument. To make the student understand the word, grammatical notes were given; to make the meaning of the sentence clear to him, the relations of words, phrases and parts therein were shown by filling up gaps or supplying ellipses and by explaining allusions. Lastly, the idea of the passage was made clear by setting forth the argument as explicitly as possible and by relating it to the previous as well as to the following points. Hence one well-versed in the text was called 'Pada-vākya-pramāṇagña,' 'proficient in the three parts.'

It is interesting to find that the explanation of the text was almost on the same lines as at present. According to Vāchaṣpatimiśra[943] the adhyayana (the hearing of words), śabda (apprehension of meaning), uha (reasoning leading to generalisation), suhṛtprāpti (confirmation by a friend or teacher), and dāna (application) are the five steps for

941 Śls. 81-82. 942 II. 27.

943 Quoted by Mahāmahopādhyāya C. K. Tarkalaṅkāra in his "Lectures on Hindu Philosophy (1st year) pp. 299-301.

the realisation of the meaning of a religious truth. Curiously enough these steps correspond wholly with those of Dewey. In his book "How we think" he gives the following steps :—

(1) A problem and its location (adhyayana and śabda).
(2) Suggested solutions and selection of a solution (uha and suhṛtprāpti).
(3) Action (application) [dāna].

The following śloka gives steps similar to those of the Herbertians :—

"Śuśruṣā śrabaṇañchaiba grahaṇaṃ dhāraṇaṃ tathā
Uhapohārta bijñānaṃ tatvajñānaṃcha dhīguṇaḥ."
—Kāmandakī.

Dhīguṇa includes the following qualities :—(1) śuśruṣā (desire to listen), (2) śrabaṇam (act or process of hearing) (3) grahaṇam (accepting, taking in), (4) dhāraṇam (digestion of what has been taken in) (5) uhāpoha (discussion) (6) arthavijñānam (grasping the correct sense) (7) tatwajñānam (knowledge of profound truth).

The western method of lecturing to advanced students was unknown to the teachers of Brahminic schools but free discussions with the teacher, questions and answers from either side, concrete illustrations and references to the practical details of daily life, allowing some discount for the dogmatic mysticism of the sacred texts—form a clear evidence of the rational method of education obtaining in those times. Indeed, the Upaniṣads often fall into the form of a dialogue,[944] which shows that the method of teaching was catechetical, like that of explaining a subject by an intelligent and graduated series of questions and answers which is associated with the great Greek teacher Socrates. In the Mahābhārata (specially in the Śānti and Anuśāsana parbas) we find how the method of teaching through questions and answers was resorted

[944] Dṛptabalaki—Gargya and Ajātaśatru in Bṛhad. Up., II. 1; Yājñabālkya and Maitreyī in Bṛhad. Up., 2. 4; Yājñabālkya and and Janaka in Bṛhad. Up., 1-5; IV. 3; Janaśruti and Raikava in Chāndogya Up., IV. 1-3; Uddālaka Āruṇi and the five great householders in Chāndogya Up., 11-23; Śvetaketu Āruṇeya and his father in Chāndogya Up., VI; Nārada and Sanatkumāra in Chāndogya Up., VII; Vṛgu Varuṇi and his father in Taittirīya Up., III. 1-8; Nachiketas and his father in Kaṭha. Up., II.

to by Viṣma, Sanatsujāta and Bidur. The pupil asked questions (there is no lack of boldness in some of these questions);[945] and the teacher discoursed at length on the topics referred to him (e. g., in the Kena and Kaṭha Upaniṣads). In these discourses are found utilised all the familiar devices of oral teaching such as apt illustrations,[946] stories[947] and parables.[948]

It is not to be understood that these discourses leave nothing for the pupil to think out for himself. Manu says:

"Āchāryāt pādamādatte pādam śiṣyāḥ swamedhayā
Pādam sabrahmachāribhyaḥ pādam kālakrameṇa tu."

"The student learns only a fourth part from his teacher, a fourth by self-study, a fourth from his fellows, and the last fourth by experience in after life" Indeed the need for introspection and contemplation, on the part of the student, is never overlooked. Manana or cogitation, as a means of convincing oneself of the truth of what he has learnt and thus fortifying himself against possible future doubts, is specially prescribed. Even as regards the initial teaching it is usual for the preceptor to furnish only broad hints and ask the pupil to work them out fully. The most interesting instance of this method of teaching is found in the Tattirīya Upaniṣad (III) where Varuṇa while instructing his son Vṛgu, contents himself with indicating only in general terms the features of the Absolute and leaves to his son the discovery by reflection of His exact content. This method of giving general hints and directions is repeated four times and it is only on the fifth occasion that Vṛgu is able to comprehend the nature of the Absolute.

A spirit of enquiry and criticism was expected and encouraged. The aspirants for learning were asked to put questions *ad libitum.*[949] The Tamil Nannul[950] emphasises the need for discrimination and reflection in the student and appreciates spontaneity and originality:

'The swan, the cow, the earth, the parrot, the pot with holes,
The browsing goat, the buffalo, the straining fibre;
These, the first, the middle sort, and the last, of scholars shadow forth.'

945 Compare Praśña, III. 2. 946 Praśña, II. 947 Kaṭha.
948 Kena III. 949 Yathā Kāmam praśñān pṛchhata in Praśnopañiṣaḍ.
950 Quoted by S. V. Venkateśwara in his Indian Culture Through the Ages, Vol. I. p. 252.

The swan discriminates; the cow ruminates at leisure; the earth yields in proportion to labour bestowed; the parrot merely repeats; the pot with holes loses all; the goat eats with the tips only; the buffalo makes the water in the pond muddy and drinks it; the strainer lets all the water out and retains only the dregs. Though thus the spirit of discrimination and reflection was looked on with favour, hyper-criticism was put out of countenance. Yāska lays down that a śāstra should not be taught to a fault-finding or prejudiced person.

The method of teaching the Vedic hymns was purely oral. This might have been due to the absence of a script in those early times but to our mind this oral teaching stands on some rational principles. According to the orthodox Hindus the ṛṣis knew the hymns by internal inspiration and the swaras (accents) were best learnt from the teacher orally. Moreover, learning committed to memory was of the greatest use at the sacrifice, school or assembly. In the Ṛgveda[951] there is an allusion to pupils reciting the syllables dictated by their teacher, who carefully saw that not a single accent (swara) was wrongly pronounced. The Prātiśākhya[952] also contains a number of minute rules as to the repetition of words etc. According to Kautilya[953] "he (the prince) shall not only revise old lessons but also *hear* over and again what has not been clearly understood". In this connection it is interesting to find that the oral method of teaching has been advocated by some Western educators of modern times. The eminent French educationists of the 17th century, Port Royalists, made it a point to bar books as far as possible and laid great stress upon conversation as a means of developing mental faculties. Pestalozzi and Frœbel were even more emphatic on this point so far as primary education was concerned. Locke ranked "instruction" 'last' and 'least' in his 'accomplishments' of gentlemen's sons—virtue, wisdom, breeding and learning; and Rousseau would have no use of books at all in any stage of education. Taking these views exaggerated in some cases, with due discount, we see that oral methods of teaching are considered to be an effective means of training up the understanding of children.

---

[951] VII. 103, 5. [952] Ch. 15. [953] Arthaśāstra (R. Śyāmaśāstrī's Eng. Trans., p. 11.

The study of any subject carried on with sufficient attention and necessary motive and in graded steps not only imparts proficiency in that line but also trains up the mental powers for general use and application in other branches as well. This psychological principle was also verified in this ancient system of education. Memorising was undoubtedly greatly insisted on and the secret of memory was repetition. Pupils who could repeat correctly after a single repetition by the teacher (Ekasañdhagrāhi) were rare, and the usual number of repetitions by the teacher was five[954] which enabled the pupil to repeat without any mistake. The success of a student was judged from his capacity to repeat the whole Veda thus learnt without any fault whatever. There were some who made mistakes, and they were nick-named after the number of mistakes they committed, ranging from one to fourteen.[955] Max Muller[956] quotes Professor R. G. Bhāṇḍārkār with regard to the wonderful arrangements which the Hindus devised for the accurate preservation of the sacred text. These were far more complicated than anything the Massorites ever dreamed of. In the Saṃhitā arrangement the words were in their natural order and joined together according to the sanskrit rules of sañdhi. In the Pada arrangement the words were separate, that is, not united by sañdhi, and the compounds also dissolved. In the Krama arrangement the words were in the following order: 1, 2; 2, 3; 3, 4; 4, 5; etc., with sañdhi between them. In the Jatā arrangement the order was 1, 2, 2, 1, 1, 2; 2, 3, 3, 2, 2, 3; 3, 4, 4, 3, 3, 4; etc. In the Ghana, 1, 2, 2, 1, 1, 2, 3, 3, 2, 1, 1, 2, 3; 2, 3, 3, 2, 2, 3, 4, 4, 3, 2, 2, 3; etc. This must have greatly added to the burden upon the pupil's power of memorising and we must wonder how pupils could have got by heart such an enormous mass of material—a task which most English boys would find unbearable. But we should bear in mind that though the study started with repeating it was soon followed by explanation. Illustrations were freely used in giving pupils the necessary ideas as is seen in the Brāhmaṇas and the Upaniṣads.

---

[954] Pāṇinī V. 1. 58. [955] Pāṇinī IV. 4, 63, 64.

[956] Lectures on the Origin of Religion, (New Impression, 1901) pp. 169-70.

Kautilya[957] also refers to the teaching of the principles of Polity to the King with illustrations taken from Itihāsa and Purāṇa.

The pupils were to read among themselves the texts they had learnt and to reflect on the meaning of what they had learnt.[958] Even the Ṛgveda contains flings at parrot-like or frog-like reciters, and clear indications of the futility of learning by rote. "They consider one man as firmly established in the friendship of speech; another bears speech without fruit, without flowers."[959] The latter is compared to a pillar supporting a hall and styled a bearer of Vedic burden, while the knower of the meaning and significance is said to attain all happiness. The Brāhmaṇas declare that the man who knows the meaning and the significance of the ritual attains as high an end as the performer of the ritual. By Pāṇini's time there was so much of subsidiary Vedic studies, that there was a clear differentiation of the passages to be learnt by rote from the subjects to be known.[960] That memory was not the only mental power trained up or relied on, is also evident from the very first lesson, the Gāyatrī, in which the reciter prays for the stimulation of his understanding. Montaigne rightly says that judgment is of greater importance than reading and that learning is of no use if understanding be not with it. Even in the case of the Classics memorising was insisted on though it was not without understanding. No doubt Kālidās often refers to repetition as the 'mother of study', but in Subhāṣita we are told: "Whoever learns by heart, writes, observes, asks questions (to get his difficulties solved), and waits upon the learned, has his intellect developed like a lotus by the Sun's rays." Thus, side by side with memorising we find 'observing' and 'questioning' described as leading to the development of the intellect. Illustrations and similes are so common in Sanskrit literature specially in the Classics, that we can safely say that the teachers used those teaching devices in their daily lessons. In Uttara-Rāma-Charita[961]

---

957 Arthaśāstra (R. Śyāmaśāstrī's Eng. Trans.), p. 318.

958 Yāska: Nirukta I. 18.

959 Ṛgveda X. 71, 5.

960 Hence the sūtra "tadadhīte tadveda"—"That he learns by heart, that other he understands".

961 Belvarkar's Eng. Trans., p. 71.

prince Lava is told by his companions in the hermitage that they saw an animal commonly known as the 'horse'. Then he says : "You fools, have you not studied in that part describing Aśvamedha?" Was this recognising so common an animal by the help of Vedic texts? Was this the method of teaching in Bhavabhūti's time? The generalisation would be too sweeping; but it is clear that teaching was purely humanistic even then—from books to nature and not vice versa. Much was left to the teacher's discretion but in general, it seems that the modern principles of teaching (like, 'from the simple to the complex', 'from the known to the unknown', 'from the concrete to the abstract') were followed by them.

The testimony of Hiuen Tsang about the method of teaching in Brahminical schools is highly interesting. The method of teaching was meant more "to rouse the disciples to mental activities than to instruct them in dogma. They instruct the innert and sharpen the dull, and the teachers doggedly persevere in giving instruction to those who are addicted to idleness".[962] Unfortunately for us the pilgrim who was more interested in the doctrines and the teaching of Buddhism than in the methods of Brahminical education, has given us only a meagre description of the method that brāhmaṇa teachers followed. But considering the fact that when Hiuen Tsang visited India, Brahminism had almost regained its predominance in Northern India, it is certainly improbable that its educational organisation could have been in any way inferior to that of the Buddhists. It must also be remembered that the great intellectual awakening of the preceding two centuries was closely associated with the revival of Brahminism.

In the Upaniṣads we find that the philosophic teaching given there is often illustrated by parables from Nature or stories like that of Nachiketas visiting the abode of the dead. And in the later works like the Pañchatantra and the Hitopadeśa we find stories and fables given a very important place in the inculcation of moral truths. India is in fact the home of fables and allegory. If the Hindu teachers, as seems likely, made use of this form of teaching in instructing their pupils, then this must have gone a great way in relieving the monotony

---

962 Watters—Yuan Chwang, p. 159; Beal—Buddhist Records, Vol. I. p. 78.

of the laborious process of learning by heart. In this connection it is interesting to note Frœbel's words :—" Children feel an intense craving for all kinds of stories and legends, because they have a desire to have some knowledge of the nature, cause and effect of their individual life by comparing it with some thing and some one else.........Comparison with somewhat remote objects is more effective than that with near objects ".

The lecture method is not necessarily an ideal one. Really when a lecture is given to a class of say fifty students it is useless to some of them who may be insincere. Its necessity is not felt by some others and a few of the rest probably cannot follow it. This method is again one-sided, because the lecturer alone is put to exertion. In the ancient Hindu schools the pupils would approach the teacher with questions to be solved and the answers were to be rightly appreciated. The system of teaching was individual and each pupil was separately instructed by the teacher, though there were occasions when the teacher explained something to all the pupils at the same time. The teacher was appealed to every now and then and he had sufficient opportunities to judge their capacities and to influence their activities. On the other hand, the tendency in modern schools, run on the lines of the class system, is to avoid the teacher, who then cannot so well understand and impress his pupils. In this sense the Dalton plan may not sound to be an invention to the student of Ancient Indian Education. The modern school does little for the bright children and it is admittedly on them that the future of the society depends. In the ancient Indian schools every child received individual attention, was encouraged and promoted from grade to grade in due consideration of his ability. There was no necessity to detain the clever one for the dull, or to yoke on the latter to the former. There was thus no waste of energy and no waste of time.

Again, the doctrine of Adhikārabāda shows that the ancient Hindu philosophers, like the educators of the present century used to take into consideration the capacity and fitness (adhikāra) of the pupil. The Bhāgabad Gitā[963] says :—

" Ārūrūkṣormmuneryogaṃ karma kāraṇmuchyate
Yogārūḍhasya tasyaiba śamaḥ kāraṇamuchyate "

[963] VI. 3.

"To the sage who wishes to rise to devotion, action (without attachment) is said to be the means and to him, when he has risen to devotion, serenity is said to be the means". Indeed the modern principle of suiting matter and method to the nature and needs of the pupil was not unknown in Ancient India. Viṣṇu Śarmā, a brāhmaṇa teacher had the charge of the ignorant and vicious sons of Sudarśana, king of Pātaliputra. The princes had an inordinate liking for the rearing of pigeons. When the teacher observed this and saw that they attended to nothing else, he told them that he would do nothing but fly pigeons, feed them and look after them in the pigeon-house. The princes were overjoyed to hear that. As the number of pigeons increased they had to name and count them. Viṣṇu Śarmā was clever enough to put peculiar red marks on the wings of the pigeons and called them ka, kha, ga, etc. The princes thus learned the letters of the alphabet and to join the letters into syllables and syllables into words. The foundation of a knowledge of Arithmetic was laid in counting the pigeons, in telling how many there were in two or three adjoining cots, how many remained in the cots after so many were on the wing. By this novel method was taught not only notation, numeration, addition and subtraction but also something of drawing, engineering and house-building which were required in planning and constructing the dove-cots. Not only this but Ethics and Politics were also taught in this fashion as the tales of Pañchatantra and Hitopadeśa testify to this day. In fact such manuals were written by teachers who had to educate some ill-behaved children of the rich in such an interesting disguise.

We have already seen that most of the branches of knowledge known to the Hindus were the offshoots of their great sacred project, sacrifice. The pupils were taught to work at it and it was a sufficient field for their native activities from brick-laying to drawing, from counting to reciting, from measuring to chiselling. The kṣhatriya and the vaiśya pupils had more practical projects before their eyes in the form of warlike feats and industrial arts respectively and their training was sufficiently concrete, though rather emperical in the beginning. When we add to this the many story-projects to be found in the Hitopadeśa and the Pañchatantra we can easily find that the 'project' method of teaching is not quite a modern invention.

We have one Jātaka[964] which shows how Nature-study was insisted on as the best means of awakening a healthy curiosity, a spirit of observation and enquiry which are indispensable aids to intellectual culture. In the story, a world-renowned Professor of Benares "had five hundred young brāhmaṇas to instruct", one of whom "had always foolish notions in his head and always said the wrong thing; he was engaged with the rest in learning the scriptures as a pupil, but because of his folly could not master them. The teacher was at pains to consider what method of instruction would be suitable for that 'veriest dullard' of all his pupils. And the thought came to him that the best way was to question him on his return from gathering firewood and leaves, as to something he had seen or done that day, and then to ask him what it was like. 'For' thought the master, 'this will lead him on to making comparisons and giving reasons and the continuous practice of comparing and reasoning on his part will enable me to impart learning to him.'"

Again, the monitorial system was an Indian invention. To manage a school with an evergrowing number of students sometimes ranging upto to 500[965] was no easy task for an individual teacher. He was therefore helped by a staff of Assistant Masters (pitthiāchāriya) appointed from amongst the most advanced or senior pupils. Assistance in teaching was also rendered by the senior pupils as such, for, we are told of a teacher appointing his eldest disciple to act as his substitute. Another teacher of Taxila, while going to Benares on some mission, appointed his chief pupil to take charge of his school during his absence, saying: "My son, I am going away from home; while I am away, you are to instruct these my pupils" (numbering 500). We read of Prince Sutasoma of the Kuru country who "being the senior pupil soon attained to proficiency in teaching" and "becoming the private teacher" of his comrade in the school, "soon educated him, while the others only gradually acquired their learning."[966] The position of a senior

---

964 Jātaka No. 123.

965 Jātaka I. 239, 317, 402; III. 18, 235, 143, 171 etc.

966 Jātaka II. 100; V. 457; I. 141; IV. 51; V. 457-58.

pupil to a 'mahāvaḍḍhaki' is indicated by Buddhaghoṣa.[967] Viṣṇu Saṃhitā[968] says : "On a preceptor's son, junior or equal to him in years, happening to be his tutor, he shall pay the same respect to him as to his own preceptor." Manu[969] speaks in the same strain : "A preceptor's son, if he be his younger or equal in age, or if he be a disciple of his in respect of the celebration of a religious sacrifice, he (the pupil) shall respect as his own preceptor, in the event of that (son) having taught him the Vedas." These passages seem to imply that the son of the teacher sometimes helped the father by teaching in his stead. This monitorial system has its own advantages : the responsibility thrown on a particular pupil trains him up for that (teaching) work and makes him bold and well-behaved; the leaders among the pupils are marked out, who may become the leading spirits in the society; the spirit of public service and self-sacrifice is cultivated; and the democratic discipline is inculcated as boys understand boys better than others. "The monitorial system of Bell and Lancaster, which Bell is said to have devised by seeing the method used in schools in India, is but a caricature of the Indian ideal. In English schools the prefectual system has associated the elder boys with the masters in the government and discipline of the school and it is generally recognised as being one of the most valuable parts of their training. According to the Indian ideal the more advanced scholars are associated with the master in the work of teaching and though the system may have been originally devised to help the master in solving the problem of teaching several pupils at different stages at the same time, it must have been a valuable training for the monitors themselves. In India the bullying of younger boys by older ones is almost unknown and the respect shown by the younger boys to the older boys is very marked. The resusciation of this ancient Indian ideal of monitors would therefore be worth a trial, and it is not unlikely that it might show very excellent results if the conditions were also fulfilled, that the class should be small and it was composed of pupils all at different stages of progress."[970]

---

967 Aśl., 111, 112. 968 XXVIII. 31. 969 II. 208.

970 F. E. Keay—Ancient Indian Education, pp. 179-80.

Again, there is a marked difference between the Hindu and the European theories of sense perception. "They agree with regard to the mind receiving the knowledge of the external world through the senses. The divergence is to be noted regarding the way to stimulate the mental process. According to European educationists the pupils must be given a good deal of exercise in observation, *i. e.*, in the use of their senses, because intelligence depends upon the cultivation of a keen sensory capacity. Hindu teachers, on the other hand, believed in the reverse order of dependence. According to them the cultivation of a keen sensory capacity depended on intelligence and the all-pervading nature of the human mind. They, therefore, tried to develop the pupil's mind in such a way as to use the the pre-conscious thought as early as possible and thus to take the line of greatest connection in preference to the line of least resistance followed by the Western thinkers. The Hindu pupils were taught to go to the root of the mind by means of prayers, meditation and righteous conduct and thus to stimulate and sharpen all its activities that are more or less correlated or co-ordinated. According to the Hindu theory, to confine one's study to matter directly bearing on the particular subject, in which one is anxious to excel, is not always the best way to develop fresh brain-power. Some noted occidentals have acted on a similar principle. Sir Humphry Davy is said to have attended Coleridge's lectures on poetry to stimulate his imagination for his scientific work. Gladstone used to read the Bible before delivering his epoch-making speeches to throw into broad relief his political ideas in contrast with theology. There is, therefore, no fear of the development resulting from the study of texts like these extending merely a better comprehension of abstractions. The student will gain a wider grasp and a harder grip. The judgment in every phase of life will be improved. Though water poured into a tank may flow in at one spot, it finds its level and eventually fills up the tank evenly and smoothly. Similarly, the Hindu system improves not one special part of the mind but the whole more or less together. The Hindu method added nothing from outside to the mind but removed something detrimental to powerful personality. This was similar to the hypnotic treatment of a patient, during which the physician disentangles his confused mental processes. The Hindu pupil was trained to reach the fountain of all inspiration (jñānādhikaraṇātmā) in the pre-conscious state of his mind and not to hover about the sprays in the form of its external working. This pre-conscious state as the Hindus believed and has now been corroborated, is the source of all powers physical and spiritual and the sooner it is sought for, the better. The mind is like an iceberg: nine-tenths of it are below the conscious state. If the thoughts lying in the pre-conscious state are occasionally brought to the surface as they can be by the Hindu system of mind-training, a connecting link between the every day commodity and its greatest store-house is established. He who is in closest touch with the pre-conscious state solves difficult questions speedily, for, all solutions which are called inspirations really come from within and the pre-conscious in constant touch with the conscious mind makes the most successful combination useful for all purposes. Hence the Hindu teacher tried to nourish the child-mind from within by religious exercises and moral tales and to prepare it for work in worldly life".[971]

Study and teaching, however, can only lead to a mediate knowledge. For an immediate knowledge of the intimate Truth and Reality, the pupil must depend upon himself. The knowledge of the Ātman cannot be gained by mere speculation concerning it, but only by revelation as the result of the proper degree of self-growth. The acquisition of such knowledge, which means emancipation, is not a matter of study but of life. It presupposes two things: (1) annihilation of all desires and (ii) annihilation of "the illusion of a manifold universe, of the consciousness of plurality". The means evolved to secure these two ends are what are popularly known as the system of (i) Sannyāsa and (ii) Yoga. The former means the 'casting off' from oneself of his home, possessions and family and all that stimulates desire. It thus "seeks laboriously to realise that freedom from all the ties of earth in which a deep conception of life in other ages and countries also has recognised the supreme task of earthly existence, and will probably continue to recognise throughout all future time".[972] The system of

[971] S. M. Mitra—Hindu Mind-Training, pp. 15-21.

[972] Deussen—Philosophy of the Upaniṣads.

Sannyāsa as a means of attaining the knowledge of the Brahman and emancipation is completely developed in a series of later Upaniṣads such as the Brahma, Sannyāsa, Āruṇeya, Paramahaṃsa, etc., with which we are not concerned here for the present.

Yoga teaches the withdrawing of the organs of sense from their objects and concentrating them on the inner self, endeavours to make one's self free from the world of plurality and to secure union with the Ātman.

In Post-Vedic times the practice of Yoga was developed into a formal system with its own text-book, the sūtras of Patañjali. Its first beginnings are, however, shown in Kaṭha (III & VI) Śvetāśvatara (II) and Maitrāyaṇa (VI). The system implies the following eight members (angas) of external practices: (1) yama or discipline consisting in abstinence from doing injury, honesty, chastity, poverty (2) niyama or self-restraint (purity, contentment, asceticism, study and devotion) (3) āsanam, sitting (in the right place and in the correct bodily attitude) (4) prāṇāyāma, regulation of the breath (5) pratyāhāra, withdrawal of the senses from their objects (6) dhāraṇā, concentration of the attention (7) dhyānam, meditation and (8) samādhi, absorption.

As has been already indicated, both the systems are a perfectly intelligible consequence of the doctrine of the Upaniṣads according to which the highest end is contained in the knowledge of self-identity with the Ātman. As a means to the attainment of that end, we must purposely "dissolve the ties that bind to the illusory world of phenomena" (implied by Sannyāsa) and practice self-concentration (Yoga). Thus arose two remarkable and characteristic institutions of Indian culture through which emancipation was sought to be attained and expedited by processes and disciplines invented by the spiritual genius of the people. The first seeks by calculated methods to annihilate desires and the second the consciousness of plurality.

§ 16. Was there any examination?

As there was no class system, no annual examinations were required for the formation of fresh classes. The pupils received individual instruction and the teacher could see in fresh lessons whether they followed him or not. This was thought quite sufficient. "It is no use putting to test what has not quite settled in the mind" says Kālidās. Much depended, therefore, on the judgment of the teacher: if he found that a particular boy was quite well up, he was encouraged and led onwards. On the completion of the higher course some regular examination was necessary and this was arranged by presenting the pupils before an assembly of the learned or at royal sacrifices. In a hymn of the Ṛg-veda[973] there is a reference to such an assembly of the learned meeting together for debate :—

> "All friends are joyful in the friend who cometh in triumph having conquered in assembly.
>
> He is their blame-averter, food-provider; prepared is he and fit for deed of vigour.
>
> One plies his constant task reciting verses; one sings the holy psalm in Sakvari measures.
>
> One more, the brāhmaṇa, tells the lore of being, and one lays down the rules of sacrificing."

We have references to Brahmavādin, with the variants Brahmavādya and Brahmodya. The title of Vipra or Kabi was the reward of a scholar who had beaten the others. Such debates and disputations are mentioned in the Atharvaveda, where the opener, (Prāśa) and the opponent (Pratiprāśa) are contrasted. The questioner, the cross-questioner and the judge at a disputation are mentioned in the Brāhmaṇa literature.[974] The success in a such a debate refers to the passing of some test required before a young brāhmaṇa was considered eligible to take part in a sacrificial ritual or be a teacher himself.[975]

---

[973] X. 71.

[974] Atharvaveda XI. 3; XV. 1; Taitt. Saṃ., II. 5, 9, 1; Atharvaveda II. 27. 1 and 7. Śatapatha Brāhmaṇa XI. 4. 1, 1, Kauśitakī Brāhmaṇa XXVI. 5; Br. Up., III. 3, 1; III. 6, 4; Taitt. Br., III. 4.

[975] Compare the "Responsio" of the Middle Ages in Europe.

These examinations were mostly oral. They tested memory-work rather than intelligence ordinarily; but in the higher stages where there was specialisation full scope was given to originality. This is evident from the descriptions preserved in the Brāhmaṇas and the Upaniṣads, of animated debates held at royal sacrifices.

In course of time when the sciences arose, examinations of a more practical nature were held. The famous physician Jīvaka[976] received his medical education in Taxila for seven years after which he had to undergo an examination in which he was asked to describe the medicinal use of all the vegetables, plants, creepers, grass, roots, etc., that could be found within a radius of fifteen miles round the city of Taxila. Jīvaka examined them for four days and then "submitted the results informing his professor that there was hardly a single plant which did not possess some medicinal property."

§ 17. Teacher's duties to the student.

The relation between the teacher and the taught was of the happiest kind. In the Sāvitṛī verse to be recited at the beginning and end of each day's study, the teacher and his pupil both prayed: "May He protect us two; may we both enjoy happiness; may we both perform heroic deeds." Thus the teacher and his pupil were united by a common aim of preserving and propagating the sacred learning and to show its worth in their life and conduct. The pupil looked up to his preceptor as his father.[977] The teacher was also under an obligation to fulfil his duty towards the pupil. "He is to teach him the truth exactly as he knows it."[978] "He should not conceal anything from him, for, such concealment would spell ruin to him."[979] The Taittirīya Āraṇyaka[980] lays down that the teacher must teach with all his heart and soul. He was bound also according to the Śatapatha Brāhmaṇa[981] to reveal everything to his pupil who at any rate lived with him for one whole year (saṃvatsaravāsin). According to Āpastamva[982]

---

976 Mahāvagga (Vinyapītaka, edited by Oldenburg) VIII. 3.

977 Praśña Up., V. 8.

978 Muṇḍakopaniṣad I. 2. 23.

979 Praśña Up., VI. 1.

980 VII. 4.

981 XIV. 1. 1. 26, 27.

982 I. 2.

"not only was the teacher to love the pupil as his own son but also to give him full attention in the teaching of the sacred science and withhold no part of it from him." The teacher, however, was quite free to impart to his pupil only the knowledge that he was fit for and reserve subjects to which he was not equal. There are on record certain cases of learning kept secret and revealed only to special persons.[983]

Manu[984] says : "Having initiated a pupil, let the preceptor teach him the rules of purification and good conduct as well as the mode of doing burnt offerings and sañdhyās." "To a brāhmaṇa duly initiated with the thread, shall be given instructions, regarding the practice of vows gradually and in conformity with the regulation; he shall be made to get by heart the (different portions of the Vedas)."[985] "But if the teacher neglects to teach (the Veda) the pupil should forsake him."[986] Kautilya[987] says : "When between..............teacher and student, one abandons the other while neither of them is an apostate.................the first amercement shall be levied." Again, "the teacher was not to use the pupil for his own purposes except in times of distress."[988]

§18. Discipline.

In Manu Saṃhitā[989] we find a passage which according to Kulluka's interpretation defines the behaviour of the teacher to his pupil. The literal English translation of the passage runs thus :—

"The good of creatures should be effected with kind sympathetic means; desiring virtue, one shall use sweet and gentle words under the circumstances."

"He whose speech and mind are always pure and fully restrained derives all the benefits enumerated in the Vedānta."

---

983 For instance, the Vaśiṣṭhas and Stombhāgas in Pañchaviṃśa Brāhmaṇa XV. 5. 24; Taittirīya Āraṇyaka III. 5. 2. 1; Kaṭha Saṃ., XXXVI. 17; Pravahana Jaivāli and his knowledge of Brahman in Bṛhad. Up., VI. 1. 11.

984 II. 69.

985 Manu II. 173.

986 Vaśiṣṭha Saṃhitā, Ch. XI.

987 Arthaśāstra (R. Śyāmaśāstrī's Eng. Trans.,) p. 251.

988 Āpastamva I. 2.

989 II. 159-61.

"Persecuted or oppressed, one must not hurt the feelings of others. Let him wish or do no injury to anybody. Let him not use a harsh word that bars the gate of heaven, to any body."

The text has "Bhūtānām......................śreyonuśāsanam." Kulluka explains 'bhūtānām' by 'śiṣyānām', of pupils) and 'śreyo' by 'instruction;' the whole meaning according to him, is that 'instructions should be given with the help of compassionate means.' Śukrāchārya[990] also says: "Towards the disciple no one obeying my command should be harsh and cruel in words."

According to Yājñabālkya Saṃhitā,[991] however, "one can reprove a son or disciple at the time of teaching." Gautama[992] says: "A preceptor should admonish his pupil without beating him or inflicting any kind of corporal punishment on him. In case of emergency he may be chastised with a cut piece of rope or with a bamboo-twig without leaves. A king shall punish a preceptor for chastising his pupil in any other way." Manu is in favour of punishment but of a mild type; says he: "Let him not raise a club to anybody nor strike anybody with a club, except his son and disciple for the sake of discipline."[993] "A wife, son, servant, brother or disciple found guilty of an offence should be punished with a chord or with a (foliated) bamboo-stick. They shall be beaten on the lower parts of the body and never on the upper limbs. For having flogged them in any other fashion one shall be liable to punishment for theft."[994] Āpastamva[995] seems to be more harsh and lays down a list of punishments that could be used by the teacher at his discretion—frightening, fasting, bathing in cold water, striking with a cane and banishment from school (literally, from the teacher's presence.) The offences of royal pupils also did

---

990 Śukranītisāra, Ch. I. line 589. 991 I. 155.

992 Ch. II. 993 Manu IV. 164.

994 Manu VIII. 299-300. Compare in this connection the passage given to a Theban school-boy for exercise in calligraphy in the second millenium B. C.: 'Pass not a day in idleness or thou wilt be beaten........The ear of a boy is in his back; he listens when he is beaten'—Blackman; Luxor and Its Temples, p. 176.

995 I. 2.

not escape their usual punishment even in those early days represented by the Jātakas. On the offence of a prince being reported to the teacher (the offence being taking some sweets from a vendor's basket without paying for them), "he caused two lads to take the young fellow by his two hands and smote him thrice upon the back with a bamboo-stick bidding him take care not to do so again."[996] Still the general feeling was towards mildness as may be gathered from Kautilya's dictum, which has passed into a proverb, that the period of discipline for a boy terminates at the age of sixteen and that he should henceforth be treated as a friend.

Rupture of this relationship was the result of failings on the part of the teacher or offensive conduct on the part of the pupil. There were cases of pupils who did not take seriously to study but were with the teacher only for securing some worldly advantage. There were Tīrthakākas who frequently changed their teachers; Odanapāṇinīyas, who studied Pāṇini only to earn a livelihood; Ghṛtarandhryas and Kambalachārāyaṇīyas, anxious only to secure ghee or some comfortable covering blankets by taking to the life of studentship. There were also students who did not keep the whole term, but entered life before their studies were over (Khaṭvārūdha). But these were apparently exceptional cases,[997] laughed at by the literary world of the time. There were also cases of rebellious students whom the Jaina Sūtras compare to "bad bullocks."[998] The great Yājñabālkya of Mithilā disagreed with his teacher of the Yajurveda Vaiśampāyana by name, and repaired in disgust to the Himālayās and compiled a new system, known as Śukla Yajurveda. Another dissentient pupil was Āpastamva, whose differences with his teacher Baudhāyana are narrated in the Purāṇas.

The student was also allowed to desert his teacher under certain contingencies.[999] One of these was incompetence or lack of knowledge

---

[996] Jātaka No. 252 (Tilmukhi Jātaka).

[997] Pāṇini I. 4, 26, 28 ; II. 1. 41 ; II. 1. 26.

[998] Jacobi : Jaina Sūtras, pp. 149 and 152.

[999] Āpastamva I. 5, 26, ; I. 4, 25.

on the part of the teacher. Another was the transgression of the law by him. A teacher could be deserted also if he used his pupil's time to the detriment of his studies. Other legitimate reasons for giving up one teacher and taking to another was the teacher's neglect of his study and rituals, his negligence in imparting instruction, and commission by him of cardinal sins. But these contingencies were the exceptions which prove the general rule that the pupil was well cared for by his teacher from whom he parted on the most cordial terms.

The foregoing account shows us an interesting and pleasing picture of the life of the pupil and the teacher in India dating back to many centuries before Christ. The pupil was under a somewhat rigorous discipline but there was nothing harsh or brutal about it and a high ideal of moral life and character was held before the pupil and the teacher. The latter usually had no mercenary motive to impel him to teach but was to perform his work solely as a duty which he owed towards others and his pupil in particular. Parental love on the one hand and deep respect on the other made a sweet combination of feelings that had

"Less of earth in them than heaven."

It is laid down in Kautilya's Arthaśāstra[1000] that if a teacher and a student sue each other (paraṣparāviyoga) they shall be punished with the highest amercement." The pupil's relation to the teacher has indeed been sometimes so developed that it had led to the teacher or guru, receiving divine honours from his pupil or disciple, in some forms of Hinduism and in some sects that have sprung from it. In a more sober conception of this relationship it is thought of as that of father and son[1001] and so far was this idea carried out that the pupil was considered to be in a closer relation to the teacher than to his own father. It is no wonder, therefore, that the parting scenes (for example, between Kṛṣṇa and Sandipani) are full of overwhelming sentiments. The whole family felt as if some intimate relation was leaving them

---

1000 R. Śyāmaśāstrī's Eng. Trans., p. 224.

1001 In the Rāmāyaṇa (Kiṣkindhyākāṇḍa, 18th sarga) we are told that a younger brother, a son and a meritorious pupil are all sons.

and the student felt as if he was going away from his real home to that of his worldly father. It is no wonder, therefore, that the teacher felt very happy when he heard that his pupils were doing quite well, particularly when one of them became more learned and famous than he himself. Rev. F. E. Keay[1002] rightly observes: "In the West, it is the institution rather than the teacher which is emphasised and it is the school or college which a student regards as his *alma mater*. In India it is the teacher rather than the institution that is prominent and the same affection and reverence which a Western student has for his *alma mater* are in India bestowed with a life-long devotion to the teacher. Even the introduction of Western education with its many teachers and many classes, has not entirely broken down this ideal, inspite of the complications which it produces. To an Indian student a teacher who only appears at stated hours to teach or lecture and is not accessible at all times to answer questions and give advice on all manner of subjects is an anomaly. Such a relationship, no doubt, throws a greatly increased responsibility upon the teacher and where the teacher is not worthy of his position may be attended with grave dangers. But where the teacher is a man who reaches a high intellectual, moral and spiritual standard, there is much to be said for the Indian ideal. There is no country in the world where the responsibilities and opportunities of the teacher are greater than they are in India.''

§ 19. THE COMPLETION OF STUDENTSHIP AND THE PARTING SPEECH OF THE TEACHER.

The completion of formal studentship was signalised by a great ceremonial bath at Samābartana, which put an end to the vows the pupil had taken as a brahmachārin. He sacrificed in the water his sacred girdle, staff and sacred thread, which he had been using all these years. He parted with the teacher after making him a suitable present. Lest his specialised knowledge and erudition shall fill him with spiritual pride, we have this provision in Āpastamva[1003]: "The knowledge which śūdras and women possess is the completion of all study.

[1002] Ancient Indian Education, pp. 178-79.

[1003] Āpastamva II. 11, 29.

They declare it a supplement to the Atharvaveda". The Taittirīya Upaniṣad[1004] has preserved for us a specimen of the parting words which a teacher generally addressed to his student when the latter was permitted to return home after the completion of his studies :—

"Say what is true! Do thy duty! Do not neglect the study of the Veda! After presenting gifts to thy teacher, take care that the thread of thy race be not broken! Do not swerve from truth, from duty! Do not neglect your health! Do not neglect your worldly prosperity! Do not neglect the learning and the teaching of the Veda!

"Do not neglect the (sacrificial) works due to the gods and the manes! Let thy mother be to thee like unto a god! Let thy father be to thee like unto a god! Let the guests be to thee like unto a god! Whatever actions are blameless, those should be regarded, not others. Whatever good works have been performed by us those should be observed by thee—

"Not others. There are some Brahmins better than we. To those you should show proper reverence. Whatever is given should be given with faith, with joy, with modesty, with fear and from a sense of duty. If there be any doubt in the mind with regard to any sacred act or with regard to conduct—

"In that case conduct thyself as brāhmaṇas who possess good judgment conduct themselves therein, whether they be appointed or not, as long as they are not too severe, but devoted to duty. And with regard to things that are doubtful, as brāhmaṇas who possess good judgment conduct themselves therein, whether they are appointed or not, as long as they are not too severe, but devoted to duty.

"Thus conduct thyself. This is my admonition. This is the teaching. This is the true purport (upaniṣad) of the Veda—this is the command. Thus should this be observed".

"These words read almost like the Chancellor's Convocation Address to the students of a modern University passing out of its portals on their admission to their degrees. It will be noticed that in this ancient

---

1004 I. 11.

valedictory address, emphasis is laid upon several interesting points. In the first place, entering upon the householder's life and fatherhood are enjoined as a compulsory religious duty in the interests of the continuity of the race. In the second place, is enjoined the duty of studying and teaching the Veda in the interests of the continuity of culture. In the third place, the duties of domestic and social life are indicated. They are: to honour father, mother, teacher and guest as gods; to honour superiors; to give in proper manner and spirit, in joy and humility, in fear and compassion, so that it may bless both "him that gives and him that takes"; to perform sacrifices and in all doubtful cases, to order himself according to the judgment of approved authorities. Lastly, the pupil is also admonished not to neglect health and possessions. We may in passing note the spirit of humility, characterising the teacher, as shown in asking his pupil to imitate his good points and ignore his bad ones and recognising his superiors". [1005]

[1005] Sir Aśutoṣa Mukerjī Silver Jubilee Volumes, Vol. III. Part. I. Orientalia, pp. 230-31.

CHAPTER VII.

SECONDARY AND HIGHER EDUCATION IN THE BUDDHIST SEATS OF LEARNING.

I. THE BUDDHIST MONASTERIES AS SEATS OF LEARNING.

The character of Buddhist education of which the monastery was the centre will be evident from the fact that Buddhism included in it the non-recognition of the Vedas and of the brāhmaṇa hierarchy as well as of the religious aspect of the caste system. Buddha carried no crusade against any of these but the opposition was implicit in his system. Hence the Buddhist education was not based on Vedic study and its teachers were not brāhmaṇas, except those who had become converted to Buddhism.

§ 1. THE SELECTION AND ADMISSION OF STUDENTS.

The Buddhist monastery was open to all comers and not merely to the three twice-born castes. There was, however, exception to the general principle and the following classes of persons were excluded from admission into the monastery: (1) one affected with the five diseases viz., leprosy, boils, dry leprosy, consumption, and fits;[1006] (2) one who is in the royal service;[1007] (3) a proclaimed robber;[1008] or one who has broken out of jail;[1009] or wears the emblems of his deeds;[1010] (4) one who has been punished by scourging;[1011] or branding;[1012] (5) a debtor;[1013] (6) a slave;[1014] (7) one under fifteen years of age;[1015] (8) a eunuch;[1016] and (9) one deformed in person or any of whose limbs was cut off.[1017]

The ceremony of admission is thus described in the Vinaya Pitaka:[1018] "Let him who desires to receive ordination first cut off

---

1006 Mahāvagga I. 39.
1007 Ibid., I. 40.
1008 Ibid., I. 43.
1009 Ibid., I. 42.
1010 Ibid., I. 41.
1011 Ibid., I. 44.
1012 Ibid., I. 45.
1013 Ibid., I. 46.
1014 Ibid., I. 47.
1015 Ibid., I. 50.
1016 Ibid., I. 61.
1017 Ibid., I. 71.
1018 Ibid., I. 38.

his hair and beard; let him put on yellow robes, adjust his upper robe so as to cover one shoulder, salute the feet of the bhikṣus with his head; and sit down squatting; then let him raise his joined hands and tell him to say 'I take my refuge in the Buddha, I take my refuge in the Dharma, I take my refuge in the Saṃgha.'" This act of admission was called pabbajja. A new form was substituted at a later date for the upasampadā ordination. The upajjhāya from whom the new convert—saddhivihārika—received the ordination played the most important part in the system. He must be a learned competent bhikṣu who has completed ten years since his upasampadā.[1019] The procedure of choosing an upajjhāya is laid down as follows:—"Let him (who is going to choose an upajjhāya) adjust his upper robe so as to cover one shoulder, salute the feet (of the intended upajjhāya), sit down squatting, raise his joined hands and say (thrice): "Venerable Sir, be my upajjhāya." (If the other answers) "well" or "certainly" or "good" or "all right" or "carry on (your work) with friendliness (towards me)" or should he express this by gesture (lit., by his body), or by word, or by gesture and word, then the upajjhāya has been chosen." The upajjhāya alone[1020] could confer on his saddhivihārika the upasampadā ordination but the latter must be possessed of a certain standard of education and moral practices.[1021] Several formalities were also required. Thus it was necessary that the candidate should formally ask for being ordained and provide himself with alms and robes. Then it must be ascertained by formal questioning in an assembly of bhikṣus whether he labours under any of the disqualifications mentioned above and whether his parents have given their consent to his adopting the life. The candidate was instructed beforehand by a learned competent bhikṣu as to the manner in which to reply to those formal questions.[1022] After the instruction was over, the instructor came

---

1019 Sūtra-nipāta, Nābāsūtra, verses 316-22.

1020 A particular individual not the saṃgha or a part of it could serve as an upajjhāya. Several classes of persons could not serve as an upajjhāya. These are described in detail in Mahāvagga I. 68.

1021 The details are laid down in Mahāvagga I. 36. 2ff.

1022 For details compare Mahāvagga I. 76.

to an assembly of the bhikṣus, not less than ten in number[1023] and asked its formal permission for the candidate to appear, in the following terms:

"Let the Saṃgha, reverend sirs, hear me. N. N. desires to receive the upasampadā ordination from venerable N. N.; he has been instructed by me. If the Saṃgha is ready, let N. N. come." On the permission being granted, the candidate appeared before the assembly, adjusted his upper robe so as to cover one shoulder, saluted the feet of the bhikṣus with his head, sat down squatting, raised his joined hands and thrice uttered the formula: 'I ask the Saṃgha, reverend sirs, for the upasampadā ordination: might the Saṃgha, reverend sirs, draw me out (of the sinful world) out of compassion towards me."

Then a learned competent bhikṣu moved the following resolution (ñatti): "Let the Saṃgha, reverend sirs, hear me. This person N. N. desires to receive the upasampadā ordination from the venerable N. N. If the Saṃgha is ready, let me ask N. N. about the disqualifications." Permission being granted he addressed the candidate as follows:

"Do you hear, N. N. This is the time for you to speak the truth and to say that which is. When I ask you before the assembly about that which is, you ought, if it is so, to answer 'It is'; if it is not so, you ought to answer 'It is not.'

Then followed the string of questions: "Are you afflicted with the following diseases? leprosy, boils, dry leprosy, consumption, fits? Are you a man? Are you a male? Are you a freeman? Have you no debts? Are you not in the royal service? Have your father and mother given their consent? Are you full twenty years old? Are your alms-bowl and your robes in due state? What is your name? What is your upajjhāya's name?."

After satisfactory answers were received, a learned competent bhikṣu proclaimed the following ñatti before the Saṃgha: "Let the Saṃgha reverend sirs, hear me. This person N. N. desires to receive the

---

[1023] In border countries the assembly could be composed of four bhikṣus and a chairman (Mahāvagga V. 13. 11).

upasampadā ordination from the venerable N. N.; he is free from the disqualifications; his alms-bowl and robes are in due state. N. N. asks the Saṃgha for the upasampadā ordination with N. N. as upajjhāya. If the Saṃgha is ready, let the Saṃgha confer on N. N. the upasampadā ordination with N. N. as upajjhāyā."

" Let the Saṃgha, reverend sirs, hear me. This person N. N. desires to receive the upasampadā ordination with the venerable N. N. The Saṃgha confers on N. N. the upasampadā ordination with N. N. as upajjhāya. Let any one of the venerable brethren who is in favour of the upasampadā ordination of N. N. with N. N. as upajjhāya, be silent and any one who is not in favour of it, speak."

'And for the second time I thus speak to you: Let the Saṃgha etc., (as before).

"And for the third time I thus speak to you: Let the Saṃgha etc., (as before).

" N. N. has received the upasampadā ordination from the Saṃgha with N. N. as upajjhāya. The Saṃgha is in favour of it, therefore, it is silent. Thus I understand."

Two classes of persons had to pass through an intermediate stage of discipline before being formally admitted. These were persons who (1) formerly belonged to a heretic (Titthiya) school or (2) were between 15 and 20 years of age.

A probation (parivāsa)[1024] of four months was imposed upon the former by a formal act of the Order on his making the threefold declaration of taking refuge. If he failed to satisfy the bhikṣus by his character and conduct[1025] during the period, the upasampadā ordination was refused him.

A person between 15 and 20 years of age could receive only the pabbajja ordination and had to wait till his twentieth year for the

[1024] Exception was made in favour of the fire-worshippers, the Jatilas and heretics of Śākya birth. They received the upasampadā ordination directly and no parivāsa was imposed upon them (Mahāvagga I. 38. 11).

[1025] The details are given in Mahāvagga I. 38. 5-7).

upasampadā. The novice (śramanera) as he was called during this intermediate period had to live a life of strict discipline under an upajjhāya.[1026] He had to keep the ten precepts,[1027] viz., abstinence from (1) destroying life, (2) stealing, (3) impurity, (4) lieing, (5) intoxicating liquor, (6) eating at forbidden times, (7) dancing, singing, etc., (8) garlands and scents, (9) use of high beds, and (10) accepting gold or silver. He was expelled from the fraternity if he violated any of the first five precepts or if he spoke against the Buddha, the Dharma, and the Saṃgha or if he held false doctrines or had sexual intercourse with bhikṣuṇīs.[1028] In five other cases he was liable to be punished.[1029] The punishment could be inflicted by any bhikṣu, with the consent of the upajjhāya.[1030] I-Tsing observes : "In the case of a śramanera a transgression of the twelve particulars set forth in the Vinaya texts does not involve guilt ; for a śikṣamānā (fem.) however, there are some modifications of the rule. Now what are the twelve particulars ? (1) One must distinguish between legal and illegal robes (Nissaggiyā 1—10), (2) one must not sleep without garments, (3) one must not touch fire (probably Pākittiyā 56), (4) one must not eat too much food (Pākittiyā 35, 36 and 34), (5) one must not injure any living things (Pākittiyā 61), (6) one must not throw filth upon the green grass (Pākittiyā 11 and 20), (7) one must not recklessly climb up a high tree (unless in emergency), (8) one must not touch jewels (Pākittiyā 84 ; Nissaggiyā 18 and 19), (9) one must not eat food left from a meal (Pākittiyā 38), (10) one must not dig the ground (Pākittiyā 9), (11) one must not refuse offered food, (12) one must not injure growing sprouts. The two lower classes of members (*i. e.*, śramaneras and śramaneris need not conform to the twelve, but the śikṣamānās (fem.) incur guilt if they fail to keep the last five particulars (8—12 above). These three lower members also have to observe the summer-retreat (Varsha)."[1031]

1026 Sūtranipāta, Tubataka sūtra, verses 922-932.

1027 Mahāvagga I. 36.

1028 Mahāvagga I. 60.

1029 Mahāvagga I. 57.

1030 Mahāvagga I. 58.

1031 Takakusu's Eng. Trans., p. 97.

The Vinaya-saṃgraha[1032] Chapter XII (Nanjio's Catalogue, No. 1127) gives the six rules and the six minor rules for the female members :— The six important rules are :—(1) A female must not travel alone; (2) she must not cross a river alone, (3) she must not touch the body of a man, (4) she must not have the same lodging with a man, (5) she must not act as a match-maker, (6) she must not conceal a grave offence committed by a nun. The six minor rules are :—(1) A female must not take gold or silver which does not belong to her, (2) she must not shave the hair in any place but the head, (3) she must not dig up an uncultivated ground, (4) she must not wilfully cut growing grass or a tree, (5) she must not eat food which is not offered, (6) she must not eat food which has once been touched.

As soon as the ceremony of ordination was over "some such thing as a girdle or a filter should be brought and offered to the teachers who are present in the place of the ordination (and take part in it), in order to show sincere gratitude."[1033] Then a prospect of the life he was going to lead was held out before the new bhikṣu. The four Resources of the brotherhood were proclaimed to him, so that he might be prepared beforehand for the worries and troubles of the life to come. "I prescribe, O bhikṣus" said Buddha,[1034] "that he who confers the upasampadā ordination (on a bhikṣu) tell him the four Resources :—

(1) "The religious life has morsels of food given in alms for its resource................."

(2) "The religious life has the robe made of rags taken from a dust-heap for its resource................"

(3) "The religious life has dwelling at the foot of a tree for its resource................."

[1032] Quoted in Takakusu's I-Tsing, p. 97, foot-note 3.

[1033] Takakusu's I-Tsing, p. 103.

[1034] Mahāvagga II, 77.

(4) " The religious life has decomposing urine as medicine for its resource................."

" Thus must the new bhikṣu endeavour to live all his life; better food, robes etc., which it might be his lot to enjoy from time to time, being only looked upon as extra allowances (atirekalābho)."

An idea of the stern moral life he was expected to lead was at the same time conveyed to him in the shape of the following four Interdictions :—[1035]

(1) " A bhikṣu who has received the upasampadā ordination, ought to abstatin from all sexual intercourse even with an animal."

(2) " A bhikṣu.................ought to abstain from taking what is not given to him and from theft, even of a blade of grass."

(3) " A bhikṣu ....ought not intentionally to destroy the life of any being down to a worm or an ant."

(4) " A bhikṣu.................ought not to attribute to himself any super-human condition."

According to Sūtranipāta[1036] the bhikṣu (1) should not be greedy about casting a look at personal beauty of a person, (2) should not lend his ears to gossips of the townsfolk, (3) should not be greedy about sweet things, (4) should never save articles of food, drink, clothing etc., (5) should not be anxious to get such articles of food, drink, clothing etc., (6) should not indulge in idle talks, (7) should never behave wrongly, (8) should not sleep too much, (9) should forsake idleness, dishonesty, gaudy dress, indecent talks, gambling and idle jokes, (10) should not study black art, astrology, and lakṣaṇatatwa, (11) should not have a fancy for the chirping of birds, (12) should remain unaffected by praise or calumny, (13) should forsake anger, calumny, greed, and desire, (14) should not engage himself in buying and selling, (15) should give up pride, bragging and quarreling, (16) should not tell a lie nor think of evil thoughts and (17) should never utter harsh words to anybody.

1035 Mahāvagga I. 78. Compare Sūtranipāta, Samyaka-paribrājanīyasūtra, verses 359-73.

1036 Tubatakasūtra, verses 922-932.

In course of time when the Buddhist monasteries began to admit advanced students who did not desire to be ordained as monks, the system of admission was different. Thus, at Nālandā and Vikramaśīlā monasteries the students were admitted by the dwārapaṇḍits or gate-keepers (one at Nālandā and six at Vikramaśīlā). Hiuen Tsang[1037] says: "If men of other quarters desire to enter............the keeper of the gate (at Nālandā) proposes some hard questions; many are unable to answer and retire. One must have studied deeply both old and new (books) before getting admission. Those students, therefore, who come here as strangers, have to show their ability by hard discussion; those who fail compared with those who succeed are as seven or eight to ten." This examination at the gate was thus the Matriculation of the scholars to enable them to enter the portals of these Universities. Thenceforth their name had no concern with the register of the state; for there was a register-book of the assembly on which their names were written down.[1038]

§2. Classes of Teachers and Qualifications Required of Them.

There seems to have been a system of gradation of Buddhist scholars and teachers. 'The brother who expounds orally one treatise (or class of scripture) in the Buddhist Canon, whether Vinaya, Abhidhamma or Sutta is exempted from serving under the Prior; he who expounds two is invested with the outfit of a Superior; he who expounds three has brethren deputed to assist him; he who expounds four has lay servants assigned to him; he who expounds five, rides on an elephant and has a surrounding retinue.' 'An ordained priest is Dahara (small teacher); after passing ten summer retreats, (one becomes) a Sthavira (settled one) who could be trusted to live by himself without a teacher's supervision. But the Upādhyāya and the Āchārya are the most important classes of teachers. According to I-Tsing[1039] " 'upādhyāya' is to be translated by 'teacher of personal instruction; 'achāryā'[1040] is translated 'teacher of discipline,'

1037 Beal—Buddhist Records of the Western World, Vol. II., pp. 170-71.

1038 Takakusu's I-Tsing, p. 65.

1039 Takakusu's Eng. Trans., pp. 117-18.

1040 Ibid.

'it means one who teaches pupils rules and ceremonies' ".[1041] I-Tsing observes: "Any one who becomes an upādhyāya must be a sthavira, and must have passed the full ten summer-retreats. The age of a Karmāchārya and private instructor, and of other teachers who are witnesses, is not limited; they must be fully acquainted with the Vinaya, being themselves pure; and must be either in the full or in the half number."[1042]

§3. Relation between the teacher and the pupil.

It was ordained that the novice should live for the first ten years in absolute dependence upon his upajjhāya.[1043] The relation between the two is described in minute detail in the Vinaya texts[1044] and may be somewhat understood from the following general principle laid down by Gautama Buddha:[1045]

"The upajjhāya, O bhikṣu, ought to consider the saddhivihārika as a son; the saddhivihārika ought to consider the upajjhāya as a father. Thus, these two, united by mutual reverence, confidence and communion of life, will progress, advance and reach a high stage in this doctrine and discipline."

The Sigalovāda Sutta[1046] contains a section which details the duties of pupils and teachers. The pupil should honour his teacher by rising in his presence, by ministering to him, by supplying his wants and by attention to instruction. The teacher should show his affection to his pupils, by training them up in all that is good, by teaching them

---

[1041] For the relation of Āchārya to Upādhyāya see Mahāvagga I. 32, 1 note, S. B. E., Vol. XIII. pp. 178, 179.

[1042] Takakusu's Eng. Trans., pp. 104-05.

[1043] Mahāvagga I. 32. 1. It was prescribed on a later occasion that a learned competent bhikṣu had to live only five years in dependence on his upajjhāya and an unlearned one all his life (Mahāvagga I. 53. 4). In some cases a bhikṣu was authorised to live without a Nisaya i. e., independent of upajjhāya (Mahāvagga I. 53. 5ff).

[1044] Mahāvagga I. 25. 7ff; I. 32. 1ff.).

[1045] Mahāvagga I. 25. 6.

[1046] Translated into English by Childers in the Contemporary Review, February, 1876.

to hold knowledge fast, by instructing them in science and lore, by speaking well of them to their friends and companions and by guarding them from danger.

The saddhivihārika was to act as a personal attendant to the upajjhāya. Sūtranipāta[1047] says: "One should serve his preceptor just as the devas serve Indra". "Let him arise betimes; and having taken off his shoes and adjusted his upper robe so as to cover one shoulder, let him give to the upajjhāya the teeth-cleanser and water to rinse his mouth with. Then let him prepare a seat for the upajjhāya. If there is rice-milk, let him rinse the jug and offer rice-milk to the upajjhāya. When he has drunk it, let him give water to the upajjhāya, take the jug, hold it down, rinse it properly without damaging it by rubbing and put it away. When the upajjhāya has risen, let him take away the seat. If the place is dirty, let him sweep the place. After this he was to help the preceptor to dress and to get the alms-bowl ready if he wished to go out to beg. If the preceptor desired it, the pupil was to follow him as his attendant on the begging tour, keeping not too far away and not too near him. If the preceptor speaks, he is not to interrupt him. After the begging is over the pupil was to get back quickly to the monastery, prepare a seat, get water for the washing of his feet, a foot-stool and a towel. Then he must go and meet the preceptor and take his bowl and robe for him. He must fold up the robe and attend to the clothes of the preceptor. If the preceptor wishes to eat the food in the alms-bowl, he must bring him water and then offer him food. After the meal the pupil must wash and dry the bowl and put it away and also put away the robe. After the preceptor has risen, the pupil must take away the seat and put away the water for the washing of feet, the footstool and the towel. If the place was dirty he was to sweep it. Then he was to help the preceptor to bathe, getting for him cold or hot water or accompanying him to the bathing place if he wished to go there. The pupil also bathed at the same time but had to dry and dress himself quickly so as to be ready to help the preceptor. After the bathing was

---

[1047] Nābāsūtra, verse 315.

completed he was to ask the preceptor for a discourse or ask him questions. Elaborate directions are given as to the procedure to be followed by the pupil in cleansing the monastery—the cell, store-room, refectory, fire-room etc. The pupil must also see that there is drinkable water, food and water for rinsing the mouth. He was also to be a monitor and a helpmate to his preceptor. If he became discontened the pupil was to try and appease him or get some one else to do this. If indecision arose in his mind or he had become tainted with false doctrines the pupil was to try and win him back. If the preceptor is in danger of committing an offence by the words he says, let the pupil keep him back. If the precepter be guilty of a grave offence and ought to be sentenced to 'parivāsa', 'mānatta' or 'penal discipline', let the pupil take care that the Saṃgha impose it upon him and that he was rehabilitated after the penance was complete. Again, if the Saṃgha wishes to proceed against the preceptor by the Tajjaniya kamma (or other disciplinary proceedings mentioned in the first book of Chullavagga) let the pupil do what he can in order that the Saṃgha may not proceed against the preceptor or may mitigate the proceeding. Or if the Saṃgha has instituted a proceeding against him, let the pupil do what he can in order that the preceptor may behave himself properly, live modestly and aspire to get clear of his penance and that the Saṃgha may revoke its sentence. The pupil was also to see that the robe of the preceptor was washed or made or dyed, according to need. He was not to accept presents or give presents or wait on any one else or go out, without the permission of the preceptor. If the preceptor was sick he was to wait upon him and nurse him dilligently ".[1048]

The preceptor too had corresponding duties. Thus we read: "The upajjhāya, O bhikṣu, ought to observe a strict conduct towards his saddhivihārika. Let the upajjhāya, O bhikṣu, afford (spiritual) help and furtherence to the saddhivihārika by teachings, by putting question to him, by exhortation and by instruction. If the upajjhāya has an alms-bowl (or robe or other articles required for a bhikṣu) and the saddhivihārika has not, let the upajjhāya give the same to the

[1048] Mahāvagga I. 25.

saddhivihārika or take care that he gets one. If the saddhivihārika is sick, let the upajjhāya arise betimes and give him the teeth-cleanser and water to rinse his mouth with (and so on with the other duties prescribed for the saddhivihārika). He was to see that the pupil washed his robe and to show him how to make and dye it".[1049]

The Milindā-Pañha[1050] thus enumerates the duties of the teacher: 'He must always keep guard over his pupil. He must teach him what to cultivate and what to avoid; about what he should be earnest and what he might neglect. He must instruct him as to sleep and as to keeping himself in health and as to food he may take and what to reject. He should teach him discrimination (in food) and share with him all that is put as alms in his own bowl. He should encourage him by saying 'Be not afraid, you will gain advantage (from what is taught here)'. He should advise him as to the people whose company he should keep and as to the villages and vihārs he should frequent. He should never indulge in foolish talk with him. When he finds any defect in him he should easily pardon it. He should be zealous; he should teach nothing partially, keep nothing secret and hold nothing back. He should look upon him in his heart as a son, saying to himself 'I have begotten him in learning'. He should strive to bring him forward, saying to himself 'How can I keep him from going back?'. He should resolve to make him strong in knowledge saying 'I will make him mighty'. He should love him, never desert him in necessity and always befriend him when he goes wrong'. I-Tsing[1051] says: "It is wrong for a teacher not to impart the ten precepts to one who has become a priest and not to communicate the complete precepts out of fear that one should transgress them. For in such a case the novice falsely bears the name (of śramanera which means) 'seeking rest' and vainly embraces the appellation (of pravragīta *i. e.*, one) "who has gone forth from his home".

The upajjhāya could turn away a saddhivihārika for improper conduct[1052] but if the latter begged for pardon, he should be

1049 Mahāvagga I. 26. 1050 IV. 1. 8. 1051 Takakusu's Eng. Trans., p. 98.

1052 What is meant by improper conduct is explained in detail in Mahāvagga I. 27. 6-8.

forgiven.[1053] In case the upajjhāya had gone away or returned to the world or died or gone over to a schismatic faction, the saddhivihārikas had to choose an āchāriya who stood in the same relation to them as the upajjhāya.

I-Tsing (who was in India between 673 and 687 A. D.) shows us how the system was working at the time of his visit. He says: "When one has shaved the head, worn a 'pata' (simple garment) and received the upasampadā ordination after having become 'homeless', one need not tell one's teachers the five things as is ordained in the Vinaya[1054] but must tell everything else; if not, one will be faulty. The five things to be confessed are: (1) the chewing of tooth-wood; (2) drinking water; (3) going to stool; (4) making water; (5) chaitya-vandanā or worshipping of a chaitya within forty-nine fathoms in the sacred boundary. When, for example, the novice is about to eat, he should go near his teacher, and having saluted according to the rule, announce to him as follows: 'Let my upajjhāya be attentive; I now announce to you that I wash my hands and utensils, and wish to have a meal'. The teacher should say 'Be careful'. All other announcements should be made according to this example. The teacher will then tell his pupil what to do, concerning the matter and time of announcement. When there are many things to announce the pupil can do so all at once. After the lapse of five summers from the time the pupil masters the Vinaya, he is allowed to live apart from his upajjhāya. He can go about among the people and proceed to pursue some other aim. Yet he must put himself under the care of some teacher wherever he goes. This will cease after the lapse of ten summers, *i. e.*, after he is able to understand the Vinaya. The kind object of the Great Sage is to bring one up to this position. If a priest does not understand the Vinaya, he will have to be under another's care during the whole of his life-time. If there be no great teacher, he must live under the care of a sub-teacher. In this case the pupil should do all but salutation, for he cannot

---

[1053] Mahāvagga I. 27. In some cases the expulsion of the saddhivihārika and his re-habilitation was compulsory.

[1054] In the Mūlasarvāstivādanikāya-vinaya-saṃgraha, Book XIII.

salute his teacher in the morning, or ask his health, since he must always act in accordance with the Vinaya, with which he is unacquainted; and even if it be necessary to announce any matter, how can he do so when he himself does not understand the way. Sometimes he receives from the sub-teacher instruction in the morning and in the evening. Even though the sub-teacher instructs such a pupil, the meaning of the Vinaya text may not be understood as it ought to be. For, if he who confesses (*i. e.*, the pupil) cannot rightly indicate his point how can he who answers (*i. e.*, the teacher) give a proper command. A full confession is, therefore, not to be made".[1055]

I-Tsing continues: "The following is also the manner in which a pupil waits on his teacher in India. He goes to his teacher at the first watch and at the last watch of the night. First, the teacher bids him sit down comfortably. Selecting some passage from the Tripitaka, he gives a lesson in a way that suits circumstances and does not pass any fact or theory unexplained. He inspects his pupil's moral conduct and warns him of defects and transgressions; whenever he finds his pupil faulty, he makes him seek remedies and repent. The pupil rubs the teacher's body, folds up his clothes or sometimes sweeps the apartments and the yard. Then having examined water to see whether insects be in it, he gives it to the teacher. Thus if there be anything to be done, he does all on behalf of his teacher. This is the manner in which one pays respect to his superior. On the other hand, in the case of a pupil's illness his teacher himself nurses him, supplies all the medicine needed and pays attention to him as if he was his child."[1056] The main ideas of this relation of teacher and pupil are taken over from the Brahminic education and are in close similarity with it.

Indeed the Buddhist system of education shows an imitation of the early Hindu institutions. We are reminded of the anadhyāya days when Yuan Chwang tells us that the eighth, fourteenth and fifteenth of each fortnight were fast days, six days in each month when the

---

[1055] Takakusu's Eng. Trans., pp. 119-20.

[1056] Ibid., p. 120.

Sūtras forbid Vedic study and recitation.[1057] We are again reminded of the four monthly ceremonies (chāturmāsya), where he describes the first, fifth and nineth months of the year as 'the three long fasts.' Similarly, the winter-retreat or Varsha was strictly observed[1058] but the Buddhist Varsha was shorter than the Hindu. It extended from the first day of Śrāvaṇa to the last day of Āśvayuja. In I-Tsing's time it was four months, from mid-June to mid-October.[1059] As in the Hindu system, classes were held only in the morning and evening hours and never during the heat of the day.[1060]

We observe great similarity in the details of the daily life of the monks as noticed by I-Tsing. 'The Buddha ruled that a priest should never wear sandals before teachers or images'[1061] 'It is mean not to use a tooth-wood, not to wash after evacuation, and not to distinguish between clean and unclean food'.[1062] There were special instructions regarding the morning bath and ablutions and the keeping of the system cooled by oil and other artificial appliances.[1063] "When a meal is finished, do not fail to cleanse the hand.................chew tooth-wood in the mouth; let the tongue as well as the teeth be carefully cleansed and purified."[1064] "Nor is it right to eat next morning the soup and vegetables that have been left, or to partake later of the remaining cake or fruits."[1065]

In this connection it may be noted that Kulapati which according to the Hindu commentator denotes a teacher who maintains ten thousand pupils became a word of scorn among monastic Buddhists, for, says I-Tsing: "If any priest decided anything by himself alone or treated the priests favourably or unfavourably at his own pleasure, without regarding the will of the assembly, he was expelled (from the monastery) being called a Kulapati."[1066] A Hindu religious student is known as

---

1057 Watters: Yuan Chwang I. 302.

1058 Ibid., I. 145.

1059 Takakusu's I-Tsing p. 21.

1060 Ibid., p. 119.

1061 Ibid., p. 22.

1062 Ibid., pp. 24-25.

1063 Ibid., Ch. XX.

1064 Ibid., p. 26.

1065 Ibid., p. 25.

1066 Ibid., p. 63.

a brahmachārin but according to the Buddhists 'brahmachārin' denoted a student of secular literature and 'mānava' a student of the scriptures who would be tonsured and black-robed later on.[1067]

§4. Curriculum of studies.

I-Tsing gives us a very nice idea about the curriculum of studies in the Buddhist monasteries. "Throughout India every one who becomes a monk is taught Mātriketa's two hymns as soon as he can recite the five and ten precepts (Śila). This course is adopted by both the Mahāyāna and the Hīnayāna schools. There are six reasons for this. Firstly, these hymns enable us to know the Buddha's great and profound virtues. Secondly, they show us how to compose verses. Thirdly, they ensure purity of language. Fourthly, the chest is expanded in singing them. Fifthly, by reciting them nervousness in an assembly is overcome. Sixthly, by their use life is prolonged, being free from disease. After one is able to recite them, one proceeds to learn other śutras."[1068] "In India students learn this epistle in verse (Suhṛtlekhā of Bodhisattva Nāgārjuna) early in the course of instruction, but the most devout make it their special subject of study throughout their lives................There is another work of a similar character called Jātakamālā................The object of composing the Birth-stories in verse is to teach the doctrine of universal salvation in a beautiful style, agreeable to the popular mind and attractive to readers."[1069] Mahāsattva Chandra's song about Prince Viśwāntara and Aśwaghoṣa's poetical songs and Sūtrālaṅkāra-śāstra and Buddhacharit-kābya were widely read and sung throughout India.[1070]

In a previous chapter, we have seen that the Buddhist monasteries began in course of time to impart secular instruction as well. We have seen that there was a long course of grammatical study, beginning when the boy was six years of age and lasting till he was twenty, which was

---

1067 Takakusu's I-Tsing, pp. 105, 155 note.

1068 Ibid., pp. 157-58.

1069 Ibid., pp. 162-63.

1070 Ibid., pp. 164-66.

a preliminary to the study of higher subjects. With regard to this further study I-Tsing observes : "After having studied this commentary (on Pāṇinī's grammar called Kāśikāvṛtti), students begin to learn composition in prose and verse and devote themselves to logic (hetuvidyā) and metaphysics (Abhidharma-koṣa). In learning Nyāya-dvāra-tarka-śāstra (introduction to logic) they rightly draw inferences; and by studying Jātakamālā their powers of comprehension increase. Thus instructed by their teacher and instructing others they pass two or three years, generally in the Nālandā monastery in Central India or in the country of Valabha (Walā) in Western India." (Takakusu's Eng. Trans., p. 176).

If the students wanted to distinguish themselves in Yoga then they had to read—[1071]

(1) 'The Chūrṇi' (i. e., Patañjali's great commentary on Pāṇinī's sūtras.

(2) 'The Bhartṛhari śāstra' which treats of principles of human life as well as of grammatical science.

(3) 'The Vākya discourse' a treatise on the inference supported by the authority of the sacred teaching and on inductive arrangement.

(4) 'The Pei-na' (perhaps Sanskrit Veda) which they evidently studied to oppose the heretics.

"The priests learn besides all the Vinaya works and investigate the Sūtras and Śāstras as well."[1072]

"After having learnt the Yogāchārya-śāstras, he ought to study thoroughly Asaṇga's eight śāstras. These eight śāstras are :—

1. Vidyāmātra-viṃśati (gāthā)-śāstra or Vidyāmātrasiddhi (by Vasubandhu. (Nanjio's Catalogue of the Chinese Tripitaka No. 1240).
2. Vidyāmātrasiddhi-tridaśa-śāstra-kārikā by Vasubandhu (Nanjio's Catalogue No. 1215).

1071 Takakusu's I-Tsing, pp. 178-80.
1072 Ibid., p. 181.

3. Mahāyāna samparigraha-śāstramūla by Asanga (Nanjio's Catalogue, Nos. 1183, 1184, 1247).
4. Abhidharma (-saṃgīti)-śāstra by Asaṅga (Nanjio's Catalogue, No. 1199; commentary by Sthiramati, No. 1178).
5. Madhyāntavibhāga-śāstra by Vasubandhu (Nanjio's Catalogue, Nos. 1244, I248).
6. Nidāna-śāstra (Nos. 1227, 1314 by Ullangha, No. 1211 by Śuddhamati).
7. Sūtrālaṅkāra-tīkā by Aganga (No. 1190).
8. Karmasiddha-śāstra by Vasubandhu (Nos. 1221, 1222).

"Although there are some works of Vasubandhu among the above-mentioned śāstras, yet the success (in the Yoga system) is assigned to Asanga (and thus the books of Vasubandhu are included among Asanga's".[1073]

"When a priest wishes to distinguish himself in the study of Logic he should thoroughly understand Gina's eight śāstras. These are :—

1. The śāstra on the meditation of the Three Worlds (not found).
2. Sarvalakṣaṇa-dhyāna-śāstra (kārikā) by Gina (Nanjio's Catalogue No. 1229).
3. The śāstra on the meditation on the object (by Gina). Probably Ālambanapratyaya-dhyāna-śāstra (Nanjio's Catalogue No. 1173).
4. The śāstra on the Gate of the Cause (Hetudvāra) (not found).
5. The śāstra on the gate of the resembling cause not found.
6. The Nyāya-dvāra (tarka)-śāstra by Nāgārjuna (Nanjio's Catalogue Nos. 1223, 1224).
7. Pragñapti-hetu-saṃgraha (?)-śāstra by Gina (Nanjio's Catalogue No. 1228.
8. The śāstra on the grouped inferences (not found).

[1073] Takakusu's I-Tsing, p. 186.

"While studying the Abhidharma (metaphysics) he must read through the six Pādas, and while learning the Āgamas, he must entirely investigate the principles of the four classes (Nikāya). When these have all been mastered, the priest will be able successfully to combat heretics and disputants and by expounding the truths of the religion to save all."[1074]

In later years Tāntric philosophy came to be studied at Nālandā, Vikramaśilā and other monasteries. Dr. P. C. Roy has proved in his History of Hindu Chemistry[1075] that the tantras were the repositories of chemical knowledge and observes: "From the fifth to the eleventh century A. D. the colleges in connection with the monasteries of Pātāliputra, Nālandā, Vikramaśilā, Odantapura etc., were the great seats of learning as the temples attached to the pyramids in ancient Egypt and alchemy was included in the curricula of studies".

The foregoing account would show that some of these monasteries stood for the ideal of freedom in learning and welcomed knowledge from all quarters, from all sects and creeds. Indeed some of them were genuine universities in the universal range of their studies and not mere sectarian denominational schools. Thus at Nālandā at the time of Hiuen Tsang "the priests belonging to the convent or strangers (residing therein) always reach to the number of ten thousand who all study the Great Vehicle, and also (the works belonging to) the eighteen sects (of Buddhism) and not only so, but even ordinary works such as the Vedas and other books, the hetuvidyā, śabdavidyā, the chikitsāvidyā, the works on magic and the Sāṃkhya; besides these they thoroughly investigate the miscellaneous works".[1076] There were one hundred pulpits whence the teachers discoursed on their subjects, so that there were one thousand men who could explain twenty collections of sūtras and śāstras; five hundred who could explain thirty collections and perhaps ten men, including the Master of the Law, who could explain fifty collections.[1077] Hiuen Tsang himself "whilst he stopped in the convent,

---

1074 Ibid., pp. 186-87.

1075 Vol. I., pp. LXXI-LXXVIII.

1076 Beal—Life of Hiuen Tsang, p. 112.

heard the explanation of the Yoga-śāstra, three times; of Nyāya—Anusāra-śāstra once; the Hin-hiang-tin-fa-ming once; the Hetuvidyā-śāstra and the Śabda-vidyā and the tsah liang śāstras twice; the Prāṇamūla śāstra-tikā and the śata-śāstra thrice. The Koṣa, Vibhāsa and the Shaṭpadābhidharma śāstras he had already heard explained in the different parts of Kashmere; but when he came to this convent he wished to study them again to satisfy some doubts he had: this done, he also devoted himself to the study of the brāhmaṇa books and the work called Vyākaraṇa".[1078] He also "thoroughly investigated the language (words and phrases) and by talking with those men on the subject of the 'pure writings' he advanced excellently in his knowledge. Thus, he penetrated, examined completely, all the collection (of Buddhist books) and also studied the sacred books of the brāhmaṇas during five years".[1079]

The courses of study were perhaps less comprehensive at Vikramaśilā than at Nālandā. The most important branch of learning taught here was the Tantras. Next to the Tantras there were studied Grammar, Metaphysics and Logic. The fact that the dwāra-paṇḍits were eminent logicians goes to prove that Logic was evidently a popular subject.[1080] Here as at Nālandā and other monasteries the teachers and the students occupied themselves with copying manuscripts.[1081]

It will be noticed that the curriculum in these monasteries excluded all technical sciences. It was therefore a deterioration from Taxila where the curriculum was more varied. But there is nothing strange in this when we bear in mind that the monks in them had no care about food, lodging and clothing which were supplied to them gratis. In fact the monks had hardly any secular care and their whole endeavour was given to intellectual and spiritual improvement. Moreover, there is no evidence that Law, Mathematics and Astronomy were cultivated in these monasteries. Probably Law was already regarded too much as an exclusive possession of the Brahmins to make intrusion by others

---

1077 Ibid. 1078 Beal—Life of Hiuen Tsang, p. 121.

1079 Beal—Life of Hiuen Tsang, p. 125.

1080 S. C. Vidyābhūṣaṇa—Mediæval Logic, p. 150.

1081 J. R. A. S., 1010, p. 151.

possible, while Buddhism would not have the need of astronomy that Brahminism had for ascertaining auspicious times for sacrifices and other ceremonials.

We find that exercise was encouraged in the Buddhist monasteries in India. I-Tsing[1082] says: "In India both priests and laymen are generally in the habit of taking long walks, going backwards and forwards along a path, at suitable hours, and at their pleasure; they avoid noisy places. Firstly, it cures disease and secondly, it helps to digest food. The walking hours are in the forenoon and late in the afternoon. They either go away (for a walk) from their monasteries or stroll quietly along the corridors. If any one neglects this exercise he will suffer from ill health and be often troubled by a swelling of the legs or of the stomach, a pain in the elbows or on the shoulders. A phlegmatic complaint likewise is caused by sedentary habits. If any one, on the contrary adopts this habit of walking he will keep his body well, and thereby improve his religious merit............When anyone walks towards the right round a temple or a chaitya, he does it for the sake of religious merit; therefore he must perform it with special reverence. But the exercise (I am now speaking of) is for the sake of taking air, and its object is to keep oneself in good health or to cure diseases".

II. Hermitages of Buddhist saints as seats of learning.

Secondary and Higher education were also imparted in the hermitages of Buddhist saints frequently referred to in Pāli and Sanskrit literature. Thus we read in Losaka Jātaka[1083] that Bodhisattva was a teacher of world-wide fame in Benares with five hundred young brāhmaṇas to teach. "In those times the Benares folk used to give day by day commons of food to poor lads and had them taught free." In the same Jātaka we are told how the villagers appointed a teacher by paying his expenses and giving him a hut to live in. In the Tittīra Jātaka[1084] we read that "a world-renowned Professor of Benares

---

[1082] Takakusu's I-Tsing, p. 114-15.

[1083] Jātaka I. 234.

[1084] Jātaka III. 537.

gave instruction in science to five hundred young brāhmaṇas. One day he thought: So long as I dwell here, I meet with hindrances to the religious life and my pupils are not perfected in their studies. I will retire into a forest-home on the slopes of the Himalayas and carry on my teachings there". He told this to his pupils and bidding them bring sesame, husked rice, oil, garments and such like, he went into the forest and building a hut of leaves took up his abode close by the highway. His pupils too each built a hut for himself. Their kinsfolk sent rice and the natives of the country saying 'a famous professor, they say, is living in such and such a place in the forest, and giving lessons in science' brought presents of rice and the foresters also offered their gifts while a certain man gave a milch cow and a calf to supply them with milk".

Hiuen Tsang refers to such an institution maintained by Jayasena. We are told: "He (Hiuen Tsang) went again to the hill called Yaṣṭivana and stopped with a householder who was a native of Suratha and a kṣhatriya by caste—his name was Jaysena, a writer of śāstras. As a youth he was given to study and first under Bhadra-ruchi, Master of Śāstras, he had studied the hetuvidyā-śāstra; then under Sthiramati Bodhisattva, he had studied the śabdavidyā-śāstra (and others), belonging to the Great and Little Vehicle. Again under Śilabhadra, Master of the Law, he had studied the yogaśāstra. And then again, with respect to the numerous productions of secular (outside) writers: the four Vedas, works on astronomy and geography, on the medicinal art, magic and arithmetic, he had completely mastered these from beginning to end: he had exhausted these inquiries root (leaf) and branch; he had studied all of them both within and without. His acquirements (virtue) made him the admiration of the period. Purṇavarmā rāja, lord of Magadha, had great respect for learned men and honoured those distinguished as sages: hearing of this man's renown, he was much pleased, and sent messengers to invite him to come to his court and nominated him kwo-sse (Master of the kingdom) and assigned for his support the revenue of twenty large towns. But the Master of śāstras declined to receive them. After the obsequies of Purṇavarmā, Śilāditya rāja also invited him to be " the Master of the country" and assigned him the revenue of eighty large towns of Orissa. But again the Master declined the offer. The king still urged him repeatedly to acquiesce, but he as firmly refused. Then addressing the King he said: "Jayasèna has heard, that he who receives the emoluments of the world (men), also is troubled with the concerns of life; but now my object is to teach the urgent character of the fetters of birth and death; how is it possible then to find leisure to acquaint myself with the concerns of the king?" So saying he respectfully bowed and went away, the king being unable to detain him. From that time he has constantly lived on the mountain called Yaṣṭivana, where he takes charge of disciples, teaching and leading them on to persevere and expounding the books of Buddha. The number of laymen and priests (religious men) who honour him as their Master is always a large one, amounting to several hundred."[1085] "The master of the Law (Hiuen Tsang) remained with him first and last for two years and studied a treatise on the difficulties of the Vidyā-matra-siddhi śāstra, the I-i-lu-lun, the Shing-wu-wai-lun, the puh-chu-ni-pan-shih-i-yin-un-lun, the chwong-yan-king-lun; and he also asked explanations of passages in the yoga and the hetuvidyā śāstras which yet caused him doubt."[1086]

Comparable to Nālandā in the freedom of its academic life and the variety and catholicity of its studies, as described by Yuan Chwang, there was another seat of learning, the hermitage of the sage Divākaramitra, described by Bāṇa in his Harṣacharita.[1087] Originally a follower of Vedic religion and of the Maitrāyaṇī śākhā, he turned a Buddhist and according to Bāṇa had his part in the conversion of Harṣa and his sister into Buddhism. To his calm sylvan retreat in the depth of the Viñdhyā hills were admitted students differing widely and radically in doctrines and practices, followers of all possible sects and schools of thought, gathered together in a common fellowship in the quest of Truth, the supreme object of a University. There came Arhats (Digāmbara Jains) Maskaris (brāhmaṇical ascetics) Śvetapatas (śwetāmbara Jains), White-clothed vikṣus, Bhāgabatas, Vanīs

[1085] Beal—Life of Hiuèn Tsang, pp. 153-54. [1086] Ibid.

[1087] English Trans., by Cowell and Thomas, pp. 236-37.

(brahmachārins), Keśaluñchakas (those who rooted out their hairs), Kapilas (Sāṃkhyas) Lokāyātikas (Chārvākas or atheists) Jains,[1088] Kāṇaḍas (followers of Kaṇada's Vaiśeṣika philosophy), Aupaniṣadas (Vedāntins) Aiśavara karanikas (Naiyāyikas) Kārandhamins[1089] (metallurgists) Dharmaśāstrins[1090] (experts in law), Pourāṇikas, Śapta-tantavas (experts in rituals), Śaivas, Śābdikas (grammarians), and Pañcharātrikas (followers of the Pañcharātra sect of Vaiṣṇavas). Nor were Buddhist learning and culture less in evidence there: the followers of the Three Refuges (Triśaraṇa) were busy performing the ritual of the chaitya (chaitya-karma); there were students well-versed in the Śākya-śāsanas (Buddhist Law); discourses were also forth-coming on Vasubandhu's Koṣa or Bauddhasiddhānta; while there were others who specialised in the study of Bodhisattva-jātakas which they were always muttering. These different sects and schools of thought were "all diligently following their own tenets, pondering, urging objections, raising doubts, resolving them, giving etymologies, disputing, studying and explaining."[1091]

"The Supreme Buddhist Avalokiteśwara, compacted of all the letter-atoms of all the śāstras,—absorbed without faltering in penances,—revealing the real nature of all things to the student, like the light,—one whom Buddha himself might well approach with reverence, Duty herself might worship, Favour itself show favour to, Honour itself honour, Reverence itself revere,—the very source of muttered prayer, the circumference of the wheel of religious observance, the essence of asceticism, the body of purity, the treasury of virtue, the home of trust, the standard of good conduct, the entire capital of omniscience, the acme of kindness, the extreme limit of compassion, the very

---

1088 According to Professor C. V. Vaidya "the Buddhists are here called Jainas, Jīna being a name of Buddha while what are now called Jainas are called Arhats" (History of Mediæval Hindu India, Vol. I., p. 111).

1089 Philosophers of Dhātuvāda or elements (Ibid.).

1090 The Mīmāṃsakas are probably intended for they based their arguments on revelations (Ibid.).

1091 Harṣacharita—English Trans., by Cowell and Thomas, p. 236.

finality of happiness—Divākaramitra"[1092] was the teacher in this hermitage and students belonging to the above-mentioned sects and schools of thought—"all gathered here as his disciples."[1093]

III.—Method of teaching in the Buddhist seats of learning.

I-Tsing[1094] observes:—"In the fundamental principles of the Law of Buddha, teaching and instruction are regarded as the first and foremost, just as King Kakravartin very carefully protects and brings up his eldest son; so carefully is a pupil instructed in the Law." Again "the instruction of pupils (saddhivihārika) is an important matter for the prosperity of religion. If this is neglected, the extinction of religion is sure to follow."[1095] The manner of teaching is thus indicated: "Early every morning a pupil, having chewed tooth-wood, should come to his teacher and offer him tooth-wood and put a washing-basin and a towel at the side of his seat. Having thus served him, the pupil should go and worship the holy image and walk round the temple. Then returning to his teacher, he makes a salutation, holding up his cloak, and with clasped hands, touching (the ground with his head) three times, remains kneeling on the ground. Then with bowed head and clasped hands, he enquires of the teacher, saying: "Let my upādhyāya be attentive or let my āchārya be attentive; I now make enquiries whether upādhyāya has been well through the night, whether his body (lit. four great elements) has been in perfect health, whether he is active and at ease, whether he digests his food well, whether he is ready for the morning meal." Enquiries may he short or full according to circumstances. Then the teacher answers these enquiries concerning his own health. Next, the pupil goes to salute his seniors who are in the neighbouring apartments. Afterwards he reads a portion of the scripture, and reflects on what he has learnt. He acquires new knowledge day by day, and searches into old subjects month after month, without losing a minute."[1096]

1092 Ibid., p. 237.

1093 Ibid., p. 236.

1094 Takakusu's Eng., Trans., pp. 120-21.

1095 Ibid., p. 116.

1096 Takakusu's I-Tsing, pp. 116-17.

The method of teaching seems to have been chiefly oral. The Buddha did not put his teachings into writing and it was handed down by word of mouth as was the ancient custom.[1097] Teaching through questions and answers was the usual rule. This is quite clear from the lessons in the Dialogues of the Buddha and the Milindā-Pañha.[1098] The Mahāmangala Sūtra[1099] recommend intercourse with śramaṇas and religious conversations at due seasons. Hindu books analyse the latter into vāda or Saṃvāda, like that between Arjuna and Kṛṣṇa in the Gitā, Jalpa or the raising of difficulties to be cleared up and vitanda-vāda or casuistry and sophistry.[1100] By these conversations every confusion was unravelled, every lurking error dragged to light, and enquiry on the right lines stimulated and directed. But the most valuable result was obtained by the close association with the teacher that these discussions entailed, and the realisation that virtue was no mere subject for speculation or 'academic' discussion but had to be practised with consistency of aim and power of will. Indeed as the education imparted laid stress on the formation of habits and character rather than on mere intēllectual sword-play a higher place was naturally given to the āchārya, explained by I-Tsing as teacher of discipline than to the upādhyāya who conveyed oral instruction. Hence the Bodhicharyā insists that one must act upto, not merely read, the scriptures, for, "the mere reading of pharmaceutical works will not effect a patient's cure."[1101]

Buddhist methodology in regard to moral instruction becomes clear in the works of the age of Aśwaghoṣa. In the Sūtrālaṅkāra we have first a moral theme propounded, then a story in illustration and then another moral, if necessary, and lastly the conclusion. We have the

---

1097 Dwīpabaṃśa XX. 21.

1098 The Buddha and King Ajātaśatru in Digha-Nikāya, Sāmaññaphala Sutta, 13-101; The Buddha and Ambathha in Digha-Nikāya, Ch. I. 10-28 and Ch. II. 1-12; Nāgasena and King Milindā in Milindā-Pañha IV. 7. 69; IV. 7. 70; VII. 5. 41; IV. 1. 8; IV. 6-60.

1099 S. B. E., X. p. 43.

1100 Compare Vātsyāyana on the Nyāyasūtras of Gautama.

1101 Pañchatantra I., pp. 166 and 167.

play of emotion evoked after, as in the 43rd story and dramatic effect aimed at, as there and in the 20th.[1102] The Abadāna stories are also arranged after a definite plan. They begin and end in quite similar ways, and the moral is invariably pointed out.

It is interesting to find that the Buddha adapted his teachings to the needs and capacity of his disciples. As Watters well puts it: "The Buddha suited his sermons and precepts to the moral and spiritual attainments and requirements of his audience." Those who were low in the scale were led on gradually by the setting forth of simple truths, by parables and lessons and by mild restrictions as to life and conduct. At a later period of his ministry he taught higher truths and inculcated a stricter purity and more thorough self-denial.

The 'project' method of teaching was also employed by the Buddha in the case of the brāhmaṇa Varadwāja. The latter ploughed and sowed for his livelihood and the Buddha therefore converted him by the parable of the sower presented as follows: "Faith is the seed, devotion the rain, modesty the plough-shaft, the mind the tie of the yoke, mindfulness the ploughshare and goad, truthfulness the means to bind, tenderness to untie and energy the team and bullock".

Another characteristic feature of the Buddha's method of teaching and debate was to put and examine his opponent's position first. The Buddha is questioned and he puts a counter-question. Nigrodha the wanderer who had a following of 3000 thought about the Buddha, that by his habit of seclusion "his insight was ruined, he is not at home in conducting an assembly, nor ready in conversation, but occupied only with the fringes of things" and to prove the truth of his opinion asked the Buddha to expound his doctrine. The Buddha, not to be outwitted said: "Difficult is it, Nigrodha, for one of another view, without practice or teaching, to understand that wherein I train up my disciples", and turning the table thus said: "Come now, Nigrodha, ask me a question about your own doctrine." Upon this his followers shouted out: "Wonderful, Sir, the great gifts and powers of the

---

1102 Sylvain Levi: Sūtrālaṅkāra (Nariman's Trans.), Op., Cit., pp. 190 and 191.

samana Gotama in withholding his own theories and inviting the discussion of those of others!" Thus by way of criticising his opponent's doctrine he established his own.

In the Buddha's method of teaching as preserved in the Pāli works we find that sometimes parables alternate with doctrine and didactive discourse. He employs similes drawn from the life of man and the life of nature of which he was such a keen observer. From similies there is sometimes a natural transition to fable and romance. Aśoka also added concrete visual illustrations for teaching the Dhamma. [1103]

According to I-Tsing "there are two traditional ways in India of attaining to intellectual power: (1) committing to memory; (2) the alphabet fixes one's ideas. By this way, after a practice of ten days or a month, a student feels his thought rise like a fountain and can commit to memory whatever he has once heard. This is far from being a myth, for I myself have met such men".[1104] The meaning of this passage is by no means clear, but it certainly brings out the prevalent practice of learning by heart and shows what facility students seem to have gained in doing this. But it is interesting to find that side by side with memorising, thinking and questioning are described as leading to the development of the intellect. Milindā-Pañha[1105] says:—

> "By growth in reputation and in years,
> By *questioning* and by the master's aid,
> By *thoughtfulness* and by converse with the wise,
> By intercourse with men worthy of love,
> By residence within a pleasant spot—
> By these nine is one's insight purified,
> They who have these, their wisdom grows".

Great store was thus set by memorising; but it was learning by heart for constant pondering over the meaning rather than learning by rote.

1103 Rock Edict, IV. Vimānadaśanā hastidaśanā cha aṇighamdhāni cha ananicha divyāni rūpani daśayitvā.

1104 Takakusu's Eng. Trans., pp. 182-83.

1105 IV. 1, 8.

I-Tsing[1106] also says: "He (the pupil) reads a portion of the scripture, and *reflects* on what he has learnt. He acquires new knowledge day by day, and *searches into old subjects* month after month without losing a minute." There were thus three steps in the practice of wisdom: study (śruta), thought (chintā) and meditation (bhāvanā).

The method of teaching at Nālandā seems to have been both tutorial and professorial. "They arrange every day about 100 pulpits for preaching and the students attend these discourses without any fail, even for a minute".[1107] Such lecturers were greatly honoured: "When such men gave daily lecturers, they were freed from the business imposed on the monastics. When they went out, they could ride on sedan-chairs but not on horse-back".[1108] Nevertheless there was close touch between the professors and the students. I-Tsing[1109] observes: "I, I-Tsing used to converse with these teachers so intimately that I was able to receive invaluable instruction *personally* from them". He further says: "I have always been very glad that I had the opportunity of acquiring knowledge from them (teachers) *personally* which I should otherwise never had possessed and that I could refresh my memory of past study by comparing old notes with new ones".[1110]

A great place was also given to discussion and debate, at least in the higher part of the course as is evident from the following account of Hiuen Tsang about Nālandā: "The brethren are often assembled for discussion to test intellectual capacity, to reject the worthless and advance the intelligent".[1111] Again, "the day is not sufficient for asking and answering profound questions. From morning till night they engage in discussion; the old and the young mutually help one another. Those who cannot discuss questions out of the Tripitaka are little esteemed and are obliged to hide themselves for shame. Learned men from different cities, on this account, who desire to acquire quickly a renown in discussion, come here in multitudes to settle their doubts

---

1106 Takakusu's Eng. Trans., p. 117.

1107 Beal—Life of Hiuen Tsang, p. 112.

1108 Takakusu's I-Tsing, p. 64.

1109 Takakusu's Eng. Trans., p. 184.

1110 Takakusu's I-Tsing, p, 185.

1111 Watters: Yuan Chwang, p. 162.

and then the streams (of their wisdom) spread far and wide".[1112] Hiuen Tsang records actual cases of such discussions. Once while he was deputed by Śīlabhadra to expound some aspects of Yogaśāstra, another learned man Siṃharaśmi was discoursing on quite contrary doctrines in the monastery, when he silenced him by his questions and drove him in shame to leave Nālandā and repair to the Bodhi monastery at Gayā, thence to bring his fellow-student Chandrasiṃha of Eastern India to Nālandā for dicussion with Hiuen Tsang but Hiuen Tsang prevailed over him at once.[1113] I-Tsing[1114] speaks in the same strain :—"Thus instructed by their teachers and instructing others, they pass two or three years, generally in the Nālandā monastery in Central India or in the country Valabha (Walā) in Western India...........There (in these places) eminent and accomplished men assemble in crowds, discuss possible and impossible doctrines and after having been assured of the excellence of their opinions by wise men become far-famed for their wisdom. To try the sharpness of their wit, they proceed to the king's court to lay down before it the sharp weapon of their abilities; there they present their schemes and show their political talent, seeking to be appointed in the practical government. When they are present in the House of debate, they raise their seat and seek to prove their wonderful cleverness. When they are refuting heretical doctrines all their opponents become tongue-tied and acknowledge themselves undone. Then the sound of their fame make the five mountains of India vibrate and their renown flows as it were over the four borders. They receive grants of land and are advanced to a high rank; their famous names are as a reward, written in white on their lofty gates. After this they can follow whatever occupation they like".

1112 Beal—Buddhist Records of the Western World, Vol. II. p. 170.

1113 Beal—Life of Hiuen Tsang, pp. 157-58.

1114 Takakusu's Eng. Trans., pp. 176ff.

CHAPTER VIII.

VOCATIONAL EDUCATION IN ANCIENT INDIA.

In modern days society is no longer a cosmos but has fallen into chaos and this disorder must be remedied if modern civilisation is to survive. As society in the Indian ideal was a community of rational beings, not a fortuitous concourse of atoms, it was regarded as an organism, a body-politic with definite organs, each discharging a definite function for the benefit and health of the whole community. Under this ancient system, youths were trained up for their future functions in society on a caste-basis and this is re-appearing in the West, as specialised and vocational training. Thus while Vedic study is binding on all belonging to the three twice-born castes, a life of learning or an intellectual career was reserved for the brāhmaṇa. The kṣhatriya is destined for the political and military and the vaiśya for the economic career. In Adam Smith's phraseology, the former is for 'defence' and the latter for 'opulence.' It is no wonder, therefore, to find Brahminical texts never tired of dilating upon the merits to be acquired by following the duties of one's own caste. On the other hand, the Dharmaśāstras[1115] predict in an equally positive manner, grave misfortunes, in the life to come, for those who neglect the duties of their caste. The Śāstrakāras, however, did not rely upon these injunctions alone for the due observances of caste-duties. They armed the royal authority with specific powers to enforce the same.[1116]

[1115] Āpastamva II. 11. 10 ; II. 2-3. Gautama XI. 29 ; Manu X. 130. See also **Kautilya's Arthaśāstra** (R. Śyāmaśāstrī's Eng. Trans.), p. 8 ; Vātsāyana's **Kāmasūtra, Bk. I.** Ch. II. śl. 34.

[1116] Āpastamva II. 10. 12-16 ; II. 11. 1-4 ; II. 27. 18 ; Gautama XI. 31 ; **Kautilya's** Arthaśāstra (R. Śyāmaśāstrī's Eng. Trans.), p. 8 ; Manu VIII. 418 ; Viṣṇu III. 2 ; Yājñabālkya I. 361 ; Śukranītisāra Ch. IV. Section IV. lines, 82-83. **Refer in this** connection to the execution of Śūdra Śambuka by Rāma in the Rāmāyaṇa **and to** the Nasika Cave Inscription which tells us that Gautamīputra "**stopped the** contamination of the four varṇas" (Ep. Ind. VIII. pp. 60-61).

§ 1. The education of the priest.

In dealing with the education which will fit a man for his vocation as a priest it is necessary that we should divest our mind of prejudices and guard ourselves against associating modern ideas with the old state of things. We are accustomed to say that the brāhmaṇas alone could be priests, they alone could teach the Vedas, whereas we have evidences which tend to prove that at least in the earliest times they alone were 'brāhmaṇas' who possessed a knowledge of the Vedas and could perform the function of a priest. Rules were indeed laid down that nobody should serve as a priest who could not prove his descent from three (according to Kauśitakī Sūtra) or ten (according to Latyāyana Sūtra) generations of ṛṣis.[1117] But these very rules prove indirectly that the unbroken descent in a brāhmaṇa line was yet an ideal and not an actuality. It further shows the conscious attempt towards a closer corporation of priests.

We have, however, not to depend upon negative proof alone to establish our thesis. Authentic ancient texts repeatedly declare that it is knowledge and not descent, that makes a brāhmaṇa. Taittirīya-Saṃhitā[1118] declares: "eṣa bai brāhmaṇa ṛṣirārṣeyo yaḥ śusruban." "He who has learning is the brāhmaṇa ṛṣi." Again we have in Kāthaka[1119] and Maitrāyanīya[1120] Saṃhitās:

> " Kiṃ brāhmaṇasya pitaram kiṃ u pṛchchasi mātaram
> Śrutam ched asmin bedyam sa pitā sa pitāmaha."

"What do you ask about brāhmaṇa father, what do you ask about brahāmaṇa mother? Since one who knows the Veda is the father." We are further told: "The brahminhood of a brāhmaṇa is encompassed by both the Vedas and the Dharmaśāstras; and not by the Vedas only. The divine Atri has said so."[1121] "He who daily studies the Vedānta, gives up companionship and discusses the Sāṃkhya yoga

---

1117 Weber—Ind. Stud. Vol. X. p. 70.
1118 6. 6. 1. 4.
1119 30. 1.
1120 48. 1; 107. 9.
1121 Atrī Saṃhitā I. 346.

is called a Dwija."[1122] Śukrāchārya[1123] says: "Not by birth are the brāhmaṇas, kṣhatriyas, vaiśyas, śūdras and mlechchas separated but by virtue and work. Are all descended from Brahmā to be called brāhmaṇa? Neither through colour nor through ancestors can the spirit worthy of a brāhmaṇa be generated. The brāhmaṇa is so called because of his virtues, e. g., he is habitually a worshipper of the gods with the knowledge, practices and prayers and he is peaceful, restrained and kind." "Again the man who has mastered the sciences and the arts should be the preceptor of all. But one who is unlearned cannot be a preceptor because of birth."[1124] These and similar passages seem to indicate that knowledge was looked upon as the primary qualification of a person as brāhmaṇa.

As a matter of fact we find the Pañcha-viṃśa Brāhmaṇa speaking of certain persons as royal seers and the later tradition preserved in the Anukramaṇi or index to the composers of the Ṛgveda ascribes hymns to such royal seers. Viśwāmitra, Devapi and Janaka became brāhmaṇas through learning.[1125] Kavasha, son of Illusha, a low-caste woman, was admitted as a ṛṣi for his purity, learning and wisdom.[1126] "Perhaps the most notable feature of his life is that he, śūdra as he was, distinguished himself as a ṛṣi of some of the hymns of the Ṛgveda"[1127] viz., Ṛg. X. 30-34. Viśwāmitra, the Purohit of King Sudas mentioned in the Ṛgveda is described in the Pañchaviṃśa and Aitareya Brāhmaṇas as of royal descent, of the family of Jahnus. Yāska represents a prince Devapi as sacrificing for his brother Śāntanu, the king. Similarly, King Viśwāntar sacrifices without the help of a priest in the Aitareya Brāhmaṇa. The Upaniṣads tell us of kings like Janaka of Videha, Aśwapati, King of the Kekayas in the Punjab, Ajātaśatru of Kāśī and Prabahana Jābāla of Pāñchāla disputing with and even instructing Brahmins in the lore of the Brahmā. Similarly,

---

1122 Ibid., I. 367.

1123 Ch. I. lines 75-80.

1124 Śukranītisāra, Ch. IV. lines 43-44.

1125 Śatapatha Brāhmaṇa XI. 6. 2. 1.

1126 Ait. Brāh., II. 3. 19.

1127 Swāmī Kṛṣṇavarṇa in his paper on "Sanskrit as a living language in India" read before the International Congress of Orientals held in Berlin on the 14th September 1881.

the Jaiminīya Upaniṣad speaks of a king becoming a seer. Satyakāma Jābāla, son of a slave-girl was the founder of a school of the Yajur Veda.[1128] Similarly ṛsi Vālmiki, the author of the Rāmāyaṇa was but a śūdra.[1129] If then the brahminhood depended upon the knowledge and learning mainly requisite for Vedic worship, there must have been some specific method by which it was obtained. The method is fortunately referred to in Kauśitakī, 55, from which we learn that the teacher had the power to confer ārṣeyam or brahminhood upon his student, apparently if the latter were inclined to adopt the profession of a priest and had, in the opinion of the teacher, capacity required for the same. This is beautifully illustrated by a passage in the Aitareya Brāhmaṇa[1130] quoted by Muir.[1131] We are told: "Sacrifice fled from the Kṣhatriya, Vaiśya and Śūdra and approached to Brahman. Wherefore now also sacrifice depends upon Brahman, upon the brāhmaṇas. Kṣhattra then followed Brahman, and said 'invite me (too to participate) in this sacrifice. Brahman replied 'So be it: then laying aside thy own implements (bows, arrows etc.,) approach the sacrifice with the implements of Brahman, in the form of Brahman and having become Brahman.' Kṣhattra rejoined 'Be it so' and laying aside his own implements, approached the sacrifice with those of Brahman, in the form of Brahman and having become Brahman. Wherefore, now also a kṣhatriya, when sacrificing, laying aside his own implements approaches the sacrifice with those of Brahman, in the form of Brahman and having become Brahman." There was thus no inherent distinction between a kṣhatriya and a brāhmaṇa and the one might have been changed into the other by a change in the mode of life and profession. The same idea also occurs in Aitareya Brāhmaṇa:[1132] "He a king when consecrated (dīkṣamāṇaḥ) enters into the condition of a brāhmaṇa" and also in Śatapatha Brāhmaṇa.[1133] On the authority of these

---

[1128] Chāndogya Upaniṣad V. 4.

[1129] Compare: "Viśwāmitra, Vaśiṣṭha, Mātanga, Nārada and others became elevated by special penances and not by birth" (Śukranītisāra Ch. IV. Sec. IV. lines 80-81).

[1130] VII. 19.

[1131] Original Sanskrit Texts, Vol. I. p. 368.

[1132] VII. 231.

[1133] III. 2. 1. 39 ff.

and other texts Weber[1134] concludes: "Thus every rājanya and vaiśya becomes, through the consecration for sacrifice (dīkṣā) a brāhmaṇa during its continuance and is addressed as such." Again we have in the Śatapatha Brāhmaṇa:[1135] "Whosoever sacrifices, does so after having become as it were a brāhmaṇa." So also Kātyāyana says in his Śrauta Sūtra:[1136] "The word brāhmaṇa is to be addressed to a vaiśya and a rājanya also," on which the commentator annotates: "The formula 'this brāhmaṇa has been consecrated' is to be used at the sacrifice of a vaiśya and a rājanya also; and not the words 'this rājanya', 'this vaiśya' has been consecrated."[1137]

Again, as new members could be admitted to a craft-guild only by by some prescribed method, so one could be initiated into this guild of priests only after an approved term of apprenticeship with a Master. This is expressly acknowledged by the Sūtra writers. Thus Āpastamva[1138] says: "he (the āchārya) causes him (the pupil) to be born (a second time) by (imparting to him) sacred learning"; and also "this (second) birth is the best"; "the father and mother produce the body only".[1139] Again, one "whose father and grand-father have not been initiated (and his two ancestors) are called slayers of the brāhmaṇa. Intercourse, eating and intermarriage with them should be avoided."[1140] "No religious rite can be performed by a (child) before it has been girt with the sacred girdle, since it is on a level with a śūdra before its new birth from the Veda".[1141] Initiation, not birth, was thus the real claim to brahminhood and we get here a rational explanation of those elaborate ceremonies which regulated the relation between a teacher and a student.

The analogy with the guild may be carried a step further. As many of these guilds (like those of weavers, barbers, potters and oil-millers) had ultimately developed into castes so the guild of the

---

1134 Ind. Stud. X. p. 17.

1135 XIII. 4. 1. 3.

1136 VI. 4. 12.

1137 Compare Muir—Original Sanskrit Texts, Vol. I. p. 369 and foot-note.

1138 S. B. E., Vol. II. p. 3.

1139 Ibid.

1140 Ibid., p. 5.

1141 Ibid., p. 10.

priests was also converted into the brāhmaṇa a caste. We come across those craft-guilds in ancient times, and their representatives, forming so many 'castes' in modern days. It would be as much consonant to reason to say, that the membership of the primitive guilds depended upon birth, as to predicate the same of the ancient brāhmaṇa class. It may be noted, however, that the brāhmaṇas of those days did not confine their activities to the function of a priest alone. As we have seen some of them were fighters too, and it is certain that many also followed other professions. But the prohibition to carry arms which we find in the Kauśitakī[1142] is probably a typical example of the gradual restriction in this respect. Here again we find that conscious attempt towards making the corporation a closer one to which reference has already been made.

We have all along used the expression "guild of priests". It would perhaps be more correct to say "guilds of priests". For we cannot very well believe that all the brāhmaṇas in different parts of the country formed only one guild. Although there must have been some general similarity in their aims, pursuits and manner of living (as is evident from the Kauśitakī),[1143] the more coherent organisation could embrace only a limited section. As a matter of fact we hear of various schools of brāhmaṇas at this period, such as the Yajurvedīs, Māndhyandins, Maitrāyaṇīs, Ṛgvedīs, Āpastamvas, Āpastamva Hiraṇyakeśins, etc. These very names indicate that the differentiating factors were connected with the Vedic authorities relied upon by them and this, in a manner corroborates the theory that it is not birth but knowledge required by a priest which formed the basis of the guilds of priests. The divisions of brāhmaṇas according to 'śākhā' and 'charaṇa' also leads to the same conclusion. Indeed when learning requisite for the functions of a priest, formed the basis of the guilds, it is natural that groups would be formed according to the special subjects of study. But when in course of time birth took the place of learning, there must have grown up distinctions based upon locality. Already in the

[1142] 93. 104.

[1143] Compare Weber—Ind. Stud. X. 41-160.

Jātakas[1144] we meet frequently with the terms "Udichcha brāhmaṇa" and phrases conveying distinct pride in birth in such a family. This was the forerunner of the later Kanuaj, Gauḍa, Konkanasth and Tailanga Brahmins.

The nature of the education imparted to a would-be priest and teacher has already been described in Chapter I, Section 4 on "The Religious Factor in Ancient Hindu Education". As we have already remarked, a brāhmaṇa did not always receive only a priestly education. Sanskrit and Pali works as also the inscriptions refer to many brāhmaṇas who were proficient in all the branches of learning. Thus Droṇa, taught military arts not only to the Kauravas and the Pāṇḍavas but also to a king of the Andhaka family and many other princes. The brothers of Draupadī were taught Bṛhaspati-nīti by a Brahmin resident-tutor. Kanaka, the uncle of Kalhana, the Brahmin author of Rājataranginī gave lessons in music to King Harṣa of Kashmere. The Jātakas are replete with the stories of brāhmāṇa youths going to famous teachers to study sabba sīppāni and aṭṭhārasa Vijjāṭhānani. Regarding the significanae of these evidences from the Jātakas Dr. Fick aptly observes: "The three Vedas were manifestly not the sole subject which the brāhmaṇas were taught during their student days; in several places 'all the sciences' are mentioned as what the brāhmaṇa has to learn and by this are to be understood, over and above the three Vedas, eighteen branches of science.........(which) coincide approximately with the eighteen divisions which are mentioned in the Brahminical systems".[1145]

That the Brahmins studied also profane literature and Vārttā will be evident from the testimony of Manu[1146] who lays down that a brāhmaṇa should daily study the śāstras such as the Vedas, the Nigamas and other beneficial ones (danyāni cha hitānī) that lead to an increase of intellect. Such a study of profane literature need not necessarily be for fitting the brāhmaṇa student for following the

---

[1144] II. 82ff., 438ff; I. 356ff., 371ff.

[1145] Fick—Social Organisation in N. E. India in Buddha's time (Eng. Trans. by Prof. S. K. Maitra), p. 131.

[1146] IV. 19.

occupation leading to the production of wealth. It might well have been that he studies the various vidyās to make his education complete and allround. Dr. Narendra Nath Law assigns another reason for the Brahminical study of Vārttā. According to him the brāhmaṇas learn the subject sometimes perhaps for the sake of teaching it to their pupils. Says he: "The brāhmaṇas were not merely teachers of theology and philosophy but also of Economics, Polity including even the art of warfare, and use of weapons, also practical and fine arts and accomplishments".[1147]

§ 2. Education of the soldier.

The kṣhatriyas who ordinarily followed the profession of a soldier no doubt represented the nobility, the descendants of the ancient tribal chiefs but there is no reason to suppose that their rank was a closed one or that there was any social exclusiveness about them. The injunction in the Kauśitakī[1148] that a brāhmaṇa shall not carry arms proves indirectly that formerly even brāhmaṇas accepted the profession of a soldier. Armies of brāhmaṇas existed even in the days of Kautilya.[1149] From Rājataranginī[1150] we find that through the might of the wise king Yaśaskara (939-948 A. D.) "the Brahmins devoted (solely) to their studies, did not carry arms". The existence of armies of vaiśyas and śūdras is proved by Kautilya's Arthaśāstra.[1151] Indeed even when the caste system became rigid, the śāstric injunction[1152] that though ordinarily it is the duty of the kṣhatriya to embrace the profession of arms, it was yet the duty of all the twice-born classes to take up arms when Dharma is in danger shows that military training was not the monopoly of a class.

The admission into this guild of warriors was marked by the initiation ceremony. The education of such warriors commenced with Vedic learning in general and was then specialised in the study of Dhanurveda and Rājanīti. The later age at which the kṣhatriyas were

---

1147 Indian Antiquary, 1918, p. 240.
1148 93. 104.
1149 Arthaśāstra (R. Śyāmaśāstrī's Eng. Trans., p. 417.
1150 VI. 9.
1151 R. Śyāmaśāstrī's Eng. Trans., p. 417.
1152 Śukranītisāra Ch. IV., line 599.

supposed to start their schooling must be taken to indicate that its character was for them somewhat different from the instruction which the young novice for priesthood received. The latter was at school to be prepared for his future vocation as a priest and teacher and much that he would require to know would be useless to the youths of other professions. The study of the Vedas by the kṣhatriya may have included the memorising of the Vedic hymns, an acquaintance with the philosophic teachings of the Upaniṣads and certain parts of the six Vedāngas such as were necessary for the understanding of the Vedic texts or for an acquaintance with the duties to be performed in after life. Greater emphasis was undoubtedly laid on his military training.

In the Rāmāyaṇa[1153] we find a reference to the military exercises of soldiers which were, however, stopped for a few days on the death of King Daśaratha. That the troops were regularly trained in military arts is evident from the Ayodhyākāṇḍa 67th sarga where we are told that the sages who have assembled in the royal assembly on the death of Daśaratha said in the course of their address to Vaśiṣṭha on the evils that would befall a kingless state, that no body hears any longer the sound of the feet of heroes who are engaged in learning the use of arms. In the Yuddhakāṇḍa 12th sarga we are told that Rāvaṇa after casting a look at the councillers addressed Prahasta, the commander-in-Chief thus: "Hero! order my four-limbed army which is *well-trained in military arts* to defend the city carefully against the enemy" *Military tournaments* were also held for testing the military skill of soldiers. When Bharata went to Rāma in Chitrakūta, the latter asked the former the following question: "Do you show favour to those who are *skilled in war* and to those who have proved their valour in the presence of an assembled crowd?".[1154] That Rāma also took part in tournaments is evident from Ayodhyākāṇḍa 36th sarga where repentant Daśaratha orders Sumanta to send those who took part with Rāma in such tournaments to accompany Rāma in the forest. Indeed the city of Ayodhyā was filled with heroes who were proficient in Dhanurveda

1153 Ayodhyākāṇḍa, 67th sarga.

1154 Ayodhyākāṇḍa, 100th sarga.

It was three yojanas in area and nobody dared to give battle within this area and hence it was called Ayodhyā.[1155]

In the Mahābhārata[1156] Yudhiṣṭir said to Kṛṣṇa : "When the army is *welltrained* it does fighting work quite well; *untrained* soldiers are worthless; therefore considerate people properly *train* them". Maharṣi Nārada, asked Yudhiṣṭira among others the following questions : "Are you giving military training to the princes with the help of *military experts*".[1157] "Has your army succeeded in defeating the enemy, being *trained* by the commanders (balamukhyas)".[1158] Dhṛtarāṣṭra while speaking to Sañjaya about the qualities of his army says: "They (my soldiers) are experts in climbing, riding, quick march, beating, entering and in coming (out of a fort) and their skill in fighting on elephants, in horsemanship and in charioteering has been *tested*".[1159] In the Ādiparba[1160] of the Mahābhārata we are told how the Pāṇḍava and Kaurava brothers had their military skill *tested* by their tutor Droṇa and then gave a public demonstration of it before the people in a *military tournament*.

Kautilya's Arthaśāstra contains many references to military training. According to it "*footmen, horses, charioteers and elephants shall be given necessary training in the art of war at sunrise*, on all days but those of the conjunction (of planets); on these occasions of training the king shall ever be present and witness their exercise."[1161] Magasthenes remarks : "There are royal stables for horses and elephants and a royal magazine for the arms, because the soldier has to return his arms to the magazine and the horses and elephants to the stables." In the Arthaśāstra[1162] also we find mention of an Āyudhāgāra under a Superintendent. It was to this magazine that "soldiers had to return their arms after drill every morning. They could not move about with weapons without passport." "The Superintendent of

1155 Bālakāṇḍa, 6th sarga.
1156 Savāparva, 19th adhyāya.
1157 Ibid., 5th adhyāya.
1158 Ibid.
1159 Droṇaparva, 114th adhyāya.
1160 34th—37th adhyāyas.
1161 Arthaśāstra (R. Syāmaśāstrī's Eng. Trans.), pp. 309-10.
1162 Ibid., p. 310.

chariots shall also *examine* the efficiency in the training of troops in shooting arrows, in hurling clubs and cudgels, in wearing mail armour, in equipment, in charioteering, in fighting seated on a chariot, and in controlling chariot-horses"[1163] "The same rule shall also apply to the Superintendent of the Infantry."[1164] Kautilya[1165] also refers to the entire army (chaturaṅgabala) *trained* in the skilful handling of all kinds of weapons and in leading elephants, horses and chariots. In describing the qualities of the best army Kautilya[1166] says that it must be "*trained* in fighting various kinds of battles and skilful in handling various forms of weapons." In discussing the question whether a country with a large number of effete persons is better or a country with a small number of brave persons, Kautilya[1167] says that "a large number of effete persons is better in as much as they can be employed to do other kinds of work in the camp: to serve the soldiers fighting in the battle-fields and to terrify the enemy by its number. It is also possible to infuse spirit and enthusiasm, *discipline and training*." According to Kautilya[1168] the troubles of the army among others are:—"That which is specially *trained* to a particular kind of manœuvre and encampment; that which is *trained* in a particular movement in a particular place; and that which is blind (i. e., untrained)." Kautilya[1169] further observes: "Of armies which are *trained* either to a particular kind of manœuvre and encampment or a particular movement in a particular place, that which is *taught* a special kind of manœuvre and encampment may be taken to fight but not the army whose way of making encampment and marches is only suited to a particular place." Again, "of troops that have lost their leader or which are not *trained*, those that have lost their leader may be taken to fight under the leadership of a different person but not the troops which are not *trained*."[1170] Kautilya[1171] also refers to the army of kṣhatriyas "*trained* in the art of wielding weapons." He also refers to "*trained* men"[1172] as also to "men who are *trained* to fight in desert tracts,

---

1163 Ibid., p. 175. 1164 Ibid., 1165 Ibid., p. 176.
1166 Ibid., p. 321. 1167 Ibid.
1168 Ibid., p. 405. 1169 Ibid., p. 407.
1170 Ibid. 1171 Ibid., p. 417. 1172 Ibid., p. 422.

forests, valleys or plains"[1173] and to "those who are trained to fight from ditches or height during day and night."[1174] "The pay of a *trained* soldier" according to Kautilya[1175] "was 500 paṇas per annum."

The Śukranītisāra also contains many references to military training. Thus we are told that "armies are of two kinds untrained and trained."[1176] "The *trained* army is that which is skilled in vyuhas or military tactics, the opposite is the untrained."[1177] Śukra also refers to "watchmen *well-trained* in the use of arms and weapons."[1178] He further says: "the *un-trained*, inefficient and the raw recruit are all like bales of cotton. The wise should appoint them to other tasks beside warfare."[1179] "The men, however, can overpower the enemy with a small but *well-trained* army."[1180]

Parades were held twice every day under the supervision of the head of 100 soldiers. Śukrāchārya says: "The man who trains up the soldiers in the morning and in the evening in military parades and who knows the art of warfare as well as the characteristics of battle-fields is the Śatānika."[1181] According to Śukra the king should divide the day and night into thirty muhūrtas[1182] and spend one muhūrta (i. e., 48 minutes) over the *military exercises of regiments.*[1183] Again while discussing the physical advantages and disadvantages of various regions from the military standpoint he says: [1184] "That country is excellent in which there are facilities for the regular parade and exercises of one's own soldier.

Śukrāchārya has also pointed out the *proper method of developing the various methods of military strength*—(1) physical, (2) moral and (3) intellectual. Says he: "Strength of physique is to be promoted in the interest of hand-to-hand fights by means of tussles between peers, exercises, parades and adequate food. The king should promote

---

[1173] Ibid., p. 444.
[1174] Ibid.
[1175] Ibid., p. 308.
[1176] Śukranītisāra, Ch., IV., line 19.
[1177] Ibid., line 24.
[1178] Ibid., Ch., I., line 577.
[1179] Ibid. Ch., IV., lines 356-57.
[1180] Ibid., line 362.
[1181] Ibid., Ch., II., lines 286-87.
[1182] Ibid. Ch., I., line 571.
[1183] Ibid., Ch., I., line 567.
[1184] Ibid., Ch., IV., lines 454-55.

the strength of valour and prowess by means of hunting excursions against tigers (and big games) and exercises among heroes and valorous people with arms and weapons. The strength of the army is to be increased by good payments, that of arms and weapons by penances and regular exercises and that of intelligence by the companionship of (or intercourse with) the men learned in the śāstras."[1185]

"The *military regulations*" according to Śukrāchārya "should be communicated to the soldiers every eighth day."[1186] "The king" says he "should daily make the soldiers hear of the virtues that promote valour and witness the musical and dancing performances that also tend to augment prowess."[1187] That the troops[1188] and the military officers[1189] had their appropriate uniforms is evident from Śukranītisāra. Śukra even lays down rules about *tidiness and careful handling of arms and uniforms as items of military discipline.* Says he: "They (the troops) should keep the arms, weapons and uniforms quite bright (and ready for use)."[1190]

According to Śukra "full pay is to be granted to those who are *trained* soldiers. Half pay is to be given to those who are *under military training*."[1191]

According to him "the king should every morning and evening exercise himself with elephants, horses, chariots and other conveyances. And he should learn as well as teach the military arrangements of soldiers."[1192] In another place Śukra says: "The king should always practise military parades with the troops and strike the objective by means of missiles at the stated hours."[1193] In yet another place[1194] he says that the king should make the children of his family proficient in the science of archery (Dhanurveda) and in the feats of arms (Sauryavidyā). The terms 'Dhanurveda' and 'Sauryavidyā' probably refer to the theoretical and applied branches of military education.

1185 Ibid., Ch. IV. section VII., lines 32-37.

1186 Ibid., line 768.

1187 Ibid., Ch. V., lines 183-84.

1188 Ibid., Ch. IV., Section VII. line 775.

1189 Ibid., Ch. II., line 296.

1190 Ibid., Ch. IV., section VII., line 775.

1191 Ibid., lines 786-87.

1192 Ibid., Ch. I., lines 663-64.

1193 Ibid., Ch. IV., section VII., lines 779-80.

1194 Ibid., Ch. II. lines 43-46.

King Hemaṅgadā of the Kalingas bore scars on his forearm on account of the constant practice in throwing arrows.[1195] Practice of archery by King Daśaratha is also referred to in Raghuvaṃsam.[1196] We are also told of the hands of princes whose skin had become hard by the constant friction of the bow-string.[1197] Bāṇa[1198] also describes the stout forearm of Kumāragupta, a Mālava prince as "marked by the bow-string's scar". Bāṇa[1199] describes Harṣa as more delighting in the bow than Droṇa, more unerring with the arrow than Aśwatthāmā".

Even at the time of Hiuen Tsang's visit "the national guard are heroes of choice valour and as the profession is hereditary, they become adepts in military tactics.........They are perfect experts with all the implements of war *having been drilled* in them for generations".[1200]

Among the Rajputs, the youthful candidates were initiated to military fame by the ceremony of Kharg-bandāī which took place when the young Rajput was considered fit to bear arms. At the ceremony the young warrior was presented with a lance and his sword was buckled to his side.[1201] From Kalhaṇa's Rājataraṅgiṇī[1202] we find that Astrapūjā was prevalent in Kashmere in the reign of King Kalasa. Astrapūjā consists of certain rites in honour of the sword and other weapons as are performed to the present day by the Rajputs of the Dogrā country.[1203] In the Mahābhārata[1204] we find Viṣṇu advocating the worship of the sword (kharga).

William Ward referring to a work in Sanskrit on the military arts called Dhanurveda, says: "It was contrary to the laws of war to smite a warrior overcome by another or one who had turned his back or who was running away; or one fearful or he who had asked for quarter or he who had declined further fighting or one unarmed; or a single charioteer who had alone survived in the engagement: or one deranged; or females, children or old men".[1205] There were certain rules also with

---

1195 Raghuvaṃśam VI. 56.
1196 IX. 63.
1197 Ibid., XI. 40.
1198 Harṣacharita—Cowell and Thomas, p. 120.
1199 Ibid., p. 63.
1200 Watters—Yuan Chwang, Vol. I., p. 171.
1201 Tod—Annals of Rājasthān, pp. 63, 512.
1202 V. 246.
1203 Stein—The chronicles of Kashmere by Kalhaṇa, Vol. I., p. 289 foot-note.
1204 Śāntiparva, 166th adhyāya.
1205 A View of the Hindus, II. 461.

regard to combats. In fighting for instance with the club or mace, it was unlawful to strike below the navel. The spirit of chivalry thus inculcated must have set before these young soldiers a high ideal of valour and virtue.

But in the later Mediæval Hindu period, Hindu intelligence seems to have revelled more in the study of poetics and dramaturgy than in the more necessary study of the art of war. The army consisted chiefly of the quotas furnished by the Sāmantas. Such a feudal army cannot be relied on either in respect of numbers or of efficiency. The attention and affluence of kings were bestowed more upon court-poets than upon generals; the stage attracted the people more than the camp. Moreover, owing to the recrudescence of the doctrine of Ahiṃsā due to the rise of new Vaiṣṇavism and the progress and popularity of Jainism, of Lingayat and other sects, the great body of the people with the exception of the Rajputs gave up animal diet and accepted the non-slaughter of animals as a binding religious duty. Thus they became unfit as well as unwilling to fight.[1206] There are no doubt examples of Brahmin and even brave Jaina generals and soldiers in this period but the generality of the people being unaccustomed to fight and becoming by their food unagressive and docile when the Rajputs failed, all the Hindu kingdoms from the Sutlez to the Brahmaputra and from the Himalayas to the Vindhyas succumbed and almost willingly submitted to the Moslem yoke within the short period of a quarter and a century.

§ 3. Commercial education.

The vaiśyas represented the mass of the people at large from which, the two upper classes were recruited.[1207] They along with the brāhmaṇas and the kṣhatriyas were to be initiated with the sacred thread as a preliminary to entering upon the study of the Veda which was to

---

1206 Marco Polo remarks: "They (the people of the country) are most wretched soldiers. They will kill neither beast, nor bird nor anything that hath life" (George B. Parks—Travels of Marco Polo, p. 276.

1207 Compare Śatapatha Brāhmaṇa 11. 2. 7. 16; 12. 7. 3. 8; Fick, p. 163; Senart—Castes, p. 153; and Oldenburg in Z. D. M. G. Vol. Li., p. 280.

last at least twelve years.[1208] The later age at which the vaisyas were supposed to start their schooling may be taken to indicate that they were not expected to attain to the same proficiency in Vedic learning as the young novice for priesthood. Moreover, with regard to the vaiśyas trade, rearing cattle and agriculture were regarded as their special pursuits[1209] and in fitting themselves for these, they would have less benefit from the Vedic schools than even the kṣhatriyas.

Therefore, for the vaiśya boy there was a nice system of commercial education. Thus in the Mahāvagga[1210] we are told of three professions—lekhā, gaṇanā and rūpa. The Hātigumphā inscription of Khāravela, king of Kalinga also refers to these branches of learning.[1211] Lekhā signifies the art of writing which includes not only the niceties of style and diction but also the different forms of correspondence[1212] as will be seen from Ch. X. of the Adhyakṣa-prachāra of Kautilya's Arthaśāstra which in its concluding verse tells us that there were not one but many verses on the subject. Kautilya[1213] thus tell us :

" Writs are of great importance to kings, in as much as treaties and ultimata leading to war depend upon writs..............................

" As to a writ addressed to a lord (īśwara) it shall contain a polite mention of his country, his possessions, his family and his name; and as to that addressed to a common man (anīśwara) it shall make a polite mention of his country and name.

" Having paid sufficient attention to the caste, family, social rank, age, learning (śruta), occupation, property, character (śīla), blood-relationship of the addresse, as well as to the place and time of writing, the writer shall form a writ befitting the position of the persen addressed.

1208 Gautama I; Āpastamva I. 1; Manu X. 1.

1209 Manu X. 79.

1210 S. B. E., XIII. p. 201ff.

1211 Lekha rūpa gaṇanā vyavahāra vidhiviśāradena sarvavidyāvadātena. Compare—Muddagaṇanasankhalekhaśilpatthanesu in the Milindā-Pañha, 59, 13.

1212 Compare ' correspondents ' in Jātaka No. 96.

1213 Arthaśāstra (R. Śyāmaśāstrī's Eng. Trans.), pp. 80-85.

" Arragement of subject-matter (arthakrama), relevancy (sambandha) completeness, sweetness, dignity, and lucidity are the necessary qualities of a writ.

" The act of mentioning facts in the order of their importance is arrangement.

" When subsequent facts are not contradictory to facts just or previously mentioned and so on till the completion of the letter, is termed relevancy.

" Avoidance of redundancy or deficiency in words or letters; impressive description of subject-matter by citing reasons, examples and illustrations; and the use of appropriate and suitably strong words (aśrantapada) is completeness.

" The description in exquisite style of a good purport with a pleasing effect is sweetness.

" The use of words other than colloquial (agrāmya) is dignity.

" The use of well-known words is lucidity..

" The word "iti" is used to indicate the completion of a writ; and also to indicate an oral message as in the phrase " vāchikamasyeti," " an oral message along with this writ."

" Calumniation, commendation, inquiry, narration, request, refusal, censure, prohibition, command, conciliation, promise of help, threat and persuasion are the thirteen purposes for which writs are issued........

" Also writs of information, of command and of gift; likewise writs of remission, of licence, of guidance, of reply and of general proclamation are the varieties..

" Clumsiness, contradiction, repetition, bad grammar and mis-arrangement are the faults of a writ.

" Black and ugly leaf and uneven and uncoloured writing cause clumsiness (akānti).

" Subsequent portion disagreeing with previous portion of a letter, causes contradiction (vyāghāta).

" Stating for a second time what has already been said above is repetition.

" Wrong use of words in gender, number, time, and case is bad grammar (apaśabda).

" Division of paragraphs (varga) in unsuitable places, omission of necessary division of paragraphs and violation of any other necessary qualities of a writ constitute misarrangement (samplava).

" Having followed all sciences and having fully observed forms of writing in vogue, these rules of writing royal writs have been laid down by Kautilya in the interest of Kings."

Viṣṇu Saṃhitā[1214] lays down thirteen sūtras for the writing of documents which he classifies under three heads. These documents must have distinct, clear letters, page-marks and a seal affixed thereto.[1215] Śukrāchārya says: " Documents are of two kinds—for describing works or deeds and keeping accounts of income and expenditure. Each however has been greatly diversified through varieties of usage and practice ".[1216] He describes fifteen kinds of business and legal documents,[1217] the deed of compromise,[1218] the documents of private nature like kṣemapatra and vāṣāpatra.[1219] " The documents for keeping accounts are of various kinds according to the differences in amount, great and small, values and measurements ".[1220]

In this connection we may well refer to the Kharosthi inscriptions and documents that have been recovered from a large area in S. E. Turkisthan from Niya to the extremity of the Lobnor region.[1221] These may be conveniently divided into five classes according to the materials on which they were written: (1) documents on wooden tablets, with clay seals on some of them (2) documents on leather (3) paper documents (4) writings on silk (5) inscriptions on frescoes of shrines.

1214 Ch. VII.

1215 Ibid., Ch. VII. 12.

1216 Śukranītisāra, Ch. II., lines 599-600.

1217 Ibid., lines 601-28.

1218 Ibid., lines 629-30.

1219 Ibid., lines 637-40.

1220 Ibid., lines 643-44.

1221 Kharosthi Inscriptions discovered by Sir Aurel Stein in Chinese Turkisthan. 2 Vols. Transcribed and Edited by A. M. Boyer.

The interest of the first three classes lie in the fact that they are of an altogether secular character and are written in a sort of Prakrit dialect. Therein we find official advice as to the decision of different disputes or other instructions to the local officials: deeds of agreement, bonds and similar legal instruments; records of accounts, or lists, public or private; letters of information (technically known as vimnadi—lekha) etc. Similar documents on wood and paper in Chinese have been recovered from different sites in E. Turkisthan[1222] some of which have been published by M. Chavannes.[1223] Similar records on wood and paper in Tibetan[1224] have been recovered from the Miran and Mazartagh sites by Sir A. Stein. Documents of a similar nature in Khotanese[1225] and Uigurish[1226] have also been found. Documents of a similar nature are still use in Eastern Turkisthan as we know from a few extracts in R. B. Shaw's Sketch of the Turki language.

Now one may ask the question, from which country this particular mode of composing letters, both official and private, was first introduced in the far off region of Central Asia. This is not the place to discuss the much disputed theory about the possibility of an early immigration from India to this part of Asia as found in legends[1227] or to find out how far the traditional tales about Khotan handed down by the Tibetans about the invasion of Soked (Saketa) by Li (Khotan) is based on fact.[1228] But it is certain that the discovery in the Lobnor region of records which are not only written in an alphabet used in India—for Kharosthi is essentially the alphabet of Gāndhāra—but also in an Indian dialect viz., Prakrit, showing the use of this foreign language for purposes of administration even at the very threshold of China cannot be well-accounted for by these traditional tales.

1222 Serindia, General Index, pp. 15-20 and Ancient Khotan, App. A.

1223 Ibid., p. 1329.

1224 Rev. A. H. Francke, Tibetan Documents from Chinese Turkisthan, J. R. A. S. 1914, p. 37ff.

1225 Hœrnle, Reports 1902, Pt. II., p. 36ff.

1226 Serindia, pp. 84, 1175; Gruenwedel.........Bericht. p. 181ff.

1227 Ancient Khotan, I. p. 156.

1228 Sten Konow. S. B. A. W., 1916, p. 820 and J. R. A. S., 1914, p. 339ff.

But the existence of the Kushana empire which included both Chinese Turkisthan and N. W. India and the extension of Buddhism into the heart of Central Asia by this Empire seem to supply a satisfactory answer to our question. The stereotyped complimentary phrases used in the Kharosthi documents are pre-eminently Indian and sometimes Buddhistic in nature. Stein has also noticed how the style of writing in these records follows closely the instructions given in the Kashmerian manual Lokaprakāśa.[1229] It seems certain, therefore, that like the script and the language the mode of composing these letters, official and private, was introduced from India and probably from the N. W. parts.

The word 'gaṇanā' for similar reasons cannot mean 'arithmetic' but 'accounts,' corresponding to 'gaṇanākhya' of Kautilya. Even in later times this word had this meaning and we thus find the term 'gaṇanāpati' used by Kalhaṇa in his Rājataraṅgiṇī[1230] and understood correctly by Dr. Stein[1231] to denote "Head of Account Office." Kautilya[1232] says:

"The superintendent of accounts shall have the Accountants office constructed with doors facing either the North or the East, with seats (for clerks) kept apart and with shelves of *account-books* well-arranged.

"Therein the number of several departments; the description of the work carried on and of the results realised in the several manufactories (karmānta); the amount of profit, loss, expenditure, delayed earnings, the amount of vyāji (premia in kind or cash) realised,—the status of government agency employed, the amount of wages paid, the number of free labourers engaged (viṣṭi) pertaining to the investment of capital on any work; likewise in the case of gems and commodities of superior or inferior value, the rate of their price, the rate of their barter, the counter-weights (pratimāna) used in weighing them, their number, their weight and their cubical measure, the history of customs, professions and transactions of countries, villages, families, and corporations, the gains in the form of gifts to the King's

---

1229 Ancient Khotan I, p. 365, n. 8.

1230 V. 26.

1231 The Chronicles of Kashmere, Vol. 1. p. 189.

1232 Arthaśāstra (R. Śyamaśāstrī's Eng. Trans.), pp. 69-72.

courtiers, their title to possess and enjoy lands, remission of taxes allowed to them and payment of provisions and salaries to them; the gains to the wives and sons of the king in gems, lands, prerogatives and provisions made to remedy evil portents; the treaties with issues of ultimatum to and payments of tribute from, or to friendly or inimical kings—all these shall be regularly entered in prescribed *registers*.

"From these books, the superintendent shall furnish the accounts as to the forms of work in hand, of works accomplished, part of works in hand, of receipts, of expenditure, of net balance and of tasks to be undertaken in each of the several departments.

"To supervise works of high, middling and low description, superintendents with corresponding qualifications shall be employed ...."

"Accounts shall be submitted in the month of Āṣāṛdha.................

"When an accountant has not prepared the table of daily accounts (akṛtāhorūpaharam), he may be given a month more (for its preparation) ....

"If an accountant has to write only a small portion of the accounts pertaining to net revenue, he may be allowed five nights to prepare it."

In chapter II.[1233] of his Śukranītisāra, Śukrachārya also describes the *technique of keeping accounts.*

It is equally interesting to find Kautilya mentioning '*audit*'[1234] and 'examination of accounts'[1235] among the duties of the Collector-General. He also refers to *checking the accounts* kept by an accountant as the duty of the superintendent of Accounts. Says he: "The table of daily accounts submitted by him (an accountant) along with the net revenue shall be checked with reference to the regulated form of of righteous transactions and precedents and by applying such arithmetical processes as addition, subtraction, inference and by espionage. It shall also be verified with reference to (such division of times as) days, five nights, pakṣas, months, four-months and the year. The

---

[1233] Lines 747-73.

[1234] Arthaśāstra (R. Syāmaśastrī's Eng. Trans.), p. 67.

[1235] Ibid., p. 68.

receipt shall be verified with reference to the place and time pertaining to them, the form of their collection (i. e., capital, share), amount of the present and past produce, the person who has paid it, the person who caused its payment, the officer who fixed the amount payable and the officer who received it. The expenditure shall be verified with reference to the cause of the profit from any source in the place and time pertaining to each item, the amount payable, the amount paid, the person who ordered the collection, the person who remitted the same, the person who delivered it and the person who finally received it. Likewise the net revenue shall be verified with reference to the place, time and source pertaining to it, its standard of fineness and quality and the persons who are employed to guard the deposits and magazines (of grains, etc)."[1236]

The word 'rūpa' is taken by Professor Rhys Davids to mean 'money-changing' and by Dr. Buhler 'commercial and agricultural arithmetic.' But as Professor D. R. Bhāṇḍārkār[1237] has pointed out, in Chapter XII. of Adhyakṣa-Prachāra of Kautilya's Arthaśāstra, Kautilya speaks of 'rūpya-rūpa' and 'tāmra-rūpa' which cannot but signify silver and copper coins respectively. He also signifies an officer 'rūpa-darśaka," the examiner of coins, so that rūpa must be the science of coinage, a study of which is essentially necessary for a stable home and foreign trade.

Manu also lays down an ambitious scheme of commercial education as part of the education of the vaiśya. Says he: "(The vaiśya must possess the knowledge of) defects or excellences of articles, the good or evil traits of countries, profits or losses in manufactured articles............ He must know the wages of artisans and workmen and languages of different races of men, shall be able to forecast the increase or decrease in the prices, and amelioration and deterioration in the quality of an article at a particular place and time as well as the mode of selling and buying."[1238] Thus Manu's curriculum of commercial education for the vaiśya includes rudiments of commercial geography, arithmetic and some languages as well as the practical details of trade.

[1236] Ibid., p. 72. [1237] Ancient Indian Numismatics. [1238] Manu IX. 331-32.

In the Lokaprakāśa[1239] of Kṣemendra (middle of the eleventh century) we find a large number of forms for commercial contracts, huṇḍikas (bills of exchange), bonds, official orders etc. In these forms the use of the word dīnnāra (also written dinar) in the technical sense of 'cash' is extremely common. In Kalhaṇa's Rājataraṅgiṇī[1240] the terms "śreyas" and "aśreyas" are used as merchantile terms, corresponding to our 'profit' and 'loss' or 'credit' and 'debit.'[1241] Kautilya [1242] also refers to bills of exchange (ādeśa). Rājataraṅgiṇī[1243] also refers to such bills of exchange (huṇḍika). It is unnecessary to enumerate here all the numerous passages of the Lokaprakāśa in which references to commercial contracts etc., are met with. It will suffice to refer the reader to the quotations given in Professor A. Weber's Indische Studien[1244] and to the formulæ of a contract which is reproduced below as a typical example :[1245]

"Deyaṃ śrī prāpte sati biṣaya Jayavaneya (the modern Zevan) dām (ara) amukenāmuktaputreṇa keeṃ vā neśāne sati dharmataḥ dīnārasahasradaśake anke di (10,000, etc) dīnārā adyārabhya saṃvatsaraṃ tāvat prāptatavāt dī (nnāra) sahasra ekaṃ nyāyaprāyaparihāre sati ruddhā nibandhaṃ nyāytāṇḍatayā(?) yasya hasteyam huṇḍikā tasyaivaṃ."

The text of Kṣemendra represents a strange mixture of the usual Koṣa and a practical hand-book. Though a great deal of the information given in it is decidedly old and probably from the hand of our well-known Kṣemendra, there are unmistakable proofs both in the form and contents of the book, showing that it has undergone considerable alterations and additions down even to the seventeenth century. And it is just this circumstance which strengthens the assumption that the work had remained for centuries in uninterrupted use as a practical manual.

1239 Prakāśa II. and IV.

1240 VIII. 136.

1241 Stein—The Chronicles of Kashmere, Vol. II., p. 12 foot-note.

1242 Arthaśāstra (R. Śyāmaśāstrī's Eng. Trans.), pp. 189, 227.

1243 V. 266, 302.

1244 XVIII. pp. 289-412.

1245 For a similar huṇḍika form *see* Ibid., p. 342.

It may be argued with regard to the teaching of these commercial subjects that at first they were learnt by the boy from his father in the actual course of business and probably amounted in most cases to little more than the minimum which would be necessary for the successful carrying on of the particular trade in which he was engaged. Thus knowledge of the various languages of men need not have meant more than a slight acquaintance with the speech of foreigners with whom trade brought him into touch, picked up in his intercourse with them and a knowledge of the good or evil traits of countries would be gathered in the same way. Thus the commercial education of the young vaiśya would, at the earliest period at any rate, be domestic and he would learn something from his father in the actual course of business.

But evidences regarding the existence of trade-guilds with an Alderman (Jeṭṭaka, Prathama Kulika or Seṭṭhi) at its head are so copious in ancient Indian literature[1246] and inscriptions[1247] that it is not unlikely that on the analogy of the craft-guilds they might have made some provision for the education of commercial apprentices. For, Kalhaṇa in his Rājataraṅgiṇī clearly refers to the training of merchants and clerks under a teacher. Says he: "Courtesans, the official (kāyastha) the clerk (divira) and the merchant, being (all) deceitful by nature, are (in this respect) superior to a poisoned arrow that they have been *trained under a teacher's advice*."[1248] Kautilya in his Arthaśāstra

---

1246 Jātaka I. 368; II. 295; Gautama XI. 21; Chullavagga VI. 41., S. B. E., XX. p. 179; Mahāvagga VIII., 1-16ff., S. B. E. XVII., p. 181ff; Kautilya's Arthaśāstra (R. Śyāmaśāstrī's Eng. Trans.), pp. 190, 228.

1247 Pehoa Inscription, Ep. Ind. Vol. I. p. 184; Harṣa Stone Inscription, Ep. Ind. Vol. II. pp. 116ff; Belgaum Inscription, Ep. Ind. Vol. XIII. p. 18; Inscription of the tenth year of Jātavarman Vīra Pāṇḍya, Govt. Epigraphist's Report, 1915, p. 104; Inscription from Yewur, Ep. Ind. Vol. XII. p. 273; Niḍagundi Inscription, Ep. Ind. Vol. XIII. p. 12; Junnar Inscription, Luders No. 1180; Also Ep. Indica, IV. p. 296, foot-note 2; Ibid., V. p. 9; Ibid., IV. 290; Ep. Carnatica, Vol. VII. S. 118; Govt. Epigraphist's Report, 1913, pp. 99-100; Ibid., 1919, p. 5, No. 10; Ibid., 1913, p. 21, No. 141; Ibid., 1915, p. 48, No. 478; Ibid., 1916, p. 121; Ibid., 1919. p. 18, No. 216; The clay-seals discovered at Basārh, Arch. Surv. Report, 1903-04, p. 104. Seal Inscriptions discovered in Vaiśālī, Ibid., 1913-14, p. 122.

1248 Stein—The Chronicles of Kashmere, Vol. II., p. 12.

refers not only to men "possessed of the knowledge of the sciences dealing with agriculture and the plantation of bushes and trees (Kṛṣitantragulma-vṛkṣāyurvedajñaḥ)" [R. Śyāmśāstrī's Eng. Trans., p. 142] but also to men "who are *trained* in such sciences" (Ibid.).

Moreover, it is to be noted that there exist in India at the present time what are called Mahājani schools. These exist in several market-towns where the Mahājans or local traders would combine in giving employment to a teacher who would teach their sons writing and accounts, so as to prepare them to follow their own calling. These schools have probably existed from old times but like so many things in India, it is difficult to say whether they are really very ancient or not. But whenever they were started, it must have been because the traders found it more satisfactory for a boy to have acquired some education before he began actual work in the market.

§ 4. TECHNICAL EDUCATION.

The śūdras, it is claimed, have no right to approach the sacred fire (i. e., perform sacrifice) or to read the sacred texts. There are, however, passages in the early texts which clearly assert these rights.[1249]

0249 The passages are :—

(1) "Yathemāṃ bāchaṃ kalyāṇī mā badāni janevyaḥ
Brahmarājnyāvyāṃ śūdrāya chāryāya cha swāya chāraṇāya cha
Priyodevānāṃ dakṣiṇāyai dāturiha bhūyāsamayaṃ me kāmaḥ samṛdhyatāmupāmādo namatu".

—Yajurveda XXVI 2.

(2) "Satyamahaṃ gavīraḥ kābyenasatyanjātenāsmi jātavedā
Na me dāso na me Āryo mahitwā bataṃ mīmāya yadahaṃ dhariṣye."

—Atharvaveda V. 2. 11.

(3) "Brahma bai stomānaṃ tribṛit, kṣhatraṃ pañchadaśo, biśaḥ saptadaśaḥ śūdro barṇa ekabiṃśaḥ."

—Aitareya Brāhmaṇa IV. 8. 1.

(4) "Ahīti brāhmaṇasyāgahyādrabeti vaiśyasya cha rājanya bandhośchādhābeti śūdrasya"

—Śatapatha Brāhmaṇa I. 1. 1. 4. 19.

(5) "Habiṣkṛdehītiḥ brāhmaṇasya habiṣkṛidāgahīti rājanyasya habiṣ kridā drabeti vaiśysya habiṣkṛdādhābeti śūdrasya prathamaṃ bāba sarbeṣām"

—Āpastamva Śrautasūtra I. 19.

Some of the commentators,[1250] however, have entirely repudiated the right of the śūdras to Vedic study and liturgy. Nevertheless, even these authorities have frankly admitted these rights of the Rathakāras and and the Niṣādas who according to these teachers themselves, were not included in the three higher classes or are even non-Aryans as proved by Paṇḍit Vidhaśekhara Bhaṭṭāchārya.[1251]

---

(6) " Achāntodakāya gauriti nāpita strīrbruyāt muñchagā baruṇa pāśāt. Tameba nāpitaṃ muñcha gāmiti mantraṃ bruyāt. "
—Govila Gṛhyasūtra IV. 10.

(7) " Tathaibābritā niṣādasthapatiṃ yājayet ".—Āpastamva Śrautaśutra IX. 14.

(8) " Śūdrā vājasaneyinaḥ "—Vaśiṣṭha.

(9) " Śūdrobā charita brataḥ "—Gautama.

(10) " Falārthatwāt karmaṇaḥ śāstraṃ sarvādhikāraṃ syāt. "
—Jaiminī's Pūrva Mīmāṃsa VI. 1.

(11) " Kartūbā śruti saṃyogādbidhiḥ kātarsnena gamyte ".
—Jaiminī's Pūrva Mīmāṃsā VI. 1.

(12) " Sthapatirniṣādaḥ syāt śabda sāmarthāt. "—Jaiminī's Pūrva Mīmāṃsā VI. 1.

(13) Śabaraswāmī thus sums up the views of Bādari: " So it is clear that Bādari thought that everyone had a right to the scriptures ",
—Mīmāṃsā sūtra VI. 1. 27, 29.

(14) " Śrābayechchaturo barṇān kṛtwābrāhmaṇamagrataḥ Vedasyādhyayanam hidaṃ tachcha kāryam mahat smṛtam. "
—Mahābhārata, Śāntiparva, 328th adhyāya.

(15) " Chatwāro barṇāḥ yajñamimam bahanti "
—Mahābhbārata, Banaparva, 104th adhyāya.

(16) " Śūdrānām duṣṭakarmaṇāmupanayanam ".—Pāraṣkara Gṛhyasūtra II. 60.

(17) " Māskarin observes: " Thus the upanayana is only for a savarna, an ambaṣṭha and a niṣāda. It is said in a smṛti: ' Having initiated a savarṇa one should teach him the science of archery; having initiated an ambaṣṭha, the science of medicine; and having initiated a niṣāda the training of elephants. ' "

(18) " One should initiate also a well-qualified śūdra and teach him (medical science), but omitting Vedic mantras
—Suśrūta-Saṃhitā (Nirṇayasāgara edition, I. 2. 5.).

(19) " Śūdrānāṃ brahmacharyatwaṃ munivih kaiśchidiṣyate ".—Yājñabālkya.

(20) " Vidyārathaṃ brahmachārī syāt sarbeṣāṃ pālane gṛhī "—Śukranīti.

1250 Kātyāyana Śrautasūtra I. 1. 6.; Āpastaṃva's Yajñaparivāṣasūtra I. 2; Jaiminī's Mīmāṃṣāsūtra VI. 1. 25-38, etc.

1251 The Viśwabhāratī Quarterly, October 1923, pp. 270-77.

We all know that the vaisyas and the śūdras never formed any homogeneous people but remained a conglomeration of different groups of people following different professions and different rules of life. The Vedic literature alone supplies the names of a number of functional groups which correspond to recognised castes of the present day.[1252] In course of time some of these (functional groups) developed into guilds. The Mūga-Pakkha Jātaka[1253] refers to the existence of eighteen such guilds. It is not possible to determine what these conventional eighteen guilds were, but we get a considerably greater number by collecting together all scattered references in literature and inscriptions—(1) cultivators [1254] (2) traders,[1255] including caravan traders (3) herdsmen[1256] (4) money-lenders[1257] (5) workers in wood[1258] (6) workers in metal including gold and silver[1259] (7) Leather workers[1260] (8) workers fabricating hydraulic engines (odayṃtrika)[1261] (9) bamboo-workers (vāsakara)[1262] (10) braziers (kāsakara)[1263] (11) weavers[1264] (2) potters[1265] (13) oil-millers[1266] (14) painters[1267] (15) corn-dealers (dhaṃñika)[1268] (16) garland-makers and flower-sellers[1269] (17) mariners[1270] (18) robbers and freebooters[1271] (19) forest-police who guard the caravans[1272] (20) workers in stone[1273] (21) ivory-workers[1274] (22) jewellers[1275] (23) rush-workers and basket-makers[1276] (24) dyers[1277] (25) fisher folk[1278] (26) butchers[1279] (27) barbers and shampooners.[1280]

1252 Vedic Index, II. pp. 585-86.

1253 Jātaka VI. 1; compare Jātaka VI. 427.

1254 Gautama XI. 21.

1255 Gautama XI. 21; Jātaka I. 368; II. 295.

1256 Gautama XI. 21.

1257 Ibid.

1258 Jātaka VI. 427.

1259 Ibid.

1260 Ibid.

1261 Nāsika Inscription (Luders No. 1137; Ep. Ind. VIII., pp. 82-86.

1262 Junnar Inscription (Luders No. 1165.

1263 Ibid.

1264 Nāsika Inscription (Luders No. 1137; Ep. Ind. VIII., pp. 82-86.

1265 Ibid.

1266 Ibid.

1267 Jātaka VI. 427.

1268 Luders No. 1180.

1269 Jātaka III. 405.

1270 Jātaka IV. 137.

1271 Jātaka III. 388; IV. 430.

1272 Jātaka II. 335.

1273 Rhys Davids—Buddhist India, pp. 90ff.

1274 Ibid.

1275 Ibid.

1276 Ibid.

1277 Ibid.

1278 Ibid.

1279 Ibid.

1280 Ibid.

These guilds provided for an efficient system of technical education by their apprentice system. The laws relating to the apprenticeship are thus stated by Nārada :[1281]

" Swaśilpa michchhannārhatuṃ bāndhabānāṃanugyayā,
Āchāryasya basedante kālam kṛtwā suniśchitam,
Āchāryaḥ śikṣayedenaṃ swagṛha dattasoganam,
Nachānyatkārayet karma putrabatchchainamācharet,
Śikṣayantamadṛṣtaṃ ya āchāryaṃ saṃparityajet,
Balādbāsayitabyaḥ syādbadhabandhaicha sorhati,
Śikṣitopi kutaṃ kālamantebāsosamāpabruyāt,
Tatra karma cha yat kuryādāchāryasyaibatatfalam,
Gṛhitaśilpaḥ samaye kṛtwāchāchāryapradakṣiṇām,
Saktitaśchānumānyai namantebāso nibarttyante
Betanaṃ bā yadi kṛtam jñatwāśiṣyasya kauśalam
Antebāso samādadyānna chānyasya gṛhe baset ".

" If a young man wishes to be initiated into the art of his own craft, with the sanction of his relations, he must go and live with a master, the duration of his apprenticeship having been fixed. The master shall teach him at his own house and feed him. He must not employ him in work of a different description, and should treat him like a son. If one forsakes a master, who instructs him properly, he may be compelled by forcible means to remain (at the master's house) and he deserves corporal punishment and confinement. Though his course of instruction be completed, an apprentice must continue to reside at the house of his master till the fixed period has expired. The profit of whatever work he may be doing there belongs to his master. When he has learnt the art of his craft within the (stipulated) period, the apprentice shall circumambulate him and return home after taking leave of him. If, however, a salary be fixed befitting his skill, the pupil should accept it and should not go to stay (i. e., accept appointment) in the house of another (craftsman)."

The above rules bring out several important and interesting features. In the first place, there was the system of indenture under

1281 V. 16-21.

which the apprentice and the master were bound to each other for a fixed period stated in the deed. As Vīramitrodaya points out, the teacher must make an agreement in this form : 'Let this apprentice stay with me so and so long.' In the second place, the indenture emphasises equally and fairly the obligation of both the master and the apprentices. As regards the obligations of the master, he had to adopt the apprentice as his own son and treat and feed him as such. He should teach him honestly; the master was competent to make him do the work strictly related to the craft he was learning but was not competent to exploit his labour or skill by employing it for purposes unconnected with it. Kātyāyana fixed a penalty upon the master for employing the apprentice in other work. "He who does not instruct the apprentice in the art and causes him to perform other work shall incur the first amercement; and the pupil may forsake him and go to another teacher, released from the indenture."[1282] The master further, should not treat the apprentice like a hired labourer but like a son, with due tenderness and affection. Equally strict were the obligations under which the apprentice was bound to his master. He was to stay at his master's house and do work pertaining to the craft of his choice. Bṛhaspati[1283] says : "Arts (consisting of) work in gold, base metals and the like and the art of dancing and the rest, are termed human knowledge and he who studies them should do work at his teacher's house." If through the master's efficient training he attains proficiency in the craft before the expiry of the period stipulated for in the indenture, he was not competent to leave the master but had to serve out his full term, cheerfully yielding to him the fruits of his labour as the reward or compensation for the saving of time effected by the superior skill of the master in teaching. Yājñabālkya[1284] says : "Even if one has learnt the art (within the prescribed time), he must live in the house of one's teacher for the full period of contract. The student desirous of learning an art, who has received his board from the teacher, must make over to the latter the fruits of his labour (during the period of

---

[1282] Colebrooke's Digest of Hindu Law, Vol. II., p. 7.

[1283] XVI. 6.

[1284] II. 187.

his pupilage)." The master was also empowered to compel the return of a runaway apprentice, whom he could flog or confine for his disobedience. Gautama[1285] says: "The apprentice may forsake his master either of his own motion (in which case he is liable to correction) or under instructions from his kinsmen who consented to his pupilage. In the latter case, the deserted master can sue the pupil's guardians for a breach of contract." According to Nārada[1286] he who deserted a teacher who had duly discharged his duty and was in no way culpable, was to be compelled to reside with him and was liable to stripes and confinement.[1287] But it was lawful for the apprentice to disobey and even desert his master by way of protest agaist any mortal sin or other heavy crime committed by the latter. This is a characteristically Hindu provision securing the moral purity of craftsmen to which modern industrial legislation is hardly sufficiently attentive. There is again another provision for the payment of a salary to the pupil adequate to his proficiency if it was desired by the master to retain his services, in which case the first claim upon his services belongs to his master.

Lastly, the pupil is recommended to be always humble before his master in the following quaint exhortation: "For science is like a river, ever advancing to a humbler level, therefore as one's knowledge grows broader and deeper one should become ever more humble towards the source of one's knowledge."[1288]

This exhortation is indeed symbolical and characteristic of the sacred and spiritual relations that normally obtained between the master craftsman and his apprentices—relations which were the direct outcome of the peculiar educational system and environment under which they worked. To these wholesome relations and specially to the superior educational efficacy of the system which produced them, is to be traced the signal success which is admitted on all hands to have

---

1285 II. 43-44.   1286 V. 19.

1287 Compare—" Atitya bañdhūn avalanghya mitrāṇi āchāryam āgachchati śiṣyadoṣāḥ " in Bhāsa; Pāñcharātra I. 18 (Droṇabākya).

1288 Nārada V. 12.

been achieved by the handicraftsmen of ancient and Mediæval India and which so largely enabled her to command for much more than a thousand years (from Pliny to Tavernier) the markets of the East as well as the West and obtained for her an easy and universally recognised pre-eminence among the nations of the world in exports and manufacturers. We are, however, more concerned with the system than its success, with the method of training than their results, the character of the educational machinery and organisation than the record of its magnificent outputs. 'The essence of the whole system is that the young craftsman is brought up and educated in the actual workshop of his master whose disciple he is. This means that the pupil stands in a peculiar relation to his master, a sacred relation of devoted personal service and attachment in which alone can the learner best imbibe and most naturally and spontaneously assimilate the special excellences of his teacher, his true inward method, even his trade secrets which can no longer be hidden from one whom he has adopted as his son. The very intimacy and depth of the personal relationship between the teacher and the taught solves substantially the difficulties of the educative process, which is impossible in the case of the busy professor at a modern technical school where he is concerned with his students for a few hours in the week and had no opportunity of associating them with his main business in which he is called upon to show his real worth and exercise his best talent. And this brings us to the other aspect of our indigenous organisation, viz., training in the actual workshop where the teaching is learnt from the very beginning in relation to real things, difficulties and problems and primarily by service, by personal attendance on the master. And it is not only technique that is learnt but something more valuable: in the workshop there is life itself, besides mere plants and tools, for, the workshop is part of a home which relieves its mechanical monotony and places the pupil in touch with life and its difficulties, human relationships, culture, and religion, whereby his heart is trained as much as his hand—a thing which is as necessary to art as mere technique.'

There is one other noticeable feature in connection with the rules of apprenticeship as explained by Nārada. It is that considerations of caste did not affect the admission of apprentices into a craft. The only consideration that mattered was the consent of the apprentice's guardian and relations. This shows that the barriers between occupations were not so fixed and rigid as those between castes. This is proved not only by the aforesaid solitary rule stated by Nārada but by the universal permissive regulation contained in all the important law-books, authorising the twice-born classes to take to an occupation of an inferior caste, in times of distress or failure to obtain a living through lawful labour.[1289] The Pali literature, moreover, is full of much interesting evidence on this point. The evidence would show that though normally the trades and crafts were organised on a hereditary basis and technical talent descended from father to son, the way was quite open to exceptions to that rule. Thus in Vinaya[1290] we find parents discussing the best profession which their son might take such as lekhā, gaṇanā and rūpa, without a reference being made to the father's trade. In the Chullavagga[1291] the vikṣus are allowed "the use of a loom and of shuttles, strings, tickets and all the apparatus belonging to a loom." We also read of brāhmaṇas as physicians,[1292] goat-herds,[1293] merchants, hunters and snake-charmers,[1294] archers and the servant of an archer who was formerly a weaver,[1295] low-caste trappers (nesādā),[1296] even cart-wrights.[1297] Jātaka No. 495 gives a long list of the various occupations followed by Brahmins. In Jātaka V. 290-93, a kṣhatriya, a king's son named Kuśa in his infatuation for Pabhāvatī, apprentices himself *incognito* in succession to the court-potter, basket-maker, florist and cook to his father-in-law without a word being said as to his loss of caste when these vagaries became known. In Jātaka IV. 84 a prince takes to trade while in IV. 169 another resigning his kingdom goes to the frontier where he dwells "with a rich merchant's family working with his own hands." Jātaka

---

1289 Gautama VII. 6; Vaśiṣṭha II. 22; Baudhāyana II. 4. 16; Viṣṇu II. 15; Manu X. 81.

1290 I. 77; IV. 128.

1291 V. 28.

1292 Jātaka IV. 361.

1293 Jātaka III. 401.

1294 Jātaka IV. 457.

1295 Jātaka III. 219; V. 127, 128; I. 356, 357.

1296 Jātaka II. 200; VI. 170.

1297 Jātaka IV. 207, 208.

IV. 156 speaks of a Brahmin who takes to trade to be better able to afford charitable gifts. Brahmins engaged personally in trading without such pretext are also mentioned.[1298] Again, we hear of a weaver looking on his handicraft as a mere make-shift and changing it off hand for that of an archer;[1299] a pious farmer and his son with equally little ado turning to the low trade of rush-weaving.[1300] 'Stories all of these, not history; nevertheless, they serve to show that social divisions and economic occupations were far from coinciding.'

Some of the Jātaka stories throw interesting sidelight on the organisation of these guilds. Though the conditions of pupilage (as given by Nārada) are not given, the apprentice in the industrial sense frequently appears in the Jātakas. Thus in Jātaka No. 97 we have a publican and his apprentice while in Kuśa Jātaka[1301] a prince apprentices himself to a potter, basket-maker, florist etc In Jātaka III. 475 we read: "Once upon a time, when Brahmadatta was reigning in Benares his son young Brahmadatta and young Mahādhana, son of a rich merchant of Benares were comrades and play-fellows and were educated in the same teacher's house. In Jātaka IV. 38 we find that the son of a poor woman of a caravan, a merchant's son and the son of a tailor in the employ of a merchant, "all grew up together and by and by went to Taxila to complete their education." In Jātaka V. 457-9 two princes received instruction in arts at the hands of the same teacher who had besides 101 pupils. Kautilya in his Arthaśāstra[1302] also refers to apprentices. The senior pupil also acts as Assistant Master (piṭṭiāchāriya). The position of a senior pupil to a Mahā-Vaḍḍhaki is indicated by Buddhaghoṣa.[1303] The relative position of a pupil to a master wood-wright is also indicated.[1304] We have also instances of fees being paid by apprentices to teachers in the Jātakas[1305] where two merchant-sons paid 2000 pieces each.

In course of time it became normal for the craftsmen of a particular trade to belong to one caste, so that the bonds which united them

---

1298 Jātaka V. 22, 471.
1299 Jātaka II. 87.
1300 Jātaka IV. 318.
1301 Jātaka No. 531.
1302 R. Śyāmaśāstri's Eng. Trans., p. 166.
1303 Aśl., 111 112.
1304 Jātaka I. 251; V. 290f.; Atthaśālini, p. 111.
1305 Jātaka IV. 224, 225; 38, 39.

became stronger and no outsider would be admitted. There were no indentures of apprenticeship and a boy would be learning the particular craft from his father and would eventually take the place of his father as a member of the guild. The system of education was thus a domestic one. The boys had practically no choice of profession and were brought up to the same trade as their father. Where the father was living and in good health he would usually train up his son and the young craftsman was, from the very beginning, trained up in the actual workshop. Moreover, fair and proper training of apprentices was assured as the father imparts industrial skill and trade-secrets to a son more willingly than any other teacher. Moreover, this system of technical education is very cheap and the lad inherits a certain amount of skill from his father and unconsciously imbibes much of the technical knowledge from the atmosphere of the particular profession in which he is brought up. Thus the training was free from the artificiality of the school-room. In the collection of jade at the Indian museum there is a large engraved bowl on which a family in the employ of the emperors of Delhi was engraved for three generations.[1306]

But when birth came to determine the whole course of a man's occupation in life, there is little chance of his capacities being always put to the best use and each profession may have to tolerate many persons who are incompetent or useless in that particular profession but who may perhaps do better in some other. Similarly, however worthy or desirable an acquisition a man may be, he cannot enter a craft-guild unless he was born to it. "A craft-guild of Mediæval Europe may expand and develop; it gives free play to artistic endeavour. But the later craft-guilds of India based on birth is an organisation of a lower type; it grows by fission." In such a craft-guild based on birth invention or originality is checked because every craftsman's social prospects are limited to the customary position of his caste. The master craftsman's teaching merely reproduces his old fashioned knowledge and does not tend to progress; he looks askance at new knowledge and new tools and refuses to be wiser than his ancestors. In the sculptures of our old caves and temples and in our woodcarving

---

1306 Birdwood—The Industrial Arts of India, p. 142.

and metal decorations we see the same figure or design repeated *ad nauseam*. As for the training of apprentices, though father is the most willing teacher he is not always the best of tutors nor is the son always the aptest of pupils. Education does not produce best results when both teachers and pupils are chosen by accidents of birth. Denying as this system does, equal opportunities to all, it often becomes the source of grave injustice to large classes of the community.

The question now presents itself how far this system of technical education discouraged the spread of liberal education among the craftsmen. As for the religious side of their education we can pretty definitely say that it was not neglected for, though persons other than the twice-born castes were in course of time excluded from the study of the Vedas they were not shut out from participation in all religious rites. To the idealistic mind of the Hindus, art and industry are the representation of one aspect of the Divinity which pervades every department of life. They therefore transcend the limitation of beauty and form in nature and attempt to represent the ideal as the only true beauty. Beauty has an absolute existence in the ideal plane and is revealed in the mind of the Hindu artist by God. The Hindu artist thus relies more upon the inward inspiration than upon any discipline in reproducing the external form. The God who is the source of all beauty, rhythm, proportion and idea is Viśwakarman. We do not mean to say that these deep thoughts were realised and consciously expressed by every craftsman; certainly not when tradition had become a mere habit. But to adopt slightly the words of Nietzsche, those who first uttered these thoughts in stone or metal and some of those who came after them, knew as well as the wisest ones about the secret of life.

In the Mahābhārata Viśwakarman is described as Lord of the arts, the carpenter of the gods, the fashioner of all ornaments, who made the celestial chariots of the deities, on whose craft men subsist and whom a great and immortal god, they actually worship. Viśwakarmā is not only worshipped by craftsmen with offerings and ritual at the beginning of their work but there are also numerous charms and songs with which he is invoked to ward off disasters and assist them in their work. The tools and implements are also worshipped as they are considered to be gifts of Viśwakarmā whom they are meant to interpret. The artisan's work is also sacred. As it is said in Manu: "The hand of the artisan is always pure." In Eastern Bengal the women of the middle class who work at the charkā worship Viśwakarmā on the first day of the Bengali year by decorating the charkā with flowers and with their own hand-drawing and giving offerings of milk, curds and cheeṛā.[1307] The weavers particularly do not work in Vijayā Daśamī, on Ekādaśī and Dvādaśī days and worship the loom, the shuttle, and the weights and measures. On the Trayodaśī day they begin work anew. The tilis, the tāmlis and gandha-baṇiyās who deal in spices worship Gandheśwarī on the Baiśākhī Pūrṇimā day with the prayer "bāṇijya bṛddhipurbaka śrīdurgāpṛtibāmo śrīdūrgāpūjāmaham kariṣye."

Coming to the literary side of the craftsman's education we find that in many arts and crafts certain sanskrit works had to be learnt by heart.[1308] These contained traditional rules relating to the particular craft, and would not only be learnt but also explained to the novice. Thus in South India there are vastuśāstrīs, who know by heart the traditional rules regulating the building of houses, who must be consulted by those who wish to erect new houses as to all the necessary details prescribed by the ancient books.[1309] From an extract from a Śilpaśāstra quoted by Dr. Coomāraswāmī in his Arts and Crafts of India and Ceylon[1310] we learn that "the śilpī should understand the Atharvaveda the thirty-two śilpaśāstras and the Vedic mantras by which the deities are invoked."

Besides this kind of literary education the Indian craftsman also came to know something of the doctrines of Hindu religion, folklore, mythology, epic and other stories that might be handed down in the family or related as the villagers gathered for gossip and discussion in the evenings or taught by some wandering mendicant, wandering scholar or temple priest.

1307 Guruvandhu Bhattāchārya's article on "Viśwakarmā vrata" in Prativā, 1320 B. S.

1308 Coomāraswāmī—Mediaeval Sinhalese Art, Ch. VI.

1309 Padfield—Hindu At Home, p. 3.

1310 Page 33.

In this connection we may well refer to the Mandasore Stone Inscription[1311] of Kumāragupta and Bandhuvarman which relates how a guild of silk-weavers, originally settled at Lāta, immigrated into the city of Daśapura attracted by the virtue of the king of that place. Here some of them learnt archery, some adopted the religious life, some learnt astrology and astronomy, some poetry, some became ascetics while others adhered to their hereditary profession of silkweaving. This inscription invalidates the notion, too generally entertained that the guilds were stereotyped close corporations of crafts busy only with their own profession and shows that "through the autonomy and freedom accorded to them by the law of the land they became a centre of strength and an abode of liberal culture and progress which made them a power and ornament of the society."[1312]

§ 5. Medical education.

In the literature of the Hindus there is a system of medicine which is certainly of great antiquity. One of the fourteen ratnas or precious gems which the gods are believed to have produced by churning the ocean was a learned physician. In the Charaka Saṃhitā[1313] we find that Brahmā taught Dakṣa the science of medicine; Dakṣa became the preceptor of the Aświn twins; they in their turn became the teachers of Indra and Indra imparted this knowledge to Bharadwāja who was sent by a conclave of sages to learn the art for the welfare of the human race. Bharadwāja had Punarvasu, Ātreya and others as disciples. Ātreya's students were Agniveśa, Bhela, Jatukarṇa, Pārāśara, Hārīta and Kṣārapaṇi. Ātreya seems to have taught through the traditional method of questions and answers; for each chapter of Hārīt Saṃhitā, written by his pupil Hārīt ends with the words "Said by Ātreya in answer to Hārīt". Śuśrūta[1314] learned the science of medicine from Divodāsa, surnamed Dhanvantarī, King of Benares at his Himalayan retreat. According to Śuśrūta,[1315] Divodāsa was the incarnation of Dhanvantarī, the celebrated physician of the gods in heaven and he was the first to propound the art of healing in this world.

1311 Fleet—Gupta Inscrptions, No. 18.

1312 R. C. Mazumdar—Corporate Life in Ancient India, second edition, p. 68.

1313 I. 1.

1314 Ibid.

1315 Ibid.

Arrian[1316] informs us in his Indica that the study of medicine among the Brahmins was in great favour. Strabo says: "The Indians do not pursue accurate knowlege in any line, except medicine".[1317] Indeed India attracted even foreign scholars in historic times who came to study medicine under Indian teachers. Thus the ministerial family of Barmak under Harun (786-808 A. D.) sent scholars to India to study medicine and pharmacology. Even in later centuries, Moslem scholars sometimes travelled for the same purposes as the emissary of the Barmak, e. g., Almuwaffak, not long before Ālberūnī's time.[1318]

That there was a proper provision for the training of a physician will be evident from the following description of a doctor who is thought fit for service in a hospital, preserved in the Nandi Purāṇa: "The doctor should be well-versed in the religious treatises, experienced, familiar with the actions of medicines, a discriminator of the colour of the roots of the herbals and well-acquainted with the proper season of raising them from the ground, *well-trained* with the qualities of the juices, (their strength and actions), śāli rice, meat and medicaments, *trained* in compounding medicines, one who knows well of the physique of men by intelligence, one who knows the temperament and the qualities of the diet, a pathologist who is not idle, well-acquainted with the remedial agents for the premonitary signs and sequelæ of disease, proficient in the requirements of time and place, well-read in the medical text-books—the Āyurveda with its eight divisions and an expert in curing diseases by domestic remedies (prepared from handful of common ingredients)".

Such medical education was imparted to students in important centres of learning like Taxila and Nālandā even in historic times. Jivaka, surnamed Komarabhachcha, who was famous for his special proficiency in the treatment of children's diseases was brought up by Prince Abhaya, son of King Bimbisāra and sent by him to Taxila for medical studies.

1316 Indica, C. 27.

1317 McCrindle: Megasthenes and Arrian, Frag. 25.

1318 Ālberūnī—An Enquiry into India (Sachau's Eng. Trans.), pp. XXXI.-XXXII.

He studied medicine there under the great ṛṣi professor Ātreya. In the Mahāvagga[1319] we are told that after seven years' study he had to undergo an examination in which he was asked to describe the medicinal use of all the vegetables, plants, creepers, grass, roots etc., that could be found within a radius of fifteen miles round the city of Taxila. Jīvaka examined them for four days and then "submitted the results informing his professor that there was hardly a single plant which did not possess some medicinal property.[1320]

Thus the study of Medicine at Taxila seems to have had both a theoretical and a practical course. The practical course included a first hand study of plants to find out their medicinal values as shown in the above account of Jīvaka's education. We may also refer in this connection to the successful surgical operations executed by Jīvaka as soon as he left Taxila on finishing his education, for, they show that he must have had a previous practical training in such difficult operations. According to Hiuen Tsang[1321] the famous monastic university of Nālandā also made provision for the teaching of medicine.

In the Mahāvagga (VIII. 26, 6 and 8) we find the *qualities of a good nurse* thus described: "There are five qualities, O bhikṣus which, when one who waits upon the sick has, he is competent to the task— when he is capable of prescribing medicines; when he does know what (diet) is good and what is not good for the patient, serving what is good and not serving what is not good for him: when he does wait upon the sick out of love, and not out of greed; when he does not revolt from removing evacuation, saliva or vomit; when he is capable of teaching, inciting, arousing and gladdening the patient with religious discourses. These are the five qualities, O bhikṣus, which, when one who waits upon the sick has, he is competent to the task." That provision was made for the training of such nurses will be evident from the following description of the staff of a hospital, found in Charaka Saṃhitā (I. XV) :— "The staff should consist of servants and companions. The servants should be good, virtuous, pure, fond, clever, generous, *well-trained in*

1319 VIII. 3.

1320 Universities in Ancient India—S. C. Das in the Hindusthan Review, March, 1906.

1321 Beal—Life of Hiuen Tsang, p. 112.

nursing, skilful in works, able to cook rice and curries well, competent to administer a bath, expert masseur, *trained* in raising and removing a patient, dexterous in making or cleaning beds, practised in the art of compounding medicines, and willing workers not likely to show displeasure to any order."

A word with regard to the Veterinary science. We have a book on Hastī-Āyurveda, dealing with the treatment of elephants written by Pālakāpya who was a veterinary surgeon in the court of Romapāda, King of Anga. In the Mahābhārata we find references to Gajasūtra, Aśwasūtra, works on elephants and horses. In the Mahābhārata[1322] Sahadeva is described to have stayed with King Virāta as a cowherd and he is made to speak of his scientific knowledge of all cattle and of the cure of their diseases. Nakula became the manager of the horses at the same court and was an expert in the Veterinary science[1323] on which he has written several works, his "Aśwa-chikitsā" being still extant.[1324] Kautilya also refers to elephant-doctors[1325] and says: "Elephant-doctors shall apply necessary medicines to elephants which, while making a journey happen to suffer from disease, over-work, rut or old age."[1326] He also refers to Veterinary surgeons[1327] and says: "Veterinary surgeons shall apply requisite remedies against undue growth or diminution in the body of horses and also change the diet of horses according to changes in the seasons."[1328] We learn from Edict No. II of Aśoka that he established throughout his own Empire and the frontier kingdoms hospitals for the treatment of men and beasts alike. On the Veterinary science there are the works of Yogamañjari of Vardhamāna, Aśwavaidyaka of Dipāṅkara and Aśwāyurveda of Gana. A Brahmin Salotor by name wrote a book on the Veterinary art in Sanskrit which was translated into Persian under the title of "Kurrat-ul-mulk" by order of Ghays-ud-din Muhammad

---

1322 Birātaparva, 3rd adhyāya.

1323 Ibid., 3rd and 12th adhyāya.

1324 Thakore Saheb of Gondal—The History of Aryan Medical Science, p. 188.

1325 Arthaśāstra (R. Śyāmaśāstrī's Eng. Trans.), pp. 56, 169, 173.

1326 Ibid., p. 174.

1327 Ibid., pp. 52, 166.

1328 Ibid., p. 168.

Shah Khilji in 783 A. H. (*i.e.*, 1381 A. D.).[1329] The book is divided into eleven chapters and thirty sections. It is curious that without any allusion to this work, another work on the Veterinary art styled Salotari and said to comprise in the sanskrit original 16,000 ślokas, was translated in the reign of Shahjahan by Sayyid Abdullah Khan Bahadur Firoz Zung who found it among some other sanskrit books which during his expedition against Mewar, in the reign of Jahangir, had been plundered from Amar Sing, Rāṇā of Chitor. It is divided into twelve chapters and is more than double the size of the other.

Kautilya[1330] refers to men "possessed of the knowledge of the medical treatment of trees and plants" (kṛṣitantra-gulmavṛkṣāyurvedjñāḥ). He even refers to men "*trained* in such sciences."[1331] There is a chapter on Vṛkṣāyurveda in the Agni Purāṇa.[1332] Kāmandaka in his Nītisāra[1333] also refers to Vṛkṣāyurveda. There is also one chapter on Vṛkṣāyurveda in the Bṛhatsaṃhitā.[1334] Bhattapāla in his commentary on this chapter refers to three other authorities on Vṛkṣāyurveda—Kāśyapa, Parāśara and Sāraswata. Professor Winternitz[1335] contends that these references indicate the existence of a rich literature on the subject, proving thereby the later origin of the Arthaśāstra. The conclusion may be tempting but the evidences before us do not enable us to speak with certainty whether treatises actually existed, because a great part of the technical knowledge might have been in a floating state simply handed down from the experts to their pupils.

There are passages in Charaka and Śuśrūta Saṃhitās and in Bhābaprakāśa which prove the importance of the study of plants in all their aspects to the would-be physician. Hence the student of medicine

---

1329 The translator makes no mention in it of the work on the same subject, which had been previously translated from the Sanskrit into Arabic at Bagdad under the name of Kitab-ul-Baitarat (Elliot's Historians of India, Part I., pp. 263, 264.

1330 Arthaśāstra (R. Śyāmaśāstrī's Eng. Trans), p. 142.

1331 Ibid.

1332 Ch. 283.

1333 12th sarga, śl., 17.

1334 Ch. 54.

1335 "Kautilīya Arthaśāstra"—Prof. Winternitz in the Calcutta Review, April, 1924.

was enjoined to learn of the plants from those who were likely to know them—those who lived in the forests or were in some way concerned with them. Thus we are told :

" Ouṣadhirnāmarupāvyam jānantehyajapā bane
Abipāśchaba gopāścha ye chānye banabāsinaḥ—Charaka.

" Gopālāstāpasābyādhā ye chānye banachāriṇaḥ
Mūlahāraśćha ye tevyo veṣajabyektiriṣyti—Śuśrūta.

" Āvīra gopāla pulindatāpasāḥ
Pānthastathānyepi cha banyapāragāḥ
Parīkṣya tevyo bibidhauṣdhāvidhā
Rasādi lakṣyāṇi tataḥ prayojayet—Bhāvaprakāśa.

The seeker after knowledge is to learn from the shepherd, cowherd, goat-herd, fowler, the devotee and hermit in the forest, those living in or having any connection with jungles. He should learn of the plant from them, examine it and after due enquiry accept the identification (of the plant) as valid. The fact that these men were likely to talk in Prākṛt or in different dialects need not frighten him: that would not deter him in his progess; as we find—

" Prāyo janāḥ santi banecharāste
Gopādayah prākṛtanāmaḥ saṃgñāḥ
Prayogānarthā bachana prabṛittir
Yasmāt tataḥ prākṛitamityadoṣaḥ "
—Dhanwantari Nighaṇṭu.

Again—

" Ekantu nāma prathitaṃ bahūnām
ekasya nāmāni tathā bahūni
Drabyasya jātyākritibarṇabīrya-
rasapravābādirguṇairbhabanti
Bahūṇyataḥ prākṛtasaṃskṛtāni
nāmāni bijñāya bahūṃścha pṛṣtwā
Dṛṣtwā cha saṃspṛśhya cha jātilinge
badyādviṣaga veṣajamādareṇa."
—Dhanwantari Nighaṇṭu.

These may excite laughter in modern people—considering that the knowledge one may expect to learn therefrom must be of a very crude nature indeed. But a little reflection would point otherwise. Dr. George Watt has remarked in his invaluable book "The Dictionary of the Economic products of India: "There are, for example, numerous forms of Dhaturā known to the native expert that would be utterly unrecognisable in the herbariums, like the form of Aconitum Napullas, some of these are poisonous and others comparatively innocuous. The shepherd will dig up and eat one form of Aconite but eschew another, recognising it as a violent poison. But to the Botanist they are undistinguishable. This same knowledge is prevalent regarding the form of Dhaturā. That we should longer remain entirely ignorant of these facts is doubly to be regretted since we are alike unable to check criminal abuse and to take full advantage of the meritorious forms." It is no wonder, therefore, to find that the student is enjoined to go to the Himalayas[1336] and the Vindhyas in search of plants. Thus we read in Charaka and Sarangadhara :

"Ouṣadhīnāṃ parābhūmirhimabāna śailasattamaḥ"—Charaka.

"Āgnayā biṅdhyaśailādyā raumyo Himagirirmataḥ
Atastadauṣadhānisyuraṇurupāni hetuviḥ"—Sarangadhara.

We have also—

"Jivakarṣavakau jñeyau Himādriśikharodbhabau"
—Bhāvaprakāśa.

"Mahāmedāvidaḥ kāṇḍo morāngadau prajāyati"
—Bhābaprakāśa.

"Amlabetaṣaḥ chotdeśe prasiddhāḥ"—Rājanighaṇtu.

Passages like these describe at once the place of the study of Botany in the scheme of Hindu medical education as well as indicate the vast laboratory of the Indian continent which the student had to use for observation, experiment and collection of specimen.

1336 Compare: "He who thinks of the Himalayas though he should not see him, is greater than he who performs all worship in Kāśī"—Skandhapurāṇa.

CHAPTER IX.

FEMALE EDUCATION IN ANCIENT INDIA.

Scholars hold widely divergent views about female education in Ancient India. In the Ṛgveda[1337] Indra himself has said: "The mind of woman brooks no discipline, her intellect hath little weight. But there are passages in the Saṃhitā portion of the Vedas which refer to female education. Thus we read:

"Ādhenabo dhunayaṃtamiśiświḥ sabardudhāḥ śaśayā apradugdhāḥ

Nabyā nabyā yubatayo bhabantirmmahaddebānāmsuratwamekam "[1338]
"An unmarried young learned daughter should be married to a learned bridegroom. Never think of giving in marriage a daughter of very young age."

"Upāyāmgṛhitosyādityevyastwā

Viṣṇuragāyaiṣate somastaṃ rakṣyaswa mā twādavan."[1339]
"A young daughter who has observed brahmacharya (i. e., finished her studies) should be married to a bridegroom who like her is learned."

"Brahmacharyeṇa tapasā rājā rāstraṃ birakṣati
Āchāryo brahmacharyena brahmachārin michchate
Brahmacharyeṇa kanyāyubānaṃ bindyate patim."[1340]

"A king by observing brahmacharya (the vow of study) can protect his kingdom easily. An āchārya can impart education to his students if he has himself observed his brahmacharya (vow of studies). A young daughter after the observance of brahmacharya (vow of studies) should be married to a young man".

We shall now adduce evidences which go to show that women in those early days enjoyed the right to utter the sacred mantras. Thus in the Aśwalāyana Śrautasūtra (I. 11) we are told:

"Imaṃ mantraṃ patni paṭhet Vedaṃ patnai pradāya bāchayet".

[1337] VIII. 34, 17.

[1338] Ṛgveda III. 5. 55. 16.

[1339] Yajurveda VIII. 1.

[1340] Atharvaveda XII. 3. 17, 18.

"The wife (of the sacrificer) should recite in a sacrifice this mantra. Placing the Veda in the hand of the wife, have this mantra recited by her." Again—

"Patnyā api mantrapāṭhobhabatyebetyādi"

In Áśwalāyana we find—

"Agnaye swāheti sāyaṃ juhuyāt
Suryāya swāheti prātastusṇīm dwitīye ubhayatra".

Govila Gṛhyasūtra is quite explicit on the right of women to perform the Agnihotra with Vedic mantras:—

"Kāmaṃ gṛhyegnau patnījuhutāt prātarLomau
Gṛhapatnīgṛhya eṣognirbhabatīti."[1341]

Again—

"Dhrubamasi dhrubāhaṃ patikule bhūyasamamuṣyāsābitipatināma gṛṇhīyādātmanaścha"[1342]

"The wife should utter the mantra 'Dhrubāha' and then pray to God for ability to live in her husband's house in safety and steadfastness and then utter her own name as well as that of her husband."

In Pāraskara Gṛhyasūtra we are told :

"Striyopi mantreṇa tamāruhya"

"After reciting the mantra the wife should seat herself on the seat."

We are further told in the Sāṃkhāyana Sūtra—

"Ghṛtabantam kutāyinaṃ rāyaspoyaṃ sahasriṇaṃ
Vedo dadhātu bājinam, iti vedepatnīṃ bāchayati"

"The women-folk should mutter mantras beginning with Ghṛtabantam etc.".

[1341] Govil Gṛhyasūtra I. 3. [1342] Ibid., II. 3.

Again—

"Patnī pannejanīrgṛṇhāti pratyantiṣṭyantībasubhyo rudrevya āditevya iti."[1343]

"Facing the Western direction while standing with a potful of water in her hand for sacrificial purpose, the wife should utter the mantra "basuvyo rudrevya etc.".

Again—

"Sāvitrī prasūtā daibyā āpa undantu tanuḥ dīrghāyuṣ twāyarbachas iti."[1344]

"At the time of the boy's chūḍākaraṇa, the mother should utter the mantra mentioned above".

Jaiminī in his Pūrva Mīmāṃsā[1345] says:

"Tasyā yābaduktamāśīrbrahmacharyamatulyatwāt."

"Women like men can bless with Vedic mantras and observe brahmacharya (the vow of study)." In Lātyāyana Śrautasūtra[1346] we are told that even the maidservants should utter "idam madhu etc.".

Again—

"Gṛhapaterdāsyonabānudaharaṇān pūrayitwā pradakṣiṇam mārjālīyaṃ Parīṣurhaimahā idaṃ madhwidammadhwiti badantyaḥ pañchābarāddhyāḥ pañchaśataṃ parārddhyāḥ pañchbiṃśatiḥ sāmprataḥ".

Now it may be argued that the utterance of the mantras need not necessarily mean the regular study of the sacred texts. But in the commentary on Govila Gṛihyasūtra I. 3. we are told—

"Pātnīmadhyāpayet kasmāt patnījuhuyāditi bachanāt, nahi khalwanadhītya śaknoti patnī hotumiti".

"The female-folk should be taught, for without such studies they cannot perform Agnihotra".

1343 Āpastamva Śrautasūtra XII. 5. 12.

1344 Pāraskara Gṛhyasūtra IX. 2. 1.

1345 VI. 1. 24.

1346 XVIII. 4. 3.

29

Again in Govila Gṛhyasūtra[1347] we find : "Yachchāmnāyo bidagdhyāt". "The woman should read me (Veda)".

In Lātyāyana sūtra[1348] we are told : "Patnī cha". "The wife also (should sing the Sāma Veda).

That women used to read Mīmaṃsā philosophy and even to teach others is evident from Patañjali's Mahābhāṣya where after the sūtra "Anupasarjanāt" we read—

"Kāśakṛtsnena proktā mīmaṃsākāsakṛtsnī.

Kāśakṛtsnīṃ mīmaṃsāmadhītesau Kāśakṛtsnā brāhmaṇī".

"The Brahmin female who had studied the mīmāṃsā-śāstra written by the sage Kāśakṛtsna is called Kāśakṛtsnā".

Again it is written in the Vārtika after Kṛdanta (iguścha)—

"Striyāmapādāna upasaṃkhyānam

Upetyādhīyatesyāh sā upādhyāyī".

"The woman going near whom one reads is called Upādhyāyī.

There were also women or girl-students, Kaṭhī and Bahvṛchi being known by the different śākhās.[1349]

Moreover, the adhikaraṇas (aphorisms) of Jaimini in his Pūrva Mīmāṃsā[1350] which turns on the text "Darśapūrṇamāsyābhyām swargakāmo yajeta" when read in the light of the comments of Sabara Swāmī lead to the broad conclusion that in respect of rights to perform one of the Vedic commands, women are on a level with men. The way in which this commentary on the adhikaraṇa is described by Sabara Swāmī (in his Jaiminī's Mīmāṃsā-darśan) and by Mādhabāchārya (in his Jaiminī's Nyāya-mālā-vistāra) shows that the text of the Vedas "swargakāmo yajeta" is a typical command, so that all rights which

---

1347 I. 6.

1348 IV. 6.

1349 Pāṇinī IV. 1, 48, 63.

1350 Ch. IV. Pada I, adhikaraṇa III.

men have under the Vedic law are in Jaimini's view equally shared by women. Sabara Swāmī in his commentary, has headed the third adhikaraṇa of Chapter I of Jaimini's Mīmānsā Darśan as "the adhikaraṇa that deals with the equal rights of men and women in the performance of sacrifices etc." The word 'etcetra' lends corroboration to the view that the right of men and women were equal in respect of all commands contained in the Vedas. Pārtha Sārathi Miśra in his Śāstradīpikā takes the same view. Mādhabāchārya in his Nyāya-mālā-vistāra[1351] says:—"Asyaibādhikaraṇasyānusareṇa aṣṭabarṣam brāhmaṇamupanī yata tamadhyāpayīta ityachāpi striyāpyadhikārah." Thus according to Mādhavāchārya, a girl of the twice-born classes has as much right to be initiated at the age of eight years as boys of the same age and is entitled equally with them to study the Vedas.

The text of Yama quoted below shows that in very early times maidens used to tie the sacred cord (sign of initiation) to study the Vedas and to recite the Sāvitrī, the most sacred of prayers:

"Purākalpe kumārīṇā mouñjibandhanamiṣyte
Adhyāpanaṃ cha vedānāṃ sāvitrī badanaṃ tathā."[1352]

There was a similar initiation for girls in the Vedic age. The reference to the sacred vesture or triple thread of Saraswatī bears clear evidence to this effect. The girdle tied round the boys' waist at the initiation has its counterpart in the girdle tied round the wife's waist at sacrifices which represents her upanayanam according to the Brāhmaṇas.[1353] It may be noted in this connection that among the Parsis who are descended from the same Aryan stock as the Hindus the custom of tying thread both by men and women prevails.

Hārīt, one of the earliest of sages, describes that all the four stages of life including that of studentship were open to women and that both the sexes had a right to utter the mantras (Vedic texts).[1354]

[1351] Bombay edition, p. 335.

[1352] Yama quoted by Parāśara Mādhavya.

[1353] Taitt. Brah., III. 3, 2, 37.

[1354] "Dwibidhā strīyo brahmabādiṇyaḥ sadyobadhwaścha Tantra brahmabīdinīnāmunayana mouñjibandhanaṃ vedādhyayanaṃ swagṛhe vikṣācharyā iti" Hārītabachanam.

Kātyāyana Saṃhitā[1355] says: "If it (the rite of serving the sacred Fire) cannot be performed by one, they (i. e., the wives) should, either according to seniority or ability, severally or jointly, perform the rite, according to their own light and *knowledge of the scriptures.*" Dakṣa Saṃhitā[1356] says: "The household of men has the wife for its root, if she *follows the Vedas.*"

In Hemādri we read—

"Kumārim̱ śikṣayet vidyām dharmanītau nibiśayet
Dwayoḥ kalyāṇadā proktā yā vidyāmadhigachchati
Tato barāya biduṣī kanyā deyāḥ manīṣiviḥ
Eṣa sanātanaḥ panthā ṛṣiviḥ parigīyate
Ajñatapatimaryyādāmjñatapatisebanāṃ
Nodwāhayet pitā bālāmajñatadharmaśāsanām."

"The girl should be taught Vidyā and Dharmanīti. The girl who is endowed with learning brings good to the family of her father and of her husband. The parents should give a fit daughter in marriage to an educated bridegroom—this is the opinion of the sages. So long as the girl is ignorant of patimaryyādā, patāsebana and dharma-śāsana, so long her father should not give her in marriage."

Again in the Mahānirvāṇatantra—

"Kanyāpyeba pālanīyā śikṣanīyātiyatnataḥ."

"The daughter also should be properly educated and taken care of."

As a matter of fact we find that some of the hymns of the Ṛgveda were originally given through women; through their mouths the sacred mantras were spoken which in later times their daughters were not allowed to study or repeat. Viśwavārā, a lady of great learning, composed the ṛk in the 5th maṇḍala fourth aṣthaka 28th sūkta of the Ṛgveda. Lopemudrā was the author of the ṛk in the first maṇḍala second aṣtaka fourth adhyāya one hundred and seventy-nineth sūkta of the Ṛgveda. Apalā was the author of the ṛk in the eighth maṇḍala, sixth aṣtaka,

---

1355 XIX. 5. 1356 IV. 1.

sixth adhyāya, ninety-first sūkta of the Ṛgveda. Śāswatī was the author of the ṛk in the seventh maṇḍala, seventh adhyāya, twenty-fourth sūkta of the Ṛgveda. Ghoṣā, Ātrieyī and Paulāmī were also authors of mantras and rose to the rank of ṛṣis. Godhā, Brajāyā, Juhu and Devaśunī also rose to the rank of ṛṣis.

Two very interesting incidents described in the Bṛhadāraṇyaka Upaniṣad may be referred to in this connection. The great king Janaka of Videha once performed a sacrifice, at which the most learned Brahmins, including those from Kuru and Pāñchāla countries, were present. Janaka wished to know which of those brāhmaṇas was the best read. So he enclosed a thousand cows and ten pādas of gold were fastened to each pair of horns. And then Janaka spoke to the assembled brāhmaṇas: "Let the wisest among you drive away these cows." Yājñabālkya, the great philosopher, asked his pupil to drive them away. Then the other brāhmaṇas became very angry and one after another, they plied Yājñabālkya with questions. Yājñabālkya silenced them all. One of his interlocutors was the venerable lady Gārgī, the daughter of Vachakru. She stood up in the midst of the assembly and held a philosophic discussion with the great Yājñabālkya, till the latter remarked: "O Gārgī, do not ask too much, lest thy head should fall off. Thou askest too much about a deity about which we are not to ask too much." Gārgī stopped for the moment but some time after she rose again and began with the proud remark: "Venerable brāhmaṇas, now I shall ask two questions. If he will answer them, none of you, I think will then be able to defeat him in any argument concerning Brahman." The two questions were on Brahman, described as Limitless in Time and Space but in whom exist Time and Space. Yājñabālkya answered these questions.

The second incident is also connected with Yājñabālkya. "Maitreyī" said he, "verily I am going away from this my house into the forest. Let me make a settlement between thee and that Kātyāyanī, my other wife." Maitreyī said: "My lord, if this whole earth full of wealth, belonged to me, tell me should I be immotal by it." "No" replied Yājñabālkya. And Maitreyī said: "What should I do with that by which I do not become immortal? What my Lord knoweth of immortality, tell that to me." Yājñabālkya replied: "Thou who art truly dear to me, thou speakest dear words. Come, sit down, I will explain it to thee, and mark well what I say." Then followed one of the most abstruse philosophical discussions about the Universal Self, and its relation to the Individual.[1357] These two incidents eloquently testify to the high position, learning and mental equipment of women in ancient India, to which it will be difficult to find a parallel in the history of the world.

From the Kauśitakī Brāhmana[1358] we learn that an Aryan female Pathyāvasti went to the north, studied there and obtained the title of vāk i. e., Saraswatī.[1359] Two directions given in the Aitareya Upaniṣad[1360] imply that elderly married ladies were permitted to hear Vedāntic discourses. The Upaniṣads mention several other women as teachers but it is not clear whether they were married. In this connection we may note that women were taught some of the fine arts like dancing and singing which were regarded as accomplishments unfit for men.[1361]

Evidences of ladies taking part in advanced Vedic studies are found in stage directions in the Taittirīya Āraṇyaka[1362] and Aitareya Upaniṣad[1363] where ladies are directed to leave the hall of learning when some principles of gynecology came to be explained, which are indelicate for the female ear. The introduction of Umā in the Kenopaniṣad is illustrative of the great regard the poet and sage had for the educative power of woman, even as regards the highest metaphysical truths and their teaching. A kumārī Gandharvagṛhītā is quoted as viśeṣāvijñā (of excellent intellect) in the Kauśitakī[1364] and Aitareya Brāhmaṇas (V. 29). Some of the women-saints are mentioned, e. g., Gārgī, Vāchaknavī, Vaḍavā, Pratidheyī, Sulavā and Maitreyī.'[1365]

1357 S. B. E. Vol. XV., pp. 108f.

1358 VII. 6.

1359 Muir—Original Sanskrit Texts, p. 388.

1360 II. 1.

1361 Taitt. Sam., V. 1. 6. 5; Maitrā. Sam., III. 7. 3; Śat. Brāh., III. 2. 4, 3-6.

1362 I. 13.

1363 III.

1364 II. 9.

1365 Aśv. Gṛ. sūtra III. 4.

In the Rāmāyaṇa we are told that Kauśalyā at the proposal of the installation of Rāma as Yubarāja offered oblations to the Fire with mantras :—

"Sā kṣhaumabasanā dṛṣtā nityaṃ brataparāyaṇā.
Agniṃ Yuhotisma tadā mantrabatkṛt mangalā."[1366]

Similarly when Bāli was going to fight with Sugrīva the former's wife Tārā performed swastvayana with the muttering of mantras. Again we find Tārā, the widow of Bālī while asking Rāma who had killed her husband to kill her also address Rāma thus: "See, husband and wife are both not separate beings, this is proved by woman's right to sacrifice and the evidence of the Vedas."[1367] Indeed that Śitā was well-versed in purābṛtta and in dharmanīti is evident from her talk with Rāma when she is dissuading the latter from undertaking the task of ridding Daṇḍakāraṇya forest of the Rākṣasas.[1368]

In the Mahābhārata[1369] we read of Śibā, a brāhmaṇa lady who was well-versed in the Vedas—

"Atra śarmā Śivā nāma brāhmaṇī Vedapāragā."

In the Śāntiparba[1370] we are told that when on one occasion. King Janaka was intent on embracing sannyāsa, his wife dissuaded him from this resolve after proving to him the superiority of the gārhasthya āśrama from the Vedas and the śāstras. In the Śāntiparba[1371] we are also told of one princess sulavā by name, who asked by the king (Janaka) about her identity replied :

"Sāhaṃ tasmin kule jātā vartayarsati mādbiddhyo
Binītā mokṣadharmeṣu charāmyekāmunibratam."

[1366] Ayodhyākāṇḍa, 20th adhyāya, śl. 55. [1367] Kiṣkindhyākāṇḍa, 24 sarga.

[1368] Āraṇyakāṇḍa, 9th sarga. [1369] Banaparva.

[1370] 18th adhyāya. In the Ṛgveda we have a housewife reminding her husband that the ancient sages did attend to the begetting of progeny and did not consider their spiritual progress hampered thereby. (Ṛgveda VIII. 31, 9; I. 179, 2; V. 61, 8; V. 78, 4; VII. 76, 3; Taitt. Brah., III. 3. 3,

[1371] 321st adhyāya.

She then delivered to Janaka a learned discourse on Yoga, Samādhi and Mokṣa. In the Udyogaparba we are told that a woman Badulā by name taught Rajadharma to her son herself.

A brāhmaṇa lady Līlāvatī was the author of the celebrated Algebra which found its way to Europe.

From the Lalita-vistāra we learn that even at the time of Buddha girls had a right to study the śāstras and were taught to read and write. Thus Gautama says: "I shall need the maiden who is accomplished in writing and in composing poetry, who is endowed with good qualities and well-versed in the rules of the śāstras."[1372] Another passage may be cited from the same work to show that the education of girls of the highest class not only enabled them to discharge their domestic duties and to take interest in the concerns of life but also dowered them with an attitude of openness to the reception of new ideas. The wife of the Buddha was bold enough to put the question: "So long as my behaviour, my qualities, my prudence remain undisturbed, why need I a veil to cover my face with?"[1373] It must be concluded therefore that the girl of this period was no domestic drudge and had her individuality and free opinions within limits.

In course of time the right of initiation and the right to study the Vedas or sacred literature generally were denied to women. It is impossible to fix decidedly the time when such a retrograde movement commenced. But from the following aphorism of Jaiminī it is apparent that a school had in Jaiminī's time already sprung up, of which the sage Aitiśāyana was the exponent which maintained the view that women were not entitled to perform Vedic sacrifices :—

"Lingabiśeṣanirdeśāt punyuktamaitiśāyanaḥ"

"As the particular gender is specified it refers to males so says (the sage) Aitiśāyana." A study of Jaiminī's aphorisms on the Vedic text 'swargakāmo yajeta', referred to above will not fail to impress even the superficial reader with the forcible and vigorous reasoning with which Jaiminī refutes the arguments of the opposite school and claims

1372 Lalita-vistāra—R. L. Mitra, XII. pp. 199-200.

1373 Ibid., p., 199.

for women equality with men in respect of personal and proprietory rights. It also appears from the following aphorism of Jaimini that the sage Bādarāyaṇa supports the view taken by Jaiminī :—

" Jātiṃ tu bādarāyaṇobiśeṣāt tasmāt strayapi pratīyate jātyarthyasyābiśiṣtyatwāt."

Bādarāyaṇa says that any one (whether man or woman) belonging to the three regenerate classes is entitled to perform sacrifices as there is no class distinction in the word (swargakāmo); therefore, woman also is included because the three regenerate classes consist of men and women alike."

It may perhaps be objected that Jaiminī was merely fighting for a theory and that when claiming for women equality with men in the performance of Vedic sacrifices and in the study of the Vedas, he was breaking away from the conventional feeling of his time. But the objection loses all force when we turn to the evidences, to which reference has already been made, of the right of women to Vedic study furnished by the Vedas and the Sūtras both of which preceded the Smṛtis in point of time.

When we come to the Smṛtis we find that the women were thought incompetent to perform sacrifices[1374] and to read the Vedas as they could not be initiated. Manu,[1375] for instance, says that initiation of women consisted in their marriage: " The nuptial ceremony is stated to be the Vedic sacrament for women and to be equal to the initiation, serving the husband (equivalent to) residence in the house of the teacher and the household duties the same as the worship of the sacred fires."

Medhātithi and Nārāyaṇa, two of the commentators of Manu, add the gloss that by Vedic sacrament is meant the sacrament having for its object the study of Vedic texts. Kulluka in his commentary hints that by prescribing marriage in the place of upanayana, it is implied that women must not be initiated. Vijñāneśwara in his comment on

[1374] Manu IV. 205, 206.

[1375] II. 67.

śloka 15 of Yājñabālkyasmṛti in the chapter on Āchāra says that initiation for women means marriage. If they could not be initiated, it follows that they could not study the Vedas. In another verse Manu makes the position clear. In Chapter IX. verse 18 the sage says: "For women no sacramental rite is performed with sacred texts; thus the law is settled; women who are destitute of strength and destitute of the knowledge of Vedic texts are impure as falsehood itself, that is a fixed rule." In Jagannātha's opinion, this text indicates the exclusion of women from the study of Vedic texts. There is also a text of Yama which ordains that women are forbiddin to utter Vedic mantras. In his comment on śloka 30, Ch. XIII of Nāradasmṛti Asahaya remarks—

"Tathāhi śāstrādhyayanādhikāritwāt śāstramātropājivi dharmādharma-jñānābhābāt swātantryā bartamānatwena puruṣapāratantryā bhābāt tenopadeśasaṃgachcha."[1376]

"The reason for dependence is that women have no right to study the śāstras and consequently lack the knowledge to decide between right and wrong between Dharma and Adharma since such knowledge is dependent on the śāstras. We read in the Śrimat Bhāgabad Purāṇa that women in common with the śūdras were declared incompetent to hear the Vedas. This retrograde spirit is also correctly indicated by Megasthenes who came to India in the 4th century B. C. He says: "The brāhmaṇas do not communicate a knowledge of philosophy to their wives." But he admits that some women did pursue philosophy.

It is probably the early foreign invasions of India that may account for this exclusion of women from Vedic studies. In almost every nation of the world in the primitive stages of its development, the early ideas about the inferiority of the female sex prevailed; woman was not regarded as a person, she was not recognised as a citizen. "In fact, she was not a unit but a zero in the sum of human civilisation"[1377] and it is very probable that the conquering mlechchas entertained these notions. When the people of Hindusthan who had already attained

---

[1376] Jolly—Institutes of Nārada.

[1377] Mr. Cady Santon—History of Women Suffrage, Vol. III. p. 290.

to a high degree of civilisation came in contact with their first foreign rulers far less civilised than they, they might have adopted those rules concerning the position of women which belonged peculiarly to an imperfect civilisation.

From this time the education of girls came to be entirely domestic and vocational, in the sense that they were being prepared for that which was considered a woman's principal work—the duties of the household. Indeed as the men were devoted more and more exclusively to social duties, to learning or teaching or were plunged in the delights of a dreamland beyond the tomb or the cremation ghat, they had to be freed from worldly worries by their wives. Thus according to Śatapatha Brāhmaṇa[1378] weaving is the function of women. Weaving is also a domestic occupation for women in the Jātakas.[1379] Among the qualities which, according to Anguttara Nikāya[1380] every woman should be endowed with, we find that she should be skilled in spinning and weaving, must be intelligent enough to do and manage household affairs and must preserve the earnings of her husband. The Dhammapada commentary[1381] tells us that pounding rice and cooking are some of the duties of a household woman. Śukrāchārya[1382] says: "The woman should be assistants in the functions of the males, viz., agriculture, shopkeeping etc. The woman should practise music, gentle manners etc., according as the husband is master of these and perform the winning arts etc., with regard to him". Vātsyāyana in his Kāmasūtra[1383] enumerates among others the following duties of married wives :—

"She should arrange to plant in her garden rows of flower plants such as Kubjaka, Āmalaka, Mallikā, Jāti, Kuruṇḍaka, Nabamallikā, Tagara, Nandyvarta and other plants. There should also be rows of

---

[1378] Tadbā etat sṛṇāṃ karma yada ūrṇāsūtram—Śat. Br. XII. 7. 2. 11.

[1379] Jāt. VI. 26.

[1380] IV. pp. 268-69.

[1381] III. p. 41.

[1382] Śukranītisāra, Ch. IV. sec. VII. lines 54-56.

[1383] Bk. IV. Ch.I.

trees such as Bālakośiraka, Pātāleka and others and the ground should be kept attractive in appearance."[1384]

"She should secure the seeds of various medicinal herbs and vegetables such as Mūlaka and sow them in time".[1385]

"From the curds that remain after their daily consumption, she should extract its essence (butter) as also oil from oilseeds, sugar and jaggary from sugarcane, spinning of thread from out of cotton and weaving cloth with them, the securing of Sikya (a sling for placing vessels suspended from ceilings), of ropes (for drawing water) of strings (for tying cattle), of barks (for making cloth out of them), looking after pounding and grinding (of paddy, rice, etc.,) finding some use for āchama, muṇḍa (scum of boiled rice) tuṣa (husk or chaff of grain), kaṇa (broken rice), kuti (bran) and aṅgāra (charcoal), knowledge (remembering) of wages of servants and their disbursements, the care of cultivaotin and welfare of cattle, *knowledge of constructing conveyances*, looking after sheep, cocks, lavakas, parrots, cuckoos, peacocks, monkeys and deer, *the reckoning of daily income and expenditure and making up a total of them all*—all these are the duties of a wife".[1386]

"Looking after purchases and sales and incomes and expenditures—these also should be carefully looked after".[1387]

"She should consider the annual income and expenditure accordingly".[1388]

"She should excel other women of her rank and birth in cleverness, in her *knowledge of arts* (sixty-four in number) appearance, *art of cooking......*".[1389]

Manu[1390] says: "They (women) should be employed in looking after the expenses of the household, in maintaining the cleanliness of their persons and of the house and in looking after the beddings, wearing apparel and household furniture". In another place Manu[1391]

1384 Ibid., śl. 7.
1385 Ibid., śl. 29.
1386 Ibid., śl. 33.
1387 Ibid., śl. 35.
1388 Ibid., śl. 32.
1389 Ibid., śl. 31.
1390 X. 11.
1391 IX. 28.

refers to *nursing* as contingent on the wife of a man. Kautilya[1392] also refers to the cutting of wool, fibre, cotton, panicle (tulā), hemp and flax and of spinning threads by women of all classes and castes.

The training for all this began in the girl's own home under the supervision of her mother and when she was married and went to live with her husband, it would be continued owing to the Indian custom of the non-separation of the family, by her mother-in-law. The injunction that she should be employed in the collection and expenditure of her husband's wealth would mean that she had some knowledge of accounts, however elementary it may be. But as there was no school for girls and no time was fixed for the commencement of their education (the right to initiation being prohibited now) it is likely that the intellectual side of female education received no special care and was left to circumstances that might be. But although shut out from the study of the Vedas and from performing a sacrifice, apart from her husband, the performance of certain religious duties was specially enjoined for her and in addition to receiving instructions in the rites and ceremonies in which she was expected to take part a woman would become acquainted with something of the vast heap of mythological stories and folk-lore which had been handed down and accumulated in India from ancient times. Indeed, literacy and education did not go hand in hand in the case of Hindu women. Many of them were perhaps illiterate but all were well-educated inspite of that. This was a fact, strange though it may seem to the Western mind, and it was accomplished on the strength of the religious ideal of life and by means of the home as the centre of all activity.

Vātsyāyana in his Kāmasūtra has however preserved for us a liberal scheme of female education. He says :—

" A woman should study Kāmasūtra before she attains her youth. A married woman should study it with the consent of her husband. The ācharyas are, however, of opinion that because a woman is not permitted to study śāstras according to the Hindu religious texts and

---

1392 Arthaśāstra (R. Śyāmaśāstrī's Eng. Trans.), pp. 140-41.

also because she is not fit to receive this kind of learning, there is no need giving here the courses of training which a woman has to undergo."[1393]

"But Vātsyāyana considers that women should be taught the principles of these śāstras and their practical application. As the teaching of these principles to women requires the study of these śāstras on the part of the teachers the laying down in the Kāmasūtra of the method of training the women, is not out of place. And thus the practical knowledge of Kāmasūtra gained by women is dependent on this śāstra though remotely."[1394]

"Such a result is not confined to the Kāmasūtra only. The fact that a large majority of people secure a knowledge of the principles of various śāstras without themselves studying them, is observed in very many other instances. In all parts of the world there are only a few who have studied or are fit to study the śāstras. But the principles of them are intended for all people and understood by various means."[1395]

"There are however, certain women such as courtesans, princesses and daughters of noblemen who have their intellect sharpened by a *direct study* of the śāstras.[1396]

"For these reasons a woman may learn śāstras as well as the application of their principles or either of them from a person in whom she may have confidence."[1397]

"A woman should learn in her girlhood, alone in private, the sixty-four kinds of sexual knowledge which can be understood by practice only."[1398]

"The teachers of girls are:—(1) a daughter of her nurse who has been brought up with her and had intercourse with man (2) a woman friend who speaks in a frank manner and has likewise had intercourse

---

[1393] Kāmasūtra, Bk. I. Ch. III. śls. 2-4.
[1394] Ibid., śl. 5.
[1395] Ibid., śl. 6.
[1396] Ibid., śl. 12.
[1397] Ibid., śl. 13.
[1398] Ibid., śl. 14.

with man (3) her mother's sister of her own age (4) an elderly woman servant who is trusted and is to the girl like her mother's sister (5) A nun that previously had sexual intercourse with man and (6) her own elder sister, because of the trust reposed in them by the girl."[1399]

" The author enumerates hereunder the 64 kalās or arts.

1. Gītam—singing.
2. Vādyam—playing on musical instruments.
3. Nṛtyam—dancing.
4. Ālekhyam—painting.
5. Viśeṣakachhedyam—cutting of leaves etc., in the form of certain figures to serve as marks on the forehead.
6. Taṇḍula Kusumāvalivikāra—arrangement on coloured rice-grains and flowers of different colours, in various forms as an ornamental exhibit at the time of the worship (of a deity etc.).
7. Puspastaraṇam—covering the floor of a hall or room with flowers.
8. Daśana-vasanāngarāga—colouring the teeth, clothes and body.
9. Maṇibhumikākarma—in certain parts of the house studding the floor with precious stones etc.
10. Śayanarachanam—arrangement of bed according to the taste and condition of persons.
11. Udakavādyam—playing on water so as to produce a musical sound as if from a drum (jalataranga).
12. Udakaghāta—striking (at others) with handfuls of water or by squirting it through some instrument such as a syringe.

1399 Ibid., śl. 15.

13. Chitrāșcha yoga—various kinds of preparations by compounding drugs and other medicinal substances or spells against others (enemies chiefly) to disable or deform them.

14. Mālyagradhanavikalpa—stringing flowers into garlands for the purpose of wearing or worshiping (an image etc).

15. Śekharāpīḍayoga—striking flowers in the form of śekhara or āpīḍa (two kinds of head-ornaments).

16. Nepathyaproyaga—ways of dressing and decorating oneself with flowers or ornaments.

17. Karṇapatrabhanga—making some kinds of ear-ornaments out of ivory, conch, etc.

18. Gandhayukti—preparation of perfumatory articles.

19. Bhūṣaṇayojana—making of new ornaments or improving old ones with the insertion of precious stones etc., or the proper way of wearing ornaments.

20. Indrajalayoga—producing illusions by playing trickery.

21. Kanchumarścha yoga—some preparations out of drugs to increase virility and the strength of the body.

22. Hastalaghava—nimbleness of hand by which one is able to do things easily and quickly.

23. Vichitraśāka-yusha-bhakṣyakriyā—preparation of varieties of food, vegetables, soups and sweatmeats and other dishes.

24. Panakarasaragasavayojanani—preparation of different kinds of drinks including intoxicants.

25. Sūchivanakarmaṇi—needleworks of various kinds, sewing, etc.

26. Sūtrakṛḍā—playing with strings of threads. Some tricks by which threads cut or burnt are made to appear as unbroken. Or this may be interpreted like this—some plays in which dolls are made to dance and play by means of threads attached to them from behind.

27. Viṇādamaruka vādyāni—playing on Viṇā and Damaruka (a kind of drum).

28. Prahelikā—proposing and solving of riddles.

29. Pratimala—amusing way of reciting ślokas (verses). One person recites a śloka, another person following with another śloka that begins with the last letter of the previous śloka. This is commonly known as "Antadi"—i. e., the end of the one (śloka) is the beginning of another śloka.

30. Durvachaka yogaḥ—participating in reciting ślokas (verses) difficult both in meaning and pronunciation (producing harsh sounds after a laborious pronunciation of words).

31. Pustakavachanam—reading in melodious tones standard works such as the Ramāyaṇa and the Mahābhārata.

32. Nātakākhyāyikā-darśanam—knowledge of dramas and stories.

33. Kābyasamasyāpūraṇam[1400]—a quarter or part of a verse (śloka)—the last quarter generally—being given, to compose the other parts of the verse.

34. Pattikavetra vanavikalpa—making of different articles of furniture (cots, seats etc.,) from canes and reeds.

1400 Rājataraṅgiṇī (IV. 46) refers to samasyā (Stein—The Chronicles of Kashmere, Vol. I., p. 124.

35. Takṣakarmaṇi—cutting into required shapes, certain materials—wood, metal etc.; making from gold, steel, wood, silver or any other substance, unnatural forms of male organs for using them as substitutes in sexual intercourse (these are called Apadrabyās).

36. Takṣaṇam—carpentry.

37. Vastuvidyā—Engineering specially that part of the science which treats of the ways of constructing dwelling houses, the sites on which they are to be built, the materials to be used and such other matters as sanitation, connected with the subject.

38. Rupyaratnaparīkṣā—testing, valuing, etc, of precious stones.

39. Dhātuvāda—the combination, purification and precipitation of minerals; making valuable metals out of inferior kinds, as gold from iron.

40. Maṇirāgakarajñānam—knowledge of the process of dying crystals and precious stones and of the location and working of the mines.

41. Vṛkṣāyurveda—knowledge of medicines for plants.

42. Meṣa-kukkuta-lavaka-yuddhāni—training rams, cocks and lavakas (quails or some birds allied to them) to fight.

43. Śukasārikapralāpanam—teaching parrots to speak human languages and sending messages through them.

44. Utsadane, samvahane, keśamardanecha ꞉kauśalam—dexterity in the process of removing dirt from the body, in massaging (rubbing the body) and dressing the hair.

45. Akṣaramuṣtikakathanam—finding out some hidden meaning of some groups of letters ingeniously composed to mean various things, as in our "shorthand".

46. Mlechitabikalpa—varieties of cypher-languages—some newly coined expressions unintelligible to all except the initiated.

47. Deśabhāṣāvijñānam—knowledge of the languages of different countries.

48. Nimittajñānam—knowledge of good and bad omens.

49. Puṣpaśakatika—making of carts, palanquins, horses, elephants etc., out of flowers.

50. Yantramatrika—construction of machines for locomotion, pumping water etc., and of guns and other weapons for war purposes.

51. Dhāraṇamatrika—science of memory—memory-training—, so that one is able to make such feats as Śatavadhāna (attending to 100 things at the same time and answering to several questions put by many persons simultaneously.

52. Sapatyam—a feat in which one person recites a known śloka (verse) and another who does not know the śloka before, has to repeat it along with the former.

53. Manasi—another feat in which one is to fill up with appropriate words or phrases, the blanks left in a verse or sentence.

54. Kāvyakṛyā—composing poems.

55. Abhidhānakoṣachhandobijñānam—knowledge of lexicons and metre.

56. Kriyākalpa—kāvya, alaṅkāra and poetry (Poetics and Rhetoric).

57. Chhalilākayoga—Some processes of deception or fun in which voice and person are disguised so as not to be recognised.

58. Vastragopanam—covering the private parts of the body with cloth; or wearing a long cloth in such a way that it may look fit or as if it were a short cloth or wearing a torn cloth in such a way that its damaged parts are not seen by others.

59. Dyutaviśeṣa—varieties of gambling.

60. Akarsa-krīḍā—a particular kind of gambling with dice.

61. Bālakrīḍanakāni—plays for children with balls and dolls.

62. Vainayikanam vidyānam jñānam—knowledge of such arts and sciences by which good manners and obedience are learnt or knowledge of the sciences and arts which educate a person.

63. Vaijayikanam vidyānam jñānam—knowledge of such sciences as will bring victory over opponents.

64. Vyāyāmikanam vidyānam jñānam—knowledge of such sciences as are connected with the physical exercise and the development of the body.

These are the sixty-four subordinate sciences that form part of the sexual science ".[1401]

" A woman gifted with these arts will, by these means live even when her husband is on exile or when she is suffering from some great trouble or has become a widow, even if she is living in a foreign country ".[1402]

From the above it is evident that Vātsyāyana's scheme of female education was an ideal one including (1) literary accomplishments (kalās Nos. 28, 29. 30, 31, 32, 33, 45, 46. 47, 51, 52, 53, 54, 55, 56, 62), (2) knowledge of domestic arts (kalās Nos. 10, 25), (3) knowledge of

1401 Kāmasūtra, Bk. I. Ch. III. śl. 16.

1402 Ibid., śl. 23.

culinary arts (kalās Nos. 23, 24), (4) knowledge of arts relating to toilet, dress, comforts or luxuries (kalās Nos. 5, 6, 8, 14, 15, 16, 17, 18, 19, 44, 58), (5) knowledge of manual arts (kalās Nos. 7, 22, 36, 37), (6) knowledge of recreative arts (kalās Nos. 12, 20, 26, 28, 29, 30-33, 42, 43, 45, 49, 52, 53, 57, 59, 60, 61,), (7) knowledge of scientific arts (kalās Nos. 9, 13, 17, 21, 34, 35, 38, 39, 40, 41, 50), (8) knowledge of music (kalās Nos. 1, 2, 11, 27), (9) knowledge of drama (kalā No. 32), (10) knowledge of etiquette (kalā No. 62), (11) knowledge of painting (kalā No. 4), and (12) physical exercise (kalās Nos. 3, 63, 64).

It is also evident from Bk. I. Ch. III. śloka 13 of Vātsyāyana's Kāmasūtra quoted above that princesses and daughters of some noblemen received a special share of this education in the sixty-four kalās for they "have their intellect sharpened by a *direct study* of the śāstras." Vātsyāyana refers to another set of sixty-four arts taught by Pāñchāla which he has fully described in Bk. II. dealing with samprayogikam or sexual intercourse. Vātsyāyana says: "King's daughter or the daughter of a nobleman well-skilled in these arts will have her husband under her sway even when he has one-thousand wives in his harem."[1403]

In the Jaina Kalpasūtra[1404] we find the Arhat Ṛṣabha saying that during his reign he taught among other subjects the sixty-four accomplishments of ladies (chatuṣṣaṣti-mahilāguṇe).

We have already seen that singing and dancing were regarded as particularly feminine accomplishments and are dubbed as "unmanly" in the later Vedic texts.[1405] In the Rāmāyaṇa[1406] we accordingly find that the hundred daughters of Rājarṣi Kuśanāva, born of the womb of Ghṛtāchi were well-versed in dancing, singing and music. Hemā was also an expert in singing and dancing.[1407] The wives of Rāvaṇa, king of Laṅkā (Ceylon) were highly proficient in dancing and singing.[1408] To teach the girls the arts of dancing, singing, music as well as painting there were dancing halls as well as halls of music and painting. The Mahābhārata[1409] refers to a dancing hall

---

1403 Ibid., śl. 22.

1404 Text, p. 74; S. B. E., Vol. XXII. p. 282.

1405 Taitt. Saṃ., VI. 1, 6, 5. Compare Tasmāt gāyanśryaḥ pryāḥ—Maitra. Saṃ., III. 7. 3.

1406 Bālakāṇḍa, 32nd sarga.

1407 Kiṣkindhyākāṇḍa, 51st sarga.

1408 Sundarakāṇḍa, 10th sarga.

1409 Virātaparba, 22nd adhyāya.

(nṛtayaśālā) constructed by king Virāta where his daughters were taught dancing in day time. Vātsyāyana[1410] also refers to music halls. The Mālavikāgñimitra[1411] also refers to halls of music where Mālavikā was taught the arts of dancing, and acting by Gaṇadāsa. The Priyadarśikā and the Ratnābalī also refer to Chitraśālā and Gandharvaśālā. Paes (1537 A. D.) gives a vivid description of the dancing hall of the king of Vijayanagara, where the ladies of his harem were taught dancing.[1412]

Indeed the princesses and daughters of noblemen on account of their ability to pay had in some cases a private tutor to coach them. Draupadī is described as lovely, learned and chaste[1413] and her conversations with Yudhiṣṭhir, Kṛṣṇa and Satyabhāmā do credit to the best educated woman. She seems to have been a master in keeping accounts, for, she says to Satyabhāmā that she alone used to keep all the household accounts of King Yudhiṣṭhir.[1414] She explicitly says that she has learnt Bṛhaspati-nīti from a Brahmin tutor, engaged by her royal father who taught this to her along with her brothers.[1415] We are further told in the Mahābhārata[1416] that Arjuna in the disguise of an eunuch was employed by king Virāta to teach dancing, singing and music to (his daughter) Uttarā, her maids of honour and maid-servants. Similarly Mālavikā[1417] and Rajyaśrī,[1418] sister of Harṣa had Gaṇadāsa and Divākaramitra respectively as their tutors.

If we may go by the indications afforded by Indian literature it seems that some girls specially of the ruling class were not behind their brothers in education. Indian literature does not contain a direct reference to unmarried girls being sent to school but there are many references to educated women. From the Vimānavatthu

---

1410 Kāmasūtra, Bk. VII. Ch. I. śl. 15. 1411 M. R. Kale's Eng. Trans., p. 2.

1412 Sewell—A Forgotten Empire, pp. 288-89.

1413 Priyā cha darśanīyā cha paṇḍitā cha patibratā.

1414 Mahābhārata, Banaparba, 231st adhyāya.

1415 Ibid., 32nd adhyāya

1416 Virātaparba, 11th adhyāya; also 2nd adhyāya.

1417 Mālavikāgñimitra (M. R. Kale's. Eng. Trans.), pp. 2, 4, 5.

1418 Harṣacharita—Cowell and Thomas, p. 258.

commentary[1419] we learn that Latā of Sāvatthi was learned, wise and intelligent. Among the female authors quoted in Hāla's Anthology are Anulakṣmī, Mādhavī, Revā and Nāthā. That there was systematic education of girls at home is clear from the Kumārasambhava where Kālidāsa tells us that Umā acquired the Vidyās[1420] and from the Meghadūta, where the Yaṣka's wife is able to compose songs with letters drawn from her husband's name.[1421] In Kālidāsa's Avijñāna-Śakuntalam we find the heroine penning a love-letter on a lotus-leaf. Such letter-writing by females is also referred to in Vātsyāyana's Kāmasūtra.[1422] From Mālavikāgñimitra we learn that Gaṇadasa taught dancing, acting and allied arts to Mālavikā. She learnt from Gaṇadāsa the dance called Chalita[1423] and the five-limb dance (or acting consisting of five parts).[1424] When Queen Dhāriṇī enquired through a maid-servant of Mālavikā's progress, the tutor himself thus speaks of her aptitude: "Let the Queen be informed that Mālavikā is exceedingly clever and intelligent or in short, whatever movement expressive of sentiment is taught by me to her in the way of acting (or dramatic representation), the girl, as it were, teaches me the same in return, by her superior performance of it (i. e., by improving upon it)"[1425] The Mālavikāgñimitra also refers to "two girls skilled in arts" specially in music sent as a present from the Vidarbha country to Agnimitra.[1426] The Raghuvaṃśam refers to princess Indumatī as possessed of endless accomplishments[1427] who after her marriage was taught fine arts by her royal husband Aja.[1428] We are also told in Raghuvaṃśam that king Agnivarṇa imparted to the ladies of his harem the principles of the art of gesticulate dancing.[1429] Tradition tells us that Kālidāsa's wife was herself a great literary personality who had

---

1419 Page 131.

1420 Prapedire prāktanajanmavidyāḥ.

1421 Madgotāṅkam virachitapadam geyamudgātukāmā.

1422 Bk. V. Ch. IV. Śls. 51-52.

1423 Mālavikāgñimitra (M. R. Kale's Eng. Trans.), p. 2.

1424 Ibid., p. 5.

1425 Ibid., p. 4.

1426 Ibid., pp. 55, 56.

1427 Canto VI. 37.

1428 Canto VIII. 67.

1429 Canto XIX. 36.

vanquished many scholars in open debates. Tradition also tells us that Kālidāsa was unable to defeat in a debate the learned queen of the king of Karṇāta. We are told by Bāṇa that "Rajyaśrī gradually grew up in daily increasing familiarity with friends expert in song, dance, etc., and with all accomplishments."[1430] Her royal brother while engaging Divākaramitra as her tutor says: "I desire that she should remain at my side and be comforted with your righteous discourse and your passionless instruction which produces salutary knowledge and your advice which calms the disposition, and your Buddhist doctrines which drive away worldly passions."[1431] According to Hiuen Tsang "of great intelligence she was distinguished for her knowledge of the Sammatiya school doctrine of Buddhism and sitting behind the king was seen to follow with appreciation the learned discourse of Yuan Chwang on Mahāyāna doctrine."[1432] Bāṇa also describes the wives of Sāmantas coming in thousands to the royal palace at the time of Harṣa's birth and keeping the birth-festival merry by dancing.[1433] In Harṣa's drama Priyadarśikā, the king assigns to the queen the task of arranging for the instruction of the maid Priyadarśikā in dancing, singing and vocal and instrumental music (gīta-nṛtya-vādyādiṣu). The Ratnābalī[1434] represents the heroine Śāgarikā drawing the portrait of her lover on the picture-board (chitraphalākā) with brush (vartikā) and colours carried in a basket (samudagaka). In Ratnābalī[1435] Susangatā (a maid-servant of Queen Vāsavadattā and a friend of the heroine Sāgarikā) is also described as taking a pencil and drawing Sāgarikā in the pretext of Rati in representation.' In the century after Harṣa we find that Saraswatī, the learned wife of Madana Miśra adjudicated in the philosophical discussion between her husband and Śaṅkara. In the Swapnavāsabadattā[1436] Vāsabadattā is driven to weave the garland for the new Queen's marriage, she being well-versed in this art. Rajaśekhara held very forward and liberal views

---

1430 Harṣacharita—Cowell and Thomas, p. 121.

1431 Ibid., p. 258.

1432 Beal—Life of Hiuen Tsang, p. 176.

1433 Ibid., pp. 111-112.

1434 Act II. 9; also Act II. 16.

1435 Act. II. 26.

1436 III. 25.

about female education. He says[1437] that women too may become poetesses like men. Accomplishment is intimately connected with the soul but does not depend upon the distinction of the sex. Rājaśekhara quotes thrice[1438] in his Kābyamīmāṃsā the opinion of his wife Abantisundarī. It would thus appear that she was the authoress of some work on Poetics. The Karpūramañjarī was also first put on board at her desire. According to Rājaśekhara[1439] in his time daughters of princes and prime ministers, courtesans and wives of jesters were found well-versed in sciences and were poetesses too. Rājaśekhara quoted in Śūktimuktābalī praises five such poetesses—(1) Śilabhaṭṭārikā who was quite a match for Bāṇa and whose style echoes the sense in Pāñchāla fashion; (2) Vikatanitambā whose verses flowed with milk and honey; (3) Vijayāñkā of the Karṇāṭa country who was Sarasvatī incarnate, and an eminent successor to Kālidāsa in the Vidarva school of poetry, (4) Prabhudevī of Lāta who was full of the graces of rhetoric, and a mistress of all the arts, (5) the dark-complexioned, Vijjikā who described herself as having given the lie direct to Daṇḍin's description of the Goddess of Learning as all white. The Kathāsaritsāgara[1440] refers to a queen of Śātabāhana "who knew grammatical treatises." We are also told of a teacher of dancing named Labdhabara, hailing from Madhyadeśa who was appointed by king Harivara as "the instructor in dancing of the ladies of the harem." "He brought (Queen) Anangaprabhā so much excellence in dancing that she was an object of admiration even to her rival wives."[1441] Another princess Haṃsābalī of Vidiṣā gave a demonstration of "her skill in dancing which she had lately been taught" before her father and her tutor Dardura.[1442] We are further told that "king Udayatunga has a daughter named Udayābatī, well taught in all the

---

1437 Puruṣabat yoṣitopi Kabībhabeyuḥ. Saṃskāro hyātmani samabaiti na sraiṇaṃ pauraṣaṃ bā bivāgamapekṣate—Text, p. 53.

1438 Text, pp. 20, 46 and 57.

1439 Śruyante dṛśyate cha rājaputryo mahāmātraduhitaro gaṇikāḥ kautuki-vāryāścha śāstraprahatabudhwayaḥ kabayaścha—Text, p. 53.

1440 Penzer, I., p. 69.

1441 Ibid., IV. p. 156.

1442 Ibid., VI. p. 41.

sciences and he has publicly announced that he will give her to the first brāhmaṇa or kṣhatriya who conquers her in argument. And by her wonderful skill in argument she has silenced all other disputants" except Vinītamati to whom she was married.[1443] Another princess Gandharvadattā, daughter of Sāgaradattā "attained supreme skill in music." "And the princess has firmly resolved that whoever is so well-skilled in music that he can play on the lyre and sing perfectly in three scales a song in praise of Viṣṇu shall be her husband."[1444]

Among the Tāntrics there were many learned women. Kalhaṇa in his Rājataraṅgiṇī[1445] refers to women as preceptors in the Tāntric cult. Stein remarks: "The tradition of Kashmerian paṇḍits knows of cases, as alluded to by K., in which women have assumed the position of Tāntric gurus."[1446]

Buddhism produced a marvellous effect on many women who were moved by the attractive power of the Buddha's Dhamma and renounced the world to lead a pious life in the expectation of a happy rebirth or in order to annihilate rebirth altogether. Ladies of the Śākya family were naturally the earliest women to embrace the hardy life of nuns. The women appear to have enjoyed a greater amount of independence and free thinking among the Śākyas than among the peoples of the plains perhaps owing to the same scarcity of women that forced them to enact a law prohibiting multiple marriages. The change of attitude towards women is, however, apparent in the reluctance of Buddha to admit them into his religious order. His aunt Mahāprajāpati, wished to join the order but was refused three times. She appealed to Ānanda who interceded for her and at last the Buddha gave consent at the eloquent persuation of Ānanda and rationalism triumphed for the time being.[1447] But the Buddha was careful to point out that but for this concession to women now declared eligible for admission into the order

---

1443 Ibid., VI. 73-75.

1444 Ibid., VIII. 28-29.

1445 VI. 12 (Stein—The Chronicles of Kashmere, Vol. I. 237).

1446 Stein—The Chronicles of Kashmere, Vol. I. 237 foot-note.

1447 Vinaya Texts, S. B. E., Vol. XX. pt. III., pp. 302 *et seq*; Compare Monoratha Purāṇa, Sinhalese edition, 203.

"the pure religion would have lasted long, the good law would have stood fast for a thousand years; but now it will last only 500 years".[1448] It is no wonder, therefore, that the general tendency of the Buddhist canon law would be to assign a distinctly inferior position to the bhikṣuṇīs and to their saṃgha.[1449]

The bhikṣuṇīs had to undergo a period of probation for two years during which they would learn the six precepts. After this they would receive upasampadā ordination. This ordination, though carried on in the bhikṣuṇī saṃgha in exactly the same way as that of bhikṣus in the bhikṣu saṃgha had to be confirmed by the latter. They had to go twice a month to take instruction from a bhikṣu. They must not put any question without taking the bhikṣu's permission.[1450] They must not take their seat in the presence of a bhikṣu without his permission. They should receive instruction from the bhikṣu by turn.[1451] They should learn the precepts common to the bhikṣus and the bhikṣuṇīs and the precepts specially meant for the latter.[1452] Thus did the Buddhist nunneries become centres of education and culture, for, those who were admitted as nuns received instruction in the Buddhist doctrines. But we do not know whether the nunneries like the monasteries became centres of secular instruction, receiving pupils even from amongst those who were not intending to join the order. In Ceylon there are no such nunneries to-day, though there are a few girl's schools in the nunneries in Burma. Some Buddhist nuns are said to have visited women in their homes at intervals and at such meetings some oral teaching or discussion of religious precepts might have been taken up.

We hear of the intellectual attainments of the Buddhist nuns and some of their literary compositions are still preserved in the famous Therīgāthā. They are fine lyrics and in the opinion of some critics,

---

1448 Mahāparinirvāṇa Sutta V. 23.

1449 For the details of the Bhikṣuṇī saṃgha, *see* Vinaya Pītaka I. pp. 130, 167; II. pp. 253-55, 257-58; IV. pp. 211, 220-21, 247; Compare Chullavagga X. and the Bhikṣuṇī Pātimokkha.

1450 Vinaya Pītaka II. pp. 253-55.

1451 Majjima Nikāya III. 270.

1452 Vinaya Pītaka II., p. 258.

worthy of being ranked with those of Kālidāsa and Amaru. But it has been argued by some that the authorship of the verses in the Therī-gāthā cannot be ascribed to the women who sang them. "Be that as it may, there is no gainsaying of the fact, in the absence of any historical truth to the contrary that in the Buddha's days women who broke through the fetters of worldly life and gained the joys of asexual rational beings, sang extempore learned and thoughtful verses on many occasions—specially when Māra, the Buddhist Satan tried, in vain, his level best to lead astray these saintly sisters sometimes by joyful or lewd temptations and sometimes by frightful sights".[1453] As Dr. Bimalā Churn Law has pointed out, the gāthās sung by some women and the record of the intellectual attainments of certain individual ladies (mentioned by him) prove that a fairly high standard of literary culture was attained in feminine circles in the days of Gautama Buddha. Thus, Sukkā was a great preacher and one day she taught the Buddhist doctrine to the bhikṣuṇīs in such a way that everybody listened to her with rapt attention; even the tree-spirit was so much moved that it began to praise her. At this the people were excited, came to the sister and listened to her attentively.[1454] The Samyutta Nikāya also refers to her power of oratory. It says that she delivered a sermon to a big audience at Rājagṛha. A Yakkha being pleased with her declared in the streets of Rājagṛha that Sukkā was distributing honey and those who were wise should go and drink it. Buddhā Kuṇḍalakeśa entered the Order of the Nigaṇṭhas, learnt their doctrine and left their company. Thereafter she found no one equal in debate to her. But she was defeated by Sāriputra who advised her to go to the Buddha for refuge. She went to the Buddha who discerned the maturity of her knowledge.[1455] The Majjhima Nikāya[1456] speaks of Dhammadinnā who was asked one day by her husband to explain Sakkāyadiṭṭhi (belief in one's body to be soul), Sakkāya-nirodha, Ariya-aṭṭhangikomaggo, Saṃkhāras, Nirodhasamāpatti, the manner of rising up from nirodhasamāpatti

---

[1453] B. C. Law—Women in Buddhist Literature, pp. 61-62.

[1454] Therīgāthā Commentary, 57-61.

[1455] Ibid., pp. 99f.

[1456] Pt. I. pp. 299f.

and the several kinds of Vedanā. She gave satisfactory explanation to each. She was once questioned by her husband on the Khandas and the like. She answered these questions so correctly that she was praised by the Buddha and was ranked as the foremost among the sisters who could preach.[1457] She also mastered the Vinaya well.[1458] Sanghamittā, daughter of Aśoka[1459] was well-versed in the three-fold science. She knew well the magical powers.[1460] She taught Vinaya Pītaka in Anurādhapura in Ceylon and the five collections (of the Sutta Pītaka) and the seven treatises (of the Abhidhamma).[1461] From the Sutta-Nipāta[1462] we learn that Khemā was vastly learned, eloquent and full of ready wit. When king Pasenadī asked her the reason of Buddha not answering the question whether a being after death is reborn or not, she asked the king whether he had anybody who could count the sands of the Ganges and the drops of water in the sea; the king answered in the negative. Then she said : " If any being is free from attainment to five khandhas, it becomes immeasureable and fathomless like a sea. Hence rebirth after death of such a being is beyond conception". Uttarā like Sanghamittā was well-versed in the three-fold science and like her she, Mallā, Pabbatā Pheggu, Dhammadāsī, Pasādapāla and Aggimittā taught in Anurādhapura the Vinaya Pītaka, five collections of the Sutta Pītaka and the seven treatises of the Abhidharma.[1463] Hemā like Sanghamittā was well-versed in the three-fold science and like her taught the Vinaya Pītaka, the five collections of the Sutta Pītaka, and the seven treatises of the Abhidharma.[1464] Sīvalā and Mahāruhā taught in Anurādhapura the Vinaya Pītaka, the five collections of the Sutta Pītaka and the seven treatises of the Abhidharma.[1465] Añjali Samuddanāvā taught Vinaya Pītaka in Anurādhapura.[1466] Sumanā, Mahilā, Mahādevī, Padumā and Hemāsā

1457 Therīgāthā Commentary, 15; Compare Monoratha Purāṇa, pp, 360-63; Aṅguttara Nikāya I. 25.

1458 Dwīpabaṃśa, Sec. XVIII.

1459 Mahābaṃśa, p. 101.

1460 Dwīpabaṃśa, Sec. XV.

1461 Ibid., XVIII.

1462 IV. pp. 374-80.

1463 Dwīpabaṃśa, Sec. XVIII.

1464 Ibid.

1465 Ibid.

1466 Ibid.

also taught the Vinaya Pītaka in Anurādhapura.[1467] Kālī was well-versed in the whole of the sacred scriptures and taught the Vinaya Pītaka in Anurādhapura.[1468] Aggimittā was well-versed in the three-fold science.[1469] Sapattā, Channā, Upāli and Revatī were the highest among the Vinaya-studying nuns.[1470] Patācārā was the foremost of the nuns who mastered the Vinaya Pītaka.[1471] Uppalavannā, Sobhitā, Isidāsikā, Viśākhā, Sabalā, Saṃghadāsī, Nandā, Saddhammanandi, Somā, Giriddhi, Dāsī and Dhammā were also well-versed in the Vinaya.[1472] Nanduttarā was versed in Vijjā and Sippa.[1473] The Divyāvadāna[1474] refers to female students reading Buddhavachana at night. Cūlanāgā, Dhannā, Soṇā, Mahātissā, Cūla-sumanā and Mahāsumanā were learned and versed in the tradition.[1475] Jenti or Jentā developed the seven Sambojjhangas.[1476]

We learn from Kautilya's Arthaśāstra[1477] that female slaves were taught by teachers "arts such as singing, playing on musical instruments, reading, dancing, acting, writing, painting, playing on the instruments like vīṇā, pipe and drum, reading the thoughts of others, manufacture of scents and garlands, shampooing and the art of attracting and captivating the mind of others." The Therīgāthā commentary[1778] says that Puṇṇa or Puṇṇikā, the daughter of Anāthapiṇḍaka's domestic slave obtained Sotāpattiphalam after hearing the Sihānada Suttanta. She defeated a Brahmin in argument and was therefore given freedom by her master. The Dhammapada commentary[1479] says that Khujjuttarā, a maid-servant of Sāmābatī, Queen of Udena, king of Kośāmbī used to steal four out of the eight Kahāpaṇas daily given to her for buying flowers. One day she heard the sermon delivered by the Buddha in the house of the garland-

---

[1467] Ibid.

[1468] Ibid.

[1469] Ibid., sec. XV.

[1470] Ibid., Sec. XVIII.

[1471] Aṅguttara Nikāya I. 25 ; Compare Dwīpabaṃśa, sec. XVIII.

[1472] Dwīpabaṃśa, sec. XVIII.

[1473] Therīgāthā Commentary, p. 87.

[1474] Page 532.

[1475] Dwīpabaṃśa, sec. XVIII.

[1476] Therīgāthā Commentary, p. 27.

[1477] R. Śyāmaśāstrī's Eng. Trans., pp. 155-56.

[1478] Pp. 199f.

[1479] I. pp. 208f.

maker where she went to buy flowers and obtained Sotāpattiphalam. Since then she discontinued stealing and bought flowers for eight kahāpaṇas. The queen questioned her how she had bought so many flowers for eight kahāpaṇas. The girl confessed her guilt and said that after hearing the Buddha's sermon, she had come to realise that stealing a thing is a sin. The queen asked her to repeat the sermon she had heard. Since then the slave-girl was regarded as a mother and *teacher* by the queen and her 500 female attendants, who asked her to go to the Master daily to hear the Dhamma and repeat it to them. In course of time she mastered the Tripītaka.

The cultivation of the æsthetic sense in women contributed to the formation of a class of Saubhikās or Śobhānikās which existed as early as the days Patañjali. The expression lenasobhika in the Madhura inscriptions is probably also of similar reference. These inscriptions show that women actually appeared on the stage.[1480] A class of gay women is depicted in the Kāmasūtra[1481] as frequenters of goṣṭhis and ghaṭas and Bhāsa[1482] refers to the gaiety of life among these maidens. From Kautilya's Arthaśāstra[1483] we learn that actresses were taught by teachers " arts such as singing, playing on musical instruments, reading, dancing, acting, writing, painting, playing on the instruments like the viṇā, pipe and drum, reading the thoughts of others, manufacture of scents and garlands, shampooing and the art of attracting and captivating the minds of others." Kautilya also says that the wives of actors and others of similar profession were also taught " various languages and the use of signals (sanja) and that they were employed by the state in detecting the wicked and in murdering or deluding foreign spies.[1484]

In common with the other parts of the world prostitution in India dates from the earliest times; but through the clouds of myth and

---

1480 Arch. Survey Rep. for 1903-4, p. 123f.

1481 Sūtra 13.

1482 Bhāsa : Abhimāraka, pp. 69, 86f.

1483 R. Śyāmaśāstrī's Eng. Trans., pp. 155-56.

1484 Ibid., p. 156.

mystery which cover the dawn of Indian History any distinction between the secular and the sacred prostitution must be looked upon as little more than conjecture. Secular prostitution is mentioned in the Ṛgveda[1485] while in the Vājaseni Saṃhitā[1486] it seems to be recognised as a profession. In the law-books[1487] the prostitute is regarded with disfavour. The Jātakas[1488] refer to dancing girls (nātakī) who were accomplished in dancing and music (naccagīta-vāditakuśalā). The dancing women employed to keep prince Siddhārtha in hilarity were skilful in dancing, singing and in playing on musical instruments.[1489] They seem to have lived a more intellectual life than other women: Ambapālī invited the Buddha, Aspasia received Socrates in her house. We are told that Ambapālī was so well-versed in dancing, singing and lute-playing that she charged fifty kahāpaṇas for one night.[1490] Sālavatī was installed as a courtesan by a merchant of Rājagaha. She was an expert in dancing, singing and lute-playing and her fee was one hundred kahāpaṇas for one night.[1491]

Kautilya[1492] refers to "prostitutes whether or not of a prostitute's family" "noted for their beauty, youth and *accomplishments*" and lays down that the Superintendent of Prostitutes should employ such women at the king's court on a salary of Rs. 1000 paṇas per annum. Vātsyāyana in describing the qualities to be possessed by a courtesan says that she must possess "*a knowledge of Sexual science and its attendant arts*[1493] *and a taste for arts* (*sixty-four in number*)."[1494] In another passage Vātsyāyana[1495] says that she (the prostitute) should seek help from "those that are *learning arts* (*sixty-four in number*) *from her*".

1485 Macdonell and Keith—Vedic Index, 1912, I. p. 365; II. p. 480 *et seq.*; R. Pischel and K. F. Geldner—Vedische Studien, 1881-99, I. pp. 196, 275, 306 *et seq.*; II. p. 120.

1486 Ibid.

1487 Manu IX. 259; IV. 209, 211, 219, 220; V. 90.

1488 Fausball, Jātaka II. p. 328; V. p. 249.

1489 Rhys Davids—Buddhist Birth Stories, p. 171.

1490 Vinaya Texts, Part II. p. 171.

1491 Ibid., p. 172f.

1492 R. Śyāmaśāstrī's Eng. Trans., p. 153.

1493 Kāmasūtra, Bk. VI. Ch. I. śl. 14.

1494 Ibid., śl. 13.

1495 Ibid., śl.9.

That they also used to hold *discussions on arts* is also referred to by Vātsyāyana.[1496] Vātsyāyana is more explicit in Bk. I. Ch. III. of his Kāmasūtra regarding the education of prostitutes. After enumerating the 64 kalās which every woman should learn he says—

"There is another set of 64 arts different from the foregoing taught by Pāñchāla and these will be shown in the next book—Samprayogika—each in its proper place. For, this section treats of the actual courses of sexual intercourse and the Pāñchāla arts are nothing but these acts. A courtesan who has good character, beauty and virtue, will get, on account of her increased worth due to a knowledge of these 64 kalās, the rank of gaṇikā (a more honourable class among veśyās) as well as an honourable place in a gathering of persons. Such a woman will always be rewarded by kings and praised by gifted persons and her connection will be sought by many people. She thus becomes an example to be followed by the women of her class."[1497]

Kautilya is no less explicit about the education of prostitutes. According to him *prostitutes were taught by teachers "arts such as singing, playing on musical instrument, reading, dancing, acting, writing, painting, playing on the instruments like lute, pipe, drum, reading the thoughts of others, manufacture of scents and garlands. shampooing and the art of attracting and captivating the minds of others"*[1498] and he says that these teachers are to be "endowed with maintenance by the state."[1499] Kautilya also refers to rūpadāsīs who were experts in making garlands, scents and the like.[1500] Kautilya further says: "They (the teachers of prostitutes) shall train up the sons of prostitutes to be chief actors (rangopajīvi) on the stage."[1501] Vātsyāyana also lays down rules for the *education of the daughters of the prostitutes and Natas.* Says he—

"The necessity for initiating her (courtesan's) daughter in love affairs having arisen, the mother should allow her to be *trained* in these

1496 Ibid., śl. 25.

1497 Ibid., Book I. Ch. III. śls. 17-21.

1498 Kautilya's Arthaśāstra (R. Śyāmaśāstrī's Eng. Trans.), p. 155.

1499 Ibid., p. 156.

1500 Ibid., p. 154.

1501 Ibid., p. 156.

matters by a female friend or by a clever woman-servant of hers. After she (the daughter) has thus gained the *knowledge of* sexual science and been trained in the different postures in copulation and finding her arrived at the lovely youthful age, she should be proclaimed as a clever lovely girl and thus gain voluptuous youths for her. These are the ways current from ancient times."[1502]

"The cases of the daughters of Natas (those men that have as their profession dancing and singing) may similarly be understood. She should be given to the one who would *train her up in the arts of dancing and singing*."[1503]

Kalhaṇa also refers to the education of courtesans. Says he: "*Courtesans*, the official (kāyastha), the clerk (divira) and the merchants being all deceitful by nature, are (in this respect) superior to a poisoned arrow that they have been *trained under a teacher's advice*."[1504]

Daṇḍin in his Daśakumāracharita narrates the story of a famous dancer, who was also a prostitute who suddenly pretended to feel the desire of becoming a devotee. She accordingly went to an ascetic to carry out her purpose. Soon, however, her mother follows to dissuade her from her intention and addressed the holy man as follows:—"Worthy sir,..................as soon as she (this daughter of mine) was old enough *I had her carefully instructed in the arts of dancing, acting, playing on musical instruments, singing, painting, preparing perfumes and flowers, in writing and conversation and even to some extent in grammar, logic and philosophy. She was taught to play various games with skill and dexterity, how to dress well and show herself off to the greatest advantage in public*................Yet after all the time, trouble and money which I have spent upon her, just when I was beginning to reap the fruit of my labours, the ungrateful girl has fallen in love with a stranger, a young Brahmin without property and wishes to marry him and give up her profession.........and because I oppose this marriage she declares that she will renounce the world

[1502] Kāmasūtra Bk. VII. Ch. I. śl. 20. [1503] Ibid., śls. 23-24.

[1504] Stein—The Chronicles of Kashmere, Vol. II. p. 12.

and become a devotee."[1505] The Kathāsaritsāgara[1506] refers to "Rūpaṇikā's mother Makaradaṃṣtrā, who had *trained up many courtesans.*"

The dancing girls who are often attached to temples were generally called Devadāsīs (maid-servants of the god). Kautilya in his Arthaśāstra Bk. II. Ch. XXIII. refers to Devadāsīs.[1507] Kalhaṇa in his Rājataraṅgiṇī[1508] and Kālidāsa in his Meghadūta refers to devadāsīs. Ibn Asir also refers to 300 females singing and dancing at the gate of the temple of Somanāth. From the story of Rūpaṇikā in Somadeva's Kathāsaritsāgara[1509] it is quite clear that Rūpaṇikā combined the professions of a prostitute and a temple-servant. The Chinese traveller Chau Ju-kwa in his work, Chu-fan-chi, dealing with the Chinese and Arab trade of the twelfth and thirteenth centuries refers to "four thousand Buddhist temple buildings (in Gujrat) in which live over twenty-thousand dancing girls who sing twice daily while offering food to the Buddha (i. e., the idols) and while offering flowers."[1510] He also speaks of similar customs in Cambodia.[1511] Marco Polo (about 1290 A. D.) refers to such dancing-girls attached to temples in the "Province of Maabar" (i. e., Tanjore).[1512] Some Tamil inscriptions[1513] refer to such devadāsīs. One of these inscriptions shows that in 1004 A. D. the chief temple at Tanjore had four hundred tali-cheri-peṇḍugal or "women of the temple" attached to it. The whole Chola country was full of temples with devadāsīs in attendance, as is clear from this inscription, which

---

1505 "Anaryan" (F. F. Arbuthnot)—Early Ideas: A group of Hindoo Stories, 1881, p. 76.

1506 Penzer, Vol. I. p. 140.

1507 R. Śyāmaśāstrī's Eng. Trans., p. 140.

1508 Stein—The Chronicles of Kashmere, Vol. I. p. 148.

1509 Penzer, Vol. I. p. 139.

1510 Eng. Trans., by Hirth and Rockhill, 1911, p. 92.

1511 Ibid., p. 53.

1512 Yule and Cordier—The Book of Marco Polo, 1903, Vol. II. pp. 345-46; G. B. Parks—The Travels of Marco Polo, pp. 279-80,

1513 E. Hultzsch—South Indian Inscriptions, Vol. II. part III. pp. 259-303.

gives a long list of the dancing girls who had been transferred to the Tañjavūr (Tanjore) temple. After each name details are added showing among others from what temple the girl originally came. Paes also refers to such devadāsīs in the temples of Vijayanagar. Travellers like Linschoten (1598), De Bry (1599), Gouvea (1606), Bernier (1660), Thevenot (1661), Fryer (1673), Wheeler (1701), a writer in Letters Edificantes (1702), Orme (1770), Sonnerat (1782) and Moor (1794) also refer to such devadāsīs.[1514]

This ancient connection of dancing girls with temple worship is nothing peculiar to India. Among the ancient Jews harlotry appears to have been connected with religious worship and to have been not only tolerated but also encouraged. In Egypt, Phœnicia, Chaldæa, Cannan, Persia, the worship of Isis, Moloch, Baæl, Astarte, Myletta and other deities consist of the most extravagant social orgies and temples were the centres of vice. It is, needless for our present purpose to speculate about the genesis of this custom. Female artists were possibly introduced in temples more for the performance of certain specified duties, than for the purpose of pandering to the libidinous taste of those who frequent such places of worship. The dancing girl is not necessarily bad, but there is in her life much temptation to do evil and little stimulus to do right and where one may live a blameless life, many others go wrong and drop below the margin of respectability. Thus in time, harlotry came to be regarded as inseparably connected with the vocation of dancing girls and as an essential feature of temple worship.

Coming to our subject proper we find that these devadāsīs received some training to enable them to perform their work of dancing, reciting and singing. Jayāpīḍa of Kashmere in the course of his tour of adventure entered the city of Paundrabardhana and saw dancing and singing (performed there in the temple) in accordance with the precepts of Bharata.[1515] One of these dancing girls was Kamalā who

[1514] *See* Hobson Jobson, Yule and Burnell, under "dancing girl", "devadāsī", "bayadere", "nautch girl" and "cunchurree".

[1515] Stein—The Chronicles of Kashmere, Vol. I. p. 160.

was "*versed in (all) arts.*"[1516] A Tamil Inscription[1517] dated 1004 A. D. gives the names and shares of the *dancing-masters*, musicians, singers etc. Abbe J. A. Dubois in his famous Hindu Manners, Customs and Ceremonies says: "Every temple of any importance has in its service a band of eight, twelve or more.............. They......are the only women in India who *enjoy the privilege of learning to read, to dance and to sing.*"[1518] According to Dr. John Shortt[1519] these devadāsis begin a strenuous three-year course of singing and dancing at the early age of five. According to Mr. N. S. Aiyar in ancient days the devadāsis of Travancore who became experts in singing and dancing received the title of Rāyar (queen) which appears to have been last conferred in 1847 A. D. According to Syed Siraj Ul Hassan the training of the bogams (the usual term for Telegu dancing girls) is most thorough and complete. Says he: "Commencing their studies at the early age of seven or eight, they are able to perform at twelve or thirteen years of age and continue dancing till they are thirty or forty years old.[1520]

That the institutions of both secular and sacred prostitution were utilized by the state as secret service agents is evident from Kautilya's Arthaśāstra. According to it women of accomplishments should be employed as spies inside the houses of kings who are inimical, friendly, intermediate, of low rank, neutral and in the houses of the superintendent of such Kings' eighteen Government departments.[1521] According to him "women artisans or prostitutes should be employed to convey information to its destined place under the pretext of taking in musical instruments or through cipher-writing (guḍhalekhya)".[1522] Thus even women artisans, not to speak of prostitutes, knew the art of reading signs, of cipher-writing and probably that of playing on musical

1516 Ibid., p. 161.

1517 E. Hultzsch—South Indian Inscriptions, Vol. II. Part III. pp. 259-303.

1518 Eng. Trans., by Henry K. Beauchamp, 1906, Third Edition, pp. 585-87.

1519 Paper on the Bayadere or Dancing girls of South India, Memoirs read before the Anthropological Society of London, 1867-69, Vol. III. London 1870, pp. 182-94.

1520 The Tribes and Castes of H. E. H. the Nizam's Dominions, 1920, Vol. I. p. 94.

1521 R. Śyāmaśāstrī's Eng. Trans., p. 25.

1522 Ibid., p. 24.

instruments. It is probably on account of this service obtained from them by the state that Kautilya lays down that the Superintendent of weaving should employ mothers of prostitutes and devādāsis who have ceased to attend temples on service to cut wool, fibre, cotton, panicle (tūlā), hemp and flax and pay them wages according to the quantity and quality of their work.[1523]

It is no less interesting to find that some women had also some knowledge of military arts and sciences. From the hymns of the Ṛgveda we find that non-Aryan girls joined the army in large numbers. In their case some military training may be presumed, as they played their part so well that men of the time did not regard it as easy or ungallant to war with women.[1524] It would appear that some military training was not barred to women as might be inferred from the mention in Patañjali of Śāktikī, which means a female spear-bearer[1525] and from the story in the Rāmāyaṇa of Kaikeyī saving her husband Daśaratha, by fighting against his enemies. Military arts have been enumerated by Vātsyāyana in his list of 64 kalās to be learnt by women in general (*See* kalās Nos. 50 and 63). This is corroborated by Kautilya who says: "On getting up from the bed, the king shall be received by the troops of women armed with bows." "The Karpūramañjarī of Rājaśekhara[1526] refers to girls with names ending in kelī, Anagakelī, Barkarakelī, Sundarakelī, Rājakelī and Kandarpakelī as holding shields and swords and thus guarding the prison of Karpūramañjarī. An inscription[1527] of Mihira Bhoja discloses bands of women who gloried in the military profession. Paes[1528] who came to India in 1531 A. D. says: "They also say that each of them (queens of the king of Vijayanagara, has sixty maidens.........within, with these maidens, they say there are twelve thousand women; for you must know that there are *women who handle sword and shield and others who wrestle* and others who blow trumpets and others pipes and other instruments which are different from ours".

1523 Ibid., p. 140.

1524 Rgveda V. 61; 80, 6; VII. 78, 5; VIII. 33, 19; 91.

1525 Pāṇini IV. 1, 48, 63; Patañjali on IV. 1, 15.

1526 Konow and Lanman's edition, p. 279.

1527 Ep. Ind., Vol. XVIII. No. 13.

1528 Sewell—A Forgotten Empire, pp. 248-49.

The above survey makes it clear that the education of girls in Ancient India fitted them for the role they were to play in life as a good housewife, an expert actress or a trained dancing girl attached to temples for religious functions. We have seen that the Vedic girl received a fair share of masculine attention and liberal education. The frequent prayers for the concord of husband and wife in the Vedic texts are certain proof that feminine subservience could not be taken for granted and co-operation had to be prayed for. But in course of time the normal woman came to have her girlhood education in which emphasis was laid on her modesty, regard for family life, care of religion, children and the kitchen and on domestic management and husbanding of resources. Henceforward we rarely have figures like Vedic Maitreyī's, hidden behind philosophical theories or Buddhist nuns poring over Buddha's words by midnight. It is rarely, too, we have a Vasantasenā, the hataera of the Mṛchchhakatikā, as full of the intensity of life as man, sparkling, scintillating and businesslike. What a contrast is presented to the passing student, by the lady-hymnists of the Vedic period, and their self-conscious sweetness and self-assertion in the Upaniṣads where women vie with men in intellectual striving and outlook on life; and by the patient Griseldas of the Epic and Sūtra periods however intelligent and cultured, whose delight lay not in inroads into the citadels of masculine rights and privileges but in the routine duties of domestic husbandry and the fashioning of future men. Thus the sexes came to regard their functions in life as complementary and not competitive. The queen of the house knew not unwilling child-bearing, unwanted babes or the need for the exercise of a modern 'dreadful patience'. Her work was one round of self-denial and social service, the coping-stone of India's structural edifice.

CHAPTER X.

THE EDUCATION OF THE PRINCE IN ANCIENT INDIA.

In the Ṛgvedic Age the sons of rājanyas undoubtedly shared with the other Aryans the knowledge of the Veda but the incessant struggle with the non-Aryans must have made their education more military in character. There is a passage in the hymns of the Ṛgveda[1529] which refers to military combats among young warriors and as the rājanyas became marked off from other classes of society as those whose function was to fight for their protection, the practice of arms must have become specialised.

But in the Brāhmaṇa period when with the progress of Aryan colonisation in the East, the battle cries were drowned in the peaceful avocations of life, the princes had enough leisure to devote their attention to Vedic studies. In the Atharvaveda[1530] there is a reference to the king guarding his country by brahmacharya, though it lends itself to a different interpretation. To this may be added the evidence of the Kāṭhaka Saṃhitā[1531] in its reference to the rite intended to benefit one, who, although not a brāhmaṇa, had yet studied (vidyām anūcya) but had not acquired fame. More conclusive, however, is the evidence of the Brāhmaṇas and the Upaniṣads regarding learned kṣhatriyas and princes who studied the Vedas and attained proficiency in the sacred lore.

Thus among the princes, Janaka, king of Videha had the highest reputation as a master of Brahmavidyā. He had learnt portion of the subject from the various brāhmaṇa āchāryas viz., Udaṇka, Barku, Gardabhīvipīta, Satyakāma and Vidagdha Sākalya.[1532] We find in the Śatapatha Brāhmaṇa[1533] that King Janaka, meets with some travelling brāhmaṇas named Śvetaketu Āruṇeya, Somaśusma Satyayajñi and Yājñabālkya and asks them how they offered the Agnihotra but with

---

1529 IV. 42, 5.
1530 XV. 5. 17.
1531 IX. 16.
1532 Bṛhad. Up., IV. 1.
1533 XI. 6. 2. 1.

regard to the answer of Yājñabālkya, the king compliments him by saying: "Thou O Yājñabālkya, hast approached very close to the solution of the Agnihotra," pointing out at the same time the incompleteness of his answer in certain respects. The brāhmaṇas then said amongst themselves: "This rājanya has surpassed us in speaking, come let us invite him to a theological discussion". Yājñabālkya however interposed: "We are brāhmaṇas and he a rājanya; if we overcome him, we shall ask ourselves, whom have we overcome? But if he overcome us, men will say a rājanya has overcome brāhmaṇas. Do not follow this course". In the end the Agnihotra was explained by Janaka and on Yājñabālkya offering him a boon, he replied: "Let mine be the privilege of asking questions of thee when I list," thus showing his thirst for knowledge. "Like the traveller furnishing himself with a ship or wagon for a long journey, the king (Janaka) had his mind equipped for the eternal journey of the soul with upaniṣads or doctrines". His former teachers (mentioned above) had taught him respectively six definitions of Brahman as Speech, Breath, Eye, Ear, Manas and Heart. Yājñābālkya further develops these definitions by pointing out the upaniṣads or hidden attributes belonging to those six appearances as their supports (āyatana) viz., Prajñā, belonging to Vāk (for, knowledge is conveyed by speech), Priyam to Prāṇa (for, life always seeks its self-preservation), Satyam to Eye (which conveys truth better than the ear), Anantam to ear, Ānanda to Manas (for, thought is the source of Bliss) and Sthiti to Hṛdaya (for, in heart rests every thing). At the conclusion of each lesson, the king offered the gift of 1000 cows with big bulls like elephants; but Yājñabālkya each time declined the offer on the ground that, under his father's instruction, a teacher could not accept it before he had completed the teaching of his pupil On another occasion King Janaka leaving his throne approached Yājñabālkya and bowing to him requested instruction. Yājñabālkya hailed the king as one who was self-collected by the study of the Upaniṣads, worthy of honour like the gods, and yet learned by studying the Vedas and listening to Upaniṣadic discourses. Therefore to such a competent person he put the most difficult question: "Whither will you go after death?" The question could not be answered by the king and was made the basis of further abstruse instruction by Yājñabālkya upon a theme which baffles human thought to this day.[1534] The substance of his instruction is that "the soul after death goes nowhere whence it has not been from the very beginning nor does it become other than that which it has always been, one eternal omnipresent Ātman."[1535] At the conclusion of the instruction, the king was so much moved as to lay at the feet of his preceptor the gift of his entire kingdom with himself as his slave. There is recorded a third occasion on which Janaka received instruction from Yājñabālkya. Here the king first proposes the question: "What serves man for light?" Yājñabālkya explains that, when external light such as Sun, Moon or fire fails, there shines the inner light of his self or Ātman. This self is defined as "the spirit behind the organs of the sense which is the essential knowledge and shines within the heart." That spirit at birth assumes a body and becomes united with all evils, but the evils are left behind at death. A person, as Yājñabālkya further explains, consists of desires. As is his desire, so is his will; as is his will, so is the deed; and whatever deed he does, that he will reap. To whatever object a man's own mind is attached, to that he goes strenuously together with his deed; and having obtained the complete consequences of whatever deed he does on earth, he returns again from that world (which is the temporary reward of his deed) to this world of action. But as to the man who does not so desire, who, not desiring, freed from desires, is satisfied in his desires, or desire the Self only, his vital spirit does not depart elsewhere—being Brahman he goes to Brahman. When all desires which once entered his heart are undone, then does the mortal become immortal, then he obtains Brahman, with his body cast off like the slough of a snake. If a man understands the self, thus saying "I am He" what could he wish or desire that he should pine after the body? Knowing this the people of old did not wish for offspring. What shall we do with offspring, they said, we who have this Self and this world of Brahman? At the end of these words, "than which deeper, finer, more noble were never uttered by human lips"

1534 Compare Deussen's candid confession: "Nor have we even to-day any better reply to give" (Philosophy of the Upaniṣads, p. 90).

1535 Deussen—Philosophy of the Upaniṣads, p. 348.

(as remarked by Deussen) the king repeated his precious gift, saying: "Sir, I give you the Videhas and also myself to be together your slaves.[1536]

Similarly, we find that king Bṛhadratha of the Ikṣvāku race learnt Brahmavidyā from the brāhmaṇa ascetic Sākāyana.[1537] King Janaśruti was at great pains in searching for the brāhmaṇa Raikva to learn from him the Brahmavidyā.[1538]

Again in the Chāndogya[1539] we find that Pravahana Jaivāli, king of the Pāñchālas gave evidence of greater knowledge of Sauravidyā than Śilaka and Dālbhya. Again according to the Bṛihad.[1540] and Chāndogya[1541] Upaniṣads the aforesaid king of Pāñchāla silenced Śvetaketu Āruṇeya and his father and treating them as disciples communicated to them the knowledge of Pañchāgnividyā.[1542]

A narrative in the Kauśitaki[1543] and the Bṛhad.[1544] Upaniṣads relates that once a brāhmaṇa youth Gārgya Bālāki came to king Ajātaśatru of Kāśī to speak to him regarding Brahman. What Bālāki said did not meet with the King's appreciation. Then the son of Bālāki approached the king with fuel in his hand and said: "Let me attend thee (as thy pupil)."[1545] The king replied : "I regard it as an inversion of the proper rule that a kṣhatriya should initiate a brāhmaṇa".[1546] "But" continued he: "Come, I will instruct thee." Then taking him by the hand he departed.

Another learned king was Aśwapati Kaikeya. To Uddālaka Āruṇi came five brāhmaṇas named Prācinaśāla, Satyayajña, Indradyumna, Jana and Buḍila to learn Vaiśwānaravidyā. Āruṇi, diffident as to the fullness of his knowledge of the subject, asked them to go to king Aśwapati Kaikeya with fuel in their hands. The king said: "How is this, venerable

---

1536 Bṛhad. Up., IV. 1-4.

1537 Maitrā. Up., 1f.

1538 Ibid.

1539 I. 8f.

1540 VI. 2. 1f.

1541 V. 3. 1f.

1542 It treats of the paths along which men depart after death and so forth.

1543 IV. 1.

1544 II. 1.

1545 Samitpāṇi pratichakrame upāyānit—Kauś. Up., IV. 1. 19.

1546 Pratilomarūpameba brāhmaṇamupanayeta—Kauś. Up., IV. 1. 19.

sirs, when ye are learned in the scriptures and sons of men learned in the scriptures ?" They said : "Venerable Sir, thou knowest Vaiśvānarā throughly: teach us Him." He said: "I do indeed know Vaiśvānarā throughly : put your fuel on (the fire), ye are become my pupil."[1547]

It is no less interesting to find that there were also some royal sages, rājanya-ṛṣis as they are called (in the Pañc. Br. XII. 12. 6.). We may also refer to the tradition preserved in the Nirukta[1548] relating how Devāpi, a king's son became the purohita of his younger brother Śāntanu. From the Raghuvaṃśam of Kālidāsa we learn that king Kārtyabīrya was engaged in metaphysical learning.[1549] Similarly, king Brahmaniṣṭha was well-versed in metaphysics.[1550] In the Śatapatha Brāhmaṇa[1551] we find a rājanya as a lute-player and singer at the Aśvamedha sacrifice, probably the forerunner of kṣhatriya bards from whom sprang the Epics.

Despite their military character it is quite clear from the Epics that the princes received a liberal education. The educational attainments of the princes mentioned in the Epics would show that they studied Dhanurveda, the lore of elephants[1552] and chariots,[1553] langhaṇa (jumping) and plavana (swimming)[1554] and also subjects like the Vedas, Vedāngas, Nītiśāstra, Arthabivāga, Vārttā, Daṇḍaniti, Music and Poetry, Lekhya (writing)[1555] and Ālekhya (painting).[1556] In the Rāmāyaṇa[1557] we find Rāma asking Bharata whether he studies the three Vidyās (tisravidyāḥ) where as is apparent Ānvīkṣikī has been dropped from the curriculum of studies as not of much importance to princes. Bhīṣma says to Yudhiṣṭhir that the king should study the Vedas and Rājanīti.[1558] Devarṣi Nārada enquired of king Yudhiṣṭhir whether he is giving military

---

[1547] Chāndogya Up., V. 11 ; Śat. Brāh., X. 6. 11.

[1548] II. 10.

[1549] Canto VI. 38.

[1550] Canto XVIII. 28.

[1551] XIII. 4. 3. 5.

[1552] Rāmāyaṇa, Bālakāṇḍa 80, 27f.

[1553] Ibid.

[1554] Ibid.

[1555] Ibid.

[1556] Ibid.

[1557] II. 100. 68.

[1558] Mahābhārata, Śāntiparba, 63rd adhyāya.

training to the princes through experts in military science.[1559] Bhīṣma says to Yudhiṣṭhir: "Dharma—(Law) is of four kinds—that laid down by the Vedas, by the Smṛtis, by sages and that determined by self-examination. The king should be conversant with all these. That king is really proficient in Law who knows it as sanctioned by Tarka-śāstra, Veda-śāstra, Vārttā-śāstra and Daṇḍanīti".[1560] Professor Hopkins observes: "How are we to interpret this? The science of arms required years of patient study. Is it conceivable that a boy otherwise occupied in physical training should by the age of sixteen be master of the special skill that gave him power on the battle-field and at the same time have found time to commit to memory even one Vedic collection? It is clear that the law is later than the epic on this point; and even there such knowledge is only to be assumed as is desirable for the warrior in general. The active young knight and busy trader must have performed their duties towards the Veda in a very perfunctory way, if at all."

In the Rāmāyaṇa[1561] we are thus told about the education of Rāma and his brothers: "All of them were versed in the Vedas and heroic and intent upon the welfare of others. And all were accomplished in knowledge and endowed with virtues and among them all, the exceedingly puissant Rāma, having truth for prowress, was the desire of every one and spotless like unto the Moon himself. He could ride on elephants and horses and was an adept in managing cars (chariots) and he was ever engaged in the study of arms and aye occupied in ministering unto his sire................ Those best of men ever engaged in the study of the Vedas, were accomplished in the art of archery and always intent upon ministering unto their father."

In due course Rāma had his initiation,[1562] observed the vow of celibacy as a student[1563] in the house of his guru[1564] and on finishing his education took the ceremonial bath.[1565] Rāma was endowed with knowledge; he has seen the end of the Vedas and Vedāngas; he

---

1559 Ibid., Savāparba, 5th Adhyāya. 1560 Ibid., Śāntiparba, 132nd adhyāya.

1561 Bālakāṇḍa (M. N. Dutt's Eng. Trans.), pp. 51f.

1562 Ramāyaṇa, Ayodhyākāṇḍa, 20th sarga. 1563 Ibid., 82nd sarga.

1564 Ibid., 1st sarga. 1565 Ibid., 1st and 82nd sargas.

was well-versed in Dhanurveda and all the śāstras. (Bālakāṇḍa, 1st sarga). From childhood he has studied the Vedas, observed the vow of brahmacharya, served his gurus and has thus grown lean and thin.[1566] He is well educated[1567] and "Learning resides in him."[1568] He is the strongest and most learned of all and is well-versed in the use of weapons and is the repository of penance.[1569] He learnt from Viśwāmitra two mantras called Balā and Atibalā which are the mothers of all learning.[1570] He also learnt from Viśwāmitra the use of innumerable weapons.[1571] He used to cultivate the śāstras to find out their profound truths, being surrounded by aged and learned sādhus of good conduct during the intervals of the practice of weapons.[1572] "He has returned home after finishing his education in the house of his guru being a master of Vedas and Vedāngas. He has mastered the use of all kinds of missils and weapons of magical potency or not............... His teachers are aged Brahmins who have seen the true import of Dharma. He is endowed with genius and memory and proficient in the three Vargas... .... He has well mastered poetry and philosophy and all those arts that are specially suited for travelling purposes. He is proficient in Arthavivāga. He is a passed master in riding on horses and elephants and in training them. He is an expert in constructing phalanx, in marching against the enemy and in killing them. He is an expert charioteer and is the best of all those who are proficient in Dhanurveda."[1573] "He has mastered the use of all kinds of missils and weapons that are known to Suras, Asuras and men. He has acquired all learning and knows the Vedas along with their Angas. He is profoundly proficient in music."[1574] He is also well-versed in Nitiśāstra[1575] and in all the śāstras.[1576] Reference to military

---

1566 Ibid., Ayodhyākāṇḍa, 12th sarga.

1567 Ibid., 8th sarga.

1568 Ibid., 12th sarga.

1569 Ibid., Bālakāṇḍa, 21st sarga.

1570 Ibid., 22nd sarga.

1571 Ibid., 27th and 28th sargas.

1572 Ibid., Ayodhyākāṇḍa, 1st sarga.

1573 Ibid., Ayodhyākāṇḍa, 1st sarga.

1574 Ibid., 2nd sarga.

1575 Ibid., Yuddhakāṇḍa, 32nd sarga.

1576 Ibid., 18th and 108th sargas.

tournaments where Rāma used to play with other warriors for testing his military skill is also to be found.[1577]

Lakṣmaṇa was also well-versed in all the śāstras[1578] and in Nīti and in the art of warfare.[1579] He can throw 500 arrows by bending the bow once.[1580] His wielding of arms was extraordinary and without any defect and in the use of arms he displayed fastness, variety and beautiful skill.[1581]

Bharata was also well-versed in the three Vedas, Vārttā (Economics) and in Polity (Daṇḍanīti).[1582]

Yuvarāja Angada of Kiṣkiñdhyā was well-versed in sāma, dāna, bheda and nigraha and in the eight angas of knowledge (viz., śuśrūṣā, śrabaṇa, grahaṇa, dhāraṇa, tarka, bitarka and arthatatvajñāna). He was more skilled in warfare than Bālī.[1583]

Rāvaṇa's son Indrajit was also skilled in the art of warfare.[1584] He was well-versed in the use of all heavenly weapons[1585] and any one in the three worlds who is not aware of his military prowess and skill in arms is infamous.[1586] Indeed like Lakṣmaṇa his wielding of arms was extraordinary and without any defect and in the use of arms he displayed fastness, variety and beautiful skill.[1587]

Prince Akṣa, another son of Rāvaṇa, was also skilled in the art of warfare and was highly proficient in aiming and throwing arrows and in hitting the mark.[1588]

" Prince Atikāya, another son of Rāvaṇa, was well-versed in all the śāstras. He was an expert in riding on horses and elephants, in the use of swords, bows and arrows. He was proficient in sāma, dāna, sandhi and bigraha and the whole city of Lañkā is without any fear owing to the prowess of his arms."[1589]

1577 Ibid., Ayodhyākāṇḍa, 30th sarga.

1578 Ibid., Uttarakāṇḍa, 58th sarga.

1579 Ibid., Yuddhakāṇḍa, 29th and 88th sargas.

1580 Ibid., 49th sarga.

1581 Ibid., 88th sarga.

1582 Ibid., Ayodhyākāṇḍa, 100th sarga.

1583 Ibid., Kiṣkiñdhyākāṇḍa, 55th sarga.

1584 Ibid., Yuddhakāṇḍa 88th sarga.

1585 Ibid., Sundarakāṇḍa, 48th sarga.

1586 Ibid.

1587 Ibid., Yuddhakāṇḍa, 88th sarga.

1588 Ibid., Sundarakāṇḍa, 47th sarga.

1589 Ibid., Yuddhakāṇḍa, 70th sarga.

About the education of Kuśa and Laba, the twin sons of king Rāma we are told thus:—"Maharṣi Vālmikī finding Kuśa and Laba who were talented, well-versed in Dharma, endowed with sweet voice and able to comprehend the meaning of kābya began to teach them the Vedas and the whole Epic Rāmāyaṇa .... They have completely mastered the art of music and sthāna and mūrchhanā-tatva."[1590] In the Uttarakāṇḍa 94th sarga we find Vālmikī saying to Kuśa and Laba: "Sing every day 24 sargas full of ślokas in the manner I have shown you before..................... If Rāma be pleased to ask you whose sons you are, say that you are the students of Vālmikī.) In the Raghuvaṃśam we are told that Vālmikī taught Kuśa and Laba the Vedas and the Vedāngas,[1591] as also the art of singing.[1592]

Rājarṣi Daśaratha was well-versed in the Vedas and the Vedāngas.[1593] The contemporary king of Magadha was also well-versed in all the śāstras.[1594]

Rāvaṇa, king of Lañkā (Ceylon) also observed the vow of celibacy as a student, resided in the house of his teacher and after finishing his Vedic education, performed the ceremonial bath and leaving the house of his guru became a householder.[1595] He has thus seen the end of the Vedas and Vedāngas.[1596]

We also find Hanumāna, the minister of Sugrīva well-versed in the Vedas, the śāstras, nīti, grammar and the art of war. "Rāma after his first talk with him thus speaks of him to Lakṣmaṇa: 'One who has not mastered Ṛk, Yajur and Sāma Vedas cannot talk in this way. He must have heard the whole of Vyākaraṇa many times, for, he talked a great deal but no apaśabda fell from his lips.......... He did not fail to utter every word in its proper place and made me understand the theme of his talk by uttering words which carried comprehension into my mind.'"[1597] His power of elocution is also referred to elsewhere.[1598]

1590 Ibid., Bālakāṇḍa, 4th sarga.

1591 XV. 33.

1592 XV. 69.

1593 Ibid., 6th sarga.

1594 Ibid., 13th sarga.

1595 Ibid., Yuddhakāṇḍa, 92nd sarga.

1596 Ibid., 110th sarga.

1597 Ibid., Kiṣkindhyākāṇḍa, 3rd sarga.

1598 Ibid., 55th sarga.

He was well-versed in the art of warfare[1599] and in all the śāstras[1600] " In this earth nobody can surpass Hanumāna in valour, enthusiasm, intelligence, prowess, good conduct and knowledge of Nīti, gravity, cleverness and fortitude. When this hero of extraordinary strength reads grammar, he with a view to understand the meaning of the grammatical text, takes the book in hand and facing the Sun moves from Udayagiri to Astāchala. He is exceptionally proficient in Sūtra, Bṛtti, Arthapada, Mahāvāṣya and Saṃgraha. He stands unrivalled in scholarship and in ability to find out the profound truths of the Vedas. He has seen the end of all the śāstras. He has surpassed even Bṛhaṣpati, the guru of the Suras in learning and in tapobidhāna ".[1601]

In the Ādi Parba[1602] of the Mahābhārata we get the following account of the education of the Kauravas and the Pāṇḍavas: " Mahātmā Bhīṣma expressed the desire to entrust the proper training in good conduct and education of his grandsons in the hands of an intelligent teacher well-versed in various śāstras. He then brought to his palace the Vedic scholar Droṇāchārya, son of Varadwāja and after according fitting reception, put him in charge of the education of his grandsons. Satisfied with the solicitude of Bhīṣma for the proper education of the princes he accepted them as his disciples; and with very great care and attention began to teach them with a special emphasis on Dhanurveda. The pupils were all intelligent and within a short time they became proficient in all the śāstras and endowed with unbounded valour ". " Duryodhana and Bhīma who were prone to anger, both practised mace-fighting under Droṇa's instructions.........Nakula and Sahadeva became expert swordsmen. Dharmarāja Yudhiṣṭhir became a first class charioteer.........and of all the royal pupils Arjuna alone became an unrivalled bowman ".[1603] Droṇa himself tested their military skill[1604] and then with the permission of Dhṛtarāṣtra arranged for a military tournament where the princes gave a public demonstration

---

[1599] Ibid., Sundarakāṇḍa, 47th sarga.

[1600] Ibid., Kiṣkiṅdhyākāṇḍa, 55th sarga and Yuddhakāṇḍa, 17th sarga.

[1601] Ibid., Uttarakāṇḍa, 36th sarga.

[1602] 130th adhyāya.

[1603] Ibid., 132nd adhyāya.

[1604] Ibid., 132nd and 133rd adhyāyas.

of their military skill.[1605] It is interesting to find that Droṇa, the tutor of the princes was a Brahmin. The purpose of the author may have been to exalt the dignity of the brāhmaṇa caste by showing how the kṣhatriyas learnt even military skill from the brāhmaṇas. But we can point out that it is distinctly stated in the Mahābhārata that Droṇa accepted the employment to have his vengeance on king Drupad who taunted him for his poverty.[1606]

The Pāṇḍavas studied all the Vedas and the various śāstras.[1607] Of them Yudhiṣṭhir was versed in the Vedas and the science of war and highly skilled in driving horses and chariots.[1608] Nakula was an expert in fighting with swords[1609] while Arjuna was not only an unrivalled bowman[1610] but was also versed in Dharmārthatatwa and Arthaśāstra.[1611]

The upanayana ceremony of the sons of the Pāṇḍavas was performed by Maharṣi Dhaumya and after finishing the study of the Vedas they learnt Dhanurveda and the use of all the weapons from Arjuna.[1612]

The brothers of Draupadī had a Brahmin resident-tutor appointed by their royal father, who taught them Bṛhaṣpati-nīti.[1613]

Bhīṣma was proficient in the use of all kinds of astras[1614] and śāstras,[1615] an unrivalled bowman and was equal to Indra as a warrior.[1616] From Vaśiṣṭha he had learnt all tho Vedas and the Vedāngas.[1617] He has got by heart all the śāstras which Śukrāchārya has read.[1618] He has mastered all the śāstras[1619] and knows the true import of Dharma.[1620]

1605 Ibid., 134th—137th adhyāyas.

1606 Ibid., 137th adhyāya ; also 133rd, 138th and 166th adhyāyas.

1607 Ibid., Anukramaṇikādhyāya.

1608 Ibid., Udyogaparba, 28th adhyāya.

1609 Ibid., Śāntiparba, 166th adhyāya.

1610 Ibid., Ādiparba, 132nd adhyāya.

1611 Ibid., Śāntiparba, 167th adhyāya.

1612 Ibid., Ādiparba, 221st adhyāya.

1613 Ibid., Banaparba, 32nd adhyāya.

1614 Ibid., Ādiparba 100th adhyāya.

1615 Ibid., 67th adhyāya.

1616 Ibid., 100th adhyāya.

1617 Ibid., 100th and 103rd adhyāyas.

1618 Ibid., 100th adhyāya.

1619 Ibid.

1620 Ibid., 103rd adhyāya.

Dhṛtarāṣtra was proficient in many śāstras[1621] while Bidur was was versed in all the śāstras.[1622] In the Ādiparba[1623] we are told that 'Bhiṣma had Dhṛtarāṣtra, Pāṇḍu and Bidur taught by a competent tutor and made them experts in physical culture. When these princes came of age they became versed in Dhanurveda, mace-fighting, swordsmanship, gajaśikṣā, nītiśāstra, itihāsa, Purāṇas, Vedāngas etc. Of them Pāṇḍu became an unrivalled bowman, Dhṛtarāṣtra became famous for his physical strength and Bidur for his piety'.

The king of the Kekayas was proficient in Vedic learning[1624] while Yayāti studied all the Vedas and the Vedāngas.[1625] Ambariṣa studied the Vedas and Rājanīti.[1626]

The Mahābhārata[1627] also refers to a king of the Andhaka family and other princes as pupils of Droṇa who taught them military science.

The Śākya prince Gautama was taught the three R's under a teacher named Viśwāmitra whom according to tradition, he confounds by his knowledge already possessed of various styles of writing. He is next taught by eight other brāhmaṇa teachers viz., "Rāma and Dhaja, Lakṣmaṇa and Manti, Yañña and Suyāma, Subhoga and Sudatta" and also the brāhmaṇa Sabbamitta of high lineage in the land of Udichcha, a philogist and grammarian, well-read in the six Vedāngas, whom Śuddhodhana sent for and handed over the boy to his charge to be taught".[1628] From the Antagada Dasao[1629] we learn that when Goyame was past eight years he was sent to a teacher of the arts on an auspicious day. He learnt from him the eighteen vernaculars, delighted in song, music and dance, was able to fight on horse, elephant and chariot and became clever in boxing and night-sallying (nagara-vaccham). Indeed he was not inattentive to physical culture. The legends represent him as skilled in the twelve arts and especially in archery, like Arjuna of old and he proved his superiority to all Śākya youths in open challenge.

1621 Ibid., Udyogaparba, 29th adhyāya.

1622 Ibid., Ādiparba 206th adhyāya.

1623 109th adhyāya.

1624 Ibid., Śāntiparba, 17th adhyāya.

1625 Ibid., Ādiparba, 81st adhyāya.

1626 Ibid., Śāntiparba, 98th adhyāya.

1627 Ādiparba, 132nd adhyāya.

1628 Milindā-Pañha, IV. 6, 3.

1629 Barnett's Antagada Dasao, p. 81.

As in the story of Arjuna, the price of his victory was the hand of Yaśodharā, daughter of his cousin, Suprabuddha, to whom he was married at sixteen. One of the beaten youths was another cousin of his, Devadatta, who could never forget this discomfiture and grew up to be the chief enemy of the Buddha in the world.

From the Jaina sūtras[1630] we learn that Mahābīra was proficient in the eighteen scripts corresponding to the eighteen vernacular tongues.

In conformity with the later injunction of Manu[1631] to the effect that the king should learn "from the people the trades and the professions"[1632] we find that the practice of a craft was not considered derogatory to the dignity of a prince. The Kuśa Jātaka,[1633] for instance, mentions a prince who only consents to marry when a princess is found exactly like a golden image which he himself had fashioned and which was far superior to that made by the chief smith employed for the purpose. From the Mahāvaṃśa we find that king Jetthatissa of Ceylon was a "skilful carver and painter who wrought a beautiful image of the Bodhisatwa and also a throne, a parasol, and a state-room with beautiful work in ivory made for it and who himself taught the arts to his subjects". In the story of Jīvaka we are told that even in royal families idlers were not tolerated and that it was not easy to eke out one's living without the knowledgė of some art. In the Hātigumpha Inscription of Khāravela we read of a prince who claims to have been proficient in lekhā, gaṇanā and rūpa. In Bāṇa's Harṣacharita[1634] it is stated how on the occasion of the marriage of a princess "even kings girt up their loins and busied themselves in carrying out decorative work set as tasks by their sovereign. In Jātaka (IV. 84) we are told of a prince who took to trade. According to Kalhaṇa,[1635] Lothana, a prince of the Lohara family maintained himself by agriculture, trade and other means.

1630 Samavāya Sūtra p. 54; Nandi Sūtra pp. 376ff.

1631 VII. 43.

1632 Vārttāramvāścha lokataḥ.

1633 Jātaka No. 531.

1634 Eng. Trans., by Cowell and Thomas, p. 124.

1635 Rājataraṅgiṇī VIII. 2482.

Coming to the Dharmasūtras and the Dharmaśāstras we find that according to Gautama[1636] the king shall be fully taught the three-fold sacred science and Ānvīkṣikī.[1637] In another passage Gautama[1638] says: "The administration of justice shall be by the Veda, the Dharmaśāstra,[1639] the Angas and the Purāṇa"; so that it may be presumed that the princes were expected to be acquainted with these also during their student-life. That the princes used to have their initiation which marked the beginning of their student-life is evident from Manu.[1640] "After his initiation" says Manu,[1641] "let him learn from those well-versed in the three Vedas, the three-fold sacred science, the eternal principle of punishment, the science of reasoning, the science of self-knowledge and from the people the principles of trade, agriculture and cattle-rearing and the science of wealth".[1642] In another passage Manu[1643] says: "Each day conformably to the rules of the śāstras and usages of the country, he (the king) shall severally adjudicate the eighteen sources of law-suits"; so that it may be presumed that the king was expected to be acquainted with these in his student-life. Manu[1644] enjoins the prince, however, to refrain from singing, dancing and music, for, by addicting to them he becomes dissociated with virtue and wealth. According to Yājñabālkya Saṃhitā[1645] the king should be well-versed in Logic, Polity and Vārttā (the principles of trade, agriculture, cattle-rearing and interest) and Trayī (the triple Vedas). According to Hārita Saṃhitā[1646] the king should be proficient in the laws of Polity and well-versed in the true spirit of making peace and dissensions.

1636 XI. 1.

1637 Dr. Buhler seems to have wrongly translated, the word as logic in S. B. E., Vol. II; for, according to Kautilya's Arthaśāstra (R. Śyāmaśāstrī's Eng. Trans.), p. 6) it comprises the philosophy of Sāṃkya, Yoga and Lokayāta (atheism.)

1638 XI. 19.

1639 Dr. Buhler considers this word as probably an interpolation, for, it was then included in the Angas as Kalpa.

1640 VII. 2.

1641 VII. 43.

1642 The same verse also exists in the Matsya Purāṇa 215. 53 and in the Agni Purāṇa 225. 21-22; *see* also Gautama Dharmasūtra, XX. 3.

1643 VII. 3.

1644 VII. 46-47.

1645 I. 311.

1646 II. 4.

In the age represented by Kautilya's Arthaśāstra there seems to have been a considerable development of royal education. The number of authorities whose different opinions Kautilya quotes in his Arthaśāstra and sometimes refutes while discussing the educational programme for princes shows among other things that there was considerable interest as to what was the best kind of education for a young prince to receive. It is not impossible that this development of royal education may have been the result of the desire of some Indian rulers to improve the efficiency of their kingdoms in view of the possibilities of foreign invasions like those of Darius (521 B. C.) and Alexander the Great (327 B. C.). But whether this was so or not, it seems certain that a considerable development of royal education took place in the age of Kautilya and we get a valuable picture of this education in his Arthaśāstra.

In Bk. I. Ch. XVII. of Kautilya's Arthaśāstra,[1647] entitled 'Protection of Princes' we are told :—

"Ever since the birth of princes, the king shall take special care of them.

"For" says Bharadvāja, "princes like crabs have a notorious tendency of eating up their begetter. When they are wanting in filial affection, they shall better be punished in secret."

"This is" says Viśālākṣa, "cruelty, destruction of fortune and extirpation of the seed of the race of kṣhatriyas. Hence it is better to keep them under guard in a definite place."

"This" says the school of Parāśara, "is akin to the fear from a lurking snake, for, a prince may think that apprehensive of danger, his father has locked him up and may attempt to put his own father on his lap. Hence it is better to keep a prince under the custody of boundary guards or inside a fort."

"This" says Piśuṇa, "is akin to the fear (from a wolf) of a flock of sheep; for, after understanding the cause of his rustication, he may avail

---

[1647] R. Śyāmaśāstrī's Eng. Trans., pp. 37-40.

himself of the opportunity to make an alliance with the boundary guards (against his father). Hence it is better to throw him inside a fort belonging to a foreign king far away from his own state."

"This" says Kauṇapadanta, "is akin to the position of a calf; for, just as a man milks a cow with the help of her calf, so the foreign king may milk (reduce) the prince's father. Hence it is better to make a prince live with his maternal relations."

"This" says Vātavyādhi, "is akin to the position of a flag; for, as in the case of Aditi and Kauśika, the prince's maternal relations may, unfurling this flag, go on begging. Hence princes may be suffered to dissipate their lives by sensual excesses in as much as revelling sons do not dislike their indulgent father."

"This" says Kautilya, "is death in life; for no sooner is a royal family with a prince or princes given to dissipation attacked, than it perishes like a worm-eaten piece of wood. Hence when the queen attains the age favourable for procreation, priests shall offer to Indra and Bṛhaspati the requisite oblations. When she is big with a child, the king shall observe the instructions of midwifery with regard to gestation and delivery. After delivery, the priests shall perform the prescribed purificatory ceremonials. When the prince attains the necessary age, *adepts shall train him up under proper discipline.*"

"There can be" says Kautilya, "no greater crime or sin than making wicked impressions on an innocent mind.................. Hence he shall be *taught only of righteousness and of wealth* (*artha*) but not of unrighteousness and non-wealth.................... When under the temptation of youth, he turns his eye towards women, impure women under the guise of Āryas shall, at night and in lonely places, terrify him; when fond of liquor, he shall be terrified by making him drink such liquor as is adulterated with narcotic (Yogapāna); when fond of gambling, he shall be terrified by spies under the disguise of fraudulent persons; when fond of hunting, he shall be terrified by spies under the disguise of highway robbers; and when desirous of attacking his own father, he shall, under the pretence of compliance, be gradually persuaded of the evil consequences of such attempts."

Kautilya further says: "Sons are of three kinds: those of sharp intelligence: those of stagnant intelligence; and those of perverted mind. "Whoever carries into practice whatever he is *taught* concerning righteousness and wealth is one of sharp intelligence; whoever never carries into practice the good instructions he has been *taught* is one of stagnant intelligence; and whoever entangles himself in dangers and hates righteousness and wealth is one of perverted mind............... Never shall a wicked and an only son (of the last type) be installed on the throne."

From the above it is evident what a great emphasis Kautilya laid on the proper education of a prince. In another passage[1648] we are told: "The king who is *well-educated and disciplined in sciences,* devoted to good government of his subjects and bent on doing good to all people will enjoy the earth unopposed." Again, according to Kautilya the king should possess among other qualities, "sharp intellect, strong memory, keen mind, *traninig in all kinds of arts,* cleverness to discern the causes necessitating cessation of treaty or war with an enemy or to lie in wait keeping treaties, obligations and pledges or to avail himself of the enemy's weak points and to observe custom as *taught* by aged persons."[1649]

Coming to Kautilya's curriculum for the education of the prince we find that it included four sciences: Ānvīkṣikī, Trayī, Vārttā and Daṇḍanīti.[1650] We have already seen that according to Kautilya "he (the prince) shall be taught only of righteousness and wealth"[1651] and he expressly says that "these can be learnt only from the four sciences."[1652] It appears, however, that the authorities are not agreed as to the number of sciences to be taught, for, we are told:—[1653]

"The school of Manu hold that there are only three sciences: the triple Vedas, Vārttā and the science of government, in as much as the science of Ānvīkṣikī is nothing but a special branch of the Vedas.

1648 Ibid., p. 11.
1649 Ibid., p. 319.
1650 Ibid., pp. 10-11.
1651 Ibid., p. 38.
1652 Ibid., p. 6.
1653 Ibid.

"The school of Bṛhaspati say that there are only two sciences: Vārttā and the science of government, in as much as the triple Vedas are merely an abridgment for a man experienced in affairs temporal.

"The school of Uśanā declare that there is only one science and that the science of government; for, they say, it is in that science that all other sciences have their origin and end."

"But Kautilya holds that four and four only are the sciences; wherefore it is from these sciences that all that concerns righteousness and wealth is learnt, therefore they are so called."

But although Kautilya prescribes four sciences for the prince, he admits the supreme importance of Daṇḍanīti as a subject for royal education. For says he:—

"The first three sciences (out of the four) are dependent for their well-being on the science of government."[1654]

"The sceptre on which the well-being and progress of the sciences of Ānvīkṣikī, the triple Vedas and Vārttā depend is known as Daṇḍa. That which treats of Daṇḍa is the science of government, Daṇḍanīti."[1655]

"A king of unrighteous character and vicious habits will, though he is an emperor, fall an easy prey either to the fury of his own subjects or to that of his enemies. But a wise king, *trained in politics*, will, though he possesses a small territory, conquer the whole earth with the help of the best-fitted elements of sovereignty and will never be defeated."[1656]

"Whoever, *well-versed in polity*, thus acquires friends, wealth and territory with or without population will overreach other kings in combination against him."[1657]

"Even if the king is held by the chiefs under their influence, the minister may, through the medium of king's favourites *teach him the principles of polity* with illustrations from the Itihāsa and Purāṇa."[1658]

[1654] Ibid., p. 10.
[1655] Ibid., p. 9.
[1656] Ibid., p. 321.
[1657] Ibid., p. 365.
[1658] Ibid., p. 318.

The Nitisāra of Kāmandaka has a description of a tree of Polity of which the four vidyās have been called the four roots. Says he: "He is indeed a real politician who knows the tree with eight branches, four roots, sixty leaves, two props, six flowers and three fruits."[1659] Similarly, in the Yuktikalpataru the different vidyās have been compared to the branches and flowers of a true. In the beginning of the work, the reason why it has been called a tree has been thus explained: "The root of this tree is Daṇḍanīti (Polity), the stem is Jyotiṣa, the various Vidyās are its branches and flowers, its fruits are unknown and its sap is nectar to the good (i. e., promotes their welfare)."[1660]

But Kautilya rightly observes: "Daṇḍa (punishment) which alone can procure safety and security of life is, in its turn, dependent on discipline."[1661] "Hence *the king shall keep up his personal discipline by receiving lessons in sciences.*"[1662] Now "discipline is of two kinds: artificial and natural; for instruction can render only a docile being conformable to the rules of discipline and not an undocile being.[1663]

1659 Kāmandakīya, Nītisāra VIII. 42.

1660 Yuktikalpataru, slokas 6-7.

1661 Arthaśāstra (R. Śyāmaśāstrī's Eng. Trans.), p. 10.

1662 Ibid., p. 13.

1663 Kriyā hi drabyam binayati nādrabyam—Arthaśāstrā Bk. I. Ch. V.

In Bhababhūti's Uttara-Rāma-charita Ātreyī says: "Now with these two boys possessed of exceedingly brilliant power of comprehension and retentiveness as they are, students like us cannot keep pace in the studies. For, the preceptor imparts unto the clever, instructions just the same as unto the dull and in no wise doth he their power of comprehension either make or thwart; and yet there does result a vast difference as to the outcome; for we know that only a pure crystal is able to take in images and not a mere lump of clay." (Uttara-Rāma-chārita—Belvalkar's Eng. Trans., p. 32).

Kālidāsa in his Raghuvaṃśam speaks in the same strain: "Nisarga-saṃskārabinītaḥ; swāvbhābikaṃ binītatwaṃ teṣām; mūmurṣu ṣahajaṃ tejo habiṣeba habibhujam".

In Bāṇa's Kādambarī Śukanāsa says to Chandrāpīḍa: "Men such as thou art, are the fitting vessels for instruction. For, on a mind free from stain the virtue of good counsel enters easily, as the moon's rays on a moon crystal. The words of a guru, though pure, yet cause great pain when they enter the ears of the bad as water does; while in others they produce a nobler beauty, like the ear-jewel on an elephant" (Kādambarī—C. M. Ridding's Eng. Trans., pp. 76-77).

The study of sciences can tame only those who are possessed of such mental faculties as obedience, hearing, grasping, retentive memory, discrimination, inference and deliberation but not others devoid of such faculties."[1664] It follows from the above that for those who have not this natural disipline, there is the artificial discipline of punishment.

"Sciences" he continues:[1665] "should be studied and their precepts strictly observed under the authority of specialist teachers. Having undergone the ceremony of tonsure, the student shall learn the alphabet (lipi) and arithmetic. After investiture with the sacred thread[1666] he shall study the Triple Vedas, the science of Ānvīkṣikī under teachers of acknowledged authority (siṣṭa), the science of Vārttā under government superintendents and the science of Daṇḍanīti under theoretical and practical politicians."[1667]

With regard to the length of the course we are told: "The Prince should observe celibacy till he becomes sixteen years old. Then he shall observe the ceremony of tonsure (godāna) and marry." If the investiture with the sacred thread took place in accordance with the regulations laid down in the Dharmasūtras in the eleventh year after conception the course would thus last six years. But we know that to learn one Veda twelve years were prescribed for the brahmachārin by the Dharmasūtras. It thus seems that the study of Vārttā and Daṇḍanīti may have been continued even after marriage. For, while dealing with the life of a saintly king Kautilya says that among other things the king should "acquire wisdom by keeping company with the aged and keep up his personal discipline by receiving lessons in the sciences."[1668] Again, while dealing with the duties of a king Kautilya says: "He shall divide both day and night into eight nālikas ($1\frac{1}{2}$ hrs.) ....during the second (one-eighth) part of the day he shall not

---

1664 Ibid., 10.

1665 Ibid., pp. 10-11.

1666 Compare the custom in ancient Persia where according to Alcibiades the princes were given over to royal tutors only at fifteen.

1667 Vātsyāyana in his Kāmasūtra Bk. I. Ch. II. refers to Arthachintakāḥ (Professors of Arthaśāstra).

1668 Arthaśāstra (R. Śyāmaśāstrī's Eng. Trans.), p. 13.

only bathe and dine but also *study* .... During the second (one eighth) part of the night he shall attend to bathing and supper and *study*................. During the sixth (one eighth) part of the night he shall recall to his mind the injunctions of sciences."[1669] From the Māhābhārata[1670] we learn that King Janadeva of Mithilā had in his palace one hundred āchāryas who used to teach him the duties of the men living in the different āśramas (stages) of life. We similarly find that kings Dhṛtarāṣtra and Yudhiṣṭhira were regularly taught by Bhīṣma and Bidur respectively.[1671] Even in the course of their flight to the forest from the city of Baraṇabata the Pāṇḍavas used to read the Upaniṣads, the Vedāngas and Nītiśāstra.[1672] Śukrāchārya also while dealing with the daily routine of the king says that the king should take two muhūrtas (i. e., 96 minutes) for prayers, *study* and charity[1673] and another muhūrta for observing (i. e., *studying*) old and new things.[1674] Yājñabālkya[1675] also enjoins the king to *study* the Vedas after taking his evening meal.

Some further particulars with regard to Kautilya's scheme of education are forthcoming. "For acquiring efficiency in the skill of shooting arrows at moving objects, he shall engage himself in sports only in such forests as are cleared by hunters and houndkeepers from the fear of highway robbers, snakes and enemies."[1676]

During the period of study the young prince was to be placed under the strict supervision of his teachers. "In view of maintaining efficient discipline, he shall ever and invariably keep company with aged professors of sciences in whom alone discipline has its firm root."[1677]

The hours of study were thus planned out. "He shall spend the forenoon in receiving lessons in military arts concerning elephants, horses,

---

1669 Ibid., Bk. I. Ch. XIX.

1670 Śāntiparba, 218th adhyāya.

1671 Ibid., 227th adhyāya and Anuśāsanaparba.

1672 Ādiparba, 156th adhyāya.

1673 Śukranītisāra, Ch. I. line 558.

1674 Ibid., line 564.

1675 I. 330.

1676 Arthaśāstra (R. Śyāmaśāstrī's Eng. Trans.), pp. 49-50.

1677 Ibid., p. 11.

chariots and weapons and the afternoon in hearing Itihāsa......... During the rest of the day and night, he shall not only receive new lessons and revise old ones but also hear over and again what has not been clearly understood".[1678]

The above outline of royal education gives greater importance to practical wisdom than to theoretical philosophy and religious instruction. Kautilya has included the study of the three Vedas in the curriculum of royal studies but in later details it is curious to find no reference to their study. Moreover, the injunction referred to above that the science of Vārttā is to be studied under Government superintendents and the science of Daṇḍanīti under theoretical and practical politicians shows that these two subjects were learnt in very close contact with their practice in actual life. We have also seen that in the opinion of Kautilya, of the three kinds of princes, *whoever carries into practice whatever he is taught* concerning righteousness and wealth is the best.[1679]

That a thorough grasp of the subject was the objective is evident from the following: "He (the prince) shall not only..............revise old lessons but also hear over and over again what has not been *clearly understood.* For, from hearing (sūtra) ensues knowledge, from knowldge steady application (yoga) is possible; and from application self-possession (ātmavattā) is possible. This is what is meant by efficiency of learning (vidyāsāmarthyam).[1680]

Kāmandaka in his Nītisāra is equally emphatic on the education of the prince. Says he: "The King for the sake of attaining progress should train up his sons with proper education (śikṣā); for, uneducated princes bring ruin on the family".[1681] He further says: "If the king be trained up by proper education (vidyā) then he is never depressed by dangers and difficulties".[1682] Again: "The king who daily receives a proper training in the 64 kalās like dancing, singing, music etc., daily impoves his position like the Moon

---

1678 Ibid., p. 11.

1679 Ibid., p. 39.

1680 Ibid., p. 11.

1681 Kāmandakīya Nītisara, 7th sarga, śl. 5.

1682 Ibid., 1st sarga, śl. 59.

in the lunar fortnight".[1683] His scheme of royal education as outlined in sarga two of his Nītisāra is almost wholly copied from that of Kautilya. It thus includes the study by the prince of Ānvīkṣikī, the Trayī, Vārttā and Daṇḍanīti.[1684] According to him the king should also be proficient in the śāstras and in Vyabahāra[1685] as also in the 64 kalās.[1686]

Śukrāchārya has also drawn up in his Nītisāra a syllabus of intellectual training for princes. Says he: "Association with the guru is for the acquisition of śāstras, the śāstras are calculated to increase knowledge: the king who is trained up in the branches of learning is respected by the good and does not incline to wrong deeds even if impelled by evil motives".[1687] "Ānvīkṣikī, the Trayī, Vārttā and Daṇḍanīti—these four branches of learning the king should always study. The science of discussion and Vedānta are founded on the science of Ānvīkṣikī; virtue and vice, as well as interests and injuries of man are based on the Trayī; wealth and its opposite on Vārttā; good and bad government on Daṇḍanīti. Thus all the castes of men and the stages of human life are built upon these sciences. The six Angas, the four Vedas, Mīmāṃsā (system of philosophy), Nyāya (system of philosophy), Dharmaśāstras as well as the Purāṇas—all these constitute the Trayī. In Vārttā are treated interest, agriculture, commerce and preservation of cows. The man who is well up in Vārttā need not be anxious for earning. Daṇḍa is restraint and punishment, thence the king is also known to be Daṇḍa. The Nīti that regulates punishment constitutes Daṇḍanīti, so called because it governs and guides. Man gives up both pleasure and pain through Ānvīkṣikī and the science of Self (metaphysics) and gets both temporal and spiritual self-realisation through the Trayī".[1688]

Śukrāchārya, however, lays the greatest stress on the study of Nītiśāstra by the prince. Says he: "As Nītiśāstra is considered to be the spring of virtue, wealth, enjoyment and salvation, the ruler should ever carefully *peruse* it; by *knowing* it, rulers can be victorious

1683 Ibid., śl. 61.
1684 Ibid., 2nd sarga, śl. 1.
1685 Ibid., 6th sarga, śl. 1.
1686 Ibid., 1st sarga, śl. 61.
1687 Śukranītisāra, Ch. I. lines 295-97.
1688 Ibid., lines 303-16.

over foes, affectionate and conciliatory towards subjects and well up in the arts of state-craft ".[1689] "Nītiśāstra conduces to the desires and interests of all and hence is respected and followed by all. It is also indispensable to the prince since he is the lord of all men and things. Just as in the case of the sick persons who take unprescribed food (apathya), the diseases come immediately and do not delay in manifesting themselves, so also in the case of the princes who are *unschooled* in the principles of Nītiśāstra, the enemies make their appearance at once and do not delay in declaring themselves. The two primary functions of the king are the protection of subjects and constant punishment of offenders; these two cannot be achieved without Nītiśāstra ".[1690] "The king who always *studies* the abridged text of Śukra becomes competent to bear the burden of state-affairs ".[1691]

Śukra also includes *manly exercises and military training* in his scheme of education for the prince. Says he: "The king should always practise military parades with the troops and strike the objective by means of missiles at the stated hours ".[1692] "He should every morning and evening exercise himself with elephants, horses, chariots and other conveyances ".[1693] This "exercise over elephants, horses and carriages" should be taken by the king at dawn and for one muhūrta (=48 minutes) only;[1694] for, "excessive walking...............and over-exercise soon bring about men's old age ".[1695] "And he should learn as well as teach the military arrangements of soldiers ".[1696] "He should sport with tigers, peacocks, birds and other animals of the forest and in the course of hunting kill the wild ones ".[1697] Śukra explains his reasons for including manly exercises as an integral part of royal education thus: "The advantages of hunting are the growth of ability to strike the aim and agility in the use of arms and weapons but cruelty is the great defect ".[1698]

[1689] Ibid., lines 10-13.

[1690] Ibid., lines 23-28. Compare Ibid., lines 29-38; Ibid., lines 301-02; Ibid., Ch. IV. Sec. VII. lines 857-58.

[1691] Ibid., Ch. IV. Sec. VII. lines 853-54.

[1692] Ibid., lines 779-80.

[1693] Ibid. Ch. I. line 663.

[1694] Ibid., line 559.

[1695] Ibid., Ch. III. lines 603-04.

[1696] Ibid., Ch. I. line 664.

[1697] Ibid., lines 665-66.

[1698] Ibid., lines 667-69.

In another place Śukra says: "The king should make the children of his family well-up in 'Nītiśāstra, proficient in archery (Dhanurveda), capable of undertaking strains and of bearing harsh words and punishments, habituated to the feat of arms (Śauryavidyā), master of all arts and sciences, upright in morals as well as discipline through his ministers and councillors."[1699] Thus the course of instruction for the children of the royal household was at once physical, intellectual, moral, military as well as political. Moreover, the terms "Dhanurveda" and "Śauryavidyā" refer perhaps to the theoretical and applied branches of military education. The former indicates proficiency in the science of archery i. e., military tactics and implements generally, while the latter refers to actual field-work, parade, mock-fights, assaults-at-arms etc.,—practices that call forth martial enthusiasm and develop warlike aptitudes.

The curriculum of royal studies, according to Aśwaghoṣa comprised a number of subjects—the Veda, sacrifices, the performance of sacrifices; archery, the training of elephants, the domesticating of horses, the carrying of the lance, jumping, running, massage, fording a river, strategy, the rules of battle array; music, dancing, the art of playing on the tambourine, the art of playing on the conch, sculpture, painting; sewing, weaving, sealing, wax-work, the making of garlands of flowers, arrangement of garlands, examination of precious stones and valuable materials for clothing; grammar, literature, the origin of writing, eloquence, rhetoric; the study of origins, heredity and eugenics; astronomy, casting horoscopes of boys and girls, interpretation of dreams and of the flight of birds; computation, interest; the arts of love and laughter, conjuring tricks, chess, dice etc. This list agrees in the main with what we find in the Lalitavistāra and compares well with what we find described in the Jaina texts as the the curricula of studies of Mahābīra.

In the Milindā-Pañha we are told that "the business of the princes of the earth is to learn all about elephants, horses, chariots, rapiers and the documents and the law of property"[1700]

1699 Ibid., Ch. II. lines 43-46.

1700 S. B. E., Vol. XXXV. p. 247.

The Matsya Purāṇa[1701] says that "the king should have his prince instructed by learned teachers in Dharmaśāstra, Kāmaśāstra, Arthaśāstra, Dhanurveda as also in the knowledge of elephants and chariots. He should regularly take physical exercises and learn the śilpas."

In the Bhāgabad Purāṇa[1702] we read that the youthful Kṛṣṇa and Balarāma studied the Vedas with their Angas, Upaniṣads, Dhanurveda, Dharmaśāstra, Mīmāṃsā, Ānvikṣikī, Rājanīti and the sixty-four kalās.

It is to be presumed that as in the case of the ordinary twice-born student, the prince's training of the sciences and arts was based on a knowledge of the grammar of the Sanskrit language. The story contained in the Kathāsaritsāgara[1703] of the king who did not know Sanskrit grammar seems to show that some royal pupils did not always find it easy to master all its intricacies.

With regard to the text-books, those used by the ordinary twice-born students for Vedic study would serve also for the princes in so far as they studied the same subjects but there were two developments which arose to meet the needs of the special training required for them. We have already referred to the Arthaśāstra as a subject to be studied by the prince. Kāmandaka in his introduction to the Nitisāra also refers to the Arthaśāstra of Kautilya as a favourite learning of kings. Says he: "From the scientific work of that learned man who had reached the limits of knowledge, *the favourite learning of the kings,* brief yet intelligible and useful in the acquisition and maintenance of the earth, we are going to extract and *teach kings* in the manner acceptable to those learned in the science of Polity." Daṇḍī in his Daśakumārcharita[1704] says: "Learn then the science of Polity. Now this has been by the revered teacher Viṣṇugupta abridged into six thousand ślokas *in the interest of the Maurya (king)* that when learnt and well-observed, it can produce the results expected from it."

The scope of this subject (Arthaśāstra) has been thus laid down by Kautilya: "The means of subsistence of mankind is termed Artha.

1701 Ch. 220. 2-3: 24, 2-3.
1702 X. 45. 25-27.
1703 Penzer, Vol. I. p. 71.
1704 II. 8.

The earth which contains mankind is also termed Artha. The science which treats of the means of acquiring and maintaining the earth is Arthaśāstra."[1705] From this it follows clearly that Arthaśāstra really treated of Artha in the sense of earth, and not in its primary sense of wealth which was the subject that properly pertained to the field of Vārttā. Kautilya's Arthaśāstra mentions the same fact in another place, for, it actually commences with the statement that it was composed by the author as a 'compendium of almost all the Arthaśāstras written by prior teachers for the *acquisition and maintenance of the earth.*'[1706] From this it follows that Arthaśāstra was really a very comprehensive science as its data were drawn from a wide variety of of sources, for, any subject that had more or less intimate bearing upon the means of acquiring and maintaining the earth could not but naturally fall within its scope. Thus, Daṇḍanīti was the most important branch, in fact the fundamental basis, of Arthaśāstra, for, Daṇḍanīti "upon which the progress of the world depends"[1707] was of the utmost importance to princes in their efforts to acquire and maintain the earth. Vārttā also supplied no mean quota to the science, for, it was through Vārttā and Vārttā alone that two of the seven limbs of the state, viz., Koṣa and Daṇḍa could be acquired. The Śukranīti recognises this double aspect of Arthaśāstra when it defines it as the science which describes the actions and administration of kings, as well as the means of livelihood in a proper manner.[1708] In fact, this double aspect of the Arthaśāstra has often given rise to a confusion of ideas and has led to its being designated sometimes as Polity and sometimes as Economics by writers at different times. Later on Arthaśāstra was devested of its economic topics and became simply the political science. In later Sanskrit literature this use is made of the word Arthaśāstra and the terms Nītiśāstra, Arthaśāstra, Daṇḍanīti and Rājanīti are used indiscriminately to represent the science of Polity.

Vārttā was another subject of royal study. The word is derived from the root 'vṛt' by the addition of the suffix 'n'. Thus Vārttā

[1705] Arthaśāstra, Bk. V. Ch. I.

[1706] Ibid., Bk. I. Ch. I.

[1707] Tasyāmāyattā lokayātrā—Bk. I. Ch. IV.

[1708] Bk. IV. Sec. III, lines 110-111.

etymologically represents vṛtti or means of livelihood. Along with the use of the term Vārttā as a collective name for occupations, it was also used as the designation of a division of learning, pertaining to knowledge relating to those occupations. According to Kautilya gain and loss of wealth[1709] are to be known from Vārttā. In Śukranīti[1710] we are told that profit and loss of wealth are based on Vārttā. Kāmandaka in his Nītisāra[1711] merely repeats the words of his political guru about the nature of Vārttā. Vārttā was thus the branch of learning that had wealth for its subject of study. It at first included three subjects—agriculture, cattle-breeding and trade.[1712] Kāmandaka writes to the same effect.[1713] Vāya Purāṇa[1714] also says :

> " Kṛṣibāṇijyā tadbartu tṛtīyaṃ paśupālanam
>
> Vidyāhyotā mahāvāga Vārttā vṛttiayāśāyaḥ"

In course of time Vārttā came to include usury as well. As Bhāgabad Purāṇa[1715] says :

> " Kṛṣibāṇijyagorakṣā kuṣīdaṃ turymuchyate
>
> Vārttā chaturvidyā tatra bayaṃ gobṛttayoniśm."

Śukranīti[1716] also says that in Vārttā are treated interest, agriculture, trade and preservation of cows. In the Devīpurāṇa[1717] we find that even Karmānta, i. e., manufacture has been added to Vārttā while in the Mahābhārata[1718] the various arts and crafts (bibidhāni śilpāni) were included in it.

Kautilya describes the merits of Vārttā as a subject of royal study in no uncertain words. Says he: " It is most useful in that it brings in grains, cattle, gold, forest produce and free labour. It is by means

---

1709 Arthānarthau.

1710 Ch. I. lines 305—08.

1711 II. 7 ; also Agnipurāṇa 238. 9.

1712 Kṛṣipaśupālye bāṇijyā cha vārttā—Arthaśāstra, Bk. I. Ch. IV.

1713 II. 14.

1714 V. 10. 28.

1715 X. 24. 21.

1716 Ch. I. lines 311-12.

1717 67. 13.

1718 XII. 167. 10-11.

of the treasury and the army obtained solely through Vārttā that the king can hold under his control both his and his enemy's party."[1719]

The study of Itihāsa by the prince included the study of Purāṇa, Itibṛtta, Ākhyāyikā, Udāharaṇa, Dharmaśāstra and Arthaśāstra.[1720] It is when we look at this comprehensive sense of Itihāsa that we can understand why products of imagination have been incorporated in history.[1721] The Purāṇas resemble more than any other of these six branches, history (in the modern sense of the word). The five subjects that form the subject-matter of these Purāṇas may be regarded as their five characteristics. They are sarga, pratisarga, vaṃśa, vaṃśānucharita and manvantara. Under vaṃśa and vaṃśānucharita were recorded the names of kings, the periods for which they reigned and noteworthy events connected with the distinguished reigns. The nature of Udāharaṇa will be clear from two passages in the Arthaśāstra of Kautilya[1722] and Vātsyāyana's Kāmasūtra.[1723] It seems that Udāharaṇa embodies facts and not mere imagination. As regards the nature of Itibṛtta, probably it dealt at length with events.[1724] The mention of Itibṛtta of kings and ṛṣis as well as the sacred Purāṇa Saṃhitā embodying Dharma and Artha in the same verse supports the same view. Ākhyāyikā included moral fables and stories such as were collected (afterwards) in the Pañchatantra and the Hitopadeśa.

The Dharmaśāstras as a general rule contain groups of laws, religious and civil and about atonement (āchāra, byābahāra and prāyaśchitta).

Ānvīkṣikī—was another subject of royal study. According to Kautilya[1725] it comprised the philosophy of Sāṃkhya, Yoga and Lokāyata. In Śukranītisāra[1726] we are told that the science of discussion and Vedānta are founded on Ānvīkṣikī. According to Kautilya "the

---

[1719] Arthaśāstra, Bk. I. Ch. IV.

[1720] Kautilya's Arthaśāstra (R. Śyāmaśāstrī's Eng. Trans.), p. 11.

[1721] Padma Purāṇa II. 85, 15; Vāyu Purāṇa 55, 2.

[1722] Bk. I. Ch. VI; R. Śyāmaśāstrī's Eng. Trans., pp. 12-13.

[1723] Bk. I. Ch. II; K. Rangaswāmī Iyenger's Eng. Trans., p. 16.

[1724] Mahābhārata I. 1. 16. [1725] Bk. I. Ch. II. [1726] Ch. I. lines 305-08.

science of Ānvīkṣikī is most beneficial to the world, keeps the mind steady and firm in weal and woe alike and bestows excellence of foresight, speech and action. Light to all kinds of knowledge, easy means to accomplish all kinds of acts and receptacle of all kinds of virtues, is the science of Ānvīkṣikī ever held to be".[1727]

In course of time the four sciences of Trayī, Daṇḍanīti, Vārttā and Ānvīkṣikī came to be known as Kulavidyās of princes. From Raghuvaṃśam[1728] we find that a king wed his sons first to the Kulavidyās (which the commentator explains as Trayī, Daṇḍanīti, Vārttā, and Ānvīkṣikī) and then to princesses.

But the preceptors, finding perhaps that their royal pupils did not always take kindly to the effort studying the political wisdom of the Arthaśāstra, devised the plan of using fables and stories as vehicles for teaching this science. The Pañchatantra existed in the first half of the sixth century A. D. but the Tantrākhyāyikā which is considered to be its most original and earliest form was composed many centuries earlier.[1729] It is introduced with the story of a certain king who had three particularly idle and stupid sons. He wished to find a teacher for them and at last met with a certain brāhmaṇa, who promised to give the young princes such instruction in six months that they would surpass all others in the knowledge of right conduct. For the accomplishment of his object he composed the Pañchatantra. The Hitopadeśa is a similar collection of fables much later than the Pañchatantra on which it is based. There are also other collections of fables like them, as for instance, the Kathāsaritsāgara. The Mahābhārata contains a great deal of didactic material embedded in the story and this may also have been used in the instruction of princes. For stories of heroes they had the epic poems like the Rāmāyaṇa and and the Mahābhārata and at a later date the bardic chronicles (like Chānd-Rāisā) of Rājasthān written in the vernaculars.

1727 Bk. I. Ch. II. 1728 Canto XVII. 3.

1729 J. R. A. S., 1910, pp. 966f. Dr. Hertel thinks that the Tantrākhyāyikā was composed between 300 B. C. and 570 A. D. and nearer the earlier limit. Dr. F. W. Thomas takes it be as old as 300 A. D.

The education of the prince was in course of time made more individualistic than ever as is evident not only from Indian literature but also from inscriptions and coins. The Milindā-Pañha[1730] thus describes the attainments of Milindā (Menander the Great):—"Many were the arts and sciences he knew—holy tradition and secular law; the Sāṃkhya, Yoga, Nyāya and Vaiśeṣika systems of philosophy; arithmetic: music; medicine; the four Vedas; the Purāṇas and the Itihāsas; astronomy, magic, causation and spells; the art of war; poetry; conveyancing—in a word, the whole nineteen. As a disputant, he was hard to equal, harder still to overcome; the acknowledged superior of all the founders of the various schools of thought. And as in wisdom so in strength of body, swiftness, and valour, there was found none equal to Milindā in all India." From the Mṛchhakatika we learn that Śūdraka was a scholar in Ṛgveda, Sāmaveda, Mathematics, the arts regarding courtesans and the science of elephants.

Samudragupta was noted not more for his conquests than for his proficiency in the humanities of the times. The Allahabad Pillar Inscription describes how he was well-versed in the śāstras.[1731] But his learning was not confined to the sacred lore alone. He was the prince of poets (kavirāja) whose various poetical compositions were fit to be the means of subsistence of learned people[1732] and gave him an empire of fame for his enjoyment.[1733] Altogether his sharp and polished intellect put to shame Kāśyapa, the preceptor of Indra.[1734] Besides poetry he also cultivated the sister arts of music. He "put to shame Nārada by his choral skill and musical accomplishment."[1735] The Lyrist type of his coins represent Samudragupta as playing on the lyre or lute (viṇā). He was no less proficient in the sterner arts of the warrior. He depicts himself as an archer on some of his coins which represent him as holding a bow in his left hand and an arrow in his

---

1730 S. B. E., Vol. XXXV. pp. 6-7.

1731 Allahabad Pillar Inscription, line 5; śāstratatwārthabharttuḥ—Ibid., lines 15 and 30.

1732 Ibid., line 27.

1733 Kirtirājyaṃ bhunakti—Ibid., line 6.

1734 Ibid., line 27.

1735 Gāndharva-lalitāḥ lalitaiḥ—Ibid., line 27.

right with the head of the arrow resting on the ground. On other coins he stands out as the invincible hunter and takes the title Vyāghra-parākrama, of which the meaning is visible on the obverse, representing the king as trampling on a live tiger, which falls back as he shoots it. Wearing only waist cloth, turban and some jewellery he stands as the very picture of energy.

As to Harṣa Śilāditya, Bāṇa distinctly says that Harṣa was a poet. " In poetical contests he poured out a necter of his own which he had not received from any foreign source;"[1736] " his poetical skill finds words fail;"[1737] " his knowledge cannot find range enough in doctrines to be learned ; "[1738] " all the fine arts are too narrow a field for his genius."[1739] This might be the exaggerated estimate of a courtier composing the panegyric of his patron but we have some evidence in its support from an external source. I-Tsing[1740] says that Harṣa " versified the story of the Bodhisattva Jīmutabāhana (cloud-borne) who surrendered himself in place of a Nāga. Historians of Sanskrit Literature credit Harṣa with the authorship of two dramas, the Ratnābalī and Priyadarśikā together with a grammatical work. That literary criticism in Ancient India at least, thought highly of Harṣa is evident from the fact that Jayadeva, the author of Gītagovindam names him along with Bhāsa and Kālidāsa as one of his illustrious predecessors.[1741] Harṣa is also stated to have taken part in dramatic performances.[1742] Moreover, Harṣa was a skilful calligraphist if it is his autograph which is seen in the Banskhera Plate Inscription, the last line of which consists of the sign-manual

---

1736 Harṣacharita—Cowell and Thomas, p. 58.

1737 Ibid., p. 65.

1738 Ibid.

1739 Ibid.

1740 Takakusu's Eng. Trans., p. 163.

1741 " Yasyā corāśchikura nikarāḥ karṇapuro mayūro
Bhāso hāsaḥ Kavikulaguru Kālidāso vilāsaḥ
Harṣo harṣo hṛdayavasatiḥ pañchabāṇastu Bāṇaḥ
Kīsam naisā kathaya kavitā kāminī kautakīya."

Corā is the mass of locks, Mayūra the ornament of the ear, Bhāsa is the smile and Kālidāsa, the master of all poets is the charm, Harṣa is pleasure and Bāṇa is the five-arrowed Cupid. How could the damsel of Poetry be other than charming ?

1742 Panikkar—Śrī Harṣa of Kanauj, p. 68.

of the king written in elaborately ornamented characters. That Harṣa was also taught archery is evident from Bāṇa who describes Harṣa as "more delighting in the bow than Droṇa, more unerring with the arrow than Aśwatthāmā."[1743]

Bāṇa also describes the stout forearm of Kumāragupta, a Mālava prince as "marked by the bow-string's scar"[1744] showing that the princes of the time practised archery.[1745] According to Bāṇa "with an intellect unwearied in political science and a deep study of the law-books he (king Tārāpiḍa of Ujjain) made in light and glory a third with the Sun and the Moon."[1746]

That the princes also used to take physical exercise in the hall of exercise attached to the palace is evident from Bāṇa's Kādambarī where we are told that the king entered the private apartments and "there laying aside his adornments, like the Sun divested of his rays or the sky bare of moon and the stars, he entered the *hall of exercise*, where all was duly prepared. Having taken pleasant exercise therein with the princes of his own age, he then entered the bathing place."[1747]

An idea of the character of and care for the education of the princes of the age will be evident from the following account given by Bāṇa about the education of prince Chandrāpīḍa, son of king Tārāpīḍa of Ujjain :—"As Chandrāpīḍa underwent in due course all the circle of ceremonies, beginning with the tying of his top-knot, his childhood passed away; and to prevent distraction, Tārāpīḍa had built for him a palace of learning outside the city, stretching half a league along the Siprā river, surrounded by a wall of white bricks like the circle of peaks of a snow-mountain, girt with a great moat running along the walls, guarded by very strong gates, having one door kept open for ingress, with stables for horses and palanquins close by, and a gymnasium constructed beneath—a fit palace for the immortals. He took infinite pains in gathering there teachers of every science, and having placed the boy there, like a young lion in a cage, forbidding all egress,

---

1743 Harṣacharita—Cowell and Thomas, p. 63.

1744 Ibid., p. 120.

1745 Compare Raghubaṃśam, VI. 56, IX. 63; XI. 40.

1746 Ibid., p. 48.

1747 Kādambarī—C. M. Ridding's Eng. Trans., p. 13.

surrounding him with a suite composed mainly of the sons of his teachers, removing every allurement to the sports of boyhood and keeping his mind free from distraction, on an auspicious day he entrusted him, together with Vaiśampāyana, to masters, that they might acquire all knowledge. Every day when he rose, the king with Vilāsabatī and a small retinue, went to watch him, and Chandrāpīḍa undisturbed in mind kept to his work by the king, quickly grasped all the sciences taught him by his teachers, whose efforts were quickened by his great powers, as they brought to light his natural abilities; the whole range of arts assembled in his mind as in a pure jewelled mirror. He gained the highest skill in word, sentence, proof, law and royal policy; in all kinds of weapons such as the bow, quoit, shield, scimitar, dart, mace, battle-axe and club; in driving and elephant-riding; in musical instruments, such as the lute, fife, drum, cymbal and pipe; in the laws of dancing laid down by Bharata and others and the science of music such as that of Nārada; in the management of elephants, the knowledge of a horse's age and the marks of men; in painting, leaf-cutting, the use of books and writing; in all the arts of gambling, knowledge of the cries of birds, and astronomy; in testing of jewels, carpentry, the working of ivory, in architecture, physics, mechanics, antidotes, mining, crossing of rivers, leaping and jumping and sleight of hand; in stories, dramas, romances, poems; in the Mahābhārata, the Purāṇas, the Itihāsas and the Rāmāyaṇa; in all kinds of writing, all foreign languages, all technicalities, all mechanical arts, in metre and in every other art. And while he ceaselessly studied, even in his childhood an inborn vigour like that of Bhīma shone forth in him and stirred the world in wonder. For, when he was but in play the young elephants, who had attacked him as if he were a lions' whelp, had their limbs bowed down by his grasp on their ears and could not move; with one stroke of his scimitar he cut down palm-trees as if they were lotus-stalks; his shafts, like those of Paraśurāma when he blazed to consume the forest of earth's royal stems, cleft only the loftiest peaks; he exercised himself with an iron club which ten men were needed to lift".[1748] "The king learning that

[1748] Ibid., pp. 59-61.

Chandrāpīḍa had grown to youth and had completed his knowledge of all the arts, studied all the sciences and won great praise from his teachers, summoned Balāhaka, a mighty warrior and with a large escort of cavalry and army sent him on a very auspicious day to fetch the prince. And Balāhaka, going to the palace of learning............... approached Chandrāpīḍa and respectfully gave the king's message: 'Prince, the king bids me say: "Our desires are fulfilled; the śāstras have been learnt; thou hast gained the highest skill in all the martial sciences. All thy teachers give thee permission to leave the house of learning. Let the people see that thou hast received thy training, like a young royal elephant come out from the enclosure, having in thy mind the whole orb of the arts like the full moon, newly risen. Let the eyes of the world, long eager to behold thee, fulfil their true function; for, all the zenanas are yearning for thy sight. This is now the tenth year of thine abode in the school and thou didst enter it having reached experience of thy sixth year. This year, then, so reckoned, is the sixteenth of thy life, Now, therefore, when thou hast come forth and shown thyself to all thy mothers longing to see thee and hast saluted those who deserve thy honour, do thou lay aside thy early discipline, and experience at thy will the pleasures of the court and the delights of fresh youth. Pay thy respects to the Chiefs; honour the brāhmaṇas; protect thy people; gladden thy kinsfolk."[1749]

Relying on inscriptions Prof. Dubreuil describes Mahendrabarman, Pallava of Kāñchi (618 A. D.) as one who glorified poetry and music. It appears that he was the composer of some swaras. A burlesque (prahasana) has been found at Travancore written by Mahendrabarman. Prof. Dubreuil has found confirmation of this fact from an inscription on a cave at Māmandūr and which he reads as Mattavilāsādipadam prahasanam, Mattavilāsa being a title Mahendrabarman I. According to Hiuen Tsang Aṃśubarman a recent king (of Nepal) had written a treatise on Etymology. This report of Hiuen Tsang about Aṃśubarman's learning receives corroboration from an Inscription[1750] (dated S. 39 i. e., 635 A. D.) where the following epithet is applied to him: "niśi niśi

[1749] Ibid., pp. 61-62.

[1750] No. 7 (Ind. Antiquary, IX. p. 170).

chānekaśāstrārtha bimarśābasāditāsaddarśanatayā dharmādhikārasthitekāraṇamebātatsa bamanatiśayam manyamānaḥ." Parameśwarabarman Pallava, king of Kāñchi (674 A. D,) is described in the Kuram Pallava grant[1751] as fond of poetry. King Jayāpīḍa of Kashmere (751-782 A. D.) was well-versed in the śāstra on dancing and acting composed by Bharata muni.[1752] "Receiving instruction from a master of grammatical science, called Kṣīra, the learned Jayāpīḍa gained distinction with the wise. He was proud of being able to compete with the learned. So much greater was his fame from the title of scholar than from that of king that notwithstanding his various faults it has not faded like other (things) subject to time."[1753] Jaydeva of Nepal (759 A. D.) is mentioned to have composed certain verses contained in the Inscription dated S. 153. The Eastern Chalukya king Vinayāditya III (766-809 Saka) was specially proficient in Mathematics and hence was called Guṇaka. An idea of the training imparted to King Śañkarabarman of Kashmere (883-902 A. D.) by his royal father can be obtained from the following words of Śañkarabarman himself, preserved in Kalhaṇa's Rājatarañgiṇī: "I was taken about by my father, on foot and without shoes, dressed in heavy armour when it was hot and in transparent thin cloth when it was cold. When those who went before the king saw me as I was running by the side of the horses during the chase and elsewhere, torn by the thorns and with tears in my eyes, they made representation to him. He replied to them: 'Since I have attained the throne from common rank, I know the hardships (experienced) by attendants at different times during their services. After undergoing such misery, this (son) will be sure to know the troubles of others when he comes to the throne. Otherwise, he may remain ignorant (of them), being born on the throne."[1754] Mahendrapāla (890-908 A. D.) and Mahīpāla (910-940 A. D.) of Kanauj also had as their teacher the famous poet and dramatist Rājaśekhara who in his works always describes himself as such. Kṣhemagupta (940-958 A. D.) of Kashmere is described by Kalhaṇa as trained by his teacher in the art of drawing darts.[1755] Abhimanyu of

---

[1751] Hultzch—South Indian Inscriptions, Vol. I. pp. 148-50.

[1752] Rājatarañgiṇī, IV. 423.

[1753] Ibid., IV. 489-91.

[1754] Ibid., V. 196-99.

[1755] Ibid., VI., 180-81.

Kashmere (958-972 A. D.) was a learned king, well-versed in the śāstras.[1756] Bhoja Paramāra of Dhara (c. 1010-1055 A. D.) was a great author himself and a master of many subjects. He studied Astronomy, Alaṃkāra (poetics), Architecture, Yoga and Grammar and on each of these subjects, he has left works which are still treated as authoritative. His Saraswatikaṇṭāvaraṇa on poetics, Rājamārtaṇḍa on Yoga and Rajamṛgāñkakaraṇa on astronomy are well-known and speak of his high proficiency in these sciences. Bhoja is mentioned by several well-known writers as an author on Hindu Law as well, though no work of his on that subject is extant. He is so mentioned by Sūlanātha in the Prāyaśchittaviveka, by Raghunandana and even by Vijñāneśwara in his famous Mitākṣarā. Rājendra Chola of Tanjore (1014-44 A. D.) was not only a great military commander but also a learned man as the title paṇḍit is found prefixed to his name in many inscriptions. King Eraga of the Raṭṭas of Saundatti is described in one of his inscriptions (dated 1040 A. D.) as a Vidyādhara in singing.[1757] Abhimanyu of the Kachhaghāta dynasty of Dubkhund was famous for his skill in horsemanship and archery which was extolled even by Bhoja, king of Malwa.[1758] Kalasa (1063-1089 A. D.) of Kashmere is described by Kalhaṇa as having learnt diplomacy and bravery from Jindurāja.[1759] Anantabarman Choḍaganga (1076-1142 A. D.) of the Eastern Ganga dynasty of Trikalinga and Orissa is described as learned in the Vedas and the śāstras and even in architecture and fine arts as if Saraswatī herself was his nurse.[1760] Lakṣhamaṇadeva Paramāra of Dhar

---

1756 Ibid., VI. 290.

1757 I. A., XIX. p. 161.

1758 Yasyātyadrutabāhabāhana mahāśastraprayogādiṣu prābipyam prabikatthitam pṛthumati śrībhojapṛthwibhujā—Dhubkund Inscription—E. I., III.

1759 Rājataraṅgiṇī, VII. 577.

1760 " Dhātrī tasya Saraswatīsamabhbabannunaṃ nachetpītabāna talsāraswatamārya-bālakatamaḥ śrī choḍagangeśwaraḥ.

Tādṛkvedamatiḥ kathaṃ nipuṇatā śāstreṣu tādṛkkathaṃ tādṛkkābyakṛtiḥ kathaṃ pariṇateḥ śilpeṣu tādṛkkātham ".

—J. R. A. S. B., LXV. p. 331.

(1081-1104 A. D.) was also a great poet.[1761] Harṣa of Kashmere (1089-1101 A. D.) was the embodiment of all sciences.[1762] "Knowing all languages, a great poet in all tongues and a depository of all learning, he became famous even in other countries. He was an expert singer as well."[1763] Bilhaṇa in his Vikramāñkacharita[1764] praises Harṣa of Kashmere for his personal bravery in battle, for his skill as a poet by which he surpassed even Śrī Harṣa of Kanuaj. He also refers to his power of composing sweet songs in all languages (sarvavāṣā-kavitwa). "Surely" says Kalhaṇa, "not even Bṛhaṣpati is able to name clearly all the sciences in which he was versed. Even to this day, if one of the songs which he composed for the voice is heard, tears roll on the eye-lashes even of his enemies."[1765] He was eminent by his knowledge of all sciences.[1766] From Kanaka, Kalhaṇa's own uncle, Harṣa took lessons in song and for his services as tutor in music he gave a lac of gold dīnnārs.[1767] Harṣa himself used to teach the dancing girls of his palace how to act.[1768] He was also skilled in athletic exercises.[1769] Naravarmadeva Paramāra of Dhara (c. 1104-1133 A. D.) was like his father Udayāditya a poet and was the author of the fragment of an unpublished praśasti found in the Mahākāla temple in Ujjain.[1770] In the Bhojaśālā at Dhara and in Umā and Mahākāla temples in Ujjain inscriptions have been found in serpentine form giving the sanskrit noun and verb terminations of Pāṇini, accompanied by verses containing the names of Udayāditya and Naravarman and making punning allusions to their valour and learning.[1771] Govindachandra (1114-1155 A. D.) of the Gāhadavāla dynasty of Kanauj is described in most Gāhadavāla records as "Vividha-vichāra-vidyā-vāchaṣpati," a very Bṛhaṣpati (teacher of gods) in different

---

1761 Nāgpura Praśasti.

1762 Rājataraṅgiṇi, VII. 319.

1763 Ibid., 613.

1764 XVIII. 64-66.

1765 Rājataraṅgiṇī, VII. 941-42.

1766 Ibid., 970.

1767 Ibid., 1117-18.

1768 Ibid., 1640-41.

1769 Ibid., 1704.

1770 Luard and Lele—The Paramāras of Dhar, p. 29.

1771 Udayādityanāmāṃkabarṇanāgakṛpāṇikā ....maṇiśreṇī sṛṣṭā sukabibandhunā...............kabiṇāṃ cha nṛpānāṃ cha hṛdayeṣu nibeśitā—Luard and Lele's The Paramāras of Dhar, p. 30.

sciences and philosophies. King Bhikṣācara (1120-22 A. D.) when a boy was trained in arms and taught sciences by Naravarman, the ruler of Malwa.[1772] Someśwara III (1126-37 A. D.) of the later Chālukya dynasty of Kalyan was the author of Mānasollāsa or Abhilaṣitārtha-chintāmaṇi which is a compendium of military art, political science, horse and elephant rearing, poetry, dialectics, music, astronomy—in short, all sciences which lead to the happiness of men. In Astronomy he gave the Dhruvāṅkas (constants to be added). Vijayāditya Kadamba of Goa (1158 A. D.) was also a very learned prince and earned the title of Vāṇībhuṣaṇa. The praise bestowed on him in an inscription is well worth quoting below :—

" Vṛgan kunti prāse dhanusi biṣame chāṣifalake bare bādye gīte
sarasakabitāśāstrabisare
Tumragādyārohe smṛtiṣu cha purāṇeṣu purujit parijñānādhobhuj
jagati vahuvidyādhara iti."

Ballālasena (1159-70 A. D.) of Bengal was also a learned man, being the author of Dānasāgara and he commenced another work which his son Lakṣamaṇasena finished. Aparāditya II Śilāhāra of Thana (1175-1200 A.D.) was also a great scholar, being the author of the well-known commentary on Yājñabālkyasmṛti known as Aparāka, a work of recognised authority on Hindu law and recognised as such even in far off Kashmere. Arjunabarmadeva Paramāra of Dhar (1210-16 A. D.) is described in his court-poet Madana's drama which is inscribed on slabs, found at Dhar by Lele, as not only a poet but also an author.[1773]

It is thus evident that even in the Mediæval Hindu period the Indian princes were taught as before, not only the śastras but also the śāstras. Al Beruni's statement[1774] that "the Brahmins teach the Vedas to the kṣhatriyas.................. the vaiśyas and śūdras are not allowed to hear it, much less to pronounce and recite it" proves not only the later origin of the dictum "Kalābādyantayoḥ sthitiḥ"

1772 Rājataraṅgiṇī, VIII. 228.

1773 Kāvyagāndharvasarvasyanidhinā yena sāmpratam
Vārābatāraṇaṃ devyāśchakre pustakabinayoḥ
—Ep. Ind., IX. p. 108.

1774 Sachau's Eng. Trans., Vol. I, p. 125.

but also the study of the Vedas by the kshatriyas. And we have already seen how noted kings like Samudragupta, Harṣa Śīlāditya, Harṣa of Kashmere, Bhoja, Govindachandra and Vijayāditya were as learned in the sacred and profane lore as the Brahmins. But the above survey makes it clear that in the later (Mediæval) Hindu period, although there were princes well-versed in military science like Muñja and Bhoja of Dhar, Harṣa of Kashmere, Abhimanyu of Dhubkhund and Rājendrachola of Tanjore Indian princes in general, revelled more in the study of poetics than in the more necessary study of the science of war and of the science of the state. The distinctions of heroines in love and despair, the essentials of poetry, poetical blemishes and embellishments and the figures of speech engaged the intelligence of the princes and some of them even wrote elaborate treatises on poetics and dramaturgy. This, no doubt, made princely education individualistic and liberal in character but the minute study of poetics led to the deterioration of taste and morals and the increase of voluptuousness can be marked from the Karpūramañjarī of Rājaśekhara to the Ramvāmañjarī of Nyāyachandra. The stage attracted the princes more than the camp and the way was thus paved for foreign domination and rule.

In the Bhagalpur grant[1775] of Nārāyaṇapāla and in the Deo-Barnak Inscription[1776] (of Bengal) we find the mention of an officer over king's sons, designated respectively as Kumārāmātya and Mahākumārāmātya, but we do not know whether the education of the princes was among their functions. Nevertheless on account of their ability to pay most of the princes seem to have engaged private tutors. Viṣma learnt the Vedas and the Vedāngas from his tutor Vaśiṣṭha[1777] and had Dhṛtarāṣtra, Pāṇdu and Bidur taught by a competent tutor.[1778] He also appointed Droṇāchārya to coach his grandsons—the Pāṇḍavas and the Kauravas.[1779] King Drupad also appointed a Brahmin resident-tutor who taught among other subjects

---

[1775] Ind. Ant., XV

[1776] Corp. Ins., Vol. III. p. 216.

[1777] Mahābhārata, Ādiparba, 100th and 103rd adhyāyas.

[1778] Ibid., 109th adhyāya.

[1779] Ibid., 130th adhyāya.

Bṛhaspati-nīti to the princes.[1780] King Suddodhana[1781] appointed Sabbamitta as tutor to his son Gautama. Similarly, Balāditya (Samudragupta ?) and Mahīpāla had Vasubandhu[1782] and Rājaśekhara respectively as their tutors. King Harṣa of Kashmere appointed Kanaka, (Kalhaṇa's uncle) as his tutor in music to whom he gave a lac of gold dīnnāras as tuition-fee (Rājataraṅgiṇī, VII. 1117-18). King Jayāpīḍa of Kashmere had Kṣīra as his tutor in grammar (Stein—The Chronicles of Kashmere, Vol. I. p. 165 and 165 foot-note).

The education of the prince was kept by the Brahmins closely in their hands. According to Manu[1783] teaching the Vedas shall never revert to the kṣhatriya as against the brāhmaṇa. The injunction of Manu[1784] that the king should learn from the people the theory of the various trades and professions seems to imply that in the subject of Vārttā others besides Brahmins might be called in to give instruction to the young princes and this would seem probable also in the matter of military skill. Viśwāmitra thus gave to Rāma a training in the use of missiles and weapons ;[1785] yet brāhmaṇa control dominated throughout. We are told that Rāma's teachers are aged brāhmaṇas who have seen the true import of Dharma.[1786] Droṇa a Brahmin taught military arts to the Kauravas and the Pāṇḍavas.[1787] Droṇa also taught military art to a king of the Andhaka family and to many princes.[1788] Bhiṣma was taught the Vedas and the Vedāngas by Vaśiṣṭha, a Brahmin. (Mahābhārata, Ādiparba, 100th and 103rd ādhyāyas). The brothers of Draupadī were taught Bṛhaspati-nīti by a brahmin resident-tutor.[1789] King Janaka learnt Brahmavidyā from various brāhmaṇa āchāryas.[1790] King Bṛhadratha learnt Brahmavidyā from the brāhmaṇa ascetic Sākāyana.[1791] King

---

1780 Ibid., Banaparba, 32nd adhyāya.

1781 Milindā-Pañha, IV. 6, 3.

1782 Paramārtha's Life of Vasubandhu.

1783 X. 77.

1784 VII. 43.

1785 Rāmāyaṇa, Bālakāṇḍa, 27 and 28th sargas.

1786 Ibid., Ayodhyākāṇḍa, 1st sarga.

1787 Mahābhārata, Ādiparba.

1788 Ibid., 132nd adhyāya.

1789 Ibid., Banaparba, 132nd adhyāya.

1790 Bṛhad. Up., IV. 1.

1791 Maitrā. Up., 1f.

Janaśruti learnt Brahmavidyā from the brāhmaṇā Raikva.[1792] Prince Gautama was taught by nine teachers all of whom were Brahmins.[1793] In Kautilya's Arthaśāstra[1794] we are told: "That kshatriya breed which is *brought up by Brahmins*, is charmed with the counsels of good councillors and which faithfully follows the precepts of the śāstras becomes invincible and attains success, though unaided by weapons". Kanaka, the uncle of Kalhaṇa, a Brahmin gave lessons in music to king Harṣa of Kashmere.[1795] Kṣīra, Jayāpīḍa's teacher in grammar was a brāhmaṇa of the Rājanaka family of Kashmere.[1796] Al-Beruni[1797] speaks in the same strain: "The *Brahmins* teach the Veda to kṣhatriyas. The latter learn it but are not allowed to teach it even to a brāhmaṇa.[1798]

In his town-planning scheme Kautilya has reserved for the royal teachers' residence a good site. Says he: "Royal teachers, priests, sacrificial place, water reservoir and ministers shall occupy sites east by north to the palace".[1799] According to him 'they are to receive the sum of 48,000 paṇas per annum' which was also the pay of the minister, the commander of the army, the heir-apparent prince, the mother of the king and the queen.[1800] With this amount for their subsistence, they will se ·tely yield themselves to temptation and hardly be discontented.[1801]

Tod in his Rājasthān[1802] in referring to these purohita teachers gives rather a bad opinion of them as men who took advantage of their position to get gain for themselves by working on the superstition of their employers. But we need not suppose that this was generally the case and many of them were men of high character whose moral influence on their pupils was distinctly good. India has had many famous rulers, who were educated under this system and many who also attained to literary merit. Among these princes there also grew up a

---

1792 Ibid.

1793 Milindā-Pañha, IV. 6, 3.

1794 R. Śyāmaśāstrī's Eng. Trans., p. 17.

1795 Rājataraṅgiṇī, VII. 1117.

1796 Stein—The Chronicles of Kashmere, Vol. I. p. 165 and 165 foot-note.

1797 Sachau's Eng. Trans., Vol. I. p. 125.

1798 Compare the remark of king Ajātaśatru: Pratilomaı ūpameba brāhmaṇamupanayeta (Kauś. Up., IV. 1. 19).

1799 Arthaśāstra (R. Śyāmaśāstrī's Eng. Trans.), p. 61.

1800 Ibid., p. 307.

1801 Ibid.

1802 Page 407.

spirit of chivalry, very much like that which prevailed in Europe in the Middle Ages.[1803] Tod mentions that amongst the Rajput tribes, youthful candidates were initiated to military fame in much the same way as young men in Europe in the Middle Ages became knights. The ceremony of initiation was called *Kharg bandai* or binding of the sword and took place when the young Rajput was considered fit to bear arms. The spirit of chivalry thus inculcated must have set before these young princes and nobles a high ideal of valour and virtue and this is reflected in the Epics and in the bardic chronicles of Rājasthāna which contain many stories of noble deeds and knightly heroism.

Indeed, the education of the Indian princes was not inferior to that of the European Knights in the Age of Chivalry. No doubt the note of personal ambition and of adventure for adventure's sake seems much less prominent in the Indian ideal than in the European but the gentler virtues such as patience and filial devotion were much more emphasised as we see in the story of Rāma. The idea that the king and the prince had a duty to perform to society in the protection of the weak and that their position was not one so much of glory and of ease as of service to others, is very prominent. Thus Viśwāmitra in exhorting Rāma to kill Tāṛakā says : "Do not feel it impious to kill a female. For the good of the four varṇas this is enjoined for the princes. One who has taken over the charge of the protection of the people should perform all kinds of deeds, however cruel, sinful and infamous they might be, if thereby, he would keep in safety his subjects".[1804] Rāma on hearing Sītā's words dissuading him from undertaking the task of ridding Daṇḍakāraṇya of Rākṣasas who are killing innocent hermits living therein, thus says to her: "You yourself have just said that the kṣhatriya should take the bow and the arrow so that the word 'ārtta' (unprotected) should not remain in this earth. Now these hermits of Daṇḍakāraṇya have approached me seeking my protection against these Rākṣasas".[1805] No doubt many of them failed to live up to this noble ideal but in formulating it and holding it before the young princes India has much of which to be proud.

[1803] Rājāsthān, pp. 63, 512.

[1804] Rāmāyaṇa, Bālakāṇḍa, 25th sarga.

[1805] Ibid., Āraṇyakāṇḍa, 10th sarga.

CHAPTER XI.

The Educational institutions in ancient India.

§ 1. The Parisads.

From the most ancient times there existed in India Brahminic settlements and in connection with them Pariṣads or assemblies of learned brāhmaṇas who gave decisions on all points connected with the Brahminic religion and learning. We have already referred (*ante*, pp. 55-57) to these Pariṣads as seats of learning and have seen that not only were different faculties represented but even a student was a member of the Pariṣad. The settlement of brāhmaṇas proficient in different branches of the ancient learning in various centres must have meant the gathering together also of a number of students who received instruction from them and thus these Pariṣads would form the nucleus of something corresponding to a University.

§ 2. Taxila.

An instance of an early Brahminic intellectual centre was Takṣaśilā. This town is now represented by more than twelve square miles of ruins to the north-west of Rawalpindi and the south-east of of Hasan Abdal.[1806] The site according to Sir John Marshall, embraces three separate cities namely, the Bir Mound to the south which was in occupation from the earliest times say 1500 B. C. until the close of the Maurya domination about 180 B. C.; secondly, the city known as Sir Kap further north, which is believed to have been founded by the Greek invaders in the first half of the second century B. C. and to have been occupied by the Greeks and their successors, the Scythians and Parthians until about 70 A. D.; and thirdly, the city of Sir Sukh, still further north, to which there is reason to believe the capital was transferred from Sir Kap by the Kushanas. Thus, within four centuries, Taxila became subject to five different empires—the Macedonian, the Mauryan, the Bactrian, the Parthian and the Kushana

[1806] V. A. Smith—Early History of India, third edition, p. 61.

and from these widely different civilisations, extending from Greece to Western China and from the steppes of Russia to the Bay of Bengal it must have inherited much of the culture and of the arts peculiar to each. We are told in the Rāmāyaṇa[1807] that Vyabahāra (Law) was a specialised subject at Taxila. The Mahābhārata also refers to Takṣaśilā as a noted seat of learning. The story is told of one of its teachers named Dhaumya who had three disciples named Upamanyu, Aruṇi and Veda. Aruṇi hailed from Pāñchāla and was an ideal student in respect of devotion to his teacher under whose orders, in order to stop a leakage in the water-course in his field, Aruṇi, finding every other means unavailing, threw his body into the breach. We learn from the Dhammapadātthakathā[1808] that a student went to Taxila from Benares for studying the śilpas and had 500 class-mates. According to the same work[1809] Pasenadī, king of Kośala was educated at Taxila. The Mahāvagga[1810] has reference to teachers at Taxila, to whom students were going for the study of the śilpas. From the Mahāvagga[1811] we also learn that Jīvaka, the renowned physician at at the court of Bimbisāra, was educated in medicine and surgery at Taxila. So much reputation had been gained by Taxila as a centre of learning that we are told by Pāṇinī[1812] that Takṣaśilā as the surname of a person denoted that his ancestors had lived at Taxila, while the Mahābhārata[1813] declares the men of Taxila to be unrivalled in discussions on matters of learning. The Jātaka stories are equally full of references to the fame of Taxila as a University town.[1814] The great grammarian Pāṇinī and Chāṇakya, the minister of Chandragupta Maurya are said to have had their education in Taxila. Here at the time of Alexander's invasion the Greeks first came into contact with the brāhmaṇa philosophers and were astonished at their asceticism and strange doctrines. In the days of Aśoka the Great, Taxila was "one of the greatest and most splendid cities of the East and enjoyed special

---

[1807] Uttarakāṇḍa, 101, 11.

[1808] Pali Text Society's edition, I. 250.

[1809] Ibid., I. p. 211.

[1810] Mahābaṃśa, VIII. 1, 5 and 6.

[1811] VIII. 3.

[1812] Pāṇinī, IV. 3. 93.

[1813] Ādiparba, III. 172.

[1814] I. 273, 317, 402, 406, 431, 447, 463; II. 277; IV. 38; V. 127; VI. 347 etc.

reputation as the headquarters of Hindu learning. The sons of peoples of all the upper classes, chiefs, brāhmaṇas and merchants flocked to Taxila as to a University town, in order to study the circle of Indian arts and sciences, especially Medicine." At the time of Hiuen Tsang's visit "the brāhmaṇas of this town are well-grounded in their literary work and are of high renown for their talents, well-informed as to things (men and things) and of a vigorous understanding (memory)."

The fame of Taxila as a seat of learning was mainly due to that of its teachers. Of one such teacher we read: 'youths of the warrior and the brāhmaṇa caste came from all India to be taught the arts by him.'[1815] They are always spoken of as being 'world-renowned,' being authorities, specialists and experts in the subjects they taught. And it was the presence of scholars of such acknowledged excellence and wide-spread reputation that caused a steady movement of qualified students drawn from all classes and ranks of society towards Taxila from far off Benares,[1816] Rajagṛha,[1817] Mithilā,[1818] Lālhya country,[1819] Ujjain,[1820] Kośala,[1821] and the Sivi and Kuru Kingdoms in the 'North Country',[1822] thus enabling it to exercise a kind of intellectual suzereignty over the wide world of letters in India.

The students are always spoken of as going to Taxila to 'complete' their education and not to begin it.[1823] They are invariably sent at the age of sixteen[1824] or when they 'come of age.' This shows that Taxila was the seat not of elementary, but of secondary and higher education. The age limit for admission there was curiously enough the same as is prescribed by modern Universities. Moreover, only

---

1815 Jātaka III. 158.

1816 Jātaka I. 272, 285, 409; II. 85, 87; IV. 50, 224; V. 263, 127 etc.

1817 Ibid., III. 238; V. 177, 247.

1818 Ibid. IV. 316; VI. 347.

1819 Ibid., I. 447. Lālya has been identified by Mr. Nandalal De with the Hugly district in Bengal. (J. A. S. B., New series, Vol. VI., 1910. p. 604.

1820 Ibid., IV. 392.

1821 Ibid. III. 115.

1822 Ibid., V. 210; V. 457; III. 399; I. 356.

1823 In Jātaka IV. 38 we are told that the son of a poor woman of a caravan, a merchant's son and the son of a tailor in the employ of the merchant "all grew up together and by and by went to Taxila to *complete* their education".

1824 Jātaka I. 285.

the students of a maturer age could be sent so far away from their homes for the furtherence of their studies.

The students of Taxila were quite a heterogenous lot, drawn from all ranks and classes of society and representing diverse social conditions. Chaṇḍālas, however, were not admitted as students, for, we are told in the Cittasambhūti Jātaka[1825] that two Chaṇḍāla boys who disguised as brāhmaṇas came to Taxila to study law but betrayed themselves by their coarse language and manners when one of them burnt his mouth at a dinner were at once expelled.

While all castes except the Chaṇḍālas were admitted to instruction it seems that the castes so admitted did not always confine themselves to their traditional subjects of study. We read of a Brahmin boy of Taxila who learnt divination under his teacher. Another Brahmin boy studied magic charms. Another is spoken of as having gone in for the liberal arts and ultimately specialised in archery. It is again a Brahmin boy that studies 'the charm which commands all things of sense.' There is a reference to a Brahmin boy choosing 'science' for his study and to another mastering the three Vedas and the eighteen accomplishments.[1826]

No doubt the poorer students who could not pay their tuition fees had to undergo a course of menial service for the school (see *ante*, pp. 119-20) but the recognition of the dignity of all honest labour secured to them a status of equality with its aristocratic section. What further levelled down all distinctions within the school was the insistence upon certain standards of simplicity and discipline in life to which all its members had to submit. The Prince Brahmadatta of Benares[1827] is sent on to Taxila for his studies with the modest equipment given him by his royal father of "a pair of onesoled sandals, a sunshade of leaves, and a thousand pieces of money" as his teacher's fees, of which not a single pice he could retain for his private use. Thus the prince enters his school as a poor man, divested of all riches. The same fact is pointed out by the story of Prince Junha of Benares,[1828] who accidentally

---

1825 Jātaka IV. 391.

1826 Jātaka II. 200; II. 99; III. 219; IV. 456; III. 18; II. 87; III. 115, 122.

1827 Jātaka No. 252.

1828 Jātaka IV. 96.

breaking the alms-bowl of a Brahmin by colliding with him in nocturnal darkness, was asked to pay him the price of a meal as compensation. The prince then said to the Brahmin: "I cannot now give you the price of a meal, Brahmin; but I am Prince Junha, son of the king of Kāśī, and when I go to my kingdom, you may come to me and ask for the money." Thus while at school a king's son was as poor as the son of a peasant.

Of the subjects taught the three Vedas and the eighteen vijjās (vidyās) are frequently mentioned. In the Bhīmsena Jātaka[1829] there is a description of how the Bodhisattva learnt the three Vedas and the eighteen vijjās. In the Kosiya Jātaka[1830] we are told that Bodhisattva being born in a Brahmin family studied the three Vedas and the eighteen vijjās at Taxila. In the Dhummedha Jātaka[1831] it is stated that at the age of sixteen Bodhisattva went to Taxila and mastered the eighteen vijjās. In the Asadisa Jātaka[1832] we find that the Bodhisattva mastered the three Vedas and the eighteen vijjās. In many other Jātakas,[1833] we find that Bodhisattva studied the three Vedas and the eighteen vijjās. The invariable mention of the three Vedas shows that the study of Atharvaveda was not included in the curriculum of studies. The Vedas were of course to be learnt by heart. We are told of a teacher of Taxila from whose lips 500 brāhmaṇa pupils learnt the Vedas.[1834]

Of the conventional eighteen vijjās archery was one. In the Bhīmsena Jātaka[1835] we learn that Bodhisattva learnt archery at Taxila. In the Asadisa Jātaka[1836] we are told that Bodhisattva learnt archery at Taxila and got himself appointed as the archer of a king at whose orders he brought down a mango from the top of a tree with his bow and arrow. From the Sarabhanga Jātaka[1837] we learn that Bodhisattva learnt archery at Taxila and gave exhibition of many feats

---

1829 Jātaka I. 356.
1830 Jātaka I. 463.
1831 Jātaka I. 285.
1832 Jātaka II. 87.
1833 Jātaka I. 505, 510; III. 115, 122; IV. 200.
1834 Jātaka I. 402.
1835 Jātaka I. 356.
1836 Jātaka II. 87.
1837 Jātaka V. 127.

before the king of the country of his birth. He pierced a plank eight fingers thick, an iron sheet one finger thick, a cart full of earth and sand, etc. He was further requested to show more feats, viz., śaralaṭṭhi (stick of arrows), śararajjum (a rope of arrows) śaraveṇi (a row of arrows) śarapāsāda (a palace of arrows), śaramaṇḍapa (a pavilion of arrows), śarasopāna (a ladder of arrows), śarapokharaṇi (a tank of arrows), śarapadumam (a lotus of arrows) and śaravassam (a flight of arrows). The Pañchavyūha Jātaka[1838] also refers to the military training of Bodhisattva, a son of Brahmadatta, king of Benares. Indeed Taxila was famous for its military schools. One such school[1839] could boast of counting all the then princes throughout India numbering 103 as its students. In this connection we may refer to the story of the brāhmaṇa boy of Benares Jyotipāla by name who was sent to Taxila at the king's expense for education in archery. When he had finished his training and was returning home, the teacher presented him with his own sword, a bow and arrow, a coat of mail and a diamond and asked him to take his place as the head of 500 pupils to be trained up by him in the military arts as he was himself old and wanted to retire.[1840]

Another branch of learning taught at Taxila was snake-charming. In the Compeyya Jātaka[1841] it is stated that a young Brahmin learnt Alambanamantam (mantra for charming snakes) at Taxila.

Religious ceremonials seem to have been taught at Taxila. In the Susīma Jātaka[1842] we are told that Bodhisattva was once born as the son of a hatthimangalakārako. When the king wished to perform hatthimangala ceremony, his ministers requested him to choose a priest from among the elderly Brahmins. Upon this Bodhisattva's mother became sorry and young Bodhisattva coming to know the cause of his mother's sorrow enquired as to where he would be able to learn Hattisuttam. Being told about Taxila he went there, learnt Hattisuttam and took part in the royal ceremony.

1838 Jātaka I. 273.

1839 Jātaka V. 457.

1840 Jātaka V. 127

1841 Jātaka IV. 456.

1842 Jātaka II. 47.

Certain occult sciences were also taught. In the Vrahāchatta Jātaka[1843] it is related how a son of the king of Kośala leart Nidhi-uddhāraṇamantam at Taxila and then found out the hidden treasure of his father with which he hired mercenaries and reconquered the lost kingdom of his father. We hear of pupils at Taxila, learning magic charms, spell for bringing back the dead to life, spell for understanding animal cries, the art of prognostication, charm for commanding all things of sense and divining from the signs on the body.[1844]

According to the Rāmāyaṇa[1845] Vyabahāra (Law) was a specialised subject of study at Taxila. This is also evident from the Chittasambhūti Jātaka[1846] where we learn of two chaṇḍāla boys who came from far off Ujjain to Taxila to learn Law in the guise of brāhmaṇa pupils.

Taxila, however, was specially reputed for its school of Medicine.[1847] Jīvaka,[1848] the physician of Bimbisāra, studied Medicine here under the great ṛṣi professor Ātreya.[1849] The study of Medicine seems to have had both a theoretical and practical course. The theoretical course consisted of a study of the texts on Medicine and Surgery while the practical course included a first hand study of plants to find out their medicinal values, as shown in the account of Jīvaka's education. We may also refer to the successful surgical operations executed by Jīvaka as soon as he had left Taxila on finishing his education, for they show that he must have had a previous practical training in such difficult operations.

The colleges at Taxila seem to have had a number of sittings every day. The poorer students who paid for the expense of their education by the performance of menial work for the school during the day could find time for study only in the nights when accordingly the

---

1843 Jātaka III. 115-116.

1844 Jātaka II. 100; I. 510; III. 415; III. 122; IV. 465; II. 200.

1845 Uttarakāṇḍa 101, 11.

1846 IV. 391 (Jātaka No. 498).

1847 Jātaka IV. 171.

1848 Mahāvagga (Vinaya Pītaka edited by Oldenbuŋg), VIII. 3.

1849 The Chinese literature, as pointed out by the author of "Bauddha Bhārata" (in Bengali) refers to a Chinese prince who came to study Medicine at Taxila.

teacher imparted instruction to them.[1850] It was probably convenient for the day-scholars to attend night classes: We read of Prince Junha who "one night, after he had been listening carefully to his teacher's instructions, left the house of his teacher in the dark and set out for home."[1851] Another student of Benares who went to Taxila for a particular instruction implored his teacher thus: "Give me your time for this night only. I will learn the whole after one lesson."[1852] As regards the students who paid their teachers fees, they were given 'schooling on every light and lucky day'.[1853]

We have already referred to the theoretical and practical courses in Medicine at Taxila. Similarly, a practical turn was given to all instruction as a pedagogic principle. Thus we read of a brāhmaṇa student of a market-town in the North country who specialised in the science of archery at Taxila and after finishing his education went as far as the Andhra country in prosecution of the practical application of his art.[1854] A prince of Kośala is also mentioned who after studying the three Vedas and eighteen liberal arts at Taxila left the place to study the practical uses of these sciences learned.[1855] Lastly, there is an instance in which a student, on the completion of his education in the arts at Taxila and returning home to Benares had to exhibit before his parents a practical demonstration of the technical knowledge he had acquired. Thus the University reacted on the villages and preserved the artistic capacities and traditions of the people.

Many other educational institutions are frequently referred to in the Jātakas e. g., in I. 234 (Losaka Jātaka); I. 317: I. 402; I. 447; I. 463; I. 510; II. 48; III. 122; III. 537 (Tittira Jātaka); IV. 391; V. 128; V. 457. From the Jātakas we learn that some these institutions were maintained partly by the honorariums paid by the sons of the wealthy members of the society[1856] and partly by the scholarships awarded to students by the states to which they belonged.[1857] Sometimes

---

[1850] Jātaka II. 278.
[1851] Jātaka IV. 96.
[1852] Jātaka II. 47.
[1853] Jātaka No. 252.
[1854] Jātaka I. 356.
[1855] Jātaka III. 115.
[1856] Jātaka I. 272, 285; IV. 50, 224 etc.
[1857] Jātaka V. 263; III. 238, V. 247; V. 127.

the students had a common mess[1858] but when they were too poor a charitable community came forward to provide for them a free education.[1859] It is worthy of note that not only religious treatises like the three Vedas[1860] but also the various secular arts and sciences were cultivated in these centres of education. Instead of the three Vedas, we sometimes find mention of sacred texts,[1861] holy books[1862] or the law.[1863] Some of these terms may indicate the sacred literature of the Buddhists. We find even the direct mention of a Vinaya scholar and a Sūtra scholar.[1864]

Side by side with institutions of a heterogenous composition, we also find references to colleges of particular communities only. Teachers with 500 pupils all Brahmins are frequently mentioned. Sometimes teachers would have only brāhmaṇa and kṣhatriya pupils. We also read of a teacher at Taxila whose school had on its rolls only princes as pupils—"*all princes* who were at that time in India to the number of 101", besides two other princes newly admitted from the kingdoms of Kuru and Benares.[1865]

§ 3. The Hermitages.

Other centres of learning were the hermitages of one or more renowned sages living in the forests.

The hermitage of Vālmīki was at Chitrakūta hill.[1866] It was situated on the bank of the river Tamasā.[1867] According to Bhababhūti[1868] it was situated on the Ganges. According to Somadeva[1869] it was situated not far from a spot called Pañchabaṭī. Here Rāma and his party were entertained.[1870] When Śatrughna

1858 Jātaka I. 317; IV. 391.

1859 Jātaka I. 239 (Losaka Jātaka); I. 317; III. 171.

1860 Jātaka I. 402; I. 259.

1861 Jātaka III. 235.

1862 Jātaka IV. 293.

1863 Jātaka IV. 392.

1864 Jātaka III. 486.

1865 Jātaka I. 317, 402, 436; III. 158; V. 457.

1866 Rāmāyaṇa, Ayodhyākāṇḍa, 56th sarga.

1867 Ibid., Uttarakāṇḍā, 45th sarga.

1868 Uttara-Rāma-Charita, Acts. IV. and V; Belvalkar's Eng. Trans., pp. 31-33.

1869 Kathāsaritsāgara, Penzer's edition, Vol. I. p. 166.

1870 Rāmāyaṇa, Ayodhyākāṇḍa, 56th sarga.

came to stay here for one night while on his expedition against Lavaṇa, Vālmīki related to him how this hermitage was connected with King Saudāsa of the family of Raghu.[1871] Many students resided in this hermitage of whom Varadwāja who was proficient in śāstric knowledge was one.[1872] In this hermitage Kuśa and Lava were taught the Vedas, the art of music, sthāna and murchhanā-tattva and the Rāmāyaṇa.[1873] The Raghuvaṃśam of Kālidāsa also refers to this hermitage of Vālmīki[1874] whose pupils brought Sītā before king Rāma.[1875] In this hermitage Vālmīki taught the twin sons of Rāma the Vedas and the Vedāngas[1876] as also the art of singing.[1877] In Act IV. Scene I of Bhababhūti's Uttara-Rāma-Charita,[1878] one of the pupils admires the beauty of the hermitage which is now putting on its best appearance to welcome some venerable guests. The other is delighted at the thought that the guests bring with them also a holiday for the school. In the course of their conversation it transpires that the guests are no other than Arundhatī, Vaśiṣtha and the Queen-mother, who on the conclusion of Ṛsyśringa's twelve year sacrifice have repaired to Vālmīki's hermitage. Among the day's guests there is also Janaka, Sītā's father, come on a friendly visit to Vālmīki. In Act II. Scene I we are told that Ātreyī was a fellow-student of Kuśa and Lava in this hermitage. She tells us that "as soon as Kuśa and Lava had gone through the chaula ceremony Vālmīki assiduously grounded them with the exception of the three Vedas—in the three other branches of knowledge. And then when the boys had reached the eleventh year from their conception, they were invested with the sacred thread and instructed in the knowledge of the three Vedas also".[1879]

The hermitage of Anangadeva was at the confluence of the Ganges and the Saraju. The virtuous munis living there were the students of Anangadeva. It was visited by Viśwāmitra, accompanied by Rāma and Lakṣmaṇa.

1871 Ibid., Uttarakāṇḍa, 66th sarga.

1872 Ibid., Bālakāṇḍa, 2nd sarga.

1873 Ibid., 4th sarga.

1874 Canto XIV. 38.

1875 Canto XV. 74.

1876 Canto XV. 33.

1877 Canto XV. 69.

1878 Belvalkar's Eng. Trans., p. 60.

1879 Ibid., p. 32.

The hermitage of Vaśiṣṭha was also visited by Viśwāmitra who accepting the hospitality enquired about the welfare of Agnihotra students, their penance, and the trees.[1880] It was also visited by King Daśaratha.[1881] The pristine grandeur of this hermitage is evident from its graphic description preserved in the Bālakāṇḍa, 51st Sarga. The Mahābhārata[1882] also refers to this hermitage.

The hermitge of Varadwāja was near the confluence of the Ganges and the Jumna.[1883] The way to Ayodhyā from this hermitage was only three yojanas off.[1884] Chitrakūta hill was only twenty miles off from this place.[1885] Rāma and his party stayed here on their way to Chitrakūta.[1886] On their way to Ayodhyā after undergoing their period of banishment Rāma and his party stayed here.[1887] When Bharata and his councillors reached this hermitage on their way to Chitrakūta in search of Rāma, Varadwāja ordered his students to make arrangements for their reception.[1888] Varadwāja had a great friend in king Pṛsathanāmā whose son Drupad was sent to this hermitage for education. Varadwāja was succeeded in this hermitage by his son Droṇa. The latter was a fellow-pupil of Drupad and was taught the Vedas and Vedāngas in this hermitage.[1889]

The hermitage of Śukra was in the kingdom of Rājā Daṇḍa which was situated between the Vindhyā mountain and Śaivala.[1890] Śukra lived in this place, accompanied by many students.[1891] King Daṇḍa himself was one of Śukra's students.[1892]

The hermitage of Rājarṣi Tṛṇabindu[1893] was by the side of the great mountain Sumeru. In this place Brahmarṣi Pulastya who was

---

1880 Rāmāyaṇa, Bālakāṇḍa, 51st and 52nd sargas.

1881 Ibid., Uttarakāṇḍa, 51st sarga.

1882 Banaparba, 101st adhyāya.

1883 Rāmāyaṇa, Ayodhyākāṇḍa, 54th and 89th sargas.

1884 Yuddhakāṇḍa, 125th sarga.

1885 Ayodhyākāṇḍa, 54th sarga.

1886 Ibid.

1887 Yuddhakāṇḍa, 125th sarga.

1888 Ayodhyākāṇḍa, 90th sarga.

1889 Mahābhārata, Ādiparva, 130th and 166th adhyāyas.

1890 Uttarakāṇḍa, 79th sarga.

1891 Uttarakāṇḍa, 81st sarga.

1892 Uttarakāṇḍa, 80th sarga.

1893 Uttarakāṇḍa, 2nd sarga.

proficient in Vedic learning (swādhyāya) used to recite the Vedas. His son Viśrabā was like him proficient in the Vedas.

The hermitage af Agastya was on the bank of the Saraju near its confluence with the Ganges.[1894] When Rāma and his party visited it, Agastya, being informed of their arrival by one of his students, received them, being surrounded by his students.[1895] The Mahābhārata also refers to this hermitage which was visited by King Yudhiṣṭhir.[1896] The Raghuvaṃśam[1897] also refers to this hermitage and locates it near Pañchavaṭī on the banks of the Godāvarī.[1898] Bāṇa in his Kādambarī locates it in the Vindhyan forests and says that the hermitage has long been empty.[1899] Bhababhūti in his Uttara-Rāma-Charita[1900] also refers to this hermitage and locates it in the Daṇḍaka forest. " Here in this region are dwelling—with Agastya at their head—many scholars learned in the Sāmaveda. To acquire from them Upaniṣad lore, hither have I come " says Ātreyī. She then explains why although studying at Vālmīki's she is compelled to travel southwards in search of instruction : because (1) she could not keep pace with Kuśa and Lava and (2) Vālmīki himself was much occupied with the composition of a new poem, the Rāmāyaṇa. Rājaśekhara is his Karpūramañjurī[1901] also refers to this hermitage.

The Daṇḍakāraṇya forest was studded with many such hermitages.[1902] They are resounding with the incessant muttering of the Vedas.[1903] Thus in this forest there were the hermitage of Swarabhanga,[1904]

[1894] Āraṇyakāṇḍa, 12th sarga. The Bombay edition of the Rāmāyaṇa (IV. 41. 15) locates the hermitage of Agastya on a crest of the Mālābār range but a later stanza (34) of the same canto puts the dwelling of Agastya on Mount Kuñjara in Ceylon.

[1895] Āraṇyakāṇḍa, 12th sarga.

[1896] Banaparva, 96th, 97th, 98th and 99th adhyāyas.

[1897] Canto XIII. 36.

[1898] Raghuvaṃśam, Canto XIII. 34-36.

[1899] C. M. Ridding's Eng. Trans., pp. 18-20.

[1900] Belvalkar's Eng. Trans., pp. 31-33.

[1901] Konow and Lanman's edition, p. 228.

[1902] Rāmāyaṇa, Āraṇyakāṇḍa, 1st, 8th and 11th sargas.

[1903] Ibid., 1st sarga.

[1904] Ibid., 5th sarga ; Kālidāsa in his Raghuvaṃśam (Canto XIII. 45) also refers to this hermitage.

the hermitage of Sutīghna,[1905] the hermitage of Maharṣi Idhmabāha,[1906] Nyagrodhāśrama,[1907] the hermitage of Bāmanadeva[1908] which Viśwāmitra made his own (otherwise known as Siddhāśrama),[1909] the hermitage of Maharṣi Mātanga[1910] the hermitage of tāpasī Śabarī on the western bank of the river Pampā[1911] and the hermitage of the seven sages called Saptajana.[1912]

Besides these there were the hermitages of Gautama in the forest near Mithilā, the capital of King Janaka,[1913] the hermitage of Maharṣi Atrī, not far off from Chitrakūta hill,[1914] and the hermitage of Maharṣi Niśākara.[1915]

In the opening verses of the Mahābhārata, there is a reference to the hermitage of Vyāsa, the son of Satyabatī and author of the Mahābhārata. In this hermitage "Vyāsa taught the Vedas to his disciples. Those disciples were the highly blessed Sumanta, Vaiśampāyana, Jaiminī of great wisdom and Paila of great ascetic merit." They were afterwards joined by Śuka, the famous son of Vyāsa.[1916] After composing the Mahabhārata Vyāsa was thinking how he could teach it to his pupils. At last he taught it to Vaiśampāyana who recited it at the snake-sacrifice performed by Janmejaya.[1917]

In Vyāsa Saṃhitā[1918] we find a reference to the hermitage of Vedavyāsa at Benares where a body of sages asked the latter questions regarding the duties of the members of different social orders (varṇas). The answers are embodied in the Vyāsa Saṃhitā.

1905 Rāmāyaṇa, Āraṇyakāṇḍa, 5th, 7th, 8th and 11th sargas; Kālidāsa in his Raghuvaṃśam (Canto XIII. 41) also refers to this hermitage.

1906 Ibid., Āraṇyakāṇḍā, 11th sarga.

1907 Ibid., 13th sarga.

1908 Ibid., 38th sarga.

1909 Ibid., Bālakāṇḍa, 29th sarga.

1910 Ibid., Āraṇyakāṇḍa, 73rd sarga; Kiṣkiñdhyākāṇḍa, 11th sarga. The Kathāsaritsāgara (Penzer, V. 202; VII. 144, 145, 149, 151, 152, 156) also refers to this hermitage.

1901 Ibid., Kiṣkiñdhyākāṇḍa, 13th sarga.

1912 Ibid.

1913 Ibid., Bālakāṇḍa, 48th sarga.

1914 Ibid., Ayodhyākāṇḍa, 117th sarga,

1915 Ibid., Kiṣkiñdhyākāṇḍa, 61st sarga.

1916 Mahābhārata, XII. 328.

1917 Mahābhārata, Anukramaṇikādhyāya.

1918 Ch. I. śls. 1-2.

The Parāśara Saṃhitā[1919] refers to the hermitage of the holy Vyāsa in the forest of Devadāru on the summit of the Himalayas where he was asked by a body of sages to relate to them the rules of good conduct, cleanliness and religious rites which may be beneficially followed and observed by men in this age of Kali.[1920] Vyāsa, well-versed in the Śrutis and Smṛtis asked them to go to his father Parāśara's hermitage at Badarikā. Then the sages with the holy Vyāsa at their head went to Parāśara and the latter's reply to their questions is embodied in the Parāśara Saṃhitā.[1921]

A beautiful description of the hermitage of Parāśara at Badarikā is preserved in the Parāśara Saṃhitā.[1922] The Mahābhārata[1923] refers to Bhagwāna Viṣṇu's hermitage at Badarikā which was visited by Yudhiṣṭhir and his party. Bāṇa's Kādambarī[1924] and Somadeva's Kathāsaritsāgara[1925] also refers the hermitage of Badarikā.

There was also the hermitage of Devaśarmā whose favourite pupil was Bipula.[1926] Another hermitage was that of Śamika, one of whose pupils was Gouramukha.[1927] Another hermitage was that of Maharṣi Uddālaka one of whose pupils Kahoṛa read with him for many years and served him so faithfully that Uddālaka gave him his own daughter in marriage.[1928] The hermitage of Viśwāmitra was on the banks of the Kauśikā.[1929] The hermitage of Maharṣi Baka was resounding with the recitation of Vedic hymns.[1930] The hermitage of Subrata was in the land watered by the Dṛsadbatī.[1931] There were also the hermitages of Saradbāna,[1932] Chyaban,[1933] Śvetaketu,[1934] Maharṣi Sthūlaśira,[1935] Maharṣi

---

1919 Ch. 1 śl. 1.
1920 Ibid., śl. 2.
1921 Ch. I. śls. 4-5, and 18.
1922 Ibid., śls. 6-7.
1923 Banaparba, 144th adhyāya.
1924 C. M. Ridding's Eng. Trans., p. 216.
1925 Penzer, Vol. I. pp. 58, 59, 79; Vol. II. p. 36.
1926 Mahābhārata, Anuśāsanaparba, 40th adhyāya.
1927 Ibid., Ādiparba, 41st adhyāya.
1928 Ibid., Banaparba, 131st adhyāya.
1929 Ibid., Ādiparba 71st and 72nd adhyāyas; Banaparba, 109th adhyāya.
1930 Ibid., Śalyaparba, 42nd adhyāya.
1931 Ibid., Banaparba, 90th adhyāya.
1932 Ibid., Ādiparba, 130th adhyāya.
1933 Ibid., Banaparba, 101st adhyāya.
1934 Ibid., 131st adhyāya.
1935 Ibid., 133rd adhyāya.

Raivya,[1936] Yavakṛta,[1937] Baiśrabaṇa,[1938] Bṛṣaparbā,[1939] and Āstirṣeṇa.[1940] The Mahābhārata also refers to many hermitages on the banks of the Bhogabatī,[1941] the Godāvarī, [1942]Beṇwā,[1943] the Bhāgīrathī,[1944] the Payoṣṇī[1945] the Narmadā,[1946] and the Viśwāmitra (river).[1947]

The hermitage of Kāśyapa was situated on the bank of the Kauśikī, near Viśwāmitra's hermitage[1948] and Kāśyapa's son Ṛṣyaśringa used to study the Vedas under his father.[1949] The Kathāsaritsāgara[1950] also refers to this hermitage.

The hermitage of Kakṣasena was on the bank of the Viśwāmitra river.[1951]

We get, however, a somewhat detailed account of the hermitage of Maharṣi Kaṇva. It was situated on the bank of the Mālinī river[1952] (*ante*, p. 59). The Mahābhārata has preserved a beautiful description of the natural beauty of the hermitage. The course of studies carried on here has been described in a previous chapter. The Kathāsaritsāgara[1953] narrates the story of king Chandrāvaloka who on reaching this hermitage in the course of a hunting expedition was advised by Kaṇva to give up "the cruel sport of death"; on the king's promise to renounce hunting Kaṇva gave his daughter Indībarapravā in marriage to the king. The Kathāsaritsāgara[1954] also narrates the story of Vyāghrasena, minister of king Mṛgāṅkadatta who came to this hermitage and was advised by Kaṇva not to be cowed down by misfortunes and was told that "those who endure with resolute hearts terrible misfortunes hard to struggle through, attain in this way the objects they most desire; but those others whose energies are paralysed by loss of courage, fail".

1936 Ibid., 134th and 135th adhyāyas.

1937 Ibid., 137th adhyāya.

1938 Ibid., 155th adhyāya.

1939 Ibid.

1940 Ibid.

1941 Ibid., 24th adhyāya.

1942 Ibid., 88th adhyāya.

1943 Ibid.

1944 Ibid.

1945 Ibid.

1946 Ibid., 89th adhyāya.

1947 Ibid.

1948 Ibid., 109th and 110th adhyāyas.

1949 Ibid., 110th adhyāya.

1950 Penzer, Vol. I. p. 161.

1951 Mahābhārata, Banaparba, 89th adhyāya.

1952 Ibid., Ādiparba, 70th adhyāya.

1953 Penzer, Vol. VII. pp. 89-90.

1954 Ibid., p. 161; *see* also Ibid., III. p. 130.

The Mahābhārata[1955] also refers to the hermitage in the Naimiṣa forest which was like a University. The presiding personality of the place was Saunaka to whom was applied the designation of kulapati, sometimes defined as the preceptor of ten thousand disciples.[1956] Saunaka attracted to Naimiṣa a vast concourse of learned men by his performance of a twelve years' sacrifice of which the most essential accompaniment was the discourses and disputations of learned men on religious, philosophical and scientific topics.

The wide range and variety of their studies are also indicated. There were specialists in each of the four Vedas; in sacrificial literature and art; in kalpasūtras; in the art of reciting the Saṃhitās, in ortheopy generally and in Śikṣā (phonetics) Chhanda (metrics) Śabda, Vyākaraṇa and Nirutka. There were philosophers well-versed in Ātma-vijñāna (science of the Absolute), in Dharma (the way to salvation) and in Lokyāta Vaiśeṣika. There were Logicians knowing the principles of Nyāya and of Dialectics (the art of establishing propositions, solving doubts and ascertaining conclusions). There were also specialists in the physical sciences and arts, for example, experts in the art of constructing sacrificial altars of various dimensions and shapes (on the basis of a knowledge of Solid Geometry); those who had knowledge of the properties of matter (drabyguṇa), of physical processes and their results, of causes and their effects; and zoologists having a special knowledge of monkeys and birds. It was thus a forest University where the study of every branch of learning known and developed in those days was cultivated.

Among other hermitages noticed by the Mahābhārata may be mentioned that in the forest of Kāmyaka on the banks of the Saraswatī.[1957] But a hermitage near Kurukṣetra[1958] deserves special notice for the interesting fact recorded that it produced noted women hermits. There " leading from youth the vow of brahmacharya a Brahmin maiden was crowned with ascetic success " and ultimately acquiring yogic powers she become a tapas-siddhā, while another lady, the daughter

---

[1955] Mahābhārata I. 1. 1.

[1956] *See* the commentary of Nilakaṇṭa.

[1957] III. 183.

[1958] IX. 54

not of a Brahmin but of a kṣhatriya, a child not of poverty but of affluence, the daughter of a king, Sāndilya by name, came to live there the life of celibacy and attained spiritual pre-eminence.

We have already referred (*ante*, pp. 57-58) to the hermitage of Ālāra Kālāma where Gautama learnt some philosophical doctrines.

The Tittīra Jātaka, as we have already seen, refers to such a hermitage. Such schools of spiritual culture are also referred to as being composed of the standard number of 500 ascetics gathering round the personality of an individual hermit.[1959] We have, however, references to schools of larger sizes. We read of one which was so overcrowded with zealous pupils that the chief had to get other hermitages established by his seven senior pupils to relieve the congestion but to no purpose, for the original or parent hermitage continued to be crowded as before with aspirants after the religious life.[1960]

The hermitages were generally established in the Himalayas. Sometimes, however, bands of ascetics would establish themselves near the centres of population in view of the facilities so afforded for attracting recruits. We read of Śvetaketu who after receiving his education first at Benares and then at Taxila comes in the course of his travel to a village where he meets a group of 500 ascetics who after ordaining him taught him all their "arts, texts and practices".[1961]

The Raghuvaṃśam of Kālidāsa has preserved a description of the hermitage of Atrī[1962] whose wife Anusūyā was very kind to Sītā[1963] whom she gave very wholesome advice on the virtues of chastity.[1964]

Bāṇa in his Harṣa-Charita refers to the hermitage of Bhairavāchārya which was situated near the city of Thāneśwara in a Bel-tree plantation, contiguous with the woods on the banks of the Saraswatī.[1965] This sage is described by Bāṇa as "a second overthrower of Dakṣa's

---

1959 Jātaka I. 141 etc.
1960 Jātaka V. 128.
1961 Jātaka I. 406, 431; III. 143; IV. 74; III. 115; IV. 193; III. 235.
1962 Canto XIII. 50-52.
1963 Ibid., Canto XII. 27; XIV. 14.
1964 Rāmāyaṇa, Ayodhyākāṇḍa, 118th adhyāya.
1965 Harṣacharita—Cowell and Thomas, pp. 86-87.

sacrifice;" "whose powers, made famous by his excellence in multifarious sciences, were like his many thousands of disciples, spread abroad over the whole sphere of humanity."[1966] King Puṣpabhūti visited this hermitage where the king and his retinue were welcomed by the sage and his students.[1967]

Bāṇa in his Kādambarī has given a graphic description of the hermitage of a great ascetic named Jābāli. "Its precints were filled by munis entering on all sides, followed by pupils murmuring the Vedas, and bearing fuel, kuśa grass, flowers and earth."[1968] "The young brāhmaṇas were eloquent in reciting the Vedas; the parrot-race was garrulous with the prayer of oblation that they learnt by hearing it incessantly..................... Leafy huts were being begun; courts smeared with paste and the inside of the huts scrubbed. Meditation was being firmly grasped, mantras duly carried out, Yoga practised and offerings made to woodland deities. Brahminical girdles of muñja grass were being made, bark garments washed, fuel brought, deer-skins decked, grass gathered, lotus-seed dried, rosaries strung and bamboos laid in order for future need. Wandering ascetics received hospitality and pitchers were filled."[1969] "Here the performance of śrāddha rites was taught; the science of sacrifice explained;[1970] the śāstras of right conduct examined; good books of every kind recited; and the meaning of the śāstras pondered."[1971] After speaking of Jābāli's penance Bāṇa observes: "Happy is the hermitage where dwells this king of brāhmaṇas. Nay rather happy is the whole world in being trodden by him who is the very Brahmā of earth: Truly these sages enjoy the reward of their good deeds in that they attend him day and night with no other duty, hearing holy stories and even fixing on him their steady gaze, as he were another Brahmā. Happy is Saraswatī who, encircled by his shining teeth and ever enjoying the nearness of his lotus mouth,

---

1966 Ibid., p. 85.

1967 Ibid., pp. 87-88.

1968 Kādambarī—C. M. Ridding's Eng. Trans., p. 38.

1969 Ibid., p. 39.

1970 The Rāmāyaṇa (Bālakāṇḍa, 14th sarga) refers to men versed in Yajña-śāstra who are constructing altars on the occasion of the celebration of a sacrifice by Daśaratha who was desirous of sons.

1971 Kādambarī—C. M. Ridding's Eng. Trans., p. 39.

dwells in his serene mind, with its unfathomable depths and its full stream of tenderness, like a haṃsa on the Mānasa lake. The four Vedas that have long dwelt in the four lotus-mouths of Brahmā, find here their best and most fitting home. All the sciences which became turbid in the rainy season of the Iron age, become pure when they reach him, as rivers coming to autumn. Of a surety holy Dharma, having taken up his abode here, after quelling the riot of the Iron Age, no longer cares to recall the Golden Age."[1972]

Hiuen Tsang also refers to such forest hermitages as seats of learning. The hermitage of Jayasena as described by him has already been referred to (*ante*, pp. 171—72). We are thus told of another hermitage: "On the west of the city (probably Lahore) on the north side of the road, there is a great forest of An-lo (Āmra) trees; in this forest dwelt a brāhmaṇa of 700 years who in appearance was but thirty years old. His form and complexion were perfect. His understanding was of a divine character; his reasoning powers, superabundant. He had thoroughly investigated the *Chung and Pih* śāstras (the Prāṇyamula and the Śataśāstra); he was eminent in the study of the Vedas and the other books. He had two followers, each of whom was aged 100 years or more.............. Here he (Hiuen Tsang) remained for one month studying the Sūtras, the *Peh-lun* (Śataśāstra), the *Kwang-peh-lun* (Śataśāstra vāipulyam). The author of this work (i. e., Deva Bodhisattva) was a disciple of Nāgārjuna who himself having received the doctrines of his master explained them with clearness."[1973]

§ 4. Schools attached to Hindu Temples.

Besides these institutions there were also numerous schools attached to temples. One of the most interesting of such schools is mentioned in No. 202 of 1912[1974] which registers the gift of some land for the maintenance of a grammer-hall in the temple at

---

1972 Ibid., p. 41.

1973 Beal—Life of Hiuen Tsang, pp. 74-76.

1974 Madras Epigraphist's Report for 1912-13, p. 110.

Tiruvorraiyūr called "Vyākaraṇa-dāna-vyākhyāna maṇḍapa" for the upkeep of teachers and pupils who should study grammar there, and for the worship of the god "Vyākaraṇa-dāna-perumal" (i. e., Śiva) who in that very maṇḍapa was pleased to appear before Pāṇinī for fourteen continuous days and to teach him the first fourteen aphorisms (with which Pāṇinī's grammar begins) known as the Maheśwara sūtras. In this temple Śaiva religion and philosophy (Śivadharma and Siddhānta) were also taught. This famous school of grammar is referred to in other later records. No. 110 of 1912, assigned to the thirteenth year of Sundara Pāṇḍya-deva III, registers an agreement by which the residents of Pularkottan submit to a special tax levied in the northern and southern divisions of Tiruvorraiyūr for maintaining the same historic maṇḍapam and other similar buildings of the temple. No. 201 of 1912 in the thirty-eighth year of Kulottuṅga Chola III, registers the gift of a village for the same grammar-hall and refers to the king's declaration making the village rent-free. No. 120 of 1912 again registers the gift of a village and some gold ornaments to the god of the temple by king Kulottuṅga Chola III.

Similarly No. 182 of 1915[1975] refers to the establishment of a school, a hostel for students and a hospital in the Jananātha-maṇḍapa of the Venkateśwara Perumāl temple at Tirukkuḍal by the royal grant of Vīrarājendra-deva (1062 A. D.). In this school were taught the Vedas, śāstras, grammar, Rūpāvatāra (probably name of a grammatical work recently discovered) etc.

We find reference to another school[1976] attached to the Nāgeśwara temple at Kumbakonam which taught among other subjects the Mīmāṃsā philosophy of the school of Prabhākara, thus proving that even courses of study which were not in strict accord with the views of the founder of the temple were not regarded with disfavour.

An inscription dated 153 Saka (=1068 A. D.) records a royal grant for the feeding and clothing of the students of the local Siddheśwara temple.

[1975] Ibid., for 1916, p. 119.

[1976] Ibid., for 1912, p. 651.

Another inscription dated 94 Saka (=1093 A. D.) records a grant for feeding pupils of the local temple.

Another inscription dated 132 Saka (=1072 A. D.) mentions twelve teachers, (vyākhyātā) in the local Kriyāśakti temple.

Another inscription mentions a Vyākhyānaśālā as built near a Saiva temple (Epigraphica Indica, Vol. II. p. 310).

THE SANSKRIT COLLEGE AT ENNĀYIRAM.

Reference to an educational institution with an attached hostel for students is to be found in an inscription[1977] of the time of Rājendra Choladeva I (1018-1035 A. D.). It records that in order to assure success to the arms of the above king, the village Assemby made an endowment to the Lord in the temple of Rāja-rāja-viṇṇagara, mainly intended for maintaining a hostel and a college for Vedic study. In the college there were 340 students who resided in the hostel attached thereto where the following arrangements were made for feeding them :—

(*a*) Six nāli of paddy was alloted to each of the following students per day :—

(1) Seventy-five studying the Ṛgveda.
(2) Seventy-five studying the Yajurveda.
(3) Twenty studying the Chāndoga Sāma.
(4) Twenty studying the Talavakāra Sāma.
(5) Twenty studying the Vājasenīya.
(6) Ten studying the Atharva.
(7) Ten studying the Baudhāyanīya Gṛhyakalpa and Gaṇa.
(8) Forty studying Rūpāvatāra (probably name of a grammatical work recently discovered).

(*b*) One kuruṇi and two nāli of paddy were allotted to each of the following students per day :

(1) Twenty-five learning the Vyākaraṇa.
(2) Thirty-five learning the Prabhākara and
(3) Ten persons learning the Vedānta.

The students were further encouraged in their studies by the present

---

[1977] Inscription No. 333 of 1917.

of half a kalañju of gold to each one of them. The Instructive staff comprised the following :—

Three to teach the Ṛgveda.

Three to teach the Yajurveda.

One to teach the Chāndoga.

One to teach the Talavakāra Sāma.

One to teach the Vājaseniya.

One to teach the Baudhāyaniya Gṛhya and Kalpa and Kāṭhana.

One to teach Vyākaraṇa.

One to teach the Pravākara.

One to teach the Vedānta.

The fee attached to each chair which is given in detail and the allowances granted to the students described above, enable us to judge of the relative importance attached to the different subjects in this period. The teacher of Vedānta, for instance, got a *tuni* of paddy more per day than the teacher of Vyākaraṇa and Mīmāṃsā.[1978] It is no less interesting to note that the teachers in some of the subjects were paid according to what economists call the "piece-work" system. Thus the teacher of Vyākaraṇa was paid one Kalañju of gold per adhyāya taught.

ANOTHER SANSKRIT COLLEGE IN S. INDIA.

Similarly, inscription No. 176 of 1919 refers to another Sanskrit College with 260 students on the rolls. The Instructive staff comprised the following :

Three to teach the Ṛgveda.

Three to teach the Yajurveda.

One to teach the Sāmaveda.

One to teach the Chāndoga.

[1978] Ibid., for 1918, pp. 145f.

One to teach the Talavakāra.

One to teach the White Yajurveda.

One to teach Mīmāṃsā.

One to teach Baudhāyana Gṛhyasūtra.

One to teach Satyāshāḍha Sūtra.

Here were also taught the Mahābhārata, the Rāmāyaṇa, Vyākaraṇa, Rūpāvatāra, Vedānta and the Vaikhānasa śāstra.[1979]

This institution was maintained out of the endowment of 72 *veli* of land yielding annually 12000 *kalam* of paddy, out of which 9,525 *kalam* was reserved for this College. This land of 75 *veli* was free from rent and the teachers and the students enjoyed special exemptions.[1980] It may also be noted that the teachers here received four *kalam* of paddy daily as against one at Eṇṇāyiram.

The Sthānagundūru Agrahāra.

Another inscription at Taldaguṇḍy No. 103 [1981] belonging probably to the 12th century A. D. records that in the Sthānagundūru Agrahāra "were professors skilled in medicine, in sorcery (or magic), in logic, in poetry, in the art of distorting people by incantation, in poetry, in the use of weapons, in sacrificing....................and in the art of cookery to prepare the meals. While its groves put to shame the groves of Nandana, such was the glory of that great agrahāra that all the surrounding country prayed to be taught in the four Vedas, the six Vedāngas, the three rival divisions of Mīmāṃsā, the tarka and other connected sciences, the eighteen great Purāṇas, the making of numerous verses of praise, the art of architecture, the arts of music and dancing and in the knowledge of all the four divisions of learning which were possessed by the brāhmaṇas of the Sthānagundūru agrahāra." The four divisions of learning mentioned in the passage imply Vārttā as one of them, so that the agrahāra was the repository not only of sacredotal learning but also of the secular arts and sciences.

[1979] This seems to be the first epigraphic evidence of priest-craft as a regular subject of instruction.

[1980] Madras Ep. Rep. for 1919, p. 96.

[1981] L. Rice—Mysore Inscriptions, p. 197.

The Sanskrit College at Dhar.

Another great educational establishment was the famous college for Sanskrit studies at Dhar established by King Bhoja Paramāra (c. 1010-1055). Col. Luard and Mr. Lele in "The Paramāras of Dhar and Malwa" give us interesting details about this college. In this college sanskrit aphorisms on various subjects were inscribed on stone. A drama composed by the Gauḍa Brahmin Madana, commemorating the victory of his patron Arjunabarman Paramāra over the king of Gujrat was also inscribed on slabs. When the college was converted into a mosque by the Moslem conquerors all these slabs of stone were used for flooring and are now so rubbed over that almost nothing inscribed thereon is now legible. Madana's drama, however, has been deciphered and edited in Epigraphica Indica, VIII. This drama, we are told, was staged in the college on the occasion of a spring festival. Close to this college there is an old well called Akkal-kūvī or 'well of wisdom'; and it reminds us of the famous Chandra's well in Nālandā Vihāra and of the time when learned men who studied in this college and held disputations in its hall, drank water from this well and advanced in wisdom and knowledge. This Sanskrit college was known as Sarasvatī-sadana or Bhāratī-bhuvana and still subsists as the Kamāl Maula Mosque.

That such centres of learning flourished in the Hindu kingdom of Vijayanagara late in the fifteenth century is known to us. Mr. Sewell[1982] observes: "Here and there (in the city of Vijayanagara) were wonderfully carved temples and fanes to Hindu deities, with Brahminical colleges and schools attached to the more important amongst the number."

§5. The Ghatikās.

The South Indian inscriptions refer to various other educational institutions. Thus Tālaguṇḍa Pillar inscription of Kākusthavarman refers to an institution known as the Ghatikā at Kāñchipura patronised

---

[1982] A Forgotten Empire, p. 82.

by the Western Kṣhatrapas. We are also told that a brāhmaṇa Mayūraśarman by name entered with his teacher Vīraśarman this ghatikā with a view to acquire mastery over all the sacred lore.[1983] From the Velūrpālayam plates we learn that this ghatikā was captured by the Pallava King Skandhaśiṣya from the Western satrap Satyasena.[1984] As a result of this political turmoil the ghatikā had to suspend its work for a time and hence the lamentation of Mayūraśarman:

> " Kaliyugesmin aho bata kṣhatrāt pipelavā vipratā yāta
> Brahmasiddhiḥ kṣhatrādhinā."

" Alas! although they work ever so hard, the final fruits of Brahminical learning depend for their realisation, on the mood of the kṣhatriyas." The Kāśakudi plates of Nandivarman refers to such a ghatikā where he had all the four Vedas discussed and their injunctions explained.[1985] We find many other references to such institutions in the South Indian inscriptions.[1986]

§ 6. Hostels, messes and halls for students.

The Jātakas[1987] clearly prove that the students had a common mess. Hostels for students are mentioned in many South Indian inscriptions. Inscription No. 182 of 1915[1988] refers to a hostel (and a hospital) for students of the school attached to the Venkateśwara Perumāl temple at Tirukkuḍal established by the royal grant of Vīrarājendradeva (1062 A. D.) In this hostel the students were provided with food, bathing oil on Saturdays and with oil for lamps. The staff and establishment for the school-hostel and hospital comprised one physician, one surgeon, two servants who fetched drugs, supplied fuel and did other services for the hospital, two maid-servants for nursing the patients (for whom there were fifteen beds) and one

---

1983 Prabashanam nikhilam. Dr. Kielhorn incorrectly reads nikhilām and takes it with ghatikām making no sense.

1984 Ep. Ind., VII.

1985 South Indian Inscriptions, II. 349 and 356.

1986 Ep. Ind., III. 36; IV. 196; VI. 241; Ep. Carnatica III. 108; V. 178; VII. 197.

1987 IV. 391; I. 317.

1988 Madras Ep. Rep., for 1916, p. 119.

general servant for the hostel and the hospital. Another inscription[1989] which comes from Paṇaiyavaram refers to a hostel where there was provision for an oil bath for the students every week. Similarly No. 343 of 1917 refers to a hostel attached to a temple where provision was made for feeding 506 brāhmaṇas and the Śrivaiṣṇavas. The number probably included the 340 students of the Sanskrit College at Eṇṇāyiram. It is stated in the inscription that the members of the Village Supervision Committee were made responsible for the daily supply of the firewood required for the hostel. The husking of paddy for the hostel was to be done at the rate of two measures of rice per five measures of paddy. It is further stated that brāhmaṇa merchants were lent some money by the village Assembly, the interest on which was paid by them in kind, in the shape of supplying sugar and other necessaries; and half the surplus quantity of clarified butter, milk and curds left after meeting the requirements of worship was made over to the hostel. Brahmin bachelors were appointed as watermen and as cooks for the hostel. Buddhist monasteries like Nālandā and Vikramaśīlā (as we shall see later on) had satras (for students) attached to them. Side by side with these hostels and messes we find also the existence of halls for students. Sussala, the wife of Rilhana, the chief minister of king Jayasiṃha of Kashmere (1128—49 A. D.) constructed *halls for students.*[1990]

§7. The Tols.

Other schools of Sanskrit learning were the tols. It generally consists of a thatched chamber in which the paṇḍita (teacher) and his students met and a collection of mud huts round a quadrangle in which the students lived in the simplest manner. The huts were built and repaired at the expense of the paṇḍit. The paṇḍita provided the pupils with shelter, free tuition, and food and clothes they obtained from him and also from the rich men of the locality and by begging at the chief festivals.

[1989] Ibid., No. 323 of 1917.

[1990] Rājataraṅgiṇī, VIII. 2416; Stein—The Chronicles of Kashmere, Vol. II. p. 187.

Sometimes in a town of special sanctity or even of political importance, numbers of such tols were established side by side and constituted a kind of University. Examples of these are Benares and Nadīā. Nadīā survived the shock of the Muhammadan invasion under Bakhtyar and during the Mediæval period taught a number of subjects e. g., (1) Logic, (2) Smṛti, (3) Jyotiṣa, (4) Grammar, (5) Kāvya, and (6) Tantra. But the greatest achievements of the University were in the field of Logic. Dialectical discussions were held specially at a festival and the ambition of the student was to gain success by adroit and hair-splitting arguments. Professor Cowell, who visited the schools at Nadīā in 1867 says : "I could not help looking at these unpretending lecture-halls with a deep interest, as I thought of the Paṇḍits lecturing there to generation after generation of eager, inquisitive minds. Seated on the floor with the "corona" of listening pupils round him, the teacher expatiates on those refinements of infinitesimal logic which make a European's brain dizzy to think of, but whose labyrinth a trained Nadīā student will thread with unfaultering precision."[1991]

Among its famous teachers may be mentioned the names of Abdihodha Yogī who is said to have founded there the first school of Logic and Vāsudeva Sārbbabhauma. Its distinguished alumni are Raghunātha Śiromaṇi, the author of the Didhiti and the commentary on Gautamasūtra, Raghunandan, the most renowned teacher of Law in Bengal, Kṛṣṇānanda, the famous Tāntric philosopher and Śrī Chaitanya, the great Vaiṣṇava leader of the sixteenth century.

§ 8. The Tamil Academy.

Another educational institution though of a different type altogether was the Tamil Academy or Sangam.[1992] The first Academy was held at Mādurā, the second at Kavāṭapuram and the third at Uttar Mādurā. These were associations of learned men summoned by kings from time to time to set the standard in Tamil style, to regulate state

---

[1991] Quoted in Nadīā Gazeteer (Bengal District Gazeteer No. 24), 1916, p. 182.

[1992] M. Śrīnivāsa Aiyanger—Tamil Studies.

patronage and to set the stamp of approval on works conforming to the standard. They remind us of the Babylonian Academy (the Metibta) which convoked a general Assembly (the Kalla) twice a year, when a treatise previously announced was brought and discussed. Among the titles bestowed by the Tamil Sangam we find Āśiriyar (Sanskrit, ācārya) Pulavar (paṇḍita) and Kavi-chakravartī (prince of poets). It also made gifts of land and money. The Padiṟṟuppattu states that Kaṇṇanār got five hundred villages, Kāppiyanār ten lacs of rupees and Nacchellai one lac of gold coins and solid gold for jewels.

§ 9. LITERARY EXAMINATIONS.

Rājaśekhara[1993] who lived about 880—920 A. D. says that "the king-poet should have a special chamber for testing literary compositions. The chamber should have sixteen pillars, four doors and eight turrets. The pleasure-house should be attached to this chamber. In the middle of the chamber there should be an altar one hand high with four pillars and jewelled floor. Here the king should take his seat. On its northern side should be seated Sanskrit poets and behind them Vaidikas, Logicians, Paurāṇikas, Smārtās, physicians, astrologers and such others; on the eastern side the Prākṛta poets, and behind them actors, dancers, singers, musicians, bards and such others; on the western side vernacular poets and behind them painters, jewel-setters, jewellers, gold-smiths, carpenters, black-smiths and such others; and on the southern side Paiśācha poets and behind them paramours, courtesans, rope-dancers, jugglers, wrestlers and professional soldiers."[1994]

In another place Rājaśekhara[1995] says that "the king should hold assemblies for the examination of the works of poets. He should patronise poets, become the Savāpati (President) like the ancient kings Vāsudeva, Śātabāhana, Śūdraka and Sāhasāñka, and honour and give donations to the poets whose works stand the test. Assemblies of learned men

---

1993 Kābyamīmāṃsā in the Gaekwad Oriental Series, Text, pp. 54-55.

1994 Ibid., Introduction, p. XX.

1995 Ibid., Text, p. 55.

(Brahmasabhās) should be held in big cities for examining poetical and scientific works; and the successful candidate should be conveyed in a special chariot (Brahmaratha) and should be crowned with a fillet. Such assembles for examining in poetry were held in Ujjainī. Kālidāsa, Menṭha, Amara, Rūpa, Sūra, Bhārabi, Harichandra and Chandragupta were examined here. Pātaliputra was the centre for examinations in sciences. It was after passing from here that Upavarṣa, Varṣa, Pāṇinī, Piñgala, Vyādi, Vararuchi, and Patañjali got fame as śāstrakāras."[1996]

§10. The Maṭhas.

We have already seen that in the Buddhist system of education it was the monastery, which was the principal centre of learning. Monasteries have never had such an important place in Hinduism as in Buddhism but they have existed and are still to be found. From Amarakoṣa[1997] we learn that a maṭha was a hostel or hall for students. Teachers are also mentioned in connection with them. Thus inscription Nos. 205 of 1913 and 371 of 1911 refer to Vāgiśwara Paṇḍita, No. 477 of 1912 refers to Nirvāṇadeva and Nellore No. 525 mentions Dattātreyaswāmin "the excellent guru."

(i) Śaiva Maṭhas.

The earliest monasteries or maṭhas of which we have clear record in epigraphy are those associated with Jñāna-Sambandha (seventh century A. D.) which in the next few centuries had branches in numerous tracts of the Chola and Pāṇḍya countries. Hiuen Tsang has recorded that the Śaiva anchorites lived in maṭhas which were probably copied from the Buddhist Vihāras. One inscription registers the gift to a temple of a maṭha in the western street for reciting the Veda.[1998] Another refers to the maṭha of Āṇḍār Sundaraperumāl at Kāñchipuram.[1999] A third inscription registers a house and a house-garden for purposes of a maṭha, together with some land mortgaged to it as a guarantee for the regular supply of rice.

1996 Ibid., Introduction, p. XXI.

1997 Maṭhaśchchātrādi-nilayaḥ.

1998 Madras Ep. Rep. 1908-09, p. 125.

1999 Ibid., p. 123.

The succession of the pupils (of the donee) shall enjoy the maṭha as long as the Sun and the Moon exist. No. 181 of 1912 refers to a maṭhapati, who is an important functionary frequently appearing on temple councils in later records. No. 509 of 1912 records the sale of land belonging to a temple for a maṭha.[2000] Another important maṭha was that of Mahāvratins mentioned in No. 423 of 1914.[2001] An inscription of Amoghavarṣa refers to the existence of five maṭhas one of whose donees was surnamed Traividya, showing that these were the seats of orthodox Hinduism and Vedic learning. Inscriptions Nos. 212 and 269 of 1911 refer to a maṭha built in honour of Midadudayār in the second year of King Āditya Chola I of Tanjore. Inscriptions Nos. 127 and 132 of 1912 and 373 of 1913 refer to the foundation at Tiruvāriyūr of a maṭha by a Brahmin lady of Mercara. Inscription No. 504 of 1909 refers to a maṭha at Karungulam. Inscription No. 119 of 1911 refers to the foundation of another maṭha in honour of Iśwaradeva by one of his lady-disciples. From the Mysore Inscription we get a glympse of the universal range of studies carried on in the maṭhas at Belgame which were mostly founded by Kālāmukha ascetics from Kashmere. In the Koḍiya maṭha instruction was given in the Vedas, Vedāngas, grammar of Kumāra, Pāṇinī and Śākatāyana, Śabdānuśāsana and other works; the six Darśanas, the Yoga-śāstras of Lakula, Patañjali and others; the eighteen Purāṇas, Dharmaśāstras, Kāvyas, Nātakas and other śāstras.[2002] The third pontiff of this maṭha was proficient in Siddhānta, Tarka, Vyākaraṇa, Kāvya, Nātaka, Bharata-śāstra and other sciences connected with Sāhitya and in Jainism, Lokayāta, Buddhism and Lakula Siddhānta. Another pontiff was not only well-versed in Vedānta, Siddhānta, Āgama etc., but was also clever in explaining the origin of words and in devising new metres. There were many under him who observed the vow of studentship for life. Other such maṭhas in Belgame were the Pañchalinga maṭha, the Pañchamaṭha, the Hiraṇyamaṭha and the Tripurāntaka, all of which find mention in the epigraphs of the twelfth century. The

---

[2000] Madras Ep. Rep. 1913, p. 57. [2001] Ibid., 1915, p. 42.

[2002] Epigraphica Carṇatica. VII. Sk. 102.

educational character of these maṭhas is clear also from the reference in one of the inscriptions to the Koḍiyamaṭha as "our hereditary Gurukula" (seat of learning).

A series of epigraphic records in South India relates to maṭhas connected with Śaivism which grew in power and popularity under the Chola Kings. No. 467 of 1908 refers to a maṭha called Tiruvāgīśam-Rājendraśolan at Tirucchattimuram and another maṭha at Śembaikkuḍi.[2003] Other maṭhas connected with the Śivayogins or Maheśwaras are mentioned in Nos. 164, 177, 402 and 583 of 1908. Rājendra Chola set up images of some Śaiva saints and a maṭha at Tanjore. There were Śaiva maṭhas in Kovilūr in the Trichinopoly district and in Maḍipaḍu in the Guntūr district[2004] and at Kariśūḷṇdamangalam on the Tāmraparṇī river. The mismanagement and misappropriation of the revenues of the last maṭha by one of the managers led to the dismissal of the recalcitrants after due enquiry and to the handing over of the properties to the Venkaṭāchalapati temple of the place, subject to certain restrictions as regards the audit of accounts and the general maintenance of the maṭha.[2005] Other Śaiva maṭhas were founded by Tirujñāna Sambandha and his followers, one of which was at Tiruvānaikāval. It was known as the maṭha of 48,000 (villages or families) which was later superseded by tnat of Śaṅkarācārya, apparently a branch of that at Kāñchipuram.

The Pillar Inscription at Malkāpuram in the Guntūr taluk of the Guntūr district[2006] records that Viśweśvara-Śivāchārya of the Gauḍa country, a highly learned scholar and religious leader used one of the many gifts bestowed on him by the Kākatīya kings to found at Mandaram (the Mandadam) monastery, a feeding house, schools of students of Śaiva Puritans, together with a maternity and a hospital. Three teachers were appointed for teaching the three Vedas and five for Logic, Literature and the Āgamas. There were also appointed one doctor and one accountant (kāyastha). For the maṭha and feeding house were provided six brāhmaṇa servants. It was directed that the presiding teacher

2003 Madras Ep. Rep., 1908-09, p. 103.
2004 Madras Ep. Rep., No. 187 of 1917.
2005 Madras Ep. Rep. No. 576 of 1916.
2006 Ibid., for 1917, p. 122.

appointed to supervise these charities should be liable to removal for neglect of duty or misconduct by the entire Śaiva community (sāntānikā). There are other inscriptions to show that the same strict regulations applied to Śaiva teachers appointed as heads of the maṭhas.[2007]

Kalhaṇa in his Rājataraṅgiṇī[2008] also refers to the establishment of innumerable maṭhas for Brahmins, Śaivas and Pāśupatas in Kashmere.

(ii) Vaiṣṇava Maṭhas.

References to Vaiṣṇava maṭhas are also to be found. No. 465 of 1909 assigned to Kālaśekhara I records a gift of two villages for a Vaiṣṇava maṭha, where learned brāhmaṇas from eighteen Vaiṣṇava countries are to be fed. An interesting series of inscriptions from the Kurnool district, assigned to the middle of the thirteenth century A. D. refers to a famous Vaiṣṇava maṭha named Golaki maṭha at Mannikoil which is stated to have wielded its spiritual influence over three lacs of villages under a succession of famous teachers. Inscriptions at Shermadeva[2009] refer to Vaiṣṇava and Śaiva maṭhas flourishing side by side.

§ 11. Vidyāpīṭhas.

For the conversion of the common mass Śaṅkarācārya is said to have founded Vidyāpīṭhas with a great teacher presiding over each. One such was the Kāñchipuram Vidyāpīṭha. Others were at four important corners of India—Sāradā (Badarikā) in the North, Purī in the East, Dwārakā in the West and Sringeri in the South. In theory the Vidyāpīṭha was an expansion of the old Gurukulas but in practice it was modelled on the Śaiva maṭhas. Logic and Grammar were taught free as also Vedic and Vedāntic lore. Students were fed free of cost in most cases by liberal endowments made by the generous public. The Conjeveram Copper Plate of

---

[2007] Ibid.; *also* Ep. Ind., Vol. XII. pp. 290f.

[2008] I. 170, 195, 335; II. 135; III. 8, 460, 476; IV. 512, 696; V. 38, 244, 245; VI. 87, 88, 99, 104, 300, 304, 305, 307; VII. 120, 142, 149, 180, 182, 183, 214, 608, 961, 1678; VIII. 243, 246, 247, 673, 2401, 2408, 2419, 2420, 2421, 2422, 2423, 2426, 2431, 2433, 2434, 2439, 2443, 2447, 3316, 3350, 3354, 3356, 3359.

[2009] Madras Ep. Rep. for 1916, Nos. 567, 579.

Vijayagaṇḍa Gopāla[2010] records the grant of a village in Chingleput to the head of the maṭha of Kāñchipuram, when a follower of Śaṅkarācārya "was pleasing religious students by daily gifts of food and expounding to them treasures of the Vedānta". The grant was intended to cover the cost of feeding either 108 or 800 brāhmaṇas daily. The teachers and pupils of these Vidyāpīṭhas were often sent out among the remote villagers to win them to the ways of goodness and truth. Sannyāsī Sureśwarācārya alias Madana Miśra, the renowned teacher of Mīmāṃsā, is mentioned as the first successor of S'ankarācārya on the gaddi of the Sringeri maṭha. Mādhavācārya, prime minister of Bukka I of Vijayanagara and author of Sarvadarśanasaṃgraha was elected in 1331 A. D. the head of this Vidyāpīṭha.[2011]

§ 12. The Jaina Monasteries.

The Jaina monasteries were built on the model of the Buddhist Vihāras (or monasteries) and there the members of the Order prosecuted their studies and became learned men. This is proved from the references to debates at important centres where Jaina monks known as Tīrthāṅkaras are said to have taken part in discussions. Hiuen Tsang refers to some discussions among Brahmins, Bhikṣus and Tīrthāṅkaras in some Buddhist monasteries. The Jaina monasteries were scattered in Behar, Gujrat and the Carnatic. Kumārapāla Chālukya of Anhilwad (c. 1143—1173) and his ministers are said to have built many Jaina Vihāras. The Tamil epics[2012] give us a picture of Jaina monasteries at Kāveripaṭṭṇam, Uriyūr and Mādurā, filled with both monks and nuns, surrounded by high walls, painted red and overlooking little flower-gardens.

§ 13. The Buddhist Monasteries.

We get a valuable account of innumerable Buddhist monasteries in India from the itineraries of many Chinese pilgrims who visited

---

[2010] Ep. Ind., Vol. XIII. No. 16.

[2011] P. C. Roy.—History of Hindu Chemistry, Vol. I. p. LXXVIII.

[2012] Venkateśwara—Indian Culture Through the Ages, Vol. I. p. 251.

India in the fifth and seventh centuries A. D. Their long, toilsome and dangerous journeys would hardly have been undertaken unless the fame of the Buddhist monasteries in India as places of learning had reached as far as China.

Fa-hsien who was in India between 339 and 414 A. D. makes frequent references to monasteries. In the country of Udyāna there were five hundred monasteries, all belonging to the Lesser Vehicle.[2013] In a country called Bhida (in the Punjab) there were many monasteries, containing in all ten thousand priests.[2014] In a country called Muttra or Mandor on the right and left banks of the Jumna there were twenty monasteries with some three thousand priests.[2015] Fa-hsien refers to three monasteries in Kapitha of which the monastery called Fire Domain was one.[2016] "Tradition says that near about this time the Shrine of the Garden of Gold in Śrāvastī was surrounded by ninety-eight monasteries, all inhabited by priests except one which was vacant".[2017]

THE MṚGADĀBA MONASTERY.

Another seat of learning was the Isipatana or Mṛgadāba (Deer Park) Saṃghārāma, near Benares. A bath or washing was customary for the inmates of the Buddhist monasteries[2018] and accordingly we find here a plastered brick-lined reservoir or kuṇḍa with sloping sides, about seven feet square and five feet deep, with a flight of steps.[2019] Fa-hsien found here 1500 monks studying the Sammatīya branch of Hīnayāna Buddhism. Hiuen Tsang gives a more detailed description of this place where he found 1500 monks all of the Sammatīya school. There were cloisters (kañkrama) in this Deer Park where the World-honoured used to walk. They are about two cubits wide, fourteen or fifteen cubits long and two cubits high, built with bricks.[2020] I-Tsing visited this monastery[2021] and seems to have been much impressed by it, for says he: "I would sometimes direct my thoughts far away to the Deer Park."[2022]

[2013] Giles—The Travels of Fa-hsien, p. 11.

[2014] Ibid., pp. 19-20.

[2015] Ibid., p. 20.

[2016] Ibid., pp. 27-28.

[2017] Ibid., p. 35.

[2018] Takakusu's I-Tsing, p. 107.

[2019] Arch. Surv. of India, Annual Report for 1921-22, p. 44.

[2020] Takakusu's I-Tsing, p. 114.

[2021] Ibid., Introduction, XXXIII.

[2022] Ibid., XXIX.

A monastery at Patna.

In the city of Pātaliputra "by the side of king Aśoka's pagoda, a monastery under the Greater Vehicle was built, very imposing in appearance; and also one under the Lesser vehicle, the two together containing six to seven hundred priests, grave and decorous, each in his proper place,—a striking sight. Virtuous śramaṇas and scholars from the four quarters, wishing to investigate the principles of duty to one's neighbour all came to the latter monastery. There is resident in the former a brāhmaṇa teacher, who is named Mañjuśrī (after the famous Bodhisattva) and who is very much looked up to by the leading śramaṇas and religious mendicants under the Greater Vehicle throughout the kingdom.[2023]

The Jetavana monastery.

In Fa-hsien's time the chief place for higher Buddhist education was the Jetavana monastery near Pātalīputra. 'There were chapels for preaching and halls for meditation, mess-rooms and chambers for monks, bath-houses, a hospital, libraries and reading rooms, with pleasant shady tanks and a great wall encompassing all. The libraries were richly furnished not only with orthodox Buddhist literature but also with Vedic or other non-Buddhistic works and with treatises on the arts and sciences taught in India at the time. The monastery was well-situated, being conveniently near the city, and yet far from the distracting sights and noises of the world. Moreover, the park afforded a perfect shade, and was a delightful place for walking in, during the heat and glare of the tropical day. It had streams and tanks of cool clear water; it was free from noxious stinging creatures; and it was a favourite resort of the good and devotional people of all religions.'[2024]

The city of Rājagṛha contained two monasteries.[2025] "Where Buddha attained his Buddhaship (in the city of Gayā) there are three monasteries each with resident priests.................. The strictness with which, while Buddha was still in the world, the holy brotherhood

[2023] Giles—The Travels of Fa-hsien, p. 46. [2024] Watters—Yuan Chwang, I. 386.

[2025] Giles—The Travels of Fa-hsien, p. 49.

observed their vows and disciplinary regulations and the gravity of their deportment when sitting, rising or entering an assembly, persist down to the present day."[2026] In the city of Benares there are now two monasteries in the deer-forest, both with resident priests.[2027]

Monastery at S'rī-Parvata.

In the Deccan "there is a monastery dedicated to Kāśyapa Buddha made by hollowing out a great rock. It has five storeys in all; the lower being in the form of an elephant with five hundred stone chambers; the second in the form of a lion, with four hundred chambers; the third in the form of a horse with three hundred chambers; the fourth in the form of an ox with two hundred chambers; and the fifth in the form of a dove, with one hundred chambers. At the very top there is a spring of water which runs in front of each chamber, encircling each storey, round and round, in and out, until it reaches the bottom storey where, following the configuration of the excavations it flows out by the door. In all the priests' chambers, the rock has been pierced for windows to admit light, so that they are quite bright and and nowhere dark. At the four corners of these excavations the rock has been bored and steps have been made by which top can be reached..................."[2028]

Dr. Beal thus discusses the situation of this monastery in his "Life of Hiuen Tsang": "The king (Sadvāha) prepared the cave-dwelling for him (Nāgārjuna) of which we have a history in the 10th book of the "Records." This cave-dwelling was hewn in a mountain called Po-lo-mo-lo-ki-li i. e., Bhramarāgiri, the mountain of the black bee (Bhramarā=Durgā). Dr. Burgess has identified this mountain with the celebrated S'rīśailas, bordering on the river Kṛṣṇā called by Scheifner S'rīparvata. Doubtless it is the same as that described by Fa-Hien in the 35th Chapter of his Travels. He calls it the Po-lo-yue Temple, which he explains as "the Pigeon (Pārābata) monastery. But a more probable restoration of the Chinese symbols

---

[2026] Ibid., p. 55-56.

[2027] Ibid., p. 61.

[2028] Ibid., pp. 62-63.

would be the Pārbatī or Parvata, monastery. The symbol *yue* in Chinese Buddhist translations is equivalent to *va* (or vat). We may therefore assume that the Po-lo-yue monastery of Fa-Hien was the Durgā monastery of Hiuen Tsang, otherwise called S'rī-parvata. This supposition is confirmed by the actual history of the place; for Hiuen Tsang tells us that after the Buddhists established themselves in the monastery, the brāhmaṇas by a stratagem took possession of it. Doubtless, when in possession, they would give it a distinctive name acceptable to themselves; hence the terms Bhramarā or Bhramarāba."[2029]

This spot 'S'rīparvata' is also referred to in the Ratnābalī[2030] as being the place whence the Tāntric magician S'rīkhaṇḍa Dāsa came to Kauśāmbī to teach Udayana the art of making flowers blossom at any season. In Bhababhūti's Mālatīmādhava[2031] frequent mention has been made of S'rīparvata which was the residence of the Tāntric priest Aghoraghaṇṭa, priestess Kapālakuṇḍalā, the Buddhist S'rāvikā Saudāminī and others. In the Kathāsaritsāgara[2032] we read of an ascetic who went to S'rīparvata and performed a course of asceticism there for propitiating S'iva. In Tibetan the mountain is called Dpal-gyi-ri (Fortune-her-mountain) which according to Tibetan authorities[2033] was situated in Southern India where Nāgārjuna Bodhisattva (33 B. C.) spent his last days absorbed in deep meditation.

Hiuen Tsang thus writes about this Śrīparvata monastery: "The king Sadvāha……. ……….tunnelled out this rock through the middle and built and fixed thereon (in the middle) a Saṃghārāma; at a distance of 10 *li*, by tunnelling, he opened a covered way (an approach). Thus by standing under the rock (not knowing the way in) we see the cliff excavated throughout and in the midst of long galleries (corridors) with eaves for walking under and high towers (turrets), the storeyed building reaching to the height of five stages, each stage with four halls with vihāras enclosed (united)……………… From the high peak

---

2029 Introduction p. XXI.

2030 Act. II. Prabeśaka.

2031 Acts I, IX., X. etc.

2032 Ch. LXXXIII.

2033 Tārānāth's Geschichte des Buddhismus Von Schiefner, p. 84.

of the mountain descending streamlets, like small cascades, flow through the different storeys, winding round the side-galleries and then discharging themselves without. Scattered light-holes illumine the interior (inner chambers)."[2034] Neither Fa-Hien nor Hiuen Tsang personally visited the spot. It would seem to have been utterly deserted and waste even in Fa-hsien's time. This favours the record of its early construction in the time of Nāgārjuna (about the 1st century B. C.).[2035]

Fa-hsien refers to a monastery of the Greater Vehicle in Central India where he obtained copies and extracts of several sacred texts.[2036] He stopped here for three years, learning to write and speak Sanskrit (or Pali) and copying out the Disciplines.[2037] In the country of Tamluk he found twenty-four monasteries, all with resident priests. He stayed here for two years, copying out śāstras and drawing pictures of images.[2038]

Sung-yun (518 A. D.) refers to two monasteries to the north of the royal city of Udyāna country.[2039] He also mentions another monastery in this country with three hundred priests and more.[2040] In this country there was another monastery where formerly dwelt a śramenera who being constantly occupied in sifting ashes (belonging to the convent) fell into a state of spiritual ecstacy.[2041] He also refers to another monastery in this country with about eighty priests in it. He took up his quarters in a monastery in Gāndhāra.[2042]

Hiuen Tsang who was in India from 629-645 A. D. refers to the monastery of Kū-chī, in the extreme north-west, which was a resort "for men of eminence from distant lands, who were hospitably entertained by the king, officials and people."[2043] The Buddhist brethern at at Srughna were lucid expounders of abstract philosophical doctrines and distinguished brethern from other lands came to them to reason out their doubts.[2044] In Lamghan there were ten monasteries.[2045]

2034 Beal—Buddhist Records of the Western World, Vol. II. pp. 214-15.

2035 Ibid., p. 215 footnote.

2036 Giles—The Travels of Fa-hsien, p. 64.

2037 Ibid., p. 65.

2038 Ibid., p. 66.

2039 Beal—Buddhist Records of the Western World, Vol. I. p. XCVI.

2040 Ibid., p. XCVII.

2041 Ibid., p. XCIX.

2042 Ibid., CI.

2043 Watters—Yuan Chwang I. 63.

2044 Ibid., p. 318

2045 Beal—Life of Hiuen Tsang, p. 57.

In the town of Dīpañkara there was one.[2046] Four or five *li* to the north of the town of Puṣkalābatī there was another monastery.[2047] In the Udyāna country there were formerly 1400 monasteries with 18,000 priests;[2048] but now all is desert and depopulated.[2049] In the valley of Daril in Udyāna, however, there was then one large monastery.[2050] In Taxila there was another.[2051]

The Jayendra convent.

In Kashmere there were formerly 500 monasteries but there are now only 100 with about 5000 priests.[2052] The most important of these was the *Che-ye-in-to lo* (Jayendra) convent. "Before noon he (the chief of the priests of that establishment) explained the Koṣa-śāstra. Afternoon he explained the Niyāya-anusāra-śāstra—after the first watch of the night he explained the Hetuvidyā śāstra. On these occasions all the learned men within the borders (of the kingdom) without exception, flocked together (to hear the discourse). The Master of the Law, following the words of his teacher, grasped thoroughly the entire subject—he penetrated all the obscure passages and their sacred mysteries completely".[2053] "Then there was in the congregation certain priests versed in the doctrine of the great Vehicle—viz., Pi-shu-to-sang-ho (Viśuddhasiṃgha), Chin-na-fan-tu (Jinabandu); and of the Sarvāstavādin school, the following: Su-kia-mi-to-lo (Sugatamitra), Po-su-mi-to-lo (Vasumitra); and of the school of the Mahāsañghikas, the following: Su-li-ye-ti-po (Sūryadeva), Chin-na-ta-lo-tu (Jinatrāta)".[2054] "This country from remote times was distinguished for learning and these priests were all of high religious merit and conspicuous virtue as well as of marked talent and power of clear exposition of the doctrine; and though the other priests (i. e., of other nations) were in their own way distinguished, yet they could not be compared with these—so different were they from the ordinary class".[2055] "Having halted here, first and last,

2046 Ibid., p. 60.
2047 Ibid., p. 64.
2048 Ibid.,
2049 Ibid.
2050 Ibid., p. 66.
2051 Ibid., p. 67.
2052 Ibid., p. 68.
2053 Ibid., p. 70.
2054 Ibid.
2055 Ibid., p. 71.

for two years and having studied the sūtras and the śāstras and paid reverence to the sacred traces the Master took his leave ".[2056]

In Sakala there was one monastery with about a hundred priests. "In the old days Vasubandhu Bodhisattva here composed the treatise Shing-i-tai-lun ".[2057] In the kingdom of Chīnapati there was a "convent called Tu-she-sa-na (?). Here there was a renowned priest named Pi-ni-to-poh-la-po (Vinītaprabha). He was of a good reputation and had mastered the three piṭakas. He had himself composed a commentary on the Pañchaskhanda śāstra and in the Nidyāmātrasiddhi-tridaśa śāstra. On this account the Master remained there fourteen months. He studied the Abhidharma śāstra, the Abhidharma-prakaraṇa-śāsana-śāstra, the Nyāyadvāra-tarka -śāstra, and others ".[2058] Then there was the Tāmasavana monastery with some 300 priests.[2059]

In the kingdom of Jālandhara there was "the Nagaradhana convent where there was an eminent priest called Chandravarmā who was thoroughly acquainted with the Tripiṭaka. On this account he (Hiuen-Tsang) rested here four months, studying the Prakaraṇa-pāda-bivāsa-śāstra."[2060] In the kingdom of Mathurā there was a mountain monastery founded by the venerable Upagupta.[2061] In the kingdom of Matipura there were ten monasteries.[2062] "In this kingdom there was an eminent priest called Mitrasena, ninety years of age. He was a disciple of Guṇaprabha and deeply versed in the Tripiṭakas. The Master of the Law stopped with him half the spring and the summer following, studying the Tattvasatya-śāstra, the Abhidharma-Jñāna-prasthāna-śāstra and others."[2063]

In Kapitha there was one monastery.[2064] In Kanauj there were 100 monasteries and 10,000 priests.[2065] In the kingdom of Ayodhyā there were 100 monasteries with several thousand priests.[2066] Hiuen Tsang[2067] makes particular mention of one monastery in Ayodhyā where

---

2056 Ibid., p. 72.
2057 Ibid., p. 73.
2058 Ibid., p. 76.
2059 Ibid.
2060 Ibid., p. 77.
2061 Ibid.
2062 Ibid., p. 79.
2063 Ibid., p. 81.
2064 Ibid.
2065 Ibid., p. 82.
2066 Ibid., p. 85.
2067 Watters—Yuan Chwang, Vol. I. pp. 355-56.

Maitreya is reported to have communicated the materials of three Buddhist treatises[2068] to Asanga while the latter was living in the monastery. In Prayāga there was one monastery.[2069] In Kauśāmbī there were ten monasteries.[2070] In the kingdom of Viśākhā there were about 20 monasteries and some 3,000 priests.[2071] In S'rāvastī there were 100 monasteries.[2072] In Rāmagrāma there was one monastery.[2073] In Benares there were thirty monasteries and 2,000 priests.[2074] In the kingdom of Magadha there were about fifty monasteries.[2075] In Pātalīputra there were the Kukkutarāma and Tilaḍaka convents.[2076]

In the country of Hiraṇya there were ten monasteries and about 5,000 priests.[2077] "Recently there was a frontier king who deposed the ruler of this country and bestowed the capital on the priests; in it moreover he built two convents each containing 1000 priests. There are two eminent brothers here, one called Tathāgatagupta, the other Kṣāntisiṃha, both belonging to the Sarvāstavādin school. Here the Master stopped one year and read the Vibhāsha and the Nyāya-anusāra, śāstras and others."[2078]

In the kingdom of Champā there were some ten monasteries with about 300 priests.[2079] In the kingdom of Kajūghira there were six or seven monasteries with about 300 priests.[2080] In Pauṇḍrabardhana there were about twelve monasteries.[2081] In Karṇasuvarṇa there were ten monasteries and 300 priests.[2082] Besides these there were in this country two monasteries "where they did not use either butter or

---

2068 These treatises are: Śaptadaśabhūmiśāstra-yogācārya, Sūtrālañkāra-tīkā, and Madhyānta-vibhāga-śāstra.

2069 Beal—Life of Hiuen Tsang, p. 90.

2070 Ibid., p. 91.

2071 Ibid., p. 92.

2072 Ibid., p. 92 footnote; *compare* Beal—Buddhist Records of the Western World, Vol. II. p. 2.

2073 Beal—Life of Hiuen Tsang, p. 96.

2074 Ibid., p. 98.

2075 Ibid., p. 101.

2076 Ibid., pp. 102-03.

2077 Ibid., p. 127.

2078 Ibid.

2079 Ibid., p. 128.

2080 Ibid., p. 131.

2081 Ibid.

2082 Ibid.

milk—this is the traditional teaching of Devadatta."[2083] In Samatata there were twenty monasteries with 3000 priests.[2084] In the kingdom of Tāmralipti there were ten monasteries and a congregation of about 1000 priests.[2085] I-Tsing[2086] gives us a detailed description of Bha-ra-ha monastery[2087] of Tāmralipti whose monks were strict observers of precepts. In this monastery there lived the famous Buddhist teacher Rahula-mitra. "He was then about thirty years old................ Every day he read over the Ratnakūtasūtra which contains 100 verses. He was not only versed in the three collections of the scriptures but also, thoroughly conversant with the secular literature on the four sciences. He was honoured as the head of the priests in the eastern districts of India."[2088] In Orissa there were about 100 monasteries and ten thousand priests or so[2089] who studied the Great Vehicle.[2090] In Kalinga there were about ten monasteries occupied by some 500 priests who studied the Law according to the Sthavira school.[2091] In southern Kośala there were 100 monasteries and 10,000 priests.[2092] In the kingdom of Andhra by the side of the capital there is a large monastery.[2093] In Dhanakataka there was a monastery called Pūrvaśilā.[2094] To the west of the capital resting against a mountain there is a monastery called Avaraśilā.[2095] Hiuen Tsang heard that there were at that time in Ceylon 100 monasteries with 10,000 priests.[2096] In Kongkaṇapura there were about 100 monasteries and ten thousand priests.[2097] In Mahārāṣtra there were about 100 monasteries and 5,000 priests.[2098] Hiuen Tsang[2099] makes particular mention of Ācāra's monastery in Mahārāṣtra where Dignāga, the Buddhist 'Bull in discussion' is said to have resided frequently. According to him, south of Kāñchipuram there was "a large monastery which was a rendezvous

---

2083 Ibid.

2084 Ibid. p. 132.

2085 Ibid., p. 133.

2086 Takakusu's I-Tsing, pp. 62-65.

2087 Barahat or Varāha ?

2088 Takakusu's I-Tsing, pp. 62-64.

2089 Beal—Life of Hiuen Tsang, p. 134.

2090 Ibid.

2091 Ibid.

2092 Ibid., p. 135.

2093 Ibid., p. 136.

2094 Ibid.

2095 Ibid.

2096 Ibid., p. 144.

2097 Ibid., p. 146.

2098 Ibid., p. 147.

2099 Watters—Yuan Chwang, Vol. II. p. 122.

of the most eminent men of the country." In Mālava there were about 100 monasteries and 20,000 priests who studied the Little Vehicle and belonged to the Sammatīya school.[2100] "The people of this country in their manners are polished and agreeable. They exceedingly love the fine arts. In all the five Indies, Mālava on the south-west and Magadha on the north-east alone have the renown of loving the study of literature, of honouring virtue (or goodness) and of polite language and finished conversation."[2101] In the kingdom of Vallabhi there are about 100 monasteries and 6000 priests who study the Little Vehicle according to the Sammatīya school.[2102]

A MONASTERY IN PARVATA.

In the country of Parvata by the side of the capital there is a great monastery with about 100 priests, all of whom study the Great Vehicle.[2103] "It was here that Jinaputra master of śāstras, formerly composed the Yogāchārya-bhūmi-śāstra-kārikā. Here also the Master of S'āstras Bhadraruchi and the Master of S'āstras Guṇaprabha, originally became disciples. Because this country had two or three leading priests whose claims for learning might serve for guidance, the Master of the Law stopped here for two years and studied the Mulāvidharma-śāstra and the Saddharma-sampārigraha-śāstra and the Prasikṣā-satya-śāstra, as received in the Sammatīya school".[2104]

MAHĀBODHI MONASTERY.

In Gayā, a king of Ceylon Meghabarṇa by name built with the permission of the Gupta Emperor Samudragupta a monastery of three storeys, six halls and three towers, enclosed within a wall 30 or 40 feet high. The establishment is called Mahābodhi Saṃghārāma by Hiuen Tsang who saw it accomodating nearly "1000 ecclesiastics, all Mahāyānists of the Sthavira school".[2105] This Vihāra belonged to the Theravāda, yet adhered to the Mahāyāna.[2106] It was visited by I-Tsing who

---

2100 Beal—Life of Hiuen Tsang, p. 148.
2101 Ibid.
2102 Ibid., p, 149.
2103 Ibid., p. 152.
2104 Ibid., pp. 152—53.
2105 Watters—Yuan Chwang, Vol. II. p. 136.
2106 Hiuen Thsang, III. p. 487 *Seq.*

worshipped here the image of the real face of the Buddha.[2107] He also refers to the miraculous power possessad by the Nāga Mahāmukilinda of this vihāra.[2108] For the purpose of announcing hours to the monastics there was a clepsydra in this monastery where a bowl is immersed sixteen times between morn and midday.[2109] This monastery was visited by the Chinese pilgrim Hiuen-Chiu in the middle of the seventh century who remained here for four years[2110] It was also visited by the Chinese pilgrims—Taou-le,[2111] Hiuen-Ta'i[2112] Hiuen-hau,[2113] Taou-sing[2114] and Yuan-hwui.[2115] Mocha-deva, a Cochin-chinese also visited it and died here.[2116] Saṃghavarmā, a man of Samarkand also visited it.[2117] Hwui Lun, a Corean pilgrim otherwise called Prajñāvarmā also refers to this monastery.[2118] It was also visited by the Chinese pilgrim Wu-hing.[2119] During his residence here Atisa "thrice defeated the Tirthika heretics in religious controversy and thereby maintained the superiority of Buddhism over all other religions in Magadha".[2120] When Abhayakara Gupta was at the head of the Buddhist hierarchy of Magadha (that is, towards the end of the eleventh and the beginning of the twelvth century) there were no less than one thousand monks at Mahābodhi as compared with three thousand at Vikramaśilā and one thousand at Odantapurī.[2121]

Tildhaka monastery.

There was another monastery at Tiladhaka in Magadha.[2122] It is referred to as Tilḍaka by Hiuen Tsang.[2123] I-Tsing mentions this monastery as two yojanas distant from Nālandā.[2124] Tildhaka has been

---

2107 Takakusu's I-Tsing, p. XXXII.
2108 Ibid., p. 39.
2109 Ibid., p. 145.
2110 Beal—Life of Hiuen Tsang, Introduction, p. XXVIII.
2111 Ibid., XXIX.
2112 Ibid., XXX.
2113 Ibid.
2114 Ibid., XXXI.
2115 Ibid., XXXII.
2116 Ibid., XXXIV.
2117 Ibid., XXXVI.
2118 Ibid., XXXVII.
2119 Chavannes, Memoirs of I-Tsing, p. 144.
2120 S. C Das—Indian Pandits in the Land of Snow, p. 51.
2121 Phaṇīndranāth Bose—Indian Teachers of Buddhist Universities, pp. 84, 157-58.
2122 Takakusu's I-Tsing, p. 184.
2123 Beal—Life of Hiuen Tsang, pp. 102-03; *see* ante, p. 347.
2124 Chavannes, Memoires, p. 146 note.

identified with modern Tillāra, west of Nālandā.[2125] A famous Buddhist scholar and a Master of the Law Jñānachandra by name was in this monastery when I-Tsing visited it.[2126] This monastery was visited by another Chinese pilgrim Wu-hing.[2127] Near Tiladaha lived a teacher of Logic, from whom Wu-hing learned the logical systems of Jīna and Dharmakīrti etc.[2128]

There was the Pan-da-na (Bandana) monastery, a spot where the great Nirvāṇa was preached by the Buddha.[2129] This is no doubt the monastery in Mukuta-bandhana in Kuśinagara referred to in Mahāparinirvāṇa-sūtra.[2130]

There was another monastery called the 'Temple of the Heavenly Kings' which was visited by 'two men who lived in Nepal and were the children of the wet-nurse of the Duke-Prince of Tibet'.[2131]

There was another monastery called the 'Sin-che Temple' in the Western country which was visited by the pilgrims Sin-chiu and Chi Hing both of whom lived and died there.[2132] It was also visited by the Corean pilgrim Hwui Lun who lived here for five years.[2133]

There was a monastery at Tāmralipti where the pilgrim Tang came and "resided for twelve years, having perfected himself in Sanskrit".[2134]

There was another monastery at Tāmralipti where the pilgrim Hiuen-ta "remained for one year learning Sanskrit and practising himself in the śabda-śāstra".[2135]

There was another monastery at Kuśinagar called the 'Parinirvāṇa Temple' where the pilgrim Tang died.[2136]

2125 Cunningham—Ancient Geography of India, I. 456.

2126 Takakusu's I-Tsing, p. 184.

2127 Chavannes, Memoires of I-Tsing, p. 144

2128 Ibid.

2129 Takakusu's I-Tsing, p. 38.

2130 IV. 45; S. B. E., Vol. XI. p. 129.

2131 Beal—Life of Hiuen Tsang, Introduction, p. XXXIII.

2132 Ibid., XXXIV.

2133 Ibid., XXXVI.

2134 Ibid., XXXV.

2135 Ibid., XL.

2136 Ibid., XXXV.

Then there was the monastery called Tu-ho-lo (Tukhara Temple) which was visited by the Corean pilgrim Hwui Lun.[2137]

There was another monastery called the Kapisa Temple which was also visited by the Corean pilgrim Hwui Lun.[2138] The priests of this establishment studied the Little Vehicle.[2139]

Another monastery was called Kiu-lu-kia Temple. "It was two stages to the east of the Mahābodhi monastery. It was built long ago by a king of the Kiu-lu-ka country, a southern Kingdom (Kurukṣhetra country ?)."[2140] "Recently" says the Korean pilgrim Hwui Lun, "a king called Sun-Army (Ādityasena) built by the side of the old temple another which is now newly finished".[2141]

Hwui Lun also refers to two monasteries called the Deer Temple and the Tchina (or China) Temple. The latter according to tradition was built by a Mahārāja called S'rīgupta for the use of Chinese priests.[2142]

Another Chinese pilgrim Tan-Kwong arrived at A-li-ki-lo (Arakan?) where he was reported to have found much favour with the King of that country who built for him, a monastery with books and images.[2143]

Oukong another Chinese pilgrim visited (759-763 A. D.) Kashmere and took there the final vows of a Buddhist monk and spent fully four years engaged, as his itinerary tells us, in pilgrimages to holy sites and in the study of Sanskrit. Though he is said to have studied from day break to nightfall his diligence does not seem to have brought him much literary culture. This is curiously shown by the popular apavraṃśa forms in which he records the names of monasteries he specially singles out for notice. He mentions two Buddhist monasteries in Udyāna called Sukhāvatī and Padmāvatī.[2144] While Hiuen Tsang mentions only about one hundred convents in Kashmere, Oukong found more than three hundred.[2145]

2137 Ibid., XXXVI.
2138 Ibid.
2139 Ibid.
2140 Ibid.
2141 Ibid.
2142 Ibid.
2143 Ibid., XXXIX.
2144 Levi and Chavannes—L' Itineraire d' Oukong, Journal Asiatique, 1895, VI. pp. 341 *Sqq.*
2145 Ibid.

Monasteries in Kashmere.

Kalhaṇa's Rājataraṅgiṇī also refers to a large number of monasteries in Kashmere. King Surendra of this country built in the country of the Darada a vihāra called Narendrabhabana[2146] and in his own kingdom built a vihāra called Saurasa.[2147] King Jalauka built the vihāra of Jalora.[2148] Kalhaṇa refers to the Dharmāraṇya vihāra in Vitastatra.[2149] King Jalauka also built the Kṛtyāśrama vihāra.[2150] Dr. Stein in his "Notes on Oukong's Account of Kashmere" has identified this vihāra with the "monaste'-re du mont ki-tche" visited by Oukong. King Juṣka built Juṣkapura with its vihāra.[2151] Kalhaṇa refers to a vihāra at Kinnaragrāma.[2152] Kalhaṇa refers to the burning by king Nara of thousands of vihāras.[2153] King Meghabāhana's queen Amṛtaprabhā built a vihāra called Amṛtabhavana.[2154] In his Notes on Oukong[2155] Stein has identified this vihāra with the monastery of Ngo-mi-to-po-wan mentioned by the Chinese pilgrim. Yukādevī, another wife of king Meghabāhana built at Nadavana a vihāra of wonderful appearance.[2156] Indradevī, another wife of King Meghabāhana built another vihāra called Indradevībhabana.[2157] Many vihāras of renown were built by other queens of Meghabāhana such Khādanā and Sammā, under their own names.[2158] Jayendra, the maternal uncle of king Pravarasena II (of Kashmere) built the illustrious Jayendravihāra.[2159] Hiuen Tsang also visited and halted at this vihāra for purposes of study.[2160] The queen of king Durlabhaka, Prakāśadevī by name, founded the Prakāśikā-vihāra.[2161] In the reign of King Kṣemagupta (950—958 A. D.) Damara Saṃgrāma when attacked by assasians entered this monastery and the king Kṣemagupta therefore had the latter burned down without

---

2146 Rājātaraṅgiṇī, Bk. I. 93; Stein, The Chronicles of Kashmere, Vol. I. p. 17.

2147 Rājatar., I. 94; Stein, I. 17.

2148 Rājatar., I. 98; Stein, I. 18.

2149 Rājatar., I. 103; Stein, I. 19.

2150 Rājatar., I. 147; Stein, I. 26.

2151 Rājatar., I. 169; Stein, 1. 30.

2152 Rājatar., I, 199; Stein, I. 34.

2153 Rājatar., I. 200; Stein, I. 34.

2154 Rājatar., III. 9; Stein, I. 73.

2155 pp. 9 *Sqq.*

2156 Rājatar., III. 11; Stein, 1. 73.

2157 Rājatar., III. 13; Stein, I. 74.

2158 Rājatar., III. 18; Stein, I. 74.

2159 Rājatar., III. 355; Stein, I. 103.

2160 Beal—Life of Hiuen Tsang, pp. 69-70; *see* ante, pp. 345-46.

2161 Rājatar., IV. 79; Stein, I. 126.

mercy. Taking from this vihāra which was entirely burnt down the brass image of Sugata (Buddha) and collecting a mass of stones from the decaying temples he erected the temple of Śiva.[2162] He also took thirty-six villages from the burnt vihāra and gave them into the tenure of the Khāsa ruler.[2163] In the reign of Pravarsasena II the minister Morāka built the Morākabhabana monastery.[2164] The ministers of King Yudhiṣṭhira II named Sarvaratna, Jaya and Skandagupta built many vihāras.[2165] Bhinnā, wife of King Meghabāhana built a vihāra.[2166] Galūn, minister of King Vikramāditya of Kashmere built a vihāra under the name of his wife Ratānbalī.[2167] The wife of king Durlavabardhana built the Anangabhabana vihāra.[2168] King Lalitāditya-Muktāpīḍa built while at play (kṛḍan) the vihāra of Kṛḍārāma.[2169] At Huṣkapura Lalitāditya-Muktāpīḍa built a large monastery.[2170] In his Notes on Oukong,[2171] Dr. Stein suggests the identification of this vihāra with the Moung-ti vihāra mentioned by the Chinese pilgrim. This king also built the ever-rich Rājavihāra. He also built the wonderful and famous Kayya-vihāra.[2172] Tuhkhāra Caṇkuṇa, the chief minister of Lalitāditya Muktāpīḍa founded the Caṇkuṇa Vihāra.[2173] In his Notes on Oukong,[2174] Dr. Stein identifies it with the monastery which figures as "le monastere du general." A second vihāra built by Caṇkuṇa at S'rīnagara is referred to in IV. 215.[2175] This too bore the founder's name as seen from VIII. 2415 *sqq*. Which of these two vihāras Oukong may have meant cannot be determined. Caṇkuṇa's vihāra at S'rīnagara was repaired by Sussala, the wife of the minister Rilhaṇa under king Jaysiṃha.[2176] The physician Iśānachandra, a son-in-law of the minister Caṇkuṇa built a

---

2162 Rājatar., VI. 171-73; Stein, I. 248.

2163 Rājatar., VI. 175; Stein, I. 249.

2164 Rājatar., III. 356; Stein, I. 103.

2165 Rājatar., III. 380; Stein, I. 105.

2166 Rājatar., III. 464.

2167 Rājatar., III. 476; Stein, I. 114.

2168 Rājatar., IV. 3; Stein, I. 120.

2169 Rājatar., IV. 184; Stein, I. 139.

2170 Rājatar., IV. 188; Stein, I. 140.

2171 pp. 3 *Sqq*.

2172 Rājatar., IV. 200; Stein I. 142.

2173 Rājatar., IV. 211; Stein, I. 143.

2174 pp. 19 *Sqq*.

2175 Stein, Vol. I. p. 143.

2176 *See* Rājatar., VIII. 2415 *Sqq*.

vihāra.[2177] King Jayāpīḍa built a large vihāra.[2178] In the reign of King Nandigupta (972—973 A. D.) his grandmother Diddā built a vihāra with a high quadrangle.[2179] Queen Jayamatī, wife of King Uccala (1101-11) built a vihāra.[2180] King Uccala also built in honour of his sister Sulla a vihāra.[2181] Kalhaṇa mentions another monastery Skandhabhabana vihāra in S'rīnagara where Sussala's queens burnt themselves when the rebels hovering round the city made the usual burning ground at Mākṣikasvāmin.[2182] Ratnādevī, queen of king Jayasiṃha (1128-49 A. D.) built a vihāra.[2183] Rilhaṇa, the chief minister of Jayasiṃha had a vihāra constructed at the place called Bhalerakaprapā (fountain of Bhaleraka) in honour of his deceased wife Sussala. "This (vihāra) became known by the name of her cat which had followed her dead mistress into death instead of forgetting her attachment as is the wont of animals".[2184] Rilhaṇa's wife Sussala also built a vihāra. It covered the whole ground of the residence of former royal dynasties and made the whole city a joy to look at.[2185] Bhuṭṭa, a minister of Jayasiṃha founded a town called Bhuṭṭapura which is adorned by great houses with vihāras and maṭhas.[2186] King Jaysiṃha completed the Sullavihāra founded by his uncle.[2187] In the reign of Jayasiṃha Dhanya commenced the construction of a vihāra which was to bear the name of Bijjā (vihāra) in honour of his deceased wife (Bijjā).[2188] Cinta, the wife of the commander-in-chief of Jayasiṃha Udaya by name adorned the bank of the Vitastā by a vihāra. The five buildings within her vihāra appear as if they were the five high fingers of the upraised arm of Law.[2189] There was in Kashmere the monastery of Ratnaraśmi where in the reign of Śrī Harṣa of Kashmere Dharmottarācārya's Pāralokasiddhi was translated into Tibetan.[2190]

[2177] Rājatar., IV. 216; Stein, I. 144.

[2178] Rājatar., IV. 507; Stein, I. 167.

[2179] Rājatar., VI. 303; Stein, I. 261.

[2180] Rājatar., VIII. 246; Stein, II. p. 21.

[2181] Rājatar., VIII. 248; Stein, II. 22.

[2182] Rājatar., VIII. 1442; Stein, II. 113.

[2183] Rājatar., VIII. 2402; Stein, II. 186; Compare VIII. 2433; Stein, II. 189.

[2184] Rājatar., VIII. 2410-11; Stein, II. 186.

[2185] Rājatar., VIII. 2417; Stein, II. 187.

[2186] Rājatar., VIII. 2431; Stein, II. 189.

[2187] Rājatar., VIII. 3318; Stein, II. 259.

[2188] Rājatar., VIII. 3343; Stein, II. 261.

[2189] Rājatar., VIII. 3352-53; Stein, II. 262.

[2190] S. C. Vidyābhūṣaṇa—Med. Logic., p. XX. footnote No. 3.

From the Chacha-nāmā we learn that there was a monastery in Sind called Navavihāra. The story (related in the Chacha-nāmā) of the S'ramaṇa of this vihāra shows how Buddhism had drifted by this time into the grossest superstitution and idolatry. An ancestor of the ministerial family of Barmak[2191] was an official of this Nauvihāra.

There was another monastery built in Kalinga by the great Buddhist scholar and logician Dharmakīrti (about 635—650 A. D.).[2192]

Then there was the monastery of Kṛṣṇagiri where Dīpāñkara S'rī Jñāna received his lessons from Rāhulagupta. Here he was given the sacret name of Guhyajñāna Vajra and initiated into the mysteries of esoteric Buddhism.[2193]

From the Moslem accounts of the conquest of Sind we learn that there was a nunnery at Debal in Sind, containing " 700 beautiful females under the protection of Buddha ".

From an inscription of King S'ivadeva of Nepal, dated 143 S. (=749 A. D.) we learn of a monastery called S'ivadeva vihāra for the maintenance of which he assigned lands.

From the Sārnath Inscription of Kumāradevī, queen of Govinda-chandra Gāhāḍavāla of Kanuaj (c. 1114-1155) we learn that the queen founded a Buddhist vihāra commemorated by the inscription.[2194]

KAṆIṢKA MAHĀVIHĀRA.

The Ghosrawan Inscription states that one Bīradeva after having completed the study of all the different Vedas repaired (in the 9th century A. D.) to Kaṇiṣaka Mahāvihāra in the neighbourhood of Peshwar for further study. In an earlier period this vihāra was famous for its school of sculpture. The famous Buddhist relic-casket exhumed from the ruins of the great stupa of Kaṇiṣka near Peshwar bears the inscription

---

2191 "The name Barmak is said to be of Indian descent, meaning Paramaka i. e., the superior (abbot of the vihāra)".—Sachau's Alberuni, Preface, p. XXXI.

2192 S. C. Vidyābhūsaṇa—Med. Logic, p. 104.

2193 S. C. Das—Indian Pundits in the Land of Snow, pp. 50-51; Phaṇīndranāth Bose—Indian Teachers of Buddhist Universities, p. 67.

2194 Ep. Ind., Vol. IX. p. 319.

"Dāsa Agisāla navakarmi Kaṇiṣkasa vihāre Mahāsenasa saṃghārāme" (the slave Agisāla, the overseer of works at Kaṇiṣka's vihāra in the saṃghārāma of Mahāsena). Thus even foreign artists were accepted as teachers by the local Indian sculptors who in their usual way adopted the new methods to their own purposes.

As a result of the explorations carried on at Mathurā we learn that the Katra was the site of a Buddhist monastery name Yasi-vihāra which was still extant in the middle of the sixth century.

On Jāmālpur site there once stood a Buddhist monastery founded by Huviṣaka in the year 47 of Kaṇiṣka's era.

As a result of recent excavations carried on at Nagar Junikonda (Nagārjuna's Hill) we learn that this ancient Buddhist site on the right bank of the Kṛṣṇā river in the Palnad taluk of the Guntur district of the Madras Presidency contained four Buddhist monasteries.[2195]

Nālandā monastery.

But the crest-jewel of Buddhist monasteries was the University of Nālandā of which we possess a somewhat detailed account from the Tibetan and Chinese sources.

Scholars are divided their opinion regarding the date of its foundation. Tārānāth says: "Here in Nālandā was in former times, the birth-place of the venerable Sāriputra and it is also the place where, he with 80,000 arhats, attained nirvāṇa. In course of time, only the chaitya of the venerable Sāriputra remained at which King Aśoka gave great offerings to the gods and to which he erected a Buddhist temple. ....In this way the first founder of the Nālandā vihāra is Aśoka". In one of the sculptures at Nālandā, Cunningham found inscribed Ārya Sāriputra and Ārya Maudgalayana. But judging from the fact that there is no mention of it by Fa-hien it would be very hard to accept this version of the Tibetan historian regarding the foundation of the University. Fa-hien,[2196] however, speaks of the village of Nālo which some scholars have identified with Nālandā. But this identification is not universally accepted.

[2195] Liberty, Sunday, Feb. 2. 1930, p. 9.

[2196] Beal—Buddhist Records of the Western World, Vol. I. p. LVIII.

General Cunningham observes: "From the total silence of Fa-hien regarding any of the magnificient buildings at Nālandā, which are so minutely described by Hiuen Tsang, I infer that they must have been built after 410. Surely if the lofty temple of Bālāditya which was 300 feet in height had then existed, it seems scarcely possible that Fa-hien should not have noticed it". He then points out that according to Hiuen Tsang[2197] four out of the six monasteries at Nālandā were founded by Bālāditya, the King of Magadha and his three immediate predecessors. Bālāditya was a contemporary of Mihirakula, the Huna ruler of Western India. Mihirakula began his reign in 510 A. D.[2198] and therefore his contemporary Bālāditya also lived about that time. Before Bālāditya his three immediate predecessors viz., Tathāgata, Buddhagupta and Śakrāditya each built one monastery at Nālandā. If we take 25 years as the average of each reign then Śakrāditya can be said to have reigned about 435 A. D. The date of the temple may therefore be about 435 A. D. General Cunningham would therefore "assign the probable date of the temple and monasteries to the two centuries between the visits of Fa-hien and Hiuen Tsang or from A. D. 425 to 625".[2199]

Hiuen Tsang records that the great temple of Bālāditya was similar to that of the Bodh Gayā temple. As similarity of style may be taken as denoting proximity of date the erection of Bālāditya's temple may, with great probability, be assigned to the same century in which the Vajrāsana temple (built by king Vajra of Magadha) at Nālandā was built. Dr. Spooner during his excavations at Pātaliputra has made the discovery of a terra-cotta plaque which bears the illustration of a temple. Dr. Spooner supposes this to be the illustration of the temple of Bodh Gayā. The plaque also contains some characters in Kharosthi. Now the Kharosthi script was introduced into India in the second century A. D. and so it may be surmised that the Bodh Gayā temple was built during the Kushana time.[2200] Hence the Bālāditya temple at Nālandā was also built during the Kushana time.

2197 Watters—Yuan Chwang, I. p. 289.

2198 V. A. Smith—Early History of India, p. 316.

2199 Arch. Survey Reports, Vol. I. p. 29.

2200 Annual Report of the Archæological Survey, Eastern Circle, 1913-14, p. 71.

According to Professor S. V. Venkateśwara.[2201] "it is likely that Śakrāditya is another name of Chandragupta II Vikramāditya of the Gupta lineage, who appears in some records as Devarāja (Śakra). If so, the monastery was built by that king, who as we know, had Buddhist subordinates. The result would tally with Yuan Chwang's description of Nālandā as having been planned after Bodh Gayā, and with the archæological view that it was modelled on Sārnāth. Dr. Spooner[2202] would place the ruins of Sārnāth as early as the Kushana period. He assures us that there are four monasteries of different periods built one over the ruins of another".

Hwui-li in his Life of Hiuen Tsang remarks that the Nālandā monastery was founded 700 years before the time of Hiuen Tsang.[2203] "This remark clears up the date of Śakrāditya, the founder of the first monastery at Nālandā. The expression, therefore in the Si-yu-ki 'not long after the Nirvāṇa of Buddha'[2204] must be taken, *cum grano*, to mean 'a good while after'.[2205] The foundation of the Nālandā monastery would then be about 80 B. C."[2206]

All that we can say is that no definite conclusion can be arrived at unless there is thorough excavation of the sites; and until we see the actual plinth of the temple itself, it would be hazardous to come to a definite conclusion.

Regarding the name of the monastery Hiuen Tsang observes: "The old accounts of the country say that to the south of this Saṃghārāma, in the middle of an āmra grove, there is a tank. The Nāga of this tank is called Nālanda. By the side of it is built the Saṃghārāma, which, therefore, takes the name (of the Nāga). But the truth is that Tathāgata in old days practised the life of a Bodhisattva here, and became the king of a great country and established his capital

---

2201 Indian Culture Through the Ages, Vol. I. pp. 228-29.

2202 Archæological Survey (Eastern Circle): Annual Report for 1916-17 pp. 2 and 43.

2203 Beal—Life of Hiuen Tsang, p. 112.

2204 Beal—Budhhist Records of the Western World, Vol. II. p. 168.

2205 Beal—Life of Hiuen Tsang, p. 112 footnote.

2206 Ibid., Introduction, p. XX footnote.

in this land. Moved by pity for all living things he delighted in continually relieving them. In remembrance of this virtue he was called "Charity without intermission"—Na-alam-da—and the Saṃghārāma was so called in perpetuation of this name."[2207] According to I-Tsing the name of Nālandā is derived from Nāga Nanda.[2208] Hwui Lun, a Korean pilgrim to India observes: "The temple is called S'rī Nālandā Vihāra after the name of the Nāga called Nanda."[2209]

This famous University was situated in the modern village of Bargaon about eight miles from Rājgīr in Behar. The identification of Nālandā with Bargaon tallies with the description of the site in the Buddhist scriptures[2210] as a yojana distant from Rājagṛha, where was a mango park in Buddha's time and with Hiuen Tsang's location of it as five miles distant from New Rājagṛha. Inscriptions found in the ruins at Bargaon[2211] name it Nālandā, which means 'insatiable in giving' or 'not giving enough' as curiosity once excited and thought once stimulated could not be satisfied. The derivation is, in any case, a commentary on the ideal of University education—not cramming the mind with knowledge, but creating an insatiable thirst for it.

The University consisted of six monastic colleges. 'King Śakrāditya built the first monastery. After his decease his son Buddha-gupta-rāja continued the vast undertaking and built towards the south another monastery. Then his son (successor) Tathāgata-rāja built a monastery to the east. Next his son (or direct descendant) Bālāditya built a monastery to the north-east. His son Vajra built another monastery to the north. After him a king of Mid-India built by the side of this another monastery. Thus six kings in connected succession added to these structures.'[2212] "Moreover, the whole

2207 Beal—Buddhist Records of the Western World, Vol. II. pp. 167-68; *Compare* Beal—Life of Hiuen Tsang, p. 110.

2208 J. R. A. S., New Series, Vol. XIII. p. 571.

2209 Beal—Life of Hiuen Tsang, Introduction, p. XXXVII.

2210 Majjhima Nikāya, I. 371; Digha Nikāya, I. 211, 212; II. 81, 86.

2211 Annual Report of the Arch. Surv. of India for 1915-16, Part I. pp. 12 and 13.

2212 Beal—Life of Hiuen Tsang, pp. 110-11.

establishment is surrounded by a brick wall,[2213] which encloses the entire convent from without. One gate opens into the great College, from which are separated eight other halls, standing in the middle of the convent. The richly adorned towers and the fairy-like turrets, like pointed hill-tops, are congregated together. The observatories seem to be lost in the vapours (of the morning) and the upper rooms tower above the clouds. From the windows one may see how the winds and the clouds (produce new forms) and above the soaring eaves the conjunction of the Sun and the Moon (may be observed). And then we may add how the deep, translucent ponds, bear on their surface, the blue lotus intermingled with the Kie-ni (Kanaka) flower, of deep red colour and at intervals the Āmra groves spread over all, their shade."[2214]

" All the outside courts, in which are the priests' chambers, are of four stages. The stages have dragon-projections and coloured eaves, the pearl-red pillars, carved and ornamented, the richly adorned balustrades, and the roofs covered with tiles reflect the light in a thousand shades, these things add to the beauty of the scene."[2215]

From the Tibetan accounts[2216] we learn that Nālandā had a fine library situated in the quarter known as Dharmagañja (Piety Mart). It consisted of three splendid buildings called Ratnasāgara, Ratnadadhi and Ratnārañjaka, all associated with Ratna, i. e., Jewels, these being the three Jewels of Buddhism—Buddha, Dharma and Saṃgha. Ratnadadhi was nine-storeyed and in it were kept the sacred scripts called the Prajñāparāmitā Sūtra and Tantric works such as Samāj-guhya etc.

There were also Satras (free-board hostels) where the resident pupils were entertained free and supplied with necessaries out of the endowments to the University.[2217]

[2213] According to *Si-yu-ki* this wall was built by a king of Central India.

[2214] Beal—Life of Hiuen Tsang, p. 111.

[2215] Ibid., pp. 111-112.

[2216] S. C. Vidyābhūṣaṇa—Mediæval School of Indian Logic, Appendix A.

[2217] Beal—Life of Hiuen Tsang, pp. 112-13.

From I-Tsing's account we learn that there was a stone path at Nālandā with lotus flowers carved on it.[2218] During his time there were eight halls and three hundred apartments.[2219]

I-Tsing says: "There are more than ten great pools near the Nālandā monastery and there every morning a ghaṇṭi is sounded to remind the priests of the bathing hour. Every one brings a bathing sheet with him. Sometimes a hundred, sometimes a thousand (priests) leave the monastery together, and proceed in all directions towards these pools, where all of them take a bath."[2220]

There was a famous well in Nālandā vihāra reputed as Chandra's well.[2221] It was so called because Chandragomin thinking that his own commentary on Pāṇini's grammar was no better than the one written by Chandrakirti threw it into this well whence it was afterwards recovered and found to be superior to Chandrakīrti's. The water of this well was used to be drunk by people in the belief that their intellect would become sharp thereby.[2222] This well reminds us of the famous Akkal-kūvi (well of wisdom) in the Sanskrit College in Dhar.

Hwui Lun, a Korean pilgrim to India, thus describes Nālandā: "This building of Nālandā stands four square, like a city precinct. The gates (porches) have overlapping eaves covered by tiles. The buildings (gates ?) are of three storeys, each storey about twelve feet in height. Outside the western gate of the great hall of the temple is a large stupa and various chaityas, each erected over different sacred vestiges, and adorned with every kind of precious substance."[2223]

Again, according to Hwui Lun "this (Nālandā) is the only temple in which by imperial order, a water-clock is kept to determine the right time. The night is divided into three watches, during the first and

---

2218 J. R. A. S., New Series, Vol. XIII. p. 571.

2219 Takakusu's I-Tsing, p. 154.

2220 Takakusu's Eng. Trans., pp. 108-09.

2221 In Sanskrit Chandra-kūpa; in Tibetan Tsandrahi-khron-pa.

2222 S. C. Vidyābhūṣaṇa—History of the Mediæval School of Indian Logic, pp. 122-23.

2223 Beal—Life of Hiuen Tsang, Introduction, p. XXXVII; *Compare* Takakusu's I-Tsing, p. 145.

last of which there are religious services; in the middle watch, as the priests may desire, they can watch or repose."[2224] The regulation of the clepsydra at Nālandā is fully described by I-Tsing and distinguished from that of the clepsydras in the monasteries of Mahābodhi and Kuśinagara.[2225]

Hence the remark of Hiuen Tsang: "The Saṃghārāmas of India are counted by myriads but this is the most remarkable for grandeur and height."[2226] In the Si-yu-ki we are told: "A long succession of kings continued the work of building, using all the skill of the sculptor, till the whole is truly marvellous to behold."[2227] And recent excavations[2228] have shown how the buildings were made of bricks of a very good quality and admirable texture—"fitted together so perfectly that in some places the joints between the bricks are altogether inconspicuous." As Dr. Spooner has observed: "As brick work, the construction is remarkable, far superior to any modern work that I have seen in recent years."[2229] Indeed it does not require any great gift of imagination to reconstruct in mind what marvels these colleges would have been architecturally. To students familiar with the remains of Buddhist art either in the form of massive structural work as at Boro Budur in Java or in the form of fresco-painting such as have been preserved at Ajantā, Sigri and other subterranean monasteries, it is easy to realise what magnificent edifices would have housed the great University which was the pride of the Buddhist world.

On account of the rich endowments to the University (which we shall describe in a later chapter) "the students here (at Nālandā), being so abundantly supplied do not require to ask for the four requisites (i. e., clothes, food, bedding and medicine). This is the

---

[2224] Beal—Life of Hiuen Tsang, Introduction, p. XXXVII.

[2225] Takakusu's I-Tsing, p. 145. [2226] Ibid., p. 112.

[2227] Beal—Buddhist Records of the Western World, Vol. II. p. 170.

[2228] Annual Report of the Arch. Survey, Eastern Circle, for 1915-16, pp. 115-118.

[2229] Ibid.

source of the perfection of their studies to which they have arrived".[2230] Hiuen Tsang while at Nālandā received each day 120 Jambiras (a fruit); 20 Pin-long-tseu (areca nut), 20 tau-k'au (nutmegs), an ounce (tael) of camphor and a ching (peck) of Mahāśāli rice".[2231] "Every month he was presented with three measures of oil and daily a supply of butter and other things according to his need".[2232] "In the Nālandā convent the abbot entertains a myriad priests after this fashion, for, besides the Master of the Law (Hiuen Tsang) there were men from every quarter: and where in all their wanderings have they met with such courteous treatment?"[2233]

In a previous chapter (see *ante*, p. 157) we have referred to the rigid test for admission into the University held by the dwārapaṇḍita. We have also already described the curriculum of studies (see *ante*, pp. 66—70) and the method of teaching at Nālandā (see *ante*, pp. 178—79). Hiuen Tsang during his visit to Kāñchipura met two eminent Ceylonese priests with 300 other priests who, however, when asked to explain some choice passages of the Yogaśāstra "were not able to explain any of them as S'ilabhadra (of Nālandā) did."[2234] I-Tsing also had a similar favourable impression of Nālandā. He stayed in this monastery for ten years, studied for a considerable time and collected some four hundred Sanskrit texts amounting to 500,000 ślokas. He mentions by name many distinguished teachers with whom he conversed and says: "I have already been very glad that I had the opportunity of acquiring knowledge from them personally *which I should otherwise never have possessed.*"[2235] Besides such studies the teachers and students of Nālandā occupied themselves with copying manuscripts Thus, in the Bodelian Library, Cambridge there is an Aṣtasahasrikā Prajñāparāmitā copied at Nālandā in the fifth regnal year of Mahīpāla.[2236] In the Library of the Asiatic Society

[2230] Beal—Life of Hiuen Tsang, p. 113. Thus there was no need for teachers following some vocation like Johanen the shoe-maker, Simon the weaver or Joseph the carpenter.

[2231] Ibid., p. 109.

[2232] Ibid.

[2233] Ibid., p. 110.

[2234] Ibid., p. 140.

[2235] Takakusu's I-Tsing, pp. 184, 185.

[2236] Bendell's Catalogue.

of Bengal there is a fine manuscript, Aṣṭasahasrikā Prajñāparāmitā, copied at Nālandā by Kalyāṇamitra Chitāmaṇi in the sixth regnal year of Mahīpāla which was discovered in Nepal by Mahāmahopādhyāya Haraprosād S'āstrī.[2237] In the Library of the Royal Asiatic Society of Great Britain and Ireland there is a manuscript Aṣṭasahasrikā Prajñāparāmitā copied at Nālandā in the fourth regnal year of Govindapāla.[2238] In the Bedelian Library, Cambridge there is a manuscript Aṣṭasahasrikā Prajñāparāmitā copied at Nālandā by Grahaṇakuṇḍu in the fourth regnal year of Rāmpāla.[2239]

In Nālandā besides the Dwāra-paṇḍita there were among others three important officers: the Ching-fa-tsong (treasure of the good law), corresponding to the Chancellor of a modern University; the Karmadāna, sub-director of the monastery and the Sthavira (presiding priest).[2240] Hwui Lun, a Korean who visited Nālandā after Hiuen-Tsang remarks: "The superior is a very old man; the Karmadāna or Vihāraswāmī or Vihārapāla is the chief officer after the Superior and to him the utmost deference is paid."[2241] From I-Tsing's account we learn that the Karmadāna had to exercise a general superintendence over all monastic works,[2242] to arrange the order of seats to be occupied by the priests[2243] and to announce the time according to the clepsydra from sunset till dawn.[2244]

The head (i. e., Chancellor) of the Nālandā monastery in Hiuen-Tsang's time was S'īlabhadra who was preceded in this office by Dharmapāla.[2245] In the middle of the eighth century the great Tantric scholar Kamalaśila by name (728-776 A. D.) was at the head of this

---

2237 Proceedings of the Asiatic Society of Bengal, 1909, p. 69.

2238 J. R. A. S., New Series, VIII. 1876, p. 3.

2239 Catalogue of Sanskrit Manuscripts in the Bodelian Library, Vol. II. p. 250.

2240 Beal—Life of Hiuen Tsang, p. 106.

2241 Ibid., Introduction, p. XXXVII.

2242 Takakusu's I-Tsing, p. 84.

2243 Ibid., p. 102.

2244 Ibid., p. 145

2245 Beal—Buddhist Records of the Western World, Vol. II. p. 171.

establishment.[2246] In the reign of Nyāyapāla (—1042) Dīpāṅkara S'rījñāna was the Chancellor.[2247] From the Ghosrawan Inscription[2248] we find that Vīradeva, an inhabitant of Nagarhara was installed by king Devapāla as the High-priest of Nālandā.

The number of students residing here amounted to 10,000 in Hiuen-Tsang's time[2249] while in I-Tsing's time the number (of students) exceeded three thousand.[2250] In the time of Hiuen Tsang out of the 10,000 inmates of the convent 1,510 were teachers who between them delivered 100 different discourses on diverse subjects every day.[2251]

There were many eminent teachers at Nālandā, famous for their 'conspicuous talent, solid learning, great ability and illustrious virtue.'[2252] S'araha, the tutor and spiritual guide of Nāgārjuna increased very much the splendour and usefulness of this University.[2253] Nāgārjuna,[2254] the founder of the school of Madhyamikā philosophy was one of the early founders of this vihāra. Deva or Āryadeva[2255] was a pupil of Nāgārjuna and a great paṇḍita of Nālandā. He was the author[2256] of three Sanskrit books one of which he wrote at Nālandā vihāra. According to Hiuen Tsang[2257] he visited the countries of Mahākos'ala, Srughna, Prayāga, Chola and Vais'ālī, in all of which he won great renown by defeating the Tīrthikas and preaching the true doctrines of Buddha. Ārya Asanga also lived as a paṇḍita in Nālandā

2246 S. C. Vidyābhūṣaṇa—Med. Logic, pp. 129-30; P. N. Bose—Indian Teachers of Buddhist Universities, pp. 131-32; Waddel—Lamaism, p. 31; Journal of the Buddhist Text Society, Vol. I. Part I. p. 10.

2247 S. C. Das—Indian Pundits in the Land of Snow, pp. 51f.

2248 Ind. Ant., XVII. pp. 307-12.

2249 Beal—Life of Hiuen Tsang, p. 112.

2250 Takakusu's I-Tsing, pp. 65, 154.

2251 Beal—Life of Hiuen Tsang p. 112.

2252 Beal—Buddhist Records of the Western World, Vol. II. p. 171.

2253 S. C. Das—Indian Pundits in the Land of Snow, p. 48.

2254 Geschichte des Buddhismus Von Schiefner, pp. 66, 69-73.

2255 Ibid., pp. 83-86, 93.

2256 S. C. Vidyābhūṣaṇa's "Indian Logic as preserved in Tibet" No. 3, in the J. A. S. B., New Series, Vol. III. No. 7, 1907.

2257 Beal's Buddhist Records of the Western World, Vol. I. Bk. IV. pp. 186-190; Bk. V. p. 231; Vol. II. Bk. X. pp. 210, 227; Bk. XII. p. 302, Bk. VIII. pp. 98-102.

for some years.[2258] He wrote twelve works, most of which still exist in their Chinese and Tibetan versions.[2259] Vasubandhu[2260] like his elder brother Asanga was a follower of the Yogācāra school of the Mahāyāna and the author of a large number of books[2261] including the Tarkaśāstra. Three other works on Logic called in Chinese Ronki, Ronshiki and Ronshin are also attributed to him.[2262] Dharmapāla, a native of Kāñchipura was a student of Nālandā of which he subsequently became the head. He was a famous logician and grammarian and wrote a Sanskrit commentary on "Chandra grammar" and four Buddhist books in Sanskrit. S'īlabhadra, a native of Samatata (Lower Bengal) was a pupil of Dharmapāla at Nālandā of which he subsequently became the head. While yet a student at Nālandā he defeated in a debate a proud Brahmin who came from S. India to engage his guru[2263] Dharmapāla in a discussion. Both I-Tsing and Hiuen Tsang[2264] refer to his profound learning and it was under him that the latter learnt Sanskrit at Nālandā.[2265] He wrote many books, only one of which—that on Logic—has come down to us. Sthirmati was a famous scholar at Nālandā[2266] where at the temple of Tārābhaṭṭārikā he translated a Sanskrit book into Tibetan.[2267] He was particularly proficient in the Kalāpa system of Sanskrit grammar. He wrote nine books, translated into Tibetan seven and undertook the revision and correction of the Tibetan version of ten books.[2268] Chandragomin,[2269] a native Varendra, was a pupil of Sthirmati at Nālandā and the author of about sixty works, five of which were on Buddhist Tantricism. S'ānta Rakṣita[2270] was a professor at

---

2258 Geschichte des Buddhismus Von Schiefner, p. 122.

2259 Bunyiu Nanjio's Catalogue of the Chinese Tripītaka, Appendix I. No. 5.

2260 Beal—Bud. Records of the Western World, Vol. II. p. 171.

2261 Bunyiu Nanjio's Catalogue of the Chinese Tripītaka Appendix I. No. 6.

2262 Dr. Sugiura's "Hindu Logic as preserved in China and Japan", p. 32.

2263 Takakusu's I-Tsing, p. 181.

2264 Watters—Yuan Chwang II. p. 168.

2265 Ibid., p. 109.

2266 Ibid.

2267 Cordier—Catalogue du Fond Tibetain, II. p. 26.

2268 P. N. Bose—Indian Teachers of Buddhist Universities pp. 133-36.

2269 Ibid., pp. 116-123.

2270 Ibid., pp. 123-26 ; S. C. Vidyābhūṣaṇa—Med. Logic, pp. 124-25.

Nālandā whence at the request of the Tibetan king Khri-sron-deu-tsan he visited Tibet where he worked for thirteen years and helped the king to build the first Buddhist monastery in Tibet after the model of Odantapurī. He was the author of two works on Logic. Padmasambhaba,[2271] a native Udyāna was a pupil of Śānta Rakṣita and an expounder of the Yogāchāra school of Tantricism at Nālandā whence he went at the request of the Tibetan King Khri-sron-deu-tsan to Tibet where he introduced the Tantric element in Tibetan Buddhism and helped Śānta Rakṣita in the construction of the Sam-ye monastery. Vinīta Deva[2272] was another teacher at Nālandā who wrote the famous Samayabhedoparacana-chakra and six books on Logic.[2273] Kamalaśīla[2274] was for sometime a professor of Tantras at Nālandā whence at the request of the Tibetan King Khri-srong-deu-tsan he went to Tibet where he vindicated the religious views of his guru Padmasambhaba and Śānta Rakṣita by defeating and expelling a Chinese monk Mahāyāna Hoshang. He was the author of five works, two of which are on Logic. Buddhakīrti[2275] who translated a Sanskrit book on Tantricism into Tibetan was associated with the University of Nālandā and when Abhayakaragupta of Vikramaśīlā came here he helped him in translating a Sanskrit book into Tibetan. Kumāra S'rī, Karṇa S'rī, Sūryadhwaja and Sumati Sena were other teachers associated with Nālāndā vihāra.[2276] Acārya Devavid Siṃha[2277] was another teacher of Nālandā under whom Thon-mi the Tibetan messenger of King Sron-tsan-gampo of Tibet studied the sacred literature of the Brahmins and the Buddhists. Another teacher of Nālandā was Prabhākaramitra who was taken to China in 627 A. D. by a Chinese embassy to organise the work of the translation of sacred texts there.[2278] Jīnamitra[2279] was another

---

2271 Ibid., 126-31.

2272 Geschichte des Buddhismus Von Schiefner, pp. 195-98 ; 272.

2273 S. C. Vidyābhūṣaṇa—Med. Logic, pp. 119-21.

2274 Ibid., pp. 129-30 ; P. N. Bose—Indian Teachers of Buddhist Universities, pp. 131-32.

2275 P. N. Bose—Indian Teachers of Buddhist Universities, p, 137.

2276 Ibid., 138-42.

2277 S. C. Das—Indian Pundits in the Land of Snow (1893) p. 48.

2278 Dr. P. C. Bagchi—India and China, p. 14; Dr. U. N. Ghosal—Ancient Indian Culture in Afganisthan, p. 27.

teacher of Nālandā who visited Tibet[2280] and helped the Tibetans in the work of translating Sanskrit books into Tibetan.[2281] Hiuen Tsang[2282] mentions the names of many other teachers: 'Chandrapāla who excited by his bequeathed teaching the thoughtless and the worldly; Guṇamati the streams of whose superior teaching spread abroad even now; Prabhāmitra with his clear discourses; Jñānachandra, Śighrabuddha and other eminent men whose names are lost.' "These illustrious personages known to all, excelled in their attainments all their distinguished predecessors and passed the bounds of the ancients in their learning. Each of these composed tens of treatises and commentaries which were widely diffused and which for their perspecuity are passed down to the present time."[2283]

The fame of these teachers helped in attracting students and scholars from all parts of India and even from abroad. Hiuen Tsang says: "Learned men from different cities, on this account, who desire to acquire quickly a renown in discussion, come here in multitudes to settle their doubts and then (the streams of their wisdom) spread far and wide".[2284] Some of these came even from Mongolia[2285] and Korea.[2286] Thus Nālandā was an international educational centre in in the seventh century, when Europe was in the darkest watch of the long night of the Middle ages, when even the Saracenic schools and Arabic seats of learning had not yet been founded. And so great was the value of the hall-mark of this University that according to Hiuen Tsang "some persons usurp the name (of Nālandā students) and in going to and fro receive honour in consequence".[2287] The enthusiasm of the Chinese pilgrim Hiuen Tsang and I-Tsing for their Alma Mater may have been coloured but the conscientous and upright monks and the

---

2279 Beal's Buddhist Records of the Western World, II. p. 171.

2280 Geschichte des Buddhismus Von Schiefner, p. 226.

2281 S. C. Vidyābhūṣaṇa—Med. Logic, p. 135.

2282 Beal—Bud. Records, II. p. 171. 2283 Ibid., II. pp. 171-72.

2284 Ibid., Vol. II. p. 170.

2285 Takakusu's I-Tsing, p. 26.

2286 Beal—Life of Hiuen Tsang, Introduction, pp. XXIX, XXX and XXXVI,

2287 Beal—Buddhist Records of the Western World, Vol. II. p. 170.

careful and painstaking students whose lives were one long record of perseverance in the cause of learning are certainly not to give anything but a strictly honest description of what they saw. In the case of Nālandā especially, their testimony is one of the highest value as both of them were in residence in the University for a considerable period.

Many other foreigners also came to Nālandā. Thus Thon-mi who was sent to India by king Sron-tsan-gampo of Tibet after learning from Lipidatta the sections of Nāgri and Gāthā characters came to Nālandā where under Āchārya Devavid Siṃha he studied the sacred literature of the brāhmaṇas and the Buddhists.[2288] Hiuen-Chiu, a Chinese pilgrim remained in Nālandā for three years in the latter half of the seventh century.[2289] Another Chinese Taou-hi studied books of the Great Vehicle and wrote (copied ?) some four hundred chapters of sūtras and śāstras whilst at Nālandā.[2290] Āryabarman, a man of Sin-lo (Korea) dwelt in the Nālandā Temple, copying out many sūtras.[2291] Hwui-nieh, another Korean, studied the sacred books at Nālandā (about 638 A. D.).[2292] Buddha-dharma, a man of To-ho-shi-li (Tushara or Taurkhāra) was found by I-Tsing at Nālandā.[2293] A Chinese Taou-sing also visited Nālandā (about 649 A. D.).[2294] Tang also went to Nālandā.[2295] Hwui Lun, a Korean refers to Nālandā.[2296] Taou-lin studied the Koṣa at Nālandā for a year or two.[2297] Hiuen-ta remained in Nālandā for ten years.[2298] Wou Hing studied the Yoga, Koṣa and other works at Nālandā where he died in the end.[2299]

Dr. Kielhorn has calculated on palæographic grounds from the Ghosrawan Inscription which refers to the appointment of Viradeva as High-priest of Nālandā by Devapāla (825-50 A. D.) that the glories of Nālandā vanished from the latter half of the nineth century.[2300] But we

---

2288 S. C. Das—Indian Pundits in the Land of Snow, p. 48.

2289 Beal—Life of Hiuen Tsang, Introduction, p. XXVIII.

2290 Ibid., p. XXIX.

2291 Ibid., pp. XXIX—XXX.

2292 Ibid., p. XXX.

2293 Ibid.

2294 Ibid., pp. XXX—XXXI.

2295 Ibid., pp. XXXIV—XXXV.

2296 XXXVII.

2297 Ibid., XXXVIII.

2298 Ibid., XL

2299 Ibid., XLI.

2300 J. A. S. B., VII. Part I. pp. 492-501; also J. A. S. B., Vol. XII. pp. 268-74.

shall presently adduce evidences which go to show that Nālandā was in a flourishing condition even in later years. Thus in the fifth regnal year of Mahīpāla (980-1026 A. D.) Aṣṭasasrikā Prajñāparāmitā was copied at Nālandā which is now preserved in the library at Cambridge.[2301] The same manuscript was copied at Nālandā in the sixth regnal year of the same king which is now preserved in the Library of the Asiatic Society of Bengal.[2302] In the reign of Nyāyapāla (—1042) Dīpāñkara Śrijñāna, the head of this convent went to Tibet at the request of its king.[2303] In the fourth regnal year of Rāmapāla (ac. 1084) a manuscript was copied at Nālandā by one Grahaṇakuṇḍu.[2304] In the fourth regnal year of Govindapāla (ac. 1164) a manuscript was copied at Nālandā.[2305] That these manuscripts were copied at Nālandā and that its head in the reign of Nyāyapala (—1042) went to Tibet at the request of the Tibetan king shows that Nālandā was able to retain its fame as a centre of culture at least as late as the middle of the eleventh century.[2306] When Vikramaśilā rose as a rival and while its head Atisa was proceeding towards Tibet, the latter's Tibetan interpreter was staying at Nālandā.[2307] Again the Tibetan monk who was sent by the king of Tibet to take Atisa there from Vikramaśilā stayed on his way at Nālandā.[2308] After Nyāyapāla Nālandā's decadence commenced. Lāmā Tārānāth remarks that the professors of Vikramaśilā watched over the affairs of Nālandā.[2309] In Tārānāth we are also told of one āchārya who was a dwāra-paṇḍita at both Vikramaśilā and Nālandā.[2310] Two causes contributed to Nālandā's decay :—(i) its buildings despite repairs and reconstructions at

---

[2301] Bendell's Catalogue.

[2302] Proceedings of the Asiatic Society of Bengal, 1909, p. 69.

[2303] S. C. Das—Indian Pundits in the Land of Snow, pp. 51f.

[2304] Catalogue of Sanskrit Manuscripts in the Bodelian Library, Cambridge, Vol. II. p. 250.

[2305] J. R. A. S., New Series, VIII. 1876, p. 3.

[2306] *Compare* the view of M. M. H. P. Śāstrī in his Rāmacharita, p. 12.

[2307] S. C. Das—Indian Pundits in the Land of Snow.

[2308] Ibid.

[2309] Geschichte des Buddhismus Von Schiefner, p. 218.

[2310] Ibid., p. 236 ; *See* also Ibid., p. 250.

intervals[2311] must have become old and dilapidated and (ii) the rival University of Vikramaśilā which became the premier educational establishment of Northern India seemed to have monopolised all royal patronage. The Turuṣka invaders gave a crushing blow to Nālandā but it survived these Muhammedan raiders, for, we are told by the Pag-jon-sam-Zang that its temples and chaityas were repaired by a sage named Mudita Bhadra.[2312] Soon after this Kukutasiddha, a minister of the king Magadha erected a temple at Nālandā. When a sermon was being delivered in the temple two very poor Tīrthika mendicants appeared on the scene. Some naughty young novice monks threw some dirty water on them in disdain. Angry at this treatment these mendicants after propitiating the Sun for twelve years, performed a fire sacrifice and threw living embers and ashes from the sacrificial pit into the Nālandā temples. This produced a great conflagration which destroyed among others the fine library.[2313] That Nālandā was destroyed by fire is proved by the Bālāditya inscription discovered in 1864 by Captain Marshall among the ruins of Nālandā. This inscription is now preserved in the Calcutta Musuem and it refers to the re-building of a temple after its destruction by fire.[2314]

The Vikramaśilā Monastery.

The monastic University of Vikramaśilā according to Tibetan chronicles, was situated in Behar on a hill on the right bank of the Ganges[2315] but its precise position is not certain. Mr. Cunningham suggested the village of Silāo near Borgaon.[2316] This is out of the question as the Ganges could never have been near it, nor is there

---

2311 Dr. Spooner observes : "It can now be demonstrated that upon this one spot four separate and successive monasteries have been erected through a series of centuries, each being erected over the ruins of the previous one and the second in date enveloping the oldest." (Arch. Surv. Report, Eastern Circle, 1916-17, p. 2).

2312 S. C. Vidyābhūṣaṇa—History of the Mediæval School of Indian Logic, p. 147.

2313 Ibid., Appendix A.

2314 Journal and Proceedings of the Asiatic Society of Bengal, IV. (New Series), p. 106, *See* also Arch. Surv. Report, III p. 122.

2315 Geschichte des Buddhismus Von Schiefner, pp. 234-42.

2316 Arch. Surv. Report, Vol. VIII. p. 83.

any hill near to it. Mr. Nundo Lal De's identification with Pātharghātā hill, twenty-four miles to the east of Bhāgalpur seems to be right, for, it is on the right bank of the Ganges and has a sufficient space for many temples and buildings and a quadrangle accommodating 8,000 men.[2317] There are also ruins of Buddhist images at Pātharghātā.

According to tradition the vihāra was named after a Yakṣa called Vikrama who was suppressed here.[2318] As it was founded by King Dharmapāla of the Pāla dynasty, it was known as the *Royal* University of Vikramaśīlā.[2319]

Dharmapāla furnished it with four establishments each consisting of 27 monks belonging to the four principal sects of Buddhism. Later on other buildings were added so that it came to have six colleges, a central hall called the House of Science and four Satras or free-board hostels. There was also a large quadrangle which could accommodate an assembly of 8,000 persons. There was in the centre the temple with Mahābodhi images. Within the enclosure fifty-three smaller temples of a private character and fifty-four ordinary temples were set up. Thus the total number of temples within the compound of the monastery was one hundred and eight.[2320] There was also a "house assigned for the use of the Tibetans" in this monastery.[2321] It was surrounded by a wall, with six gates which opened on its six colleges. In its front wall, on the right of the principal entrance, was painted the likeness of Nāgārjuna, once the head of the Nālandā monastery and on the left, the portrait of Atisa, the head of this (Vikramaśila) monastery. At the gate outside the wall, there was a dharmaśālā for strangers who arrived late after the closing of the gate.[2322] It is no wonder, therefore, that the Tibetans would take Vikramaśīlā as a model for one of their monasteries.

It was managed by a board of six members presided over by the High-priest. There were six dwāra-paṇḍitas at the six gates who used

---

2317 J. A. S. B., Vol. V. No. 1. p. 7.

2318 S. C. Das in the Journal of the Buddhist Text Society, Vol. I. pp. 10-11.

2319 Ibid., p. 11.

2320 P. N. Bose—Indian teachers of Buddhist Universities, p. 34.

2321 S. C. Das—Indian Pundits in the Land of Snow, p. 58.

2322 Ibid.

to examine the candidates for admission in the same way as the dwārapaṇḍita at Nālandā did. Probably these six dwāra-paṇḍitas were the Principals of the six colleges and they collectively formed the Managing Board of six members with the High-priest as their President. According to Lāmā Tārānāth[2323] this board of management kept watch over the affairs of the Nālandā vihāra as well. 'If we accept his statement it must be admitted that a spirit of cooperation prevailed between these sister universities. Both were directly under King Dharmapāla who might have asked the board of the new university to watch over the older university. Sometimes we find men like Dīpāñkara and Abhayakara Gupta working in both the universities. We, however, do not know whether the Nālandā university was conducted under the direction of the paṇḍitas of Vikramaśīlā. What Tārānāth says is this: "Der vorstand dieser Lehrstatte hutette auch Nālandā."'[2324] According to Tārānāth in the reign of Canaka (955–983 A. D.) there were Prajñākaramati at the southern gate, Ratnākara Śānti at the eastern gate, Vāgīsvarakīrti at the western gate, Naropanta at the northern gate Ratnavajra at the first central gate and Jñāna-śrī-mitra at the second central gate. The last two paṇḍitas who taught theology in the central college were called the first and second "pillars" of the University. The Central hall called the House of Science was used for studying the Prajñāparāmitā scriptures. The Managing Board of six members granted the diploma of 'paṇḍita' to all distinguished alumni, the diploma being conferred by the reigning king.[2325] The distinguished logicians ācārya Jetāri of Varendra and Ratnabajra of Kashmere were granted such a diploma.[2326] Yamāri who lived in the time of Nyāyapāla also received the royal diploma of Vikramaśīlā.[2327] Moreover, the paṇḍitas who were eminent for their learning and character were rewarded by having their images painted on the walls of the monastery as in the case of Nāgārjuna and Atisa,[2328] referred to above.

2323 Geschichte des Buddhismus Von Schiefner, p. 218.
2324 P. N. Bose—Indian Teachers of Buddhist Universities, p. 36.
2325 S. C. Vidyābhūṣaṇa—History of the Mediæval School of Indian Logic, p. 79.
2326 Ibid., p. 151. 2327 Geschichte des Buddhismus Von Schiefner pp. 247, 253.
2328 S. C. Vidyābhūṣaṇa—Med. Logic, Appendix C.

King Dharmapāla, the founder of this monastic University realised that temples and hostels alone would not make the new vihāra a centre of culture. Something more was needed—professors. Accordingly he made provision[2329] for no less than one hundred and eight professors and also for a wood-offering (streu opfer) ācārya,, an ordination ācārya a fire-offering (brand-opfer) ācārya, a superintendent of works (bya-ba-bsruṇ-ba), a guard of pigeons and a supplier of temple servants. In course of time each of the six colleges came to have 108 Professors. Dharmapāla endowed it with rich grants out of which Satras were established for supplying gratis food and other necessaries to the inmates including the professors and the students. There were also establishments for temporary residents.[2330] It may be mentioned that the cost of the maintenance of each of these one hundred and and eight professors, three ācāryas and three superintendents was ordinarily equivalent to that of four men. We shall see in a later chapter that a Satra was added by one of the sons of King Sanātana of Varendra.

In a previous chapter (see *ante*, pp. 168, 169—70) we have described the course of studies carried on at Vikramaśilā. Among its illustrious alumni we may mention the names of Ratna Vajra, (an inhabitant) of Kashmir the author of Yukti-prayoga, who was afterwards made a dwāra-paṇḍita of his *alma mater*;[2331] Jñana-śrī-mitra the author of Tarka-bhāṣā, Kārya-kāraṇa-bhāva-siddhi and Pramāṇā-viniścaya-tīkā, who also became one of its dwārapaṇḍitas and even its High-priest when Atisa vacated this office in responding to the invitation of the king of Tibet,[2332] and Ratnakīrti, author of Pramāṇa-viniścaya, Kalyāṇa-kāṇḍa, Apohasiddhi and kṣaṇabhañga-siddhi, who also became one of its dwārapaṇḍitas.[2333] Similarly there was Jetāri author of Hetu-tattva-upadeśa, Dharma-dharmi-viniścaya and Bālāvatāra-tarka who counted Dīpāñkara or Atisa as one of his pupils.[2334] We may

2329 P. N. Bose—Indian Teachers of Buddhist Universities, p. 35.

2330 S. C. Das in the Journal of the Buddhist Text Society, Part I. pp. 1—10.

2331 S. C. Vidyābhūṣaṇa—Med. Logic, p. 139.

2332 Ibid., p. 138.

2333 Ibid., p. 140 footnote No. 2.

2334 Ibid., pp. 136-37.

also mention the names Ratnākara Śānti, author of Chhanda-ratnākara, Vijñapti-mātra-siddhi and Antara-vyāpti, who became one of its dwāra-paṇḍitas and afterwards gave an impetus to the Buddhist doctrine in Ceylon where he went at the invitation of its king[2335] and of Jamāri, author of Pramāṇa-vārtikālaṅkāra-tīkā who lived during the reign of Nyāyapāla.[2336]

Like Nalandā Vikramaśilā was famous for its eminent teachers. Tārānāth[2337] mentions Acārya Buddha Jñānapāda as associated with this University in the early stages of its development. After the death of his guru Siṃhabhadra he was engaged as the Ordination Priest of Vikramaśilā. Afterwards he was drawn into the cult of Vadschrātschārja (vajrācārya) in the same University. He was a follower of Tantricism and composed in Sanskrit several books on Tantra, twelve of which now remain only in their Tibetan translations. Another teacher was Mahāpaṇḍita (or Mahācārya) Voirochana Rakṣita (A. D. 728—864 A. D.) who after finishing his education under Padmasambhaba of Tibetan fame joined the University of Vikramaśilā and there engaged himself in composing Buddhist books in Sanskrit and translating twelve books (including two of his own) into Tibetan. Acārya Jetāri who flourished in the early part of the tenth century, was himself a student of Vikramaśilā and became a professor there. It was from him that Ratnākara Śānti learnt the texts of Sūtra and Tantra at Vikramaśilā and Dīpāñkara or Atīsa the five minor sciences. According to Tārānāth[2338] he wrote one hundred books, including Tantras and Sūtras of which only twenty-two are preserved in their Tibetan versions. Śrī Mahāpaṇḍita Prajñākaramati who flourished in the reign of Canaka (955—83 A. D.)[2339] was called in Tibetan *Nub-kye sgo-glegs-pa* which M. P. Cordier[2340] translates as 'gardien de la porte occidentale, du monastere de Vikramaśilā' (guardian of the western gate

---

2335 Ibid., p. 140.

2336 Geschichte des Buddhismus Von Schiefner pp. 247, 253.

2337 Schiefner's Tārānāth, p. 220.

2338 Ibid p. 230.

2339 Cordier—Catalogue du Fond Tibetain, III, p. 279.

2340 Geschichte des Buddhismus Von Schiefner, p. 135.

of the monastery. Lāmā Tārānāth,[2341] however, makes him the gate-keeper of the southern gate. Only two books are ascribed to him in the whole of the Tibetan Tripitaka collection. Mahācārya Ratnākara S'ānti received his ordination in the school of Sarvāstivāda in the Odantapura University and afterwards joined the Vikramaśilā University, where he was taught as we have seen the Tantra and Sūtra texts by Jetāri. On finishing his education here he was appointed in the reign of King Canaka (A. D. 955—983) as dwārapaṇḍita of the eastern gate. He afterwards gave an impetus to the Buddhist doctrine in Ceylon where he went at the invitation of its king.[2342] We do not know whether he went to Tibet, but his religious writings were eagerly sought by the Buddhists there, who translated all his thirteen books written in Sanskrit into Tibetan. Lāmā Tārānāth[2343] speaks of another famous teacher Mahāpaṇḍita Jñāna-śrī-mitra who hailed from Gaṇḍa and was the guardian of the second central gate of Vikramaśilā in the reign of King Canaka (A. D. 955—983). According to M. M. S. C. Vidyābhūṣaṇa[2344] he was the same person as Jñāna-śrī-bhadra who worked in Kashmere. He was the author of Sanskrit works, three of which are on Logic. To spread the genius of India in Tibet he learnt Tibetan and translated one of his books into Tibetan. Mahāpaṇḍita Ratnavajra, a Brahmin of Kashmere, after studying upto his thirty-sixth year, not only the Buddhist sūtras and mantras but also most of the Buddhist sciences, visited Vajrāsana (Bodh Gayā) where he mastered all the Buddhist śāstras in a very short time and then came to Vikramaśilā for further study. After he finished the course of studies here, the royal diploma of paṇḍita was awarded to him and soon after he was appointed as keeper of the middle gate[2345] by King Canaka (A. D. 955—983). After some time he went back to Kashmere where he defeated many Tīrthikas in discussion. From Kashmere he went to the country of Udyāna, whence towards the end of his career he visited Tibet to spread Buddhism there. He was the author of fourteen Buddhistic books in

---

2341 Ibid., pp. 234, 235, etc.

2342 S. C. Vidyābhūṣaṇa, Mediæval School of Indian Logic, p. 140.

2343 Schiefner's Tārānāth, pp. 235—42.

2344 Vidyābhūṣaṇa—Med. Logic, p. 137.

2345 Schiefner's Tārānāth, p. 240.

Sanskrit which found their way to Tibet through translations. When in Tibet he learnt Tibetan and translated several books into that language, four of which had come down to us. Mahāpaṇḍita Vāgīśvara-kīrti was an inhabitant of Benares and the author of a Sanskrit book on Tantra which now remains only in its Tibetan translation. He was appointed as dwāra-paṇḍita of the western gate of Vikramaśilā by King Canaka (A. D. 955-983). Dīpāñkara Srī Jñāna or Atisa like Lord Buddha came of a royal family (of Gaṇḍa), a kingdom to the east of Vajrāsana (Bodh Gayā) and like him renounced the ease and pleasure of the world and entered the monastery of Kṛṣṇagiri, where he was trained by Rahula-gupta. At the age of nineteen he took the sacred vows from from Śīla Rakṣita, who was the Mahāṣāñghika ācārya of Odantapurī University. At the age of thirty-one he was ordained by Ācārya Dharma Rakṣita in the highest order of vikṣus. He learnt all the mysteries of Buddhism from Ācārya Chandrakīrti, the High-priest of Suvarṇadwīpa[2346] which was considered the head quarters of Buddhism in the East. After residing there for twelve years, he returned to India, visiting Ceylon on the way. Attracted by the versatility of this profound Buddhist scholar king Nyāyapāla (1030—) appointed him to the post of High-priest of Vikramaśilā At the call of the Buddhist King of Tibet, Chan Chub, he left Vikramaśilā after much hesitation, for Tibet to reform the Buddhist religion there.[2347] An escort of three hundred horsemen took the sage to the Tibetan King, who welcomed him warmly and surnamed him Jovo Je.[2348] He was the real founder of Lāmāism and perhaps the greatest writer of Tibetan Buddhism. About two hundred books—both original and translations—are ascribed to him among which eighty-three are Tantric books in Sanskrit. Vīryasiṃha who popularised Buddhist literature in Tibet appears to have been connected with Vikramaśilā; for he helped Atisa in the Tibetan translation of two books, made at the vihāra of Vikramaśilā.[2349] Abhayakara-gupta who came

---

2346 Identified by Mr. S. C. Das with Sudharmanagar in Pegu Called Thaton.

2347 S. C. Das—Indian Pundits in the Land of Snow (1893) pp. 50-76. Waddell—Lāmāism.

2348 Sans. Prabhu Swāmi.

2349 Cordier—Catalogue du Fond Tibetain, II. p. 257 ; Ibid. III. p. 338.

from Gaṇḍa was a famous teacher at Vikramaśilā in the reign of King Rāmapāla (A. D. 1084-1130). He was proficient in the five sciences and while at Vikramaśilā used to write śāstras in the first two watches of the day and explain the principles of Dharma in the third. In his day the University had three thousand monks and was under the protection of King Subhaśrī of Eastern India. We learn on the authority of Tibetan writers, that a Turuṣka war took place at this time in which he played an important part and was ultimately able to drive out the Turuṣkas.[2350] He was a great Tantric scholar and besides writing two works on Śūtra group he composed in Sanskrit twenty-seven and translated into Tibetan seven books on Tantra. Mahāpaṇḍita Tathāgata Rakṣita who came of a Kāystha family of Orissa is mentioned by Tārānāth as a Tantrācārya of Vikramaśilā.[2351] He composed in Sanskrit nine books, mostly on Tantra, seven of which he himself translated into Tibetan. He also translated into Tibetan four works written by others. Mahāpaṇḍita Ratnakīrti was also associated with the University of Vikramaśilā[2352] and it was from him as from Jetāri that Ratnākara Śānti learnt the Sūtra and the Tantra. He was the author of four Buddhist books in Sanskrit, three of which he himself rendered into Tibetan. Paṇḍita Mañjuśrī, a great Tibetan and Sanskrit scholar, translated three Sanskrit books into Tibetan and happily the scene of his work on these translations was the University of Vikramaśilā. Dharmakīrti who was helped by Abhayakara-gupta in translating 'Kāla-cakrāvatāra-nāmā' was associated with Vikramaśilā where he translated into Tibetan the Sanskrit book 'Samaya-Pañcha' of Ācārya Padmasambhava.[2353] He was a native of Khams-pa which according to Mr. S. C. Das is the eastern part of Tibet. He is also described as a Lotsaba, that is, a Tibetan scholar versed in the Sanskrit language and he wrote about sixteen Sanskrit books. Mahāpaṇḍita Śākya Śrī Bhadra was a native of Kashmere and a famous logician. When he was at Vikramaśilā the vihāra was invaded and destroyed along with

---

[2350] S. C. Das—"Contributions on the Religion and History of Tibet" in J. A. S. B., 1882, p. 18.

[2351] Schiefner's Tārānāth, p. 259.

[2352] Catalogue du Fond Tibetain, III. p. 391.

[2353] Ibid., II. pp. 75-76.

Odantapura by a Turuṣka king (Bakhtyar Khilji). He then fled to the monastic University of Jāgaddala whence he visited Tibet.[2354] He wrote seven books in Sanskrit and translated two others into Tibetan. Relying on Tibetan sources Mr. S. C. Das also refers to two other famous teachers associated with Vikramaśilā. One was Vidyā Kokila who was a lineal disciple of ācārya Chandrakīrti and teacher of Atisa. The other was the famous Naropanta "who for his scholarship in the sacred literature has no equal among the Buddhists. He too was Atisa's tutor." Tārānāth also mentions the name of Naropa who was the dwāra-paṇḍita of the northern gate of Vikramaśilā in the reign of King Canaka (A. D. 955—983). When Nag-tcho was staying at Vikramaśilā as the messenger of Prince Chan Chub to take Atisa to Tibet Naropanta came on a visit to Vikramaśilā and after handing over the ministry of the religion of Buddha to Atisa, proceeded towards the south where he died soon afterwards. Some relics of his remains were brought to Tibet by Atisa and they are said still to exist, being preserved in the sacred stupa of Hor at Nethan.[2355] Tārānāth mentions Ācārya Kamala Rakṣita who was at the head of the Vikramaśilā University and was able to repel a Turuṣka attack on the University.[2356] According to Dr. S. C. Vidyābhūṣaṇa[2357] Kamala Kuleśa, Dāna Rakṣita, Śubhakara-gupta and Sunāyakaśrī also belonged to this University.

This University was visited by eminent Tibetan scholars like Rinchhen Zan-po and Legs-pahi Serab who came under the instruction of the Tibetan King "Lha Lama Yes'e hod" to invite to Tibet a saintly Buddhist scholar for the reformation of Buddhism in Tibet.[2358] It was soon visited by another Tibetan scholar Gya-tson Senga who came to Vikramaśilā under the instructions of the same king to take Atisa to Tibet.[2359] Another Tibetan scholar Nag-tcho visited

---

[2354] Schiefner's Tārānāth, p. 255.

[2355] S. C. Das—Indian Pundits in the Land of Snow (1893), p. 60, 63-64

[2356] Geschichte des Buddhismus Von Schiefner, pp. 266, 261. Quoted in S. C. Vidyābhūṣaṇa's Med. Logic, pp. 151-52 footnote No. 2.

[2357] Vidyābhūṣaṇa—Med. Logic p. 151.

[2358] S. C. Das—Indian Pundits in the Land of Snow, p. 52.

[2359] Ibid., pp. 52-53.

Vikramaśilā as a messenger of Prince Chan Chub to invite Atisa to Tibet. Nag-tcho met on his way a party of a Nepalese prince consisting of about ten men who were proceeding to Vikramaśilā.[2360] Nag-tcho remained here for full three years and applied himself with assiduity in studying the sacred books and reading Sanskrit Buddhist literature under Sthavira Ratnākara. While at Vikramaśilā he translated six books into Tibetan two of which he did with Atisa's help.[2361] "The pundits of Vikramaśilā were teaching a certain Buddhist work which in Tibet was very little appreciated. There was a very good commentary upon it called Suddha Vindu (drops of nectar). Nag-tcho translated it into Tibetan".[2362] He attended a grand congregation of eight thousand monks of all classes living in Vikramaśilā, a graphic description of which as preserved by him is given by Mr. S. C. Das in his "Indian Pundits in the Land of Snow."[2363]

According to the Muhammadan historian Minhaz in the eightieth regnal year of Lakṣmaṇasena (i. e., Lakṣmaṇasena era 1119 A. D.+80= 1199 A. D.) Magadha was invaded by Bakhtyar who especially attacked the Buddhist monasteries including Vikramaśilā. Tārānāth also refers to the destruction of Vikramaśilā along with other monasteries by the Turuṣka king. According to Tārānāth[2364] the king of Magadha had fortified Vikramaśilā and stationed some soldiers there so that it easily attracted the attention of the Moslem conqueror. Moreover, as Dr. P. C. Roy,[2365] relying on manuscripts, observes: "The monasteries had degenerated into hotbeds of corruption, so much so that the Mussalman conquerors felt little compunction in putting the inmates thereof to the sword."

ODANTAPURĪ MONASTERY.

Another monastic University was that of Odantapurī[2366] which was established by Gopāla, the first king of the Pāla dynasty about the middle of

---

2360 Ibid., p. 57.
2361 Ibid., p. 66.
2362 Ibid., p. 64.
2363 pp. 59-60.
2364 Geschichte des Buddhismus Von Schiefner, pp. 259-61.
2365 History of Hindu Chemistry, Vol. I. p. LXIX.
2366 or Odantapura.

the eighth century A. D.[2367] But according to the writer of "Universities in Ancient India[2368] it was established long before the Pāla dynasty came to power in Magadha. It was situated near Pātalīputra but it is difficult to identify its exact site. This vihāra served as a model for the great monastery of Sam-ye in Tibet which was built by its king with the assistance of Śānta Rakṣitā.[2369] It was famous as a stronghold of of Tantric Buddhism. Ratnākara Śānti, one of the dwāra-paṇḍitas of Vikramaśilā was ordained in the Sarvāstivāda school of Odantipura.[2370] Even Atisa, the High-priest of Vikramaśilā took the sacred vow at his nineteenth year from Śīla Rakṣita, the Mahāsaṅghika āchārya of Odantapura University.[2371] When Abhayakara-gupta was at the head of the Buddhist hierarchy of Magadha (that is, towards the end of the eleventh and the beginning of the twelvth Century A. D.) there were no less than one thousand Buddhist monks at Odantapurī as compared with three thousand monks at Vikramaśilā and one thousand at Mahābodhi.[2372] A monk of Odantapurī vihāra, Prabhākara[2373] by name was the translator of "Sāmudṛka—vyañjanu—varṇana" into Tibetan. This vihāra contained a splendid library which was destroyed by Bakhtyar and his troops. According to Tārānāth,[2374] the King of Magadha fortified the monastery and stationed some troops with whom the monks joined in repulsing the invaders. The University was totally destroyed in 1199 A. D., for, the colophon of Pañchakara in the library of the University of Cambridge refers to the destruction of Odantapura in the thirty-eighth regnal year of Govindapāladeva who ascended the throne in 1161 A. D. Tārānāth observes: "The Turuṣka king................ conquered the whole of Magadha, killed many clerics at Odantapurī, destroyed this as well as Vikramaśilā and on the spot of the old vihāra

[2367] V. A. Smith—Early History of India, p. 398.

[2368] J. B. T. R. S., Vol. VII. Part IV. (1906) p. 21.

[2369] S. C. Das in J. A. S. B., 1881, Part I. p. 226; Waddell's Lāmāism p. 28; Cosma de Koros—Tibetan Grammar, p 183.

[2370] S. C. Vidyābhūṣaṇa—Med. Logic, p. 140.

[2371] S. C. Das—Indian Pundits in the Land of Snow, p. 51.

[2372] P. N. Bose—Indian Teachers of Buddhist Universities, pp. 84, 157-58.

[2373] Ibid., pp. 156-58.

[2374] Schiefner's Tārānāth, pp. 259-61.

a fortress of the Turuṣkas was erected." Minhaz mentions Odantapurī as Adwand Vihar and writes : "Muhammad-i-Bakhtyar threw himself into the postern of the gateway of the place and gained possession of the place................. Most of the inhabitants of the place were Brahmins with shaven heads (Buddhist monks). They were all slain. There was a great number of books which came under the observation of the Mussalmans. They summoned a number of Hindus that they might give them information respecting the import of these books but all the Hindus had been killed. On becoming acquainted, it was found that the whole of the fortress and city was a college and in the Hindi tongue, they called a college Vihāra".[2375]

The Jāgaddala vihāra.

The Rāmacharita speaks of the Jāgaddala Mahāvihāra built by king Rāmapāla[2376] in the city of Rāmābatī founded by him on the banks of the Ganges and the Karatoyā in the country of Varendra.[2377] Being thus founded in the beginning of the twelvth century this University lasted only for a century till the Muhammadan invasion of Bengal by Bukhtyar in 1203 swept it away. After the destruction of the monastery of Vikramaśilā, Śakya S'rī Bhadra came to this vihāra whence he visited Tibet.[2378]

One of the great scholars of this University was Māhapaṇḍita Bibhūtichandra. He was the author of six books in Sanskrit which he himself translated into Tibetan. He also translated into Tibetan about eighteen Sanskrit books written by others. He translated two of these books at Din-Ri, a plateau of Southern Tibet which shows that he visited that country.[2379] Ācārya Dānaśila otherwise known as Dānaśrīla also belonged to this University. He was born in Kashmere when Mahīpāla was reigning in Bengal. He composed four books in Sanskrit, one of which

---

2375 Tabakāt-i-Nāṣari (Eng. Trans., by Major H. G. Raverty), 1881, Vol. I. p. 552.

2376 Memoirs of the Asiatic Society of Bengal, Vol. III. p. 47; Rāmacharita—M. M. Śāstrī, Ch. III. 5, 7.

2377 Ibid., p. 14.

2378 Schiefner's Tārānāth, p. 255.

2379 Cordier—Catalogue du Fond Tibetain, pp. 19, 20; Kern—Manual of Indian Buddhism, p. 134.

was on Logic and translated fifty-four books into Tibetan without aid and four more with the help of Jinamitra. The place where he translated "Kāka caritra" was the vihāra of Yar-kluns-than-poche in Central Tibet, which shows that he visited Tibet. Another scholar Paṇḍita Subhākara, otherwise known as Sumbhakara was the spiritual guide of Śākya Śrī probably Śākya S'rī Bhadra, the abbot of Vikramaśīlā and while at Jāgaddala wrote in Sanskrit "Siddhaika-vīra-tantrā-tikā"[2380] Another scholar belonging to this vihāra was Mahāpaṇḍita Mokṣākara-gupta, the author of a famous book on Logic named "Tarka-bhāṣā".

Śākya monastery.

Another great monastery was that of Śākya. It was built after the model of Odantapura which it followed in the details of monastic discipline and education. It became the seat of the first grand hierarchy of Tibet about 1202 A. D.

S'rīdhanya Kataka.

Similary there was S'rīdhanya Kataka which was situated on the banks of the Kṛṣṇā in Vidarva (modern Amraoti). It attained the height of its fame as a seat of Brahminical and Buddhist learning during the time of siddha Nāgārjuna. The great monastic University of Du-pong near Lhasa with its six colleges was built after its model.

The Muhammadan conquest, however, led to the destruction of these monasteries in N. India. Kern[2381] observes: "The learned Śākyaśrī went to Orissa and afterwards to Tibet; Ratna Rakṣita to Nepal; Buddhamitra and others sought refuge in Southern India while Sangama-śri-jñāna and several of his followers betook themselves to Burma, Camboja etc............Many emigrants from Magadha rejoined their brethren in the south and founded colleges on a modest scale in Vijayanagara, Kalinga and Konkan. The comparatively satisfactory condition of Buddhism in the Deccan about this time is attested by the

---

2380 Catalogue du Fond Tibetain, II. p. 293.

2381 Kern—Manual of Indian Buddhism, p. 134.

rich donations to the monastery at Dambal". Thus the monks of the monasteries of Vikramaśilā and Odantapura on their dispersion carried with them their learning and arts in the same manner as the Byzantine Greeks on their expulsion from Constantinople bore with them their intellectual treasures to the Italian cities. In the kingdoms of the Deccan,[2382] in Nepal and in Tibet, the Buddhist scholars found hospitable asylums just as the Greek philosophers did in the Florentine Republic under the Medicii.

§ 14. SEATS OF LEARNING.

(i) BENARES.

Benares is one of the oldest seats of learning in India. In the Tittira Jātaka[2383] we read that "a world-renowned professor of Benares gave instruction in science to five hundred young Brahmins" and afterwards repaired to a forest-home on the slopes of the Himalayas to carry on his educational work in that calm sylvan retreat. In the Kosiya Jātaka[2384] it is stated that in the reign of king Brahmadatta of Benares Bodhisattva being born in a Brahmin family became a renowned teacher at Benares and used to teach the three Vedas and the eighteen vijjās to Brahmin boys and kṣhatriya princes. In the Jātaka period Benares was, however, largely the creation of the ex-students of Taxila. We find established there schools for the teaching of spells and magic charms by students trained in Taxila. For the study of the ordinary subjects there were of course already many schools.[2385] Benares, however, was not without its own alumni as educationists. There are several references to teachers of world-wide fame with the usual number of 500 pupils to teach. The son of a Brahmin magnate is educated in Benares. There were again certain subjects in the teaching of which Benares seems to have specialised.

[2382] *Compare* "The Deccan, which from the eleventh century was the refuge and centre of literary activity generally. In Hindusthan it had been substantially arrested by the inroads and the ravages of the Muhammadans"—Weber's History of Indian Literature, p. 283.

[2383] Jātaka III. 537.

[2384] Jātaka I. p. 463.

[2385] Jātaka Nos. 130, 185 etc.; Jātaka II. 99; I. 464.

There is a reference, for instance, to a school of music presided over by an expert who was the chief of his kind in all India.[2386] Again it was at Benares that Paṇinī wrote his famous grammar, that Kapila evolved his Sāṃkhya philosophy, that Yāska wrote his Nirukta and Gautama wrote his Nyāya-śāstra.[2387] Śaṅkarāchārya is said to have studied at Benares "the accepted touch-stone of all new doctrines from the ancient days even from the days of Buddha. There in Benares, Śaṅkara published his new doctrine of Vedānta and convinced the pundits of Benares of its truth".[2388] Al Beruni[2389] says: "The most generally known alphabet is called Siddhamātṛka............the people of Kashmere use it. But it is also used in Vārāṇasī. This town and Kashmere are the high schools of Hindu sciences". According to Al Beruni,[2390] owing to the plundering exploits of Mahmud "Hindu sciences have retired far away from those parts of the country conquered by us and have fled to places where our hand cannot yet reach, to Kashmere, Benares and other places". In the days of Al Beruni[2391] astronomy was specially cultivated at Benares where Vijayanandin composed his astronomical handbook entitled Karṇa-tilaka. It appears from the Āin-i-Ākbari[2392] that Benares continued to be a flourishing seat of Hindu learning even in the sixteenth century.

(ii) Ujjain.

According to Bāṇa[2393] the inhabitants of Ujjain "are connoisseurs in all arts...............skilled in foreign languages, clever at subtleties of speech, versed in stories of all kinds, accomplished in letters, having a keen delight in the Mahābhārata, the Purāṇas and the Rāmāyaṇa, familiar with the Bṛhat-kathā, masters of the whole circle of arts...........lovers of śāstras, devoted to light literature". Ujjain's fame as a great centre of learning attracted Śaṅkarāchārya who defeated here in argument a

---

2386 Jātaka I. 239; III. 18 and 233; IV. 237; Jātaka No. 243.

2387 Nagendra Nāth Som—Bārāṇasī (in Bengali), p. 21.

2388 C. V. Vaidya—Mediæval Hindu India, Vol. II. p. 214.

2389 Sachau's Eng. Trans., Vol. I. p. 173.

2390 Ibid., I. 22.

2391 Ibid., I. p. 156.

2392 Gladwin's Eng. Trans., p. 560.

2393 Kādambarī—C. M. Ridding's Eng. Trans., p. 212.

Pāśupatāchārya. Al Beruni[2394] relates the story of the alchemist Vyādi who was a veritable martyr to the science of alchemy. Ujjain was however famous for the study of astronomy and it became the meridian from which the Hindus counted the longitude of other places.[2395]

(iii) KANAUJ.

From the reign of Yaśovarman (675-710 A. D.) Kanauj became specially famous for its study of Pūrva Mīmāṃsā or the philosophy of Vedic ritual. Yaśobarman was the patron of Bhababhūti whose guru was the great apostle of Pūrva Mīmāṃsā, Kumārila Bhatta, as is evidenced by a colophon of Bhababhūti's drama Mālatīmādhava. This together with the story that five Brahmins were sent from Kanauj to Bengal to revive orthodox Hindu customs there shows that Kanauj was a centre of Brahminical learning.

(iv) TANJORE.

Tanjore was famous for the cultivation of Nātyaśāstra and the sister arts of music and dancing. Rājarāja Chola (985-1014 A. D.) built music-halls for this purpose and invited and settled in Tanjore female dancers as also singers, pipers and drummers. Colleges were also built and learned teachers were appointed who taught literature and śāstras to students.[2396]

(v) KALYāṇa.

Kalyāṇa was an ancient seat of learning, specially famous for its study of Law and Astronomy. At Kālyaṇa Vijñāneśwara composed the famous commentary on the Yājñabālkya Smṛti, called Mitākṣarā which is recognised even to this day as the leading authority on Hindu Law all over India except Bengal. King Someśwara III (1126-1138 A. D.) himself wrote the Mānosollāsa a compendium of many sciences and made a solid contribution to the science of Astronomy by giving the Dhubāñkas (constants to be added).

2394 Sachau's Eng. Trans., Vol. I. p. 189. 2395 Ibid., I. pp. 304, 311.

2396 Aiyar's Historical Sketch of the Ancient Deccan, p. 251.

(vi) Kāñchī.

Kāñchīpuram was another great centre of learning and Hiuen Tsang had conversation with monks from Ceylon on Yoga philosophy here. Dharmapāla of Kāñchī defeated a hundred Hīnayāna sūtrakāras in a discussion lasting for seven days. The Jaina Rājāvalikathā mentions Sāmantabhadra as having gone to Kāñchīpuram a number of times and a Mysore inscription bears this out.[2397] South of it there was "a large monastery which was a rendezvous of the most eminent men of the country".

(vii) Paithan.

Under the Śātabāhanas Paithan became one of the chief seats of learning in India. Its pre-eminence remained so far recognised that even during Muhammadan and Maharatta times complicated cases were settled at Paithan under the Panchayets of its learned men. That Paithan was famous for the cultivation of sciences is evident from Kathāsaritsāgara[2398] where we are told of one Devadatta by name who went to an old preceptor named Mantraswāmin in Pratiṣṭhāna and acquired a perfect knowledge of the sciences.

Besides these, there were in Northern India Peshwar, Mathurā[2399] and Sārnātha famous for their schools of sculpture, Multan famous for its study of Astronomy and Mithilā and Navadwīpa for their schools of Logic. In Southern India Karavir, Giri and Vijayanagara were also famous seats of learning.

[2397] Inscription of Śrāvaṇa Belgolā in Ep. Carn., Vol. II. Revised No. 44, Quoted by S. V. Venkateśwara in his Indian Culture Through the Ages, Vol. I.

[2398] Penzer, Vol. I. p. 79.

[2399] Cunningham observes: "Everywhere in the north-west, I find that the old Buddhist statues are made of Sikri sandstone from which it would appear that Mathurā must have been a great manufactory for the supply Buddhist sculptures in Northern India."

CHAPTER XII.

AGENCIES OF EDUCATION.

§1. CARAKAS OR WANDERING STUDENTS.

Instruction was derived not merely from the regular teachers settled in the various seats of learning where they admitted their pupils but also from other sources. Such for instance were the Carakas or wandering students. According to Śañkara they were called Carakas because they were observing (car) a vow for the sake of learning. The word occurs in one of the inscriptions of Usavadāta at Nasik—Caraka parṣabhyaḥ—where there is a reference to Brahminical schools at four places named in the record.[2400] The Bṛhadāraṇyaka Upaniṣad[2401] refers to a band of wandering students travelling as far north as the land of the Madras. The Kathāsaritsāgara[2402] also refers to a brāhmaṇa student Śaktideva by name who "was roaming through the earth in quest of knowledge". Though not normally competent as teachers, these travelling students are yet regarded as posssible sources of popular enlightenment by the S'atapatha Brāhmaṇa.[2403]

The discussions in which these wandering students engaged themselves were not always due to accidental[2404] meetings as between Yājñabālkya and Janaka in the S'atapatha Brāhmaṇa but were sometimes deliberately challenged in a foreign region by the visiting scholars who would even throw down a prize for victory. In the S'atapatha Brāhmaṇa[2405] Uddālaka Aruṇi, a Kuru-pāñchāl Brahmin, goes north where he offers a gold coin as prize, "for the sake of calling out the timid to a disputation". Seized with fear the Brahmins of the northern country challenged him to a disputation on religious matters with Svaidāyana i. e., S'aunaka as their champion. In the end Uddālaka finds himself unable to answer all the questions put to him by S'aunaka, so he "gave

2400 Ind. Ant., 1883, p. 30.

2401 III. 3. 1. 7. 1.

2402 Penzer's edition, Vol. II. p. 174,

2403 IV. 2. 4.

2404 XI. 6. 2.

2405 XI. 4. 1f.

him the gold coin". Thus education besides that imparted by the schools, was largely spread and promoted in its higher stages by learned travelling scholars of different provinces who would seek such opportunities of establishing their philosophical positions or scientific theories and thereby their intellectual status and eminence in the realm of letters.[2406]

§2. Ascetic teachers.

Another factor of importance in the educational life of India in ancient times as to some extent even to-day was the influence of wandering monks and Sannyāsins. Hiuen Tsang was impreseed by their wide learning and spirit of self-sacrifice. "Though their family be in affluent circumstances, such men make up their minds to be like vagrants and wander here and there to get their subsistence. Though they are not moved by honour or reproach, their fame is far spread. Even kings treated them with great respect. They were greatly versed in antiquity and they devoted their time to the cultivation of knowledge".[2407] Thus could India show in abundance men who renounced the riches and the comforts of home, the many pleasures of social life and even the love of fame ('that last infirmity of noble minds') as so many impediments to the quest of Truth. Attainting truth they were anxious to impart it to their fellows. As Hiuen Tsang[2408] says: "Forgetting fatigue, they "expatiate in the arts and sciences"; seeking for wisdom while "relying on perfect virtue" they "count not 1000 *li*[2409] a long journey". With the revival of Hinduism under S'añkara, the Sannyāsins living in the convents established by him, called S'añkarāchāryas were required to tour from village to village, within their own jurisdiction, settling disputes relating to caste, conduct or creed, solving the doubts and difficulties of local priests, advising the people to follow their Dharma and at times establishing institutions for the education of the young or

2406 For an account of the *Wanderjahre* of young brāhmaṇa students *See* Dr. Buhler's Introduction to Bikramāñkacharita.

2407 Beal—Buddhist Records of the Western World, Vol. II. p. 79; Watters—Yuan Chwang, Vol. I. p. 160.

2408 Watters—Yuan Chwang, Vol. I. p. 161.

2409 1 *li*=4 miles.

for the support of Sannyāsins. Thus in these travelling bands of ascetic teachers ancient India found the real educators of thought who did more to spread education and enlightenment in the country than any paid or official agency. *The people found their own teachers irrespective of the state.*

§3. Brahmabāda or discussions near a sacrifice.

Another great educational influence in the country was the occasional concourse of learned men gathered together at the courts and palaces of kings by the sessions of sacrifices they used to celebrate with due pomp and liberality. It was customary in those days to arrange in connection with these sacrifices some interesting and instructive functions like the recitation of sacred books at some convenient hour of the day, which could be attended by the public at large. It was during sacrifices that S'ukadeva recited Bhāgabat to Janamejaya, that Sūta told the Purāṇas to ṛṣis. It was at the snake-sacrifice of Janamejaya that Vaiśampāyana recited the Mahābhārata.[2410] Similarly, at a sacrifice lasting for twelve years performed by kulapati S'aunaka in Naimiṣāraṇya Ugraśrabā recited the Purāṇas.[2411] Thus the celebration of religious sacrifices was the principal agency for the promulgation and *popularisation of original literary works of national interest and importance.*

The Upaniṣads also emphasise *the other feature* of these learned gatherings viz., that they provided the arena where scholars seeking to establish their intellectual position entered the list in tournaments of debate. These discussions were called Brahmabāda and references to to them are often met with in the S'atapatha Brāhmaṇa, Bṛhadāraṇyaka and Chhāndogya Upaniṣads. It was in such a sacrifice that Uśaṣti Chakrāyana challenged the priests to explain the nature of their deities and on their silence did so himself.[2412] This feature is also noticed in the Mahābhārata[2413] where it is stated how learned Brahmins were flocking to the sacrifice of Janaka "for the purpose of

---

2410 Mahābhārata, Ādiparba, Anukramaṇikādhyāya. *Compare* Ādiparba, 59th adhyāya,

2411 Ibid., Ādiparba, 4th adhyāya, Paulomaparbādhyāya.

2412 Chāndogya Up, I. 10, 11. 2413 III. 132-34.

listening to controversies" and the recitation of the Vedas. Thither came Aṣṭabakra but the entrance to the assembly was barred by the gate-keeper who under orders from the learned chief, Vaṇḍi, was to admit only old and learned Brahmins. Aṣṭabakra had thus first to convince the gate-keeper of his eligibility for membership of that learned assembly and addressed him as follows: "O gate-keeper, you will to-day see me engaged in a controversial fight with all the learned men and get the better of Vaṇḍi himself in argument." In the end Aṣṭabakra came out victorious, with his supremacy acknowledged by the whole assembly.

These discussions of learned men "*sitting near*" the sacrificial fire were later on written down and called Upaniṣads. Such debates at times resulted in philosophical investigations and the pompous hollowness of the ritual appealed to some thoughtful minds. They were then put down in black and white in course of time for the guidance of future generations and the writings came to be known as Āraṇyakas or discussions near Araṇi (wooden pieces by the friction of which sacrificial fire was produced) and later on probably it became traditional to read them in *sylvan* solitude and not in the presence of the common people who could appreciate the external form of anything better than the underlying truth.[2414]

Such discussions were the most *economical* and *effective* source of popular enlightenment. The kings spent little on them directly and yet encouraged a devoted class of teachers whose duty it was to lead a simple life, to cultivate high thinking, to keep learning (religious though it was) alive and to help other members of the society to follow suit. The religious commandments had a great hold on the individual mind and such progress was achieved as would have been impossible by the enforcement of secular laws. Superstition and mysticism might have been great defects in the system as propagated by the Brāhmaṇas; but the Upaniṣads marked a definite improvement upon them. In a number of places, the nature of several deities was

---

[2414] Journal of the Bombay Branch of the Royal Asiatic Society, No. XXII. p. 71.

challenged by bold seekers after the truth like Uśaṣti Chakrāyana and pure rational philosophy was taught by them instead of dogmatic explanation.

§ 4. Recitation of śāstras specially at a śrāddha.

Another agency of popular enlightenment was the recitation of śāstras on the occasion of śrāddha ceremonies. Manu[2415] says: "During the śrāddha repast Vedas, Purāṇas, Itihāsas and Khilas should be recited to brāhmaṇa guests when they would be eating." Viṣṇu Saṃhita[2416] says: "This code should be studied, remembered and recited to others. Persons, deserving good, shall hear it narrated during the celebrations of a śrāddha ceremony." In the Mahābhārata[2417] we are told that if a man arranges for the recitation of the Mahābhārata to the Brahmins at a śrāddha, then his dead ancestors get eternal food and drink. If he arranges for the recitation of the Mahābhārata on Parva days, then his sins are removed and he is assured of his residence in Brahmaloka for ever."

Aśwaghoṣa mentions a simple headman of a village listening to the recital of the Epics delivered by the Brahmins.[2418] Bāṇa[2419] also refers to Kādambarī "giving her attention to the recitation of the Mahābhārata........... by Nārada's sweet-voiced daughter, with the accompaniment of flutes soft as the murmur of bees, played by a pair of kinnaras sitting behind her." In Harṣacharita[2420] we are told of the recitation of the Vāyu Purāṇa by the reader Sudriste before Bāṇa and his relatives. A copper-plate grant[2421] of a Pāla king has been found which makes the interesting statement that a village was granted as dakṣiṇā to a Brahmin for reading the whole of the Mahābhārata to his queen Chitramaṭikā.

§5. Public Religious tournaments.

Public religious tournaments were another agency of popular education. The Indo-Aryan mind always took delight in logically

2415 Ch. III.; M. N. Dutt's Trans., p. 232. 2416 Ch. C. śl. 3.

2417 Ādiparba, 62nd adhyāya.

2418 S. V. Venkateśwara—Indian Culture Through the Ages, Vol. I. p. 212.

2419 Kādambarī—C. M. Ridding's Eng. Trans., p. 162.

2420 Eng. Trans., by Cowell and Thomas, p. 72.

2421 J. R. A. S. B., XIX., Part I. p. 66.

discussing the various questions of religion and philosophy. Buddhism specially was fond of such discussions. The development of Nyāya philosophy which Buddhism to some extent made its own lent indeed a scholastic character to such discussions and there was no criterion of truth except the opponents's defeat in discussion. Yet these discussions have an interest and a value of their own as reason was held supreme.[2422] The discussion between the Buddhist patriarch Parsva and the Brahmin scholar Aśwaghoṣa took place as early as the first century B. C. Even before this, in the age of Aśoka such discussions between scholars of different sects took place and a special edict enjoins upon them toleration, respect for the truth in each system and restraint of speech in controversy.[2423] The following dialogue[2424] between Milindā and Nāgasena is quoted to show what was thought to be the proper mode of carrying on discussions in the days of those notable persons:—

The King said: 'Reverend Sir, will You discuss with me again?'

'If Your Majesty will discuss as a scholar (paṇḍita), will; but if you will discuss as a king, no.'

'How is it then that scholars discuss?'

'When scholars talk a matter over with one another then there is a winding up, an unravelling; one or other is convicted of error; and he then acknowledges his mistake, distinctions are drawn, and contradistinctions; and yet thereby they are not angered. Thus do scholars, O king, discuss.'

'And how do kings discuss?'

'When a king, Your Majesty, discusses a matter, and he advances a point, if any one differ from him on that point, he is apt to fine him, saying: "Inflict such and such a punishment on that fellow!" Thus, Your Majesty, do kings discuss.'

'Very well. It is as a scholar, not as a king, that I will discuss. Let Your Reverence, talk unreservedly, as you would with a brother, or a novice, or a lay disciple, or even with a servant. Be not afraid?'

2422 C. V. Vaidya—Med. India, Vol. III. 2423 Rock Edict XII.

2424 Rhys Davids—Questions of King Milindā in the S. B. E. Series, Vol. XXXV., p. 46.

In the time of Chandragupta Vikramāditya of Ujjain, a great disputation between the two exponents of Hinduism and Buddhism was held on the subject of sense perceptions. Monoratha, the champion of Buddhism was worsted in the discussion owing to the Brahminical bias of the king. But in the next reign, Vasubandhu, the favourite disciple of Manoratha won the victory for Buddhism and his guru.[2425] Hiuen Tsang refers to Buddhist monasteries as the constant scenes of such discussions, for, the monks residing therein having no care for their maintenance had ample time for *study aud disputations* besides performing their religious exercises. The Buddhists themselves were divided into eighteen sects and had as many disputations among themselves as with outsiders. Hiuen Tsang himself took part in such a debate arranged by the king of Kapisa where he defeated after a five days' discussion all his opponents.[2426] He also discussed the the difficult parts of the doctrine in an open conference at the Jayendra convent.[2427] He also describes the great assemblies of learned men which were convened at the time of the quinquennial alms-giving ceremonies which Harṣa used to hold at Prayāga and at the last of which Hiuen Tsang himself was the president. The usual procedure in such assemblies was that some one made a declaration of his doctrines and called upon all present to refute them. Sometimes a written declaration was posted at the gate of a monastery calling upon adversaries to tear it. Hiuen Tsang tells us of one such declaration posted by a Brahmin opponent to the door of the Nālandā monastery which nobody daring to tear up he himself tore and then entering upon a controversy with the Brahmin defeated him.[2428] We learn from the Pattinappālai that men of learning and reputation put up flags, inviting combatants to challenge their scholarship.[2429] Again Guṇavati, a follower of Buddhism defeated a Sāṃkhya student named Mādhava in Magadha. In a seven days' discussion Dharmapāla of Kañchī silenced one hundred Hīnayāna monks in the Viśoka monastery.

[2425] Watters—Yuan Chwang p. 212.

[2426] Beal—Life of Hiuen Tsang, pp. 56-57.

[2427] Ibid., p. 69.

[2428] Ibid., pp. 161-64.

[2429] S. V. Venkateśwara—Indian Culture Through the Ages, Vol. I. p. 252.

References are found to the erection of five monasteries to commemorate the victories of five Buddhist scholars in Srughna over Jaina monks. Āryadeva,[2430] an eminent disciple of Nāgārjuna visited the countries of Mahākośala, Srughna, Prayāga, Chola and Vaiśālī in all of which he won great renown by defeating the Tīrthikas. Dignāga[2431] made the University buildings of Nālandā "resound with the exposition of the various points at issue" and defeated the Brahmin Sudurjjaya and many Tīrtha dialecticians. He travelled through Orissa and Mahārāṣtra to the south, meeting Tīrtha controversialists in discussion. For his success as a debator he was called "Bull in discussion". Dharmakīrti[2432] defeated in debates Kaṇādagupta and other followers of the Tīrtha system and when this success enraged Kumārila he defeated the latter with his five hundred followers. He further withstood the Nirgranthas, Rāhuvratin and others who lived within the range of the Vindhya mountains. In the century that followed Harṣa's death we know that Śaṅkara and Kumārila went to all the important seats of learning in order to propagate their own views after defeating their opponents. S'ilabhadra, a Brahmin prince of Magadha, conquered a South Indian scholar who had challenged the learning of his guru. I-Tsing[2433] also refers to such tournaments being held in his time. Says he: "To try the sharpness of their wit, they (eminent and accomplished scholars) proceed to the king's court to lay down before it the sharp weapon of their abilities.........................when they are present in the House of Debate, they raise their seat and seek to prove their wonderful cleverness. When they are refuting heretical doctrines, all their opponents become tongue-tied and acknowledge themselves undone. Then the sound of their fame makes the five mountains (of India) vibrate and their renown flows, as it were, over the four borders. They receive grants of land and are advanced to a high rank: their famous names are as a reward, written in white on their lofty gates". Kalhaṇa in his Rājataraṅgiṇī[2434]

2430 Beal—Buddhist Records, Vol. I. Bk. IV. pp. 186-90; Bk. V. p. 231; Vol. II. Bk. X. pp. 210, 277; Bk. XII. p. 302; Bk. VIII. pp. 98-102.

2431 S. C. Vidyābhūṣaṇa—Med. Logic, p. 80.

2432 Ibid., p. 104.

2433 Takakusu's Eng. Trans, p. 176ff.

2434 I. 178; Stein—The Chronicles of Kashmere, Vol. I. p. 32.

also refers to such tournaments between Buddhist monks and Brahmin scholars. Jaina scholars like Vijayapaṇḍita also scored eminent success in such public discussions held in various parts of Southern India. An inscription of Kubja Viṣṇuvardhana refers to youths eloquent at discussions who are honoured by the chief people of the locality who had made them serve on the committee of five.[2435] Such discussions are also referred to in many Kadamba inscriptions.[2436] The fame that followed a successful disputant in these tournaments was so great that it must have been an inducement to all scholars to persevere in the subtle theories of metaphysics and religion. This must have kept the standard of intellectual attainment very high among the theologians and professors and it must have reacted powerfully on the educational atmosphere of the country.

§ 6. Functions connected with temple worship.

With the revival of Hinduism under Śaṅkara some interesting functions came to be arranged in connection with temple worship to attract men, women and children. They took various forms and included music and pantomime, discourses by learned men on religious topics, and recitation of the śāstras and the Purāṇas. From Bāṇa's Kādambarī we learn that queen Vilāsabatī heard the recitation of the Mahābhārata in the temple of Mahākāla in Ujjain. An inscription at Śendalai[2437] provides for the reading of the Mahābhārata in the Sundareśwara temple. Objects of show and curiosity, wild animals tamed and confined to a cage, monkeys trained to perform feats, the cobra made to dance to simple music, the elephant adorned with a howdah and caprisoned in oriental fashion, horses and bullocks drawing the hackneys and stately carriages to the music of tinkling cymbals on their necks—the combination of these had the effect on the spectator of a circus, a park and a museum placed within his reach free of cost. These agencies of popular education in the broadest sense radiated from the temple as the centre of such activities.

2435 Pañchavārim Samāpayya vāragoṣṭhiṣu vāgminaḥ—Ep. Ind., V. lines 27, 28.

2436 Fleet's Sanskrit and Kanarese Inscriptions, Nos. 37 etc.

2437 Madras Ep. Rep., for 1899, para. 9.

§ 7. Buddhist agencies of education.

Other agencies of education are referred to in the Vinaya-pītaka which provide ample opportunities for the converts to come into frequent contact with the Buddhist monks. They met at the monasteries on the 8th, 14th, and 15th day of every lunar fortnight at gatherings in which the monks delivered religious discourses and dispelled doubts on the points about which questions were put to them. Fa-hsien[2438] also says that "in Ceylon on the eighth, fourteenth and fifteenth of each month, at all points where the four roads meet, a lofty dais is arranged where ecclesiastics and lay men come together from all quarters to hear the faith expounded." Every morning they came into contact with the monks begging alms from door to door. Though long religious discourses were not suitable for such occasions they could have been easily utilised for imparting to them bits of teachings intended to wear off their attachment to worldly natters and stimulate their eagerness to subject themselves rigidl, ɷo moral and religious discipline—the path to salvation. The afternoons were allowed by the rules of the monasteries to be utilised by the householders by coming there and having spiritual enlightenment from the monks through conversation and religious discourses. The householders were also permitted to invite to meals the monks singly or by batches and these occasions were similarly utilised for purposes of religious enlightenment.

In his 'sermons on stone' Aśoka gave to his subject-peoples of different communities, castes and creeds, certain common and cardinal ideals of thought and conduct which make him Humanity's first teacher of Universal Morality and Religion. These sermons meant to be read by the people at large were necessarily given at all important centres of his far-flung Empire and as they were meant to last for a long time, they were engraved on the most durable material, stone. In one of these sermons we are told that 'everywhere in his dominions his officers of all ranks—the Yuktas, the Rājukas and the Prādeśikas must go out on tours (anusamyāna), each every

---

2438 Eng. Trans., by Giles, pp. 69-70.

five years, as well for their ordinary administrative business as for the special purpose of inculcating the Dhamma".[2439] This scheme of religious tours by his officers received a further development in the institution of a special class of officers the Dharma-mahāmātras, charged with the duty of attending to the moral and spiritual welfare of his subjects.[2440] He himself would have none of the tours of pleasure of his predecessors but would instead have only "religious tours"—holding "religious conferences with the people".[2441] He thus sought occasions of personal intercourse with his subjects to *educate them to lead a better life* and not his own sport or pleasure.

§ 8. Art as an agency of education.

Where Nature failed to supply the facilities for the propagation of his Dhamma the aid of Art was invoked: huge monolithic columns were specially fashioned for the purpose and planted in places where a suitable rocky surface was not available to receive the Emperor's message in inscriptions. One of the Edicts itself informs us that "this message of the Emperor must be written on the rocks or wherever there are blocks or pillars of stone".[2442] King Bhoja had Sanskrit aphorisms inscribed on slabs in the Sanskrit College at Dhar.[2443] Moreover, both in Hindu and Buddhist art we observe a tendency to the increasing use of symbolism for making teaching concrete to the masses. Fa-hien describes a rock-cut monastery in Southern India as having five stages.[2444] The lowest is made with elephant figures and has five hundred cells in it. The second is made with lion-shapes and has four hundred chambers. The third is made with horse-shapes and has three hundred chambers. The fourth is made with ox-shapes and has two hundred chambers. The fifth has dove-shapes and has a hundred chambers in it. The animals represented in architecture are in the same order. They seem to point to the philosophical teaching of the Vedānta that the gross body, the vital

---

[2439] Rock Edict III. [2440] Pillar Edict VII.

[2441] Rock Edict VIII. [2442] Minor Rock Edict I, (Rūpanāth Text).

[2443] Luard and Lele—The Paramāras of Dhar and Malwa.

[2444] Beal—Buddhist Records of the Western World, I. pp. 68, 69.

airs (lion), the senses (horses), the mind (ox) and knowledge (dove) are in the relation of sheaths of the soul in due order.[2445] Again, as we enter a temple, the first thing that strikes us is the sculptural scenery on the walls and panelled ceiling, on the gateways and elsewhere. These pictures were designed to impart instruction in all the departments of learning which were directly or remotely connected with religion. The figures of the God-head as Creator, Preserver and Destroyer are easily recognised and explained. But there are numerous other figures of sages, heroes and devotees whose stories are familiar to the pilgrim in the legendary lore of the Purāṇas and the Epics, or even in the local legends and stories passing from the mouth to the ear. On the walls of some of the temples or on the stones paving the floor are found scenic representations of the Rāmāyaṇa, as at Kumbakonam and Tellicherry: or stories from the Mahābhārata depicted on the wooden ceiling as at Vaikam, Craganore etc. On the temple at Chidambaram[2446] we have sculptures of the various forms of dancing mentioned in the Bharata Nātyaśāstra and referred to in the Kāmasūtras. In describing the painting on the walls of the dancing-hall of the king of Vijayanagara Paes[2447] writes: "The designs of these panels show the positions at the ends of dances in such a way that on each panel there is a dancer in the proper position at the end of the dance; this is to teach the women, so that if they forget the position in which they have to remain when the dance is done, they may look at one of the panels where is the end of the dance. By that way they keep in mind what they have to do". In the basement of an old temple of Mahādeva in the fort of Dhaner in the Himalayan kingdom of Nurpur we similarly find very beautiful figures carved in stone, depicting scenes from the Purāṇas. The sculptures in the four gateways in the Sāñchi Tope "form a perfect picture Bible of Buddhism as it existed in the first century A. D.". The same principle is reflected in Iconography. "The coins of the Kushanas show Śiva, Gaṇeśa and Gajalakṣmī. The purpose of iconographic

---

2445 S. V. Venkateśwara: Symbolism in Indian Art in Rūpam for April, 1927.

2446 Madras Epigraphy Report for 1913 and Plate.

2447 Sewell—A Forgotten Empire, p. 289.

representation in this case was simply to show the regenerative power of God, of which the phallus was the most popular symbol. Generation of a newer order arises from the destruction of the older: hence the weapons in the hands of Śiva. Gaṇeśa is the god of learning, representing the mind surmounting obstacles (vighna) and developing additional power with every act of surmounting. The persistency of mental application is represented by the rat-flag, and the weight and deliberation of the matured mind by the elephant with the single tusk, as contrasted with the fleeting mind of the spiritually undeveloped, which we find represented as a horse or more often as a bull, in sculpture. It is along the lines of Tāntric symbolism that we could discover the meaning of the coin-ornaments. We have the full-fledged story of Gaṇeśa on a coin of Yajñaśrī Śātakarṇī. There is an elephant starting from a palm tree, facing a sword, with a goddess on each side. The palm-fruit with its three eyes represents Śiva, the father Gaṇeśa, the third eye being the eye of wisdom giving birth to spiritual fire. The goddesses at the sides are intellect, calm, cool and concentrated (Buddhi) and knowledge of the reality (Chit), of which the aspirant catches only a passing glimpse. These are confronted by the forces of evil, which are represented sword in hand. The Buddhist emblems of chaitya and tree, which are the generators of the wisdom of the Buddha, are more easily explained. The fire-worship of the Sassanians appears to be symbolised by the fire-altar on the Indo-Sassanian coins. Far the greatest gain to religion and philosophy was the conception and carving of Divinity as Natarāja dancing in life to the fiddling of fate; dressed in daintiness and delight illumined by flickering patches of memory that float upon the face of dark oblivion (apasmāra), which is crushed under foot—the void whose name is Death. His spouse is joy unalloyed, free from the vesture of flowing, flapping drapery, clothed in the calmness and repose of her magnetic and mastering smile. The death of the old has no terrors: it is soothing and serene when it is learnt that it is the entrance to a new life.[2448]

[2448] Contrast with the modern view: 'Death is a state of protoplasmic immobility, of infinite functional inertia ......Latent life and not sleep is the image of death...... In life the sands of time are running out rapidly; in latent life the stream has been mysteriously arrested; in death the sand is all in the lower globe, never to leave it.' (Prof. D. F. Harris in Chambers' Journal for 1926).

The savour and scent of music sets young life leaping and laughing in glee. So goes the round of dying and deathless life, changing form to adjust itself to new conditions, for, survival after fitness for use is death. Corresponding to this conception of Śiva as the master-dancer Naṭarāja, we have that of Viṣṇu as Raṅganātha, the Lord of the Stage which is this phenomenal world. The sculptures at Deogarh and Mahāmallapuram agree in painting the God Anantaśayana as the Spiritual Omega of existence resting in the lap of hydra-headed Space on the ocean of Time (Ananta). He is also the Spiritual Alpha of a new order, as life is on the dawn of bloom like the lotus of Creation, from which emerges the Creator facing all the cardinal points, and the whole gamut of gods and the Forces of Nature are wakeful and watching how the Infinite manifests itself in the new order of creation ".[2449]

§9. THE STAGE AS AN AGENCY OF EDUCATION.

That the drama was an allegory and a vehicle of high class instruction is clear from one of the fragments of two Indian dramas (probably written by Aśwaghoṣa) discovered by Luders among the Turfan palm-leaf manuscripts. One of these two contains a scene in which the allegorical figures of wisdom, endurance and fame (Buddhi, Dhṛti and Kīrti) appear to glorify the Buddha. Though the piece is only fragmentary Dr. Nirañjana Chakrabarty (in his India and Central Asia) thus gives us an idea of the nature of its contents :—

" So long as there is suffering, leading to rebirth " says the Buddha " there is nothing worth giving up, there would be nothing worth knowing whether it is constant and inconstant ? He concludes his speech by saying : 'I take pleasure in him who has gained the highest peace, the highest immortality and the truth hard to obtain."

To this answers Dhṛti : True it is. By my might is surrounded that 'Light' which bears the name 'Man' and which has now become manifest (in the world)......

[2449] Professor S. V. Venkateśwara—Indian Culture Through the Ages, Vol. I. pp. 223-25.

Dhṛti—Verily this is a couple. Where there is Buddhi there is place for Dhṛti, where Dhṛti is established, there Buddhi finds rooms to extend herself.

Kīrti—If such be the case, for you two......

B.—It is so. Again one who has no Buddhi is always like one in sleep, one who is devoid of Dhrti is always like one got drunk...one who has no fame......

K.—Where is now this Dharma, in the form of a man?

B.—Where does he not exist, he who is independent in his supernatural might?......... He flies through the air like a bird, he moves along..........................remains without being dependent (on anything), he percolates through the earth like water, he divides his form in manifold ways, he pours down showers of rain from the sky, at the same time he shines like an evening cloud, he moves about according to his free will..............................and in the right way does he pursue the Dharma.

Dh.—To him shall we then take our resort. This great sage lives at the present moment in the park of the city of Magadha................. The speech of the trio ends with this and then enters Bhagabat himself surrounded by a halo of light. We also know from the Avadānaśataka[2450] which was already translated into Chinese in the 3rd Century A. D., and therefore must have been written at a much earlier time, that a Buddha Drama was enacted by the actors of the Deccan in the presence of King Sobhavati, in which the director himself appeared as the Buddha and others as monks. Professor Sylvain Levi has also referred to another story found in the Kan-hgyur. An actor from the Deccan composed a drama containing the history of the Buddha upto his attainment of Bodhi and performed it before king Bimbisāra. Harṣa had his drama Nāgānanda (based on the story of Bodhisattva Jimūtavāhana surrendering himself in place of a Nāga) set to music and performed by a band accompanied by dancing and acting.[2451] Harṣa also had Chandradasa's

---

2450 Avadāna No. 75.

2451 Takakusu's I-Tsing, p. 163.

Viśwāntara and Aśwaghoṣa's Buddhacharita versified and set to dancing and music.[2452] All these show that already at a very early time Buddhism had given up its highly antagonistic attitude towards the theatre and even went so far as to make use of the *stage as a means of propaganda for its teachings*, nor had the Buddhists any hesitation to allow the Buddha appear on the stage impersonated by the ordinary actors.

In Bhababhūti's Uttara-Rāma-charita, Act IV, (Belvalkar's Eng. Trans., p. 69) we are told by Lava that a certain section of the Rāmāyaṇa has been turned by Vālmīki into a distinct type of work, full of sentiment and adopted to dramatic representation and sent to Bharata, the author of the aphorisms of Dramaturgy. Kṛṣṇamiśra's dramā Prabodha-Chandrodaya (based on Vedānta philosophy, all the *dramatis personæ* therein being allegorical representation of knowledge, devotion etc,) was acted about 1065 A. D. in the court of Kīrtivarman, the Chandel King of Bundelkhund. A drama composed by Madana was acted in the Sanskrit College at Dhar on the occasion of a spring festival.[2453] The Pārijātamañjurī of Vijayaśrī was acted for the first time in the Sanskrit College in Dhar at the spring festival.[2454] Rājarāja I also instituted the representation on the stage of a drama called Rājarājeśwarī nātaka.[2455] An inscription in the nineth year of Rājarāja I records a gift of land by the assembly of Śāttanūr to Kumaran Śikaṇṭan, a professional actor, for staging the seven acts of Āryakūtten. For the maintenance of a nānāvidha-nātaśālā provision is made in an inscription of Rājakeśarī Kulottunga. The performance of the Agamārgam at at Tiruvoṛṛiyūr was attended by Rājarāja III.[2456] According to Kautilya"[2457] "If a man who has not co-operated in preparing for a public play or spectacle is found hearing or witnessing it hiding.............. he shall be compelled to pay double the value of the aid due from him." That such shows were regularly held follow quite clearly from

---

[2452] Ibid., p. 165.

[2453] Luard and Lele—The Paramāras of Dhar and Malwa.

[2454] Edited by E. Hultzsch, p. 3. (verse 5).

[2455] South Indian Inscriptions, Vol. II. p. 306.

[2456] Annual Rep. Arch. Surv. of India, 1921-22, p. 117.

[2457] Arthaśāstra (R. Śyāmaśāstrī's Eng. Trans.), p. 220.

innumerable references to professional actors in Sanskrit and Pali literature.[2458]

§ 10. Travel as an agency of education.

Travel in foreign lands is also a fruitful source of education. Education in politics through taking part in administrative institutions even as audience is highly recommended in modern times. In this connection we may well quote the following lines from Śukranītisāra[2459] "One should without loth undertake travels, attend royal courts, study śāstras, see prostitutes and make friends with the learned. Through travel the numerous religious (customs), materials, animals, races of men, hills etc., come within the cognisance of man. The man who habitually attends courts and assemblies acquires knowledge as to the character of king and royal officers, the nature of justice and injustice, the men who falsely quarrel and the men who have real grounds of conflict and the procedure of cases and suits both customary and legal." In another passage, Śukrāchārya suggests the practice of undertaking distant tours. Says he: "In foreign lands, the following six are useful to men—wife without child, good conveyance, the bearer, the guard, the knowledge that can be of use in relieving other's miseries and an active servant."[2460] It appears from the Kābyamīmāṃsā[2461] that ancient poets used to travel to foreign countries and islands and utilised their experience in those countries in their works.

Indeed it was quite usual for students to go far from their homes in search of higher education. Even after finishing their education at a distant University town like Taxila or Benares the students of those days undertook an expensive travel to give a practical turn to their theoretical

---

2458 Milindā-Pañha, I. 191; Jātaka II. 12; Jātaka VI. 191; Saddharma-Puṇḍarīka, Ch. III; Manu III. 155, 158; Manu IV. 214; Manu XII. 45; Baudhāyana I. 5. 24; Vaśiṣṭha III. 3; Viṣṇu LI. 14.

2459 Ch. III. lines 260-67.

2460 Ibid., lines 595-97.

2461 Kiñchana mahākabayopi deśadwīpāntarakathāpuruṣādidarśhanena tatratyāṃ byabahṛtiṃ nibadhnantisma—p. 12 (Gaekwad Oriental Series).

Purbe hi bidwāṃsaḥ sahasraśākhaṃ saṃgam cha vedamabagāhya śāstrāṇi chābabuddhaya deśāntarāṇi dwīpāntarāṇi cha paribhramya.—p. 78 (G. O. S.).

studies at the colleges and qualify themselves for the life in the world by broadening the range of their experiences and deepening their insight into human affairs by a first hand study of the diverse manners and customs prevailing in the different parts of the country, as also to get inured to hardships. Thus a prince of Magadha after mastering all the arts at Taxila wandered through towns, villages and all the land to acquire all practical usages and understand country observances.[2462] We have mention of another student, Śvetaketu, of Taxila who similarly "wandered, learning all practical arts."[2463] There is mentioned another prince of Magadha who, being trained in all the sciences at Taxila "left that place with the intention of learning the practical uses of arts and local observances."[2464] We read again of two sons of merchants and a tailor's son travelling together to learn the customs of the country folk after finishing their education at Taxila.[2465] There is a reference to a student from Benares undertaking a travel after his education at Taxila.[2466] There is a similar reference to the Pāṇḍu brothers, who after receiving instruction at Taxila in arts "travelled about with the idea of mastering local customs."[2467] In the Yoga Vāśiṣṭha[2468] we read that after his return from his guru, Rāma went on his travels to the places of pilgrimage, the holy rivers and the hermitages of sages and the places of resort famous for their beauty or interest. It may be noted in this connection that those who planned the system of visiting places of pilgrimage selected spots, not near each other, but as far apart as the confines of India, and with a vast variety of social conditions and environments and located them on high eminences or fast by running brooks, whose blue water cut a stretch of green grass or brown gravel. Thus the eye could gaze with relief on the expanse below or the scenery around, suggesting thoughts widening the mental horizon and reaching outward to the

---

2462 Jātaka I. 238.

2463 Jātaka III. 235.

2464 Jātaka V. 247.

2465 Jātaka IV. 38.

2466 Jātaka IV. 200.

2467 Jātaka V. 426.

2468 Tīrtha puṇyāśramaśreṇīḥ draṣṭumutkaṇṭhitam manaḥ and Tīrthāni devasadmāni vanyānyāyatanāne cha.—Vairāgya Prakaraṇa.

infinite. The narrow conservatism and petty provincial prejudices attached to local and rural life, were confronted and corrected by commerce with the minds of men of piety and learning in the various regions of the Indian sub-continent.

§ 11. CLUBS AS AN AGENCY OF EDUCATION.

It is well known that there were in Ancient India institutions of various designations (sabhā, samāja or samajja and goṣṭhi) resembling very much the modern clubs.[2469] They were also possible sources of popular enlightenment, for, we are told by Vātsyāyana that "there discussions on literature, music, dancing and other arts should take place."[2470] Vātsyāyana further says: "A poor man having no other possession than his bare body....................and being well-skilled in in the kalās should lecture on these arts and make himself agreeable in a goṣṭhi."[2471] Vātsyāyana also advises the villagers to start such clubs for their own benefit[2472] and continues: "One engaged in addressing an audience in a goṣṭhi (i. e., club) should not solely speak in Sanskrit or in the vernacular. Both these languages should be adopted one now, then the other as the occasion may require. Then only he would be popular."[2473]

In Harṣacharita[2474] we find a reference to a *Logic society*. Bāṇa returning among his relatives from Harṣa's court asks of them: "Is there the old logic society, regardless of all other occupations?". In his Kādambarī Bāṇa[2475] speaks of king Śūdraka as "a founder of *literary societies*."

We know that King Pasenadi of Kośala had a picture-gallery (chittāgāra). A picture-gallery is also mentioned in Harṣa's Ratnābalī. From Kālidāsa's Mālavikāgnimitra, Act I, we find that King Agnimitra of Vidisā had his hall of painting.[2476] Act I. of Bhababhūti's

---

[2469] R. C. Mazumdar—Corporate Life in Ancient India, second edition, pp. 392-94.

[2470] Kāmasūtra, Bk. I. Ch. IV. śl. 35.

[2471] Ibid., śl. 44.

[2472] Ibid., śl. 49.

[2473] Ibid., śl. 50.

[2474] Eng. Trans., by Cowell and Thomas, p. 71.

[2475] C. M. Ridding's Eng. Trans., p. 4.

[2476] Kale's Eng. Trans., p. 3.

Uttara-Rāma-charita[2477] also refers to a picture-gallery in the corridor of Rāma's palace where by royal order scenes from king Rāma's career were painted and shown to Sītā. The Karpūramañjurī of Rājaśekhara[2478] also refers to picture-galleries. We also find a reference to a library and librarians (Saraswatī-bhāṇḍārattār) in a Brahmin village called Vikrama-Pāṇḍya-chaturvedi-mangalam.[2479] But we do not know whether or how far they were used as vehicles of education.

§ 12. The professional story-tellers etc.

The Sūta, the Māgadha, the legendary bard, the Paurāṇikas,[2480] the Bhāts[2481] of Bengal and Rājasthān, the Chāraṇas of Rājasthān[2482] and the professional story-tellers[2483] were also great sources of popular instruction. The caste of Pāṇans[2484] were also travelling minstrels who used to recite songs and lays of fighting and adventure before kings and nobles on festive and other occasions. Another agency of religious instruction was the Vairāgi[2485] of whom Abu Zaid collected an account as early as 916 A. D. They were travelling poets and reciters of old lays, the repositories of ancient folk-lore and tradition and the custodians of the ballad literature of India.

In these arrangements for the spread of knowledge among the masses the aim was to bring to the door of the humblest, though illiterate, the highest products of the human mind and heart, rather than to enable him to read, write or cipher for himself. The

---

2477 Belvalkar's Eng. Trans., pp. 18-29. 2478 Konow and Lanman's edition, p. 242.

2479 Madras Ep. Rep. for 1913-14, No. 277 of 1913.

2480 Vāyu Purāṇa I. 31-32. Padma Purāṇa V. 1. 27-28 ; Rāmāyaṇa, Ayodhyākāṇḍa VI. 6 ; Gārgi Saṃhitā, Golakakāṇḍa XII. 36 ; Rājataraṅgiṇī I. 166 (Stein, Vol. I. p. 29); Kautilya's Arthaśāstra, R. Śyāmaśāstrī's Eng. Trans., p. 476 ; *also* Ibid., p. 308.

2481 Tod—Annals of Rājasthān. 2482 Ibid.

2483 Vātsyāyana's Kāmasūtra, Bk. I. Ch. V. śl. 38 ; Ibid., Bk. VI. Ch. I. śls. 9 and 22. Kautilya's Arthaśāstra, R. Śyāmaśāstrī's Eng. Trans., pp. 277, 308 and 476; Mahābhārata. Birātaparba, 72nd adhyāya ; Kathāsaritsāgara, Penzer's edition, Vol. I. pp. 106, 120.

2484 Professor S. V. Venkateśwara—Indian Culture Through the Ages, Vol. I. p. 282.

2485 Ibid.

recitation of sacred texts and popular feasts and displays like ustava, vihāra, vimāna and agniskandha are as old as Aśoka's inscriptions as agencies of culture; while in later times the system of symbolism, of folk-songs and dances, festive gatherings at temples, processions and popular lectures on temple platforms served to enlighten the the masses and women at the circumference of culture and turn their thoughts to the larger ideas of country, humanity and religion. Indeed culture, not literacy, was the highest aim of education in Ancient India. As the Nālaḍiyār puts it, 'the uncultured may read, but are uneducated; men of culture unlettered are men well-read.'[2486] It is true that there were similar institutions in ancient and mediæval times among peoples elsewhere, and that many of them partook likewise of a sacred character; but India stands almost alone in the emphasis on śruti, learning by the ear, even long after writing came into common use.

[2486] Ibid., p. 286.

CHAPTER XIII.

EDUCATION AND THE STATE IN ANCIENT INDIA.

From the Chāndogya[2487] and the Bṛhadāraṇyaka[2488] Upaniṣads we learn that the kings used to help learned Brahmins for the cultivation of knowledge even in those early times. In the Mahābhārata[2489] Bhīṣma says to king Yudhiṣṭhir: "You should please those who are receiving education according to Vedic rules with gifts of dress etc., and by employing servants for the construction of houses for them." Yājñabālkya Saṃhitā[2490] says: "Having made suitable houses in his city the king should make the brāhmaṇas settle there. And having granted them stipends for learning the three Vedas, he should say—'Follow your own vocation'". Such settlements of the learned in parts of towns were known as Brahmapurī. There were seven such at Belgame, one of which had thirty-eight brāhmaṇa familes cultivating linguistics and letters.[2491] Similarly the village of Niranthanin is styled brahmapurī in an inscription of Madhurāntaka Potappi Chola Nallamśittaraśa who restores a grant made by Vatsarāja.[2492] Kalhaṇa[2493] refers to king Jaysiṃha of Kashmere as building houses for men of learning which "raise their terraces to such a height that the seven ṛṣiṣ (the great Bear) come to see them as they are towering above their heads."

Kautilya says: [2494] "brāhmaṇas shall be provided with forests for religious learning, such forests being rendered safe from the dangers from animate and inanimate objects and being named after the tribal names (gotra) of the brāhmaṇas resident therein". Again "those learned in the Vedas shall be granted Brahmadeya lands yielding sufficient produce and exempted from taxes and fines".[2495] Such a grant of land to

---

[2487] 5. 11. 5.

[2488] 2. 1. 1; 3. 1. 1.

[2489] Anuśāsanaparba, 60th adhyāya.

[2490] II. 188.

[2491] Ep. Carn. VII. (Sk.), 123.

[2492] Madras Ep. Rep. for 1919, No. 570 (Cndappa).

[2493] Stein—The Chronicles of Kashmere, Vol. II. p. 185.

[2494] Arthaśāstra (R. Śyāmaśāstrī's Eng. Trans.), p. 55.

[2495] Ibid., p. 52.

learned men was known as Bhattavṛtti referred to in many South Indian inscriptions.[2496] The Omgaḍu grant of Vijaya Skandavarman refers to such a bhattavṛtti while Rājarāja I (Chola) made such grants free from taxes along with Vaidyavṛttis (grants to ancestral physicians). Such grants were made not only for study but also for teaching as we learn from an inscription of Govinda IV (Rāṣtrakūta).[2497] An inscription of Āditya II (Chola) mentions to *ma* of land sold as bhattavṛtti for expounding the Prabhākaram at Kumbakonam.[2498] A Nellore inscription clearly states that bhattabṛttimānyam was for work connected with culture.[2499] Sometimes the donee is described Mahāmahopādhyāya, as in the case of Godhala Deva who was the exponent of the popular systems of Mīmāṃsā, Vyākarana, Tarka and Vedānta in the reign of Vigrahapāla of Bengal.[2500]

Endowments to learned brāhmaṇas took the form of agrahāra or village settlement. The agrahāra of Sthānā Kuṇḍūr (Tālaguṇḍa) was settled with thirty-two Brahmin families who taught the people.[2501] The Chicakole Plates of Devendravarman record the grant of a village as an agrahāra to six brāhmaṇas for supporting ascetic teachers and their pupils. The Stone inscription of Kūppatūr also refers to an agrahāra where the Mahājanas are learning, teaching, sacrificing, etc.[2502] Queen Sūryamatī of Kashmere similarly bestowed at the glorious temple of Vijayeśwara one hundred and eight agrahāras on learned Brahmins.[2503] Paramārdin Chandel of Bundelkhund gave many villages to numerous learned Brahmins.[2504] King Jayasiṃha of Kashmere made scholars and their descendants owners, as long as the planets, the Sun and the Moon should last, of villages possessing an abundance of unimpaired fields.[2505] Karṇa, king of Chedi founded the town of Karṇavatī and gave it to

---

2496 Ep. Ind., XV. 250 ; S. I. Ins., I. p. 91. 2497 Ep. Ind., XIII. 327.

2498 S. I. Ins., III. No. 200 ; and No. 223 of 1911.

2499 Nellore No. 615. 2500 Ep. Ind., XV. 301.

2501 Ep. Carn., VII. 178 (Sk).

2502 Ep. Ind., III. pp. 130-34 ; Madras Ep. Rep. for 1913. No. 144 of Saka 1069 ; Ep. Carn., VIII. (SB), 249.

2503 Stein—The Chronicles of Kashmere, Vol. I. p. 282 ; *compare* Rājatar., VII. 181.

2504 Ep. Ind., IV. p. 170.

2505 Stein—The Chronicles Kashmere, Vol. II. p. 185.

Brahmins learned in the Vedas.[2506] From Raghuvaṃśam[2507] we learn that King Kuśa gave over the whole of Kuśavatī to Brahmins versed in the Vedas.

In some cases the king used to grant stipends and liberal allowances to students and learned men. In the Mahābhārata[2508] Viṣma says to King Yūdhiṣthir: "It is highly obligatory (on you) to grant stipends to Brahmins who are well-versed in the śāstras and follow the Vedānta (Vedānta-niṣṭha)." "All kinds of teachers and learned men" says Kautilya[2509] "shall have honorariums ranging from 500 to 1000 paṇas according to their merit". According to Manu[2510] the king shall always provide for a śrotriya. "Informed of his Vedic knowledge and holy rituals, the king" says he "shall provide for his proper means of subsistence; and like a son of his own loins, he shall protect him (śrotriya) from thieves etc."[2511] Again "Let the king make gifts of all kinds of gems as well as of fees for religious sacrifices to these brahmins and to those who are well-versed in the Vedas".[2512] According to Kāmandaka[2513] the king should give money to learned Brahmins. According to Śukrāchārya "pundits, females and creepers do not flourish without resting grounds."[2514] Again, the king should have three characters—that of the Autumn Moon to the learned, that of the Summer Sun to the enemies and that of the Spring Sun to his subjects.[2515] Indeed Śukrāchārya while mentioning the ordinary political and administrative functions of the State does not forget the educational activities of what has been called the *Cultur Staat*. Says he: "The king should always take such steps as may advance the arts and sciences of the country".[2516] "He should train up the officers appointed with salaries (bhūtipoṣitām) in the cultivation of all the arts and having seen that they have finished their studies, should appoint them in their

2506 Ep. Ind., II. p. 3.

2507 Canto XVI. 25.

2508 Anuśāsanaparba, 69th adhyāya.

2509 Arthaśāstra (R. Śyāmaśāstrī's Eng. Trans.), p. 308.

2510 VIII. 395.

2511 Manu VI. 135.

2512 Ibid., XI. 4.

2513 Nītisāra, 1st sarga, śloka 18.

2514 Śukranīti (Eng. Trans., by Prof. Benoy K. Sarkar), Ch. I. line 767.

2515 Ibid., Ch. II. lines 566-67.

2516 Ibid., Ch. I. line 741.

special fields. He should also honour those every year who are very high in arts and sciences."[2517] These lines imply that the king should maintain students with scholarships for the study of the various branches of learning and when they have been sufficiently educated, should appoint them to their proper posts in Government service. Śukrāchārya further says: "Those who are proficient in revealed literature (Vedas) and the smṛtis, those who are well-versed in the Purāṇas, those who know the śāstras (other than the śrutis, smṛtis and the Purāṇas), the astrologers, those who are masters of medical science, those who are versed in religious rites and ceremonies........................ these classes of men the king should worship and maintain by stipends (bhūtyā), gifts (dāna) and honour (māna). Otherwise the king is disparaged and earns an ill-name."[2518] These lines thus suggest a sort of literary pensions granted to qualified men to enable them to devote their whole time and energy to the pursuit of their special investigations. In the Jātakas we accordingly find a class of students who paid the teacher's fee from the scholarships awarded to them by the states to which they belonged.[2519] Generally such students were sent as companions of the princes of their respective countries who were deputed to Taxila for education. We read of the sons of royal chaplains of the courts of Benares and Rājgaha accompanying their respective princes to Taxila for their education.[2520] Cases, however, are not wanting of students being sent on their own account for higher studies to Taxila at the expense of the state. Thus we read of a Brahmin boy of Benares being sent by his king at *royal* expense to Taxila for the purpose of specialising in the science of archery.[2521]

Sometimes the king helped the students in giving dakṣiṇā to their teachers on the completion of their studies. On one occasion[2522] the conventional sum of fourteen crores of rupees is said to have been paid by Kautsa to Varatantu in return for the fourteen lores he had learnt. In this story the teacher first asked for nothing and gave the

---

2517 Ibid., Ch. I. lines 737-40.

2518 Ibid., Ch. II. lines 247-51.

2519 Jātaka V. 263.

2520 Jātaka III. 238 and V. 247.

2521 Jātaka V. 127.

2522 Raghuvaṃśam, Canto V. ślokas 1-35.

pupil permission to go home saying that he was pleased with his devotion; but the latter pressed him rather in an unmannerly tone to ask for something and hence angrily the teacher asked him to produce that enormous sum. But how could the poor Brahmin pupil get it? It is described that he got it from king Raghu. In the Mahābhārata[2523] we are told how Utanka, pupil of Veda paid his guru-dakṣiṇā by begging the earring of the queen of the king.

The king we are told even at the point of death must not take any revenue from a learned (śrotriya) brāhmaṇa; nor must he suffer a śrotriya, living in his territory to be oppressed with hunger.[2524] The kingdom of a king wherein a śrotriya is oppressed with hunger, is soon consumed by that hunger.[2525] Kautilya[2526] says: "He (the king) shall avoid the property of Brahmins learned in the Vedas. He may purchase this too, by offering price to the owners." Again "learned men, orators, charitable and brave persons should be favoured (by the king) with gifts of land and money and with remission of taxes."[2527] The reasons for this exemption from taxation are thus given: "The religious rites which a śrotriya, protected by the king, performs every day, tend to increase the longevity, riches and territories of the king."[2528] Moreover, "whatever Vedic studies do his subjects do..................through his properly protecting them, he enjoyeth a sixth part of the merit thereof."[2529] "It is said" says Vaśiṣtha[2530] "that the brāhmaṇa first made the Veda known. The brāhmaṇa saves one from misfortune. Therefore a brāhmaṇa shall not be made to pay taxes." In Avijñāna-śakuntalam[2531] king Duṣmanta says that he receives from the brāhmaṇas a sixth of their penance as tax. In Raghuvaṃśam[2532] king Atithi is similarly said to receive one-sixth of the religious merit as tax from the hermit-teachers living in his kingdom. The meaning is that the hermit-teachers had

---

2523 Ādiparba, 3rd adhyāya, Pouṣyaparbādhyāya.

2524 Manu VII. 133.

2525 Manu VII. 134.

2526 Arthaśāstra (R. Śyāmaśāstrī's Eng. Trans.), p. 302.

2527 Ibid., p. 492.

2528 Manu VII. 136.

2529 Manu VIII. 305.

2530 Vaśiṣṭha Saṃhitā, Ch. I.

2531 Act V. 14; Act II. 13 and 14.

2532 Canto XVII. 65.

to pay no tax while they kept themselves engaged in educational duties.

A graphic description of *royal solicitude for the welfare of the hermit-teachers and their seats of learning* is preserved in the Raghuvaṃśam.[2533] When Kautsa after finishing his education at Varatantu's hermitage approached Raghu for money to pay his preceptor, Raghu addressed Kautsa as follows :—

"Oh thou keen-witted one ! is thy preceptor—who is the first among sages, proficient in adapting the hymns, from whom all knowledge has been acquired by thee just as all activity is gained by the world from the Sun—all hale.

"I hope the three-fold penance of the great sage which has long been hoarded up (by him) by the exercise of his body, his speech as well as by his mind and which disturbs the firmness of Indra, does not suffer waste by any kind of impediment.

"I hope there is no calamity such as a hurricane etc., in regard to the trees of the hermitage which are the beguilers of your fatigue and which have been reared up just like your children with all kinds of efforts headed by the construction of basins.

"I hope the young ones of the deer are alright—those young ones whose wish to browse the kuśa grass was not interrupted through fondness although it was a requisite for ceremonies and whose umblical cords dropped down on the laps of the sages.

"I hope the waters of your landing-place are in favourable condition—those waters in which your prescribed ablutions are performed, from which handfuls of funeral offerings are given to the manes of your ancestors and whose sandy banks are marked with the sixth part of the gleaned corn.

"I hope the crops of nibāra and other corns which are the sylvan means of the sustenance of your corporeal frames and from which portions are allotted to the guests coming at times are not attacked by domestic cattle whose natural food is husk and straw.

[2533] Canto V. 1-31.

"Have you been permitted by the great sage, after his having thoroughly educated you and being himself satisfied, to adopt the life of a householder? For, it is now time for you to enter on the second stage of life which is capable of benefitting all.

"My mind is not satisfied with the arrival of a respectable personage like thee; it is eager to be engaged in some task assigned (by thee). Is it at the desire of thy preceptor or through thy personal wish that thou hast come from the forest to do me honour?"[2534]

In the Mahābhārata we are told: "It is the bounden duty of kings to respect (literally worship) śrotriya brāhmaṇas".[2535] "If a Veda-vid snātaka brāhmaṇa without employment resorts to the profession of a thief, the king should maintain him after suggesting some occupation to him".[2536] "If a brāhmaṇa desires to leave a kingdom where he cannot get a living, the king should grant a *stipend* for the brāhmaṇa and his wife. If the brāhmaṇa still persists in leaving the kingdom, the king should approach him and say: '*Sir, if you leave my kingdom, with whose support shall my subjects live*?"[2537] In the Ādiparba of the Mahābhārata[2538] we are told how a teacher Śukra by name, angry at the insult offered to his daughter Devayoni by Śarmiṣṭhā, the daughter of king Bṛṣaparbā, threatened to leave the latter's kingdom whereupon the king appeased the wrath of the teacher by agreeing to ask his own daughter Śarmiṣṭhā to act as a maid-servant to the teacher's daughter Devayonī. The respect paid to learned Brahmins and to hermit-teachers in particular is illustrated in Daśaratha's visit to the hermitage of Vaśiṣṭha,[2539] Bharata's visit to to that of Varadwāja,[2540] Śatrughna's visit to that of Vālmīki,[2541] Duṣmanta's visit to that of Kaṇva,[2542] Rāma's visit to that of Vālmīki[2543] and Puṣpabhūti's visit to that of Vairava.[2544]

[2534] Raghuvaṃśam, Canto V. 4-11.

[2535] Anuśāsanaparba, 33rd adhyāya.

[2536] Śāntiparba, 76th adhyāya.

[2537] Śāntiparba, 89th adhyāya.

[2538] 78th, 79th and 80th adhyāyas.

[2539] Rāmāyaṇa, Uttarakāṇḍa, 51st sarga.

[2540] Rāmāyaṇa, Ayodhyākāṇḍa, 90th sarga.

[2541] Rāmāyaṇa, Uttarakāṇḍa, 65th sarga.

[2542] Avijñāna-śakuntalam, Act I.

[2543] Uttara-Rāma-charita.

[2544] Harṣacharita, III.

That only *learned* men were to be patronised by the State is clearly laid down. Thus we are told that " the king should punish with life, the village which harbours thieves by giving alms to the twice-born who do not perform religious rites and study the Vedas. The kingdom where the ignorant partake of the food which should be taken by the learned, courts drought or a great calamity appears there. There the god of rain pours down showers where the king adores these—the brāhmaṇas learned in the Vedas and well-versed in the scriptures ".[2545] Vaśiṣtha Saṃhitā[2546] speaks in the same strain: " The king shall punish the village where brāhmaṇas failing to observe their sacred duties and study the Veda, live by begging, for, it feeds the thieves ". In the Mahābhārata[2547] Bhiṣma says to Yudhiṣṭhir that the king should take taxes from those brāhmaṇas who are not śrotriyas and employ them without pay.

Royal patronage of learning in India is as old as the Ṛgveda. Numberless hymns of the Ṛgveda show the grateful dānastutis of ṛṣis in praise of their patrons. The Ikṣākus of Kośala, the Janakas of Videha and the kings of Benares were renowned patrons of learning. Indeed the patronage of learning by Janaka was on such a scale that it made his contemporary Ajātaśatru, king of Kāśī acknowledge in disappointment that he could hardly find any available learned man in the country, whom he could patronise, for all the learned men were running to the court of Janaka and settling there.[2548] His only enjoyment was not the pleasures of the usual royal hunt or chase but the company of the learned as the Emperor Aśoka in later times replaced the royal pleasure-tours by religious tours and pilgrimages. Indeed in the age of the Upaniṣads the Aristorcracies of Brain and Bullion lived in happy harmony and mutual esteem. Brahmins, proud of their intellectual lineage and attainments were not slow to receive instruction wherever they found. At the same time a large part in the intellectual life of the country was played by kings who threw themselves into it with an enthusiasm that testifies to their genuine

[2545] Atri Saṃhitā, Ch. I. śls. 22-24.

[2546] Ch. III.

[2547] Śāntiparba, 76th adhyāya.

[2548] Bṛhad. Up., II. 1. 1.

democratic feeling, their sense of universal brotherhood in the Kingdom of Spirit, of which all were entitled to be free citizens. Some of the kings were themselves leaders of thought and drew even brāhmaṇa students for instruction in the special truths of which they were the repositories. Such were Janaka of Videha, Ajātaśatru of Kāśī, Pravahana Jaibali of the Pāñchāla country and Aśwapati Kaikeya. In the Mahābhārata[2549] Arjuna told King Birāta that Yudhiṣṭhir used to maintain 88,000 snātakas. In the Banaparba[2550] Draupadī says to Satyabhāmā: " 88,000 snātaka householders were daily maintained. Dainty golden (?) dishes were daily kept ready for another batch of 10,000 snātakas. I used to receive them all by offering food, drink and clothing ". From the Jātakas we have already seen that state scholarships were awarded to some students for studies abroad.

Aśoka furthered the cause of education by establishing innumerable monasteries and nunneries throughout his Empire. He built 500 monasteries in Kashmere alone, of which 100 were seen by Hiuen Tsang[2551] and 300 by Ou-kong.[2552] Even in far off Nepal he founded such institutions specially in the city of Deo-pātan built by him after his son-in-law Devapāla who with his daughter Chārumatī chose to settle there.[2553] The existence of these institutions must be greatly responsible for the considerable extent of literacy in the country where the masses could read the edicts of Aśoka written in their own dialects and scripts. Menander the Great was an ardent patron of Buddhist learning. From the Milindā-Pañha[2554] we learn that the state encouraged very liberally the craftsmen who introduced highly trained apprentices to the king. The name of Kaniṣka is associated with three eminent Buddhist writers viz., Nāgārjuna, Aśvaghoṣa and Vasumitra. Charaka, the most celebrated author of the Indian system of medicine is reputed to have been the court-physician of Kaniṣka. His son Huviṣka also established a monastery at Mathurā. Hāla, the 17th Andhra king was

---

2549 Birātaparba, 70th adhyāya. 2550 231st adhyāya.

2551 Beal—Life of Hiuen Tsang, p. 61.

2552 Levi and Chavannes—L' Itineraire d' Oukong, Journal Asiatique, 1895, VI. pp. 341 *sqq.*

2553 Percival Landon—Nepal, Vol. I. 2554 VI. 9 and 10.

a patron of Prākṛt literature. Himself a learned man, Samudragupta was fond of the company of learned men and his name is famous as the patron of Vasubandhu the celebrated Buddhist scholar and Harisena the poet-laureate, Chandrapupta II Vikramāditya is probably the original of Rājā Vikrama of Ujjain, famous in Indian legends as the king whose court was adorned by the "nine gems" headed by Kālidāsa. Āryabhaṭṭa the mathematican, Varāhamihir, the astronomer and Brahmagupta—all received their due encouragement at the hands of Gupta emperors.

Harṣa was one of the best patrons of men of letters. As Bāṇa[2555] puts it, 'his learning at once suggests helping the learned'. He used to call forth poetical compositions by the literary men of his court who at one time presented their sovereign with the Jātakas collected into the work called Jātaka-mālā. Among examples of his patronage we know of Bāṇa. Another literary protege of Harṣa was Haridatta who is mentioned in an inscription[2556] as raised to eminence by Harṣa. Hiuen Tsang was also treated by Harṣa "with almost royal honours" "Śilādityarāja reverencing him more than ever bestowed on the Master of the Law 10,000 pieces of gold, 30,000 pieces of silver, 100 garments of superior cotton, whilst the princes of the eighteen kingdoms each presented him with rare jewels. But all these the Master of the Law declined to accept. The king then ordered his attendant ministers to place a howdah upon a great elephant, with the request that the Master of the Law would mount thereon, whilst he directed the great ministers of the state to accompany him".[2557] To Jaysena 'who had become the admiration of the age by the range of his knowledge including subjects like Hetuvidyā, Śabdavidyā, Yogaśāstra, the four Vedas, Astronomy, Geography, Medicine, Magic and Arithmetic', Harṣa made the offer of the revenue of eighty large towns in Orissa which, however, the scholar refused to accept.[2558] We may well recall in this connection the established maxim of Harṣa's policy that a fourth of the revenue from the crown lands should be spent on rewarding high intellectual eminence and another fourth on gifts to the various sects.[2559]

2555 Harṣacharita—Cowell and Thomas, p. 62.

2556 Ep. Ind., I. 180.

2557 Beal—Life of Hiuen Tsang, p. 180.

2558 Ibid., pp. 153-54.

2559 Watters—Yuan Chwang, Vol. I. p. 176.

The example of Harṣa Śīlāditya was not without its influence on some of his subordinate kings. Kumāra, king of Assam showed a commendable anxiety to profit by the learned company of Hiuen Tsang.[2560] At the time of parting with the Chinese pilgrim Kumāra-rāja addressed Hiuen Tsang thus: "If the master is able to dwell in my dominion and receive my religious offerings, I will undertake to found one hundred monasteries on the Master's behalf".[2561] When the pilgrim took his leave "the king with a large body of attendants accompanied him for several ten *lis* and then returned. On their final separation none of them could restrain their tears and sad lamentations".[2562] "Three days after the separation the king (S'īlāditya) in company with Kumāra-rāja and Dhruvadatta-rāja (of Valabhi)..............again came to accompany him for a time and to take final leave. Then he commissioned official guides to accompany the pilgrim and the escort of Udhita-rāja already attached to him with letters to the end that the princes of the countries through which the pilgrim passed might provide modes of conveyance".[2563] Thus the kings of Jalandhara, Kashmere and Kapisa honoured the pilgrim and arranged for his comforts.[2564] The king of Kashmere himself went to the river-side to pay his respects and escort him. He then sent the heir-apparent to the throne in advance to direct the people of the capital and the body of priests to prepare flags and banners and with them to march from the city to escort.[2565] A little before Harṣa, "Purṇavarmarāja, lord of Magadha, had great respect for learned men, and honoured those distinguished as sages: Learning this man's renown (Jayasena of encyclopædic knowledge) he was much pleassd and sent messengers to invite him to come to his court and nominated him "Kwo-sse" (Master of the kingdom) and assigned for his support the revenue of twenty large towns. But the Master of S'āstras (Jayasena) declined to receive them".[2566]

The Chandel king of Bundelkhund Kīrtivarman by name was the patron of Kṛṣṇamiśra whose allegorical play, the "Prabodha-chandrodaya"

2560 Beal—Life of Hiuen Tsang, pp. 170-71.

2561 Ibid., pp. 187-88.

2562 Ibid., p. 189.

2563 Ibid., pp. 189-90.

2564 Ibid., pp. 190-93.

2565 Ibid., pp. 192-93.

2566 Ibid., pp. 153-54.

was staged at his court under his patronage. The Pāla rulers similarly patronised men of learning like Atisa and Biradeva. The first Pāla king Gopāla founded the monastic University of Odantipura.[2567] Another Pāla ruler Dharmapāla founded the famous monastic University of Vikramaśilā which included several colleges.[2568] Another Pāla king Rāmapāla was the patron of Sandhyākara Nandī, the author of Rāma-charita. The Chauhan prince Prithwirāja was the patron of Chānd Bardāi, the author of the great epic 'Chānd Raisā'. The Chalukya ruler of Kalyani Vikramāñaka was the patron of the famous poet Bilhaṇa and the celebrated jurist Vijñāneśwara, author of the Mitākṣarā, the leading authority on Hindu law outside Bengal. King Yaśovarman of Kanauj was the patron of Bhababhūti, the sweet nightingale of Sanskrit literature and of Vākpati, the author of a Prakrit poem of unusual merit, called Gauḍavaho or the 'Slaying of the king of Gauḍa'. About Jayāpīḍa's patronage of learning we read in Kalhaṇa's Rājataraṅgiṇī :[2569] "By him learning which had hidden itself far away, was made to appear (again) in this land which was the original home, just as the Vitastā by Kāśyapa................ The king by bringing from abroad (competent) expositors, restored in his own country the (study of Mahāvāṣya), which had been interrupted.............. The pureminded (king) did not allow any king to compete with him but was proud of being able himself to compete with the learned................ As the king was attached to the learned, the princes who came to serve him and desired to reach his presence, frequented the houses of the scholars. The king searched for and collected all scholars to such an extent that in the lands of other kings there was a dearth of learned men. He attached to himself and elevated on account of his learning, Thakkiya............... The learned Bhaṭṭa Udbhata was this kings' sabhāpati.................. He took the poet Dāmodaragupta, the author of the (poem) Kuttinīmata, as his chief councillor as Bali (had taken) Kavi. Manoratha, Śaṅkhadanta, Cataka and Saṃdhimat were his poets and Vāmana and others his

2567 V. A. Smith—Early History of India, third edition, p. 397.

2568 S. C. Das in the J. B. T. S., Part I. p. 11.

2569 IV. 486-97 ; Stein, The Chronicles of Kashmere, Vol. I. pp. 165-66.

ministers." In the reign of Avantivarman (of Kashmere) "the minister Sūra by honouring learned men, with a seat in the (king's) sabhā, caused learning whose flow had been interrupted, to descend (again) upon this land. The scholars who were granted great fortunes and high honours, proceeded to the sabhā in vehicles (litters) worthy of kings. Muktakarṇa, Śivaswāmin, the poet Ānandavardhana (author of the Dhvanyāloka, a rhetorical treatise and the poem Deviśataka) and Ratnākara (author of the great kāvya called Harivijaya) obtained fame during the reign of Avantivarman. In the assembly-hall of the minister Sūra, the bard Kṛtamandāra recited always the following Ārya (verse) in order to remind (his master) of his resolve: This is the time for granting benefits, while fortune, fickle by nature, is present. Why should there be again time for benefits, while misfortune is always imminent?"[2570] "He (King Kalasa) and King Bhoja, both (themselves) learned and friends of poets were at that time equally renowned for their liberality."[2571] "The king (Harṣa of Kashmere) who was the crest jewel of the learned, adorned men of learning with jewels and bestowed upon them the privileges of using litters, horses, parasols etc."[2572] Harṣa was the patron of Kanaka, the learned musician who was Kalhaṇa's own uncle.[2573] Kalhaṇa's graphic description of king Jayasiṃha's patronage of learning is preserved in the following verses: "In the black darkness of ignorance, learning had shown forth at intervals, in passing lightning flahses of fortune (coming) from such clouds as Jayāpīḍa and other (royal patrons). He, however, has given permanent brilliancy to the picture of his virtue which is of wondrous variety, by bestowing wealth which last like the radiant light of a jewel. He had made scholars and their descendants owners as long as the planets, the Sun and the Moon should last, of villages possessing an abundance of unimpaired fields. The houses he has constructed for men of learning, raise their terraces to such a height that the seven ṛṣis (the great Bear) come to see them as they are towering above their heads. Safe is the journey for scholars who

---

[2570] Rājatar., V. 35-36; Stein, I. pp. 189-90. [2571] Rājatar., VII. 259; Stein, I. p. 290.

[2572] Rājatar., VII. 934; Stein, I. p. 340. *Compare* VII. 944, 948.

[2573] Rājatar., VII. 1117-18; Stein, I. p. 354.

follow him as their caravan-leader on the path on which his intuition guides, and which has been found by his knowledge. Just as Āryarāja, while lying on his bed, had chiefly found delight in (listening to) the sound arising from the flow of the water with which the Lingas were being washed, so he when about to go to sleep, dispenses with flutes, lutes and other (music) and finds his pleasure in reflecting over the talk of guileless men of learning".[2574] Bilhaṇa was made by Paramāḍi, the lord of Karṇāta, his chief paṇḍita and when he used to travel on elephants through the hill country of Karṇāta his parasol was borne aloft before the king. But when he heard that the liberal Harṣa (of Kashmere) was like a kinsman to true poets, Bilhaṇa thought even so great a splendour a deception.[2575] Kṣitirāja, lord of Lohara is praised by Bilhaṇa as a distinguished patron of poets equal in fame to Bhoja.[2576] King Muñja Paramāra of Dhar was a liberal patron of Sanskrit poets such as Padmagupta, Dhanika, Halāyudha and Dhanapāla. When Muñja died poets were in despair for the goddess of Saraswatī though not for Lakṣmī or Indrāṇī. The goddess of wealth and valour might find their favourites but the goddess of learning was now, they thought, without support.[2577] But Bhoja of Dhar falsified their misgivings. He built a college for Sanskrit studies at Dhar and patronised learned men like Rājaśekhara, the author of Karpūramañjurī and other plays whom he appointed as tutor to his son (Mahendrapāla). Dhanapāla another poet is properly associated with Bhoja and Ūvata, a native of Badnagar, wrote his commentary on Vājsenīya Saṃhitā at Ujjain during Bhoja's rule:[2578] The inscription edited at p. 209 Ep. Ind., I. tells us that "there was no trace of any quarrel under his rule for, he brought about friendship even between the goddess of learning and the goddess of wealth."[2579] King Jayasiṃha Chalukya of

---

2574 Rājatar., VIII. 2393-99 ; Stein, II. p. 185.

2575 Rājatar., VII. 949 ; Stein, I. pp. 340-41.

2576 Buhler—Vikramāñkacharita, XVIII. 47-50.

2577 Lakṣmīyārsyati govinde bīraśrībīrabeśmani
Gate muñje yaśaspuñje nirālambā saraswatī.

2578 Col. Luard and Lele—The Paramāras of Dhar and Malwa, p. 21.

2579 Paraṣparabirodhasya tasya rājye kathaiba kā
Saṃgataṃ śrīsaraswatyorapi yena prabarttitam.

Anhilwad also patronised Jain and Hindu pundits, the greatest of whom was Hemachandra, the author of the famous Sanskrit grammar Siddha Hema and of the poem Dvyāśraya. Govindachandra of Kanauj made Lakṣmīdhara, the author of Vyāvahāra-kalpataru (a treatise on law and procedure) his minister for war and peace. Jayachandra of Kanauj patronised Śrī Harṣa, the author of the epic poem Naiṣadha. Arjunavarman of Dhar patronised Madana, a dramatist and a commentator on Amaruśataka and on the works of Bhoja. Viśāladeva of Ajmere patronised Somadeva, the author of the drama Lalitavigraharāja. Lakṣmaṇasena like his father Ballālasena of Bengal was a great patron of learned men among whom Halāyudha, Umāpatidhara, Śaraṇa Govardhanāchārya, Dhoyī, Jayadeva (author of Gītagovindam) and Śrīdharadāsa were the most famous. Regarding Ānandapāla, son of Jaipāla, anecdotes are preserved showing his patronage of grammatical learning.[2580] The Chola ruler Rājarāja of Tanjore was a great patron of music and dancing. He built many colleges and appointed learned teachers in them who taught literature and śāstra to the students.[2581] Jaitugi or Jaitrapāla of Devagiri made Lakṣmīdhara, the son of the famous astronomer Vāṣkarāchārya his sabhā-paṇḍita. Pratāparudra (1316 A. D.) Kakātiya of Warangal was a famous patron of poets, in whose reign Pratāparudriya, a well-known work on poetics was written by Vaidyanātha.

There are numerous evidences to show that the kings richly endowed the seats of learning. We are told by Hiuen Tsang how "six kings in connected succession" viz., Śakrāditya, Buddhagupta, Tathāgatarāja, Bālāditya and Vajra of Magadha and a king of Central India added to the structures of the monastic University of Nālandā.[2582] At the time of Hiuen Tsang "the king of the country respects and honours the priests and has remitted the revenues of about one hundred villages for the endowment of the convent. Two hundred householders in these villages, day by day, contribute several hundred *piculs*[2583] of ordinary

---

2580 Alberuni's India—Sachau's Eng. Trans., Vol. I. p. 135 ; Vol. II. pp. 13-14.

2581 Aiyar—Historical Sketch of the Ancient Deccan, p. 251.

2582 Beal—Life of Hiuen Tsang, pp. 110-11.

2583 1 *picul* = 133⅓ lbs.

rice and several hundred *catties*[2584] in weight of butter and milk.[2585] Harṣa Śilāditya-rāja also constructed a vihāra covered with brass plates by the side of this Nālandā monastery, about a 100 feet in height.[2586] According to I-Tsing the lands in possession of this monastery contain more than two hundred villages thus showing that from the time of the visit of Hiuen Tsang the revenue of another one hundred villages was placed at the disposal of the monastery. These villages as attested by the pilgrim were bestowed by kings of many generations.[2587] Inscriptional evidences support this assertion of Chinese pilgrim. For, Mr. Hirānanda S'āstrī who was for some time in charge of the Nālandā excavations has discovered an inscription which records the grant by king Devapāla of certain villages in the Rājagṛha and Gayā districts of S'rīnagara, identified with the Patna Division, for the up-keep of the Nālandā monastery, for the comfort the vikṣus coming there from the four quarters, for medical aid, for the writing of Dharmaratnas (i. e., religious books) and for similar purposes. An undated inscription has been found at Benares which Dr. Vogel thinks to be of the eighth or nineth century in which there is a reference to a pious gift to Nālandā.[2588]

Similarly the monastic University of Vikramaśilā was furnished by its *royal* founder Dharmapāla with four establishments each consisting of twenty-seven monks belonging to the four principal sects of Buddhism. He also endowed it with rich grants, fixing regular allowances for the maintenance of the priests and the students.[2589] In the tenth century a satra (free-board hostel) was added to it by one of the sons of King Sanātana of Varendra, better known by his name of Jetāri.

As regards the management of these endowments to the monasteries I-Tsing observes: "As cultivation by the priests themselves is prohibited by the great sage they suffer their tillable lands to be

[2584] 1 *catty* = 160 lbs.

[2585] Beal—Life of Hiuen Tsang, pp. 112-13.

[2586] Ibid., p. 158-59.

[2587] Takakusu's I-Tsing, p. 65.

[2588] Arch. Surv. Rep., 1903-04, p. 219 ;

[2589] S. C. Das in the J. B. T. S., Part I. pp. 1-10.

cultivated by others freely and partake only a portion of the products. Thus they live their just life, avoiding worldly affairs and free from the faults of destroying lives by ploughing and watering fields."[2590] "The produce of the farms and gardens and the profits arising from trees and fruits are distributed annually in shares to cover the cost of clothing........................ Is it reasonable that he who gives food should wish the recipient to live without clothing?.................... Thus the Church can make use of the benefaction as it likes, without any fault, as long as it carries out the original intention of the giver. But in China an individual generally cannot get clothing from the Church-property and is thus obliged to provide for this necessity, thereby neglecting his proper function."[2591] "The secular students, however, who had no intention of joining the order "must not be fed from the permanent property of the Saṃgha, for, this is prohibited in the teaching of the Buddha; but if they have done some laborious work for the Saṃgha, they are to be fed by the monastery according to their merit. Food made for ordinary purposes presented by the giver, to be used by the students can be given to them without wrong-doing."[2592]

Similar endowments were also made by many south Indian kings. Thus, Kulottunga Chola III made the gift of a village and some gold ornaments to the god Vyākaraṇa-dāna Perumal to whom was attached the famous Grammar school of Pāṇini.[2593] In the Jagannātha-maṇḍapa by the royal grant of Virājendradeva (1062 A. D.) were established (1) a school for the study of the Vedas, S'āstras, Grammar, etc., (2) a hostel for students and (3) a hospital.[2594] A Chālukyan queen also made an endowment to the 140 mahājanas of a village belonging to her for the maintenance of the commentator on the śāstras, the reader of the Purāṇas and the teacher of the Ṛg-veda and the Yajurveda to students.[2595] The Kakātīya kings also patronised the Pāśupata teachers as also the celebrated scholar Viśeśwara-śivāchārya

[2590] Takakusu's I-Tsing, p. 62.
[2591] Ibid., pp. 193-94.
[2592] Ibid., p. 106.
[2593] No. 120 of 1912, Madras Ep. Report.
[2594] No. 182 of 1915, Madras Ep. Report.
[2595] No. 518 of 1915, Madras Ep. Report.

of the Gauḍa country who used one of the many royal gifts bestowed on him to found at Mandaran (the present Mandadam) institutions like maṭhas and schools of students of Śaiva Puritans with a staff of eight professors, three for teaching the three Vedas and five for Logic, Literature and the Āgamas.[2596]

Examples of these royal benefactions help to modify the impression that religions charities in India have always flowed in one particular channel and assumed one stereotyped form, viz., the direct furtherence of the worship of the gods, the propagation of the doctrine. The type of endowments we have just considered shows conclusively how the religious sense of the people in those ancient times was quite sound and even 'modern' in its tendencies by endowing not simply the temples of the gods but also the hardly less sacred temples of learning.

That the state in those ancieut days made some *provision for the care and education of orphans* will be evident from the Arthaśāstra of Kautilya[2597] who says: "Those orphans (asambandhinaḥ) who are to be necessarily fed by the state and are put to *study* science, palmistry (angavidyā), sorcery (māyā gata), the duties of the various orders of religious life, legardemain (jamvakavidyā) and the reading of omens and augury (antarachakra) are class-mate spies or spies learning by social intercouse (Saṃsargavidyāsatrinaḥ)." In is interesting to to find that in the Moslem period some of the (Muhammadan) rulers of the Bahamani kingdom made provision for the education of orphans, allocating funds for their support and for the learned men engaged to teach them.

The state in Ancient India seems to have made some provision for the training of spies. For, Kautilya refers to spies who are "*well-trained* in the art of putting on disguises appropriate to countries

---

2596 Madras Ep. Report, 1917, p. 122. Similarly Inscription Sk. 153 records Jayasiṃha's grant for the feeding and clothing of students in the local Siddheśwara temple. Another Inscription Sk. 94 records a grant for feeding pupils there.

2597 Arthaśāstra (R. Śyāmaśāstrī's Eng. Trans.), p. 22.

and trades"[2598] and "*taught* various languages,"[2599] "arts,"[2600] "the use of signals and cipher-writing (gūḍha-lekhya)"[2601]

The above survey certainly brings out in a very favourable light the interest in and care for the education of the people evinced by the Ancient Indian rulers. Some of them even attended the Convocation of some of the monastic Universities (S. C. Das—Indian Pundits in the Land of Snow, pp, 59-60) and conferred the diplomas on their distinguished alumni as at Vikramaśilā. (S. C, Vidyābhūṣaṇa—History of the Mediæval School of Indian Logic, pp. 79, 151 and Appendix C.) Some of them according to Rājaśekhara (Kābyamīmāṃsā, pp. 54-55) used to hold assemblies for the examination of the works of poets and to reward those whose works stood the test. (Compare for S. India, the Maṇimekhalai, Books 1 and 27, Quoted in Indian Culture Through the Ages, Vol. I. p. 218 foot-note). There was, however, no education department, no inspector of schools and colleges. None of the rulers even framed like Akbar regulations for the guidance of schools and colleges as mentioned in the Āin-i-Ākbari.[2602] But one good result emerged out of this: the educational institutions enjoyed autonomy and freedom. The rulers assigned to the educational institutions the material means for their support, gifts of land, grants of money for buildings and for the necessary equipment but did not offer strait-jackets to confine them. In the modern system, Education is under the control of a government department, the Legislature makes laws for it, the executive appoints its Directors, who are really its masters, sends the Inspectors into its schools and colleges and puts the educators in a steel-frame, which it misnames efficiency. But in Ancient India kings had been the nursing fathers of Education, they even built Universities and poured their treasures at their feet but claimed in them no control. The state did interfere in matters of discipline (Kautilya's Arthaśāstra, R. Śyāmaśāstrī's Eng. Trans., p. 224, *ante*, p. 146), but it was on the side of leniency: it sought to counteract undue severity or rigour (Manu VIII.

[2598] Ibid., p. 23.

[2599] Ibid., p. 156.

[2600] Ibid., p. 23.

[2601] Ibid., p. 24.

[2602] Blockman and Jarret's Eng. Trans., I. p. 278; Gladwin's Eng. Trans., 223.

299—300; Gautama ch. II. *ante*, p. 141) or to enforce the terms of indenture between a mastercraftsman and his apprentice (Nārada V. 19.; Bṛhaṣpati XVI. 6; Yājñabālkya II. 187; Gautama II. 43—44; *ante*, pp. 207-209). The kings, as the numerous South Indian incriptions testify, usually gave the endowments to the village assemblies who used to watch over the management of the seats of learning in the locality. (See *ante*, pp. 325-29). Even when a king wanted to bestow patronage on a poet, he did it through some village assembly. The assembly of Tribhubana Mahādevī Chaturvedimangalam awarded, under orders of Kulottunga I half a *veli* and two *ma* of land to the poet Tirunārāyaṇa Bhaṭṭan, as reward for his poem in praise of the king's exploits (Madras Ep. Rep., No. 198 of 1909). Similarly, the Tamil Academy was summoned by kings but it was the Academy and not the king who regulated state patronage and set the stamp of approval on Tamil works. Again, a monarch might enter into the Convocation of a University but no one rose to greet him and he took his seat like any other visitor, but on the entrance of its Head, the 'Venerable of Venerables (Atisa)' all rose and turned their faces towards him and in silence awaited his words.[2603] In the Avarīya Jātaka[2604] the law is taught to the King of Benares, who listens with folded hands, behind the teacher, sitting on the ground.[2605] The University was the Temple of Learning and the learned were its only Hierophants. When Learning visited Royalty, when a wise one entered a court, even Śrī Kṛṣṇa descended from his throne and bowed at the feet of the sage.

2603 S. C. Das—Indian Pundits in the Lands of Snow, pp. 59—60.

2604 Jātaka III. 229.

2605 In the Chāvaka Jātaka (Jātaka X. 309) a king of Benares is taught the sacred texts. The pupil is on a high seat, under the mango tree, the teacher on a lower seat, during the lesson. The Bodhisattva realises that it is against good form.

CHAPTER XIV.

EDUCATION AND THE SOCIETY IN ANCIENT INDIA.

We have already referred to social efficiency as the aim of Ancient Indian education. In the parting words a teacher generally addressed to his student[2606] when he was permitted to return home after the completion of his studies, we have already seen how the householder's life and fatherhood are enjoined as a compulsory religious duty in the interests of the continuity of the race, how the duty of studying and teaching the Veda is enjoined in the interests of the continuity of culture, how the duties of domestic and social life are indicated by asking the student to honour father, mother, teacher and guests as gods, to honour superiors, to give in proper manner and spirit, in joy and humility, in fear and compassion, to perform sacrifice, to look after his health and worldly prosperity and in all doubtful cases to order himself according to the judgment of approved authorities. In another passage[2607] learning and teaching the Veda are enjoined together with marriage, fatherhood, grandfatherhood, the pursuit of right, truth, penance, restraint, tranquility, consercration of fires, sacrifice, entertainment of guests and social duties. Indeed, as the student was enabled to carry on his studies with the help of the ungrudging charity of his fellow-countrymen it is quite natural that from the very beginning he would realise his duty to the society and the community at large.

Even the ascetics were not againt social service: they left the world to give the law unto the world. They did not confine their knowledge and wisdom to themselves but were anxious to impart it to their fellows in society. As Hiuen Tsang remarks: 'Forgetting fatigue', they 'expatiate in the arts and sciences'.[2608] As a concrete example we can cite the case of the Buddha whose spirituality was consistent

---

[2606] Tattirīya Upaniṣad I. 11. [2607] Ibid., I. 9.

[2608] Watters—Yuan Chwang, Vol. I. p. 161.

with the positivist ideal of social service. He was in the world and yet not of it. In the sphere of Politics and state-craft his advice was eagerly sought. If there is a feud between the Śākyas and the Koliyas which may end in bloodshed, it is the arbitration of an ascetic that is invoked and stops it: If the Emperor of Magadha has a plan to crush the liberties of a neighbouring republic, the Buddha's opinion is to be first sought on its prospects ? If there is a new chief appointed for the Śākya state, the Buddha must address him a discourse! He showed interest even in the wars of his times e. g., the two wars between Pasenadi, then king of both Kośola and Kāśī and Ajātaśatru, in the first of which the former had to retreat and in the second captured the latter, "his nephew" alive;[2609] also the war between Vidudhava of Kośala and the Śākyas which he vainly tried to prevent. Pasenadi consulted him on every point, whether it was a meal, the birth of a daughter, daily habits, the death of a grandmother at 120, law and judgment or war.[2610] Thus by instructing kings, the Buddha could influence their administration and the well-being of their subjects.

Indeed, the relation of Education to society is a vital one. 'It gives to the nation the priceless assets of learned and skilled men and women of high character to carry on the work in every department of national life. Learned men produce literature which raises the nation in the eyes of the world and far more important, spreads knowledge over the earth, literature which ennobles and inspires not only contemporaries but generations yet unborn. Science makes discoveries which add to human knowledge, increase man's power over the forces of Nature, and—if it treads only righteous paths—will preserve, uplift and strengthen human life and happiness. By education man's spiritual, intellectual, emotional and physical nature can be lifted from the savage to the saint, can poverty be abolished, can society be made fraternal instead of barbarous, can crime, the fruit of ignorance, be got ridden of, and international and social peace replace war and the strife of classes. Avidyā is the mother of poverty, of sorrow, of misery. It is darkness which the Sun of Vidyā must chase away.'

[2609] Sam. N., I. 81-83.

[2610] Ibid.

It is on account of this importance of education that the ancient Hindus laid so great a stress on the acquisition of all knowledge and specially Vedic learning. Bhartṛhari[2611] says that learning imbues a man with self-confidence and a winning personality; gives him reserve of power and resources, joy and hapiness in the exercise of these and fame and glory in the locality where he lives; and ensures him friendship and guidance when abroad. Kalhaṇa[2612] says: "The tree of learning which is ever laughed at by fools, does indeed, not show roots, blossoms and the like but bears its fruits at the time of distress by removing a man's misfortunes at one stroke". In the Mahābhārata[2613] we read: "*Learning*, bravery, skill, physical power and patience are the natural friends of a man (sahaja mitra). Through their help alone can one live happily". Śukrāchārya[2614] says: "*Learning*, valour, skill, powers and patience are the natural friends: wise men follow these". "Good *learning* always leads to human happiness". "The wealth of *learning* is superior. It grows with gifts, is not burdensome and cannot be carried away (i. e., stolen)".[2615] "The man who does not find pleasure in teaching, *learning*, preceptors, gods......... arts, music.................and literature, is either a man who has attained salvation or a beast in the form of man".[2616] In Gautama Saṃhitā[2617] we read: "Wealth, connections (rich friends) office, birth, deeds, *knowledge* and age are the factors which primarily add to the respectability of a person. But knowledge is the highest of them all, in as much as it is the source of health and virtues". Manu[2618] says: "wealth (honestly acquired), friends (relations), age, work and *erudition* (knowledge) which forms the fifth, these are the sources of honour, each succeeding one being more honourable than the one preceding (in the order of enumeration)". According to Vaśiṣṭha Saṃhitā[2619] "*learning*, wealth, age, relationship and occupation must be respected.

2611 Vidya bhogakarī yasassukhkarī vidyā guruṇāṃ guruḥ
Vidyā rājasu pūjitā na tu dhanam.—Nītiśataka.

2612 Rājatar. IV. 530 : Stein, I. pp. 170-71.

2613 Śāntiparba, 139th adhyāya.

2614 Śukranītisāra, Ch. IV. Sec. I. lines 25-26.

2615 Ibid., Ch. III. lines 360-61. *Compare* Ibid., lines 584-88.

2616 Ibid., lines 493-36.

2617 Ch. VI.

2618 II. 136.

2619 Ch. XI.

But each preceding one is more venerable (than the succeeding one)". In the Mahābhārata[2620] Aṣṭabakra says: "Age, grey hairs, wealth, friends do not make a man old. He alone is designated by the ṛṣis as old and great who has mastered the Vedas and the Vedāngas". Manu[2621] says: "Neither by years (age) nor by grey hairs, neither by wealth nor by friends (relations) does one become great. The ṛṣis made a compact of yore that, 'he of us who will study the entire Veda with the allied branches of study will be called great'". "Grey hairs do not make an old man; a young man who has studied, the Devas designate him as really old".[2622]

According to Kātyāyana Saṃhitā there is no sacrifice superior to Brahmayajña.[2623] "Constant study of the Vedas" says Manu[2624] "brings to a man the remembrances of his past experiences (Jātismara)." "Remembrance of his past births makes him apathetic to the world and its concerns and lead him to attain Supreme Brahman, and eternal happiness (beautitudes).[2625] According to Yājñabālkya[2626] "the consideration of the meaning of Vedas and other scriptural works enables a man to acquire emancipation." Again "of sacrifices, asceticism and sacred rites, the Veda alone is more powerful in bringing emancipation unto the twice-born ones."[2627] "Brahmins who study the Vedas and perform each day the religious sacrifices known as Pañcha-yajña are the wielders of the three worlds and serve as the supports of men, who are addicted to the enjoyment of the five senses."[2628] According to Yājñabālkya "a twice-born person who daily studies the Vedas, reaps the fruits of giving away thrice the earth full of riches (as well as those) of the best ascetic observances."[2629] "The twice-born one, who studies the Vedas, becomes capable of (effectively) cursing or granting boon to other

---

2620 Banaparba, 132nd adhyāya.

2621 II. 154.

2622 Manu, II. 156.

2623 Brahmayajña means the study of the Vedas with their six auxiliaries (Dakṣa Saṃhitā, II. 26).

2624 IV. 148.

2625 Manu IV. 149.

2626 III. 156-59.

2627 Yājñabālkya I. 40.

2628 Parāśara Saṃhitā, VIII. 28.

2629 I. 48.

persons and lives in the regions with the ṛṣis, after death."[2630] "Even a little study of the Vedas stand their twice-born reader in good stead both in this world and the next."[2631] "By studying all the Vedas one is immediately freed from sorrow."[2632] "As duly consecrated fires in cremation grounds consume the sins and impieties of the cremated, so the brāhmaṇas, illumined with the light of knowledge, consume all sins and become like the gods."[2633] "A learned Brahmin rescues the family by seven and seven (i. e., seven generations upwards and seven generations downwards)."[2634] "Non-study of the Vedas," on the other hand, "extinguishes the prestige of a good family"[2635] and "leads to the destruction of Brahmins."[2636]

"Hence the gift of learning is superior to all gifts."[2637] In the Mahābhārata[2638] Bhiṣma speaks to Yudhiṣthir in the same strain: "If a man imparts instruction in the Vedas to a pupil, he is making a gift equal in merit to the gifts of the whole earth and of cow." "One who gives it (the Veda) with an end in view to a non-deceitful brāhmaṇa and to one's own kinsmen headed by the son, attains to the celestial region; and if disinterestedly, to emancipation."[2639] Kātyāyana[2640] speaks in the same strain: "There is no gift superior to that of the Vedas (i. e., deliverance gratis of Vedic instructions)." According to Yājñabālkya[2641] "the Veda is the highest gift; by giving it, one acquires the undecaying region of Brahmā."

So great was the importance of studies, specially Vedic learning that even householders,[2642] not merely bonafide students, were

---

2630 Vyāsa Saṃhitā, I. 37.

2631 Ibid., I. 39.

2632 Bṛhaspati Saṃhitā, I. 79.

2633 Parāśara Saṃhitā VIII. 29; Manu XI. 246; Manu XI. 263; Manu XI. 264; Manu XII. 101; Atri Saṃhitā I. 133; Kātyāyana XIV. 14.

2634 Bṛhaspati Saṃhitā, I. 61.

2635 Manu, III. 63.

2636 Manu V. 4. For other passages extolling Vedic studies *see* Manu II. 107; XII. 102, 103; Yājñabālkya I. 41, 42, 43, 44, 45-46; III. 190. Kātyāyana XIV. 9-14; Mahābhārata, Śāntiparba 235th adhyāya; Ibid., Anuśāsanaparba, 90th adhyāya.

2637 Atri Saṃhitā, I. 333.

2638 Anuśāsanaparba, 69th Adhyāya.

2639 Atri Saṃhitā, I. 333.

2640 XIV. 18.

2641 I. 212.

2642 Mahābhārata, Śāntiparba, 191st adhyāya.

enjoined to cultivate them. Vyāsa[2643] says: "The best of brāhmaṇa (householders) should study the Vedas, Itihāsas and kindred branches of knowledge (Vedāngas) and give instructions to his own pupils." "He (the householder) should then spend the sixth and seventh part of the day in the study of the Itihāsas and the Purāṇas."[2644] The Dakṣa Saṃhitā[2645] mentions the study of the Veda as one of the nine duties which should be publicly done by a householder. Manu[2646] mentions the study of the Vedas and teaching the Vedas to pupils, as among the six duties of every brāhmaṇa (householder). According to Parāśara Saṃhitā[2647] "a brāhmaṇa (householder) who daily performs the six religious duties (mentioned by Manu) never suffers any bad luck in life." Among the six duties enjoined upon a brāhmaṇa householder by Parāśara[2648] the study of the Vedas is one. Manu[2649] says: "He (the twice-born householder) shall peruse each day, śāstras whose perusal serves to improve the intellect as well as those which treat of the art of money-getting. Likewise he shall study the Nigamas which elucidate the true import of the Vedas." "Let him not omit performing ṛṣi-yajña[2650] according to the best of his might."[2651] Vaśiṣṭha[2652] says: "(A house-holder) must be busy with reciting the Veda." Viṣṇu[2653] says: "Let him (the householder) not renounce the study of the Vedas."[2654]

Even Vānaprasthins were enjoined to study the Vedas.[2655] Yājñabālkya[2656] says: "He (the vānaprasthin) should be given to Vedic studies." According to Sāṃkhya Saṃhitā[2657] "he should daily study the Vedas." "Let him (the vānaprasthin) be always devoted to the

---

2643 III. 4. 2644 Dakṣa Saṃhitā, II. 52. 2645 III. 8-14.

2646 X. 75. 2647 I. 37.

2648 I. 38. 2649 IV. 19.

2650 The study of the Vedas is known as ṛṣi-yājña (Manu III. 81), for by such study one can repay his debt to the ṛṣis who are the founders of his religion and culture; *see* ante, p. 16).

2651 Manu IV. 20. 2652 Ch. VIII. 2653 XCIV. 6.

2654 For passages of a similar import *see* Vyāsa III. 9-10; Dakṣa, II. 52, 54; Vaśiṣṭha Ch. VIII.

2655 Mahābhārata, Śāntiparba, 191st adhyāya. 2656 III. 48.

2657 VI. 4.

study of the Vedas."[2658] Vaśiṣṭha Saṃhitā[2659] says: "Let one renounce all the religious rites but not (the recitation of) the Veda. By discarding the Veda one becomes a śūdra and therefore one shall not renounce the Veda".

Indeed, as we have already seen (*ante*, p. 181f.) knowledge, at least in the early period, was looked upon as the primary qualification for the recognition of a person as brāhmaṇa. Even in later times when Brahminhood came to depend upon birth, Vedic learning was looked upon as almost the compulsory duty of all brāhmaṇas. Thus we are told: "the S'ruti and the S'mṛti are the two eyes of the brāhmaṇas created by God. If deprived of (the knowledge of) the one, a person is called one-eyed; and if of the two, blind".[2660] The same verse is repeated in Atri Saṃhitā[2661]: "The S'ruti and the Smṛti are described as the two eyes of the bipras. One who is deficient in either of the two is described as one-eyed; and one who is deficient in the both, as stone-blind". According to Vaśiṣṭha Saṃhitā[2662] "the brāhmaṇas who *neither study nor teach the Vedas*, nor maintain the sacred fires, become of the conduct of śūdras. Without studying the Ṛk, one does not become a brāhmaṇa. They quote a śloka from Manu on this subject: 'A twice-born person who not having studied the Veda, spends his labour on another (subject), soon falls, even while living, to the condition of a śūdra and his descendants after him".

Hence even brāhmaṇas when they were unlearned were looked down upon by society "A brāhmaṇa" says Vyāsa[2663] "who has not studied the Vedas, does, like a wooden elephant, or a leather-deer, but bear the name of the genus he belongs to." "Like a deserted hamlet, like a waterless well, a brāhmaṇa, who has not read the Vedas is a brāhmaṇa only is name."[2664] "An elephant made of wood, an antelope made of leather and a brāhmaṇa indisposed to the study of the Vedas—these three have nothing but the name."[2665]

[2658] Manu VI. 8.
[2659] Ch. X.
[2660] Hārīt Saṃhitā, I. 25.
[2661] I. 344.
[2662] Ch. III.
[2663] IV. 37.
[2664] Vyāsa IV. 38.
[2665] Manu, II. 157; Parāśara, VIII. 23; Vaśiṣṭha, Ch. III.

Parāśara[2666] says: "Like a waterless well, like a deserted hamlet, like a homa done without fire, meaningless is the life of a brāhmaṇa who is without any mantram." "Like a sexual intercourse by a eunuch, like seeds cast in a barren soil, like a meritless gift made to an ignorant person, meaningless is the life of a brāhmaṇa who has not studied the Ṛk verses."[2667] Manu[2668] speaks in the same strain: "As a eunuch is sexually fruitless in respect of a woman, as (sexually) useless is the meeting of two cows, as fruitless is the gift to an ignorant, so fruitless is the life a brāhmaṇa who has not studied the Ṛks." "A brāhmaṇa who has not studied the Vedas is like unto a rush fire that is soon extinguished."[2669] Parāśara[2670] further says: "A council consisting of thousands of persons, who are brāhmaṇas only in name, should not be honoured with the dignity of a Pariṣad." Atri[2671] says: "A bipra who does not know the true nature and being of Brahman but is always proud of his sacrificial thread is for that sin called a paśu." According to Kautilya[2672] the balls of meal offered to his ancestors by a person not learned in the Vedas are unfit to be eaten by wise men."

It was, therefore, laid down that gifts should not be made to unlearned Brahmins."[2673] The wretch of a (blind) man who has no knowledge of the śruti and the smriti should not be given any present at a śrāddha."[2674] Manu says:[2675] "To a brāhmaṇa who has not studied the Vedas, oblations must not be offered, as no one casts fire-offerings in the ashes." "As a sower by sowing seeds in an alkaline soil reaps no harvest, so a giver, by giving oblations to (i. e., feeding) a brāhmaṇa, ignorant of the Vedas (in connection with a śrāddha) derives no benefit."[2676] A virtuous man, therefore, must not make even an insignificant gift to a brāhmana who is not read in the

---

2666 VIII. 24.

2667 Parāśara Saṃhitā, VIII. 25.

2668 II. 158.

2669 Manu III. 168.

2670 VIII. 22.

2671 I. 372.

2672 Arthaśāstra (R. Śyāmaśāstrī's Eng. Trans.), p. 33.

2673 Mahābhārata, Anuśāsanaparba, 37th adhyāya.

2674 Atri Saṃhitā, I. 345.

2675 III. 168. *Compare* Manu III. 131; Kātyāyana, XV. 7.

2676 Manu III. 142.

Vedas."[2677] "A gift should be made to an erudite person living at a distance in preference to an illiterate one living close by one's house. Nothing can be humiliating to an illiterate brahmana."[2678] Bṛhaṣpati[2679] says: "If an ignorant person lives in one's own house and one vastly read in the śruti at a distance, presents should be made unto the one whe is master of the Veda. There is no sin in superseding the ignorant wight." Kātyāyana[2680] says: "There is no sin in superseding a brāhmaṇa who is divorced from Vedic learning. Leaving aside a burning fire, one should not offer oblations to ashes." Vyāsa[2681] says: "By not making a gift to a brāhmaṇa, ignorant of the Vedas, one does not commit the sin of insulting a brāhmaṇa. Oblations are cast in the sacred fire, not in its ashes." "Tho cereals (food grains in one's store) begin to dance with pleasure on the arrival of a modest erudite brāhmaṇa at one's house, saying 'We shall come by a better fate.'"[2682] "Grains of rice given to a Brahmin who has neglected the study of the Vedas begin to cry in dismay 'What evils have we committed to be punished with a such a degradation?'."[2683] "Gifts made unto an illiterate brāhmaṇa, like seeds sown in a sandy soil or clarified butter kept in a pot of ashes or libations poured over burnt out cinders, prove abortive."[2684] Atri[2685] says: "Leaving aside learned brāhmaṇas one should not make any gifts to any other persons. I have neither seen nor heard of any such course."

Hārīta[2686] goes further and says: "To make gifts and offer food unto a brāhmaṇa who is ignorant of the śruti and the smṛiti encompasses the destruction of one's family." "Like a man attempting to cross (a river) with the aid of a stone-raft, both the ignorant donor and acceptor of a gift are drowned."[2687] "By giving a well-gotton wealth

---

2677 Manu IV. 192.
2678 Vyāsa Saṃhitā, IV. 33.
2679 I. 60.
2680 XV. 9.
2681 IV. 35.
2682 Vyāsa Saṃhitā, IV. 50.
2683 Ibid., IV. 51. *Compare*: In the Mahābhārata (Anuśāsanaparba, 90th adhyāya). Bhīṣma says to Yudhiṣṭhir: "A Brahmin devoid of learning is a pañkti-dūṣaka. Food taken by him at a śrāddha is food taken by a rākṣasa."
2684 Vyāsa IV. 62.
2685 I. 336.
2686 I. 24.
2687 Manu IV. 194.

to an illiterate brāhmaṇa, both the donor and the donee come to grief in the next world."[2688] According to Manu[2689] "A brāhmaṇa ignorant of the Vedas, shall have to eat as many morsels of burning spear-heads, after death, as he eats of the śrāddha oblations to the manes and deities, in life." "The life duration of an ignorant brāhmaṇa suffers, if he accepts a gift of gold or food grains; by accepting the gift of a land or a cow, he suffers in health; for accepting the gift of a horse, he is deprived of his sight, for accepting the gift of a cloth, his skin suffers, for accepting the gift of clarified butter, his energy and for accepting sesame his progeny are consumed."[2690]

In conformity with this attitude towards unlearned Brahmins it was laid down that learning could be acquired even from non-Brahmins when they are learned. Thus Manu[2691] says: "Women, gems, *knowledge* virtue, purity, good words (counsels) and the *various kinds of art* may be acquired from anywhere." "In times of distress, a brāhmaṇa student may take his lessons from a non-brāhmaṇa preceptor."[2692] Gautama[2693] speaks in the same strain: "In times of distress a brāhmaṇa may learn an art or a science from a non-brāhmaṇa teacher."

It is no wonder, therefore, that the people will be asked to show great respect to the learned. Kautilya[2694] says: "Such persons as are noted for their *learning*, intelligince, bravery, high birth or magnificent deeds shall be honoured." Manu[2695] says: "Those brāhmaṇas who are foremost (i. e., well-read) in all the Vedas and the Vedāngas and whose ten ancestors were well-conversant with the Vedas are called Paṅktipāvanas." Śukrāchārya[2696] describes learned men as ornaments in palaces, assemblies etc. The utterance of a Vedavid is sanctifying.[2697] "Ridden in the chariot of scriptures and wielding the swords of the

---

2688 Ibid.

2689 III. 133.

2690 IV. 189.

2691 II. 240.

2692 Manu II. 241.

2693 Ch. VII.

2694 Arthaśāstra (R. Śyāmaśāstrī's Eng. Trans.), p. 252.

2695 III. 184. *Compare* Manu III. 185, 186; Kātyāyana, XIV. 14; Gautama, Ch. XV.

2696 Śukranītisāra, Ch. IV. Sec. VII. lines 638-45.

2697 Atri Saṃhitā, I. 14.

Vedas in their hands, brāhmaṇas whatever they may speak even in fun is highly obligatory."[2698] That religion is to be known as the highest which a leading brāhmaṇa, knowing the Veda follows—but not that which is followed by ten thousand illiterate persons.[2699]

One who daily studies the Vedas is an apūrva atithi.[2700] One should bid farewell to a śrotriya guest by following him a little beyond the compound of one's own house.[2701] "A king or *a snātaka*, happening to call at his house, even within a year (of his last visit) on the occasion of a sacrificial ceremony, the householder shall welcome in the method of Madhuparkam and not otherwise."[2702] "Let him not wilfully leap over the shadow of his king or *preceptor* nor that of a divine image, nor that of a cow nor that of a *snātaka*."[2703] According to Yama Saṃhitā[2704] "one should give way to a wheelman, to an old man, to a bride, to a *snātaka*, to a king and to one of tender years who should be protected." Manu[2705] says: "On the road one must give way to a carter, to a man of more than ninety years of age, to a sick folk, to a carrier of weights, to a woman, to a *snātaka*, to the king and to a bridegroom." "When all these meet together (on the road), greatest preference should be shown to the king and the snātaka. *Of a king and a snātaka the first shall give way* (*show respect*) *to the last*."[2706] Yājnabālkya[2707] says: "An aged burden-carrier, a king, a *snātaka*, a woman, a diseased person, a bridegroom and a cart-man should (always) be given road; a king is adorable unto them all; *but a snātaka* (*even*) *to the king*." Viṣṇu[2708] says: "One must make way for an aged man, for one carrying a load, for a king, for *a snātaka*, for a sick person, for a woman, for a bridegroom and for a carter. All of these persons (meeting together) must make way for a king; and *even a king must make way for a snātaka*." Vaśiṣṭha[2709] says:

[2698] Parāśara Saṃhitā, VIII. 33.

[2699] Atri Saṃhitā, I. 142.

[2700] Parāśara I. 43.

[2701] Vyāsa III. 43.

[2702] Manu III. 120.

[2703] Ibid., IV. 130.

[2704] Ch. VI.

[2705] II. 138.

[2706] Manu II. 139.

[2707] I. 117.

[2708] LXIII. 50-51.

[2709] Ch. XI. *Compare* Mahābhārata, Banaparba, 132nd adhyāya.

"If one meets aged men, infants, sick-men, load-carriers and persons riding on wheels, he must give way to each of the latter. If a king and a snātaka meet, *the king must make way for the snātaka.*" The following śloka of Chāṇakya has become a common saying in India:

"Swadeśe pūjyate rājā vidwān sarbatra pūjyate"

"A king is respected in his own kingdom while a learned man is worshipped everywhere."

The śāstrakāras go even so far as to lay down that the very sight of a learned man is sacred. Thus Parāśara Saṃhitā[2710] says: "Holy is the sight of a brāhmaṇa well-versed in the Vedas, hence one should try to see him, every day." Kātyāyana Saṃhitā[2711] says: "He, who rising up in the morning, sees a śrotriya (one learned in the śruti) becomes freed from all calamities."

It is no wonder, therefore, that gifts to a learned man would be looked upon as the highest gift.[2712] "Eternal is the gift that is made unto a person who is well-read in the Vedas.................who studies the Vedas and has acquired knowledge."[2713] "The fruit of a gift is endless (when it is made unto) one who has mastered the Vedas."[2714] Parāśara[2715] says: "A gift made to a brāhmaṇa well-versed in the Vedas, tends to increase the longevity of its giver.

The society not only honoured its learned but also granted them *special privileges.* "If the king comes by any hidden treasure, he must give half of it to a brāhmaṇa. But (when) a learned Brahmin (happens to find out any) the (whole treasure) should go to him, for, he is the lord of all."[2716] Manu[2717] says: "In the absence of a

---

[2710] XII. 41. [2711] XIX. 9.

[2712] The *Psychological basis of gifts* has been thus described by Kalhaṇa: The gathering of the clouds pleases the peacocks though it spreads darkness, while the wild goose is pleased by the breaking up of the clouds which brings clearness. From the mutual regard which the giver and recipient (of a gift) show for each other, there appears in the highest degree a *resemblance of tastes.*" (Rājataraṅgiṇī, I. 308; Stein, Vol. I. p. 46).

[2713] Bṛhaspati Saṃhitā, I. 56. [2714] Dakṣa Saṃhitā, III. 26.

[2715] XII. 45. *Compare* Manu XI. 1-2. [2716] Yājñabālkya, II. 35.

[2717] IX. 187-88.

samānodaka, his preceptor, and in the absence of a preceptor, his disciple (shall inherit one's property). In the absence of all kinds of relations, brāhmaṇas, well-versed in the three Vedas, pure, with their senses fully controlled, shall take (the) estates, whereby virtue will not be impaired." Kautilya[2718] says: "Property for which no claimant is found shall go to the king but not that of a brāhmaṇa learned in the Vedas. That (the property of the learned) shall be made over to those who are well-versed in the three Vedas." "Men learned in the Vedas, persons engaged in penance as well as labourers may take with them salt for food; salt and alkalies for purposes other than this, shall be subject to the payment of toll."[2719] "Men learned in the Vedas may take from the fields ripe flowers and fruits for the purpose of worshipping their gods and rice and barley for the purpose of performing āgrayaṇa, a sacrificial performance at the commencement of harvest seasons."[2720] "Again, he alone is qualified to enter upon the life of a Yati who has studied the Vedas."[2721] He who maintains the sacred fire and studies the Vedas is purified in one day (of the impurity arising from birth or death).[2722] A Vahu-śruta, even if he has committed any delinquency, should not be punished, condemned or banished by the king from his native country."[2723]

The students also enjoyed certain *privileges*. Thus, they are exempted from paying ferry-tolls.[2724] According to Kautilya[2725] "commodities intended for the investiture of the sacred thread shall be let off free of toll". According to Viṣṇu Saṃhitā[2726] "in case where by speaking truth a student is killed, a witness may speak untruth". A person holding an uninterrupted and continuous possession of property in the face of its owner, other than an infant or an idiot, shall acquire proprietary right therein. But such a continuous possession of a property owned by a *śrotriya*, king or an itinerant *brahmachārin* or by a

---

2718 Arthaśāstra (R. Śyāmaśāstrī's Eng. Trans.), p. 205.

2719 Ibid., p. 99.

2720 Ibid., p. 146.

2721 Yājñabālkya III. 57.

2722 Dakṣa Saṃhitā, VI. 6.

2723 Gautama Saṃhitā, Ch. VIII; *compare* Atri Saṃhitā, I. 133; also Ibid., I. 113.

2724 Manu VIII. 407.

2725 Arthaśāstra (R. Śyāmaśāstrī's Eng. Trans.), p. 137.

2726 VIII. 15.

person of renowned virtues would not give rise to any title thereto in favour of the possessor ".[2727] Again, "a student does not infringe the rules of his order by carrying away, when dead, his *teacher or his sub-teacher* or his father or his mother or his guru ".[2728] On the death of one's *fellow-student* of the Vedas in the same house, the period of uncleanliness is three days; on the death of one's *disciple* he shall remain impure for two days and the night between them (pakṣini).[2729] According to Atri Saṃhitā[2730] a brahmachārin (student) becomes immediately purified. According to Manu[2731] students are never affected by death or birth-uncleanliness in as much as they are the representatives of Brahmā (on earth)".

It is no less interesting to find that in the selection of bridegrooms and government officers, *the education of the persons concerned was taken into consideration.* In the Mahābhārata[2732] Viṣma says to Yudhiṣṭhir : "If the guardian of the bride gives her in marriage to a bridegroom after making a satisfactory enquiry about the latter's *learning*, family-prestige and occupation, then it is called Brahmā marriage. Such a marriage is the most commendable form of marriage for Brahmins ". S'ukrāchārya[2733] says : "One may give his daughter even to a penniless man who possesses (proper) qualifications of age, *learning*, and beauty and should not judge a bridegroom by his beauty, age and wealth." He says further: "One should first examine the family, *then learning*, then age, then character, then wealth, then form and lastly the country of birth ; marriage is to be entered into afterwards ".[2734] Among the qualifications of an ideal bridegroom Yājñabālkya[2735] refers to his being "well-read in the Vedas." According to Yājñabālkya[2736] the Royal High priest must posses among others the qualification of being "well-grounded in the śāstras" and "well-versed in the theory of Polity." According to Kautilya[2737] the Royal

[2727] Gautama Saṃhitā, Ch. XII.
[2728] Viṣṇu Saṃhitā, XXII. 85.
[2729] Manu V. 81.
[2730] I. 97.
[2731] V. 93.
[2732] Anuśāsanaparba, 44th adhyāya.
[2733] Śukranītisāra, Ch. III. lines 344-45.
[2734] Ibid., lines 346-47.
[2735] I. 35.
[2736] I. 313.
[2737] Arthaśāstra (R. Śyāmaśāstrī's Eng. Trans.), p. 17.

High-priest ought to possess among others the qualification of being "well educated in the Vedas and the six Angas" and "well versed in the science of government." According to Kāmandaka[2738] the Royal High-priest should be well-versed in Trayī and Daṇḍanīti. According to S'ukrāchārya[2739] one who is versed in mantras and rituals, master of the three sciences (Trayī).........equipped with a knowledge of the six angas and of the science of archery with all its branches, one who knows the science of morals as well as religious interests and master of military implements and tactics is the priest (of the king)." Thus not a mere knowledge of the technique of sacrificial rites and ceremonies but a sound liberal education is expected of him. In the Mahābhārata[2740] Bhīṣma says to Yudhiṣṭhir that a minister must be well-versed in the śāstras, in military science and in nīti. Again, "he must be well-educated (suśikṣita), well-versed in tri-barga, in diplomacy, in the art of constructing phalanx and skilled in piercing through the enemy's ranks and in training and fighting on elephants."[2741] According to Manu[2742] a minister must be "conversant with the prices of lands, well-versed in the śāstras, with unmissing aims in archery or in the use of arms. According to Kāmandaka a minister must be "endowed with the knowledge of the śāstras"[2743] and "proficient in śilpavidyā."[2744] As a matter of fact we find that eminent men of learning with a deep and specialised knowledge of a particular science or art together with a general knowledge of a few other sciences were appointed as ministers. Thus Kautilya was the minister of Chandragupta Maurya. In Parāśara Saṃhitā[2745] we are told of many similarly qualified ministers: "just as the religious guide Mādhava was the mantrin of king Bukkana, so was Bṛhaṣpati to Indra, Sumati to Nala, Medhātithi to S'aibya, Dhaumya to Yudhiṣṭhir, Svaujas to Pṛthu, Vaśiṣṭha to Rāma". While enumerating the qualifications which one must possess before

---

2738 Nītisāra, 4th sarga, śl. 32.

2739 Śukranītisāra, Ch. II. lines 156-60.

2740 Śāntiparba, 84th adhyāya.

2741 Ibid., 117th adhyāya.

2742 VII. 54.

2743 Nītisāra, 4th sarga, śl. 25.

2744 Ibid., śl. 30.

2745 Bombay edition, p. 3.

he can be thought fit for councillorship S′ukrāchārya[2746] says that he must be "versed in the arts of politics". According to S′ukrāchārya[2747] a brāhmaṇa judge must be "well-versed in the Vedas". "If the brāhmaṇa be not learned enough, the king should appoint a kṣhatriya or a vaiśya who is versed in the Dharmaśāstras,'.[2748] That human affairs being very complex, cannot be investigated by a judge versed in a single science was realised by S′ukra who says: "The man who has studied only one śāstra cannot investigate a case properly. So in all cases, the king should appoint men who know good many śāstras".[2749] Similarly, a ministerial officer (amātya-sampat) must possess among others the qualification of being "well-trained in arts.[2750] According to Kāmandaka[2751] those who besides other qualifications are endowed with learning (vidyā) and proficient in śāstra, artha and vyabahāra are fit for royal service. Even the courtiers should be proficient in the Vedas and conversant with the laws of morality (Yājñabālkya, II. 2). According to Kautilya[2752] an ambassador must possess among others the qualification of being "well-trained in arts". According to Manu[2753] he must be "well-versed in all the śāstras". According to Kāmandaka an ambassador must be "proficient in the śāstras"[2754] and "conversant with mantra-śāstra".[2755] The Superintendents of Government departments must also possess among others the qualification of being "well-trained in arts".[2756] In conformity with these regulations it was laid down that the king should 'increase the subsistence and wages of his servants in consideration of their learning and work'.[2757]

Intellectual proficiency in legal and religious literature was also looked upon as one of the qualifications for every aspirant after a position in the general assembly of some of the South Indian villages.

2746 Śukranītisāra, Ch. II. lines 333-36.
2747 Ibid., Ch. IV. Sec. V. lines 23-26.
2748 Ibid., lines 27-28,
2749 Ibid., lines 65-66.
2750 Arthaśāstra (R. Śyāmaśāstrī's Eng. Trans.), p. 16.
2751 Nītisāra, 5th sarga, śls. 13-14; Ibid., śl. 67.
2752 Arthaśāstra (R. Śyāmaśāstrī's Eng. Trans.), p. 34.
2753 VII. 63.
2754 Nītisāra, 13th sarga, śl. 2.
2755 Ibid., śl. 1.
2756 Kautilya's Arthaśāstra (R. Śyāmaśāstrī's Eng. Trans.), p. 77.
2757 Ibid., p. 309.

Thus the inscription at Manur[2758] in the Tinnevelly district dated in the thirty-fifth year of the reign of Mārañjadaiyan (i. e., about the nineth century A. D.) lays down that "of the children of the share-holders in the village only one who is well-behaved and has studied the Mantra-Brāhmaṇa and one Dharma (i. e., code of law) may be on the village assembly to represent the share held by him in the village". Similarly the two Inscriptions in the Vaikuṇṭha—Perumal temple at Uttarmallūr, assigned to the tenth century A. D. lay down that a member to be eligible for nomination by his ward "must know the Mantra-Brāhmaṇa" and "if owns only ⅛th of land [the property qualification amounted to a quarter (veli) of tax-paying land] he must be proficient in one Veda and in one of the four Vāṣyas by explaining (it to others)".

[2758] Madras Ep. Report, 1906-07, No. 423 of 1906.

CHAPTER XV.

CONCLUSION: EFFECTS OF THE EDUCATIONAL SYSTEM.

It is difficult for us to determine at this distance of time what were the effects of this emphasis on knowledge and learning in Ancient India. It is no less difficult to realise the position and achievements of the educational institutions of old. The long centuries through which they have held sway show that they must have possessed elements of value and strength and that they were not unsuited to the needs of those who developed and adopted them. But the early educational system which made great contributions to the science of grammar and philosophy and other subjects became in course of time stereotyped and formal, unable to meet the needs of a progressive civilisation. For as in society, so in education it was in the ideals of the past which ever governed its development. The duty of the teacher was to pass on as nearly as he himself has received it, the mass of tradition which had been handed down from past ages. Thus in grammar, after the great work of Pāṇinī and Patañjali the science became fixed and though an enormous number of works on grammar have been written in India since, it was always recognised that these ancient authorities must not be departed from. Education also became stereotyped and the same methods which were followed hundreds of years before the Christian era continued with little change down to modern times.

Moreover, while on the one hand, the underlying philosophic thought tended towards a spirit of other-worldliness and to education being conceived as a preparation for what lay beyond the life, on the other hand, the idea of each man being born to perform certain functions in life according to his caste tended towards a narrow vocationalism and those specially who were shut out from the study of the Vedas and the higher philosophical thought received little direct religious education, save through the performance of certain religious rites, so that their training was confined to the acquisition of those subjects or mechanical arts which they needed for their caste-occupation. And when the popular elementary schools grew up to provide for the need of simple instruction, they also like the caste-training were largely utilitarian in their outlook. In this narrow vocational system there was no idea of study for the sake of study. The individual was being educated not so much for his own sake as for the sake of society and individualism came to have very little scope for development.

At the same time we should bear in mind that the ancient Indian system of education produced many great men and earnest seekers after truth and its output on the intellectual side is by no means inconsiderable. *The type of men turned out by it* may be best described in the words of Hiuen Tsang: "When they have finished their education and have attained thirty years of age, then their character is formed and their knowledge ripe. There are men who far seen in antique lore and fond of the refinements of learning are content in seclusion, leading lives of continence. These come and go outside of the world and promenade through life away from human affairs. Though they are not moved by honour or reproach, there fame is far spread. Though their family be in affluent circumstances, such men make up their minds to be like vagrants and get their food by begging as they go about. With them there is honour in knowing truth and there is no disgrace in being destitute. The rulers treating them with ceremony cannot make them come to court." They did not, however, confine their knowledge and worth to themselves but tried to share them with their fellows in society. Yuan Chwang[2759] remarks : "Forgetting fatigue" they "expatiate in the arts and sciences," seeking for wisdom, while "relying on perfect virtue" "they count not 1,000 *li* a long journey."

It is not every age, it is not every nation that can boast of the type of men described by Hiuen Tsang. But the effect of the system of education was also seen in the *high level of average men* in ancient India. The most unimpeachable testimony on this point is furnished by the foreign travellers who visited India from time to time. Strabo says: "They are so honest as neither to require locks to their

---

[2759] Watters—Yuan Chwang, I. 161.

doors nor writing to bind their agreements." Arrian says: "No Indian was ever known to tell an untruth."[2760] Megasthenes writes: "They live happily enough, being simple in their manners and frugal. They never drink wine except at sacrifices. The simplicity of their laws and their contracts is proved by the fact that they seldom go to law. They have no suits about pledges or deposits nor do they require either seals or witnesses, but make their deposits and confide in each other. Their houses and property they generally leave unguarded. Truth and virtue they hold alike in esteem". Hiuen Tsang says: "The kṣhatriyas and brāhmaṇas are clean-handed and unostentatious, pure and simple in life and very frugal. They are pure of themselves and not from compulsion. With respect to the ordinary people, although they are naturally light-minded, yet they are without craft and in administering justice they are considerate. They are not deceitful or treacherous in their conduct and are faithful to their oaths and promises. In their rules of government there is remarkable rectitude, whilst in their behaviour there is much gentleness and sweetness". Khang-thai, the Chinese ambassador to Siam says that Su-we, a relative of Fauchen, king of Siam who came to India about 231 A. D. on his return reported to the king that "the Indians are straightforward and honest".[2761] "In the fourth century Friar Jordanus tells us that the people of India are true in speech and eminent in justice".[2762] Feitu, the ambassador of the Chinese Emperor Yangti to India in 605 A. D. among other things points out as peculiar to the Hindus that "they believe in solemn oaths".[2763] I-Drisi, in his Geography (written in the 11th century) says: "The Indians are naturally inclined to justice, and never depart from it in their actions. Their good faith, honesty and fidelity to their engagements are well-known and they are so famous for those qualities that people flock to their country from every side".[2764] In the 13th century Shams-ud-din Abu

2760 McCrindle in Ind. Ant., 1876, p. 92.

2761 Max Muller—India: What Can it Teach us? p. 55.

2762 Yule—Marco Polo, Vol, II. p. 354.

2763 Max Muller—India: What Can it Teach us?, p. 275.

2764 Elliot—History Of India As Told By Her Own Historians, Vol. I. p. 88.

Abdullah quotes the following judgment of Bedi-ezr Zeman: "The Indians are innumerable like grains of sand, free from deceit and violence. They fear neither death nor life".[2765] Marco Polo (thirteenth century) says: "You must know that these Brahmins are the best merchants in the world and the most truthful, for, they would not tell a lie for anything on earth. If a foreign merchant who does not know the ways of the country applies to them and entrusts his goods to them, they will take charge of these, and sell them in the most loyal manner, seeking zealously the profit of the foreigner and asking no commission except what he pleases to bestow".[2766] The picture depicted by these accounts may be a bit overdrawn but making a due allowance for exaggeration, it is true to a great degree. As Professor Max Muller[2767] says: "There must surely be some ground for this, for, it is not a remark that is frequently made by travellers in foreign countries even in our time, that their inhabitants speak the truth. Read the accounts of English travellers in France and you will find very little said about French honesty and veracity, while French accounts of England are seldom without fling at *Perfide Albion*!".

The national character of a people necessarily suffers from the unsympathetic domination of an alien people. Successful falsehood says Bentham is the best defence of a slave; and it is no wonder that the character of the Hindus deteriorated under Moslem and British rule. The wonder is, their character is still so high. Professor Max Muller[2768] says: "I can only say that after reading the accounts of the terrors and horrors of Muhammadan rule, my wonder is that so much of native virtue and truthfulness should have survived". For, even under Moslem rule we constantly hear of brave deeds specially of the Rajputs and the Maharattas. Name a few heroes like Pratāp, Durgā Dās, Jaswānt, Hāmir, Rāj Singh, Maun, Pṛthwīrāja and Śivājī and a volume is said. The rest

"Were long to tell; how many battles fought,
How many kings destroyed and kingdoms won".

2765 Max Muller—India: What Can it Teach us?, p. 275.

2766 G. B. Parks—Marco Polo, p. 285; Yule—Marco Polo, Vol. II. p. 350.

2767 India: What Can it Teach us?, p. 57.

2768 Ibid., p. 72.

Sir Thomas Munro when asked if he thought the civilisation of the Hindus would be promoted by trade with England being thrown open, replied: "I do not exactly understand what is meant by the civilisation of the Hindus...............If a good system of agriculture, unrivalled manufacturing skill, a capacity to produce whatever can contribute to luxury or convenience, schools[2769] established in every village for teaching reading, writing and arithmetic, the general practice of hospitality and charity amongst one another and, above all, a treatment of the female sex, full of confidence, respect and delicacy, are among the signs which denote a civilised people, then the Hindus are not inferior to the nations of Europe and if civilisation is to become an article of trade between the two countries, I am convinced that this country (England) will gain by the import cargo". Thus according to the standards both of the East and of the West the character of the Indians was high and honourable. This was undoubtedly the result of the grand system of education which they had evolved, a system which produced the most comprehensive literature and the best type of men.

Indeed the very visits of the Chinese pilgrims and Arab scholars are a testimony to the educational progress and moral greatness achieved by India. It was not on a pleasure-trip upon which they came out to India. They came on a sacred mission as a seeker after the saving knowledge, of which India had then the monopoly in the whole of Asia. No amount of dangers and difficulties presented by nature and man alike in the course of their travel in those days of difficulties of means of communication could damp the ardour and enthusiasm of so many foreign scholars for learning Indian arts and sciences. Indeed from the time of Kaṇiṣka to that of Dharmapāla of Bengal, during the

---

2769 "In Bengal there existed 80,000 native schools, though doubtless for the most part of a poor quality. According to a Government Report of 1835 there was *a village school for every four hundred persons*"—Missionary Intelligencer, IX. pp. 183-93.

Sir Thomas Munro estimated the children educated at public schools in the Madras Presidency as less than *one in three*—Elphinstone's History of India, p. 205.

period of well nigh ten centuries, there had been a steady stream of Chinese students towards India, towards her many seats of learning, where they could drink at the very fountains of the wisdom which they sought. From the time of the Arab conquest of Sind there came into India from the Muhammadan kingdoms of Western Asia streams of Arab and Persian scholars like Barzouhyah,[2770] Almuwaffak[2771] and others to acquire proficiency in the Indian sciences, specially Medicine,[2772] Astronomy[2773] and Music.[2774] Their pilgrimage to the Indian seats of learning is only a tribute paid by China, Arabia and Persia to the sovereignty of Indian thought, whose influence extended beyond the geographical boundaries of India to many foreign countries and thus built up a Greater India beyond her northern mountains and southern seas. Thus her educational system, *internally* made her fit for a free and full self-expression while *externally* she was enabled to impress her thought effectively upon her neighbours who turned to her as the home of the highest learning and culture in those days.

2770 P. C. Roy—History of Hindu Chemistry, Vol. I. Introduction, p. 76.

2771 Sachau's Alberuni, Preface, p. XXXII. 2772 Ibid., p. XXXI.

2773 Weber's History of Indian Literature, p. 255; Mill's History of India, Vol.II. p. 107.

2774 Weber's History of Indian Literature, p. 272.

Index I. Sources.

A

B

C

D

E

F

G

H

I

J

M

N

T

W

Y

Z

Index I(b) Sources with the subjects.

A

B

C

D

F

G

H

I

J

K

N

O

P

S

T

Y

Index II. Subjects.

D

E

F

G

H

I

J

K

L

M

N

O

P

Q

R

S

T

U

V

W

Index III. Proper Names.

B

C

D

E

F

G

H

I

J

L

N

O

P

R

T

U

V

W

Y

[*N. B.*—The references in all these indices are to the pages of this work.]